Ultimate VMware NSX for Professionals

Leverage Virtualized Networking, Security, and Advanced Services of VMware NSX for Efficient Data Management and Network Excellence

Vinay Aggarwal

www.orangeava.com

First published: December 2023

Published by: Orange Education Pvt Ltd, AVA™

Address: 9, Daryaganj, Delhi, 110002

ISBN: 978-81-96782-62-7

www.orangeava.com

Dedicated To

My beloved Parents:

Shri Mangal Sen Aggarwal

Ritu Aggarwal

and

My wife Neha and My Son Bhavik

About the Author

Vinay Aggarwal, VCIX – NV, VCIX – DCV, CCNP – DC, CCS, has been working in IT with more than a decade of experience on different VMware technologies. Starting as a Windows Administrator at HCL Technologies, Noida, India, he ventured overseas to Birmingham, UK, partnering with TCS, before eventually returning to his roots in India as a Senior Consultant at VMware. Over the years, Vinay has gained knowledge and experience in Software Defined Datacenters (SDDC) and in recent years, has become more focused on Software Defined Networking (SDN) with VMware NSX portfolio. Vinay's dedication extends beyond his career, his contributions to the tech community have been subtle yet significant, with sessions at VMware Explore India and VMUG Delhi, India. You can keep up with Vinay's tech adventures by following him on X (formerly Twitter) at @vmvtips or delving into his day-to-day experiences with VMware technologies on his blog site, https://vmvtips.com.

About the Technical Reviewer

Sreejith works as a Consulting Architect with VMware. He has more than 15 years of experience as an information technology specialist. Indian by birth, Sreejith currently resides in the United Arab Emirates. He gathers customer requirements and creates designs of VMware Cloud Provider-based solutions that span the company's product line in order to fit the functional and business demands of businesses of all sizes and industries. He finds great delight in assisting Cloud Providers in deploying hyper-scale cloud platforms throughout Cloud Provider's datacenters using a pay-as-you-go, monthly subscription model. In addition to having multiple professional and advanced certificates, he has received seven vExpert recognitions. He is also a VMTN champion and the author of VMware NSX Network Essentials, which was published in 2016. You can find his LinkedIn ID at https://www.linkedin.com/in/csreejith/. He would like to express his profound gratitude to the VMware community and all of its members for their contributions thus far. Additionally, he would like to thank his family and colleagues at VMware for their unwavering support throughout his career.

Acknowledgements

There are a few people I want to thank for the continued and ongoing support they have given me during the writing of this book. First and foremost, I would like to thank my family for continuously encouraging me to write the book – I could have never completed this book without their support.

I am grateful to Mr. Sreejith C for his kind attention to details and his guidance during the development of this book, taking time out of his busy schedule. I am thankful to all our professional editors, especially Subha, Sonali, and Sreeja, for their patience and guidance at every step of the book process.

A special thanks to Orange AVA team for giving me the opportunity and guidance to transform a rough word document into a comprehensive book.

Preface

Welcome to "Ultimate VMware NSX for Professionals," a step-by-step guide providing understanding and mastering VMware's Network Virtualization and Security platform, NSX. In today's ever-evolving IT landscape, virtualization has become a key to build scalable and agile infrastructures. VMware NSX, a network and security virtualization platform provides strong Network Virtualization capabilities in Software Defined Datacenter.

This book is designed to provide you with a solid foundation in NSX, whether you are an IT professional looking to implement virtualized networks, a system administrator seeking to enhance your skills, or a network architect striving to design software-defined datacenter solutions. VMware NSX offers a dynamic approach to network and security management that enables organizations to efficiently utilize their network infrastructure while reducing costs and complexity.

In the pages that follow, you will embark on a journey through the core concepts and practical applications of VMware NSX. This book has been divided into 14 chapters, with each chapter covering a topic that I believe is needed to fully understand a concept. Although this book could be read cover to cover, it is designed to be flexible and allow you to move between chapters or sections of chapters to cover topics you need. However, few chapters should be read sequentially, such as Chapter 3 to Chapter 7 to understand Routing and Switching or Chapter 8 to Chapter 10 to understand security features in NSX. The details are listed below for the topics covered in each chapter.

Chapter 1 covers some key challenges with traditional networking and how Software Defined Networking can help overcome those challenges. It then introduces NSX, a VMware software defined networking solution, and covers in depth its architecture and the different key components that build the NSX environment.

Chapter 2 focuses on deployment of the first component of NSX environment, that is, NSX Manager. It covers different methods to deploy NSX Manager in vSphere environment and create an NSX Management cluster. Then focus shifts on preparing Data Plane of NSX environment, covering architecture of Transport Nodes, different pre-requisites to prepare a Transport Node and finally promoting ESXi host as an NSX Transport Node.

Chapter 3 is all about logical switching in NSX environment. This chapter deals with switching configuration in NSX environment including Geneve Encapsulation to enable Layer 2 communication on top of Layer 3 underlay networks. This chapter covers the creation and configuration of segments and segment profiles along with Layer 2 packet walks in NSX environment.

Chapter 4 marks the beginning of the first step in logical routing. This chapter covers one of the most important requirements to enable Logical Routing in NSX environment which is Edge nodes and Edge Clusters. This chapter discusses different options, design and configuration available to deploy Edge nodes in NSX environment.

Chapter 5 continues on NSX Logical Routing. This chapter delves into the world of NSX logical router and follows a packet to see how it travels within NSX environment. This chapter covers different routing topologies supported by NSX and how to configure them, along with dynamic routing protocols BGP and OSPF. Last but not least, it covers high-availability choices for routing services.

Chapter 6 covers VRF lite and EVPN to provide end-to-end isolation for different tenants in network fabric.

Chapter 7 covers logical bridging, a network service provided by NSX that can help bridge the gap between overlay networks and VLAN-backed networks to allow layer 2 communication between VMs and physical workloads or workloads running in NSX-V environment.

Chapter 8 begins the journey of security features in NSX environment. This chapter covers Micro-Segmentation with the help of Distributed Firewall that helps protect East-West traffic inside a datacenter and protect workloads from lateral attacks.

Chapter 9 builds on top of micro-segmentation and sheds light on the advanced security features provided by NSX. This chapter starts with Gateway Firewall to protect North-South traffic leaving the NSX environment and then focuses on the Intrusion Detection/Prevention System. This chapter covers the architecture and configuration of IDS/IPS along with Malware Prevention.

Chapter 10 covers the NSX Application platform and NSX Intelligence that provides recommendations for NSX DFW and detects anomalies in the network using its suspicious detectors. Also, it covers NSX Network Detection and Response which create campaigns by taking all events from Malware Prevention, Intelligence, IDS and analyzing them, reducing the burden on security administrators.

Chapter 11 covers different datacenter features, that is, NAT, DHCP, DNS, IPSec VPN, and Layer 2 VPN, and how to configure them in an NSX environment. Also, it talks about a new feature introduced in NSX which enables stateful services on Active-Active gateways.

Chapter 12 discusses the NSX Advanced Load Balancer, its features, architecture, and how it is integrated with the NSX environment.

Chapter 13 covers different NSX Multisite solution, NSX Federation, its architecture, and how it is onboarded and managed in NSX environment.

Chapter 14 covers different features provided by NSX to monitor and manage the NSX environment effectively and efficiently. It explains how to enable different authentication providers in the NSX environment to provide secure access to the environment along with RBAC to control the level of access.

Get a Free eBook

We hope you are enjoying your recently purchased book! Your feedback is incredibly valuable to us, and to all other readers looking for great books.

If you found this book helpful or enjoyable, we would truly appreciate it, if you could take a moment to leave a short review with a 5 star rating on Amazon. It helps us grow, and lets other readers discover our books.

As a thank you, we would love to send you a free digital copy of this book, and a **30%** discount code on your next cart value on our official websites:

www.orangeava.com

www.orangeava.in (For Indian Subcontinent)

☑ Here's how:

Leave a review for the book on Amazon.

Take a screenshot of your review, and send an email to **info@orangeava.com** (it can be just the confirmation screen).

Once, we receive your screenshot, we will send you the digital file, within 24 hours.

Thank you so much for your support – it means a lot to us!

Downloading the code bundles and colored images

Please follow the link or scan the QR code to download the ***Code Bundles*** of the book:

https://github.com/ava-orange-education/Ultimate-VMware-NSX-for-Professionals

The code bundles and images of the book are also hosted on ***https://rebrand.ly/bc45e5***

In case there's an update to the code, it will be updated on the existing GitHub repository.

Errata

We take immense pride in our work at **Orange Education Pvt Ltd,** and follow best practices to ensure the accuracy of our content to provide an indulging reading experience to our subscribers. Our readers are our mirrors, and we use their inputs to reflect and improve upon human errors, if any, that may have occurred during the publishing processes involved. To let us maintain the quality and help us reach out to any readers who might be having difficulties due to any unforeseen errors, please write to us at :
errata@orangeava.com

Your support, suggestions, and feedback are highly appreciated.

DID YOU KNOW

Did you know that Orange Education Pvt Ltd offers eBook versions of every book published, with PDF and ePub files available? You can upgrade to the eBook version at **www.orangeava.com** and as a print book customer, you are entitled to a discount on the eBook copy. Get in touch with us at: **info@orangeava.com** for more details.

At **www.orangeava.com**, you can also read a collection of free technical articles, sign up for a range of free newsletters, and receive exclusive discounts and offers on AVA™ Books and eBooks.

PIRACY

If you come across any illegal copies of our works in any form on the internet, we would be grateful if you would provide us with the location address or website name. Please contact us at **info@orangeava.com** with a link to the material.

ARE YOU INTERESTED IN AUTHORING WITH US?

If there is a topic that you have expertise in, and you are interested in either writing or contributing to a book, please write to us at **business@orangeava.com**. We are on a journey to help developers and tech professionals to gain insights on the present technological advancements and innovations happening across the globe and build a community that believes Knowledge is best acquired by sharing and learning with others. Please reach out to us to learn what our audience demands and how you can be part of this educational reform. We also welcome ideas from tech experts and help them build learning and development content for their domains.

REVIEWS

Please leave a review. Once you have read and used this book, why not leave a review on the site that you purchased it from? Potential readers can then see and use your unbiased opinion to make purchase decisions. We at Orange Education would love to know what you think about our products, and our authors can learn from your feedback. Thank you!

For more information about Orange Education, please visit **www.orangeava.com**.

Table of Contents

CHAPTER 1

Introduction to NSX Datacenter

Introduction

Before we start with the world of **SDN (Software Defined Networking)** or VMware's offering for SDN called **NSX,** Let's take a step back and understand the challenges with traditional physical networking. If I ask you as an application developer with you being a Network Engineer, I want to deploy multi-tier applications (could be a monolithic or container base) with components in their own broadcast domain, a firewall applied to every component with centralized management, capability for automation to provision network services on demand as and when required and ask you to prepare the underlying network infrastructure for application; these requirements from application team become very tough and challenging very soon.

But what if we had a magic wand, which we can wave and solve all these challenges? Well, cheesy lines aside, virtualization is the key to all these questions. We have solved similar challenges with compute and storage in the datacenter and by moving physical networking into software construct, we can achieve the same level of automation and flexibility with our Networking as well. So, fasten your seatbelts as we drive on the path to virtualize Networks. This chapter discusses current challenges with physical networks, how SDN can be an answer to these challenges and more specifically VMware SDN offering NSX.

Structure

In this chapter, we will discuss the following topics:

- Challenges with Physical Networks
- Introducing SDN
  - o Different models of SDN
- Introducing NSX – A VMware SDN Solution
- NSX Architecture
  - o Management Plane
  - o Control Plane
  - o Data Plane

Challenges with Physical Networks

Networks are analogous to veins in the human body like veins carry blood from different organs back and forth similarly as their core functionality, Networks provide connectivity between different components in a datacenter. Apart from connecting different components together, networks also provide some other key services in a datacenter including but not limited to:

- Layer 2 communication
- Layer 3 connectivity
- Firewall services
- NAT and VPN services
- Load Balancing services, and so on.

Initially, we started with different applications running on various physical servers housed in a datacenter. In case a developer requires to run an application on different hardware, it would take time to procure hardware, set it up in the datacenter and have the operating system ready to run the application. In such cases, physical networks were able to keep up with the speed and requirements of the application. But with the evolution of virtualization and the rise of **SDDC (Software Defined Datacenter),** physical networks are lagging behind. Make no mistake, we still require physical networks to connect different components together even in an SDDC, but like the example, in the Introduction, there are new challenges that have arisen with physical networks.

Traffic Hairpinning

Traffic hairpinning or pinning is forcing traffic to flow through a single point. This can result in a bottleneck of traffic affecting the performance of the system. In networking, devices are assigned an IP address so they can communicate with each other via IP address. If IP addresses belong to the same subnet, they can communicate with each other directly. But if their IP address belongs to a different subnet, we need a router or L3 device that can forward the packet to the correct subnet known as the default gateway. For physical workloads, it is fine to keep the default gateway on one or more routers but it becomes an issue for virtual workloads.

Imagine, two Virtual Machines sitting on the same physical server, in order to talk to each other they have to traverse the whole network path due to traffic hairpinned to the default gateway. The following *Figure 1.1* shows an example where two virtual machines are running on same hypervisor but belongs to different subnets have traffic hairpinned to default gateway.

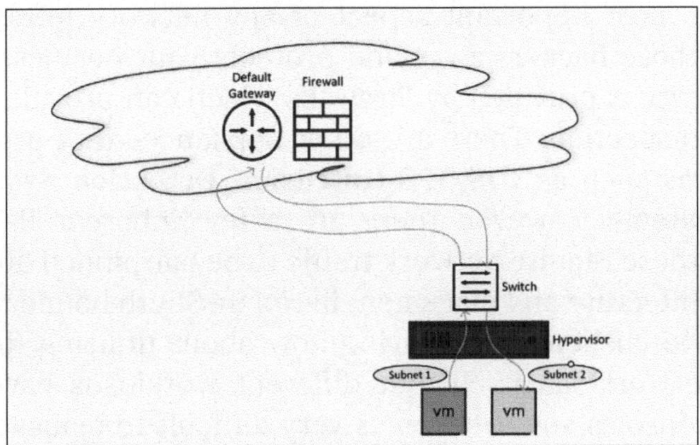

Figure 1.1: *Traffic Hairpinning in Virtual Workload*

Using firewalls or other security appliances such as IDS/IPS results in similar hairpinning of traffic affecting the performance of the application in case of non-optimal network design.

Speed and Agility

Physical networks are not capable to keep up with the speed and agility of SDDC (Software Defined Datacenter). In today's world, there is an ever-changing requirement from businesses to roll out new features and be on top of the competition. This requires faster provisioning of applications and a requirement to freely move an application from one environment to another. Server Virtualization, storage virtualization and Containers have enabled IT for faster provisioning of applications and application mobility but physical networks are holding them back. Let's take the same example from the introduction of the chapter. I need to create new subnet domains on demand for my application components, create new firewall rules and provide new load balancing services in order for the application to be up and running. How long do you think it would need to enable all these requirements; Days, Weeks or Months? It would not be an acceptable answer for businesses, they need it to be done now. What about using different devices and systems, they may use different protocols and standards, which can make it difficult for the administrator to manage all these devices. And then there is a limit to physical networks about how much can they expand, for example, 4096 VLANs limit per LAN.

Security

Security is the most important aspect of any network infrastructure. This is what keeps those hackers away and protects your business. In traditional networks, security is provided by Firewalls which can provide Layer 3, Layer 4 and Layer 7 inspection. There are other appliances that provide advanced security features such as **IDS/IPS (Intrusion Detection System/Intrusion Prevention System).** However, there are a few inherent flaws with these systems. First, these require network traffic to be hairpinned due to their non-distributed architecture and placement in North-South bound network traffic. Now, it could be challenged by saying how about utilizing firewall services directly on the workload itself. But different workloads have different OS and different consoles and it becomes very difficult to manage rules without any centralized management. Second, most of these Firewalls or Intelligent Systems are very good at acting as perimeter firewalls. They can stop most of the security attacks but not all.

Most of the cyber-attacks in recent years have a common characteristic – Lateral Movement. Once a malicious vector gets access to a system inside a datacenter, they use various vulnerabilities to exploit and move malicious code from server to server also known as East-West movement or lateral movement.

Using a perimeter-only strategy makes it extremely difficult to prohibit lateral movements, and traditional firewalling makes it exceedingly expensive to safeguard traffic across all workloads in a datacenter.

Introducing SDN

SDN or more commonly Software Defined Networking is a networking approach where Control Plane (Decision Maker) is separated from **Forwarding Plane or Data Plane** (Who transmits data). This approach is different from traditional networking in the sense that instead of using dedicated physical devices such as switches or routers to control traffic, it uses software to either create and control a new Network Infrastructure on top of physical networks known as a Virtual Network or control traditional hardware.

The key difference between SDN and traditional networking is infrastructure. While traditional networking is a hardware-based approach, SDN is a software-based approach. In an SDN architecture, the control plane is centralized and implemented in software, while the data/forwarding plane is implemented in network devices or servers. This separation allows for greater flexibility and programmability, as the control plane can be easily updated or modified without requiring changes to the physical network infrastructure. This allows network engineers to manage the entire network infrastructure from a centralized user interface and enable them to control the network, change configuration settings, provision resources or increase network capacity.

Different models of SDN

The key aspect of SDN is the separation of the Control Plane and Data Plane. This can be achieved in different ways which constitute different models of SDN.

Open SDN

Network administrators use a protocol like OpenFlow to control the behavior of virtual and physical switches at the data plane level.

SDN by APIs

Instead of using an open protocol, **APIs (Application Programming Interfaces)** controls the flow of data over the network across multiple devices.

SDN Overlay Model

Another type of software-defined networking runs a virtual network on top of an existing hardware infrastructure, creating dynamic tunnels to different on-premise and remote data centers. The virtual network allocates bandwidth over a variety of channels and assigns devices to each channel, leaving the physical network untouched.

Hybrid SDN

This model combines software-defined networking with traditional networking protocols in one environment to support different functions on a network. Standard networking protocols continue to direct some traffic, while SDN takes on responsibility for other traffic, allowing network administrators to introduce SDN in stages to a legacy environment.

Introducing NSX – A VMware SDN Solution

VMware NSX is part of a wider VMware Virtual Cloud Network framework. In essence, **VCN (Virtual Cloud Network)** is a VMware framework to apply consistent network and security policies to different types of workloads which could be virtual machines, containers or applications running on different types of platforms such as hypervisors, bare metal servers or cloud platforms. VCN is all software in nature and requires no dedicated or specialized hardware to run, as long as minimum requirements can be fulfilled VCN can be deployed as a software layer. This software layer provides connectivity between different datacenters, cloud platforms or edge infrastructure and helps in deploying consistent security policies which help in overcoming challenges posed by traditional physical networks. Apart from providing networking and security, VCN includes several other solutions which are key to providing extensibility, integration, automation and consistency. *Figure 1.2* captures key solutions part of VCN portfolio

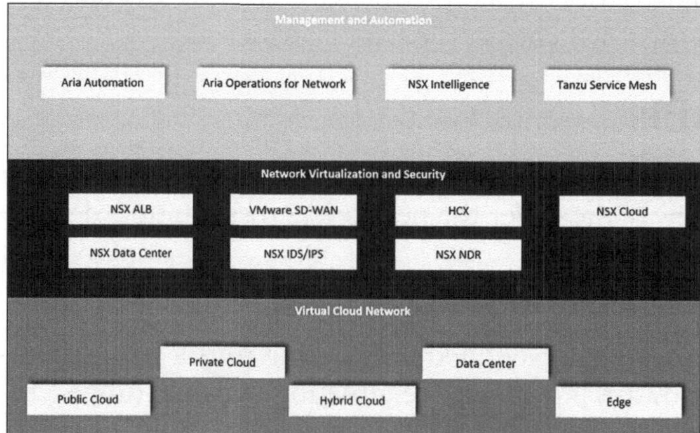

Figure 1.2: *VMware Virtual Cloud Network Portfolio*

Key solutions part of the VMware Virtual Cloud Network portfolio are:

- **NSX Data Center** – VMware solution for providing consistent networking and security policies across multiple applications and workloads running on different platforms
- **NSX Advance Load Balancer (ALB)** – VMware distributed load balancing solution for virtual machines, containers, bare metal servers or workloads running on the cloud
- **Hybrid Cloud Extension (HCX)** – Provide the capability to migrate workloads from legacy infrastructure to the cloud with minimal downtime
- **NSX Network Detection & Response (NDR)** – Advance threat detection and analysis services provided by VMware for proactive response
- **NSX IDS/IPS** – VMware advanced fully distributed Layer 7 intelligent threat detection and prevention services part of NSX solution
- **NSX Cloud** – SaaS offering for NSX services which delivers networking and security services for applications running in public cloud natively.
- **Tanzu Service Mesh** – Provide consistent networking and security management across different Kubernetes platforms from a central console
- **Aria Operations for Network** – Provide visibility, monitoring for virtual and physical networks and based on flows captured provides recommendations for distributed firewall in the NSX environment

Note: Key solutions listed above NSX IDS/IPS, NDR, and ALB are covered in this book as part of NSX and not as a standalone product. Other key solutions are outside the scope of this book.

NSX Data Center

NSX Data Center is a VMware SDN offering for networking and security and is based on four fundamental attributes:

- **Policy and Consistency** – NSX allows the user to provide desired state configuration with the help of API or UI which enables automation for fast pace business requirements. It has various controls and inventories in place to keep the system in a consistent state across different platforms.
- **Connectivity** – It provides logical switching and distributed routing capabilities separated from the management plane and control plane without being tied to a single compute domain. For example, multiple vCenter can be integrated with a single NSX to provide consistent networking across different clusters. It can further extend connectivity to different sites, public clouds or containers via specific implementations.

- **Security** – It allows for distributed security across multiple workloads but still provides centralized management for security policies. This helps in providing consistent security policy on different workloads be it Virtual machines, containers or applications running in private or public cloud to maintain correct security posture.
- **Visibility** – It provides a wide variety of toolsets such as Traceflow, Live Traffic Analysis, Spanning, metric collection, and events all available in a single place greatly reducing operation complexities.

NSX Architecture

VMware NSX Data Center is based on the Overlay SDN model and provides consistent networking and security services in the IT environment. It implements these services including but not limited to Switching, Routing, NAT, VPN, firewalling, etc. in software hence bringing networking services into software construct. Further, these services can be provisioned on demand in different combinations to create different network environments as per application requirements with tremendous agility. NSX implements all these features with the help of three different functional planes. These are:

- Management Plane
- Control Plane
- Data Plane

Figure 1.3 shows different components which made up these functional planes which are covered in depth in upcoming section.

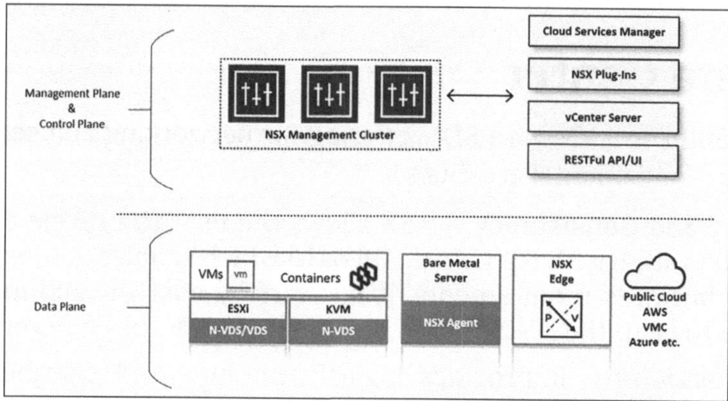

Figure 1.3: *NSX High-Level Architecture Components*

Before NSX-T 2.4 (Before version 4.x, NSX was named as NSX-T), Management plane and Control plane were deployed as separate appliance. However, starting

NSX-T 2.4, the Management plane and Control plane are merged into a single appliance known as the Manager Appliance and Data Plane is implemented with the help of transport nodes – more to be discussed in the upcoming section.

Note: Starting NSX 4.0, KVM is no longer supported as a transport node. Also, VIO is the only supported OpenStack implementation with NSX 4.0 and above.

Management Plane

The management plane is the point of entry into the NSX environment. This is where cloud platforms, management tools or API clients interact with NSX using API queries or we as a user can interact either via Graphical User Interface or API queries. The primary responsibilities of the management plane are to store user configurations, handle any queries and perform operational tasks such as pushing policies to the control plane for realization, storing configuration in the database, etc.

The management plane is implemented by NSX Manager Appliance in an NSX environment. NSX Manager provides a centralized interface to view and manage NSX deployments. As the NSX Manager appliance is the single point of entry in an NSX environment, in order to avoid a single point of failure, it is deployed as a group of three nodes to form NSX Management Cluster which provides high availability and scalability in an NSX environment.

Key functionalities of the NSX Management Cluster include:

- The entry point for user configurations either via RESTFul APIs or GUI (Graphical User Interface)
- Store desired user configuration in distributed database
- Push desired user configuration to control plane for realization
- Communicate with Data Nodes to retrieve metrics as well as realized configuration

NSX Management Cluster

As stated earlier, the NSX Management cluster is formed by grouping three NSX Manager appliances in a cluster. Prior to NSX-T 2.4, NSX Manager and NSX Controllers were separated by their roles and deployed as separate appliances. So, in total four appliances were needed, one for management and three for controllers but still it was a single point of failure of the management plane. Starting NSX-T 2.4, Management Plane components and Control Plane components merged into a single appliance eliminating a single point of failure for the management plane.

NSX Manager cluster primarily runs the following functions:

- Manager Role
- Policy Role
- Controller Role
- Distributed Persistent Database

Manager and Policy Role provides management plane functionality whereas the Controller role as the name suggests servers control plane functions. All the desired configuration is saved in a distributed database which is replicated across all three nodes, providing the same configuration view to all nodes in a cluster. *Figure* 1.4 depicts different roles which make up Management Plane and their cluster groups within a NSX Management Cluster.

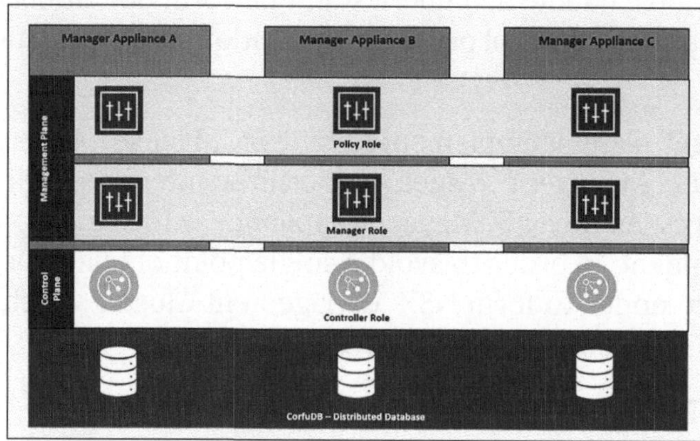

Figure 1.4: *NSX Management Cluster Components*

NSX Manager appliance is available in different sizes to be deployed based on different requirements. The following table highlights different options available to deploy an NSX manager appliance:

Appliance Size	Memory	CPU	Disk Space
Extra Small VM	8 GB	2 vCPU	300 GB
Small VM	16 GB	4 vCPU	300 GB
Medium VM	24 GB	6 vCPU	300 GB
Large VM	48 GB	12 vCPU	300 GB

Table 1.1: *NSX Manager Appliance Size*

Note: Extra Small VM resource size is only for the Cloud Services Manager appliance.

Small VM appliance is for lab or Proof-of-Concept deployment and should not be used for production deployments.

NSX Consumption Model

NSX manager provides two different models to interact with the NSX environment or consume NSX services. These two different models are handled by two different roles:

- Policy Role
- Manager Role

Primarily, you will be working with Policy Role which is a declarative state configuration model whereas the Manager role is an imperative state configuration model. Let's take an example to understand more about the Policy role and Manager role. Imagine going to a pizzeria and ordering a margarita pizza. We tell the pizzeria about our choice of margarita pizza and the size of the order whether it will be small, medium or large. We are providing the desired state of our order and we leave it up to the pizzeria to figure out the recipe, ingredients and step-by-step details to create a desired pizza. The policy role handles the desired end-state order from the user and then hands it over to the manager role to figure out the step-by-step process. So, we order through the Policy role and then the backend of the pizzeria is handled by the Manager role to figure out how to achieve the desired end state. To summarize, In Policy Model or Policy role we provide desired state whereas in the Manager role we need to provide step-by-step configurations.

NSX Policy: NSX Manager's default UI mode is policy mode. Some of the key functions provided by NSX Policy role:

- It provides a centralized interface for configuring networking and security policies across the environment
- It takes the desired state configuration from users in NSX UI or can be accessed via API URI */policy/api/*
- It enables the user to specify the final desired state of the system without worrying about the current state or underlying implementation steps

NSX Manager: NSX Manager UI is disabled by default and is deprecated from NSX-T 3.2. It is temporarily used to address deployment created via Manager mode or upgrade from older NSX-T versions. NSX-T 3.2 has introduced a policy promotion tool to migrate configuration from manager mode to policy mode. Other key functions provided by NSX Manager Role:

- It installs and prepares the data plane components
- It retrieves and validates configurations from NSX Policy and pushes the configuration to the control plane
- Also, it retrieves the metrics from data plane components

Using Policy vs. Manager UI

It is always recommended to use Policy UI for any new deployments as Manager UI is deprecated and new features are implemented in Policy UI only. However, for a few use cases, the use of Manager UI might be required. The following table highlights such use cases where Manager UI is required.

<table>
<tr><th>Policy Mode</th><th>Manager Mode</th></tr>
<tr><td>For any new deployments should use policy mode
NSX Federation is supported on Policy mode only</td><td>Any deployment created using Advanced mode</td></tr>
<tr><td>NSX Cloud Deployments</td><td>Deployment where integration with another plugin is required such as Openstack or NSX Container Plugin</td></tr>
<tr><td>Networking features - VPN, DNS Services, DNS Zones, are supported in Policy mode only</td><td></td></tr>
<tr><td>Security features available in Policy mode only:<ul><li>Endpoint Protection</li><li>Network Introspection</li><li>Context Profiles<ul><li>L7 applications</li><li>FQDN</li></ul></li></ul>New Distributed Firewall and Gateway Firewall Layout<ul><li>Categories</li><li>Auto service rules</li><li>Drafts</li></ul></td><td>Security features available in Manager mode only:<ul><li>Bridge Firewall</li></ul></td></tr>
</table>

Table 1.2: *Using Policy UI or Manager UI*

NSX Manager Communication Workflow

We have discussed a lot about different roles and components in the NSX Manager appliance, so let's map them out and see how they interact with each other. *Figure 1.5* shows key services part of NSX Manager and how they communicate with each other to take desired state configuration from user, validate it and save it in database.

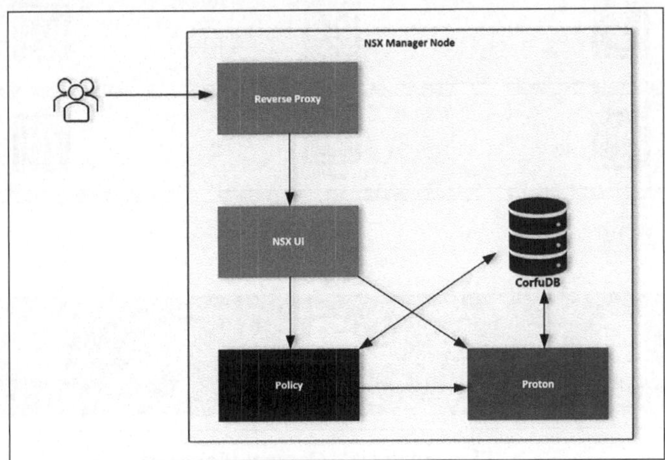

Figure 1.5: *NSX Manager Communication Workflow*

As a first step, the user accesses the UI or REST API which comes through Reverse Proxy on NSX Manager. Revery Proxy is the first point of entry with authentication and authorization capabilities. Configuration is then sent to Policy which in turn update CorfuDB which is our persistent distributed database to save desired configurations. The policy then sends configuration to Proton which is our manager role. Proton in turn validates all the configurations provided by Policy and updates the CorfuDB database. After validation and updating CorfuDB, Proton then sends the configuration to Control Plane.

Proton is one of the core components of NSX Manager and it is responsible for various key functionalities such as logical switching, logical routing, distributed firewall, etc. and both Proton and Policy save their data in CorfuDB which is replicated to other nodes in the cluster to provide consistent view to all nodes in NSX cluster.

Control Plane

Control Plane consists of the Controller role whose primary function is to maintain the realized state of the system based on desired state configuration received from the Manager role or Proton. The controller role performs this function by computing the runtime state based on the configuration from Proton and then pushing the stateless configuration to the data plane. *Figure 1.6* highlights component of control plane.

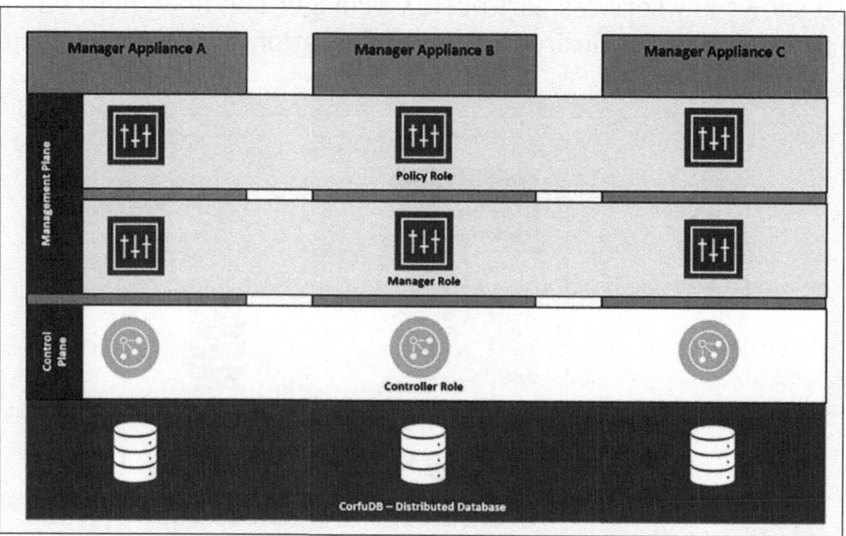

Figure 1.6: *NSX Control Plane*

Another key function of the Controller is to distribute topology information reported by data plane nodes and maintain the realized state configuration for the system. In NSX, the control plane functionality is achieved through a multi-tier approach and it is divided into two main parts, Central Control Plane and Local Control Plane as shown in *Figure 1.7*:

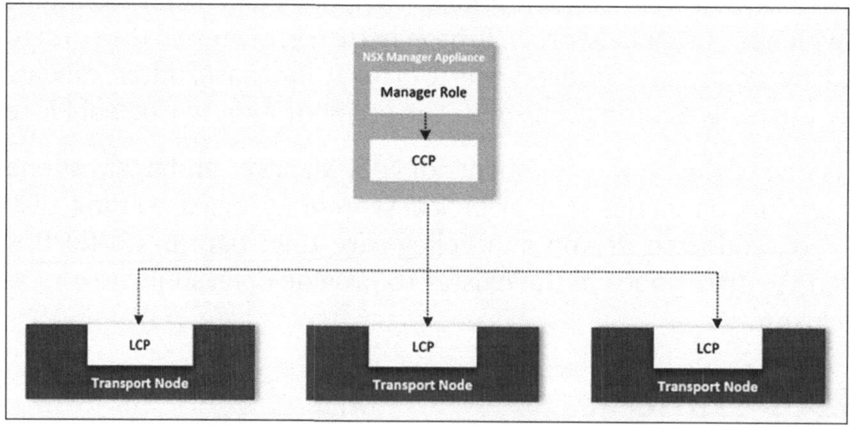

Figure 1.7: *NSX Control Plane Architecture*

- **Central Control Plane (CCP):** Central Control Plane or CCP resides on NSX Manager nodes and it is part of the Controller role. CCP is also implemented as a cluster form factor with a controller role running on all three NSX Manager nodes part of the cluster. This provides both high availability and load distribution within the control plane. As stated earlier, one of the primary functions of the controller role is to compute runtime state configuration and this is handled by CCP on NSX Manager nodes. Also, it distributes topology information reported by LCP running on data plane nodes to other CCP nodes so the same realized state is maintained across the environment.

  As CCP is logically separated from the data plane, any failure on the control plane doesn't affect data plane traffic or any user traffic is not passed to CCP avoiding any hairpinning.

- **Local Control Plane (CCP) –** Local Control Plane or LCP exists on each and every data plane node which can be ESXi host, Edge nodes or bare metal servers (more on data nodes covered in Section Data Plane). Its primary function is to program or configure kernel modules on data nodes and push stateless configuration to forwarding engines. It monitors the link status on local data nodes and provides any update in the forwarding engine to CCP.

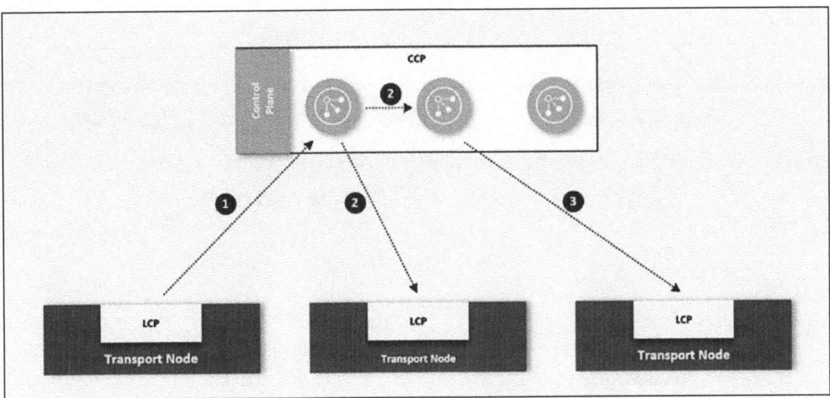

Figure 1.8: *Information distribution from LCP to CCP*

An important point to note here is each data plane node is communicating with a single control node. Any time a transport node or data node is initialized, it is assigned to a control node. CCP receives any configuration update from NSX Manager and pushes the information to the LCP of transport nodes. In *Figure 1.8*, transport node on left has a configuration update. How transport node on right receives these updates is shown in a multi-step process.

If any update or change occurs on a transport node, as a first step the LCP running on transport nodes updates its assigned control node or CCP running on a specific control node. In the second step, CCP further distributes these changes to other control nodes via the help of the distributed database. Also, any transport nodes assigned to the same CCP will receive the changes. In the last step, CCP running on other control nodes push changes to their respective assigned LCP. So, changes in any node are propagated to the entire NSX environment to keep it consistent. This distribution of workload is achieved with the help of process Sharding.

Sharding

Sharding is the process to distribute workload across multiple control plane nodes. NSX Management cluster is made up of three nodes with each node running a controller role and more specifically CCP. With the help of sharding, transport nodes or data nodes are divided equally among different CCP nodes and the CCP node is responsible for maintaining state information on data nodes that are assigned to it. This helps in dividing load across the NSX Management cluster and avoids high load or high resource usage on a specific node only. *Figure* 1.9 shows transport nodes assigned to a specific controller node to share load.

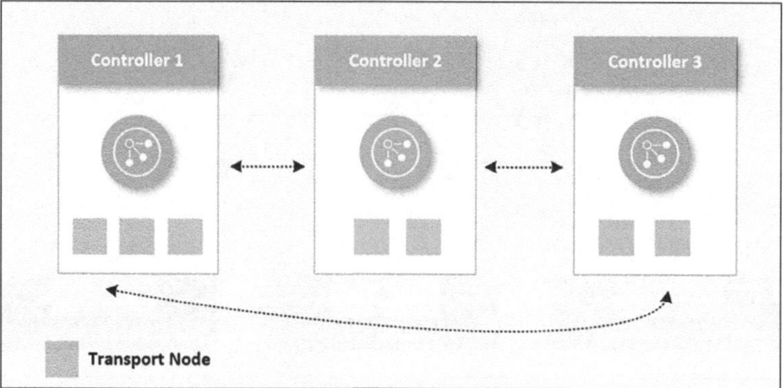

Figure 1.9: *Controller Sharding*

On a high level:

- The transport node is assigned to a specific CCP node for L2, L3 and distributed firewall rule configuration and distribution
- Each CCP node receives updates from both the Manager role and Data plane node but maintains state configuration on the specific transport node it has been assigned to.

But a question arises here – What if my controller got failed? What will happen to transport nodes assigned to failed controller node? Will it affect my data plane traffic?

The answer is pretty simple; we have separated our control plane from the data plane. So even if my controller node got failed, data plane traffic will remain unaffected and continues to flow without any effect. And there is a heartbeat running between all controller nodes so if one controller node gets failed, other controller nodes become aware of the failure and the sharding table is recalculated to again distribute the load among the remaining controller nodes.

Note: If two controller nodes or NSX Manager appliance get failed in a three-node cluster then Management Plane goes into a read-only state and no configuration changes can be performed.

Data Plane

The data plane is the most important component in the NSX environment as this is where actual packet processing is performed. It is completely distributed and stateless in nature as if any data node, for example, ESXi host gets failed all Virtual Machines running on a specific ESXi host get failed over to other hosts.

The data plane consists of Transport Nodes where TN (Transport Node) is the host who is running LCP (Local Control Plane) daemons and forwarding engines. NSX support different type of transport nodes and can be classified into two broad categories:

Host Transport Nodes

Host transport nodes are either Hypervisor or Bare metal servers which are prepared and configured for NSX to provide network and security to workloads or applications running on them. The most common host transport nodes are:

- **ESXi Host:** It provides a data plane function for different types of workloads such as VMs and containers. NSX implements a data plane on the ESXi host with the help of N-VDS (NSX Virtual Distributed Switch). Starting NSX-T 3.0, NSX can be directly installed on top of VDS v7 (vSphere Distributed Switch). Also, from NSX 4.0, N-VDS is no longer supported with ESXi.
- **KVM:** Starting NSX 4.0, KVM is no longer supported. However, in an earlier release, NSX-T installed N-VDS which is based on OVS (Open vSwitch) to provide data plane functions to VMs running on KVM.

- **Bare Metal Server:** NSX Agent or NSX third-party packages can be installed on bare metal servers running Windows or Linux to secure applications running on bare metal servers. Also, Bare Metal Server can be prepared as an Edge Transport Node to provide routing and network services to the NSX environment.

Edge Transport Nodes

Edge Nodes are special NSX appliances that are dedicated to run stateful and central network services that cannot be distributed in nature such as Gateway Firewall, N-S Routing, NAT or VPN, and so on. Edge TNs are grouped into a cluster to provide high availability and scalability for network services by abstracting and presenting compute resources as a pool of resources to centralized network services. Edge Transport Node can be deployed in two forms:

- **Edge VM Node:** As the name suggests, the Edge transport node is deployed as a virtual machine in a vSphere environment. This is the most common deployment and can cater to most business requirements.
- **Bare Metal Edge Node:** Instead of deploying a virtual machine, a bare metal server can be instantiated as an Edge transport node. Bare metal edge nodes are usually deployed where bandwidth requirements are much higher than a VM form factor can provide.

Some of the key functions provided by Data Plane are:

- It forwards the packets based on the configuration provided by the local control plane which in turn is provided by the central control plane based on the user-desired configuration
- It processes packets based on various flow tables and rules which are populated by the control plane
- It reports the topology information back to the control plane with help of the local control plane which is further distributed to other data plane nodes
- It monitors the status of links and tunnels and in case of any failure and performs failover
- Last but not least, it maintains statistics and metrics at the packet level which helps in determining resource utilization and different events

Transport Node Communication Path

As we stated earlier in Management Plane and Control Plane sections, part of their function is to communicate with data plane nodes, collect metrics or statistics and push stateless configurations respectively. Instead of the Manager from the

Management plane and CCP from the Control plane communicating directly with the data node or more appropriately transport node, they use a proxy called APH (Appliance Proxy Hub) to communicate with the transport node. *Figure* 1.10 highlights different ports and services responsible for communication between NSX Manager node and Transport node.

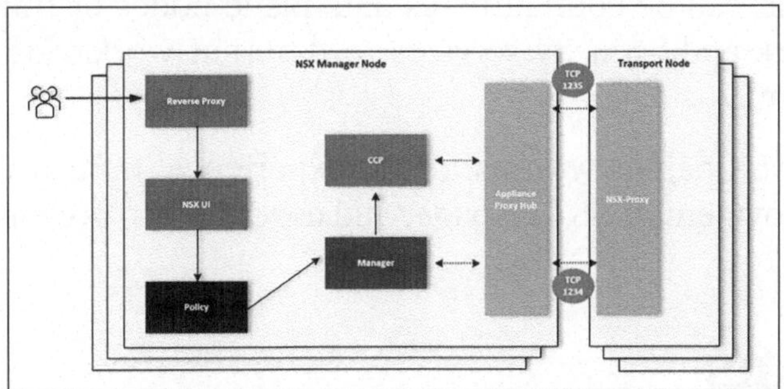

Figure 1.10: *Transport Node communication with Manager Node*

APH (Appliance Proxy Hub) runs as a service on the NSX Manager node and provides secure connectivity to the transport node based on the NSX-RPC protocol. Similar to APH on the NSX Manager node, NSX-Proxy runs on a transport node that communicates with APH to provide statistics or receive configurations. NSX preparation or initial configuration is handled by the Manager running on the NSX Manager node and when a transport node is added to NSX, it sends configuration to APH which in turn talks to NSX-Proxy over TCP Port 1234 to configure the data plane on the local node. Post preparation of NSX over data node, NSX-Proxy collects stats and metrics from the local node and sends it to APH over TCP Port 1234 for further analysis by the Manager.

Similarly, CCP pushes stateless configurations computed based on desired user configurations to APH who in turn sends it to NSX-Proxy over TCP Port 1235 for it to apply on forwarding engines. Also, any topology reported by a local node is communicated by NSX-Proxy to APH over TCP Port 1235 which further communicates information to CCP.

As there are multiple NSX Manager nodes and Transport Nodes, each establishes its own communication channel over a specified port and all traffic passing between different nodes is secure and encrypted in nature.

Conclusion

In this chapter, we discussed challenges with traditional physical networks and how VMware NSX can overcome those challenges without the need for any specific hardware with help of Software Defined Networking. Like any network device, NSX can be divided into three functional planes which are logically separated from each other to avoid effect on one plane due to the failure of another. Policy and Manager roles are key components of the Management Plane whereas CCP and LCP constituents control the plane. NSX supports a wide array of platforms that can be configured as data plane nodes or transport nodes to provide Network and Security services to different workloads or applications running on them.

Real fun with NSX begins with hands on experience. In next chapter, we will begin with deployment of NSX manager and cover how to prepare infrastructure for NSX.

Key Terms

- **VLAN (Virtual Local Area Network):** A group of devices logically segmented in same broadcast domain on a switched network
- **NAT (Network Address Translation):** It is a method to map multiple or single private IP address to a public IP address before passing traffic over network
- **SDN (Software Defined Networking):** A networking approach to separate control plane from data plane with help of software and can be implemented in different models
- **Overlay:** Virtual network created on top of physical network to create different network services with help of encapsulation and tunnels
- **NSX Manager Node:** A specialized appliance provide by VMware to implement virtual network in datacenter. Also, it serves management and control plane functions
- **NSX Manager Cluster:** A group of three NSX Manager nodes to provide high availability and scalability to management plane and control plane
- **Policy Role:** A declarative based approach which take user inputs in form of desired state configurations
- **Manager Role:** A imperative based approach which provide step by step configuration to achieve desired state configuration
- **CorfuDB:** A persistent distributed database to save configurations and inventory
- **CCP (Central Control Plane):** Controller role runs on NSX Manager node and compute stateless configurations from desired user configurations provided by manager to further push to local control plane

- **LCP (Local Control Plane):** Controller role running on transport node helps in pushing stateless configuration to forwarding engine to achieve realized state configuration
- **Transport Node:** Any host such as hypervisor or bare metal server prepared for NSX running LCP daemons and forwarding engines
- **APH (Appliance Proxy Hub):** Service running on NSX Manager node responsible for communication between NSX Manager node and transport node

Chapter 2
Deploying NSX Infrastructure

Introduction

In the previous chapter, we reviewed NSX architecture on a high level and different key components in an NSX environment such as **Manager**, **Controller** and **Transport Nodes.** This is all good but the real fun begins with deployments. This chapter covers the deployment of NSX Manager, attaching it to a **vCenter** server and most important preparing data nodes. Key steps in preparing NSX data nodes are:

- Creating Transport Zone
- Creating uplink profiles
- Preparing ESXi host for NSX

This chapter covers all the preceding steps to prepare your NSX environment in addition to deploying NSX Manager. Starting NSX 4.x, KVM is no longer supported, hence this chapter covers NSX infrastructure deployment and preparation for the vSphere environment only. KVM preparation for the NSX environment is out of the scope of this book but documentation for the same has been provided in the References section.

Structure

In this chapter, we will cover the following topics:

- Deploying NSX Manager Cluster on vSphere
- Deploying NSX Manager

- NSX Manager Base Configuration
- Deploying Additional NSX Manager Node
- Creating NSX Management Cluster using CLI
- Configuring Virtual IP for Cluster
- Validating NSX Management Cluster

- Preparing NSX Data Plane
  - Architecture of Transport Nodes
  - Transport Zones
  - Uplinks or pNICs
  - Uplink Profile
  - Transport Node Profile

  Preparing ESXi Host as Transport Node

Deploying NSX Manager Cluster on vSphere

Before configuring or utilizing NSX networking in the environment, it is important to set up a management plane as it provides entry into the NSX environment. As covered earlier, the management plane consists of three Manager appliances grouped in a cluster which are deployed as **Open Virtualization Appliance (OVA)** appliances either on standalone ESXi hosts or ESXi hosts managed by a vCenter server. The recommended way to deploy NSX Manager is through the vCenter server as the vCenter server can deploy any virtual machine that NSX Manager directs it to thus removing manual overhead. In a nutshell, first NSX Manager is deployed using the OVA file provided by VMware and post successful deployment of NSX Manager, the vCenter server is registered with NSX Manager as a compute Manager. Subsequent NSX Managers are deployed from within NSX UI to create a three-node management cluster. As a next step, prerequisites for Data Plane preparation are configured such as Transport Zone, uplink profile, etc. and ESXi host is prepared as Transport Nodes. Last but not least, edge nodes are deployed and configured in an Edge Cluster to provide centralized network services. *Figure* 2.1 shows the steps to implement NSX in the vSphere environment workflow.

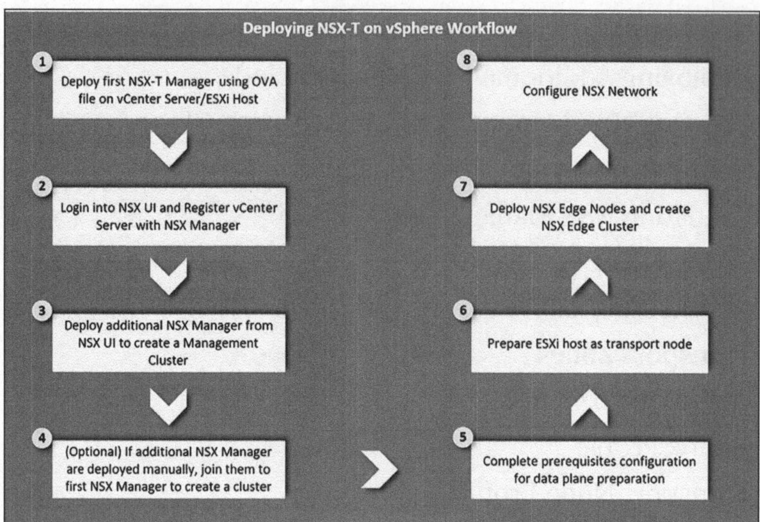

Figure 2.1: *Deploying NSX on vSphere Workflow*

All the steps mentioned in *Figure* 2.1 are covered in detail in the subsequent sections.

Note: Registration of the vCenter server is required if additional NSX Manager nodes need to be deployed from NSX UI, otherwise additional NSX Manager nodes can be deployed using the OVA file and form management cluster with help of NSX CLI.

Deploying NSX Manager

NSX Manager is provided by VMware as an **OVA (Open Virtualization Appliance)** template which can be deployed in a vSphere environment using UI or in an automated fashion through APIs or scripts. NSX Manager can be deployed either directly on a standalone ESXi host or using vCenter server-managed ESXi hosts, however appropriate permissions are required to successfully deploy NSX Manager in either option. VMware provides different components bundled together in a single appliance template, so the same template can be used to deploy CSM, NSX Manager or Global Manager (required for federation, covered in detail in *Chapter* 13, *NSX Multisite Deployment*) and once NSX Manager is deployed, Edge VM or NSX VIB installation on ESXi host can be done from same NSX Manager without the need of extra binaries. The step-by-step process to deploy the NSX Manager in the vSphere environment using the vCenter server are as follows:

Step 1: Download the **`NSX Manager OVA`** file from VMware using Customer Connect Portal.

Step 2: Login into the **`vCenter`** server with the user account assigned with proper permissions. Select the **Cluster** or **ESXi host** on which to deploy NSX Manager and either right-click or go to **`Actions`** and select **`Deploy OVF Template.`** Select **`Local File`** and browse the directory containing the OVA file. *Figure* 2.2 shows the dialog box with NSX Manager OVA selected.

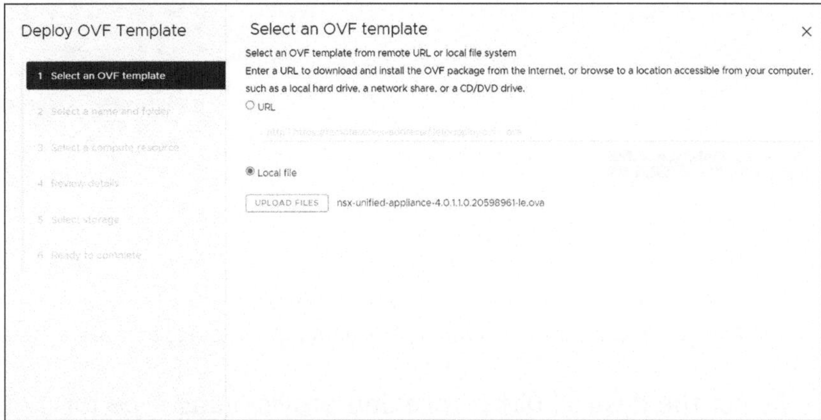

***Figure 2.2**: Select an OVF Template dialog box*

Step 3: Click **`Next`** and provide an appropriate name for NSX Manager VM which will be deployed on the ESXi host and optionally select VM folder to place NSX Manager VM.

Step 4: Click **`Next`** and select **`compute resource`** either Cluster or specific ESXi host to run NSX Manager VM.

Step 5: Clicking **`Next`** presents the **`Review`** screen with details about the OVA template file such as **`Vendor, Version, Product`** and **`Publisher`** information. Review the information and click **`Next.`**

Step 6: The next dialog box named **`Configuration`** presents four different size options to select. As covered in *Chapter 1, Introduction to NSX Datacenter*, these are:

a. **`ExtraSmall:`** Only supported for Cloud Service Manager Role

b. **`Small:`** Only supported for Global Manager production deployment. It can be used for POC or Lab deployment of NSX

Manager.

c. **Medium:** Supports up to 128 ESXi hosts (at the time of writing with NSX version 4.0.1) in a production NSX Manager cluster deployment

d. **Large:** Supports up to 1024 ESXi hosts (at the time of writing with NSX version 4.0.1) in a production NSX Manager cluster deployment

Figure 2.3 shows the **Configuration** screen with the preceding options.

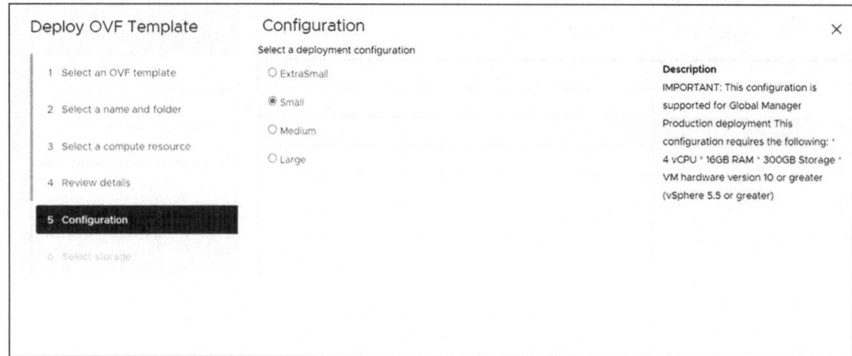

Figure 2.3: *Configuration dialog box with different size options*

Step 7: Select the desired **Datastore** and provisioning type for storage and **vSphere Port group** for network connectivity in subsequent options and click **Next.**

Step 8: The next screen named **Customize Template** is the most important screen as it will take input of all properties for NSX Manager which are:

e. **System GRUB Root User Password**: Set password for the GRUB boot menu to avoid tempering of boot options

f. **System Root User Password**: Set root password for NSX Manager appliance, provide shell access to VM

g. **CLI admin User Password**: Set admin password for NSX Manager, provide admin access to NSX environment

h. **CLI audit User Password:** Set audit user password for NSX Manager, provides read-only access to NSX environment, this can be setup later on from within NSX UI

i. **Hostname:** Hostname of NSX Manager accessible over the network

j. **`Rolename`**: Select the appropriate role to deploy NSX Manager, Cloud Service Manager or Global Manager

k. **`Management Network Details`**: Provide IP details to access NSX Manager over the network.

l. **`DNS Details`**: Setup DNS Server IP and Search List to resolve the hostname to IP within NSX Manager

m. **`Service Configuration`**: Select if SSH services should be enabled or not as per requirement. Important is to set up the NTP server correctly to avoid any issues in the network due to time drift between different components.

Step 9: Click **`Next`** and this is the final screen. Review all details and click **`Finish`** to start deployment of the first NSX Manager. *Figure* 2.4 shows the **`Ready to Complete`** screen.

Figure 2.4: *Ready to Complete screen with details entered earlier*

Step 10: It takes a few minutes depending upon the underlying hardware to complete the deployment of the NSX Manager appliance VM and after the NSX Manager is deployed, either right-click on the **`VM`** in the vCenter server or go to **`Actions, Power`** and click **`Power On`**.

Step 11: Preconfigured first boot scripts configure NSX Manager with the information provided earlier. *Figure* 2.5 shows such scripts in action.

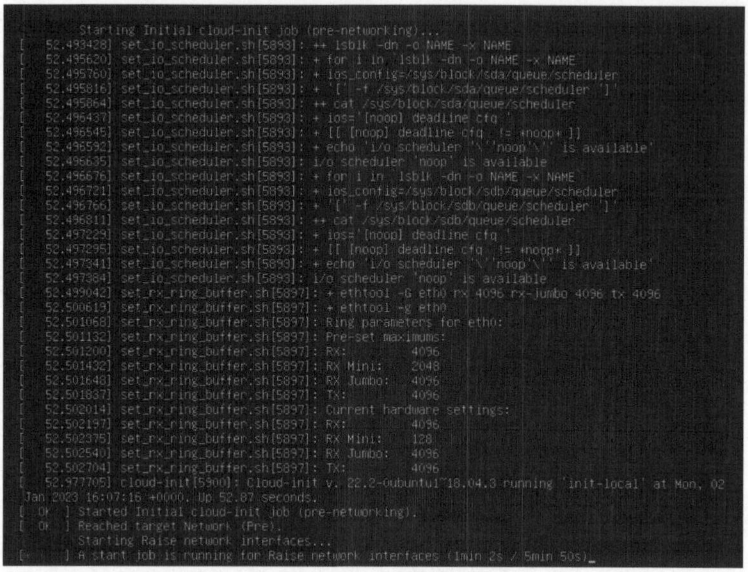

Figure 2.5: *First boot of NSX Manager Appliance*

Note: Screenshots for configurations or deployment provided in this book are based on **vSphere 7.0 Update 3** and **NSX 4.0.1.1**. There can be a few UI elements changes between different versions hence reader discretion is advised.

Congratulations! You have successfully deployed your first NSX Manager. However, we have just started with deployment and still, a long way needs to be covered. So, grab a cup of tea or coffee as in the next section we dive into base configurations of our newly deployed NSX Manager.

NSX Manager Base Configuration

After the first NSX Manager appliance is deployed there are a few initial configurations that need to be completed first before proceeding further. Some of these initial configurations are optional in nature but recommended to complete, these include but are not limited to registering the vCenter server with NSX Manager, installing licenses and deploying additional NSX Manager nodes to form a cluster. Unlike NSX-V or NSX for vSphere which support only one vCenter per NSX-V Manager in NSX Manager multiple compute Managers (or vCenter server) can be integrated up to a maximum of 16 in a Large deployment and 2 in Medium deployment. The benefit of registering the vCenter server with NSX Manager is NSX polls the vCenter server to collect cluster information for Data Plane preparation. Also, in order to deploy additional NSX Manager nodes or Edge nodes from NSX itself, it requires a compute Manager. But in order to perform these configurations, access to NSX Manager is needed which can be achieved in multiple ways.

Tip: Use VMware Configuration Maximum Tool to understand maximum supported for each component by visiting link https://configmax.esp.vmware.com/.

Accessing NSX Manager

NSX Manager can be accessed in the following ways:

- Through supported web browser by logging into NSX UI
- Through CLI
- Through API

The most commonly used method is a web browser where the user can perform configuration in an easy-to-use GUI (graphical user interface) interface. This is more involving in nature as the configuration has to be completed in a step-by-step fashion.

Accessing NSX Manager using NSX UI

Step 1: Open a web browser and enter the **FQDN (Fully Qualified Domain Name)** or IP Address of the NSX Manager appliance.

Step 2: On the `credential` prompt, provide a `username` and `password` to login into NSX Manager. If this is the first time login, provide `admin` as username and password as set earlier during deployment to log in. *Figure* 2.6 shows such a prompt in action.

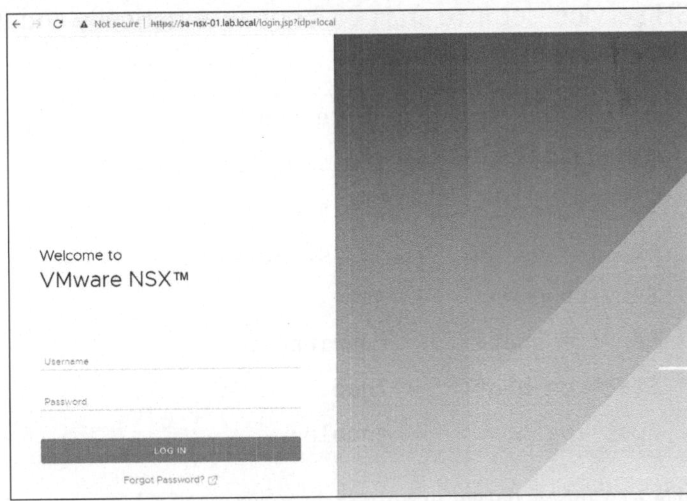

Figure 2.6: *Accessing NSX Manager using a web browser*

Step 3: First time logging into NSX Manager, accept **EULA** presented and skip the **introductory walkthrough** of UI. Also, accept either to join **VMware Customer Experience Improvement Program (CEIP)** or uncheck the box to opt out of VMware CEIP. *Figure 2.7* shows the first login screen post accepting EULA and CEIP.

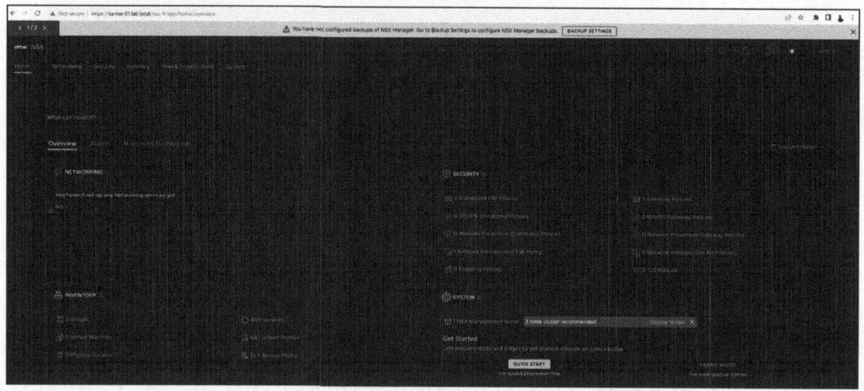

Figure 2.7: *NSX Manager User Interface*

Accessing NSX Manager using NSX CLI

In order to access NSX Manager using CLI, either an SSH session or console session needs to be opened and an admin credential needs to be provided. During deployment, NSX Manager provides an option to enable SSH session, however, if it is not selected during deployment then first SSH services need to be started and enabled in NSX Manager using Virtual Machine console from ESXi host or vCenter server. The following console output shows the commands to start the SSH service, set it to start on boot automatically and get the status of the SSH service.

```
sa-nsx-01> start service ssh
sa-nsx-01> set service ssh start-on-boot
sa-nsx-01> get service ssh
Mon Jan 02 2023 UTC 22:47:45.910
Service name:       ssh
Service state:      running
Start on boot:      True
Root login:         enabled
```

Table 2.1: *Console output to start SSH service on NSX Manager node*

NSX CLI can be accessed from an SSH client after SSH services are started on NSX Manager and use ***list*** command to show all available commands to perform retrieve information or configure the NSX environment.

Tip: NSX CLI is available across all NSX prepared infrastructure NSX Manager, ESXi host and Edge Nodes and is consistent in nature across all nodes.

Accessing NSX Manager using API

NSX Manager uses RESTful API and it drives everything, even NSX CLI and NSX UI are API clients. Usually, API is used when GUI cannot be used or certain tasks need to be automated using scripts or other tools such as Terraform or Ansible. NSX Manager accepts API requests on TCP port 443 over HTTP application protocol to perform HTTP actions such as:

- **GET**: Command to query, read and retrieve NSX objects
- **PUT, POST, PATCH**: Command to create, modify or update NSX objects
- **DELETE**: Command to delete NSX objects

A complete list of API URI path and commands can be accessed on VMware which include documentation and sample codes.

Registering vCenter Server with NSX Manager

After accessing the NSX Manager for the first time, one of the important tasks to complete is registering a vCenter server or in NSX Manager terms Compute Manager. As stated earlier, registering a vCenter server with NSX Manager provide multiple functions such as additional NSX Manager node deployment directly from NSX UI, preparing ESXi host as a Transport Node without manual registration or deeper integration with vSphere for Kubernetes. Following is the step-by-step process to register the vCenter server with NSX Manager.

Step 1: In order to register the vCenter server with NSX Manager, log in to **NSX Manager UI** with admin privileges. Navigate to **`System`** menu and in the left pane, expand **`Fabric.`** Click on **`Compute Managers`**. Any registered vCenter server will be visible here or if this is a new environment, it will be an empty screen. *Figure* 2.8 shows **`Compute Manager`** window with no registered vCenter server.

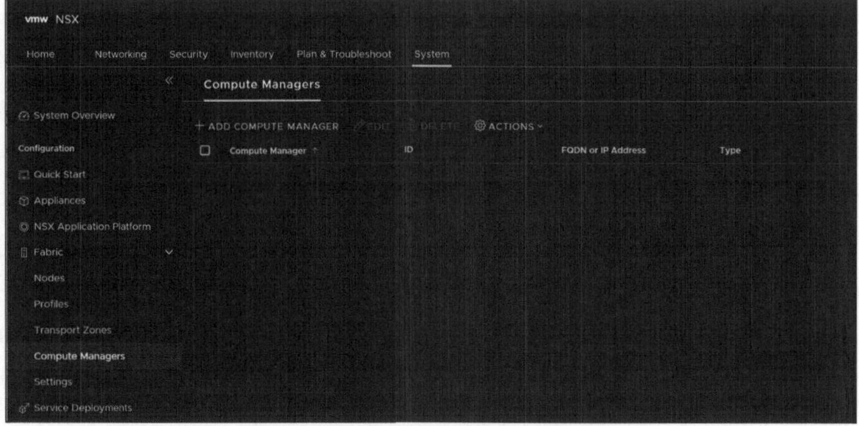

Figure 2.8: *NSX Compute Managers*

Step 2: Click on the **+ (Plus)** icon **`Add Compute Manager`** and a new dialog box with the name **`New Compute Manager`** will open as shown in *Figure* 2.9.

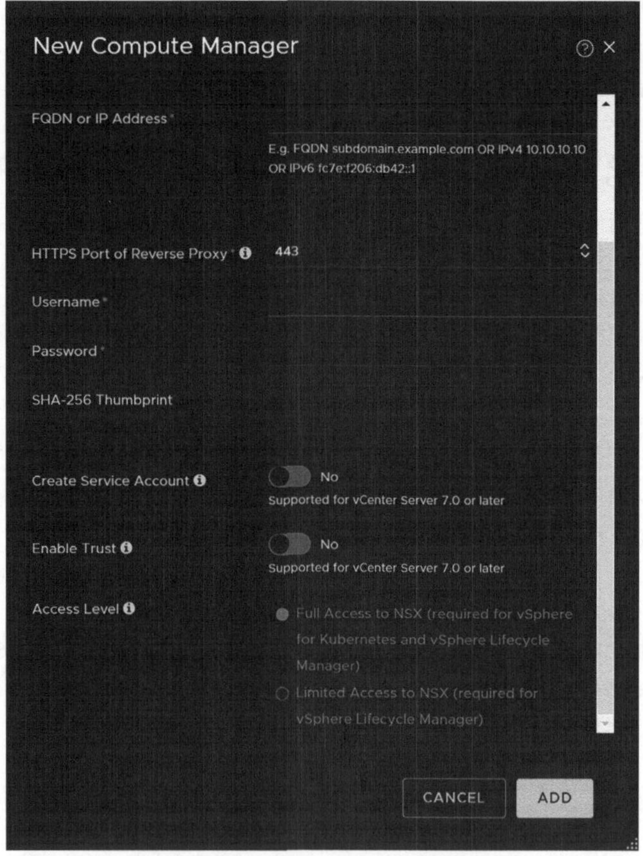

Figure 2.9*: New Compute Manager*

Step 3: Enter the required details and click on **Add**. A few key details to be entered here are:

a. **Name**: Name of Compute Manager in NSX UI

b. **Type**: vCenter

c. **FQDN or IP Address**: Either the DNS name or IP address of the vCenter server to be connected

d. **Port:** 443 (default), needs to be changed if vCenter is using a custom port

e. **Username**: User account name with required privileges to access the vCenter server (detailed list of privileges can be viewed at https://docs.vmware.com/en/VMware-NSX/4.0/administration/GUID-D225CAFC-04D4-44A7-9A09-7C365AAFCA0E.html)

f. **Password:** User account password

g. **Create Service Account**: Optional, can be enabled for vSphere 7.0 and above. If using vSphere 7.0, it is recommended to create a service account

h. **Enable Trust**: Optional, can be enabled for vSphere 7.0 and above

i. **Access Level**: It can be enabled if Trust is enabled.

   i. **Full Access**: Full access is required for the integration of NSX Manager with vSphere for Kubernetes and for using vSphere Lifecycle Manager to manage host preparation

   ii. **Limited Access**: Can be selected if only using vSphere Lifecycle Manager to manage host preparation

Step 4: A new warning prompt will pop up alerting about **Missing Thumbprint**. Validate the thumbprint and click on **Add.** *Figure* 2.10 shows such a pop-up.

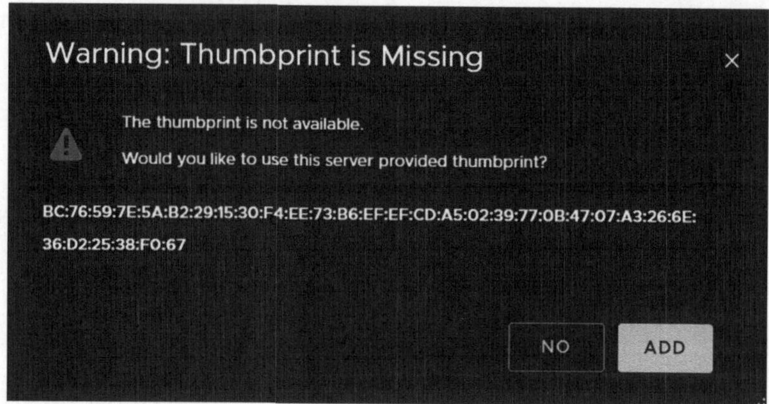

Figure 2.10: *Warning Pop-up for missing Thumbprint*

Step 5: Give it a minute or two and the vCenter server will be registered in NSX Manager with connection status as **`Up`**. *Figure* 2.11 shows the vCenter server registered with NSX Manager.

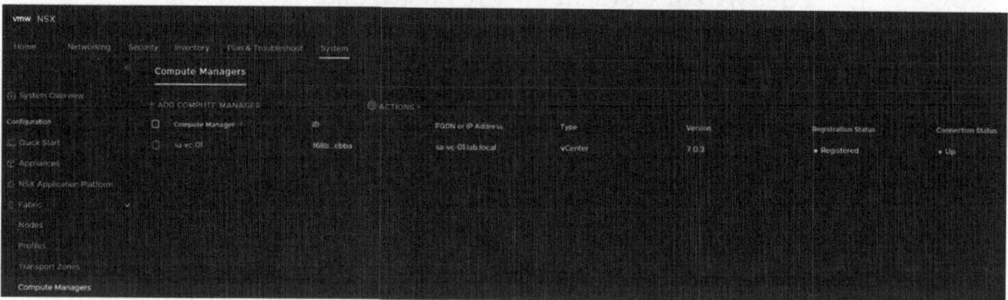

Figure 2.11: *vCenter server registered with NSX Manager*

Adding Licenses in NSX Manager

Another important task is to add licenses in NSX Manager as without adding appropriate licenses, NSX Manager will not let you prepare the ESXi host as Transport Nodes. There is an evaluation license to test NSX free of cost but it is not recommended for production deployments. To add licenses, navigate to **System** menu and in the left-hand pane, select **`Licenses`** under **`Settings.`** Click on the **+ (plus)** icon **`Add License`** and enter the license key. *Figure* 2.12 shows the license window with a newly added license key.

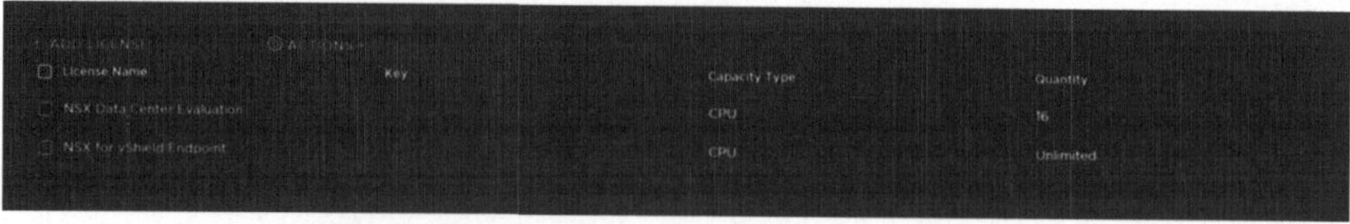

Figure 2.12: *Adding a new license key in NSX UI*

A few other important tasks are to configure Backups for NSX Manager which can be done in Backup & Restore under the System tab, replace the self-signed certificate with CA signed certificate and integrate NSX Manager with Identity providers such as Active Directory (AD). These tasks have been covered in detail with a step-by-step process in *Chapter 14, Monitoring and Managing* NSX.

Deploying Additional NSX Manager Node

After the first NSX Manager appliance is deployed, configured and the vCenter server has been registered as a compute Manager, the second and third NSX Manager nodes can be deployed directly from NSX UI to form the NSX Management cluster providing high availability and scalability in NSX environment. The step-by-step process to deploy the NSX Manager node from NSX UI are as follows:

Step 1: After logging into the first NSX Manager node, go to **`System`** tab and click on **`Appliances`** in the left-hand pane under **`Configuration.`** **`Appliances`** window shows the existing NSX Manager deployed and their status. In the same window, there are options to deploy additional NSX Manager nodes, configure Virtual IP and add NSX Advance Load Balancer appliance (covered in detail in *Chapter* 12, NSX *DataCenter Services* – 2). *Figure* 2.13 shows details of the first NSX Manager deployed earlier.

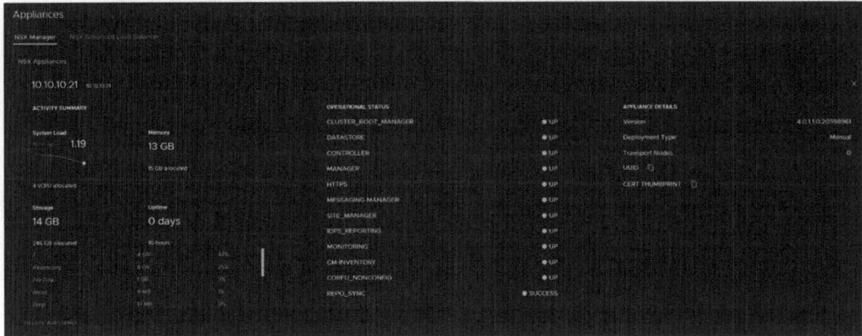

Figure 2.13: *Details of NSX Manager appliance*

Step 2: Click on **`Add NSX Appliance`** and a new window will pop up with details to be filled in:

a. **`Name:`** Provide the FQDN or hostname for the NSX Manager node

b. **`Management IP Details`**: Provide the IP details to access the newly deployed NSX Manager over the network

c. **DNS Server, NTP Server** and **Search Domains** are pre-filled by setup using the first NSX Manager. These can be overridden if required.

d. **Node Size:** Select the appropriate appliance size as per requirement. It is recommended to keep the NSX Manager size the same for all three nodes.

After providing all details it will look similar to *Figure* 2.14. Click **Next** to continue deployment.

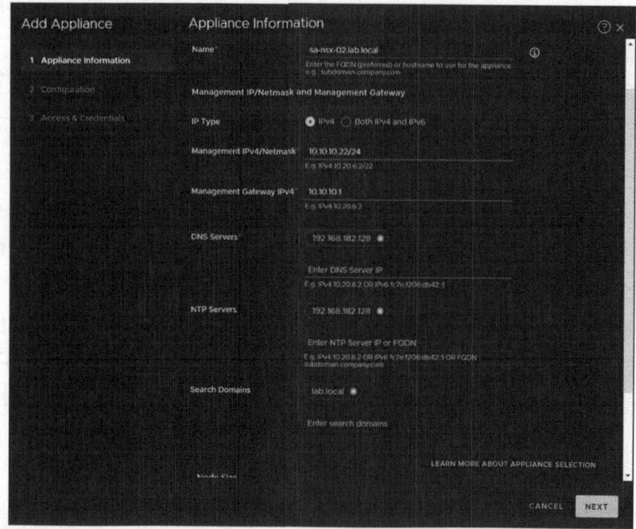

Figure 2.14: *Appliance Information for additional* NSX *Manager* Node

Step 3: The second step is about resource **configuration** where NSX Manager virtual machine will be deployed. Select the appropriate **Compute Manager, Cluster**, **Datastore** and **Network port group** to provide compute, storage and network resources to Virtual Machine. *Figure* 2.15 shows an example of such a configuration.

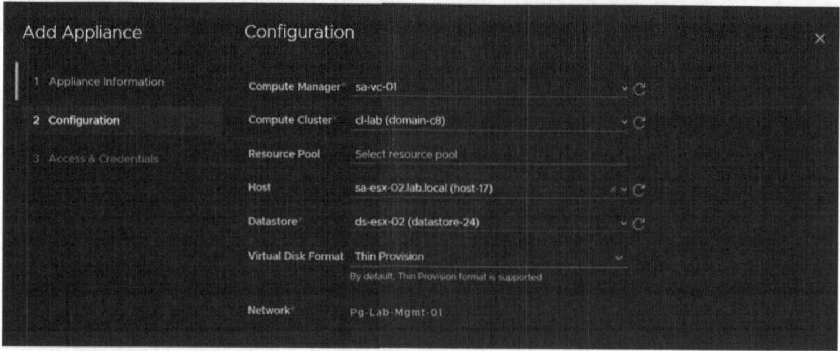

Figure 2.15: *Configuration of* NSX *Manager Virtual Machine*

Step 4: In the last step, provide the root password for the NSX Manager appliance and select if SSH login will be allowed or disallowed. Audit and Admin CLI passwords can be overridden if required. Click `Install Appliance` to start deployment of NSX Manager as visible in *Figure* 2.16. However, once a new node is joined to NSX Cluster, system root, audit and admin credentials will be overridden with the first NSX Manager node's credentials.

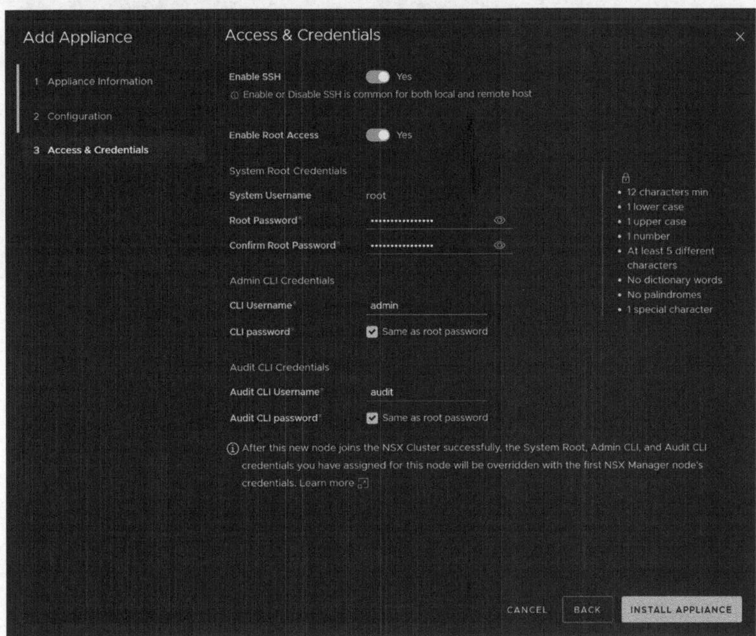

***Figure 2.16:** Final step to deploy NSX Manager from UI*

This will start the deployment of the NSX Manager node. As a first step, NSX Manager will direct the vCenter server to deploy the OVF template on selected resources. Post successful deployment of the NSX Manager template, it will be powered on and the first boot scripts will run similar to the first node. *Figure* 2.17 is a capture of vCenter tasks directed by the NSX Manager.

Recent Tasks | Alarms

Task Name	Target	Status	Details	Initiator	Queued For
Power On virtual machine	sa-nsx-02	Completed		com.vmware.nsx.management...	3 ms
Deploy OVF template	sa-nsx-02	Completed		com.vmware.nsx.management...	3 ms

***Figure 2.17:** Tasks initiated by NSX Manager in the vCenter server*

After the additional NSX Manager is fully deployed, it initiates a join request to the first NSX Manager to join the NSX Management cluster and post successful join services are distributed across all nodes in the management cluster, the cluster becomes stable as in *Figure 2.18* and additional nodes can be deployed.

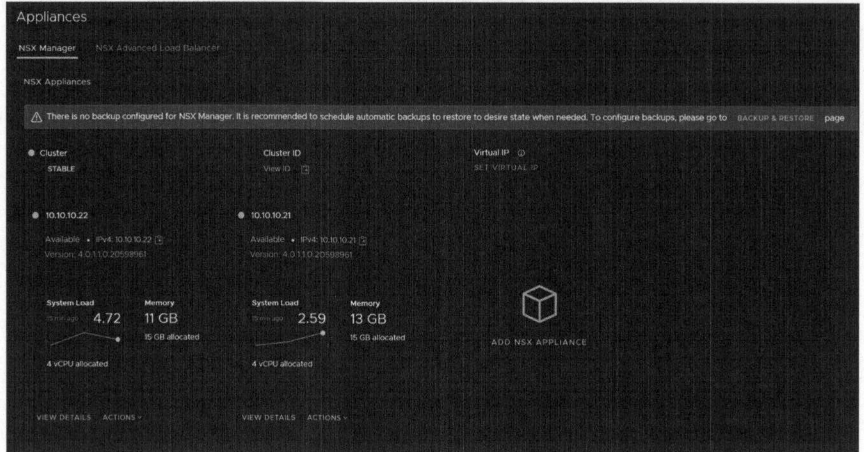

Figure 2.18: *Additional NSX node deployed successfully*

Creating NSX Management Cluster using CLI

Deploying the NSX Manager node using NSX UI takes care of forming a management cluster without the need to run any commands but this requires a compute Manager to be registered with NSX Manager. What if all three NSX Manager instances are deployed using the OVF template or a new NSX Manager instance is deployed from the OVF template instead of NSX UI? In that case, all NSX Managers nodes will be running independently not aware of each other. In such cases, NSX CLI comes to the rescue, with help of NSX CLI, independent instances can be joined together to form a management cluster.

Step 1: Open an SSH session or Console session to NSX Manager deployed first and log in using admin credentials.

Step 2: Run the following commands in sequence and capture their output:

```
get certificate api thumbprint
```

i. capture the command output string unique for this node

```
get cluster config
```

ii. capture the Cluster ID for the first node

Table 2.2 shows the console output and text in bold to be captured.

```
sa-nsx-01> get certificate api thumbprint
Tue Jan 03 2023 UTC 15:53:35.246
9b17d790b1bfd10799906649c609c4e0e02f503fc05b99e4623695e674b26b0a

sa-nsx-01> get cluster config
Tue Jan 03 2023 UTC 15:53:43.722
Cluster Id: 46231ef6-ef07-4f91-9c61-162fb1411b54
Cluster Configuration Version: 1
<-output truncated->
```

Table 2.2: *Console output on the first NSX Manager node*

Step 3: Open SSH session or Console session to new deployed NSX Manager node and log in using admin credentials.

Step 4: Run the join command in the following format to join the new NSX Manager node with the first NSX Manager instance.

```
join <Manager-IP> cluster-id <cluster-id> username
<Manager-username> password <Manager-password>
thumbprint <Manager-thumbprint>
```

Here,

i. **Manager-IP**: IP address of First NSX Manager node

ii. **Cluster-id**: Cluster ID of first NSX Manager node as captured in Step 1

iii. **Manager-username:** Admin username of first NSX Manager

iv. **Manager-password** : Admin password of first NSX Manager

v. **Manager-thumbprint**: Thumbprint of first NSX Manager as captured in Step 1

Table 2.3 provides an example output of the preceding command when run on a newly deployed NSX Manager node not part of the management cluster.

```
sa-nsx-03> join 10.10.10.21 cluster-id 46231ef6-ef07-4f91-9c61-
162fb1411b54 username admin password xxxxxxxxxxx thumbprint
9b17d790b1bfd10799906649c609c4e0e02f503fc05b99e4623695e674b26b0a
Data on this node will be lost. Are you sure? (yes/no): yes
Join operation successful. Services are being restarted. Cluster may
take some time to stabilize.
```

Table 2.3: *Console output on the new NSX Manager node*

Step 5: Log in to the first NSX Manager UI and all NSX Manager nodes will be present under Appliances in System tab.

Tip: If there is a need to change the size of NSX Manager appliances, deploy a new NSX Manager instance with desired node size. Once the new NSX Manager instance is fully deployed and part of a cluster, delete the old NSX Manager node with a smaller size. Repeat this process for NSX Manager instances until node size is uniform in the NSX Management cluster.

Configuring Virtual IP for Cluster

Now that three NSX Manager nodes are grouped together to form a management cluster, the database is replicated to all three nodes providing high availability of services. NSX management cluster serves two important functions. The first one is to provide northbound entry for system configuration to different endpoints and user access. The second one is to establish communication between different NSX components. As covered in *Chapter 1, Introduction to NSX Datacenter*, the controller role takes care of establishing communication between the controller and Transport Node and distributing Transport Nodes between different NSX Manager nodes with help of sharding. Similarly, the NSX Management cluster can provide different availability modes for northbound access to API and user access. These different models are:

- Default Deployment with no common IP address
- Configure NSX Manager with Cluster VIP
- NSX Manager with External Load Balancer

Let's discuss these different models in detail.

Default Deployment with no common IP address

In this simplistic model, all three NSX Managers are deployed without any further configuration. There is no common IP address available between different nodes. Different endpoints (Users or external systems) can connect to different NSX Manager nodes with the help of their unique FQDN or IP address. However, availability for API or GUI access is driven outside of the NSX Manager appliance. In case of failure of any node, external systems or scripts are required to point to a different healthy node which may require manual intervention. Similarly, administrator or users' needs to change their address in a web browser in order to connect to the healthy node which is not desirable for many organizations.

Configuring NSX Manager with Cluster VIP

This model works on the Active/Standby availability model where a virtual IP address is configured in the NSX management cluster. Different endpoints (users or external systems) connect to virtual IPs which provide node-level redundancy. In this model, out of three nodes in the management cluster, one node is assigned as the owner of the virtual IP. All requests hitting virtual IP/ FQDN are sent to the owner node. There is no load distribution mechanism with this approach and all northbound traffic is handled by a single node. In case of failure of owner node, a new node out of the remaining healthy nodes is selected as the owner of the virtual IP which brings to one key consideration for this model. As virtual IP remains the same, it assumes all three nodes belong to the same subnet. The cluster VIP feature uses GARP to update the mac-address and the ARP table of the upstream network devices. Hence, it is mandatory to have all NSX Manager instances in the same NSX management cluster to be in the same subnet. *Figure* 2.19 displays three NSX Manager nodes running with cluster VIP with one node selected as the owner node.

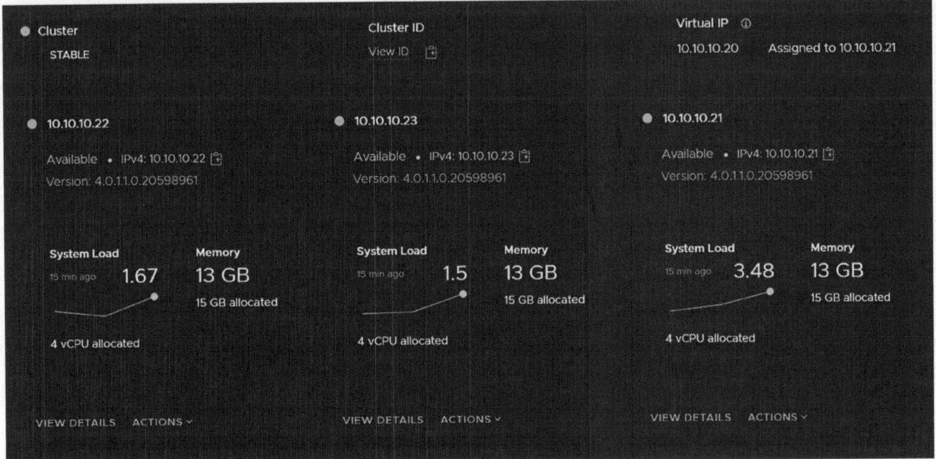

Figure 2.19: *NSX Management Cluster with Cluster VIP*

Cluster VIP can be configured in NSX UI by navigating to **`System`** tab and selecting **`Appliances`** under **`Configuration.`** Click on **`Set Virtual IP`** and then provide a free IP address from the same subnet of the NSX Manager node to configure it on the NSX management cluster. NSX UI screen will refresh and configured Cluster VIP will be visible along with the owner node IP as captured in *Figure 2.20*.

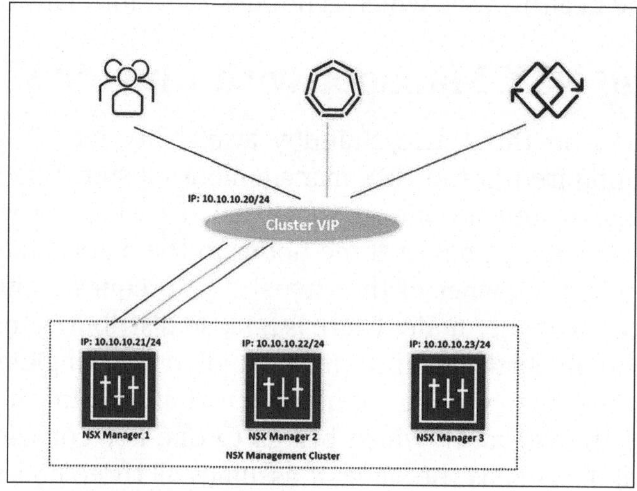

***Figure 2.20**: NSX Cluster Virtual IP with owner node information*

NSX Manager with External Load Balancer

The external load balancer can be configured with the NSX management cluster to distribute incoming requests to different NSX Manager nodes. A VIP is configured on the load balancer and NSX Manager nodes are configured as physical servers in a server pool. This model is helpful where NSX Manager nodes need to be in different subnets due to underlying physical topology (for example, could be different VLANs across different racks and the NSX Manager needs to be run in different racks). This model introduces additional components to manage and configure complexities based on different load balancer models. NSX Advanced Load Balancer (formally AVI Networks) is also supported for this type of configuration. A key point to note here is Source IP persistence is required for session-based authentication (when the NSX Manager is accessed from the web browser). Other types of authentication supported with external load balancer are:

- HTTP Basic Authentication
- Authentication using an X.509 certificate and a Principal Identity

- Authentication in VMware Cloud on AWS (VMC)

Figure 2.21 presents a scenario where NSX Manager nodes are load balanced by an external LB and source persistency is in use to redirect requests from the same client to the same NSX Manager node.

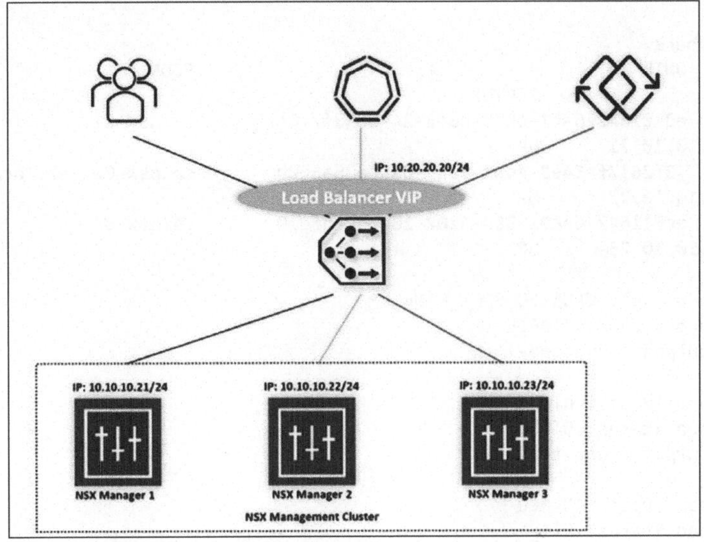

***Figure* 2.21:** *NSX Management cluster with an external Load balancer*

Validating NSX Management Cluster

Well hats off to you for coming this far! You have successfully deployed your first NSX management cluster and configured a cluster VIP to provide redundancy in the NSX environment. It's time to look behind scenes and validate what we have learned and deployed. Let's open an SSH session or Console session on the NSX Manager instance and the first command that can be run to validate the management cluster is:

```
get cluster status
```

This command provides the overall status of the management cluster, services running in the management cluster and their individual status on each node. As visible in the example output of the NSX Manager node in *Table* 2.4, different roles such as Manager, HTTPS, Controller, and Corfu running in a stable state with overall status as stable.

```
sa-nsx-03> get cluster status
Tue Jan 03 2023 UTC 18:28:00.994
Cluster Id: 46231ef6-ef07-4f91-9c61-162fb1411b54
Overall Status: STABLE

Group Type: DATASTORE
Group Status: STABLE

Members:
    UUID                                       FQDN
IP              STATUS
    e3101642-5ab1-c518-b5c3-24a8853f7f3c       sa-nsx-01
10.10.10.21     UP
    73f2617f-54e3-4d61-89c5-0a9ce75a860b       sa-nsx-02.lab.local
10.10.10.22     UP
    ec311642-6ec9-931b-2207-26dce73dfe70       sa-nsx-03
10.10.10.23     UP

Group Type: CLUSTER_BOOT_MANAGER
Group Status: STABLE
<-output truncated->

Group Type: CONTROLLER
Group Status: STABLE
<-output truncated->

Group Type: MANAGER
Group Status: STABLE
<-output truncated->

Group Type: HTTPS
Group Status: STABLE
<-output truncated->

Group Type: MESSAGING-MANAGER
Group Status: STABLE
<-output truncated->

Group Type: MONITORING
Group Status: STABLE
<-output truncated->

Group Type: IDPS_REPORTING
Group Status: STABLE
<-output truncated->

Group Type: SITE_MANAGER
Group Status: STABLE
<-output truncated->

Group Type: CM-INVENTORY
Group Status: STABLE
<-output truncated->

Group Type: CORFU_NONCONFIG
Group Status: STABLE
<-output truncated->
```

***Table 2.4**: Cluster Status output on the NSX Manager node*

Another extended version of the same command is with **verbose** option which provides leader node or owner node information for different services as shown in the example output as follows.

```
sa-nsx-03> get cluster status verbose
Tue Jan 03 2023 UTC 18:35:41.308
Cluster Id: 46231ef6-ef07-4f91-9c61-162fb1411b54
Overall Status: STABLE

<-output truncated->

Leaders:
    SERVICE                                      LEADER
LEASE VERSION
    POLICY_SVC_ADVANCELOADBALANCER               e3101642-5ab1-c518-b5c3-
24a8853f7f3c        4493
    ManualHealthCheckMonitor                     e3101642-5ab1-c518-b5c3-
24a8853f7f3c        4493
    POLICY_SVC_TAG_BULK_OPERATION                e3101642-5ab1-c518-b5c3-
24a8853f7f3c        4491
    IdfwDbDaemon                                 e3101642-5ab1-c518-b5c3-
24a8853f7f3c        4491
    POLICY_SVC_IPFIX_DFW_PROFILE                 e3101642-5ab1-c518-b5c3-
24a8853f7f3c        4493
    POLICY_SVC_IDS_PROFILE_PROVIDER              e3101642-5ab1-c518-b5c3-
24a8853f7f3c        4491
    POLICY_SVC_DFW_EXCLUDE_LIST                  e3101642-5ab1-c518-b5c3-
24a8853f7f3c        4491
    POLICY_SVC_IPFIX_L2_GLOBAL_PROFILE           e3101642-5ab1-c518-b5c3-
24a8853f7f3c        4491
    POLICY_SVC_GATEWAY_QOS_PROFILE               e3101642-5ab1-c518-b5c3-
24a8853f7f3c        4491
    MirrorStackMonitorImpl                       e3101642-5ab1-c518-b5c3-
24a8853f7f3c        4491
    POLICY_SVC_DNS                               e3101642-5ab1-c518-b5c3-
24a8853f7f3c        4491
    TNStateWorker-TransportNodeState             e3101642-5ab1-c518-b5c3-
24a8853f7f3c        4493
    POLICY_SVC_FIREWALL_CPU_MEMORY_THRESHOLDS_PROFILE_PROVIDER
e3101642-5ab1-c518-b5c3-24a8853f7f3c        4491
```

Another option to validate the management cluster is using NSX UI. In **Appliances** window under **System** tab where all three NSX Manager nodes are listed, there is a status label for **Cluster**. If all services are running on all NSX Manager nodes and no issues are present in the management cluster, it will display the status as Stable else it will change status to Degraded as shown in *Figure* 2.20. Also, by clicking on **View Details** on each NSX Manager node, the operational status of all services can be quickly reviewed as shown in *Figure* 2.13.

Preparing NSX Data Plane

Deploying NSX Manager appliances and grouping them to form a management cluster is the first step to build an NSX environment. This provides Management Plane and Central Control Plane functions in the NSX environment but the next important step is to build Data Plane where the actual processing of packets happens. A quick recap of what we covered in *Chapter 1, Introduction to NSX Datacenter* as part of NSX Architecture; Data Plane consists of different endpoints, for example, Hypervisor Host, Bare Metal server or NSX Edge nodes prepared for NSX termed as Transport Nodes which perform stateless forwarding of packet and encapsulation or decapsulation based on information provided by Control Plane. Data Plane spans across all Transport Nodes in the datacenter making it distributed in nature and it scales out every time a new Transport Node is added to the environment. In this section, we discuss in detail about how to prepare Transport Node but before we start with the implementation, it is important to understand a few key terms which make up Data Plane. *Chapter 1* introduces Transport Node and NSX virtual switch N-VDS, let's dive a little bit deeper and see how it all connects together in the physical world.

Transport Nodes are compute resources installed with NSX software components performing networking either VLAN or Overlay and security functions. Software component running on a Transport Node is a virtual switch responsible for processing traffic originating from a virtual machine or container running on a hypervisor or application in the case of bare metal server whereas Edge Nodes are special NSX appliances that are dedicated to run stateful and central network services that cannot be distributed in nature such as Gateway Firewall, N-S Routing, NAT or VPN, and so on.

Architecture of Transport Node

As we saw in previous Chapter, the Transport Node consists of a local Control Plane (LCP) daemon and forwarding engines. You might have already guessed it, NSX Virtual switch makes up the forwarding engine and if you remember from the communication path between NSX Manager and Transport Node, there is a service running locally on the Transport Node called nsx-proxy which makes up the local Control Plane. *Figure* 2.22 display both nsx-proxy and NSX Virtual Switch in action.

Figure 2.22: *Transport Node architecture for ESXi host and KVM host*

NSX-Proxy

NSX-Proxy is an agent running on each and every Transport Node and is responsible for receiving configuration from Manager and Control Plane data from CCP (Central Control Plane or Controller role on NSX Manager). It communicates with Appliance Proxy Hub (APH) service running on the NSX Manager node to provide statistics or receive configurations. This communication path has been covered in detail under Section Transport Node Communication Path in *Chapter 1, Introduction to NSX Datacenter.*

NSX Virtual Switch

NSX Virtual switch is a core Data Plane component running on the Transport node as it is responsible for forwarding traffic between logical ports and physical ports. NSX Virtual switch is called NSX Virtual Distributed Switch (N-VDS) due to its distributed nature and is based on vSphere Distributed Switch (VDS) for ESXi hosts or Open vSwitch (OVS) for other hypervisors such as KVM, bare metal servers or Edge Transport Nodes. Starting NSX-T 3.0, along with VDS (vSphere Distributed Switch) 7.0 a new model was introduced for ESXi hosts where existing VDS can be used to install NSX software components on it. This model reduced operational complexities by eliminating the need to manage two different distributed switches or avoid migrating VMkernel interfaces from VDS to N-VDS. Key considerations when configuring NSX Virtual Switch are:

- ESXi Transport Node can be configured to use either N-VDS or VDS but KVM can use only N-VDS. VDS cannot be used with KVM.

- Transport Nodes have multiple NSX virtual switches configured but each switch requires its own physical NICs or in other terms, one physical NIC on a Transport Node cannot be shared between multiple NSX virtual switches.
- Both N-VDS and VDS can be used in an NSX environment.

This enables two distinct deployment models for NSX virtual switches on Transport Nodes.

NSX on N-VDS: N-VDS is created and managed by NSX Manager only and is created and distributed across hypervisors either ESXi or KVM and NSX Edge Transport Nodes. All configurations or policies are defined and controlled from the NSX Manager for N-VDS. When N-VDS is used on the ESXi host, any network created on N-VDS is visible as an opaque port group in the vCenter server as shown in *Figure* 2.23.

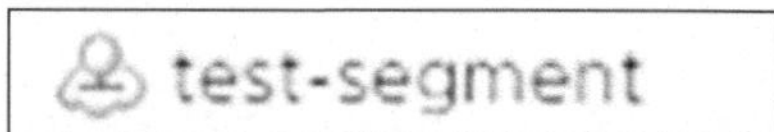

Figure 2.23: N-VDS *Opaque port group as visible in vCenter server*

Compute Manager or vCenter server has visibility into these opaque networks but a vSphere administrator cannot edit properties of the N-VDS port group directly from the vCenter server. Starting vSphere 7.0 and NSX 3.0, N-VDS is primarily used with KVM hypervisors or Edge Transport Nodes.

NSX on VDS: NSX software components can be directly installed on VDS v7.0 and above removing the need to configure N-VDS separately. This can only be configured on ESXi hosts managed by the vCenter server and supports ESXi hosts only. In the case of VDS, networks created by NSX are realized as a distributed port group in vCenter which can be distinguished by the symbol **N** in front of them. In VDS some policies are governed by the vCenter server such as NIOC (Network I/O Control) or MTU (Maximum Transmission Unit) and other policies such as security profile are controlled by NSX Manager for networks created in NSX. However, any distributed port group created in the vCenter server is fully governed by vCenter only and no control is with the NSX Manager. *Figure* 2.24 shows such a network created in NSX and realized as a distributed port group.

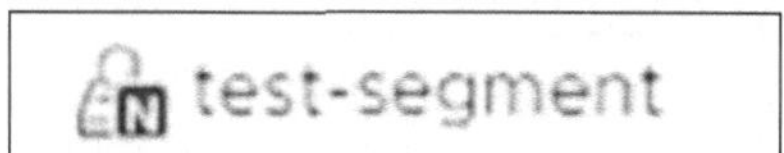

Figure 2.24: NSX *Network realized as a distributed port group in the vCenter server*

Tip: For more in-depth information about the configuration of NSX on VDS, please refer to VMware KB 79872.

N-VDS vs. VDS - Well, this begs the question of whether to use N-VDS or VDS on the ESXi host, unlike KVM where only N-VDS is supported. *Table* 2.5 provides information about the differences between N-VDS and VDS.

N-VDS on ESXi Transport Node	NSX on VDS on ESXi Transport Node
Any deployment with a vSphere version below 7.0 or an NSX version below 3.0	Any new deployments running vSphere v7.0 and later with NSX-T v3.0 and later
Require dedicated physical NICs attached to N-VDS	Require dedicated physical NICs attached to VDS
Need to migrate VMkernel interface if physical NICs are limited	No need to migrate the VMkernel interface from vSphere distributed port group to the NSX network as the same VDS can be used for the NSX network as well as vSphere distributed port groups
Can be used with standalone ESXi hosts or KVM, no vCenter server is required	Require vCenter server and few configurations rely on VDS v7

***Table* 2.5:** *Differences between N-VDS and VDS on ESXi transport Node*

Note: Starting NSX 4.0, N-VDS is no longer supported for ESXi hosts and NSX on VDS is only supported deployment for ESXi hosts.

Connecting Transport Node with Physical Network

The last bit remaining is connecting a Transport Node on a physical network. A Transport Node requires mainly two types of network connectivity - 1. Management Network, this is used to connect to the Transport Node to manage or change configuration on the node itself example taking an SSH session of the KVM host or ESXi host and 2. Transport Network, which carries the traffic from a virtual machine, container or application running on the bare metal server. A transport network is a VLAN on the physical network which carries all the overlay traffic or VLAN traffic if networking has not been fully migrated to overlay. Either a pair of dedicated physical NICs can be used to carry these two traffic or they can be logically separated with help of VLANs and trunked together on the same physical NICs. *Figure* 2.25 shows two transport with their physical NICs connected to the management network and the transport network with the management network further providing connectivity to NSX Managers.

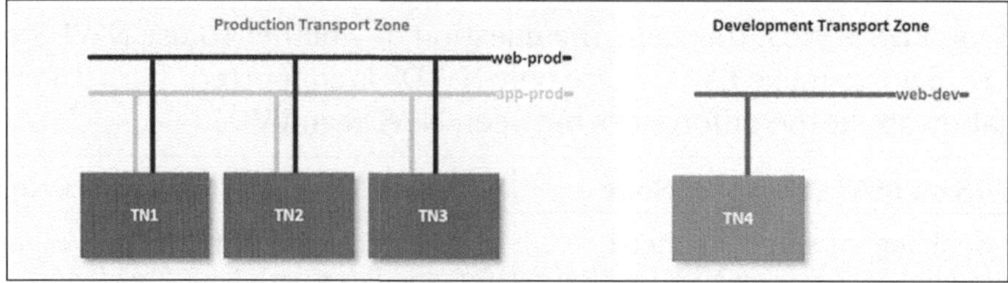

***Figure 2.25**: Transport Node connectivity with the physical network*

Transport Zones

We just learned that the NSX Data Plane exists on each and every Transport Node in the datacenter, so how do we define the scope of our NSX networks? For example, I might have a few Transport Nodes belonging to the development environment and others belonging to the production environment and if we create any NSX network in the production environment it should be visible only on the production Transport Node similarly for the development environment. So how do we define this boundary? This is where Transport Zone comes in handy. Transport Zone defines the span or scope of an NSX logical network over physical infrastructure. Think of a Transport Zone as a configuration boundary of your logical network that contains one or many Transport Nodes. In NSX, a layer 2 broadcast domain is called a segment (In Manager mode as a logical switch) and the segment spans across a Transport Zone. So, any Transport Node that attaches to the same Transport Zone will have access to the same group of segments as illustrated in *Figure* 2.26.

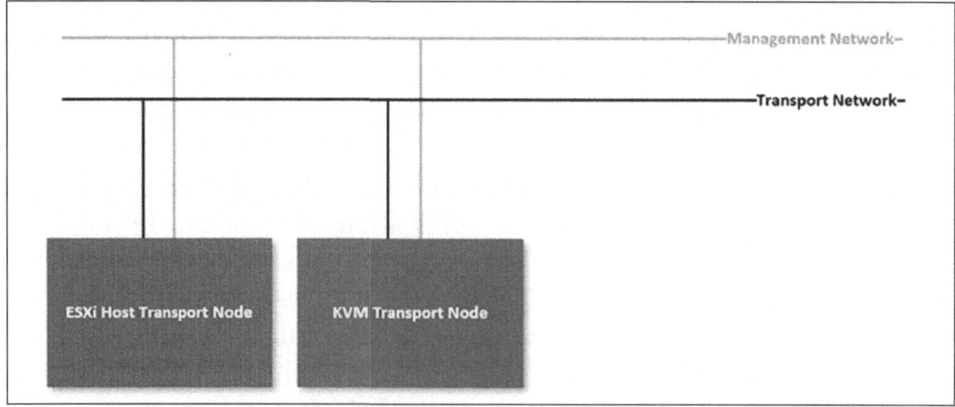

***Figure 2.26**: Transport Zone defining the boundary of the virtual network*

TN1 (Transport Node 1), TN2 and TN3 belonging to the production Transport Zone have access to segment web-prod and app-prod, whereas TN4 belonging to the development Transport Zone, have access to web-dev and cannot see segments web-prod and app-prod.

In NSX, there can be two types of Transport Zones and the difference between them is based on the type of traffic that is carried by segments.

- **Overlay Transport Zone:** Overlay backed segments are created in the Overlay Transport Zone as the name suggests. If two VMs attached to the same overlay segment running on two different hosts, their layer 2 traffic is carried by a tunnel instantiated between the two hosts by NSX without the need to make any configuration changes on physical infrastructure. Traffic in the IP tunnel is Geneve encapsulated thus decoupling NSX virtual networks from physical infrastructure. Geneve encapsulation has been covered in much detail in *Chapter* 3, *Logical Switching.*
- **VLAN Transport Zone:** VLAN segments are created in the VLAN Transport Zone which is a traditional implementation of VLAN in physical infrastructure. VLAN Transport Zone in NSX is mostly used by NSX Edge to provide connectivity to physical infrastructure or if a virtual machine requires connectivity to a traditional VLAN network.

Mapping N-VDS or VDS with Transport Zone

N-VDS or VDS is configured on Transport Node and the Transport Node attaches to one or more Transport Zone, so how do these two relate to each other? Well, the Transport Node uses N-VDS or VDS to connect to the Transport Zone, it is the N-VDS or VDS which is mapped to the Transport Zone thus providing access to VM, container or application running on the host to NSX virtual network. In older versions of NSX-T, it was required to define the name of N-VDS while creating Transport Zone and use the same name of N-VDS on Transport Node so they can map with each other but this requirement has been deprecated in the recent version of NSX 4.x and it is no longer required to define the name of N-VDS in Transport Zone. However, it is recommended to use a consistent name for Transport Zone and N-VDS/VDS as it helps in easier identification of NSX objects in troubleshooting where multiple switches and Transport Zones have been configured. *Figure* 2.27 illustrates the mapping between the Transport Zone and N-VDS/VDS.

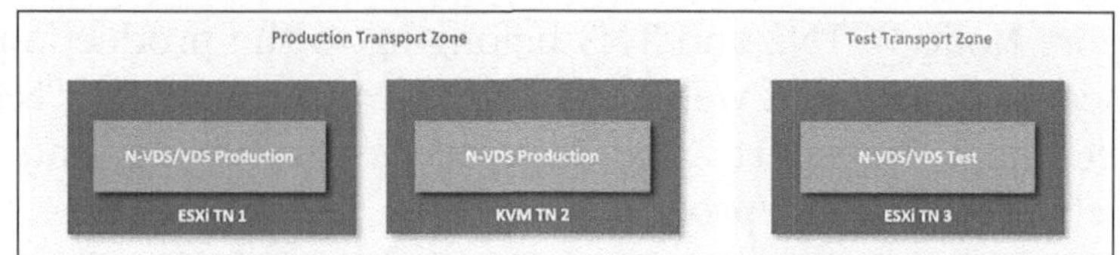

Figure 2.27: *Transport Zone and N-VDS/VDS Mapping*

A few other key considerations when designing a Transport Zone with respect to Transport Node and N-VDS/VDS are:

- A Transport Zone can have different types of Transport Nodes such as ESXi, KVM, Bare metal server or NSX Edge
- Multiple virtual switches such as N-VDS, VDS with NSX, VDS without NSX, and VSS (vSphere Standard Switch) can coexist on an ESXi Transport Node but a physical NIC can only be associated with a single virtual switch
- NSX virtual switch either N-VDS or VDS with NSX can only be attached to a single overlay Transport Zone
- NSX virtual switch either N-VDS or VDS with NSX can be attached to multiple Transport Zone
- NSX virtual switch on a single Transport Node can be mapped to a single Transport Zone only
- A Transport Node can have multiple NSX virtual switches and thus can be attached to multiple overlay Transport Zone

Note: A Transport Zone should not be considered a security boundary.

Creating Transport Zones in NSX

Let's look at the process to create a Transport Zone in NSX and what are the different inputs it requires. There are two Transport Zones that are already defined in NSX Manager, one for Overlay and the other for VLAN.

Step 1: Login into NSX Manager with admin privileges and navigate to **`System`** tab. Expand **`Fabric`** menu under **`Configuration`** and select **`Transport Zones`**. As shown in *Figure* 2.28, it will display already created Transport Zones.

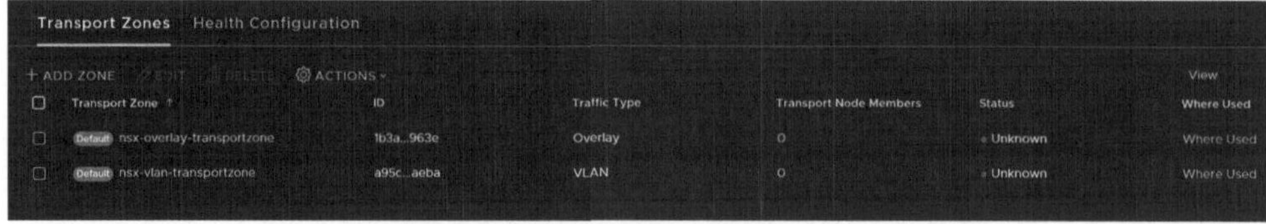

Figure 2.28: *Transport Zone in NSX*

Step 2: Click on **`+Add Zone`** button to create a **`New Transport Zone.`** Provide the following inputs and click **`Add`** (example inputs shown in *Figure* 2.29):

a. **`Name:`** Name of the Transport Zone

b. **`Description`**: Optional, remarks or notes for the Transport Zone

c. **`Traffic Type:`** Select whether it will be an Overlay backed or VLAN backed

d. **`Uplink Teaming Policy Names`**: Define the Named Teaming Policy to be used for uplinks, used for VLAN backed traffic to override default teaming policy

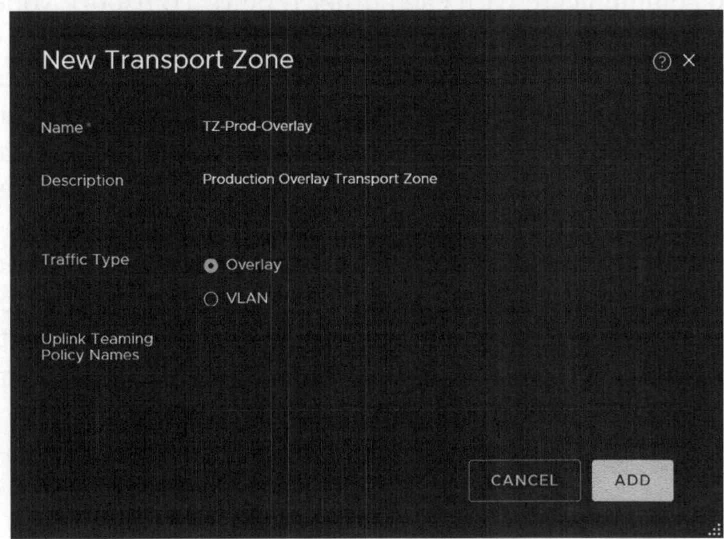

***Figure 2.29**: Create a new Transport Zone*

Step 3: The newly created Transport Zone will be visible in the list now. Optionally, it can be selected and click on **`Actions`** to set it as **`Default Transport Zone`** as illustrated in *Figure* 2.30.

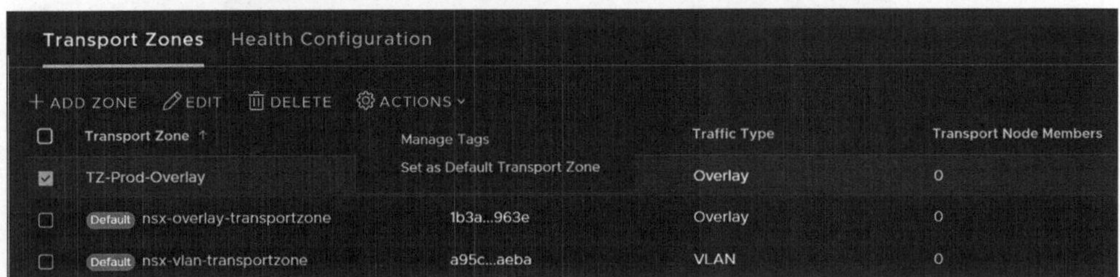

***Figure 2.30**: Set a Transport Zone as the default*

Congratulations! You are now one step closer to preparing the ESXi host as a Transport Node but like any switch, NSX virtual switch also requires uplinks to send or receive traffic to or from the physical network. So, without further ado let's dive into what are uplinks, how they differ from physical NICs, different teaming policies to provide network redundancy and scalability and how all this is tied into the NSX Manager console.

Uplinks or pNICs

In the last section, we studied how the Transport Node attaches to the Transport Zone with help of NSX virtual switch either with help of N-VDS or VDS. Any virtual machine, container or application running on different Transport Node that needs to communicate with each other require Transport Nodes to talk to each other. So NSX virtual switch needs an interface from which it can send or receive traffic to or from physical infrastructure and this interface is termed Uplink. Uplink is a logical construct that is present on NSX virtual switches that send or receive traffic physical infrastructure. Since we are talking about physical infrastructure, so there needs to be a physical interface present on the Transport Node itself and this physical interface is pNIC or physical NIC. Uplink on an NSX virtual switch maps to a pNIC present on the host to send or receive traffic, as uplink is a logical construct it can be mapped to either one physical NIC or multiple physical NICs bonded in form of **LAG (Link Aggregation Group).** *Figure* 2.31 represents uplink in the logical form present on NSX virtual switch and mapped to the physical NIC on the **Transport Node.**

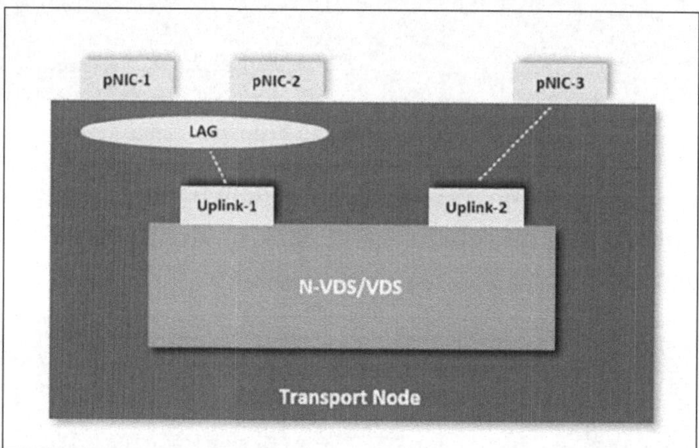

Figure 2.31: *Uplinks on N-VDS/VDS mapped to pNIC*

In the case of NSX on VDS, when the ESXi host is configured as a Transport Node, uplinks on NSX are mapped to uplinks present on VDS (vSphere Distributed

Switch) which are further mapped to vmnics (pNICs) present on the ESXi host instead of mapping directly to vmnics (pNICs) of ESXi host. It shouldn't be confused as separate uplinks for NSX as NSX is not creating a new virtual switch instead it is using the same VDS created earlier in the vCenter server. This is further explained and illustrated in later sections Creating Transport Node Profile and Preparing ESXi host as a Transport Node.

Like any other switch, NSX virtual switch also supports different teaming policies to provide redundancy and load-balancing capabilities using its uplinks. One important point to note here is NSX teaming policies are different from VDS teaming policies in vCenter and should not be confused with each other.

NSX Virtual Switch Teaming Policy

NSX support three different types of teaming policies to configure:

- **Failover Order**: As the name suggests, one uplink is designated as active whereas the other uplink remains in the standby state. If the active uplink fails, the other standby uplink will become active and takes its place. There is no distribution of traffic between uplinks and only one uplink carries all the traffic. Failover order is supported by all different types of Transport Nodes including ESXi hosts, KVM hosts and Edge Transport Nodes. Uplinks can be mapped to individual pNICs or LAGs, however, KVM supports only a single LAG configured with more than one pNICs to active. *Figure* 2.32 illustrates the failover order teaming policy between NSX virtual switch uplinks.

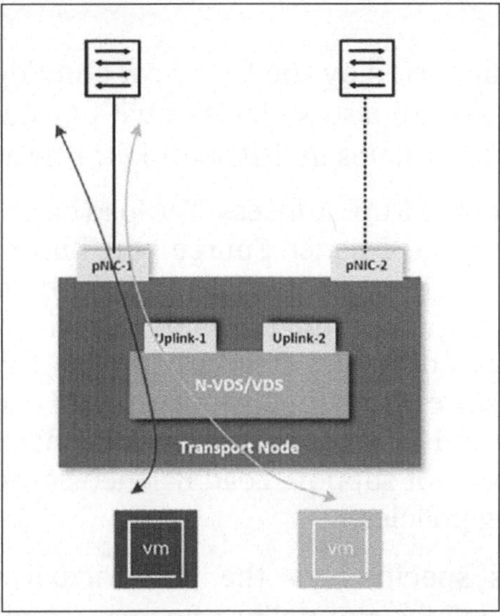

Figure 2.32: *Failover order teaming policy*

- **Load Balance Source Port:** The load balance Source port teaming policy distributes the traffic across different active uplinks based on the virtual machine source port ID and all specified uplinks act as active. *Figure* 2.33 illustrates the load balance source **port teaming policy between NSX virtual switch uplinks.**

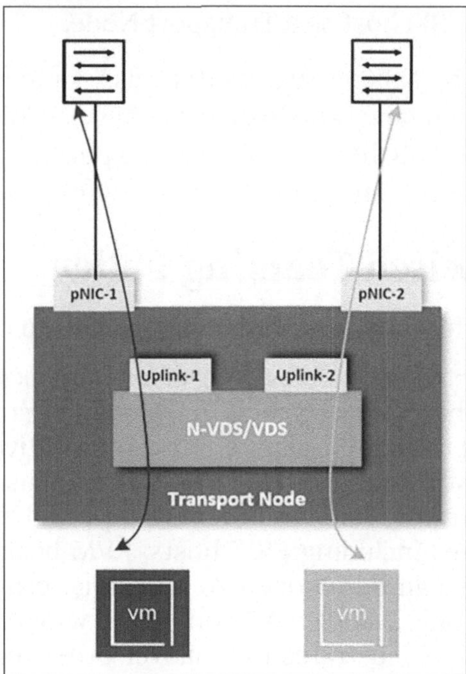

***Figure 2.33**: Load Balance Source Port teaming policy*

This policy is supported by the ESXi host and Edge Transport Node but not by KVM. LAGs are also supported with a Load Balance Source Port policy which further helps in distributing traffic across physical NICs.

- **Load Balance Source MAC Address**: The load balance source MAC address is similar to the Load Balance Source port but more granular in nature as it distributes traffic across active uplinks based on the source MAC address. Traffic initiated from the same virtual machine interface can be distributed across different uplinks based on the source MAC address of frames. LAGs are also supported with the Load Balance Source MAC Address policy and it is supported on ESXi hosts and Edge Transport Nodes. KVM does not support Load Balance Source Port or Source MAC address teaming policies.

NSX teaming policies specify how the NSX virtual switch traffic will be distributed across its uplinks and uplinks further are mapped to either pNICs or LAGs. In the case of pNICs, it's simple as traffic distributed by NSX teaming policies will be forwarded to different pNICs but with LAGs, it can have its own hashing algorithm to distribute traffic between its physical members. Also, when configuring a Transport Node, a default teaming policy must be specified which is applied to all segments present on the Transport Node. However, with ESXi hosts, this default teaming policy can be overridden with help of the Named Teaming Policy for VLAN backed segments. Please note Named Teaming policies cannot be applied to KVM hosts.

Named Teaming Policies

Overlay-backed segments always use default teaming policy, however, sometimes it is desired to override default teaming policies for specific VLAN backed segments example infrastructure traffic or steer VLAN backed traffic on separate uplinks from overlay-backed traffic. ESXi and Edge Transport Nodes allow for overriding default teaming policies by creating more specific policies based on a name, hence termed Named Teaming Policies. Named Teaming Policies can only be used to override teaming policies for VLAN backed segments only. *Figure* 2.34 shows such an example where the default teaming policy is failover order with Uplink-1 as active and Uplink-2 as standby. Another named teaming policy "ISCSI" has been created with failover order teaming policy however with Uplink-2 as active and Uplink-1 as a standby as is attached to VLAN segment ISCSI. Any virtual machine connected to segment ISCSI will use teaming policy "ISCSI" to send traffic to Uplink-2 instead of Uplink-1 thus overriding the default teaming policy.

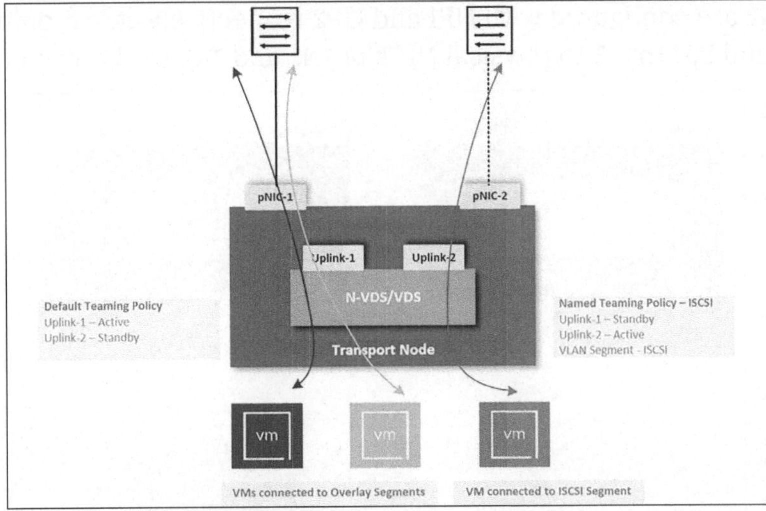

Figure 2.34: *Named Teaming Policy*

Again, an important point to remember is, named teaming policies are not supported by KVM hosts.

Uplink Profile

In order to configure the Transport Node, NSX virtual switch needs to be configured which may include defining transport VLAN for overlay traffic, MTU of uplinks, teaming policies and defining names of uplinks to be used by the NSX virtual switch. It becomes difficult to configure NSX virtual switch on each and every node independently and a hassle for an administrator. In order to avoid these issues, NSX provides an object termed Uplink Profile which can be applied to different Transport Nodes with similar configurations. The uplink profile acts as a template that includes the following information shared across Transport Nodes:

- Transport VLAN used by overlay traffic. Overlay traffic requires a tunnel to be established between Transport Nodes and any traffic on this tunnel is VLAN tagged with the ID specified in Transport VLAN in the physical infrastructure
- MTU of uplinks, default is 1700
- Name of uplinks and LAGs to be used by NSX Virtual Switch
- Default teaming policies and Named teaming policies (For ESXi or Edge Transport Nodes) to be used by uplinks

Figure 2.35 illustrates two Transport Nodes that are configured with help of Uplink Profile **UP1** and **UP2**. **Uplink-1** and **Uplink-2** defined in UP1 and UP2 are the only names given to uplinks of NSX virtual switch and when Transport Nodes **TN1** and **TN2** are configured with UP1 and UP2 respectively, it is required to map **Uplink-1** and **Uplink-2** to physical NICs of **TN1** and **TN2** as shown in the figure.

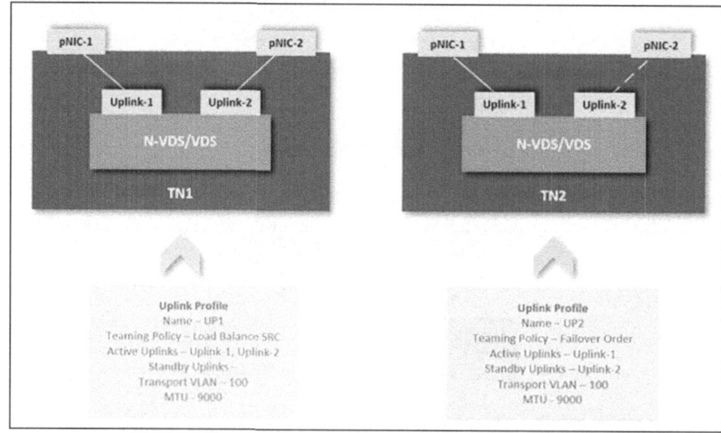

Figure 2.35: *Configure Transport Node with Uplink Profile*

If you look closely at *Figure* 2.35, you will notice that UP1 has teaming policy defined as Load Balance Source whereas UP2 has teaming policy defined as Failover Order. This allowed us to use UP1 with the ESXi host and UP2 with the KVM host instead of forcing the ESXi host to use the Failover Order teaming policy in case of a single uplink profile configuration. By creating multiple uplink profiles, a different group of Transport Nodes can be configured with a unique NSX virtual switch suitable to their requirements.

Note: In the case of NSX on VDS, MTU and LAG definitions are controlled by the vCenter server by defining it directly on VDS. It is possible to use the same uplink profile for both N-VDS or VDS but LAG and MTU definitions will be ignored in the case of VDS.

Creating Uplink Profile in NSX

NSX includes multiple uplink profiles created by default but they all have transport VLAN defined as 0 or native VLAN. It is not possible to delete or modify default uplink profiles and is advised to create new Uplink profiles based on the requirement. The process to create an Uplink profile in NSX Manager is as follows:

Step 1: Login into NSX Manager with admin privileges and navigate to **`System`** tab. Expand **`Fabric`** menu under **`Configuration`** and select **`Profiles.`** Different profiles in the environment can be configured here system-wide. Select **`Uplink Profiles`** and it will display all preconfigured profiles as shown in *Figure* 2.36.

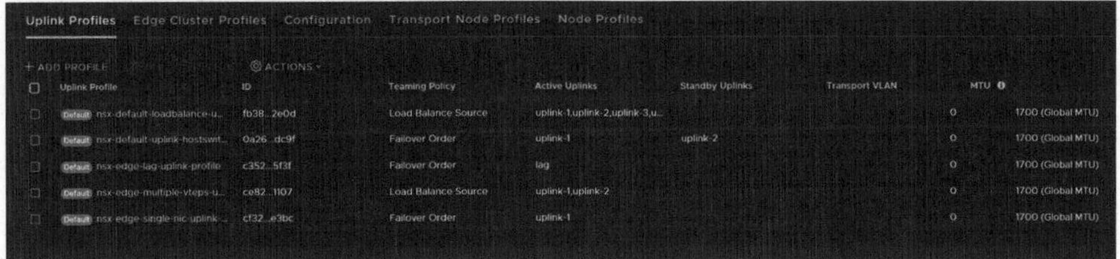

Figure 2.36: *Uplink profiles*

Step 2: Click on **`+Add Profile`** and a new screen will pop up. Provide the details listed as follows and click on **`Add`** to create a new Uplink Profile.

a. **`Name:`** Name of the Uplink profile

b. **`Description`**: Optional, any remark or note about the Uplink profile

c. **`LAGs`**: Click on **`+Add`** to create a new LAG and select LACP

Mode and Load Balancing algorithm

d. **`Teamings`**: Default Teaming is already created. Select the desired teaming policy, for example, Failover Order or Load Balance source. Under Active Uplinks, type the name of the uplink for NSX virtual switch, e.g., Uplink-1. For Load Balance Source, provide uplink names as **`Uplink-1`** and **`Uplink-2`** for 2 active uplinks.

e. **`Transport VLAN:`** Enter the VLAN ID to be used for overlay tunnel IPs

f. **`MTU:`** Enter the MTU value for uplinks, the default is 1700 but the recommended value is 9000.

Example uplink profile details are shown in *Figure* 2.37.

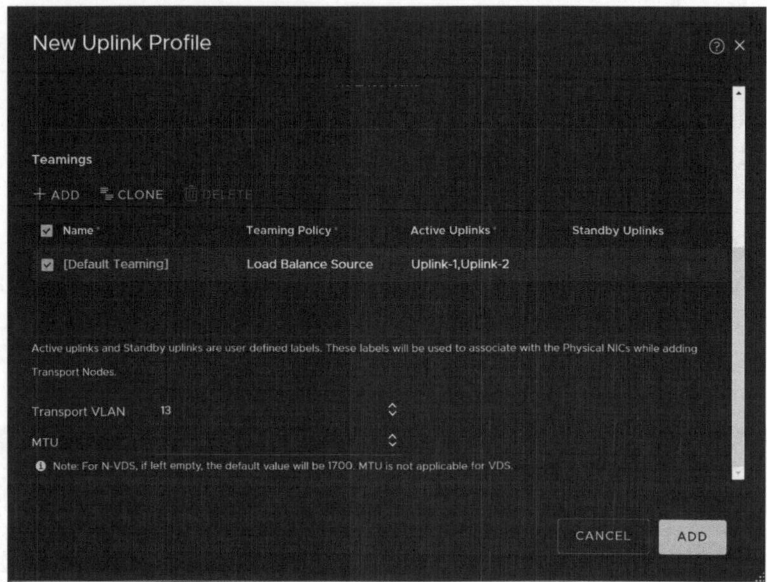

***Figure 2.37**: Details required for New Uplink Profile*

Step 3: **`Uplink Profiles`** now shows the newly created profile. It can be selected to either **`Edit`**, **`Delete`** or **`Add Tags`** as shown in *Figure* 2.38.

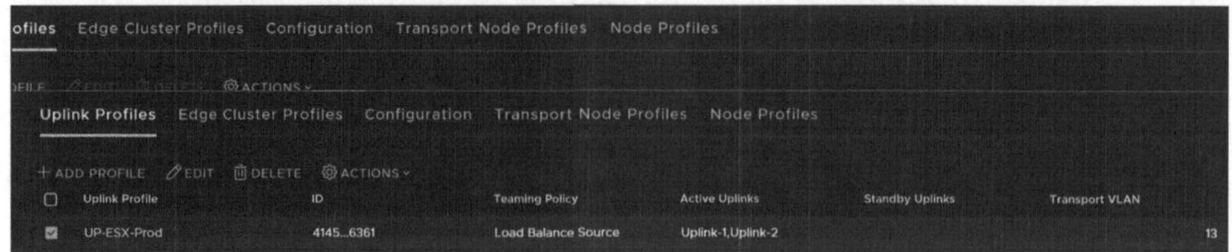

***Figure 2.38:** Newly created uplink profile*

Transport Node Profile

Similar to the uplink profile, Transport Node profiles act as a template that is used to apply the same set of configurations on ESXi hosts in a vSphere cluster. This helps in applying consistent configuration across vSphere clusters and easier management. Instead of configuring each ESXi host separately, hosts within a cluster can be configured in one go. One key point to be noted is the Transport Node profile can only be applied to vSphere clusters. While configuring the Transport Node or Transport Node profile, there are a few other profiles that need to be selected. Let's quickly cover them as well.

LLDP Profile

LLDP stands for Link Layer Discovery Protocol, which is a vendor-neutral link layer protocol that is used by network devices to advertise their identity, capabilities and neighbors. In NSX, you can either Disable or Enable the LLDP profile to send network-related information to the neighbor switch or receive information from them.

If VDS is selected as NSX virtual switch, then the option to select the LLDP profile is hidden as LLDP behavior is controlled by the vCenter server directly on VDS.

NIOC Profile

NIOC (Network I/O Control) as the name suggests allows managing traffic on uplinks in ESXi hosts with the help of shares, reservations or limiting bandwidth. It is the same as the vSphere NIOC feature used to prioritize traffic in ESXi hosts. If VDS is selected as NSX virtual switch, then the option to select the NIOC profile is hidden as NIOC is configured directly on VDS in the vCenter server. NIOC controls the traffic behavior with the help of the following three settings:

- **Shares**: Shares work only when contention is observed on uplinks and they work in a relative manner against other types of traffic. For example, if VM Traffic is assigned shares as 100 and vMotion traffic is assigned shares as 50, in case of contention, network bandwidth will be shared between them in a 2:1 ratio.
- **Reservation:** It defines the minimum bandwidth guaranteed on a single physical network adapter for traffic. If defined for System traffic, any unused bandwidth is available to other system traffic however unused system traffic reservation is not available to VM traffic
- **Limit:** It defines the maximum bandwidth a traffic type can use on a single physical network adapter. It is the opposite of reservation and is used to

limit a specific type of traffic so it doesn't exceed the defined limit, example if vMotion traffic is defined with a limit of 1 Gbps then no matter how much bandwidth is available it will never exceed 1 Gbps on an adapter.

NSX Virtual Switch Operational Mode

During Transport Node creation or Transport Node profile creation under **Advanced** configuration, NSX provides an option to choose different operational modes of NSX virtual switch (this is available for both N-VDS and VDS). These operational modes are:

- Standard
- Enhanced Data Path (EDP)

One key consideration for selecting EDP or Enhanced Data Path operational mode is that it is only available for ESXi hosts and requires NIC cards that support enhanced data path. EDP is a networking stack mode that is configured to provide network performance specifically targeting lower latency and high packet rate. It is possible that network traffic consists of a high number of smaller packets instead of a small number of larger packets as seen in the datacenter. This type of traffic is typically observed in Telco clouds such as NFV (Network Function Virtualization) workloads. EDP is best suited for NFV-type applications as EDP virtual switch has an optimized path and uses a different resource allocation model than the standard mode. EDP is not suitable for enterprise datacenter use cases or where bare metal edges are used.

NSX IP Address Pool

NSX provides an object IP Address Pool which can be used by components such as DHCP or TEP IP on Transport Nodes. IP Address pool is a range, block or group of IP addresses that are handed by the NSX Manager to different components.

While configuring a Transport Node with an overlay Transport Zone, it asks for a TEP IP. TEP IP can be configured either using DHCP, IP Address Pool or Static list. If the environment doesn't have DHCP then it becomes difficult to manage and assign an IP address to each individual Transport Node. This is where the IP Address Pool comes in handy as now it's the NSX Manager who manages the distribution and allocation of IP addresses to Transport Nodes.

IP Address pool can be configured by navigating to **`Networking`** Menu and selecting **`IP Address Pools`**. Click on **`Add IP Address Pool`** and provide a **`name`** and set the **`subnets`** to add an IP address pool which can be further used while creating a Transport Node or Transport Node profile.

Creating Transport Node Profile

Ok, so all set to create a **Transport Node** profile. However, as a quick check ensure you have a compute Manager (vCenter server) registered with NSX- T Manager and ESXi hosts on which the Transport Node profile to be applied are part of the cluster managed by the same vCenter server along with Transport Zone and uplink profiles created in NSX.

Step 1: Login into NSX Manager with admin privileges and navigate to **System** tab. Expand **Fabric** menu under **Configuration** and select **Profiles.** Select **Transport Node Profiles.** Click on **+Add Profile** icon.

Step 2: In the new window **Add Transport Node Profile**, provide the requested details and click **Add** –

a. **Name**: Name of the Transport Node profile

b. **Description**: Remark or note about the Transport Node profile

Under **New Node Switch,** configure NSX virtual switch. If required, click on **+Add Switch** to add an additional NSX virtual switch.

a. **Name**: Select the vCenter server and then select the VDS name to prepare for NSX. If selecting N-VDS, then provide the name of N-VDS

b. **Transport Zone:** Select the Transport Zone created earlier

c. **Uplink Profile**: Select the uplink profile created earlier to configure N-VDS/VDS

d. **IP Assignment (TEP):** Provide the IP Address to be used for TEP (Tunnel End Points) for the overlay Transport Zone. It can be DHCP, IP Pool Base or select Static IP List to provide IP details manually in the profile. This is only applicable if the overlay Transport Zone is selected

e. **Teaming Policy Uplink Mapping:** Map the uplinks defined in the Uplink Profile to uplinks of VDS or physical NICs of Transport Node for N-VDS

f. **Advanced Configuration**: Change the mode if required from Standard to Enhanced Datapath

Figure 2.39 shows an example Transport Node profile configuration.

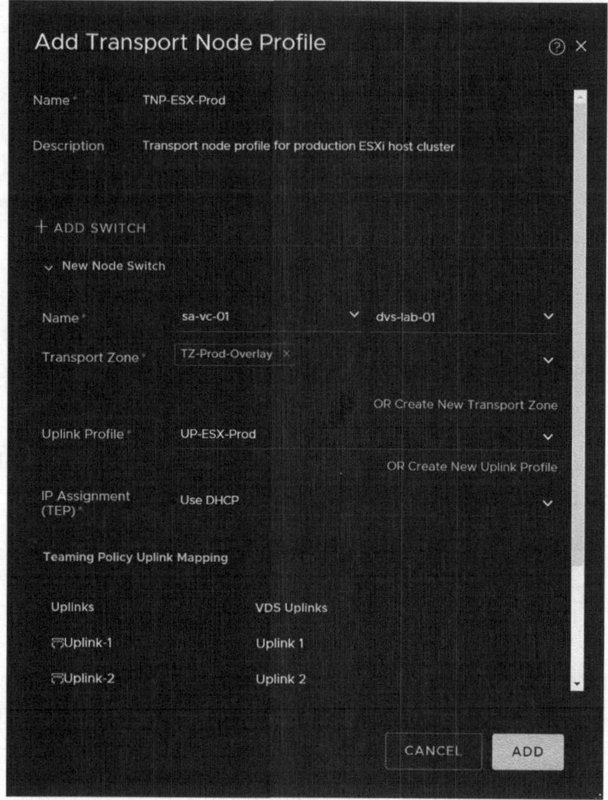

Figure 2.39: *Sample Transport Node profile configuration*

Step 3: A newly created profile appears in **`Transport Node Profiles`** which can be edited or deleted.

Preparing ESXi host as Transport Node

All steps leading up to this point are to prepare the ESXi host as a Transport Node. N-VDS/VDS configuration, Uplink profile and Transport Node profile are all preparatory requirements to configure the ESXi host as a Transport Node. ESXi host can be configured standalone for NSX or with help of the Transport Node profile, all ESXi hosts in a vSphere cluster can be configured in one go. The next steps cover how to install NSX bits on ESXi hosts either in a standalone configuration or with help of a Transport Node profile. One important point to note here, ESXi host should have minimum of 4 CPU cores and 16 GB RAM for successful installation.

Step 1: Login into NSX Manager with admin privileges and navigate to **`System`** tab. Expand **`Fabric`** menu under **`Configuration`** and select **Nodes.** The default screen shows Standalone Hosts added manually in NSX Manager. Click on the drop-down **Managed by** and select **vCenter server** to see ESXi hosts managed by vCenter server as shown in *Figures* 2.40 and 2.41.

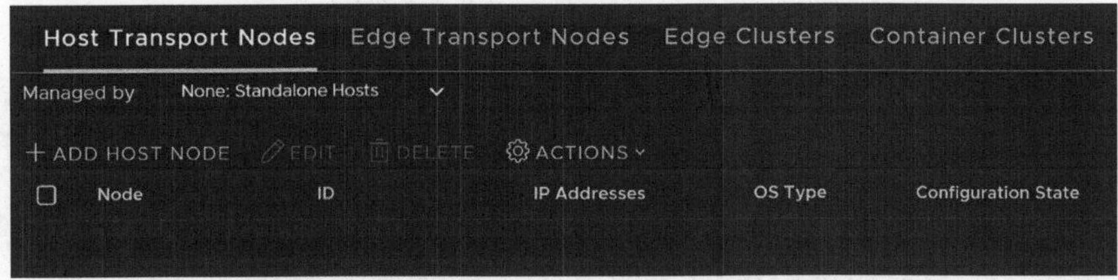

Figure 2.40: *Standalone hosts in NSX Manager*

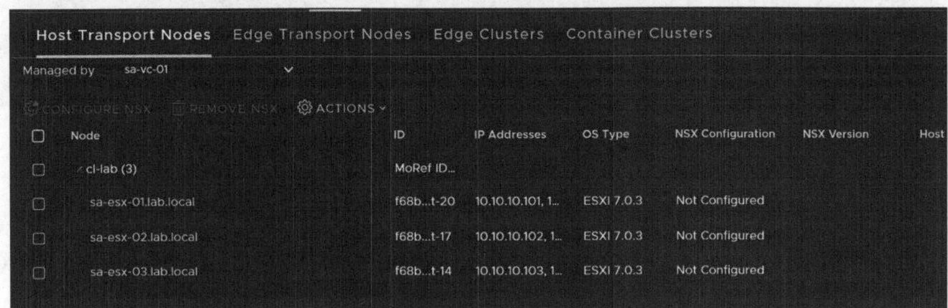

Figure 2.41: *ESXi hosts managed by vCenter in NSX Manager*

Step 2: If need to configure ESXi hosts independently or in a standalone manner, select the desired ESXi host and click **Configure NSX.** This will open a new window **NSX Installation,** click **Next** and it will request the same information as during Transport Node Profile creation. Example screenshot captured in *Figure* 2.42.

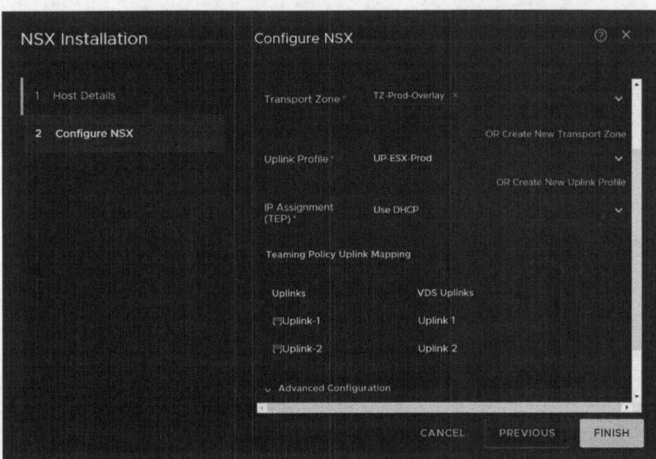

Figure 2.42: *Configure NSX on a standalone ESXi host*

Step 3: Click **`Finish`** and it will start the installation of NSX binaries on the ESXi host.

Step 4: Another way to configure ESXi hosts, instead of selecting individual ESXi hosts, select cluster and click **`Configure NSX`** as shown in *Figure 2.43*.

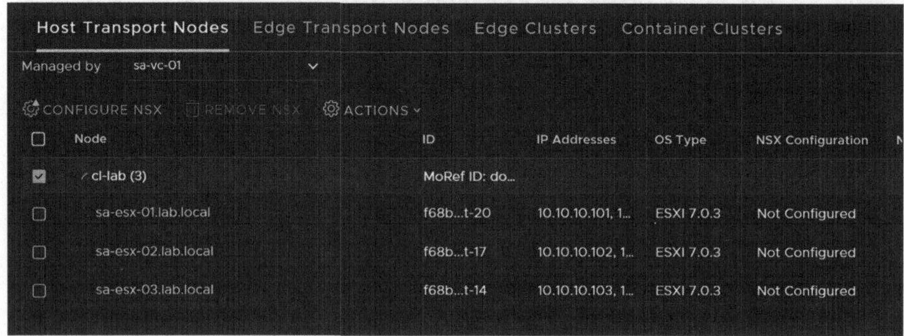

Figure 2.43: *Configure NSX on a vSphere Cluster*

Step 5: Provide the already created **`Transport Node profile`** and click **`Apply.`** This will start the installation of NSX binaries on all ESXi hosts in the cluster as shown in *Figures 2.44 and 2.45*.

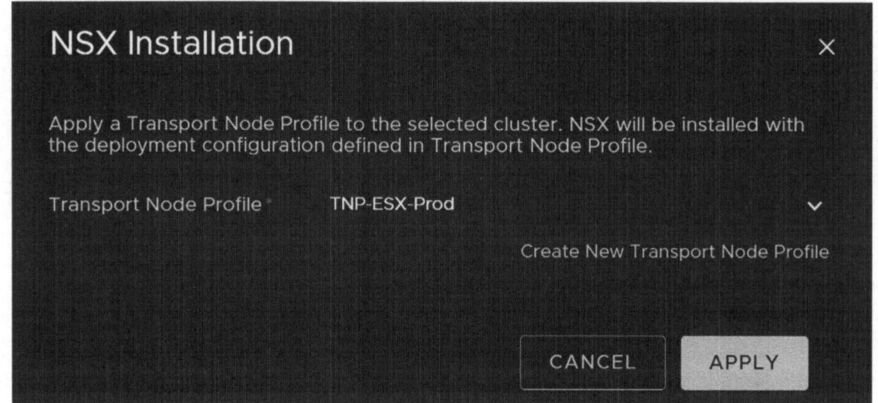

Figure 2.44: *Apply Transport Node profile on cluster*

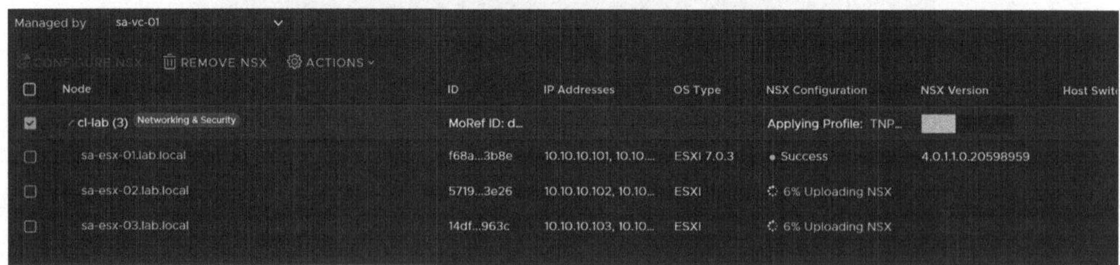

Figure 2.45: *NSX installation in progress on ESXi host*

Step 6: After all, ESXi hosts are configured and prepared for NSX, their node status will be Up and TEP IP will be listed in front of them if configured with overlay Transport Zone as shown in *Figure* 2.46

Host Transport Nodes | Edge Transport Nodes | Edge Clusters | Container Clusters

Managed by sa-vc-01

CONFIGURE NSX | REMOVE NSX | ACTIONS

Node	ID	IP Addresses	OS Type	NSX Configuration	NSX Version	Host Swit	Tunnels	TEP IP Addresses	Node Status
cl-lab (3) Networking & Security	MoRef ID: domai...			Applied Profile: TNP-ESX-Pr...					3 Hosts Up
sa-esx-01.lab.local	f68a...3b8e	10.10.10.101, 10.10.13.101...	ESXi 7.0.3	Success	4.0.1.1.0.20598959	1	Not Availa	10.10.13.101, 10.10.13.102	Up
sa-esx-02.lab.local	5719...3e26	10.10.10.102, 10.10.13.10...	ESXi 7.0.3	Success	4.0.1.1.0.20598959	1	Not Availa	10.10.13.106, 10.10.13.105	Up
sa-esx-03.lab.local	14df...963c	10.10.10.103, 10.10.13.10...	ESXi 7.0.3	Success	4.0.1.1.0.20598959	1	Not Availa	10.10.13.103, 10.10.13.104	Up

***Figure 2.46**: ESXi host with NSX installation completed in NSX*

Congratulations! You have successfully prepared the NSX Data Plane and configured virtual networking on top of it. Before, you start configuring virtual networking or NSX services, let's see how to validate NSX installation on ESXi hosts.

Validating NSX Installation on ESXi Host

There are a few options to validate NSX installation on the ESXi host. One is already covered as part of Step 6 in the previous section under the System menu within Fabric and then going to nodes. Another place within NSX UI is **Monitoring Dashboards**. Navigate to the **`Home`** menu and select **`Monitoring - System`**. It will display Transport Nodes configured in fabric. If there are any issues with Transport Nodes, it will show them as well. *Figure* 2.47 illustrates three Transport Nodes configured and their status as green as no issues observes on them. It may display Amber or Red based on degradation or error with Transport Nodes.

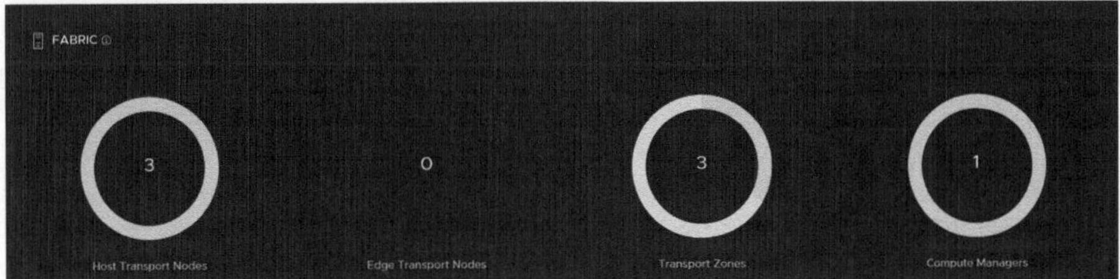

***Figure 2.47**: Monitoring Host Transport Nodes*

The second option is to login into the vCenter server and navigate to the ESXi host, Under **`Configure`** menu, select **`Virtual Switches.`** If NSX on VDS is used, vSphere distributed switch will have **`NSX Switch`** listed in front of them, for example, screenshot captured in *Figure* 2.48.

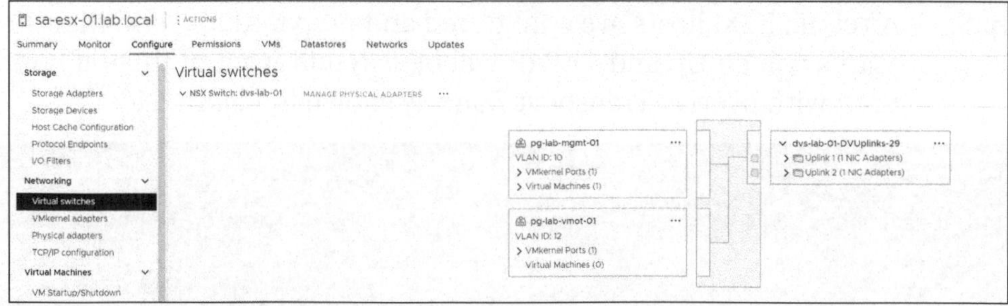

Figure 2.48: NSX *Virtual Switch in vCenter server*

If the ESXi host is configured with an overlay Transport Zone, then it uses TEP IP which is configured as **`VMkernel adapters`** in the ESXi host. Navigate to **`Configure`** and select **`VMkernel Adapters`**. It will show **`vmk10`** and **`vmk11`** configured as overlay TEPs based on teaming policies. *Figure* 2.49 shows vmk10 and vmk11 configured on the ESXi host.

VMkernel adapters

ADD NETWORKING... REFRESH

Device	Network Label	Switch	IP Address	TCP/IP Stack
vmk0	pg-lab-mgmt-01	dvs-lab-01	10.10.10.101	Default
vmk1	pg-lab-vmot-01	dvs-lab-01	10.10.12.101	vMotion
vmk10	--	dvs-lab-01	10.10.13.101	nsx-overlay
vmk11	--	dvs-lab-01	10.10.13.102	nsx-overlay
vmk50	--	dvs-lab-01	169.254.1.1	nsx-hyperbus

Figure 2.49: NSX *Overlay VMkernel adapters configured on ESXi host*

Another option to check for NSX installation on the ESXi host is using ESXCLI. With help of an SSH session on the ESXi host, run the following command to view and validate NSX VIBs successfully installed on the ESXi host which is installed on the ESXi host as part of host preparation and provide virtual networking features such as distributed firewalling, distributed routing and other NSX services on ESXi host.

```
esxcli software vib list | grep nsx
```

Table 2.6 shows an example output on an ESXi host of the preceding command.

```
[root@sa-esx-02:~] esxcli software vib list | grep nsx
nsx-adf                            4.0.1.1.0-7.0.20598959
VMware  VMwareCertified   2023-01-11
nsx-cfgagent                       4.0.1.1.0-7.0.20598959
VMware  VMwareCertified   2023-01-11
nsx-context-mux                    4.0.1.1.0-7.0.20598959
VMware  VMwareCertified   2023-01-11
nsx-cpp-libs                       4.0.1.1.0-7.0.20598959
VMware  VMwareCertified   2023-01-11
nsx-esx-datapath                   4.0.1.1.0-7.0.20598959
VMware  VMwareCertified   2023-01-11
nsx-exporter                       4.0.1.1.0-7.0.20598959
VMware  VMwareCertified   2023-01-11
nsx-host                           4.0.1.1.0-7.0.20598959
VMware  VMwareCertified   2023-01-11
nsx-ids                            4.0.1.1.0-7.0.20598959
VMware  VMwareCertified   2023-01-11
nsx-monitoring                     4.0.1.1.0-7.0.20598959
VMware  VMwareCertified   2023-01-11
nsx-mpa                            4.0.1.1.0-7.0.20598959
VMware  VMwareCertified   2023-01-11
nsx-nestdb                         4.0.1.1.0-7.0.20598959
VMware  VMwareCertified   2023-01-11
nsx-netopa                         4.0.1.1.0-7.0.20598959
VMware  VMwareCertified   2023-01-11
nsx-opsagent                       4.0.1.1.0-7.0.20598959
VMware  VMwareCertified   2023-01-11
nsx-platform-client                4.0.1.1.0-7.0.20598959
VMware  VMwareCertified   2023-01-11
nsx-proto2-libs                    4.0.1.1.0-7.0.20598959
VMware  VMwareCertified   2023-01-11
nsx-proxy                          4.0.1.1.0-7.0.20598959
VMware  VMwareCertified   2023-01-11
nsx-python-gevent                  1.3.5.py35-19972216
VMware  VMwareCertified   2023-01-11
```

```
nsx-python-greenlet            0.4.14.py35-19345965
VMware  VMwareCertified   2023-01-11
nsx-python-logging             4.0.1.1.0-7.0.20598959
VMware  VMwareCertified   2023-01-11
nsx-python-protobuf            2.6.1-19195979
VMware  VMwareCertified   2023-01-11
nsx-python-utils               4.0.1.1.0-7.0.20598959
VMware  VMwareCertified   2023-01-11
nsx-sfhc                       4.0.1.1.0-7.0.20598959
VMware  VMwareCertified   2023-01-11
nsx-shared-libs                4.0.1.1.0-7.0.20598959
VMware  VMwareCertified   2023-01-11
nsx-vdpi                       4.0.1.1.0-7.0.20598959
VMware  VMwareCertified   2023-01-11
nsxcli                         4.0.1.1.0-7.0.20598959
VMware  VMwareCertified   2023-01-11
```

***Table 2.6**: Verifying NSX VIB installation on ESXi host*

Conclusion

In this chapter, we covered the deployment of NSX Managers and preparing the Data Plane which includes creating a Transport Zone, uplink profile and Transport Node profile. It is important to understand how the Transport Zone scopes the span of the virtual network in the NSX environment and the NSX Virtual switch attaches a Transport Node to the Transport Zone. There are different teaming policies available in NSX to provide redundancy and load balancing of traffic on uplinks in the NSX virtual switch and VLAN backed segments can have their own teaming policies defined overriding default teaming policies with help of named teaming policies in the ESXi host. Finally, we discussed how to configure the ESXi host as a Transport Node.

Now that deployment is done, the next step is to create Segments or Layer 2 domains in the NSX environment and see different profiles which can be applied to segments. Also, how traffic flows between two VMs when they are connected to the same segment. Hang tight! All this will be covered in the next chapter Logical Switching.

Key Terms

- **OVA (Open Virtualization Appliance):** A template file preconfigured with the operating system and application provided by the vendor to deploy in the customer environment
- **SSH:** A cryptographic network protocol that provides network services securely over an unsecured network, operates on port TCP 22 and is mainly used for remote login
- **Nsx-proxy:** An agent running on the Transport Node responsible for communication with the NSX Manager node through APH
- **APH (Appliance Proxy Hub):** Service running on NSX Manager node responsible for communication between NSX Manager node and Transport Node
- **Transport Zone:** Define the scope of the virtual network in the NSX environment
- **NSX Virtual Switch:** Core component of Transport Node which attaches a Transport Node to the Transport Zone, acts as a forwarding engine
- **Uplink Profile:** A template to configure common settings on NSX virtual switch on different Transport Nodes
- **Default teaming policy:** A mandatory teaming policy that defines how the traffic is distributed between uplinks of NSX virtual switch.

Chapter 3

Logical Switching

Introduction

In the previous chapter, we reviewed how to prepare underlying infrastructure, deploy NSX Manager and configure Data Plane with help of ESXi hosts. Post performing these steps, we are at a stage where we can start consuming NSX services in the data center. For any data center network, switching and routing are the most important and core concepts. NSX too provides logical switching and routing services to a virtual machine, container or applications running on transport nodes.

This chapter covers logical switching, explaining Geneve encapsulation to provide an L2 subnet over L3, creating and configuring segments and their segment profile to tweak traffic behavior over a segment in order to reflect business requirements.

Structure

In this chapter, we will cover the following topics:

- Logical Switching
  - Key Terminologies in NSX Logical Switching
  - Geneve Encapsulation
- NSX Segments
  - Creation of Segments Behind the Scene
  - Configuring Segments
  - Configuring Segment Profiles
  - Configuring VNI Pool for Segments

- Logical Switching Packet Walks
  - o Segment Tables on NSX Controller
  - o Unicast Traffic Packet Walk
  - o Flooded/BUM Traffic Packet Walk

Logical Switching

NSX is entirely capable of providing switching services in a virtual networking environment. Logical switches are layer 2 broadcast domains across Transport Nodes in NSX networking which can be compared to VLAN in physical network infrastructure. But why is logical switching required? The current physical network infrastructure is very rigid and inflexible to today's workload requirements. There are multiple challenges with traditional network switching, and some of the key challenges are:

- Today's applications require network segmentation. In the multitenancy model, network segmentation for each application will require a separate set of VLANs and given the maximum limit of VLANs 4096 it can be reached very easily very soon.
- Compute virtualization and containerization have enabled to run workload anywhere and migrate it from one place to another. In order to provide continuous connectivity to the application, the same layer 2 needs to be present everywhere. This can complicate the design of data center networks and result in VLAN sprawl and STP can further complicate things.
- There will always be a limit of compute resources available on physical network hardware resulting in MAC or FIB memory table limitations.

NSX logical switching can solve these challenges presented by physical network hardware with help of segments (in Policy UI) or logical switches (in Manager UI). Some of the key benefits provided by NSX segments/logical switches are:

- With the help of overlay logical switches, there are no VLAN limitations and applications can be multi-tenant or segmented easily
- Layer 2 broadcast domain can be extended over layer 3 network with help of overlay networks resulting in workload mobility anywhere in the data center
- No need to invest in new physical network hardware as existing hardware can be used to enable NSX logical switching

- NSX segments can span across multiple switches and hypervisor hosts. It offloads MAC learning from underlying network switches for workloads to overcome hardware memory table limitations

As discussed in the previous chapter, before utilizing NSX services such as logical switching, NSX Management Cluster must be formed, stable and ready to use. Also, Transport Nodes which are going to participate in NSX networking must be prepared for NSX and present in NSX Manager.

Key Terminologies in NSX Logical Switching

Before diving deep into creating and configuring NSX logical switches there are a few key terminologies which need to be covered first:

- **Segment (Policy UI)/Logical Switches (Manager UI)**: These are layer 2 broadcast domains spanned across Transport Nodes.
- **Segment Profile (Policy UI)/Switching Profile (Manager UI):** These are configuration templates which provide more granular control over segments/logical switches.
- **Segment Ports (Policy UI)/Logical Switch Ports (Manager UI):** Logical ports which interface with the virtual NIC of VM or container applications.
- **T0/T1 Gateway:** It provides routing between segments in the NSX environment. T0 gateway also connects with the physical network to provide N-S routing between NSX virtual networks and physical networks.

Note: Depending upon the UI mode selected (either Policy UI or Manager UI), terms for a few menu items get changed such as the segment in Policy UI becomes Logical Switch in Manager UI. This book refers to Policy UI terms while discussing configurations or step-by-step guides unless Manager UI is specifically specified.

We touched base on overlay networks and their benefits over traditional VLAN-backed networks. NSX uses Geneve (Generic Network Virtualization Encapsulation) encapsulation for its overlay model. Geneve is currently in IETF Internet Draft build on top of VXLAN to provide enhanced flexibility over VXLAN.

Geneve Encapsulation

Geneve is an IETF protocol which provides a tunnel mechanism to enable layer 2 over layer 3 encapsulation similar to VXLAN. In overlay segments/logical switches, the data plane packet is encapsulated in the Geneve header before it leaves the Transport Node and encapsulated packet is transmitted to the destination Transport Node TEP IP address over UDP port 6081. These Geneve encapsulated packets are transferred between Transport Nodes with the help of tunnels established between TEP (Tunnel Endpoints). Destination Transport Node decapsulates the Geneve header and delivers the source frame to VM. *Figure* 3.1 displays the Geneve header as taken from the IETF draft.

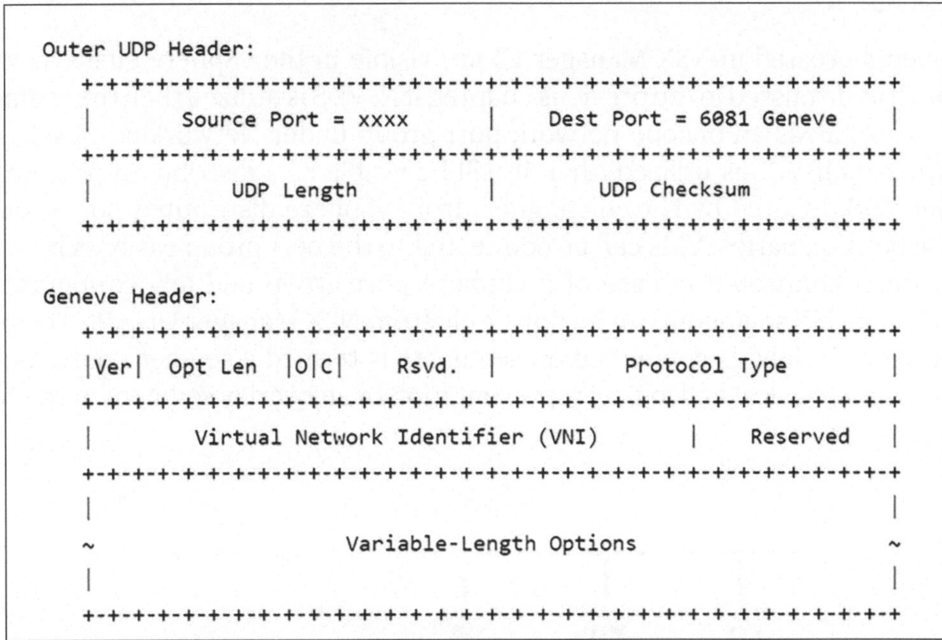

```
Outer UDP Header:
   +-+-+-+-+-+-+-+-+-+-+-+-+-+-+-+-+-+-+-+-+-+-+-+-+-+-+-+-+-+-+-+-+
   |       Source Port = xxxx      |    Dest Port = 6081 Geneve    |
   +-+-+-+-+-+-+-+-+-+-+-+-+-+-+-+-+-+-+-+-+-+-+-+-+-+-+-+-+-+-+-+-+
   |           UDP Length          |        UDP Checksum           |
   +-+-+-+-+-+-+-+-+-+-+-+-+-+-+-+-+-+-+-+-+-+-+-+-+-+-+-+-+-+-+-+-+

Geneve Header:
   +-+-+-+-+-+-+-+-+-+-+-+-+-+-+-+-+-+-+-+-+-+-+-+-+-+-+-+-+-+-+-+-+
   |Ver|  Opt Len  |O|C|    Rsvd.  |          Protocol Type        |
   +-+-+-+-+-+-+-+-+-+-+-+-+-+-+-+-+-+-+-+-+-+-+-+-+-+-+-+-+-+-+-+-+
   |        Virtual Network Identifier (VNI)       |    Reserved   |
   +-+-+-+-+-+-+-+-+-+-+-+-+-+-+-+-+-+-+-+-+-+-+-+-+-+-+-+-+-+-+-+-+
   |                                                               |
   ~                    Variable-Length Options                    ~
   |                                                               |
   +-+-+-+-+-+-+-+-+-+-+-+-+-+-+-+-+-+-+-+-+-+-+-+-+-+-+-+-+-+-+-+-+
```

***Figure 3.1**: Geneve encapsulation header (From IETF Draft)*

Geneve header provides control plane independence between tunnel endpoints and offers the following features:

- It utilizes UDP protocol to send traffic between Transport Nodes and uses port 6081.
- There is a provision of a 24-bit **VNI (Virtual Network Identifier)** field to uniquely identify segments in the NSX environment.
- This is supported by tcpdump and Wireshark tools which help in network troubleshooting by capturing traffic.

NSX Segments

As discussed earlier, segments are layer 2 subnets representing layer 2 broadcasting domain across Transport Nodes in NSX networking. Segments can be either VLAN-backed or overlay backed based on the type of Transport Zone they are part of, also Transport Zone defines the span of segments. A segment will be visible on all Transport Nodes which are attached to the same Transport Zone, so any workload such as VM, container or application can be attached to the same segment even if they are running on different Transport Nodes. Each segment is assigned an ID called VNI (Virtual Network Identifier) similar to VLAN ID but it is completely different from VLAN ID and shouldn't be confused with the same.

Segments created in NSX Manager UI are visible in the vSphere client as well. Though as discussed in the previous chapter, if N-VDS is utilized then the segment will be visible as an opaque network port group under Networking in vCenter UI whereas if VDS is utilized, then it will be visible as a distributed port group under VDS denoted by **N** to distinguish from vSphere distributed port groups. But in both scenarios, VMs can be connected to the port group easily as it would have been connected in case of a vSphere port group and any configuration change on NSX segments can be done only from NSX Manager UI/API. The port to which workload is connected on segments is termed a segment port. *Figure 3.2* shows a physical and logical representation of an overlay segment in the NSX environment.

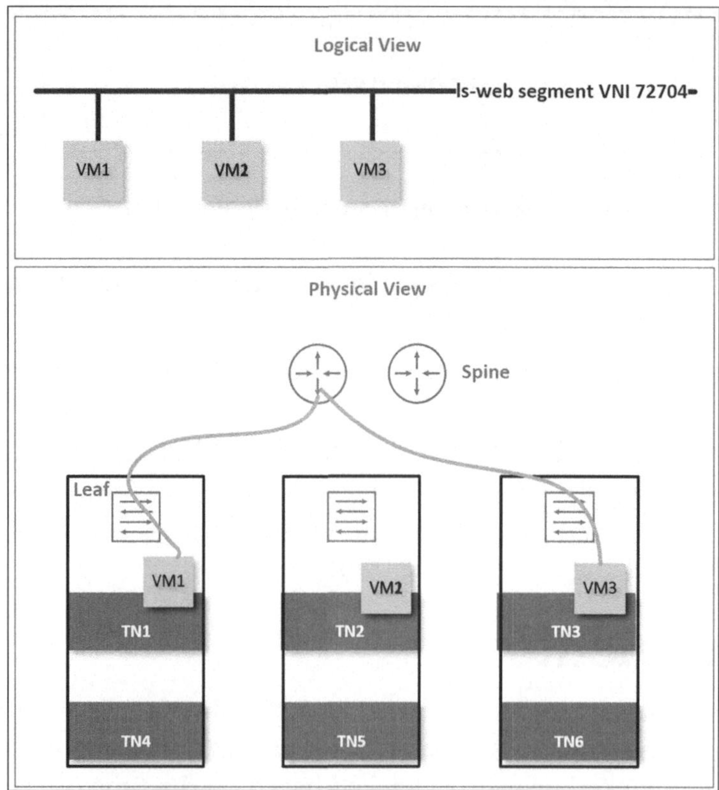

Figure 3.2: *VMs belonging to the same overlay segment running on different Transport Nodes*

A segment named ls-web is created in NSX Manager and is present on all Transport Nodes from TN1 to TN6 as they are part of the same Transport Zone. VMs are running on different Transport Nodes which belong to different underlay networks, but they are still able to communicate with each other.

In the preceding figure, all VMs belong to the same overlay segment ls-web, however physically they are spread across the environment running on different hypervisor Transport Nodes. Following a standard Leaf Spine networking model, TEP VLANs are restricted to their respective Leaf switches. Even though TEP IPs are configured with different network addresses, for VMs to communicate with each other, it doesn't matter and they do not require any special configuration on switches apart from connectivity between different TEP VLANs and Jumbo Frame support. NSX controller takes care of distributing TEP IPs between Transport Nodes to establish a tunnel between nodes and enable communication between VMs. Let's take a closer look at the communication between VM1 and VM3.

Step 1: Assuming VM1 and VM3 want to communicate with each other. Since they are sitting on the same segment ls-web, they are on the same network. Any initiation of traffic from VM1 will result in sending a frame from VM1 to VM3. So, as a first step, VM1 will send a frame on the ls-web segment destined for VM3.

Step 2: The frame will be received by hypervisor TN1 from VM1. But since VM3 is sitting on a different host, TN1 will identify that VM3's MAC address belongs to a different TEP, TN1 will encapsulate the packet in a UDP Geneve encapsulated packet and will send it on the physical network.

Step 3: The physical network receives the packet and forwards it to the destination TN3 based on the destination IP address of TN3 TEP.

Step 4: TN3 receives the packet and identifies it as a Geneve encapsulated packet and decapsulates it. Based on the information in the Geneve header, it puts the frame from VM1 on segment ls-web and uses standard switching to deliver it to VM3.

This allows end-to-end communication between VM1 and VM3. This example assumes that the MAC addresses of VM1 and VM3 are known to the hypervisor. BUM traffic (Broadcast, Unknown Unicast, Multicast) handling and ARP suppression in an NSX environment has been covered in detail in later sections of this chapter.

Creating Segments behind the Scene

Segments are created and configured from NSX UI/API interface but there are multiple agents responsible for realizing the desired configuration of a segment on all Transport Nodes configured in NSX Manager. *Figure* 3.3 displays the step-by-step process that happens within NSX Manager and Transport Nodes.

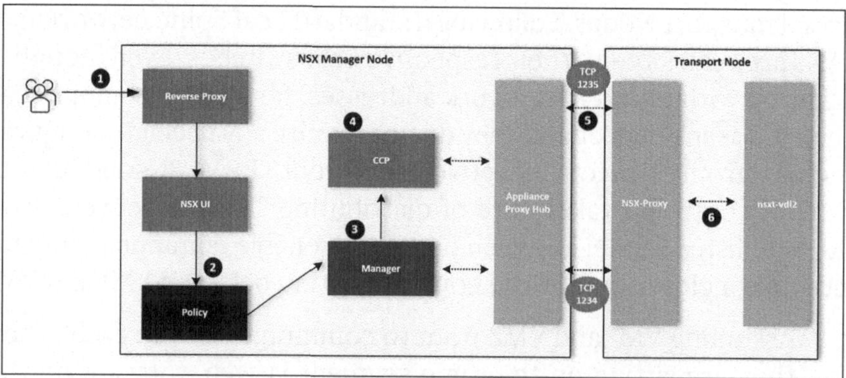

Figure 3.3: *Creating Segment in NSX environment*

As a first step, the user creates a segment in **`NSX Manager`** either through a graphical interface or programmatically using an API interface. This request is received by Reverse Proxy which then hands this over to the **`Policy role`**. In the second step, the Policy role pushes this configuration to the **`Manager role`** which translates the declarative configuration into an imperative state and saves it in distributed Corfu database. The Manager role forwards the translated configuration to **CCP (Central Control Plane)** to realize it in Transport Nodes. As discussed earlier, any communication between NSX Manager and Transport Node is taken care of by **APH (Appliance Proxy Hub),** so CCP forwards the configuration to APH to be forwarded to Transport Nodes. Now APH communicates with Transport Nodes with the help of nsx-proxy agent running on Transport Nodes on NSX-RCP communication protocol with TCP port 1235. As a last step, on Transport Nodes, the nsx-proxy agent receives the configuration from APH on NSX Manager and forwards it to the switching kernel module nsxt-vdl2 running on ESXi host or Open vSwitch running on non-ESXi nodes. These switching kernel modules create and configure the segments in Transport Nodes.

Configuring Segments

We have discussed about segments in the NSX environment theoretically in detail. So, what is required to configure segments in the NSX environment? It involved multiple steps such as creating a segment, attaching a workload such as VM to a segment, validating connectivity and configuring policies on a segment. In this section, we will cover all these steps in detail and the next section covers the Segment Profiles which are used to configure policies on a segment.

Creating a Segment in NSX

The following steps are used to create a segment in the NSX environment using GUI (Graphical User Interface).

Step 1: Login to NSX Manager UI using credentials with required privileges. Go to the **`Networking`** menu and click on **`Segments`** under **`Connectivity`** in NSX Manager. This displays all the segments created in the NSX environment. As there are no segments created in the NSX environment, a blank canvas is displayed as shown in *Figure 3.4*.

Figure 3.4: *Segments menu in NSX Manager UI*

Step 2: In order to create a new Segment, click on the **`Add Segment`** button and it will create a form with inputs on the same page as shown in *Figure 3.5*.

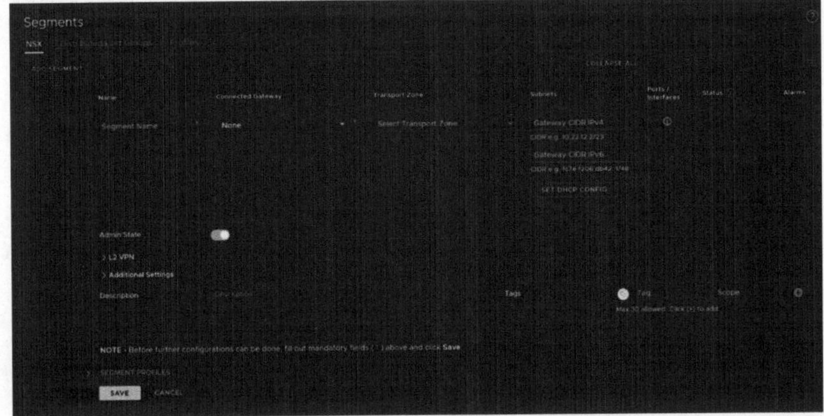

Figure 3.5: *Adding a segment in NSX UI*

Step 3: There are a few mandatory fields that need to be provided which are:

- **`Segment Name`**: Name of the segment for identification
- **`Connected Gateway`**: If it is an overlay segment, select the next hop to enable Layer 3 communication. This can be compared to the SVI (Switched Virtual Interface) of a VLAN.
- **`Transport Zone`**: Select whether it will be a VLAN-backed or overlay-backed segment
- **`Subnets:`** This defines the gateway IP address and range of broadcast domain.
- **`Admin State:`** `It` can be toggled on or off to enable or disable the segment
- **`VLAN:`** It becomes mandatory if VLAN Transport Zone is selected and VLAN ID needs to be defined here.

Figure 3.6 shows an example configuration of NSX segment ls-web with subnet 10.10.10.1/24.

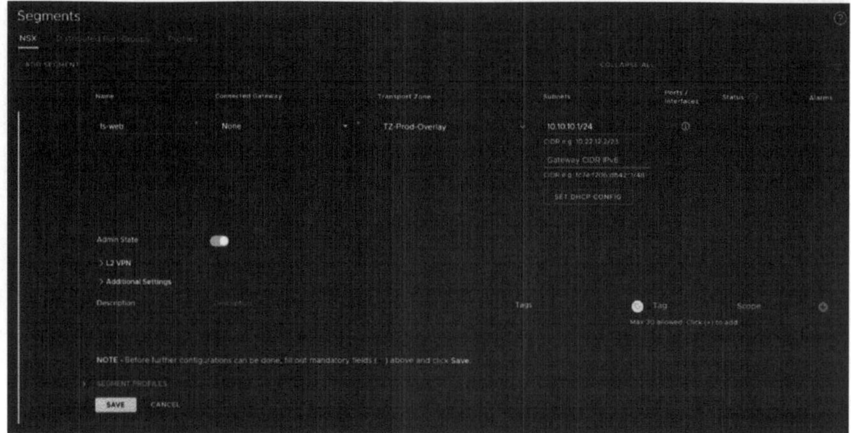

Figure 3.6*: Example snippet of segment details*

Step 4: Click **`Save`** and then select **`No`** for further configurations to finish creating a segment. *Figure* 3.7 illustrates the segment ls-web created and realized successfully. In case the segment is not realized on Transport Nodes, then the Status would be either Amber Degraded or Red Error instead of Green Success.

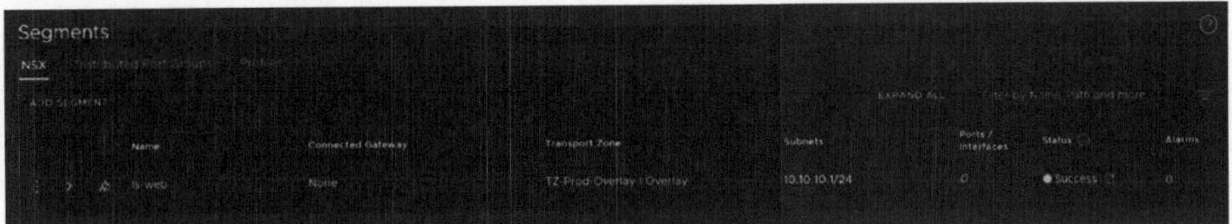

Figure 3.7: *Segment realized successfully in NSX Manager*

Connecting a VM to NSX Segment

The segment has been successfully created in NSX Manager UI and realized on Transport Nodes. The next step is to connect VMs to NSX segments. As NSX Manager is fully integrated with the vCenter server, it is possible to connect VMs directly from the vCenter server to NSX segments, however, in the case of KVM, it is more of a manual process. Attaching a VM running on KVM to the NSX segment is out of scope for this book but a reference has been provided at the end to VMware documentation. Let's see how VMs running on ESXi hosts can be connected to the NSX segment in the vCenter server.

Step 1: Login to vCenter Server UI with user credentials that have appropriate privileges. Head over to **Networking** in **Inventory** and select the **VDS** prepared for NSX. Expanding the VDS and NSX segment should be visible as a distributed port group with the denotation **N.** *Figure* 3.8 shows the details of the segment such as Transport Zone, its segment ID, number of hosts it is present on and if **Configure** tab is selected, it will be in read-only mode as any changes on the NSX segment can be done from NSX Manager only.

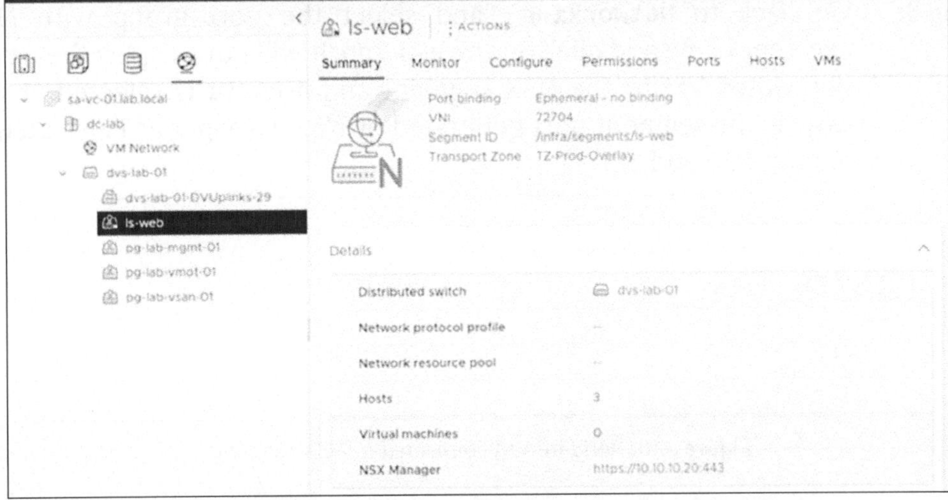

Figure 3.8: *NSX Segment in vCenter Server*

Step 2: Go to `VMs and Templates` and select the VM. Click on `Action` and then on `Edit Settings.` This opens a new dialogue box `Edit Settings.` Change the network adapter to the port group name of the NSX Segment and click `Ok` to connect the VM to the NSX segment. *Figure* 3.9 displays how to connect VM vm-web-01 to NSX segment ls-web.

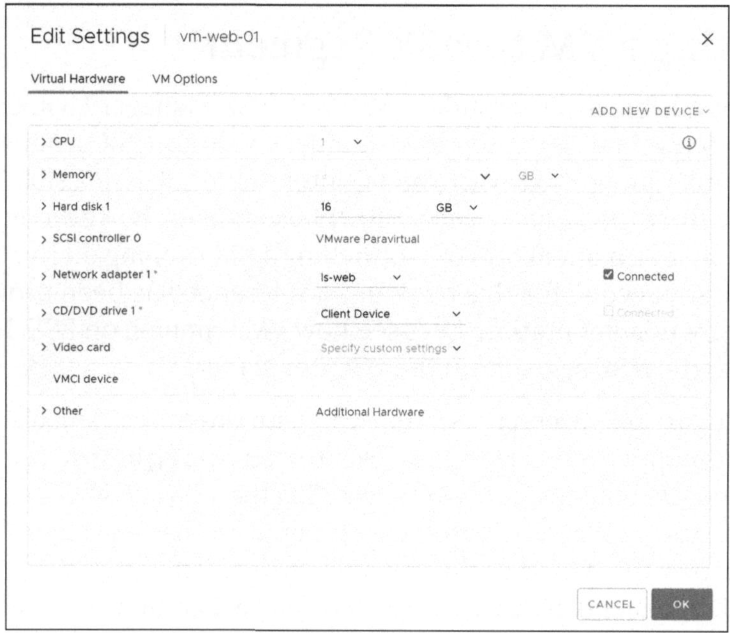

***Figure 3.9**: Connecting a VM to the NSX segment*

Step 3: Go back to `Networking` and select the port group with NSX segment name and click on the `VMs` tab. It will now display the newly connected VM to the NSX segment and if `Ports` is selected, it will display the segment port generated by NSX Manager as illustrated in *Figures* 3.10 and 3.11.

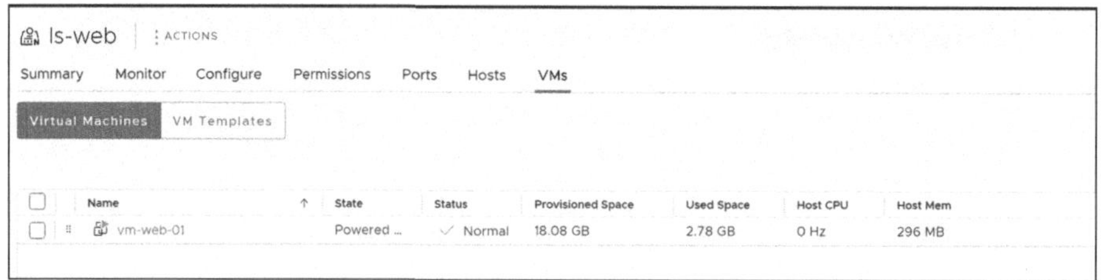

***Figure 3.10**: Validate VM connected to NSX segment*

Figure 3.10 illustrates VM with name vm-web-01 connected to NSX segment ls-web whereas *Figure* 3.11 illustrates port ID of VM vm-web-01 generated by NSX Manager when VM vm-web-01 was connected to NSX segment ls-web.

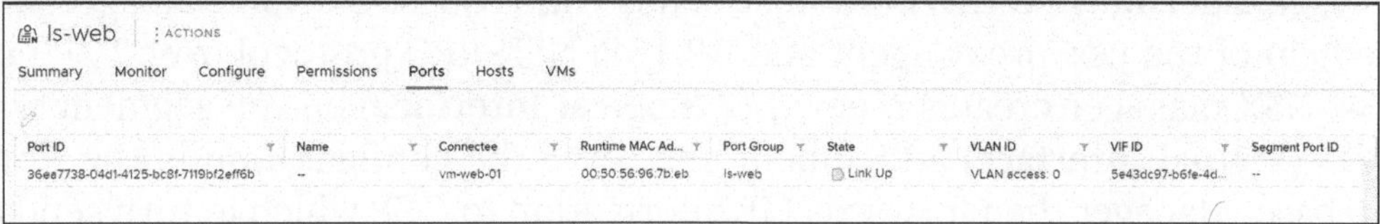

Figure 3.11: *Validate NSX segment port created by NSX Manager*

Step 4: Navigate back to NSX Manager UI and go to the **`Networking`** menu and click on **`Segments`** under **`Connectivity.`** Click on the Numeral number under Ports/Interfaces. It will display the same information as present in the vCenter server with a segment port created by NSX Manager automatically as shown in *Figure* 3.12.

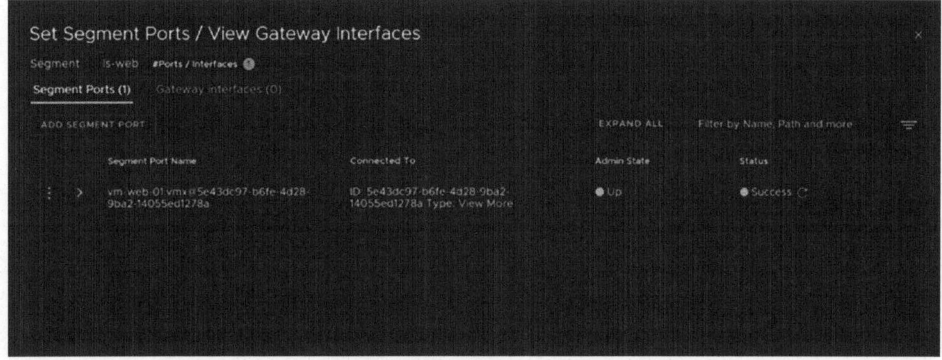

Figure 3.12: *Segment Ports as present in NSX Manager UI*

This validates the connectivity of a workload such as VM to the NSX segment and its association with help of the NSX segment port. If Admin Status or Status is other than Green or Success, it means that realization of configuration was not successful and troubleshooting is required as per error details.

Connecting a VM to NSX segment Behind the Scene

Well, we are able to successfully create the segment and connect a VM to it without any issues. But what happens behind the scenes? How does a VM get connected to the NSX segment when all the configuration needs to be done from NSX Manager only? So, *Figure* 3.13 displays the entire process and how it all happens in the backend.

The user connects a VM to an NSX segment visible as a distributed port group in the vCenter server. As the vCenter server is just a management layer, it, in turn, sends the request to the ESXi host on which VM is currently running. As we saw earlier, all the configuration changes on NSX segments are handled by NSX Manager only so the ESXi host sends the request to NSX Manager with the help of the nsx-proxy agent and APH via NSX-RPC protocol over TCP port 1234. NSX manager creates a new **LIF (Logical Interface)** on the segment with a **VIF (Virtual Interface)** attachment and saves the configuration in the Corfu database. Manager then forwards LIF information to CCP which in turn sends it to the ESXi host on which the VM is currently running via APH and nsx-proxy. This mapping of the Logical Interface and Virtual Interface is then realized on the ESXi host to allow communication from VM.

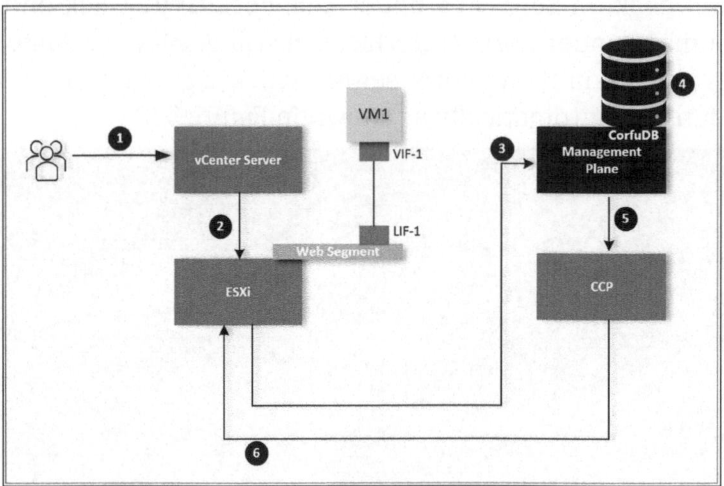

***Figure 3.13**: Connecting a VM to NSX Segment behind the scene*

Configuring Segment Profiles

Segment profiles are layer 2 configuration templates which can be applied to one or more segments for more granular control over segment policies instead of configuring each segment individually. NSX Manager provides five different types of segment profiles according to their function which are:

- **SpoofGuard**: This profile prevents a form of malicious attack called NIC spoofing either by spoofing the IP address or MAC address by validating the binding of the IP and MAC address to the virtual NIC.
- **QoS Segment Profile:** This profile provides high performance and dedicated network bandwidth for preferred traffic by prioritizing sufficient bandwidth, reducing latency, controlling jitters and reducing data loss for the preferred packet in network congestion.

- **Segment Security:** This profile provides stateless layer 2 and layer 3 security by checking ingress traffic and dropping unauthorized packets.
- **IP Discovery:** This profile helps in learning MAC and IP address with help of DHCP snooping, ARP snooping, **ND (Neighbor Discovery)** or VMware tools running on a virtual machine.
- **MAC Discovery** - This profile provides two functions namely - MAC learning and MAC address change.

NSX Manager has default segment profiles already created for each type and when a new segment is created, by default it uses these pre-created default segment profiles. However, custom segment profiles can be created which are based on the default segment profile and override any defaults. Another key point to remember is, a custom segment profile cannot be deleted if it is assigned to a segment or segment port and also a segment or segment port can be assigned only one profile of each type. For example, a segment cannot be assigned two QoS segment profiles.

Note: Default segment profiles cannot be edited or deleted. However, custom profiles can be created to override the default behavior of the segment or segment port. Also, by default for all segment profiles except Segment Security, the custom profile will inherit settings from the appropriate default segment profile.

Let's discuss each type of segment profile in more detail and how these are configured in NSX Manager.

Creating Segment Profile and Applying to Segment

Step 1: Login into NSX Manager UI using user credentials with sufficient privileges. Navigate to the **`Networking`** menu and click on **`Segments`** under **`Connectivity.`**

Step 2: Click on the tab named **`Profiles`** under **`Segments.`** It will display all the different profiles already created in the NSX environment as illustrated in *Figure* 3.14.

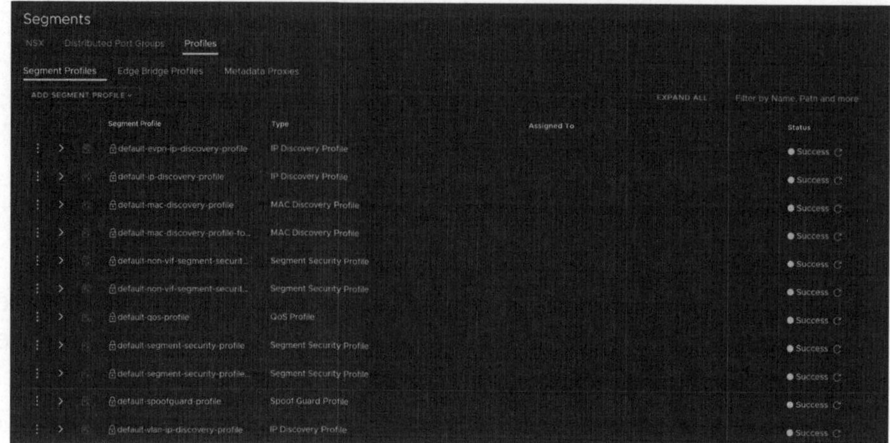

Figure 3.14: Default segment profiles present in the NSX environment

Step 3: Click on **`Add Segment Profile`** and it will ask to select the type of segment profile to be created as shown in *Figure* 3.15. According to different segment profile types, each segment profile will provide a different set of configurations that have been covered in detail in subsequent sections.

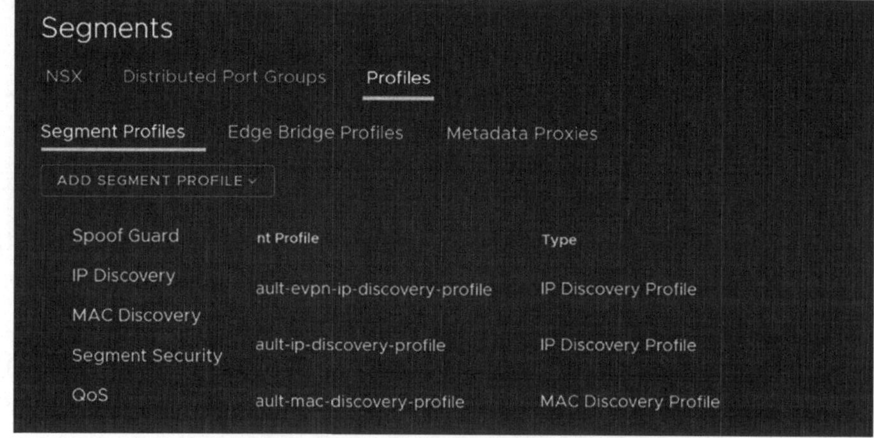

Figure 3.15: Different types of segment profiles

Step 4: After a desired segment profile is created, the next step is to assign the segment profile to the segment. In order to assign a segment profile to a segment, navigate back to **`Segments`** under **`Connectivity`** and this time select **`NSX`** instead of **`Profiles.`** This is the same place where segments are created. Click on the **`little triangle icon (>)`** to expand the desired segment details. *Figure* 3.16 displays segment ls-web expanded to show all the details.

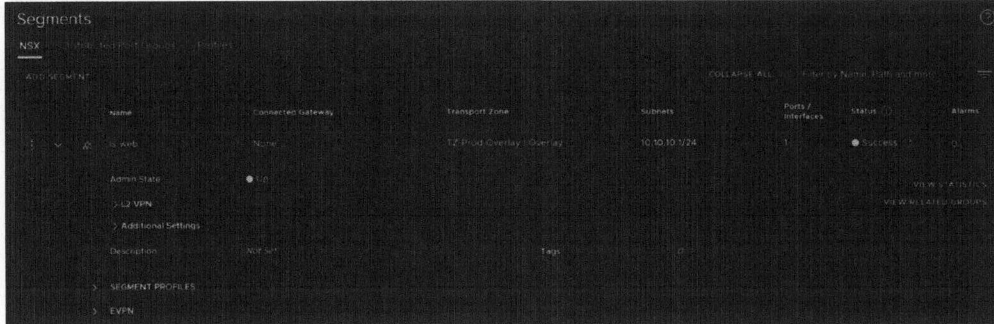

Figure 3.16: *Expanded details of a segment*

Step 5: Click on the three dots beside the name of the segment and select `Edit` as shown in *Figure* 3.17.

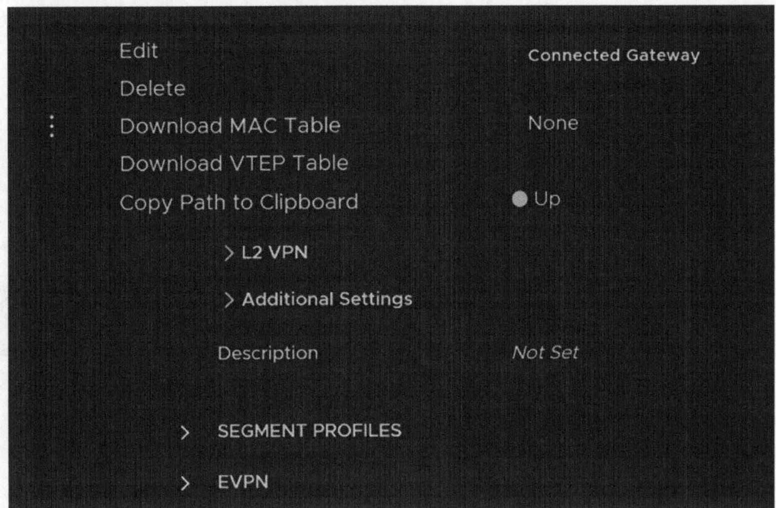

Figure 3.17: *Edit a segment*

Step 6: This action will allow the user to modify the properties of a segment. Expand the **`Segment Profiles`** by clicking on the **`triangle icon`** `(>)` and using a drop-down box against each segment profile type, segment profile can be changed. *Figure* 3.18 shows no segment profile selected for QoS.

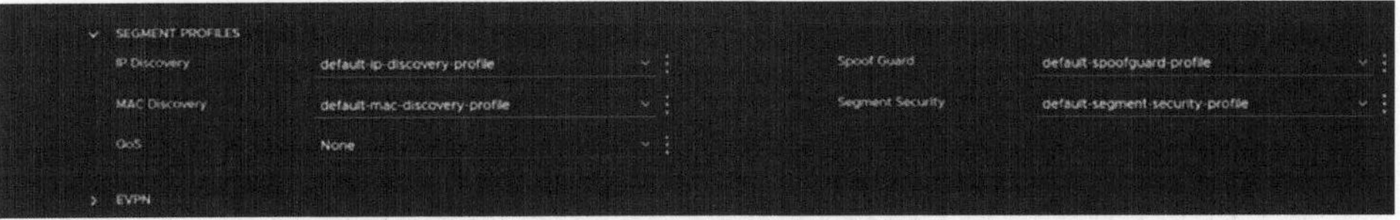

Figure 3.18: *No QoS profile selected for a segment*

Figure 3.19 shows a default QoS profile being associated by changing the option in the drop-down menu against QoS.

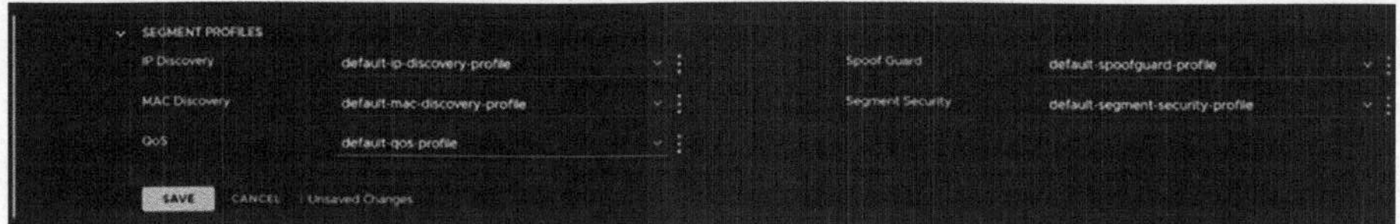

Figure 3.19: *Default QoS profile selected for a segment*

Step 7: Click on **`Save`** to commit segment profile changes and then click on **`Close Editing`** to commit changes on the desired segment.

MAC Discovery Segment Profile

MAC Discovery segment profile provides two functions which are MAC learning and MAC address change. When configuring the MAC Discovery profile, it requires the following inputs as shown in *Figure* 3.20.

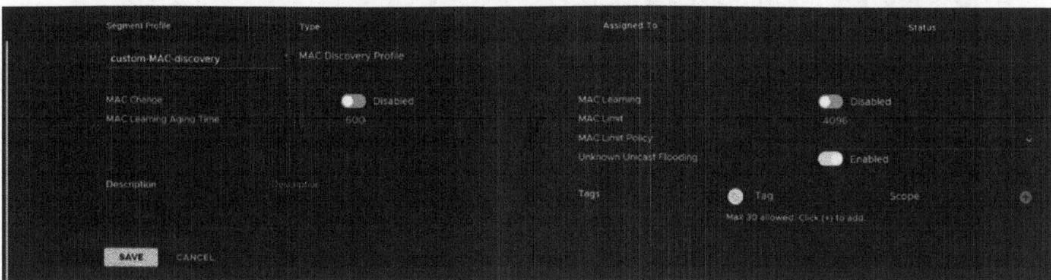

Figure 3.20: MAC Discovery Segment Profile

- **`Name`:** Segment profile name for identification
- **`Type`:** It is automatically selected as MAC Discovery Profile
- **`MAC Change`:** This property is disabled by default and it allows a virtual machine to change its MAC address. The MAC address of a VM can be changed by running an administrative command of its virtual NIC connected to a port and still sending and receiving traffic on that virtual NIC. This feature is supported on ESXi only.
- **`MAC Learning`:** This feature is disabled by default and allows network connectivity to deployments where multiple MAC addresses are configured on one virtual NIC. For example, a nested virtualization solution where ESXi is running on a VM and multiple VMs are running on nested ESXi. Without MAC learning, when the virtual NIC of the ESXi VM connects to a segment port, its MAC address is static. VMs running inside the ESXi VM do not have network connectivity because their packets have different source MAC addresses and packets from VMs running inside

nested ESXi gets dropped. With MAC learning, the vSwitch inspects the source MAC address of every packet coming from the virtual NIC of the ESXi host, learns the MAC address and allows the packet to proceed. Stale MAC addresses are removed over time if they are not used and this time period is defined by the field **MAC Learning Aging Time.** This is non-configurable and has a pre-defined value configured which is 600.

- `MAC Limit`: Maximum number of MAC addresses that can be learned is 4096. This field is configurable and can be set to lower values.
- `MAC Limit Policy`: MAC Limit Policy governs what will happen to packets coming from MAC addresses when the MAC learning Limit is reached. If it is set to **drop,** then any packet from an unknown MAC address will be dropped and if it is set to **allow** then any packet from an unknown MAC address will be allowed however their MAC address will not be learned.
- `Unknown Unicast Flooding`: MAC learning supports unknown unicast flooding when a packet is received on the segment with an unknown destination MAC address then instead of dropping the packet, it floods the packet to every port of the segment with MAC learning enabled. By default, this feature is enabled if MAC Learning is enabled.

IP Discovery Segment Profile

IP Discovery segment profile helps in learning MAC and IP address with help of DHCP snooping, ARP snooping, **ND (Neighbor Discovery)** or VMware tools running on a virtual machine. These discovered or learned MAC and IP addresses are used in ARP/ND suppression to reduce traffic between VMs connected to the same segment. The number of ARP/ND suppression cache for any port is defined by the settings in the port's IP Discovery profile which are ARP binding limit, ND Snooping limit, Duplicate IP detection, ARP ND Binding limit timeout and **TOFU (Trust on First Use).** MAC and IP address discovered with help of the IP Discovery profile is also used by SpoofGuard and NSX DFW (distributed firewall) which makes the IP Discovery profile a very significant profile. *Figure* 3.21 illustrates all the settings to be configured while creating an IP Discovery profile.

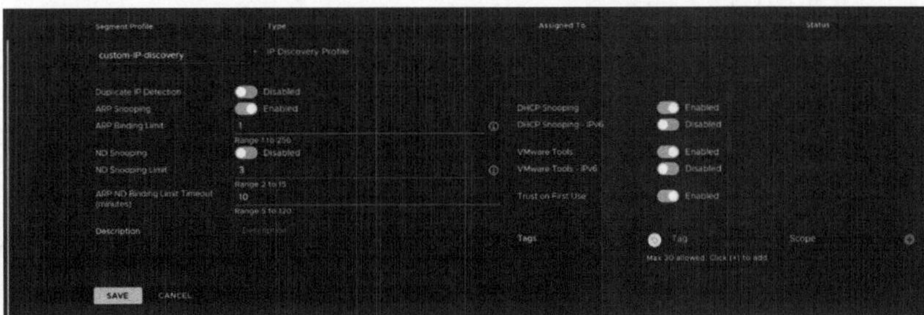

***Figure 3.21**: IP Discovery Segment Profile*

- `Name:` Segment profile name for identification
- `Type:` It is automatically selected as IP Discovery Profile
- `DHCP Snooping/DHCPv6 Snooping:` By default, IPv6 snooping is disabled and needs to be enabled with the help of a custom profile. DHCP snooping helps in learning MAC and IP addresses by inspecting packets exchanged between the DHCP server and the DHCP client.
- `ARP Snooping:` It utilizes ARP and GARP packet inspection to learn the MAC and IP address of the VM.
- `Vmware Tools/Vmware Tools - Ipv6:` As the name suggests, IP Discovery profile utilizes VMware tools running on the VM to learn its MAC address and IP address
- `ND snooping` is the Ipv6 equivalent of ARP snooping. It inspects neighbor solicitation (NS) and neighbor advertisement (NA) messages to learn the IP and MAC addresses.
- `TOFU (Trust on First Use):` In TOFU mode, when an address is discovered and added to the realized bindings list, that binding remains in the realized list forever.
- `Duplicate address detection:` It checks whether a newly discovered IP address is already present on the realized binding list for a different port. This check is performed for ports on the same segment. If a duplicate address is detected, the newly discovered address is added to the discovered list but is not added to the realized binding list. All duplicate IPs have an associated discovery timestamp. If the IP that is on the realized binding list is removed, either by adding it to the ignore binding list or by disabling snooping, the duplicate IP with the oldest timestamp is moved to the realized binding list.

Spoof Guard Segment Profile

As the name suggests, the SpoofGuard profile helps in the prevention of spoofing-type malicious attacks in the network. NSX Spoof Guard profile covers the following features:

- `MAC Spoof Guard:` SpoofGuard segment profile authenticates the MAC address of the packet.
- `IP Spoof Guard:` SpoofGuard segment profile authenticates the MAC and IP addresses of the packet.
- Dynamic ARP inspection, that is, ARP and GARP SpoofGuard and Neighbor Discovery (ND) SpoofGuard validation are all against the MAC source, IP Source and IP-MAC source mapping in the ARP/GARP/ND payload.

Figure 3.22 shows the default configuration of the Spoof Guard segment profile where the port bindings feature is in a disabled state. In order to enable port-level SpoofGuard, enable the Port Bindings feature within the profile.

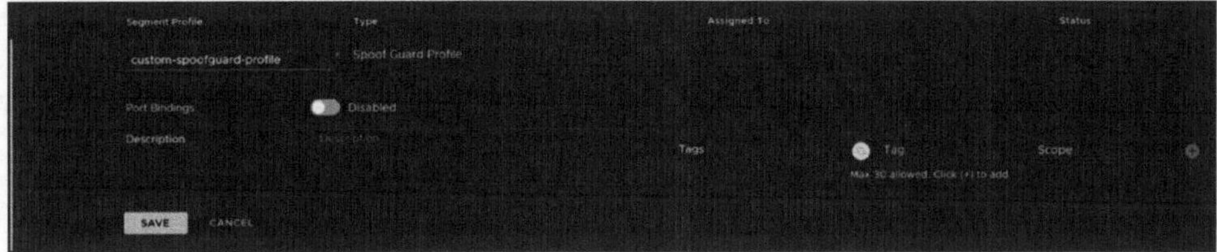

Figure 3.22: *Spoof Guard Segment Profile*

Segment Security Segment Profile

Segment security provides stateless Layer 2 and Layer 3 security by checking the ingress traffic to the segment and dropping unauthorized packets sent from VMs by matching the IP address, MAC address, and protocols to a set of allowed addresses and protocols. Segment Security profiles can be used to protect segment integrity by filtering out malicious attacks from VMs in the network.

Figure 3.23 illustrates different features which can be enabled to provide security in the segment.

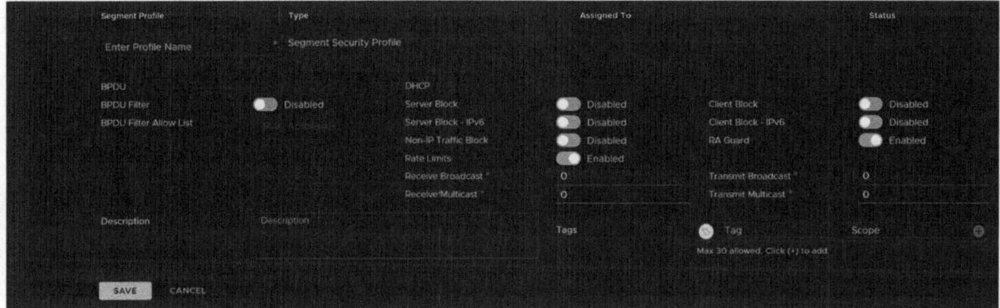

Figure 3.23: *Segment Security Segment Profile*

- **`Name`**: Name of segment profile for identification
- **`BPDU Filter`**: This feature is disabled by default. When the BPDU filter is enabled, all traffic to the BPDU destination MAC address is blocked. The BPDU filter when enabled also disables STP on the logical switch ports because these ports are not expected to take part in STP.
- **`DHCP Filter/DHCPv6 Filter`**: Server Block button and Client Block button are disabled by default. If enabled, DHCP Server Block blocks traffic from a DHCP server to a DHCP client. Note that this does not block traffic from a DHCP server to a DHCP relay agent. DHCP Client

Block prevents a VM from acquiring a DHCP IP address by blocking DHCP requests.

- **`Block Non-IP Traffic`**: This option is disabled by default and enables the Block Non-IP Traffic button to allow only IPv4, IPv6, ARP, and BPDU traffic.
- **`RA Guard:`** This feature is enabled by default and it filters out ingress IPv6 router advertisements. ICMPv6 type 134 packets are filtered out.

Note: In the Default Segment Security profile, DHCP Server Block and DHCP Server Block - IPv6 is enabled by default. If a VM connected to a segment is planning on utilizing DHCP to receive dynamic addresses, ensure to override the default Security Segment profile with a custom Security Segment profile with DHCP Server Block disabled else VM will fail to receive an IP address from the DHCP server.

QoS Segment Profile

QoS Segment profile provides high performance and dedicated network bandwidth for preferred traffic by prioritizing sufficient bandwidth, reducing latency, controlling jitters and reducing data loss for the preferred packet in network congestion. For the current release, both DSCP (Differentiated Services Code Point) and COS (Class of Service) are supported. Layer 2 COS allows specifying a priority for data packets when traffic is buffered in the segment due to congestion whereas layer 3 DSCP detects packets based on their DSCP values. COS is always applied to the data packet irrespective of the trusted mode. *Figure 3.24* shows such QoS profile options.

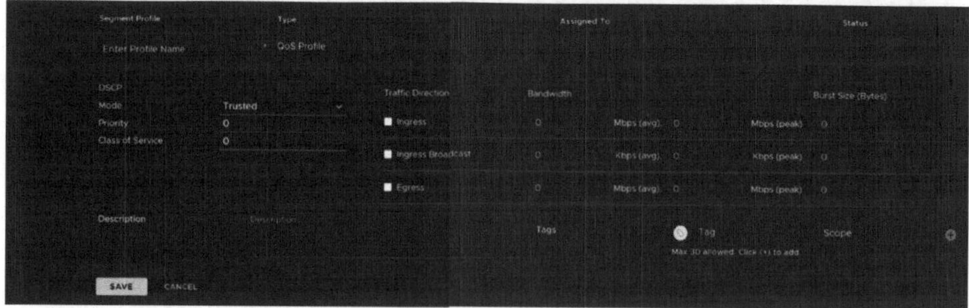

***Figure 3.24**: QoS Segment Profile*

- **`Name:`** Name of segment profile for identification
- **`Mode:`** Either Trusted or Untrusted can be selected from the drop-down menu. When Trusted mode is selected, the inner header DSCP value is applied to the outer IP header for IP/IPv6 traffic. For non-IP/IPv6 traffic,

the outer IP header takes the default value. Trusted mode is supported on an overlay-based logical port. The default value is 0. In Untrusted mode, for the overlay-based logical port, the DSCP value of the outbound IP header is set to the configured value irrespective of the inner packet type for the logical port. For the VLAN-based logical port, the DSCP value of the IP/IPv6 packet will be set to the configured value. The DSCP values range for untrusted mode is between 0 and 63.

- **`Priority`**: Set the DSCP priority value with a range from 0 to 63.
- **`Class of Service`**: It is supported on VLAN-backed logical ports and value range from 0 to 7 where 0 is the best-effort service.
- **`Ingress`**: This option defines the hard limit for ingress traffic to reduce network congestion. The default value 0 disables rate limiting on the ingress traffic.
- **`Ingress Broadcast`**: This option defines the hard limit for ingress traffic to reduce network congestion. The default value 0 disables rate limiting on ingress broadcast traffic.
- **`Egress`**: Set custom values for inbound network traffic from the logical network to the VM. The default value 0 disables rate limiting on the egress traffic.

Note: DSCP settings only work on tunneled traffic. These settings do not apply to traffic inside the same hypervisor.

Applying Segment Profile to Segment Ports

While creating segment profiles, we covered how to apply segment profiles to segments. But in NSX, it is entirely possible to override segment profiles at a port level as well for more granular control. This section covers the step-by-step process to apply and override segment profiles at a segment port level.

Step 1: Login into NSX Manager using user credentials with sufficient privileges. Navigate to the **`Networking`** menu and select **`Segments`** under **`Connectivity.`** Click on the numeral link under **`Ports/Interfaces`** of the desired segment where the segment profile needs to be overridden. This opens a new dialogue box with the name **`Set Segment Ports / View Gateway Interfaces`** as shown in *Figure* 3.25.

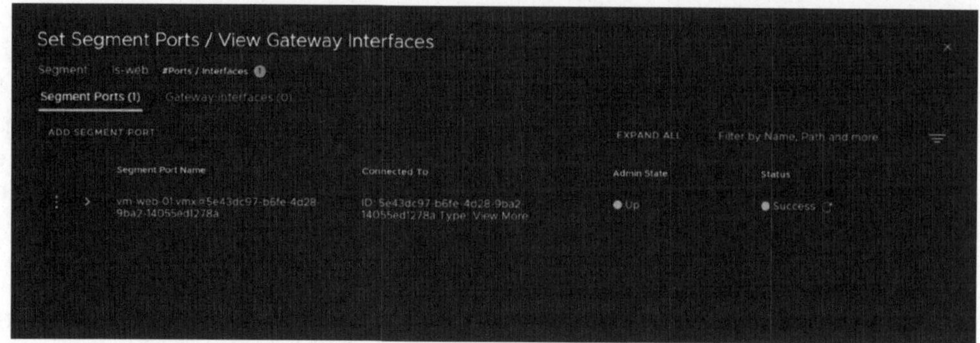

***Figure 3.25**: Set Segment Ports / View Gateway Interfaces screen*

Step 2: Click on the three dots next to the name of the segment port for which the segment profile needs to be overridden and click on **`Edit`**. Expand the **`Segment Port Profile`** using the **`small triangle (>)`** icon as shown in *Figure 3.26*.

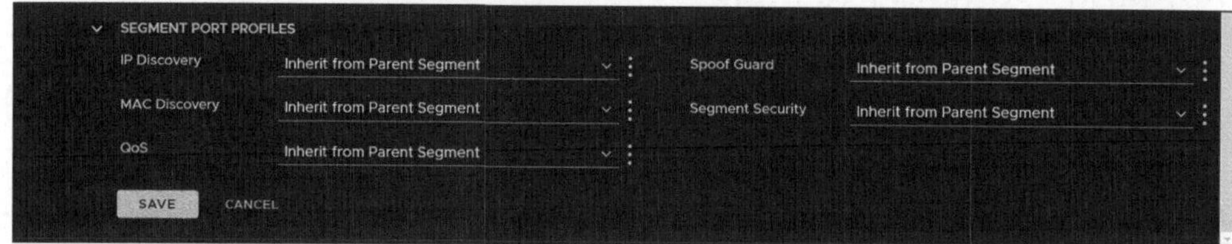

***Figure 3.26**: Segment Port Profiles menu*

Step 3: Instead of using the option **`Inherit from Parent Segment`**, use the drop-down menu to select the desired segment profile to override the segment port profile. Click **`Save`** and **`Close`** to commit the changes.

Configuring VNI Pool for Segments

NSX Manager have a VNI Pool already defined that is used to allocate unique VNI ID to NSX segments while creating them. If default VNI Pool is required to be modified, it can be done by navigating to **`System`** and selecting **`Profile`** under **`Fabric`** from the left navigation panel. Click on **`Configuration`** and it will show the VNI Pool currently configured in NSX Manager as shown in *Figure 3.27*. Click on **`Edit`** to change values for VNI Pool.

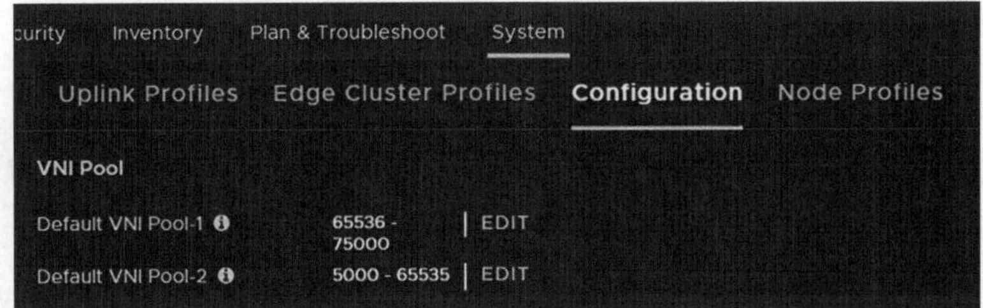

***Figure 3.27**: Configuring VNI Pool in NSX Manager*

Default VNI Pool-1 is used by default to assign VNI ID to any newly created NSX segment whereas Default VNI Pool-2 is used to assign VNI ID to NSX segments migrated from NSX-V (NSX for vSphere) using migration coordinator.

Logical Switching Packet Walks

In previous sections, we have discussed in detail how to configure segments and segment profiles, how to attach workload to a segment and what happens behind the scenes when a segment is created or a VM is attached to a segment. But still, there are multiple questions which are left unanswered such as how NSX handles the BUM traffic or how NSX achieves ARP suppression to reduce traffic between VMs in the same segment or how two VMs running on different transport nodes belonging to different underlay networks still talk to each other on the same subnet. This section covers all of these questions and many more in great depth.

Segment Tables on NSX Controller

NSX Controller maintains a central repository with help of a set of tables that are used to identify data plane components association and for traffic forwarding. These tables are

TEP (Tunnel Endpoint) Table

This table maintains the VNI to TEP IP bindings. Any ESXi host running with a workload-connected segment will have an entry of its TEP IP in the TEP table for a specific segment. For example, assuming VM1 is connected to segment ls-web and is currently running on ESXi host TN1 then the TEP table of ls-web will have an entry for TN1 TEP IP. Now, considering VM1 moved from ESXi host TN1 to TN2 due to vMotion or other circumstances, then in such cases entry of TN1 will be removed from the TEP table of ls-web. This helps to limit the flooding of traffic in case of BUM (Broadcast, Unknown Unicast and Multicast) traffic in the NSX network. *Figure* 3.28 shows such an example of a TEP table which is extracted from a transport node.

```
sa-esx-01> get logical-switch 72704 vtep-table
Mon Feb 27 2023 UTC 09:35:13.368
                              Logical Switch VTEP Table
-----------------------------------------------------------------------------------------------

                                  Host Kernel Entry
===============================================================================================
 Label        VTEP IP             Subnet IP       Is MTEP      VTEP MAC          BFD count
 35841        10.10.13.105        10.10.13.0      0        00:50:56:61:69:58        1
                                  LCP Remote Entry
===============================================================================================
 Label        VTEP IP             Subnet IP            VTEP MAC                  DEVICE NAME
 35841        10.10.13.105        10.10.13.0      00:50:56:61:69:58                 None
                                   LCP Local Entry
===============================================================================================
 Label        VTEP IP             Subnet IP            VTEP MAC                  DEVICE NAME
 86017        10.10.13.101        10.10.13.0      00:50:56:62:60:e9                 None

sa-esx-01>
```

***Figure 3.28**: TEP table example entries on ESXi host*

As illustrated in *Figure* 3.28, there is a total of three ESXi hosts which are connected to the overlay transport zone and attached to segment ls-web. But, only two ESXi hosts have a VM running on them and so only two entries are present in the LCP TEP table of ls-web and the third host entry is omitted.

Let's go a step further and see how this TEP table is updated on the ESXi host as well as CCP (Central Control Plane). *Figure* 3.29 shows an example where three VMs namely VM1, VM2 and VM3 are running on ESXi host ESXi-1, ESXi-2, and ESXi-3, respectively.

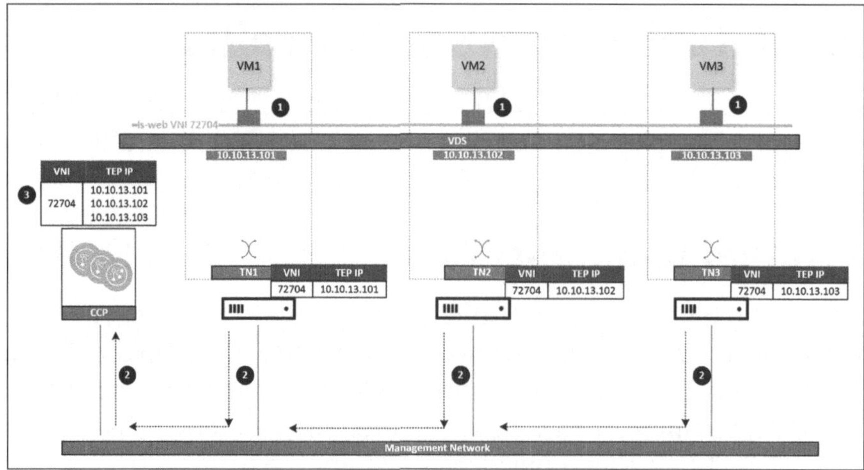

***Figure 3.29**: TEP table update in NSX environment*

All three VMs are connected to the same segment ls-web and are in a powered-on state. Assuming no communication has taken place, the TEP table will be updated in the following steps:

Step 1: VMs are powered on their respective hosts and are connected to segment ls-web. Transport Nodes, ESXi-1 – ESXi-3 register the VNI to TEP mapping on their local TEP table where VNI is the unique ID assigned to ls-web which is 72704 in this example.

Step 2: Each of the ESXi Transport Nodes sends the update of their local TEP table back to CCP (Central Control Plane).

Step 3: CCP consolidates all the updates of VNI to TEP mapping provided by Transport Nodes in a single table specific to ls-web.

Step 4: CCP then sends an updated TEP table with all the VNI to TEP mappings to all three ESXi Transport Nodes where VNI is realized (VM is connected and running on the ls-web segment).

MAC Table

MAC table maintains a list of MAC addresses to TEP IP bindings. When a vNIC of VM is connected to a segment in the NSX environment, Transport Node updates its local MAC table for a specific segment with the TEP IP and MAC address of the VM and is further communicated to CCP to maintain the global MAC table. The global MAC address table can proactively populate the local MAC address table of the different transport nodes before they receive any traffic. An important point to note here is that not all MAC addresses are reported to CCP. If a VM is allowed to send traffic from multiple source MAC addresses on a segment e.g., nested virtualization, then secondary MAC addresses are not pushed to CCP to avoid a large number of MAC addresses in the network. *Figure* 3.30 shows an example of a MAC table which is extracted from the Transport Node.

```
sa-esx-01> get logical-switch 72704 mac-table
Mon Feb 27 2023 UTC 11:30:33.089
                      Logical Switch MAC Table
---------------------------------------------------------------------------

                         Host Kernel Entry
===========================================================================
    Inner MAC            Outer MAC            Outer IP      Flags
00:50:56:96:01:db    00:50:56:61:69:58     10.10.13.105      0xd

                          LCP Remote Entry
===========================================================================
    Inner MAC            Outer MAC            Outer IP
00:50:56:96:01:db    00:50:56:61:69:58     10.10.13.105

                          LCP Local Entry
===========================================================================
    Inner MAC            Outer MAC            Outer IP
00:50:56:96:7b:eb    00:50:56:62:60:e9     10.10.13.101
```

***Figure 3.30**: MAC table example entries on ESXi host*

As illustrated in *Figure* 3.30, there are a total of three ESXi hosts which are connected to the overlay transport zone and attached to segment ls-web. But, only two ESXi hosts have a VM running on them and so only two entries are present in the LCP MAC table of ls-web for VMs under Inner MAC and the third host entry is omitted.

Let's go a step further and see how this MAC table is updated on the ESXi host as well as **CCP (Central Control Plane).** *Figure* 3.31 shows an example where three VMs namely VM1, VM2 and VM3 are running on ESXi host TN1, TN2, and TN3, respectively.

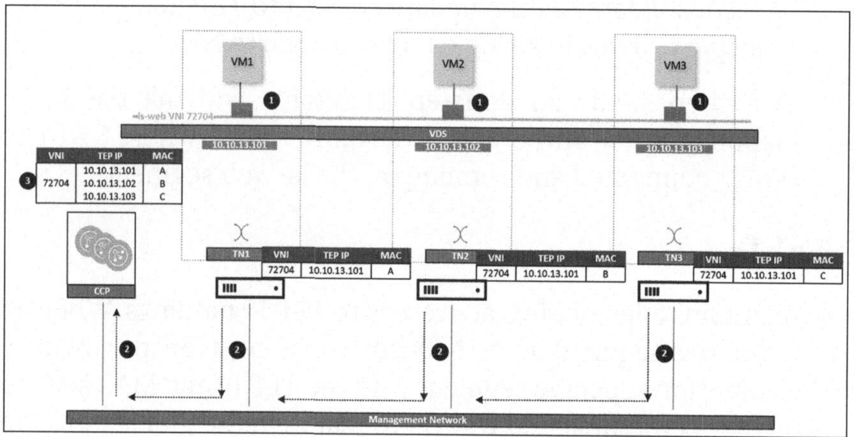

***Figure* 3.31**: *MAC table update in NSX environment*

All three VMs are connected to the same segment ls-web and are in a powered-on state. Assuming no communication has taken place, the MAC table will be updated in the following steps:

Step 1: VMs are powered on their respective hosts and are connected to segment ls-web. **`Transport Nodes, TN1 - TN3`** register the MAC to TEP mapping on their local MAC table.

Step 2: Each of the ESXi Transport Nodes sends the update of their local MAC table to CCP (Central Control Plane).

Step 3: CCP consolidates all the updates of the VM's MAC address to TEP IP mapping provided by Transport Nodes in a single MAC table specific to ls-web.

Step 4: CCP then sends an updated MAC table with all the MAC addresses to TEP mappings to all three ESXi Transport Nodes where VNI is realized (VM is connected and running on the ls-web segment).

ARP Table

NSX controller also maintains ARP tables which provide the IP address to MAC address mapping of VMs connected to an NSX segment. Its main use case of maintaining ARP tables is to implement ARP suppression in the NSX environment. NSX virtual switch with help of ARP snooping, DHCP snooping or ND snooping learns MAC address to IP address bindings which are further reported to the NSX controller in order to maintain the global ARP table which is further sent to all realized Transport Nodes. For example, assume VM1 is present on TN1 and VM2 is present on TN2. No communication has been established between VM1 and VM2 and they have just been powered on. As VM1 gets powered on TN1, using any snooping method such as DHCP snooping or VMware Tools, TN1 learns the IP1 association with MAC1 for VM1 and sends it to CCP. Next, VM2 on TN2 is powered on and would like to communicate with VM1; so either it sends a GARP packet or ARP request to learn about the MAC address of VM1. TN2 learns about IP address mapping with the MAC address for VM2 and sends it to CCP as well. NSX virtual switch also holds ARP requests from VM2 and queries CCP for the MAC address of VM1. As the MAC address of VM1 is already reported to CCP, it replies directly to the MAC address of VM1 which helps in preventing flooding on a segment for ARP requests. *Figure* 3.32 shows this process in great detail in a stepwise manner.

```
sa-esx-01> get logical-switch 72704 arp-table
Mon Feb 27 2023 UTC 11:41:41.848
                Logical Switch ARP Table
--------------------------------------------------

                    Host Kernel Entry
==================================================
          IP                  MAC            Flags
    172.16.10.1       ff:ff:ff:ff:ff:ff    0xf
    172.16.10.12      00:50:56:96:01:db    0xd

                         LCP Entry
==================================================
          IP                  MAC
    172.16.10.11      00:50:56:96:7b:eb
    172.16.10.12      00:50:56:96:01:db
```

Figure 3.32: *ARP table update in NSX environment*

Figure 3.33 shows an example of an ARP table which is extracted from the Transport Node.

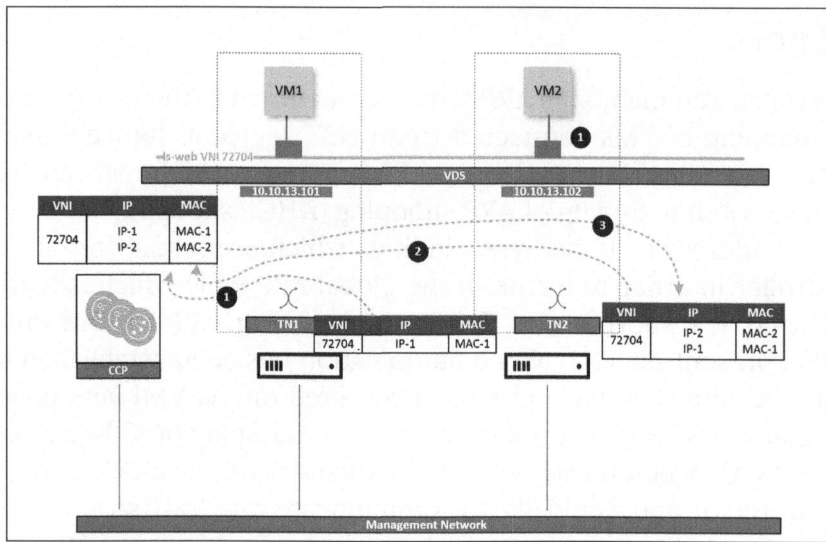

***Figure 3.33**: ARP table example entries on ESXi host*

As illustrated in *Figure* 3.33, there is a total of three ESXi hosts which are connected to the overlay transport zone and attached to segment ls-web. But, only two ESXi hosts have a VM running on them and so only two entries are present in the LCP ARP table of ls-web for VMs.

Unicast Traffic Packet Walk

When a frame has an unknown destination MAC address, it is flooded in the network and usually, switches use a MAC address table which associates the MAC address to ports in order to prevent flooding in the network. When a unicast MAC address is known in the MAC address table, it is only forwarded to a specific port and this type of traffic is known as Unicast traffic. Similarly, NSX virtual switch maintains a set of tables which are the TEP table, MAC table and ARP table for each segment in the NSX environment. ARP request flooding is avoided by the use of the ARP suppression mechanism and the MAC address of the VM is mapped with the virtual NIC of the local VM or remote TEP if VM is running on a different Transport Node and needs to be reached via the tunnel. In the NSX environment, if the MAC address of the VM is present in these tables then it is considered as Unicast traffic and the following example covers how the packet flows between two VMs attached to the same segment but running on different Transport Nodes.

Assuming VM-A and VM-B are running on ESXi host TN-A and TN-B respectively. VM-A is sending unicast traffic to VM-B. In this example, it is assumed that all tables are fully populated on both ESXi hosts. The following steps explain the packet walk when VM-A sends unicast traffic to VM-B.

Step 1: VM-A sends a frame with the source MAC address `AAAA-AAAA-AAAA` and IP address `A.A.A.A` to destination VM-B with destination MAC address `BBBB-BBBB-BBBB` and destination IP address B.B.B.B.

Step 2: ESXi host TN-A receives the frame from VM-A on segment ls-web and performs a lookup of the destination MAC address in its local MAC table. It finds that the MAC address `BBBB-BBBB-BBBB` is associated with the TEP IP address of TN-B. As the MAC address is bound to the remote TEP IP, TN-A encapsulates the frame in the Geneve packet with the destination IP address of TN-B.

Step 3: The encapsulated packet travels on the underlay physical network and is delivered to TN-B.

Step 4: TN-B receives the encapsulated packet, which is addressed to itself (TEP IP address of TN-B) and decapsulates the packet. TN-B then performs a lookup of the destination MAC address `BBBB-BBBB-BBBB in` its MAC address table and finds a hit pointing to the virtual NIC of VM-B.

Step 5: TN-B delivers the frame to VM-B.

A similar process happens when VM-B sends unicast traffic to VM-A and communication establishes between both virtual machines.

Flooded/BUM Traffic Packet Walk

Flooded traffic or BUM traffic is a type of traffic where the destination MAC address is not known or is addressed to more than one destination and NSX does not differentiate between different kinds of frames replicated to multiple destinations. It could be broadcast traffic, multicast traffic or unknown unicast traffic and all these types of traffic are replicated across the segment in a similar fashion. In the overlay segment, replication of the frame to be flooded on the segment is taken care of by different NSX components. There are mainly two ways to flood traffic on a specific segment and it can be selected on a per-segment basis.

Figure 3.34 shows an NSX environment with nine ESXi Transport Nodes each of which is hosting a virtual machine connected to the same segment ls-web. ESXi hosts TN1 – TN3 belongs to TEP VLAN A, TN4 – TN6 belongs to TEP VLAN B and TN7 – TN9 belongs to TEP VLAN C. VM1 running on TN1 needs to communicate with VM9 running on host TN9 but there is no earlier communication established.

VM1 is not aware of the MAC address of VM9. Hence BUM traffic needs to be replicated on segment ls-web.

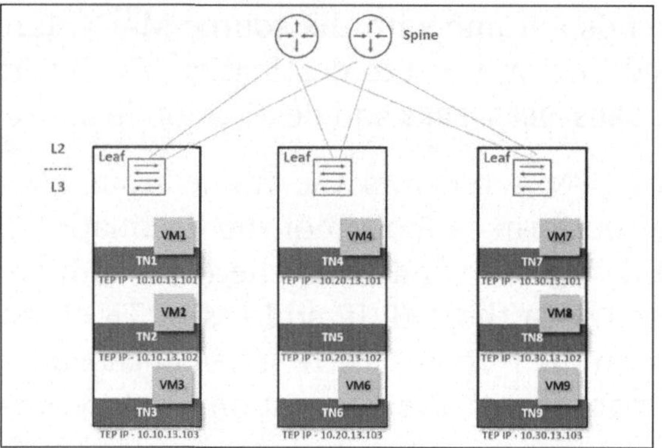

***Figure 3.34**: BUM traffic in the NSX environment*

This BUM traffic can be replicated in the segment using the following two different methods.

Head End Replication

In the Head End Replication method, it is the responsibility of the source Transport Node to send a copy of the frame to each Transport Node that is connected to the segment. As the entire burden lies on the source Transport Node then uplink bandwidth should be taken into consideration while using Head End Replication. Taking the previous example, VM1 needs to communicate with VM9 but it is not aware of the destination MAC address. Hence, the frame will be flooded by ESXi host TN1 to all the other ESXi hosts connected to segment ls-web as shown in *Figure* 3.35.

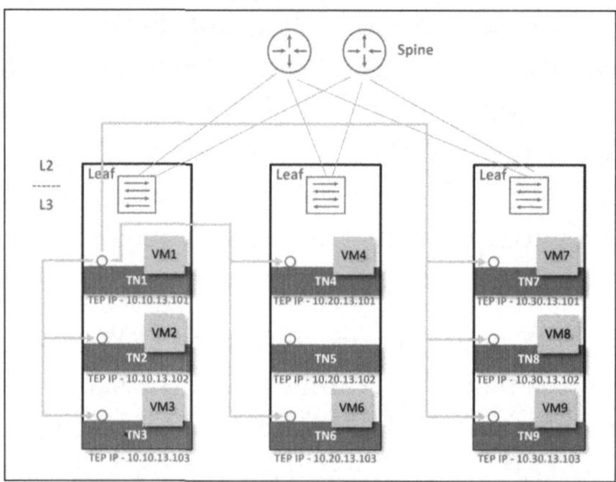

***Figure 3.35**: Head End Replication mode*

Figure 3.35 illustrates that TN1 is sending seven copies of the frame to other Transport Nodes and it skips sending a copy to ESXi host TN5 as there are no VMs connected and running on the segment. Hence TN5 does not receive a copy of the frame from TN1.

Hierarchical Two-Tier Replication

In the two-tier hierarchical mode, transport nodes are grouped according to the subnet of the IP address of their TEP network. Taking the previous example, TN1 - TN3 are grouped as one as they share TEP VLAN A, TN4 - TN6 are grouped together as one as they share TEP VLAN B, and similarly TN7 - TN9 are grouped as one. Again, VM1 needs to communicate with VM9 but it is not aware of the destination MAC address of VM9, hence traffic needs to be flooded in the segment. However, unlike Head End Replication, instead of putting all burden on source ESXi host TN1, it selects a destination Transport Node in each group and replicates the frame to designated Transport Nodes. Now, it is the responsibility of designated Transport Nodes to replicate the frame to other Transport Nodes in their respective groups as shown in *Figure* 3.36.

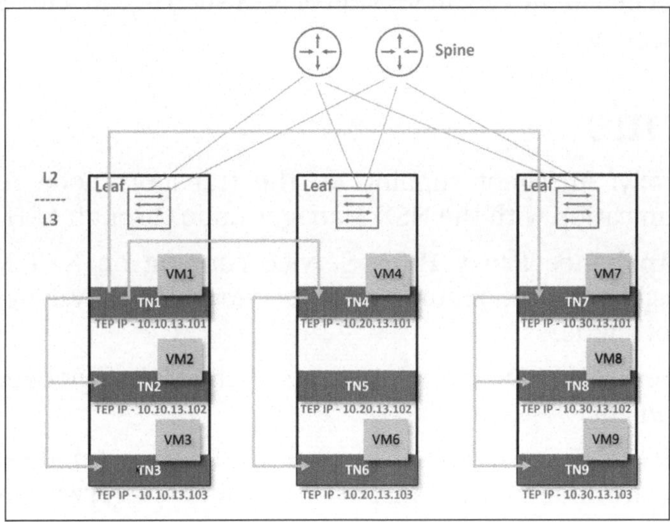

Figure 3.36: *Hierarchical Two-Tier Replication method*

Figure 3.36 illustrates that TN1 has designated TN4 to replicate the frame in group B and TN7 to replicate the frame in group C. TN1 sends a copy of the frame to its members in group A which are TN2, TN3 and also to TN4 and TN7. Further, TN4 sends a copy of the frame to TN6 but skips TN5 as there are no active connections running on the segment on TN5. TN7 send a copy of the frame to TN8 and TN9. VM9 receives a frame from TN9 and responds back to VM1.

The default two-tier hierarchical flooding mode is recommended as a best practice as it typically performs better in terms of physical uplink bandwidth utilization.

Conclusion

In this chapter, we covered the creation of Segments or Layer 2 domains in the NSX environment, and changing policies on segments with the help of segment profiles. We also covered how traffic flows between two VMs when they are connected to the same segment whether it is unicast traffic or BUM traffic. With the help of ARP tables and IP Discovery profiles, the NSX controller implements ARP suppression in the NSX environment to avoid flooding of ARP requests and covers how BUM traffic is flooded in a segment either using Head End Replication or Hierarchical Two-Tier replication method. This completes the logical switching in an NSX environment.

In the next chapter, we will see how routing is achieved in an NSX environment and what are the benefits of distributed routing. Also, we will cover the latest features introduced in the recent version of NSX such as VRF Lite, EVPN support, and OSPF adjacency.

Key Terms

- **Nsx-proxy:** An agent running on the transport node responsible for communication with the NSX Manager node through APH
- **APH (Appliance Proxy Hub):** Service running on NSX Manager node responsible for communication between NSX Manager node and transport node.
- **Transport Zone:** Defines the scope of the virtual network in the NSX environment.
- **NSX Virtual Switch:** Core component of Transport node which attaches a transport node to the transport zone, acts as a forwarding engine.
- **Segment:** Segments are layer 2 subnets representing layer 2 broadcasting domain across transport nodes in NSX networking.
- **Segment Port:** Logical port to which the virtual NIC of workload is connected on segment.
- **Segment Profile:** Configuration templates to granularly control policies on segments.
- **VNI (Virtual Network Identifier):** Unique ID assigned to segments created in the NSX environment

- **TEP (Tunnel Endpoint):** IP address assigned to Transport Nodes that enables the creation of encapsulated Geneve tunnel between nodes to allow participation in overlay networking.
- **TEP Table:** It maintains the VNI to TEP IP bindings.
- **MAC Table:** It maintains the MAC address of VMs to TEP IP bindings.
- **ARP Table:** It maintains the IP address of the VM to the MAC address of VM bindings.
- **BUM Traffic:** Broadcast, Multicast or Unknown Unicast traffic where the destination MAC address is not known or the frame needs to be flooded to multiple destinations.
- **ARP Suppression:** Method used by NSX controller to avoid flooding of ARP requests in NSX environment.

CHAPTER 4

Logical Routing – NSX Edge Nodes

Introduction

The last chapter has covered Logical Switching in the NSX environment and how Layer 2 networks can be easily extended over Layer 3 underlay physical infrastructure. But what about workloads connected to these Layer 2 segments communicating with different physical network zones or workloads connected to different networks? Introducing Logical Routing, NSX provides fully distributed East-West routing, where the hypervisor running the virtual machine performs the routing itself. It also provides highly scalable and flexible North-South routing, along with data and control plane isolation between different tenants with the help of VRFs. Sounds interesting!!! It is.

One of the most crucial prerequisites for enabling logical routing in an NSX environment is the deployment of Edge nodes and Edge Clusters. This chapter covers a few designs and configurations for deploying Edge nodes in the NSX environment.

Structure

In this chapter, we will cover the following topics:

- NSX Logical Routing
- NSX Edge Node

    - NSX Edge Form Factor
    - NSX Edge Networking
    - Deploying NSX Edge Node
    - Monitoring NSX Edge Node
- NSX Edge Cluster

NSX Logical Routing

NSX logical routing provides the capability to enable connectivity between different virtual and physical workloads in different Layer 2 subnets. In NSX, gateways are created in software as a logical construct embedded in the hypervisor at the kernel level, and they do not require any special physical appliances. This enables routing to be done closest to the source. For example, if two virtual machines are running on the same ESXi host, connected to two different overlay networks or subnets, then traffic doesn't need to leave the ESXi host and is routed within the ESXi kernel. This helps in avoiding hair-pinning of traffic. This implementation of NSX logical routing makes it suitable for containerized workloads and virtual machines.

Another key thing about NSX logical routing is its emphasis on multitenancy, which provides support for the creation of multiple isolated instances within the same NSX environment. *Figure* 4.1 illustrates an example based on NSX topology, where two virtual machines named Web-01 and App-01 are connected to two different NSX overlay networks:

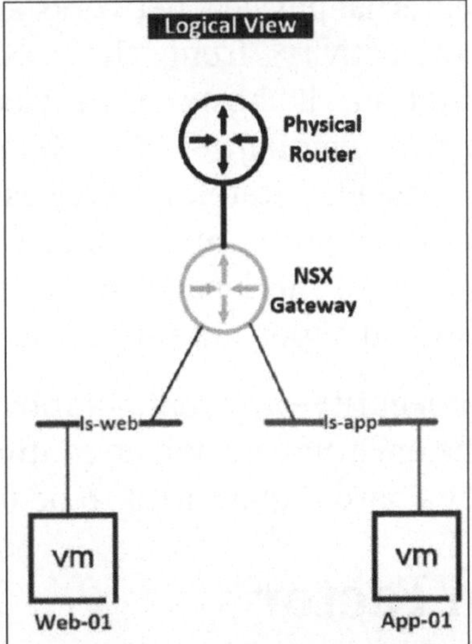

Figure 4.1: *Logical view of a routing topology in the NSX environment*

In a modern datacenter, traffic can be categorized as either East-West (E-W) or North-South (N-S) with respect to their origin and destination. If workloads present in a datacenter communicate with each other and traffic is confined within the boundaries of the datacenter, it classifies as East-West (E-W) traffic, whereas if workloads present in a datacenter communicate with external devices outside the boundary of the datacenter, it classifies as North-South (N-S) traffic. In modern datacenter, more than 70% of traffic is E-W in nature, and NSX with the help of distributed routing can help optimize it.

There are certain prerequisites before NSX logical routing can be enabled in the datacenter. These include deploying and configuring NSX Management cluster, creating overlay Transport Zones, configuring the vSphere distributed switch with NSX, and preparing Hypervisor as an NSX Transport Node with correct Transport Zones. All of these configurations were covered in *Chapter 2, Deploy NSX Infrastructure*. If you need to revisit these topics, please refer to that chapter. There is one more important prerequisite before NSX logical routing can be properly configured and used, that is, deploying and configuring NSX Edge Nodes and Edge cluster. Let's cover Edge Node and Edge cluster first without any delays.

NSX Edge Node

NSX Edge node is a necessary component in an NSX environment, which provides a pool of capacity or pool of resources. For example, CPU and memory to run centralized services with the help of container-based architecture for most of the services to share resources between them. NSX Edge node provides connectivity to external physical networks and is a must for providing North-South routing connectivity from the NSX environment to the physical network. In addition, it hosts a **Service Router (SR),** covered later in *Chapter 5, Logical Routing - NSX Gateways* a component of NSX logical router to provide stateful services such as DHCP, NAT, VPN, Gateway Firewall, and more, and enables service insertion with third-party vendors to integrate third-party services with NSX environment. Overall NSX Edge node plays an important role in the NSX environment.

Note: If NSX is running in a security-only configuration or NSX is used to provide security services only in the environment and no routing services are being used, then NSX Edge node is not a hard requirement to be fulfilled.

NSX Edge Form Factor

NSX Edge node supports two form factors as follows:

- As a virtual machine running on ESXi host, also termed as NSX Edge VM.
- As a bare-metal node, also termed as NSX Edge Bare Metal.

NSX Edge node supports Data Plane Development Kit (DPDK) for faster packet forwarding in a high-performance environment. However, the underlying platform must meet with the following requirements:

- CPU must have AESNI capability.
- CPU must have 1 GB Huge page support.

Table 4.1 lists the CPUs supported with NSX Edge node in either form factor:

CPU Vendor	CPU Family
Intel	• Intel Xeon E7-xxxx (Westmere-EX and later CPU generation) • Intel Xeon 56xx (Westmere-EP) • Intel Xeon E5-xxxx (Sandy Bridge and later CPU generation) • Intel Xeon Platinum (all generations) • Intel Xeon Gold (all generations) • Intel Xeon Silver (all generations) • Intel Xeon Bronze (all generations)
AMD	• AMD EPYC Series processors

Table 4.1: *Supported CPUs with NSX Edge node*

NSX Edge VM

NSX supports running Edge node running as a virtual machine on ESXi hosts equipped with either Intel or AMD CPU. There are different deployment sizes available for NSX Edge VM according to the requirements listed in *Table* 4.2:

Deployment Size	Memory	vCPU	Disk Space	VM Hardware Version
NSX Edge Small	4 GB	2	200 GB	11 or later (vSphere 7.0 or later)
NSX Edge Medium	8 GB	4	200 GB	11 or later (vSphere 7.0 or later)

NSX Edge Large	32 GB	8	200 GB	11 or later (vSphere 7.0 or later)
NSX Edge Extra Large	64 GB	16	200 GB	11 or later (vSphere 7.0 or later)

Table 4.2: *Resource requirement for NSX Edge VM*

NSX Edge VM small deployment is suitable only for lab or **PoC (proof of concept)** deployment and is not supported for the production environment. Certain features, such as L7 load balancing, cannot be realized on the NSX Edge node with a small size. NSX Edge Medium size is suitable for environments where the total throughput requirement is less than 2 Gbps and only L2 – L4 features, such as NAT, Routing, or L4 firewall, need to be enabled. If the total throughput requirement is from 2 Gbps to 10 Gbps, then it is recommended to go with NSX Edge Large size, and if multiple Gbps throughput is required along with VPN, North-South Malware Prevention, or L7 load balancing, it is advisable to deploy the NSX Edge Extra Large VM or use NSX Edge Bare Metal.

Note: Use VMware Configuration Maximum website (https://configmax.esp.vmware.com/home) as a guiding tool to understand different load balancer sizes and features Edge form factor can support. However, please note NSX Edge load balancer is deprecated, and it is recommended to use NSX Advanced Load Balancer.

NSX Edge Bare Metal

NSX also supports running Edge node as a bare-metal server where high performance and throughput in multiple Gbps is required. NSX Edge Bare Metal requires a minimum of 8 CPU cores, 32 GB RAM, and 200 GB storage, but it is recommended to run with 24 CPU cores, 256 GB RAM, and 200 GB storage. In addition, NSX Bare Metal Edge supports a maximum of 40 cores of CPU on a single system, meaning if a bare-metal server is running with a single socket CPU, it can have up to 40 cores, but if it is running with dual socket CPU, each socket cannot have more than 40 cores.

Note: For supported hardware configuration with NSX Bare Metal Edge v4.1, visit the link: https://ubuntu.com/certified?category=Server&release=20.04%20LTS&category=Server For supported NIC with NSX Bare Metal Edge v4.1, visit the link: https://docs.vmware.com/en/VMware-NSX/4.1/installation/GUID-14C3F618-AB8D-427E-AC88-F05D1A04DE40.html

NSX Edge Networking

NSX Edge node provides a separate TCP/IP stack for management and datapath/ fastpath interfaces. The management interface, denoted by eth0 inside the NSX Edge node, is responsible for providing management access to the NSX Edge node over the network, for example, SSH session, whereas datapath interfaces, denoted by naming scheme fp-ethx inside the NSX Edge node OS, are responsible for providing overlay tunneling and uplink connectivity to ToR switches with help of N-VDS.

NSX Edge VM Networking

Starting with NSX-T version 3.2.1, NSX Edge VM now supports up to four datapath interfaces and one management interface, whereas in the previous release, it was three datapath interfaces and one management interface. *Figure* 4.2 illustrates an NSX Edge node running on an ESXi host and different interfaces present on it:

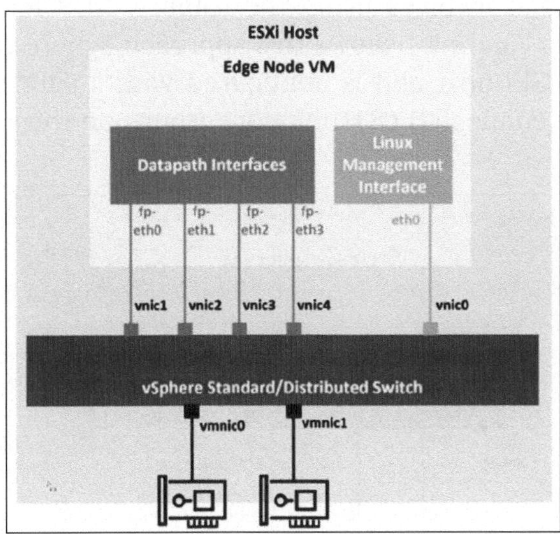

Figure 4.2: *Edge VM interfaces*

Multiple datapath interfaces enable two different N-VDS configurations on NSX Edge VM. The first approach is to use multiple N-VDS, with one N-VDS for overlay, the second N-VDS for VLAN Uplink-1, and the third N-VDS for VLAN Uplink-2. *Figure* 4.3 displays this approach where the NSX Edge node is running on an ESXi host configured with multiple N-VDS. This approach maximizes the usage of vNICs provided by the NSX Edge node and is beneficial where ESXi hosts also have multiple vmnics for dedicated traffic paths:

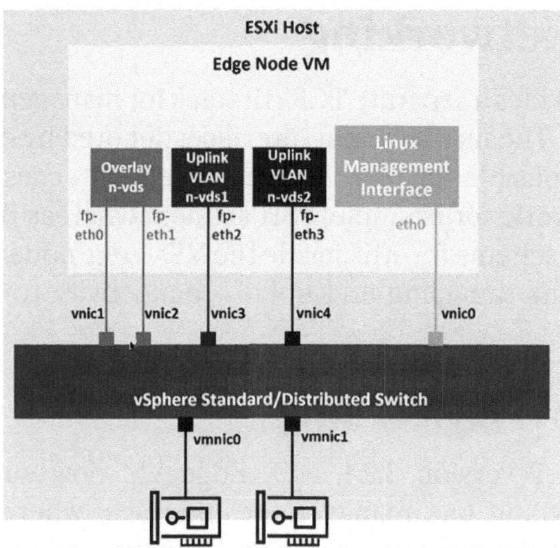

Figure 4.3: *Multi n-vds configuration on Edge node VM*

The second approach involves using the same N-VDS for both overlay and VLAN uplink traffic. *Figure* 4.4 shows this approach, where the NSX Edge node is running on an ESXi host and is configured with a single N-VDS, with two fastpath interfaces connected to trunk port groups on the vSphere distributed switch:

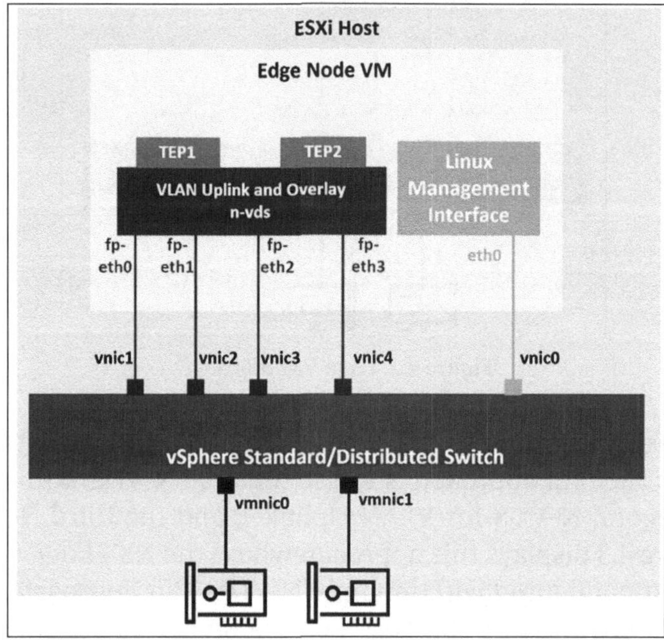

Figure 4.4: *Single n-vds configuration on Edge node VM*

This second approach is in line with the NSX Reference Design guide and is the preferred approach starting from NSX-T version 2.5 and later.

NSX Edge Bare Metal Networking

Similar to the NSX Edge VM, Bare Metal Edge is also configured with one management interface (eth0) connected to the Linux TCP/IP stack and fastpath interfaces (***fp-ethx***) for overlay and external connectivity. There are a few differences from the NSX Edge VM, especially in how NICs on bare metal are connected. Instead of connecting NICs on Bare Metal Edge to another virtual switch, they are directly connected to physical switches. In addition, the management interface can be configured as an in-band management interface, where it utilizes an interface already being used for overlay or external traffic. Another difference is that the Bare Metal Edge supports a maximum of 16 fastpath interfaces, as opposed to the limited four fastpath interfaces on the Edge VM. *Figure* 4.5 shows an NSX Bare Metal Edge configured with three physical NICs running with one management interface and two fastpath interfaces. An additional fourth NIC can be added to the Bare Metal Edge to provide redundancy for the management interface:

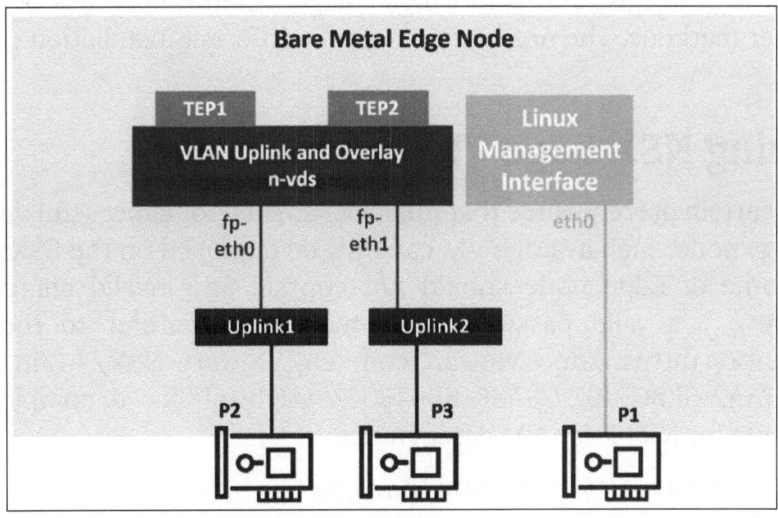

Figure 4.5*: Bare Metal Edge node networking*

Deploying NSX Edge Node

It is recommended to deploy NSX Edge VM using NSX Manager UI (User Interface); however, there are other methods available to deploy the NSX Edge node, as listed in *Table* 4.3, for both NSX Edge VM and NSX Edge Bare Metal:

NSX Edge Node Type	Supported Installation Method
NSX Edge VM	• Using NSX Manager UI (Recommended) • Using OVA file deployment from the vSphere client • Using OVA file deployment through the OVF command line tool • Using ISO file
NSX Edge Bare Metal	• Automated or Interactive mode using ISO file

***Table 4.3**: Different supported installation types for NSX Edge node*

Deployment of NSX Edge VM is recommended through NSX Manager UI because the joining of Edge node to the NSX management plane and configuration is automatically taken care of by NSX Manager and no additional commands are needed to execute. However, this requires the vCenter server to be registered as a Compute Manager in NSX. If NSX Edge needs to be deployed in a vCenter server that is not registered with NSX Manager, then it becomes necessary to utilize other methods. The next section covers different installation methods in detail.

Deploying NSX Edge VM

There are certain prerequisites that must be satisfied for successful deployment of NSX Edge node, such as Edge VM can only be deployed on the ESXi platform, the hostname of Edge node should not contain any invalid characters like underscore (_), a valid password, and more. Please refer to the VMware Documentation (https://docs.vmware.com/en/VMware-NSX/4.1/installation/GUID-11417AA2-5EBC-49C7-8A86-EB94604261A6.html) for a complete list of requirements for NSX Edge VM deployment.

Deploying NSX Edge VM using NSX Manager UI

Following these steps, NSX Edge VM can be deployed from within the NSX Manager UI. NSX Manager provides a step-by-step dialogue box to request information about the NSX Edge node:

Step 1: Log in to NSX Manager with admin privileges. Click **`System`** to open the NSX Manager **`System`** menu and select **`Nodes`** under **`Fabric`** from the left navigation panel to view **`Edge Transport Nodes`** in NSX

Manager. *Figure* 4.6 shows the **Edge Transport Nodes** view in NSX Manager. Currently, no Edge nodes have been deployed or registered with NSX Manager, hence no entries are visible here:

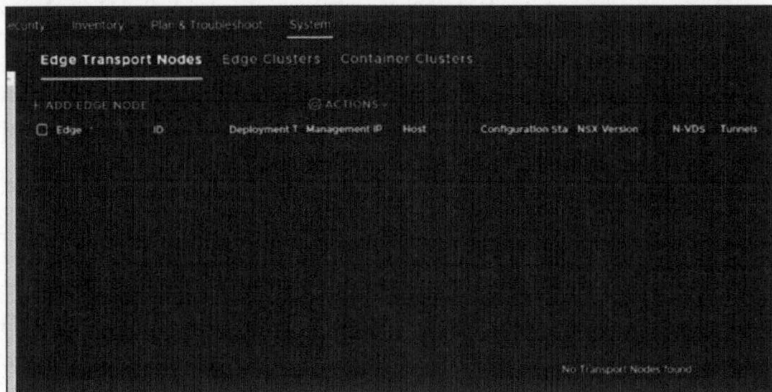

Figure 4.6: *Viewing NSX Edge Transport Nodes in NSX Manager*

Step 2: Click **Add Edge Node** to start deployment of NSX Edge node from NSX Manager. This will open a new dialogue name with the name **Add Edge Node,** as shown in *Figure* 4.7:

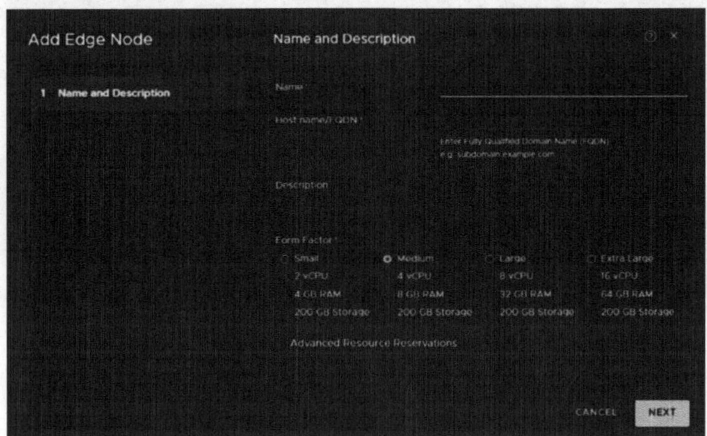

Figure 4.7: *Adding a new Edge node from NSX Manager UI*

Step 3: Provide the requested information in the Name and Description section as follows:

a. **Name**: Provide an appropriate name for the NSX Edge node.

b. **Host name/FQDN:** Provide a DNS resolvable FQDN name here. DNS A/PTR records should be created and present before starting deployment.

c. **`Description`:** This is an optional field. If required, enter your remarks or notes here.

d. **`Form Factor`:** As per requirement, select the deployment size of Edge Node, as covered earlier.

e. **`Advanced Resource Reservation`:** Expand the menu to change CPU and Memory reservations. It is not advisable to change system default values, as CPU and Memory reservations ensure that the NSX Edge node will receive resources assigned to them in case of any ESXi resource contention.

Figure 4.8 shows an example configuration for NSX Edge node sa-nsxedge-01 to be deployed from the NSX Manager UI:

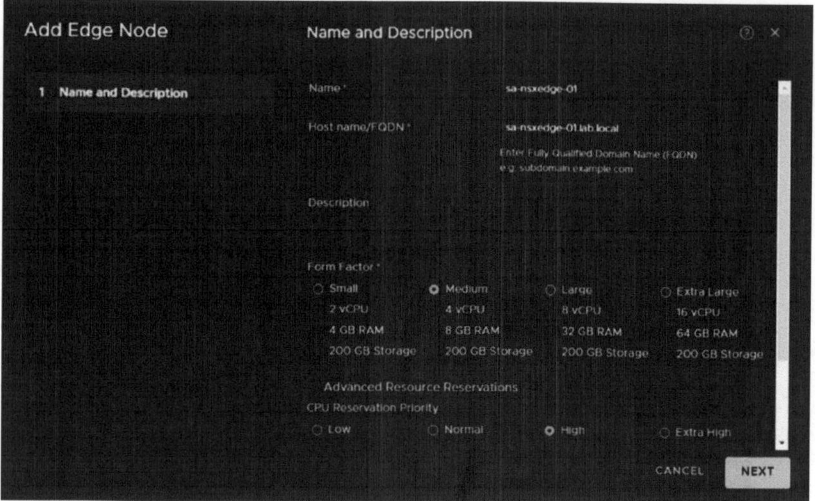

Figure 4.8: *Providing Name and Hostname to NSX Edge node*

Step 4: Click **`Next`** to continue. In the **`Credentials`** section, provide the password for Admin, Root, and optionally the Audit user. Optionally, enable SSH login for the admin and root users using the toggle button, and then click **`Next`**.

Step 5: In the third section titled Configure Deployment, select the **`Compute Manager`**, that is, vCenter server, where NSX Edge will be deployed using the drop-down menu. Using the drop-down menu, select the **`Cluster`** and **`Datastore`** to provide compute and storage to the NSX Edge virtual machine. Optionally, select the **`Resource Pool`** or **`Host`** to deploy NSX Edge virtual machine on a specific host, similar to *Figure* 4.9, and then click **`Next`** to continue deployment:

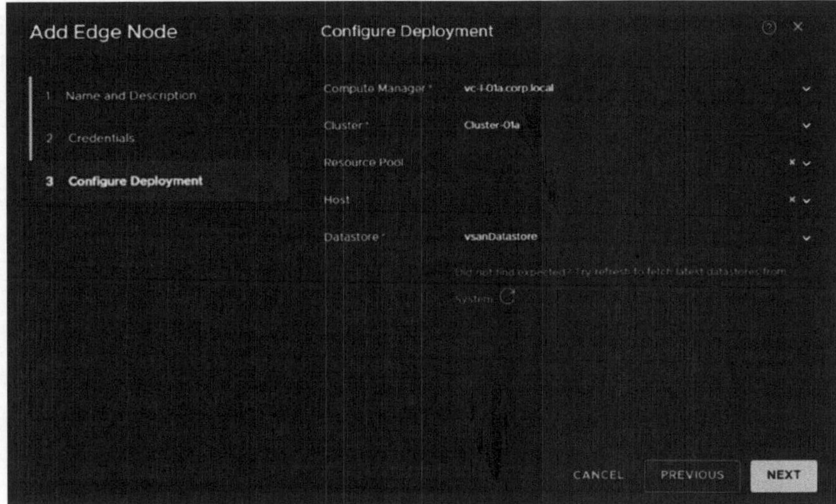

***Figure* 4.9**: *Providing compute and storage resources to NSX Edge VM*

Step 6: The next section titled **`Configure Node Settings`** is about configuring the management network. As shown in *Figure* 4.10, provide the following details:

a. **`Management IP Assignment:`** Select the type of IP address, either **`IPv4`** or **`IPv4 and IPv6`**, for the NSX Edge node management network.

b. **`Type`**: Select the type of assignment for IP address. Select **`DHCP`** for automatic assignment using a DHCP server or **`Static`** to manually enter the IP address.

c. **`Management IP:`** If static is selected, then enter the management IP address in CIDR format for NSX edge.

d. **`Default Gateway:`** Provide the default gateway for the management IP subnet.

e. **`Management Interface`**: Provide the vSphere distributed port group to which the management interface (**`eth0`**) of the NSX Edge node is connected.

f. Search Domain Names: Provide the list of DNS domain name for name resolution in NSX Edge.

g. **DNS Server**: Provide the IP address of DNS servers.

h. **NTP Server**: Provide the NTP server's IP address to sync time on the NSX Edge node. This is really important because if there is a time drift between the NSX Manager and the NSX Edge node, then it can lead to unexpected issues.

i. **Enable UPT**: As discussed in NSX Edge networking, enable UPT mode to offload packet processing to smartNICs.

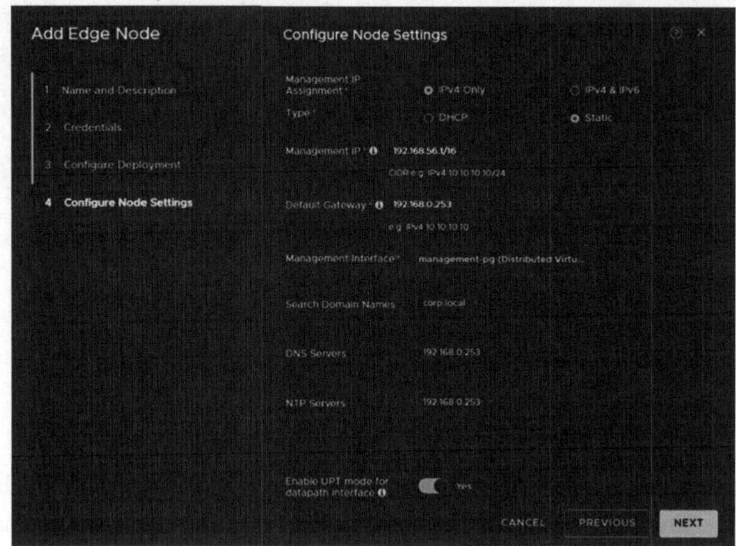

***Figure 4.10**: Configuring management network for NSX Edge node*

Click **Next** to continue to the last section for the configuration of N-VDS.

Step 7: Under the **`Configure NSX section`**, provide the following details, which define the N-VDS configuration similar to the NSX VDS configuration of an ESXi host Transport Node:

a. **`Edge Switch Name:`** The default value is nsxtHostSwitch. This can be left to default or changed to an appropriate name if required. This field defines the name of N-VDS present on the NSX Edge node.

b. **`Transport Zone:`** Similar to the Host Transport Node, the Edge node is also attached to a Transport Zone. Using the drop-down menu, select the appropriate Transport Zones. The overlay Transport Zone will remain common for both Host and Edge Transport Nodes, but the VLAN Transport Zone can be different for Edge node to make Edge-specific VLANs invisible to Host Transport Nodes.

c. **`Uplink Profile:`** Using the drop-down menu, select the Uplink Profile created earlier for the Edge Transport Node, which defines teaming policies and transport VLAN for TEP IP.

d. **`IP Address`**: Select either IPv4 to IPv6 for the TEP IP address.

e. **`IPv4 Assignment`**: Using the drop-down, select either **`Use IP Pool`** to utilize IP Pools in NSX Manager to dynamically assign TEP IP addresses or **`Static IPv4 List`** to manually define static TEP IP addresses.

f. **`IPv4 Pool:`** If Use IP Pool is selected, then select the IP Pool created for Edge nodes. Otherwise, manually define the static IP addresses.

g. **`Teaming Policy Uplink Mapping`**: Select the NSX segment or vSphere distributed port group to which NSX Edge datapath interfaces (fp-ethx) are connected.

Figure 4.11 shows an example configuration of N-VDS on NSX Edge node sa-nsxedge-01:

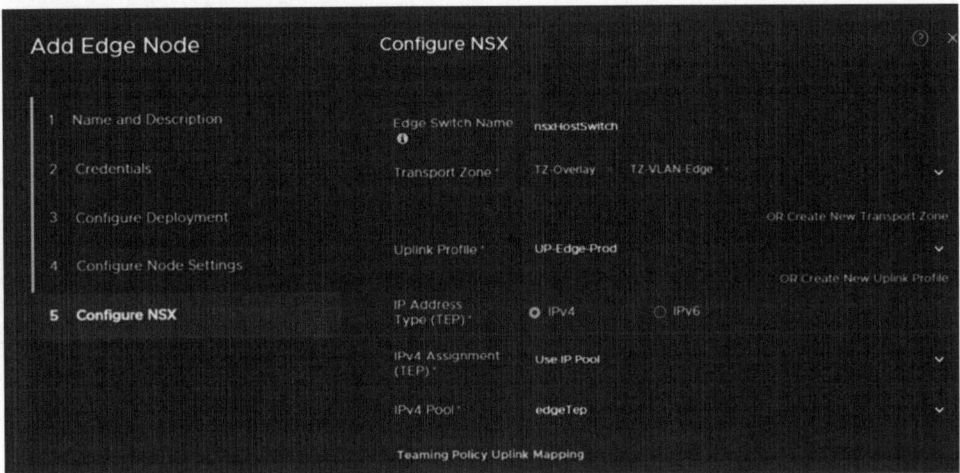

Figure 4.11: *Configure* N-VDS *on* NSX *Edge Node*

Step 8: Click **`Finish`** to save configuration and start deployment of the NSX Edge node. *Figure* 4.12 shows NSX Manager starting the deployment of NSX Edge `node sa-nsxedge-01`, with **`Configuration State`** in Deployment in Progress state:

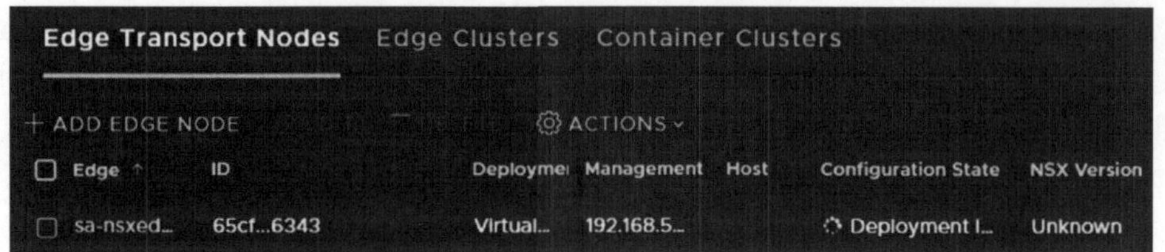

***Figure 4.12**: Deployment in Progress state of NSX Edge node*

Step 9: NSX Manager pushes the OVA file to the vCenter server, and the vCenter Server starts the deployment of the NSX Edge node using the OVA file received from NSX Manager. *Figure* 4.13 illustrates the task in the vCenter server started automatically via NSX Manager to deploy NSX Edge node sa-nsxedge-01:

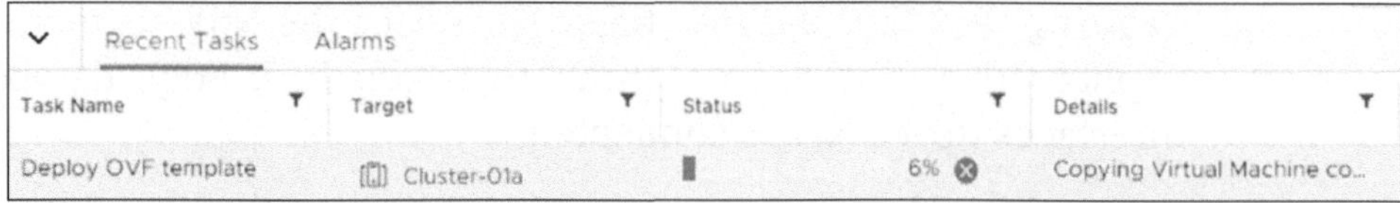

***Figure 4.13**: NSX Edge node deployment task in vCenter server*

Step 10: After the NSX Edge node is deployed successfully, it automatically gets powered on and communicates with NSX Manager to register itself with NSX Manager. After successful registration, NSX Manager configures N-VDS on the NSX Edge node and changes its `Configuration State` to `success`, as shown in *Figure* 4.14:

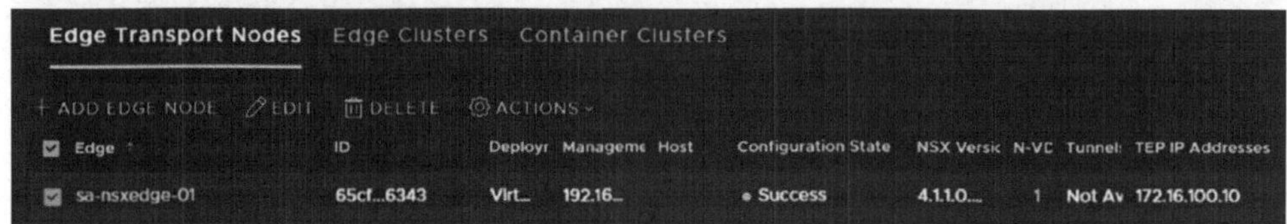

***Figure 4.14**: Successful deployment of NSX Edge node*

Deployment of the NSX Edge node from NSX Manager UI does not require any further configuration. Another benefit is that changing resource reservations or node settings can be done directly from the NSX Manager UI itself.

Deploying NSX Edge VM using OVA

If the vCenter server is not registered with NSX Manager, then NSX Manager UI cannot be used to deploy NSX Edge nodes. VMware provides NSX Edge node in an OVA file format as well that can be downloaded from the VMware portal and then deployed either from the vSphere client or using OVFTool command-line utility. In both methods, access to the vCenter server is required, so either it should be done with the help of a vSphere administrator or require access to deploy OVA file in the vCenter server.

Step 1: OVA deployment of the NSX Edge node is a standard vCenter OVA deployment process. In the first step, select the OVA file downloaded earlier. In the second step, provide the name of the virtual machine and its datacenter location. In the third step, select the cluster or ESXi host on which to deploy OVA file, and click **`Next`**. In the fifth step, **`Configuration`**, select the size of the Edge node as per your requirements, as shown in *Figure 4.15*:

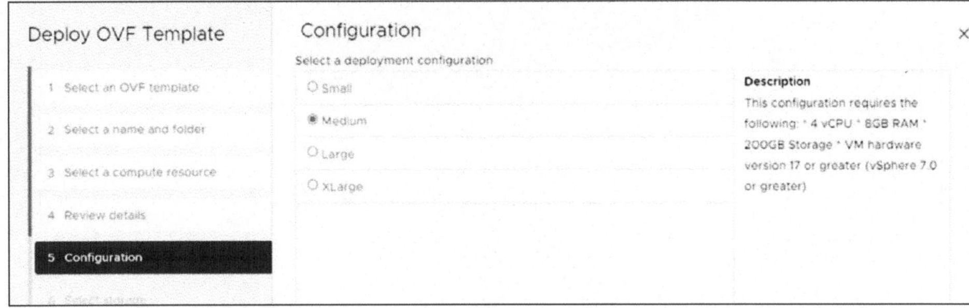

Figure 4.15: *Selecting the size of NSX Edge node during OVA deployment*

Step 2: In the next step, **`Select Networks`**, ensure that **`Network 0`** is connected to the management port group, as this will be utilized as management interface (eth0) on the NSX Edge node, and **`Network 1`** to **`Network 4`** are utilized as fp-ethx datapath interfaces, similar to *Figure 4.16*:

Figure 4.16: *Assigning networks to NSX Edge OVA*

Step 3: In the next step, **Customize Template**, provide the passwords for the admin, root, and optionally audit user. If the IP address for the NSX Edge node is not assigned by DHCP, then manually configure the Hostname, IP address, subnet mask, default gateway, DNS Server, NTP Server, and DNS search list, and enable SSH. The remaining fields can be left blank. Click **Next** to review the configuration of OVA template deployment and then click **Finish** to start OVA deployment. *Figure 4.17* shows a sample screenshot of the final step for NSX Edge OVA deployment with management network configuration:

***Figure 4.17**: Finalizing NSX Edge OVA deployment*

Step 4: After OVA deployment is complete, power on the NSX Edge virtual machine. It will take approximately 5–10 minutes to initialize networks and bootstrap configuration provided during OVA deployment depending upon the environment. Log in to the SSH session using the admin user in one of NSX Manager and run the command **get certificate api thumbprint** to retrieve certificate thumbprint, as shown in *Figure 4.18*:

```
nsx-l-01a> get certificate api thumbprint
Sat Sep 16 2023 UTC 20:18:45.013
c254a9af8e9cdada18728374eb92e60ab5ffee723019aa0fc9a3d38fd034294a

nsx-l-01a>
```

***Figure 4.18**: Retrieving certificate thumbprint from NSX Manager*

Step 5: After the NSX Edge VM is powered on and available on the network, log in to the NSX Edge node via SSH session as an admin user. Run the **command join management-plane <NSX Manager IP> thumbprint**

<NSX Manager Certificate thumbprint> username admin to join the NSX Edge node to the NSX management plane. *Figure* 4.19 shows a sample output of the command executed on the NSX Edge node sa-nsxedge-02 to join it to NSX Manager 192.168.50.1:

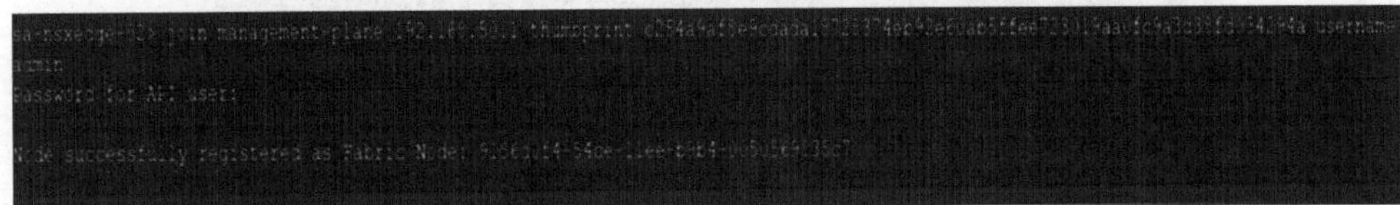

Figure 4.19: *Manually joining* NSX Edge *node to* NSX *management plane*

Step 6: Log in to NSX Manager UI with admin privileges. Navigate to **System** and click **Nodes** under **Fabric** from the left navigation panel. Under **Edge Transport Nodes,** newly joined nodes will be visible with **Configuration State** as **Not Configured**, as *Figure* 4.20 illustrates for NSX Edge node sa-nsxedge-02:

Edge Transport Nodes | Edge Clusters | Container Clusters

+ ADD EDGE NODE | EDIT | DELETE | ACTIONS

Edge	ID	Deployr	Manageme	Host	Configuration State	NSX Versic	N-VC	Tunnel	TEP IP Addresses
sa-nsxedge-01	65cf...6343	Virt...	192.16...		Success	4.1.1.0....	1	Not Av	172.16.100.10
sa-nsxedge-02.lab.local	9186...35c7	Virt...	192.16...		Not Configured	4.1.1.0....	0	Not...	

Figure 4.20: *Viewing manually joined* NSX *Edge nodes in* NSX *Manager*

Step 7: Click the checkbox to select the NSX Edge node and then click **Edit** to configure N-VDS on the Edge node. Similar to Step 7 from the previous section, provide details such as **Transport Zone, Uplink Profile**, TEP IP, and more. The only difference here is during the selection of vNICs for Uplinks defined in the Uplink Profile. NSX Manager provides NIC interfaces such as fp-ethx along with their MAC address, as shown in *Figure* 4.21, instead of NSX segment or vSphere distributed port group, as NSX Manager has no visibility into the vCenter server for a particular NSX Edge VM. NSX Administrator needs to map these MAC addresses with the vNIC of the Edge virtual machine deployed in the vCenter server for correct mapping:

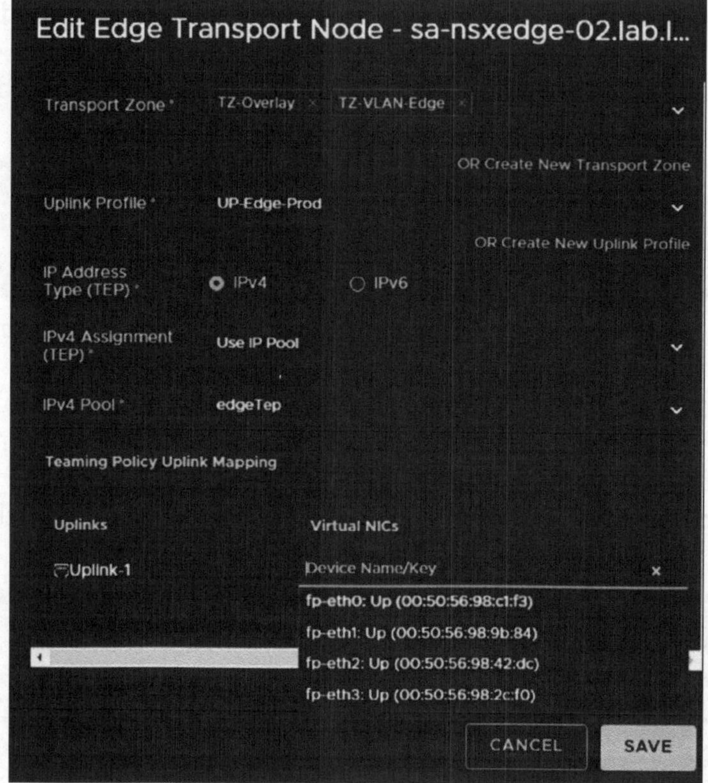

Figure 4.21: *Configuring N-VDS on NSX Edge node*

Figure 4.22 shows the MAC Address of Network adapter 2 on the NSX Edge virtual machine in the vCenter server connected to the data port group that carries Edge TEP and Uplink VLANs. This MAC Address is used to map the data interface in N-VDS during NSX Edge configuration:

Figure 4.22: *Retrieving MAC Address from vCenter server*

Step 8: Click **Save** to start configuring N-VDS on the NSX Edge node, and the **Configuration state** of the NSX Edge node will change to **In Progress** state, as shown in *Figure 4.23*:

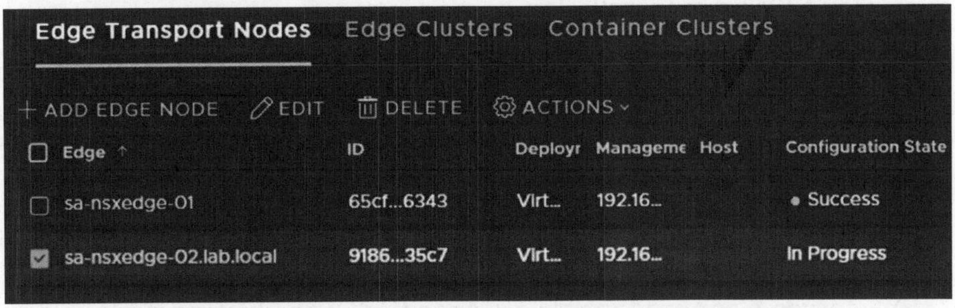

Figure 4.23: *N-VDS configuration in progress on NSX Edge node*

Step 9: After successful configuration, the Configuration State of the eNSX Edge node changes to Success. *Figure 4.24* shows NSX Edge node **sa-nsxedge-02** successfully configured in NSX Manager after deployment through the OVA file:

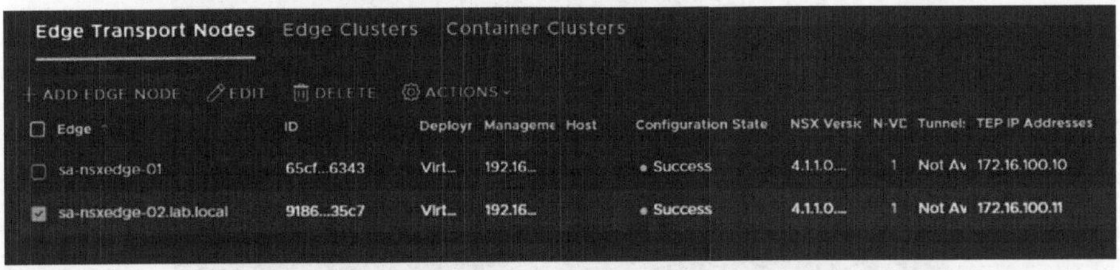

Figure 4.24: *Successfully configured NSX Edge node in UI*

Deploying NSX Edge VM using ISO

It is recommended to deploy the NSX Edge VM either from NSX Manager UI or using OVA file if the vCenter server is not integrated with NSX Manager. Generally, the ISO file installation method is used to deploy NSX Edge Bare Metal on bare-metal physical servers. If there is still a need to deploy NSX Edge VM using an ISO file, then the steps covered for Bare Metal Edge in the next section can be used to deploy NSX Edge VM as well.

Deploying NSX Edge Bare Metal

NSX Edge node can be deployed on bare-metal servers using ISO file either in an automated way or manual way. The automated installation of NSX Edge on bare-metal requires a PXE server to be set up on the network, which configures network settings such as IP Address, subnet mask, gateway, NTP, DNS servers, and more, automatically with the help of a kickstart file. Please refer to the VMware Documentation (https://docs.vmware.com/en/VMware-NSX/4.1/installation/GUID-19CF848D-51F4-40F1-9EDB-1DD3C2935F59.html) to setup PXE server for NSX Edge installation on network.

Mount the NSX Edge ISO file on the physical server, either using a virtual media console or by burning the ISO file on a physical CD/DVD disk and inserting it into the CD/DVD drive on the server. After the server boots from the NSX Edge ISO file, it provides two options, as shown in *Figure* 4.25:

- **`Automated Install`**: This option automatically configures the NSX Edge on a bare-metal server with the help of a kickstart file provided by the PXE server. User credentials are specified in the kickstart file and should be sha512 encoded.
- **`Interactive Install:`** This is a manual option and NSX Edge configuration requires to be done manually. This option is helpful when a PXE server is not present on the network.

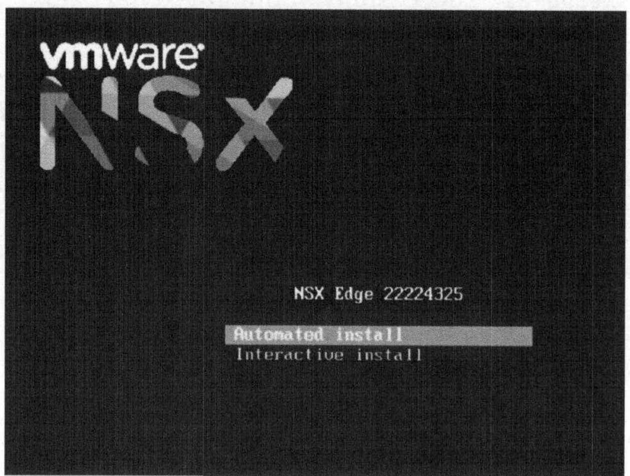

***Figure* 4.25:** *Booting physical server with* NSX *Edge* ISO

In the Interactive Install or manual installation, installation media (ISO file) verifies requirements with the help of a series of dialogue boxes requesting information such as keyboard layout option, IP configuration, hostname, and more. After verifying these requirements, the installation process starts automatically from the ISO file, and the base OS system as well as NSX Edge binaries are installed. In manual installation, the following default credentials are set up, which can be changed from the console.

- **`Username - Root, Password - vmware`**

Figure 4.26 illustrates a login attempt into the NSX Edge Bare Metal node with root credential and default password. NSX Edge will enforce changing password on the first login attempt:

```
sa-nsxedge-03 login: root
Password:
You are required to change your password immediately (administrator enforced)
Changing password for root.
Current password:
New password:
Retype new password:
```

Figure 4.26: *Logging into NSX Edge node with root credentials*

- **`Username - admin, Password - default`**

Figure 4.27 displays NSX Edge Bare Metal enforcing the user to change the password for the admin username on the first login attempt. Also, NSX dataplane services may not start unless the admin user is logged in for the first time in manual installation:

```
sa-nsxedge-03 login: admin
Password:
You are required to change your password immediately (administrator enforced)
Changing password for admin.
Current password:
New password:
Retype new password:

 * WARNING: NSX Edge is still initializing. Reboot may be performed.
```

Figure 4.27: *Changing admin credentials for NSX Edge Bare Metal*

After successful deployment of NSX Edge Bare Metal, if the manual installation method is used, then the NSX Edge node requires to be joined to the NSX management plane using the **`join management-plane`** command. Please refer to the steps covered in the previous section *Deploying* NSX *Edge* VM *using* OVA from Step 4 to Step 8 for a detailed walkthrough.

Monitoring NSX Edge Node

NSX Edge Transport Node or NSX Edge Node can be monitored directly from NSX Manager UI. While logged into NSX Manager, navigate to **`System`** and click on **`Nodes`** under **`Fabric`** and select **`Edge Transport Nodes.`** Click on any NSX Edge Transport Node, and it will open the Edge node details window, as shown in *Figure* 4.28:

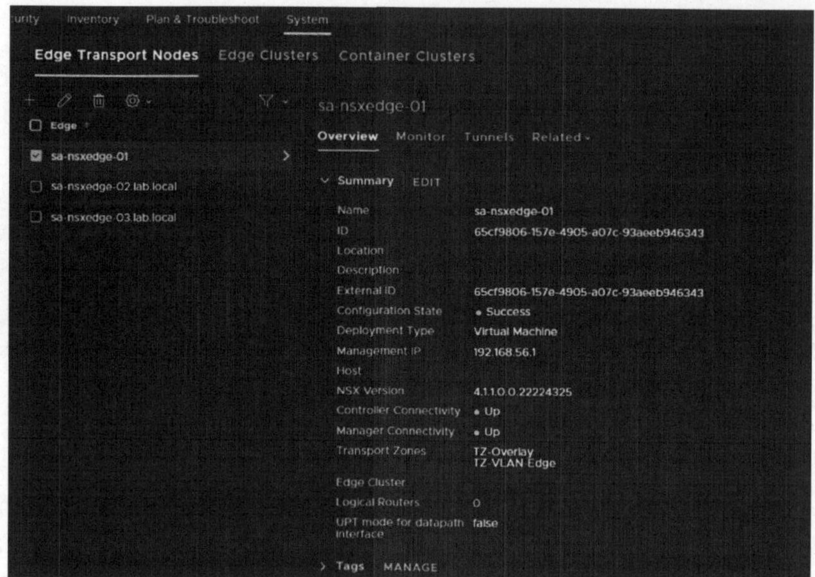

Figure 4.28: *Viewing details of NSX Edge node in NSX Manager*

The **`Overview`** tab shows the N-VDS configuration of the NSX Edge node and its connectivity status to NSX Controller and NSX Manager. Click **`Monitor`** tab to view NSX Edge health information, such as disk space, CPU and Memory usage, and NIC status, as illustrated in *Figure* 4.29:

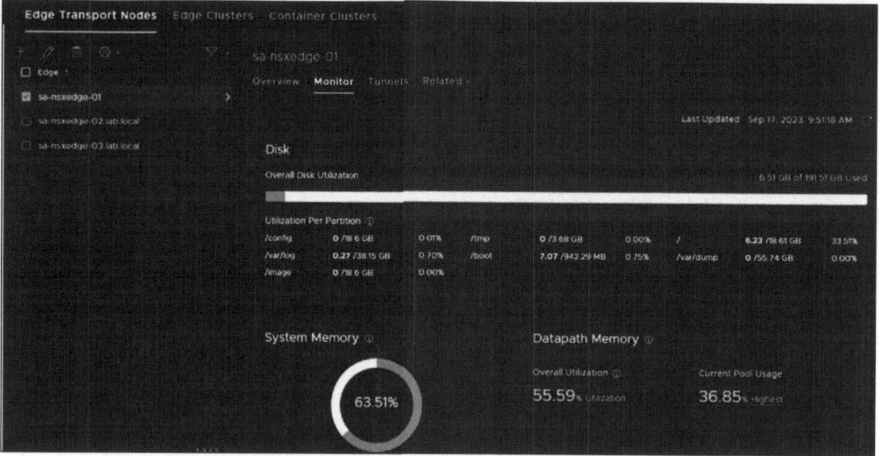

Figure 4.29: *Viewing NSX Edge system information*

This provides useful information about the health of the NSX Edge node and can be used to monitor the status information of NSX Edge nodes, as well as provides a good starting point to troubleshoot issues with the NSX Edge node.

NSX Edge Cluster

NSX Edge cluster is a group of NSX Edge nodes that provides high availability to services running on NSX Edge nodes. NSX Edge node must be joined as a member of the NSX Edge cluster before it can be used as an Edge Transport Node. NSX Edge cluster can have different form factor Edge nodes, but it is recommended to create an NSX Edge cluster with NSX Edge nodes of the same size.

A single NSX Edge cluster can contain a maximum of 10 Edge nodes with a maximum of 160 Edge clusters configured in a single NSX environment. NSX also supports failure domains within the Edge cluster, which can be mapped to NSX Edge nodes running in different racks to provide rack-level fault tolerance. As of writing till NSX release v4.1, failure domains are supported to be configured via API only. The following steps can be used to create an NSX Edge cluster in the NSX environment:

Step 1: Login into NSX Manager with admin privileges. Navigate to **`System`** menu and click **`Nodes`** under **`Fabric`** from the left navigation panel. Click **`Edge Clusters`** to view Edge clusters configured in the NSX environment. *Figure* 4.30 shows no Edge clusters as this is a new environment and no Edge clusters have been configured yet:

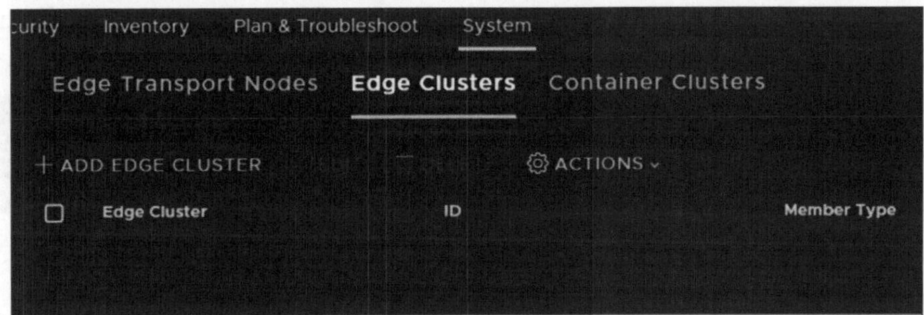

***Figure 4.30**: Viewing Edge clusters in NSX Manager UI*

Step 2: Provide an appropriate **`name`** for the Edge cluster and select the **`Edge Cluster Profile`** using drop-down menu. This profile defines the heartbeat interval and number of heartbeats between Edge nodes in the cluster to determine the liveliness of an Edge node. Under **`Transport Nodes`**, select the Edge nodes and use (>) icon to move Edge nodes from **`Available`** window to **`Selected`** window. *Figure* 4.31 shows an Edge cluster configuration with previously deployed Edge nodes, **`sa-nsxedge-01`** and **`sa-nsxedge-02`,** selected as its members:

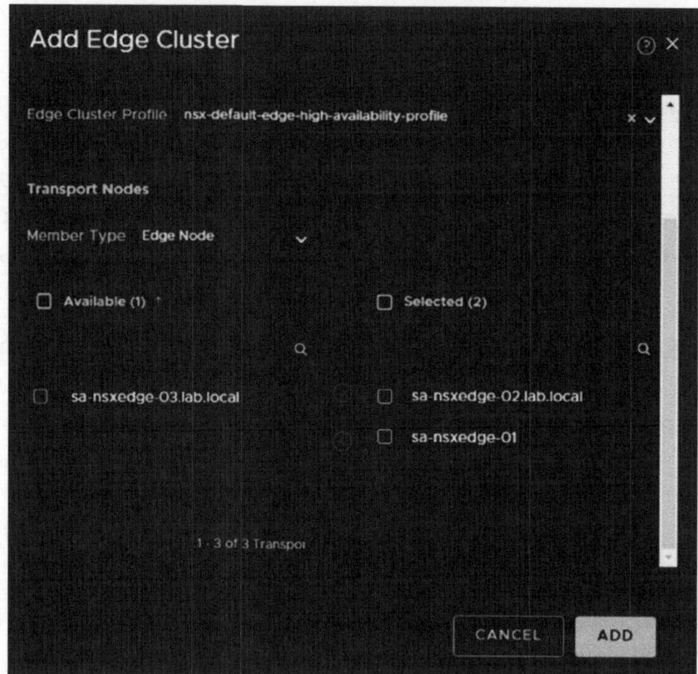

***Figure* 4.31:** *Adding an Edge cluster in NSX Manager*

Step 3: Click **Add** to create the Edge cluster and save the configuration in NSX Manager. *Figure* 4.32 shows an Edge cluster with the name EC-LAB-01 created successfully in NSX Manager:

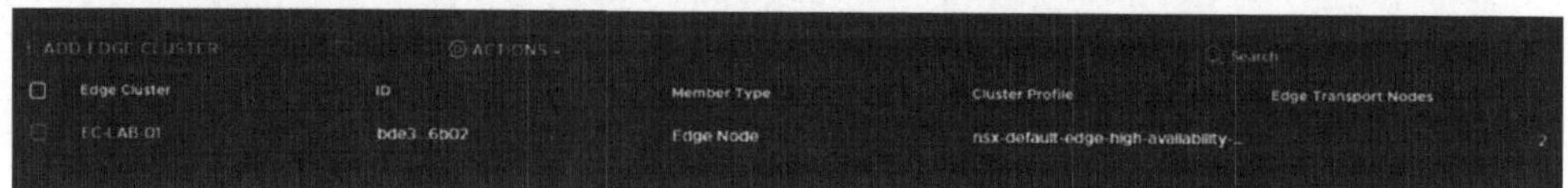

***Figure* 4.32:** *Successfully configured Edge cluster in NSX Manager*

This completes the configuration of NSX Edge nodes and NSX Edge cluster in the NSX environment. NSX Edge cluster can now be utilized to host different NSX logical routing services in the NSX environment.

Conclusion

This concludes the requirement to enable logical routing features provided by NSX. In summary, this chapter covered important components required for logical routing, namely, Edge node and Edge cluster. We covered Edge node architecture, different sizing options, and deployment options available for Edge nodes in the datacenter.

In the next chapter, we will deep dive into the world of NSX logical router. We will cover different routing topologies supported by NSX and how to configure them, along with dynamic routing protocols like BGP and OSPF. In addition, the next chapter covers high-availability options to ensure routing services are always available.

Key Terms

- **Segment:** Segments are layer 2 subnets representing layer 2 broadcasting domain across transport nodes in NSX networking
- **Edge Node:** NSX Edge node provides a pool of capacity or pool of resources, for example, CPU and memory to run centralized services.
- Edge Cluster: A group of NSX Edge nodes that provides high availability to services running on NSX Edge nodes.
- **East-West Traffic:** Workloads present in a datacenter communicate with each other, and traffic is confined within the boundaries of the datacenter.
- **North-South Traffic:** Workloads present in a datacenter communicate with external devices outside the boundary of the datacenter.
- **Single Tier Routing:** A single NSX gateway is connected to NSX logical segments in the southbound to provide E-W routing and is also connected to the physical infrastructure in the northbound direction to provide N-S connectivity.
- **Multi-Tier Routing:** Provides isolation between different gateways with a provider gateway for N-S traffic and a different tenant gateway for E-W traffic.
- **Dynamic Routing**: Enables different gateways to exchange network information with each other and is used to dynamically obtain routes from each other.
- **VRF**: Virtual Routing Forwarding (VRF) is a routing virtualization method to create multiple virtual logical routing instances on a single physical router.
- **EVPN**: Ethernet VPN, or EVPN for short, is a standards-based BGP distributed control plane for network virtualization overlay (NVO) that provides Layer 2 and Layer 3 connectivity over IP and IP/MPLS underlay networks.

Chapter 5

Logical Routing – NSX Gateways

The last chapter has covered important components required for logical routing, namely, Edge node and Edge cluster. It covered Edge node architecture, different sizing options, and options available to deploy Edge node in the datacenter. But if you have still been waiting for fully distributed East-West routing and multi-tiering architecture supported by NSX, well, wait no further as interesting stuff happens now!!!

In this chapter, we deep dive into the world of the NSX logical router and will be following a packet to see how it travels within the NSX environment. We will also cover different routing topologies supported by NSX and how to configure them, along with dynamic routing protocols such as BGP and OSPF. Last but not least, high-availability configurations are essential to any excellent design. NSX supports high-availability choices for routing services, which brings this chapter to a close.

Structure

In this chapter, we will cover the following topics:

- NSX Logical Router
    - Single-Tier Routing
    - Multi-Tier Routing
    - Creating NSX Logical Router
    - Configuring ECMP and Routing on Tier0

- NSX Routing High Availability
  - Active-Active HA Mode
  - Active-Standby HA Mode
  - High-Availability Failover Detection Mechanisms
- Conclusion

NSX Logical Router

NSX logical router or gateway provides optimized distributed routing as well as centralized routing for North-South traffic and services such as NAT, VPN, and more. This is possible due to two different components hosted in an NSX logical router or gateway, namely Distributed Router (DR) and Service Router (SR).

Distributed Router (DR) is a router that connects to multiple segments with the help of logical interfaces (LIF). It runs as a kernel module on all the NSX-prepared Transport Nodes and is distributed across all ESXi hosts and Edge nodes. It takes care of East-West routing between different segments connected to it.

Service Router (SR) is instantiated on Edge Transport nodes only and takes care of the following centralized routing services:

- Physical infrastructure connectivity
- NAT
- DHCP server
- VPN
- Gateway Firewall
- Bridging
- Service Interface

Both SR and DR are connected via an Intra-Tier transit link automatically created by NSX, and no further routing is required to be configured between them. In order to further understand connectivity and traffic flow between SR and DR, we need to first understand different routing topologies supported by NSX. These topologies define the type of NSX gateways that are deployed in the NSX environment and govern the flow of traffic. There are two routing topologies that can be implemented in the NSX environment as follows:

- Single-Tier Routing
- Multi-Tier Routing

Single-Tier Routing

In single-tier routing topology, the same NSX gateway is connected to NSX logical segments in southbound to provide E-W routing and is also connected to physical infrastructure in northbound direction to provide N-S connectivity. This NSX gateway is termed as Tier0 gateway. This Tier0 gateway consists of DR to provide E-W routing and SR to provide N-S connectivity. *Figure* 5.1 shows an example of single-tier routing topology in both logical view and physical view. It consists of two virtual machines, namely Web-01 and App-01, running on different ESXi hosts connected to overlay segments ls-web and ls-app, respectively. NSX segments ls-web and ls-app are connected to the same Tier0 gateway, which further connects to the physical router to provide connectivity to devices present in the physical network:

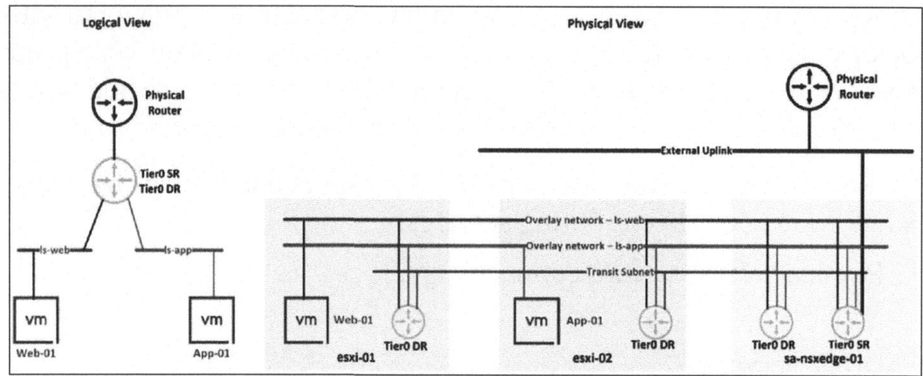

Figure 5.1: *Single-Tier Routing Topology*

As visible in topology, Tier0 DR copy is distributed across all Transport Nodes, including ESXi host and NSX Edge nodes, whereas Tier0 SR copy is present only on the NSX Edge node. Data plane functionality and ARP lookup are performed by logical interface (LIF) connected to different segments, and each LIF has an IP address assigned to it as the default gateway of the connected segment. This IP address is unique per LIF and remains the same wherever the segment exists. For example, if the default gateway of segment ls-web is assigned as 172.16.110.1, then this IP address is assigned to LIF connecting the segment to DR, and it will remain the same on esxi-01, esxi-02, and sa-nsxedge-01 nodes. In addition, MAC address assigned to LIF is termed as vMAC (02:50:56:56:44:52), which remains the same across all nodes. Let's understand this concept with the help of a packet walk for East-West routing.

East-West Routing Packet Walk

Let's further explore the previously considered topology and look at the components involved in East-West routing. *Figure* 5.2 is a subset of the topology shown in *Figure* 5.1, where it illustrates VM Web-01 configured with the IP address 172.16.110.10 and App-01 configured with the IP address 172.16.120.10, running on ESXi host esxi-01 and esxi-02, respectively. LIF1 is the logical interface connecting ls-web segment to Tier0 DR, while LIF2 is another logical interface connecting ls-app segment to Tier0 DR.

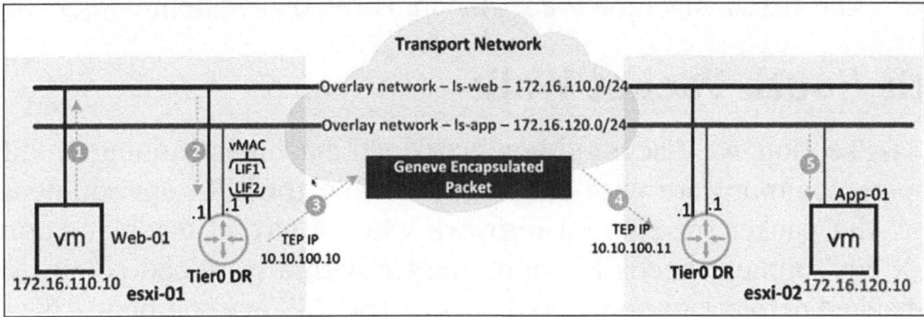

***Figure* 5.2:** *East-West Packet walk in single-tier routing*

Web-01 is trying to communicate with virtual machine App-01 running on host esxi-02. Here are the steps:

Step 1: As the IP address of App-01 belongs to a different subnet from Web-01, so in the first step, VM Web-01 sends the packet to its default gateway, with L2 header containing the source MAC address as its own and destination MAC address as vMAC of Tier0 DR. Here, vMAC remains same for all LIFs connected to DR.

Step 2: This packet is received by Tier0 DR running on host esxi-01 via its connected interface, LIF1. It performs a routing lookup locally on ESXi host itself and identifies that the destination subnet 172.16.120.0/24 is a directly connected segment on LIF2. It performs a lookup on LIF2 ARP table to determine the MAC address of the destination IP address for virtual machine App-01. With the help of logical switch ls-app MAC table, it identifies that the MAC address of App-01 is associated with the TEP IP address of host esxi-02.

Step 3: ESXi host esxi-01 encapsulates the packet and sends it to host esxi-02 with the source IP address as its own TEP IP address (10.10.100.10) and the destination IP address as remote TEP IP address (10.10.100.11). The destination VNI is of ls-app segment, as routing lookup has already been completed at the source host, esxi-01, and no further routing lookup is required at host esxi-02.

Step 4: ESXi host esxi-02 decapsulates the received packet and performs a lookup in the segment associated with LIF2, that is, ls-app MAC table.

Step 5: Subsequently, the packet is delivered to the virtual machine App-01. For return traffic, the same process happens on ESXi host esxi-02. In return traffic, a routing lookup is performed on esxi-02, and Tier0 DR running on esxi-02 makes routing decision to forward the packet to the virtual machine Web-01, connected on segment ls-web.

North-South Packet Walk

In the last section, we discussed how workload machines running on different ESXi hosts communicate with each other within the NSX environment. Let's see how the packet travels in a network when a virtual machine running in the NSX environment needs to communicate with a workload connected to a VLAN-backed network or connected outside the NSX environment. This type of network communication is designated as North-South traffic.

Figure 5.3 shows virtual machine Web-01 running on ESXi host esxi-01 connected to overlay segment ls-web and is trying to communicate with the server, phy-01, routed through a physical router on L3 physical infrastructure. There is an external connectivity setup between the Physical Router with IP 192.168.0.241 and the SR component of the Tier0 gateway, hosted on the Edge node with IP 192.168.0.240. Tier0 SR is exchanging routes from Physical Router through dynamic routings such as eBGP or OSPF. Tier0 SR learns BGP route 192.168.10.0/24 with a next hop as 192.168.0.241 through the physical router, and the physical router learns BGP route 172.16.110.0/24 with a next hop as 192.168.0.240 from Tier0 SR:

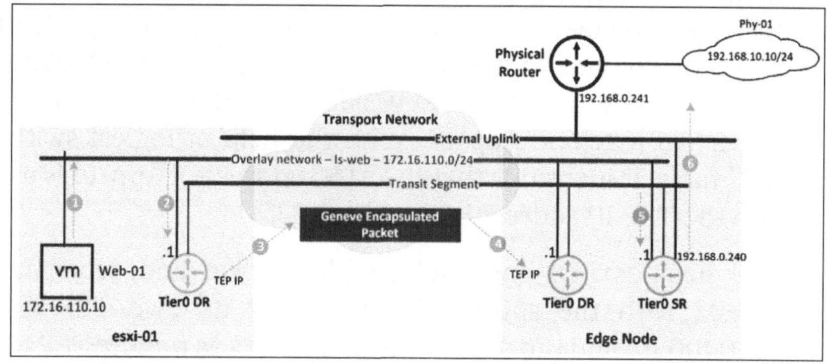

***Figure 5.3**: North-South Packet Walk in Single-Tier Routing*

Step 1: VM web-01 sends the packet destined for machine phy-01 to its default gateway 172.16.110.1. As discussed earlier, routing always happens closest to its source. Here, Tier0 DR receives the packet running on the same ESXi host, esxi-01.

Step 2: The packet is received by the local Tier0 DR. Since it doesn't have a specific route for 192.168.10.0/24, it sends the packet to its next hop via the default route. The next hop for Tier0 DR is Tier0 SR located on the Edge Node.

Step 3: ESXi host esxi-01 encapsulates the packet and sends it to the Edge Node with the source IP address as its own TEP IP address and the destination IP address as the remote TEP IP address of the Edge Node.

Step 4: Edge Node is also an NSX-prepared Transport Node, hence it decapsulates the packet and delivers it to Tier0 SR.

Step 5: Tier0 SR performs local routing lookup and identifies BGP route 192.168.10.0/24 being learned via an external interface from the Physical Router with the next hop IP 192.168.0.241.

Step 6: Tier0 SR sends the packet to the VLAN segment via External Uplink to the Physical Router, which subsequently gets delivered to server phy-01.

One important point to observe here is that routing and ARP lookup happen locally on ESXi host esxi-01, which hosts a local copy of Tier0 DR to determine that the packet must be sent to Tier0 SR. There is no further routing that happens on the Edge Node, and the packet is delivered directly to Tier0 SR.

Figure 5.4 illustrates communication from server phy-01 to virtual machine web-01 in a reverse direction:

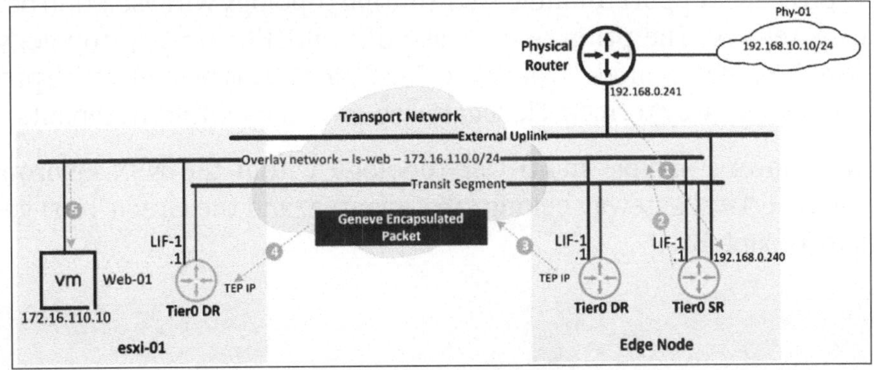

Figure 5.4: *North-South packet walk in reverse*

Step 1: An external device or server phy-01 sends the packet destined for the virtual machine web-01 to its default gateway, which in turn is received by the Physical Router. Through BGP routing, it identifies the subnet 172.16.110.0/24, and the next hop IP address is 192.168.0.240, belonging to Tier0 SR. Hence, the physical router forwards the packet to Tier0 SR hosted on Edge Node through External Uplink.

Step 2: Tier0 SR performs a routing lookup and identifies that the 172.16.110.0/24 subnet is directly connected to interface LIF-1. ARP table associated with interface LIF-1 identifies the MAC address of virtual machine web-01 corresponding to its IP address. Also, it identifies that the MAC address is being learned through remote TEP IP address of ESXi host esxi-01.

Step 3: Edge Node encapsulates the packet and sends it to ESXi host esxi-01 with the source IP address as its own TEP IP address and the destination IP address as the remote TEP IP address of esxi-01.

Step 4: ESXi host esxi-01 decapsulates the packet and performs an L2 lookup in its local MAC table associated with interface LIF-1, that is, segment ls-web.

Step 5: The packet is successfully delivered to virtual machine web-01.

Here, routing and ARP lookup happen directly on Tier0 SR, and no further routing or lookup was required to be performed on Tier0 DR hosted on ESXi host esxi-01 as interface LIF-1 is also connected to Tier0 SR, so no packet forwarding from Tier0 SR to Tier0 DR is required.

Multi-Tier Routing

NSX also provides support for multi-tier routing topology with isolation between different gateways. The primary use case of multi-tier routing topology is to enable a multi-tenancy model where the Tier0 gateway is owned by the provider, with a second gateway termed Tier1 gateway owned by different tenants.

Figure 5.5 shows a sample multi-tier topology within the NSX environment, where the Blue Tier1 gateway belongs to Tenant-A, and the Green Tier1 gateway belongs to Tenant-B:

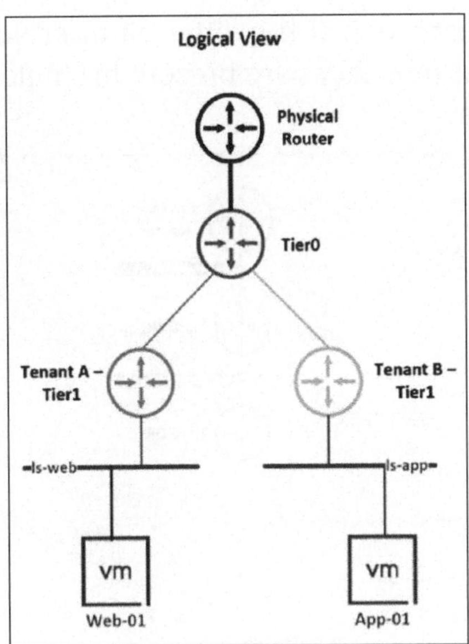

Figure 5.5: *An example multi-tier routing topology in NSX*

Tier1 gateways are used to provide East-West connectivity, and they must connect to a Tier0 gateway to provide North-South connectivity to external networks outside of the NSX environment. Also, Tier1 gateway does not support dynamic routing protocols such as BGP or OSPF unlike Tier0 gateway, and there is no ECMP routing support. Tier1 gateway can run in two different modes as follows:

- **Distributed Only**: In this mode, the Tier1 gateway only has the DR component, and no SR component is hosted on Edge nodes as the Tier1 gateway does not associate with the Edge cluster. This mode supports only East-West routing services.
- **Tier1 with Services**: In this mode, the Tier1 gateway also has an SR component hosted on Edge nodes as the Tier1 gateway associates with Edge cluster to host centralized services such as NAT, VPN, and Load Balancing. This mode is helpful where services are required and can be hosted on Tier1 instead of Tier0 gateway, providing much better throughput on Tier0 gateway.

Interfaces in Multi-Tier Routing

There are different interfaces configured automatically by NSX to connect different gateway components together, while others are configured by the administrator to provide connectivity to external networks or NSX segments. We have already discussed a few of these interfaces in our previous packet walks.

Figure 5.6 provides a closer look at the different interfaces present in multi-tier routing; however, similar interfaces are present in single-tier routing, except for the router link interface:

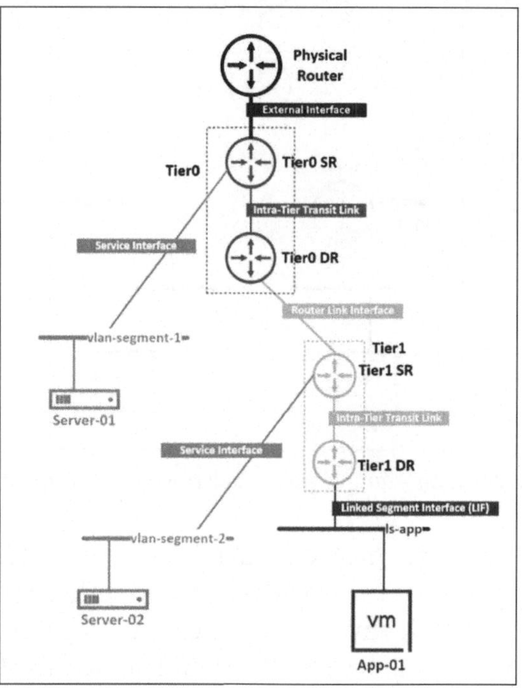

Figure 5.6: *Different types of interfaces present in routing topology*

- **External Interface:** This is the interface connecting to the physical network or physical router. This interface supports both static and dynamic routing and exists only on Tier0 gateway as it provides North-South connectivity to workloads connected in the NSX environment. Also, this interface is used to extend Virtual Routing and Forwarding (VRF) from the physical router to the NSX domain. VRF has been discussed in great detail in later section of *Chpater 6, Logical Routing – VRF and EVPN.*
- **Intra-Tier Transit Link:** This interface provides connectivity between DR and SR components of the same NSX gateway, that is, Tier0 or Tier1. A transit overlay segment is auto-plumbed by NSX between DR and SR, and it assigns IP address from range 169.254.0.0/24 by default. This range can be modified as per requirement only during the creation of the NSX gateway and cannot be modified afterward.
- **Router Link:** This interface provides connectivity between Tier0 and Tier1 gateway and is auto-plumbed by NSX when Tier1 gateway is connected to a Tier0 gateway. Each Tier0-Tier1 peer link is provided with a /31 IP address from 100.64.0.0/16 address range by default and can be

changed if required during the creation of the Tier0 gateway. However, once created, this address range cannot be modified afterward.

- **Service Interface:** This interface connects VLAN segment to the NSX gateway, providing connectivity to VLAN-backed physical or virtual servers. It is supported on both Tier0 and Tier1 gateway in Active-Standby configuration and supports static routing. It is typically used to provide connectivity to a standalone load balancer in the NSX environment.
- **Loopback:** Tier0 supports a loopback interface that can be redistributed in a routing protocol.

Tier1 DR only Packet Walk

Let's take an example to understand these different interfaces and how packet travels in a multi-tier routing topology.

Figure 5.7 shows an inside view of the example topology shown in the earlier *Figure* 5.5. It shows two Tier1 gateways, one for Tenant-A and another for Tenant-B, configured in a distributed routing-only configuration, and both are connected to the same Tier0 gateway via router link interface. This router link interface is automatically plumbed by NSX with 100.64.0.0/31 assigned to the Tenant-B Tier1 gateway link, and 100.64.0.2/31 assigned to the Tenant-A Tier1 gateway. Virtual machine Web-01 is connected to segment ls-web, which further connects to Tier1-A gateway, and virtual machine App-01 is connected to segment ls-app, which connects to Tier1-B gateway. Web-01 initiates communication with App-01. Let's see how this packet flows from Web-01 to App-01 virtual machine:

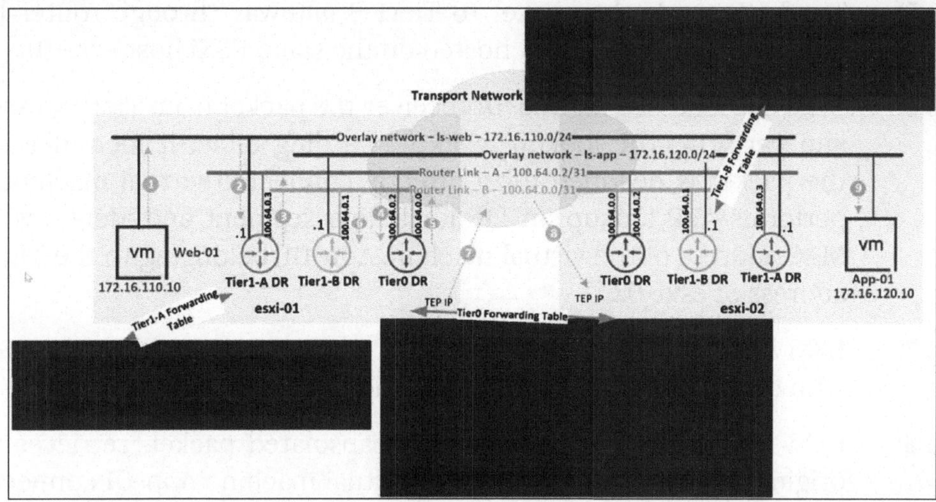

Figure 5.7: *Multi-Tier routing topology packet walk with Tier1 in DR only*

Step 1: Web-01 with the IP address 172.16.110.10/24 sends a packet destined to the virtual machine App-01 with the IP address 172.16.120.10/24 running on host esxi-02. Since the destination belongs to a different subnet, Web-01 sends the packet to its default gateway 172.16.110.1/24, which is hosted on Tier1-A gateway.

Step 2: The packet is received by Tier1-A gateway hosted on the same ESXi host esxi-01. It performs a lookup in its forwarding table and identifies that the destination subnet is not directly connected to the Tier1-A gateway. As shown in *Figure* 5.7, in the forwarding table of Tier1-A gateway, there is a default route 0.0.0.0/0 with the next hop IP 100.64.0.2/31. This IP address is the router link interface present on the Tier0 gateway.

Step 3: Tier1-A gateway sends the packet to DR copy of Tier0 gateway hosted on the same ESXi host esxi-01 via the router link interface IP address 100.64.0.3/31.

Step 4: The packet is received by Tier0 DR, and it performs a lookup in its forwarding table. If you look *Figure* 5.7 closely, there is a default route 0.0.0.0/0 with the next hop as 169.254.0.2, that is, the IP address of Intra-Tier transit link of Tier0 SR. However, there is another entry present for subnet 172.16.120.0/24 with the next hop IP address as router link interface 100.64.0.1/31, which is the IP address assigned to Tier1-B gateway.

Step 5: Tier0 DR sends the packet to Tier1-B gateway through router link interface IP 100.64.0.0/31 hosted on the same ESXi host esxi-01.

Step 6: Tier1-B DR hosted on esxi-01 receives the packet from Tier0 gateway and performs the lookup in its forwarding table. It identifies that the packet is destined for a directly connected virtual machine. It performs ARP lookup on LIF for ls-app segment and identifies the MAC address of the virtual machine App-01, belonging to the TEP IP address of esxi-02.

Step 7: ESXi host esxi-01 encapsulates the packet and sends it to esxi-02 with the destination IP address as the TEP IP address of esxi-02.

Step 8: ESXi host esxi-02 received the encapsulated packet, retrieves the original packet, and delivers it to virtual machine App-01 connected to segment ls-app.

Step 9: There is no routing lookup happening on esxi-02, as all lookups have already been done on esxi-01.

From the preceding packet walk, it is clear that all routing lookups happen locally on esxi-01. This benefits in reducing network hops between different devices and achieving fully distributed East-West routing. Now, let's take a look at what happens to the packet if Tier1 is enabled for services as well.

Tier1 with SR Packet Walk

Figure 5.8 shows the same topology discussed earlier, but this time Tier1 gateways have been attached to the Edge cluster, hence enabling the SR component of Tier1 gateway to be hosted on the Edge node. If you look closely at *Figure* 5.8, you will notice that this time there is no Tier0 DR copy present on ESXi hosts, only Tier1 DR copy hosted on ESXi hosts. This design ensures that if any centralized services are enabled on Tier1 gateway, they will process outgoing network traffic through the SR component:

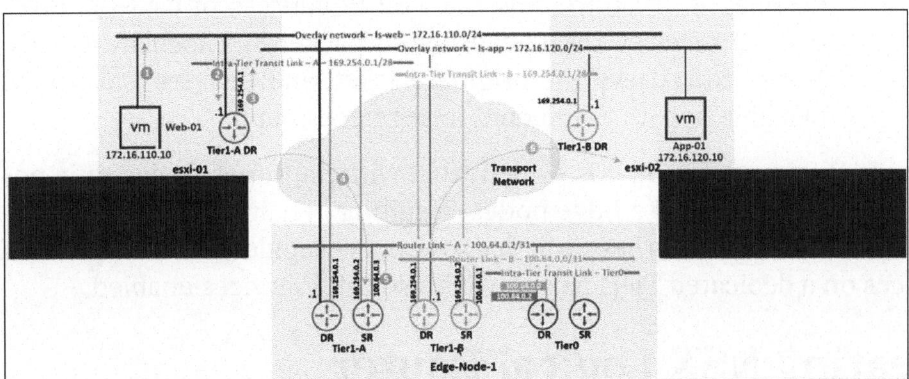

Figure 5.8: *Multi-Tier routing packet walk in Tier1 with SR*

Step 1: Web-01 with the IP address 172.16.110.10/24 sends a packet destined to virtual machine App-01 with the IP address 172.16.120.10/24 running on host esxi-02. Since the destination belongs to a different subnet, Web-01 sends the packet to its default gateway 172.16.110.1/24, which is hosted on Tier1-A gateway.

Step 2: The packet is received by Tier1-A gateway hosted on the same ESXi host esxi-01. It performs a lookup in its forwarding table and identifies that the destination subnet is not directly connected to Tier1-A gateway. As shown in *Figure* 5.8, in the forwarding table of Tier1-A gateway, there is a default route 0.0.0.0/0 with the next hop IP 169.254.0.2/28. This IP address is the Intra-Tier transit link interface of SR Tier1-A gateway hosted on Edge Node 1.

Step 3: As the packet needs to leave ESXi host esxi-01, it encapsulates the packet with the destination TEP IP address of Edge Node 1.

Step 4: The packet is sent to Edge Node 1 through the physical underlay network and is received by SR copy of Tier1-A gateway running on Edge Node 1.

Step 5: Similar to the previous packet walk, the SR copy has a router link interface attached to it, and it sends the packet to the DR copy of Tier0 gateway, which, in turn, sends the packet to the SR copy of Tier1-B gateway by performing lookups in the forwarding table. Tier1-B SR gateway forwards the packet to Tier1-B DR, which performs a lookup in the ARP table of LIF connected to the ls-app segment.

Step 6: Edge Node 1 encapsulates the packet and send it to esxi-02 with the destination IP address as the TEP IP address of esxi-02. ESXi host esxi-02 receives the encapsulated packet, decapsulate the Geneve packet to retrieve the original packet, and delivers it to the virtual machine App-01 connected to segment ls-app.

Through this packet walk, it is evident that with improper design, it is possible to pin East-West traffic to Edge nodes, resulting in hair-pinning. To avoid such non-optimal designs, it is best practice to connect segments that require stateful services on a dedicated Tier1 gateway with stateful services enabled.

Creating NSX Logical Router

A lot of concepts have been covered in the last section. Let's see how these concepts can be implemented in the NSX environment with the help of a practical example. Consider the multi-tier topology discussed earlier in *Figure* 5.5 and see how it is implemented in the NSX environment. Before adding a Tier0 gateway in NSX, ensure that an Edge cluster has been created with one or more Edge nodes, and appropriate VLAN segments have been configured to provide connectivity from the Tier0 gateway to the physical router. Another important point to remember is that a single Edge node can host only one Tier0 gateway.

Creating a Tier0 gateway

To create a Tier0 gateway in the NSX environment, follow these steps:

Step 1: Login into NSX Manager with admin privileges and navigate to the **`Networking`** menu. Click **`Tier-0 Gateways`** in the left-side navigation panel under **`Connectivity`** to view Tier0 gateways configured in the environment. *Figure* 5.9 shows an example screenshot where one Tier0 gateway is already configured and running in NSX Manager:

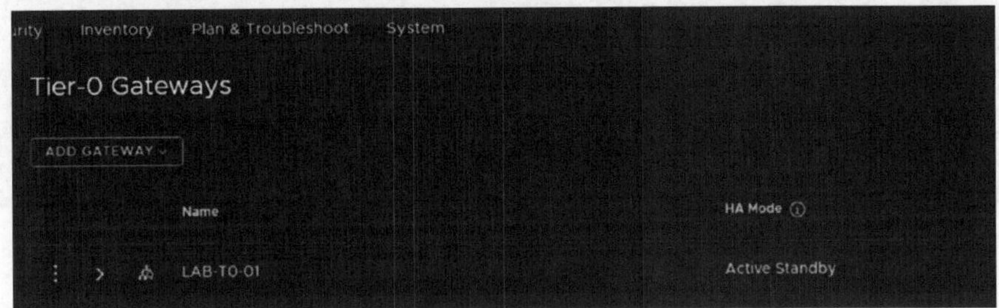

Figure 5.9: *Viewing Tier0 gateway in NSX Manager UI*

Step 2: Click **`Add Gateway`** and select **`Tier-0`**. It also gives the option to configure VRF, which is covered in the later section in *Chapter* 6, *Logical Routing - VRF and* EVPN. Provide the following required inputs:

a. **`Name`**: Provide an appropriate name for the Tier0 gateway to identify it in the NSX environment

b. **`HA Mode`**: Select either Active-Active or Active-Standby. These two modes have been explained in depth in the upcoming section.

c. **`Edge Cluster`**: Select the Edge cluster to host Tier0 gateway.

d. **`Stateful`**: This is an optional toggle button. Starting NSX release v4.0.1, the NSX gateway now supports stateful services in Active-Active configuration. *Chapter* 11, NSX *DataCenter Services* - 1, is dedicated to NSX services covers this option in great detail.

e. **`Additional Settings`**: Expand this menu to optionally override NSX default Transit subnets. After Tier0 gateway has been created, these values cannot be modified:

   i. **`Internal Transit Subnet`**: Provide IPv4 subnet to override default 169.254.0.0/24 subnet for Intra-Tier Transit links.

ii. **`T0-T1 Transit Subnet`**: Provide IPv4 subnet to override default 100.64.0.0/16 subnet for router link interface.

Figure 5.10 shows a sample initial configuration of a Tier0 gateway:

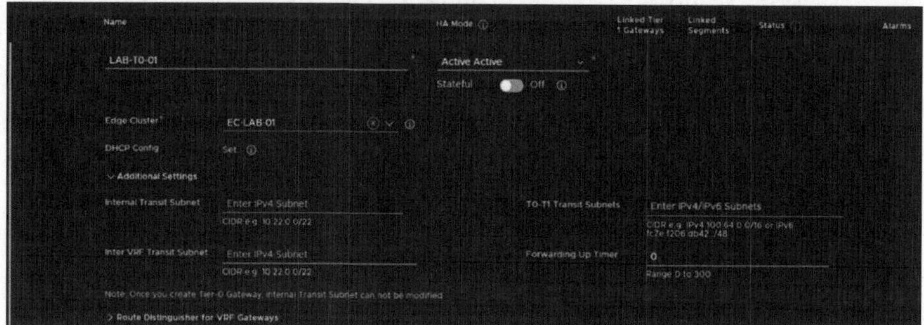

Figure 5.10*: Adding a new Tier0 gateway*

Click **`Save`** to create the Tier0 gateway. NSX Manager prompts an option to continue configuring the newly created Tier0 gateway. Click **`Yes`** to continue editing the Tier0 gateway. If click **`No`** or need to edit the Tier0 gateway, then click three dots against the Tier0 gateway name and select **`Edit`**. Expand Interfaces and click **`Set`** as shown in *Figure* 5.11. This is the first step in providing external connectivity to NSX networks:

Figure 5.11*: Configuring interfaces on Tier0 gateway*

Step 3: This will open a new window to add either External Interfaces or Service Interfaces on Tier0 gateway. Click **`Add Interface`** to a new link to Tier0 gateway. Provide the following inputs requested by NSX Manager as shown in *Figure* 5.12:

a. **`Name`**: Provide a name for the interface configured on Tier0.

b. **`Type`**: Select the type of interface; the default selection is External, but it can be changed to loopback as well.

c. **`IP Address/Mask`**: Provide the IPv4/IPv6 address in CIDR format assigned to the interface.

d. **Connected To**: Select the VLAN-backed segment configured to connect the interface.

e. **Edge Node**: Select the Edge node from the Edge cluster on which this interface will be realized.

f. **MTU**: Optionally configure MTU to support jumbo frames if required.

g. **URPF Mode**: Select either to keep URPF mode in strict mode or none. If there is asymmetric routing happening in the environment, then it is best to keep URPF as none as NSX will drop the packet in strict mode if inbound and outbound traffic communication for the same host is using different edge nodes.

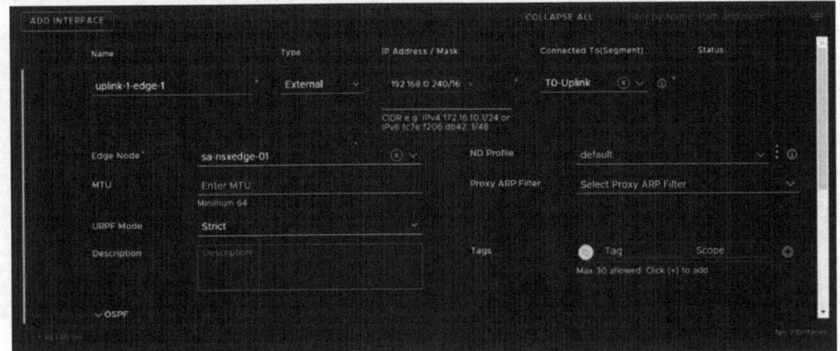

***Figure 5.12**: Adding a new External interface on Tier0 gateway*

Step 4: Click **Save** to finish adding the interface on Tier0 gateway. Add the remaining interfaces as per requirement, repeating Step 4. *Figure* 5.13 shows an example screenshot where two external interfaces have been configured on Tier0 gateway to provide external connectivity to NSX overlay networks:

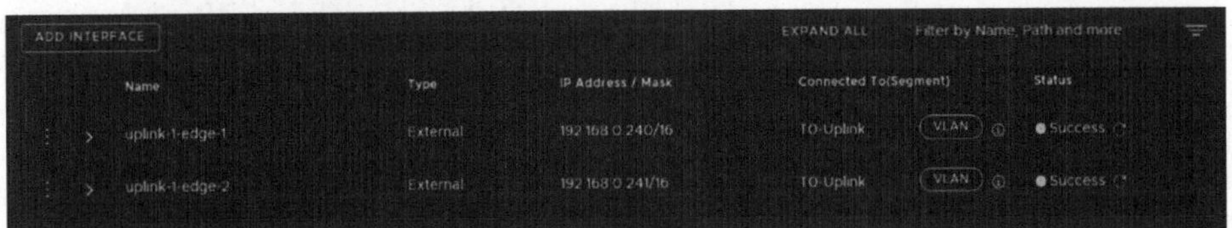

***Figure 5.13**: Viewing configured external interfaces on Tier0 gateway*

Step 5: Click `Close` and then `Close Editing` to finish the Editing Tier0 gateway.

Creating a Tier1 gateway

Continuing from creating Tier0 gateway, the next step is to create a Tier1 gateway. The following steps can be used as a reference to create a new Tier1 gateway in the NSX environment:

Step 1: Log in to NSX Manager with admin privileges and navigate to the **`Networking`** menu. Click **`Tier-1 Gateways`** in the left-side navigation panel under **`Connectivity`** to view Tier1 gateways configured in the environment. *Figure* 5.14 shows an example screenshot where two Tier1 gateways are already configured and running in NSX Manager:

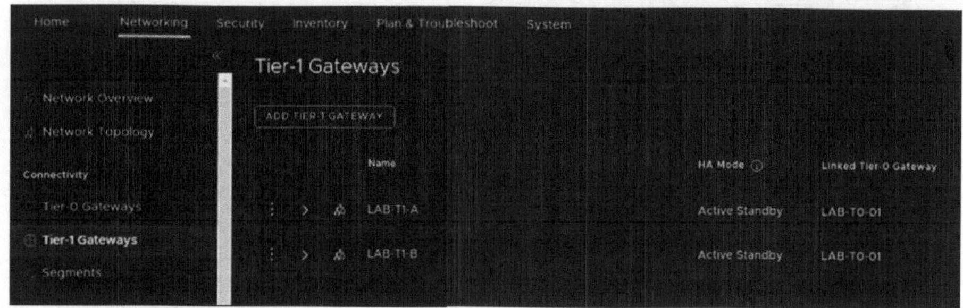

Figure 5.14: *Viewing Tier1 gateways in NSX Manager UI*

Step 2: Click **`Add Tier-1 Gateway`** and it will ask for the following inputs, as shown in *Figure* 5.15:

a. **`Name`**: Provide an appropriate name to identify Tier1 gateway in the NSX environment.

b. **`HA Mode`**: As discussed earlier, the Tier1 gateway can be configured as Distributed Only or with an SR component to host services. Use the drop-down menu to select one of the following options:

   i. **`Active-Standby`**: Configure Tier1 gateway to run in Active Standby configuration on Edge cluster to host stateful services.

   ii. **`Active-Active`**: This option was introduced post NSX release v4.0.1 to run Tier1 gateway in Active-Active configuration with stateful services.

iii. **`Distributed Only`**: This option configures the Tier1 gateway in a DR-only configuration with no SR component hosted on the Edge cluster.

c. **`Edge Cluster`**: If Active-Standby or Active-Active HA mode is selected, then it is mandatory to select Edge cluster. This is not required for Distributed-Only HA mode.

d. **`Edges Pool Allocation Size`**: Select the size of compute resources to be allocated to the Tier1 gateway from the Edge cluster. This option determines the maximum limit of stateful services.

e. **`Linked Tier-0 Gateway`**: Select the Tier0 gateway to provide North-South connectivity to physical infrastructure for connected segments to Tier1 gateway.

f. **`Route Advertisement`**: Expand this option to select which different routes to be plumbed to the Tier0 gateway. NSX automatically plumbed these enabled networks, such as Static Routes and Connected Segments, to the Tier0 gateway to avoid any manual route creation on the Tier0 gateway.

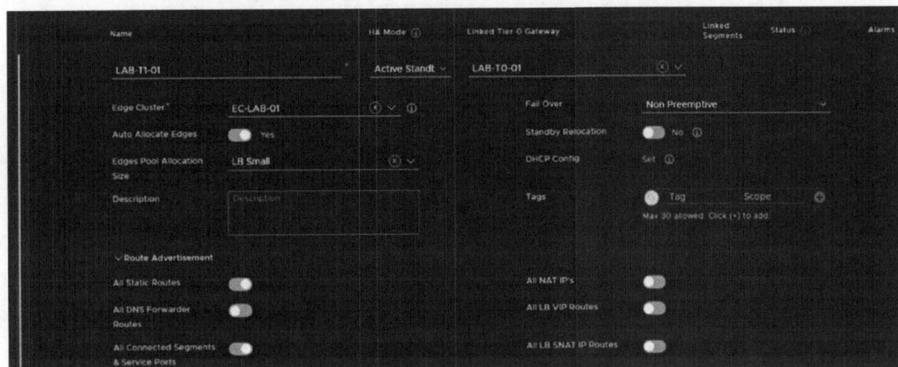

Figure 5.15: *Adding a new Tier1 gateway in NSX*

Step 3: Click **Save** to create Tier1 gateway, and then, similar to Tier0 gateway, click **Yes** to further modify the Tier1 gateway or click **No** to finish the configuration, as shown in *Figure* 5.16:

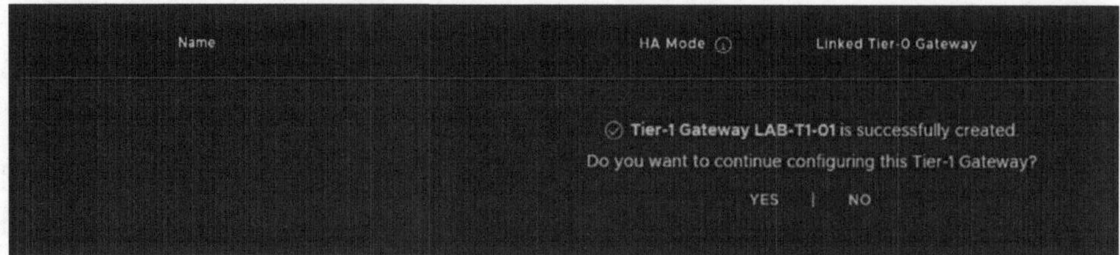

***Figure* 5.16**: *Continue editing Tier1 gateway*

Step 4: There is an additional option to apply **`Route Advertisement Rules`**. This is helpful where selected segments need to be plumbed to the Tier0 gateway instead of plumbing all networks. Click **`Set`** against **`Set Route Advertisement Rules`** to configure these filters, as illustrated in *Figure* 5.17:

***Figure* 5.17**: *Adding route advertisement rules on Tier1 gateway*

Configuring gateway on NSX Segments

Gateway on Segments is configured directly from the Segments menu. While logged into NSX Manager, navigate to the **`Networking`** menu. Click **`Segments`** in the left-side navigation panel under **`Connectivity`** to view the segments configured in the environment. Click three dots against the desired segment and select Edit. As *Figure* 5.18 illustrates, change the **`Connected Gateway`** to the desired Tier0 or Tier1 gateway, and under **`subnets`**, configure the gateway IP in CIDR format. This will configure the gateway of the subnet on the selected NSX gateway:

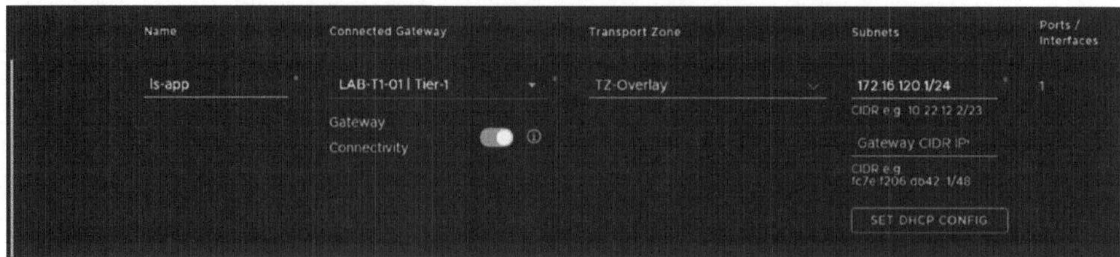

***Figure* 5.18**: *Connecting segment to NSX gateway*

Configuring ECMP and Routing on Tier0

As described previously, in multi-tier architecture, NSX automatically plumbs router link interfaces to connect the Tier1 gateway to the Tier0 gateway. There is no BGP or OSPF support on the Tier1 gateway, as northbound routing from the Tier1 gateway to the Tier0 gateway is automatically taken care by NSX by inserting a default static route with the next hop as the router link interface attached to the Tier0 gateway, as covered in packet walks. If required, static routes can be configured on Tier1 gateway pointing to the router link interface of Tier0 gateway. Additionally, southbound static routes can be configured on the Tier1 gateway with the next hop as a layer 3 device reachable via a service interface or downlink interface. As Tier1 gateway routing is mostly taken care by NSX automatically, this section focuses on Tier0 routing to the physical infrastructure and the different dynamic routing protocols supported by NSX. Tier0 gateway supports both static and dynamic routing with ECMP (Equal Cost Multipath), which is covered in subsequent sections.

ECMP routing increases North-South communication bandwidth by utilizing multiple uplinks with the help of a 5-tuple hashing algorithm that uses the source IP address, destination IP address, source port, destination port, and IP protocol. This helps in distributing traffic across multiple uplink interfaces and provides traffic load balancing. NSX supports a maximum of eight ECMP paths and is available on Tier0 external/uplink interfaces.

Static Routing

Tier0 gateway supports static routes on both external interfaces and service interfaces. A northbound static route can be configured on Tier0 gateway with the next hop IP address of the physical router on external interfaces. ECMP is supported with static routing to provide fault tolerance and load balancing of network traffic. Also, static routes can be protected via BFD with bare-metal edge nodes supporting a minimum of 50ms and Edge node VM supporting a minimum of 500 ms BFD keep-alive timers. Apart from BFD, Tier0 gateway also supports HA VIP for static routes, but it is only supported in Active-Standby mode with two external interfaces and should be considered only when the BFD option is not available.

To configure static routing, navigate to the **`Networking`** menu. Click **`Tier-0 Gateways`** in the left-side navigation panel under **`Connectivity`** to view the configured Tier0 gateways in the environment. Click three dots against the desired Tier0 gateway and click **`Edit`** to modify the Tier0 gateway. If the Tier0 gateway is configured as Active-Standby, NSX Manager will provide an option to configure HA VIP, as shown in *Figure* 5.19:

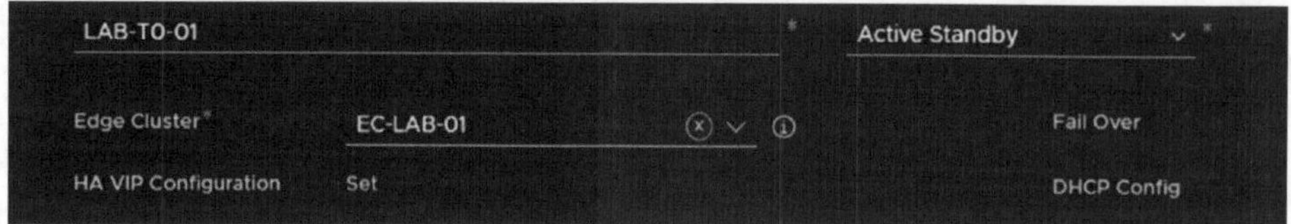

Figure 5.19*: Configuring HA VIP for static routing on Tier0 gateway*

Step 1: Click **`Set`** to configure HA VIP, and it will open a new window with the name **`Set HA VIP Configuration`** to configure a VIP for static routes. Provide an IP address in CIDR format for HA VIP and select exactly two external interfaces configured earlier, as shown in *Figure* 5.20. Click **`Add`** and then click **`Apply`** to create HA VIP. This HA VIP will be assigned to the active Edge node to receive traffic from the physical router:

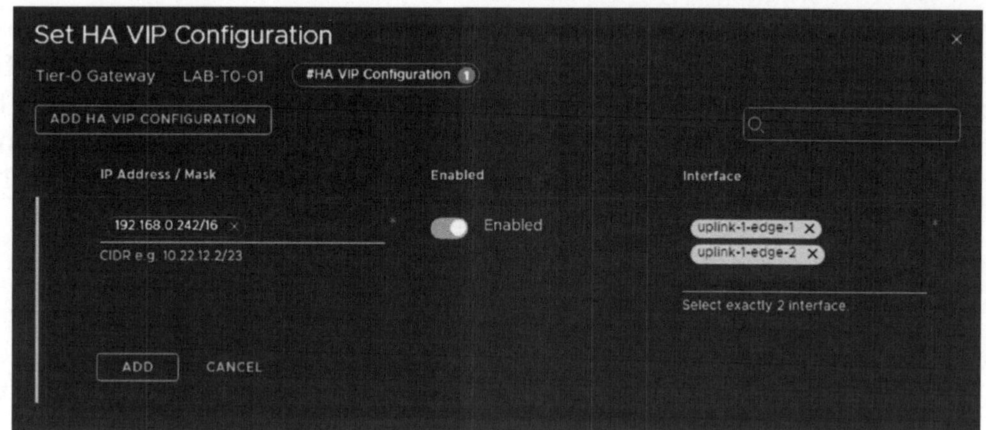

Figure 5.20*: Adding a new HA VIP for static routing*

Step 2: Scroll down a bit to view the Routing section where static routes can be configured. Click **`Set`** in front of static routes to configure static routes on Tier0 gateway, as shown in *Figure* 5.21:

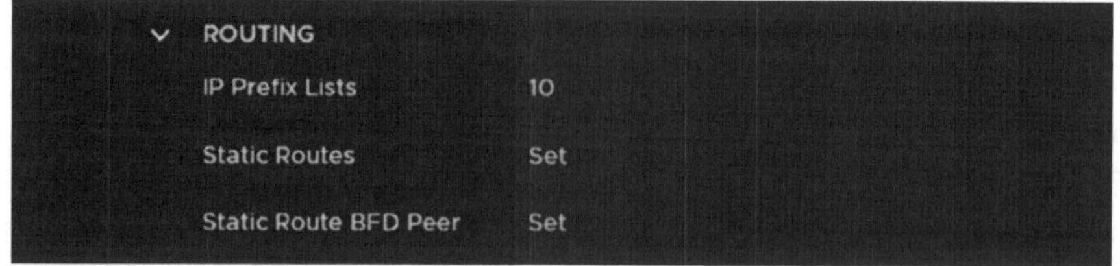

Figure 5.21: *Options to configure static routes*

Step 3: In the new window, click **`Add Static Route`** to add a new static route and provide the following information, as illustrated in *Figure* 5.22:

a. **`Name`**: An appropriate name for the static route.

b. **`Network`**: Network subnet in CIDR format for which static route needs to be configured.

c. **`Next Hops`**: Click **`Set`** to add the next hop IP address for the network subnet:

   i. **`IP Address`**: Provide the IP address of the next hop; in this example, it is the IP address of the physical router.

   ii. **`Admin Distance`**: Provide a value between 1 and 255 to set weightage to the static route.

   iii. **`Scope`**: Optionally, select the external interfaces that will be used by this static route.

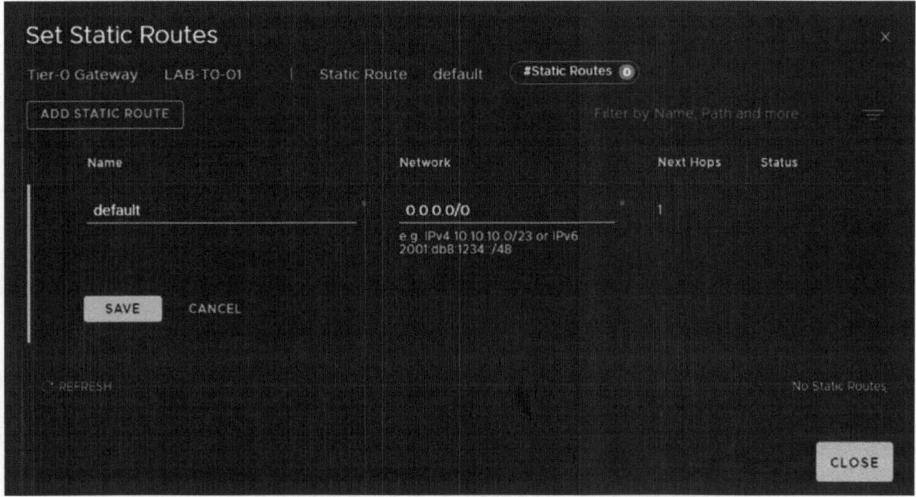

***Figure 5.22:** Adding a new static route on Tier0 gateway*

Step 4: Click **`Save`** to finish adding static route and then click **`Close`** to return to modifying Tier0 gateway. *Figure* 5.23 shows a static route successfully configured on Tier0 gateway:

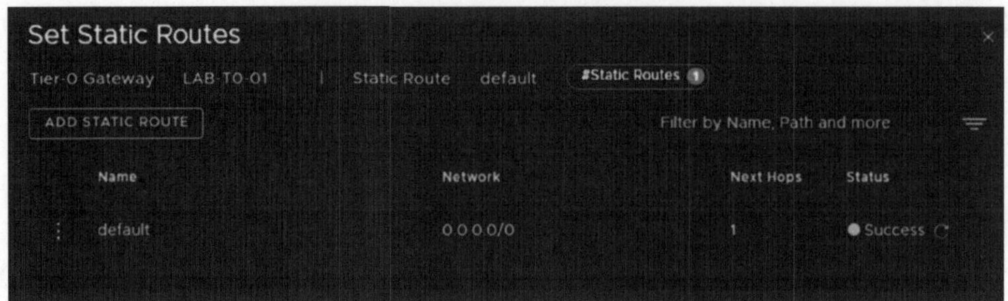

Figure 5.23: *Viewing configured static routes on Tier0 gateway*

Step 5: Similarly, click **`Set`** against **`Static Route BFD Peer`** to add BFD peers for static routes to detect any failure on interfaces and mark them down. Click **`Add Static Route BFD Peer`** to add a new peer and provide the following information:

a. **`Name`**: Name of BFD Peer to identify in NSX environment.

b. **`BFD Profile`**: Either select the default gateway BFD profile with a keep-alive interval of 500ms and retries as 3 or create a new profile as per requirement.

c. **`Peer IP Address`**: Provide the BFD peer IP address configured on the physical router.

d. **`Source Addresses`**: Optionally, provide the source IP addresses configured on Tier0 gateway.

Figure 5.24 shows an example configuration for a BFD peer with the name BFD-1 using the default BFD profile:

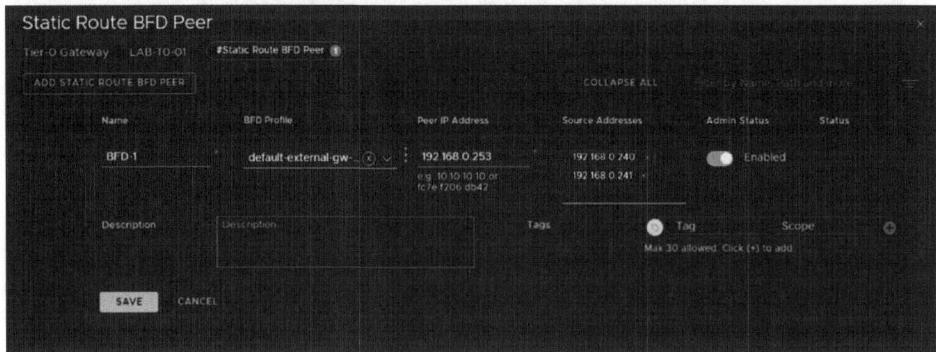

***Figure 5.24**: Adding a new BFD peer on Tier0 gateway for static routing*

Step 6: Click **`Save`** to finish adding BFD peer, and then click **`Close`** to return to Tier0 gateway. Click **`Close Editing`** to finish modifying Tier0 gateway.

This completes the configuration of static routing on Tier0 gateway. In a similar fashion, static routes need to be configured on the physical router with the next hop as Tier0 HA VIP or Tier0 external interfaces to enable southbound communication on Tier0.

Dynamic Routing

Apart from static routing, NSX also supports dynamic routing protocols, specifically BGP and OSPFv2. Dynamic routing protocols enable different gateways to exchange network information with each other and are used to obtain routes dynamically from each other. Also, if there is a change in the network, the router informs its peer router so it can update its routing table, which is a major advantage over static routing, as in static routing, any change in the network will have to be manually updated by the administrator on the router. VMware recommends configuring BGP when using dynamic routing, as BGP supports more features than OSPFv2 in the NSX environment, and it is more flexible and feature-rich than OSPFv2.

Table 5.1 highlights the different features supported by NSX between BGP and OSPFv2:

NSX Features	**BGP**	**OSPFv2**
Routing Protocol	It is a path vector routing protocol	OSPF is a link-state routing protocol
IPv6 Support	It supports MP-BGP in NSX (IPv6, IPv4, L2EVPN)	No IPv6 support
Federation	Supported	No
VRF	Supported	No
EVPN	Supported	No
BFD and Graceful restart	Yes	Yes
Route Summarization and Filtering	Yes	At ASBR level
Route Maps	Yes	Yes, but no set actions

Table 5.1: *Different features by BGP and OSPF in NSX*

BGP

NSX supports configuring external Border Gateway Protocol (eBGP) or internal Border Gateway Protocol (iBGP) on Tier0 gateway to enable North-South communication with the router in physical infrastructure. BGP works on Autonomous System (AS) number assigned to the router. If ASN of two routers is the same, they form an iBGP session, and if ASN of two routers is different, they form an eBGP session. With iBGP in NSX, redistribution of routes in BGP, prefix lists, and route maps are supported. However, Route Reflectors and BGP confederation are not supported. NSX also supports BGPv6 for both single hop and multi-hop with redistribution, prefix list, and route maps support for IPv6 address family. Apart from standard features, NSX supports both BFD and ECMP routing with BGP for faster failover and load balancing of traffic over multiple uplinks. An exhaustive list of BGP capabilities supported by NSX can be found in the VMware Documentation (https://docs.vmware.com/en/VMware-NSX/4.1/administration/GUID-7A0F6D44-4AE8-411F-8D33-2560819699CA.html).

Starting with NSX release v4.1, a few more features have been added to BGP as follows:

- **BGP ASN per neighbor and per Tier0 VRF**: Starting with NSX v4.1, it is now possible to configure a different ASN for Tier0 VRF or a different ASN on a BGP Neighbor from the global Tier0 BGP configuration. In the previous release, it was not possible to override the global BGP ASN defined at Tier0 level.
- **Autonomous System-wide Unique BGP Identifier**: NSX supports RFC6286, which relaxes the uniqueness of router ID between BGP peers across AS. It is now possible to form a BGP peer with the same router ID. This is a system default configuration and cannot be overridden.
- **Inter-VRF Routing**: It is now easier to perform Inter-VRF routing with the help of BGP route leak. This feature is covered in more detail in VRF Lite section.

Let's see the steps to configure BGP on Tier0 gateway:

Step 1: Log in to NSX Manager with admin privileges and navigate to the `Networking` menu. Click `Tier-0 Gateways` in the left-side navigation panel under **Connectivity** to view Tier0 gateways configured in the environment. *Figure* 5.25 shows an example screenshot where a previously created Tier0 gateway is present:

***Figure 5.25**: Viewing configured Tier0 gateways in NSX Manager*

Step 2: Click three dots present in front of the Tier0 gateway and then click `Edit`. This will take you into editing mode. Scroll down to the bottom of Tier0 gateway configuration, where there is a dedicated section for **BGP** configuration. By default, BGP is enabled, as shown in *Figure* 5.26:

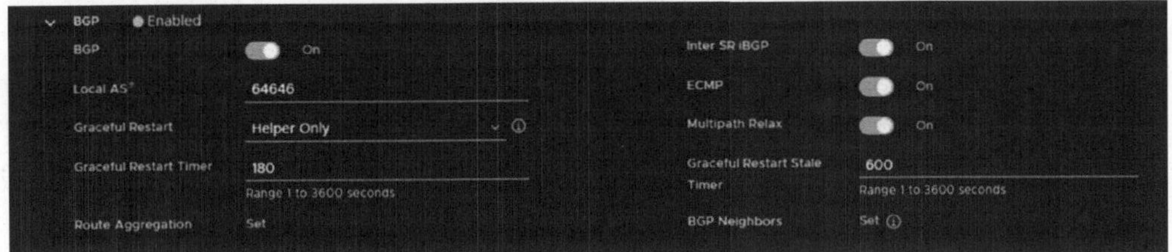

***Figure 5.26**: Configuring BGP on Tier0 gateway*

Most of the features are enabled by default; however, the same can be turned off by moving the toggle button to the off position. Different configuration options available on this screen are as follows:

a. **BGP**: Toggle the button to enable or disable BGP on the Tier0 gateway. By default, it is in the **on** state and can be turned off to enable OSPF.

b. **`Local AS`**: Provide the ASN for the Tier0 gateway. By default, value 65001 is assigned to the Tier0 gateway and can be modified as per inputs from the network administrator.

c. **`Inter SR iBGP`**: By default, this is in the on position. It creates an iBGP session running between Edge nodes of the Edge cluster in Active-Active HA mode. If gateway 1 hosted on Edge node 1 is unable to communicate northbound with the physical router, then traffic is routed via the iBGP link to gateway 2 hosted on Edge node 2 in Active-Active mode. If both gateways hosted on

Edge nodes are up, then there is no effect on traffic flow, as the route learned from the northbound physical router will always be preferred over the same route learned from inter SR iBGP. This behavior is default and cannot be overridden. If no inter SR iBGP session is required, then toggle this button to the off position. This feature is not available for Active-Standby HA mode.

d. **ECMP**: By default, ECMP is enabled. Toggle this button to turn ECMP off for BGP.

e. **Multipath Relax**: ECMP must be enabled for Multipath Relax to work. By default, it is turned on. It enables load sharing across multiple paths that differ in AS-Path attribute only but have the same AS-Path length. This behavior can be turned off by moving this button to the off position.

f. **Graceful Restart**: By default, it is set to Helper Only. It can be changed to Disable to disable graceful restart or graceful restart and Helper. It is recommended to run Tier0 gateways in Helper Only configuration.

Click **Save** to apply the changes to the BGP configuration.

Step 3: The next step is to add BGP Neighbors. This can be done by clicking **Set** in front of the **BGP Neighbors** option. This opens a new screen to add BGP peers, as shown in *Figure* 5.27:

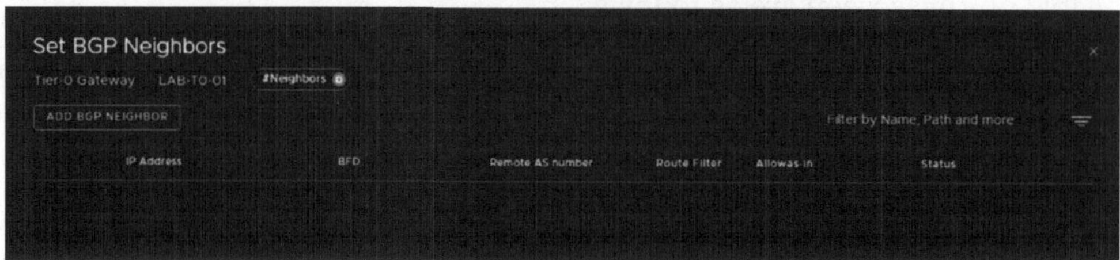

***Figure 5.27**: Adding BGP neighbor on Tier0 gateway*

Step 4: Click **Add BGP Neighbor** to add a new BGP peer by providing the following information requested by NSX UI:

a. `IP Address`: Provide the IP address of the remote BGP peer.

b. `BFD`: Toggle the button to enable or disable the BFD session.

c. `Remote AS Number`: Provide the remote ASN assigned to the BGP peer.

d. `Route Filter`: Click Set to add BGP IN or OUT route filters. You can configure IPv4, IPv6, or L2VPN EVPN type route filters. IPv4 and L2VPN EVPN route can be combined, or IPv4 and IPv6 can be combined together, but combinations of IPv6 and L2VPN EVPN route filters are not supported.

e. `Allowas-in`: Toggle the button to enable or disable BGP neighbors to receive route with the same AS. This is disabled by default.

f. `Source Addresses`: Select the IP address of external interfaces configured earlier on Tier0 gateway.

g. `Graceful Restart`: Same function as global configuration on Tier0 gateway. By default, it is set to Helper Only.

h. `Max Hop Limit`: By default, it is set to 1. The maximum it can be set to is 255.

i. `Configure Neighbor Local AS`: Toggle the button to override ASN defined at Tier0 gateway for this specific BGP neighbor. By default, it is turned off. If this is enabled, then define the following additional options:

    i. `Neighbor Local AS`: Define the local ASN different from Tier0 gateway.

    ii. `AS Path Modifier`: Select what happens to the AS Path attribute.

        1. `Default`: BGP prepends local AS of neighbor AS path for both outgoing and incoming route advertisements from the peer neighbor.

        2. `No Prepend`: The local router does not prepend the incoming advertisement from the peer with the neighbor's local AS. The advertised AS path only prepends the BGP local AS of the router.

3. **No Prepend Replace AS**: The local routes are advertised with the local AS of the neighbor instead of the local AS of Tier0 gateway to peer BGP router.

Figure 5.28 shows an example configuration for a BGP peer with the IP address 192.168.0.253:

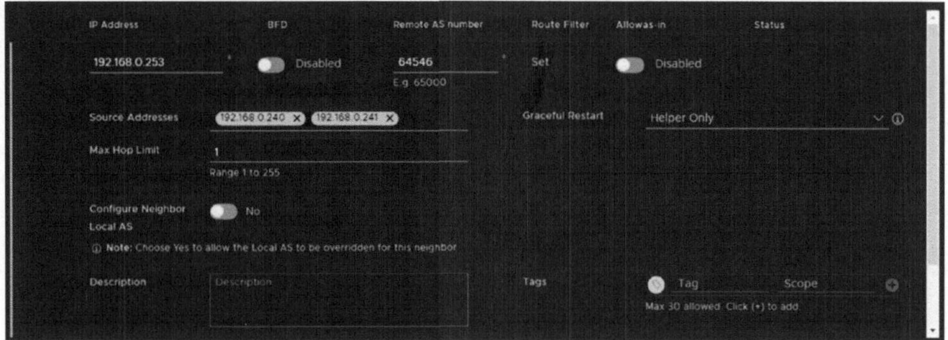

***Figure 5.28**: Configuring a new BGP neighbor on Tier0 gateway*

Step 5: Before clicking **Save**, there are a few more options to configure in BGP neighbor. Expand **Times and Password** to configure these options:

a. **Hold Down Time**: This specifies how long the Tier0 gateway will wait for KEEPALIVE message before declaring the neighbor as dead. Generally, it is set to 12 seconds.

b. **Keep Alive Time**: This specifies how frequently KEEPALIVE message will be sent. Generally, it is set to 4 seconds.

c. **Password**: Specify the password configured on the peer router for this neighbor.

Step 6: Click Save to finish configuring **BGP Neighbor**. If BGP neighbor is configured correctly and is live at the peer router, its status will show as successful, as shown in *Figure* 5.29:

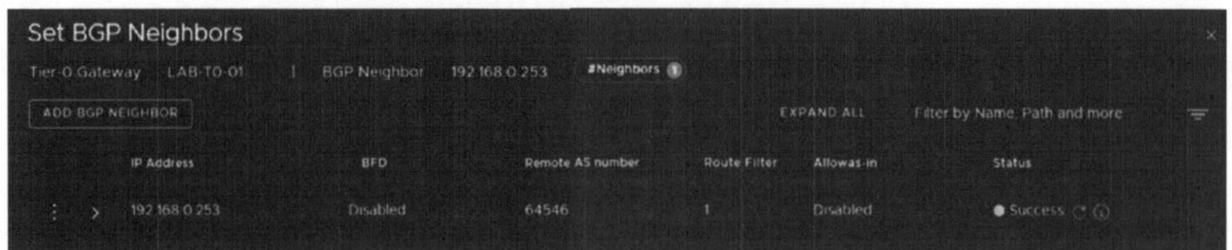

***Figure 5.29**: Successfully realized BGP neighbor*

Click on **(i)** button alongside the refresh button to view BGP session details on Edge nodes and their status, as illustrated in *Figure* 5.30. Click **`Close`** to navigate back to the Tier0 gateway screen:

BGP Connectivity Status | 192.168.0.253

Edge Node: sa-nsxedge-01

Connection Status	Established
Source Address	192.168.0.240
Local Port	179
Remote Port	43068
Messages Received	36
Messages Sent	40
Time since established	125 seconds
Total In Prefix Count	8
Total Out Prefix Count	7

CLOSE

***Figure* 5.30**: *Viewing status information of BGP neighbor*

Step 7: BGP supports route summarization as well and can be configured by clicking **Set** in front of **`Route Aggregation`**. This opens a new screen. Click **`Add Prefix`** to add a new summary route and provide a Prefix to summarize individual subnets, as displayed in *Figure* 5.31. Click **`Apply`** to save the changes and then click **`Close Editing`** to finish modifying Tier0 gateway:

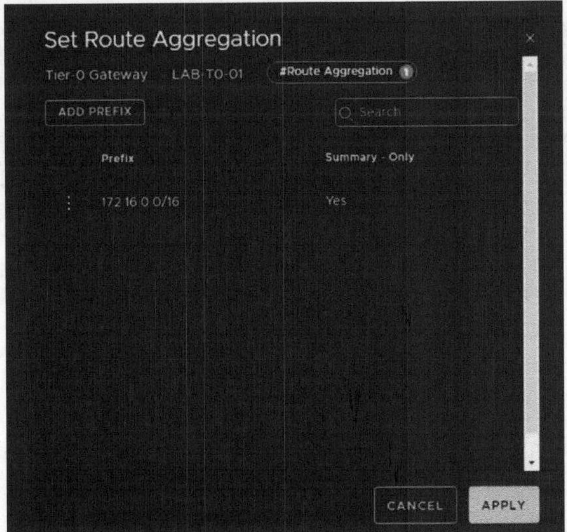

***Figure* 5.31**: *Adding summary route in BGP on Tier0 gateway*

Validating BGP Routing

Step 8: Click three dots in front of the Tier0 gateway and then click Generate BGP Summary. This will provide the BGP summary and status of different BGP sessions. *Figure* 5.32 shows an example of the BGP summary on Tier0 gateway LAB-T0-01, showing both eBGP session with physical router 192.168.0.253 and inter-SR iBGP session between the two Edge nodes:

BGP Summary

Tier-0 Gateway LAB-T0-01

Edge Node All

Edge Node	Source Address	Neighbor Address	Remote AS	Connection Status	Connection Drop Count	Established Connection Count	Address Families
sa-nsxedge-02.lab.local	192.168.0.241	192.168.0.253	64546	● Established	0	1	IPv4 Unicast In 8 | Out 5
sa-nsxedge-02.lab.local	169.254.0.131	169.254.0.130	64646	● Established	0	1	IPv4 Unicast In 15 | Out 15 and 1 More
sa-nsxedge-01	192.168.0.240	192.168.0.253	64546	● Established	0	1	IPv4 Unicast In 8 | Out 5
sa-nsxedge-01	169.254.0.130	169.254.0.131	64646	● Established	0	1	IPv4 Unicast In 15 | Out 15 and 1 More

***Figure 5.32**: Generating BGP summary on Tier0 gateway*

Step 9: Another way to validate is login into the physical router and validate if you are receiving routes from Tier0 gateway or not. In this example, physical router 192.168.0.253 is successfully receiving summary route 172.16.0.0/16 from BGP peer 192.168.0.240, as depicted in *Figure* 5.33:

```
BGP table version is 0, local router ID is 192.168.0.253
Status codes: s suppressed, d damped, h history, * valid, > best, = multipath,
              i internal, r RIB-failure, S Stale, R Removed
Origin codes: i - IGP, e - EGP, ? - incomplete

   Network          Next Hop            Metric LocPrf Weight Path
*> 100.64.0.0/31    192.168.0.240            0             0 64646 ?
*> 100.64.0.2/31    192.168.0.240            0             0 64646 ?
*> 100.64.0.4/31    192.168.0.240            0             0 64646 ?
*> 172.16.0.0       192.168.0.240                          0 64646 ?
*  192.168.0.0/16   192.168.0.240            0             0 64646 ?
```

***Figure 5.33**: Viewing routes learning from BGP on physical router*

This completes the configuration of BGP routing in the NSX environment. Let's cover the second dynamic protocol supported by NSX, that is, OSPFv2.

OSPF

NSX supports OSPFv2 on Tier0 gateway to exchange routing information with the physical router. OSPF is an Interior Gateway Protocol (IGP) that operates in a single Autonomous System. As covered earlier, there is no IPv6 support on OSPF in NSX as of writing this book. IPv6 support is introduced in OSPFv3, which is not supported by NSX.

Let's cover the steps required to enable OSPF on Tier0 gateway in NSX:

Step 1: Log in to NSX Manager with admin privileges and navigate to the **Networking** menu. Click **Tier-0 Gateways** in the left-side navigation panel under **Connectivity** to view Tier0 gateways configured in the environment. Click three dots in front of the desired Tier0 gateway and select **Edit**. Scroll to the bottom to expand the **OSPF** section. By default, OSPF is disabled, as shown in *Figure* 5.34:

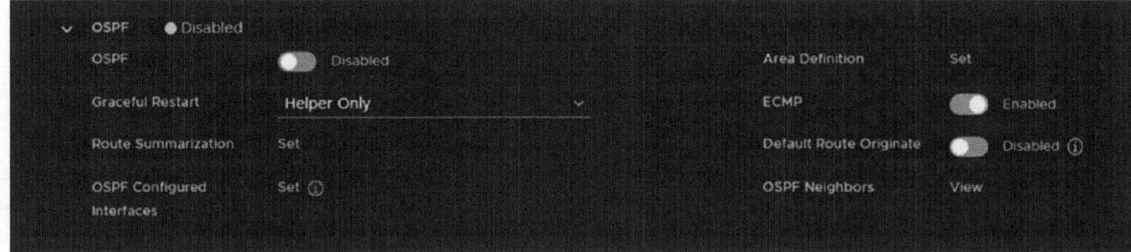

***Figure 5.34**: Configuring OSPF on Tier0 gateway*

Step 2: Move the toggle in front of OSPF to enable or disable OSPF protocol on Tier0 gateway. Click **Set** in **Area Definition** field to add OSPF Area for Tier0. NSX allows only one area definition to be added. Click **Add Area Definition** in **Set Area Definition** to add a new area by providing the following information:

a. **Area ID**: Provide a numerical value for OSPF area ID.

b. **Type**: Select either Area type is Normal or NSSA (Not so stubby Area).

c. **Authentication**: Select None if no authentication is required. Select either Password or MD5 to set authentication.

d. **Key ID**: Set the Key ID if MD5 is selected.

e. **Password**: Provide the password value if either MD5 or Password is selected.

Click **Save** to finish creating the area definition. *Figure* 5.35 illustrates an OSPF Area 10 configured successfully:

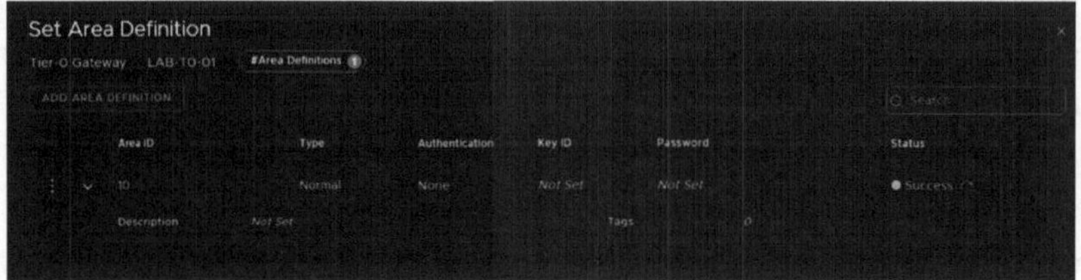

***Figure 5.35**: Adding Area definition for OSPF protocol*

Step 3: The next step is to configure OSPF interfaces. Click **Set** in **OSPF Configured Interfaces** to enable OSPF on already configured external interfaces. This will open a new screen. Click **Configure Interface** and provide the following information:

a. **Interface**: Select the external interface configured earlier from the drop-down menu.

b. **Area ID**: Select the area definition configured earlier in Step 2.

c. **Network Type**: Select if either it is a **Broadcast** or **P2P** (peer-to-peer).

d. **BFD**: Toggle the button to enable or disable BFD. By default, it is disabled.

e. **OSPF Hello Interval**: It specifies the time interval at which OSPF hello packets are sent.

f. **OSPF Dead Internal**: It specifies the total time the gateway will wait before declaring OSPF neighbor as dead.

Figure 5.36 shows an example configuration of enabling OSPF on the already configured external interface uplink-1-edge-1. Click **Save** to finish creating the OSPF interface and then click **Close** to return to the Tier0 gateway:

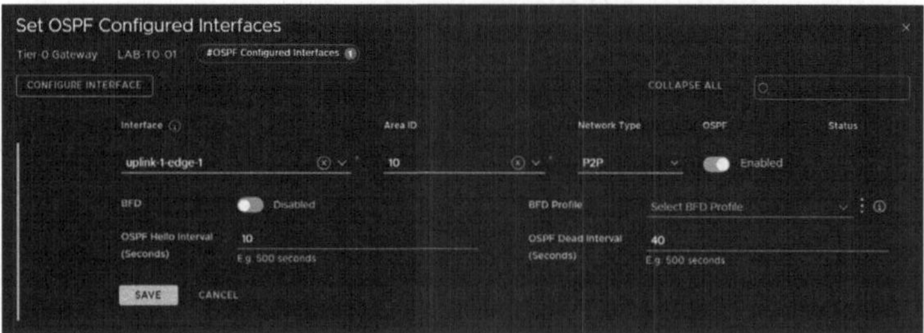

***Figure 5.36**: Adding OSPF-enabled interfaces on Tier0 gateway*

Step 4: Similar to BGP, **`ECMP`** is enabled by default for OSPF, and route summarization can be configured by clicking **`Set`** in front of **`Route Summarization`**.

Step 5: Click **`Save`** to finish setting up OSPF and save configuration. Click **`Close Editing`** to finish modifying the Tier0 gateway.

Validating OSPF Routing

Step 6: If OSPF has been configured correctly, then clicking View in the OSPF neighbors field will show all the OSPF neighbors configured and exchanging information. *Figure* 5.37 shows OSPF neighbors from Edge nodes only as there is no OSPF neighbor configured on the physical router. However, if it has been configured, then the same would have been visible here:

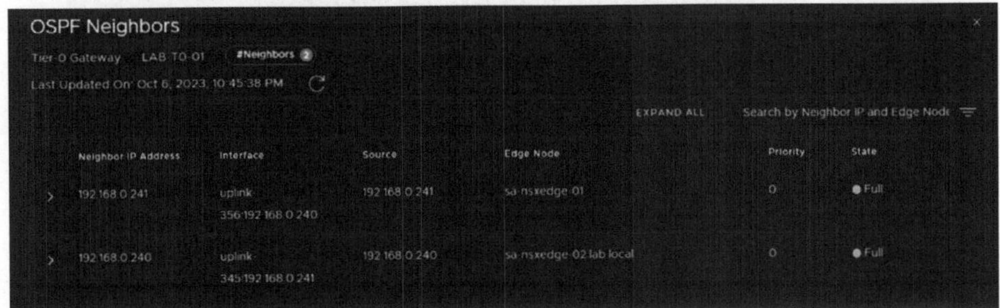

Figure 5.37: *Viewing OSPF neighbors' information*

Route Redistribution in Dynamic Routing

Well, dynamic routing is all setup and running, but for some odd reason, the physical router is not receiving routes from the Tier0 gateway. One reason for this behavior is improper or no route redistribution configured on the Tier0 gateway. For the peer router to learn routes from Tier0 gateway dynamically, route redistribution needs to be configured on Tier0 gateway.

While logged into NSX Manager, edit the Tier0 gateway by clicking three dots and selecting **`Edit`**. Scroll down to the bottom, and there is a section for **`Route Re-Distribution`**, as shown in *Figure* 5.38:

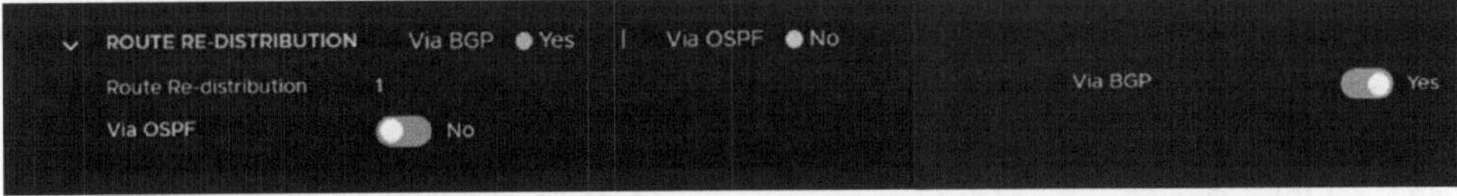

Figure 5.38: *Enabling route re-distribution on Tier0 gateway*

By default, route redistribution is enabled via BGP, but if required, it can be changed to redistribute route via OSPF by moving the toggle button to the **On** position in front of **Via OSPF**. Click **Set** or enter a numerical number in the **Route Re-distribution** field to specify which networks need to be redistributed in BGP or OSPF. Click **Add Route Re-distribution** and provide an appropriate **name**. Select the **destination protocol** and then click numerical value in the column **Route Re-distribution**. This opens another screen similar to *Figure 5.39*:

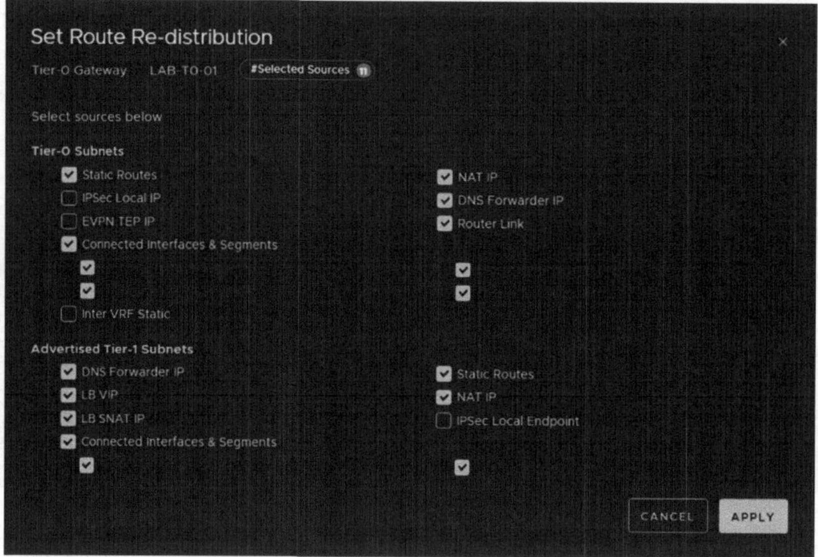

***Figure 5.39**: Different types of networks available for redistribution in dynamic routing*

Select the desired network from the list, and Tier0 gateway will redistribute those in the selected protocol. Click **Add** and then click **Apply** to save the configuration. Click **Close Editing** to finish editing the Tier0 gateway.

Woah! That's a lot of information, but this completes the configuration of dynamic routing in Tier0 gateway. In the next section, let's see how NSX handles different failure scenarios and provide high availability to gateways.

NSX Routing High Availability

NSX provides high availability to routing services with the help of multiple Edge nodes running in an Edge cluster. Services are hosted on the SR component of the gateway, hence, high-availability discussion applies to the SR component of Tier0 and Tier1 gateway. NSX supports two different modes for high availability of SR services running on Edge nodes.

Active-Active HA Mode

In Active-Active HA mode, all Edge nodes within the Edge cluster are active, and gateway services run simultaneously on all Edge nodes. This provides the distribution of load between multiple Edge nodes to prevent overutilization of a single node. By default, Active-Active HA is stateless in nature and doesn't maintain any tracking tables for the state of connections and services. Hence, it is not possible to host stateful services such as stateful firewall and stateful NAT on the Active-Active Tier0 gateway. In the previous release of NSX prior to v4.0.1, Active-Active HA mode could only be configured on Tier0 gateway, while Tier1 gateway used to run in Active-Standby mode only. However, starting with NSX v4.0.1, a new routing architecture is introduced to provide stateful services support on Active-Active HA mode. This introduced support for Active-Active HA mode for Tier1 gateway as well. This new routing architecture has been covered in great detail in *Chapter 11, NSX Datacenter Service – 1*.

Figure 5.40 illustrates two views, with the left view as the logical view of a Tier0 gateway. This shows a Tier0 gateway configured as Active-Active HA mode and connected to two physical routers via external interfaces hosted on Edge Node 1 and Edge Node 2. The right side of the diagram depicts the physical view of the topology, showing both the SR and DR components of Tier0 gateway:

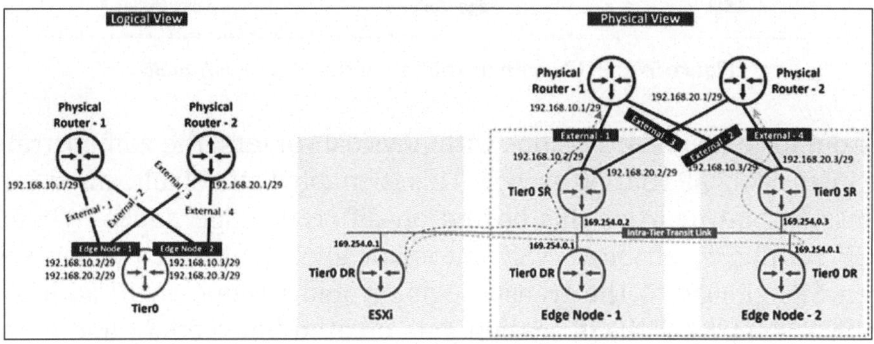

Figure 5.40: *Tier0 gateway configured in Active-Active HA mode*

Tier0 SR have different IP address on Edge Node 1 (192.168.10.2, 192.168.20.2) and Edge Node 2 (192.168.10.3, 192.168.20.3) assigned to them northbound to physical router on external interface and also have different IP addresses (169.254.0.2, 169.254.0.3) assigned southbound to Tier0 DR on Intra-Tier transit link. NSX Management plane configures two default routes on Tier0 DR with the next hop as Tier0 SR hosted on Edge Node 1 with IP address 169.254.0.2 and Tier0 SR on Edge Node 2 with IP address 169.254.0.3 to provide ECMP for overlay traffic coming from workload machines running on ESXi hosts. Both Tier0 SR are acting as active forwarders to forward traffic received from Tier0 DR to physical routers 1 and 2.

Active-Active HA mode with BGP

In Active-Active HA mode with BGP as routing protocol, all Tier0 SR form BGP neighborship with physical routers, and all paths have the same AS_PATH value, so traffic is load balanced across all paths. *Figure* 5.41 shows Tier0 SR running on Edge Node 1 and Edge Node 2, forming eBGP peering with physical routers, with all paths being treated as equal for traffic forwarding to the physical infrastructure.

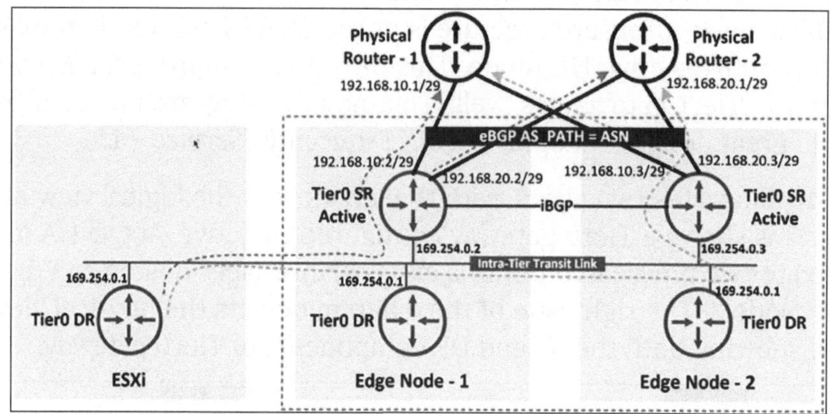

***Figure* 5.41**: *BGP configuration in Active-Active HA mode*

Apart from forming eBGP sessions with physical routers, the administrator can enable inter-SR iBGP routing as well. This is enabled by default, and it forms an iBGP session between two SRs hosted on different Edge nodes. When inter-SR iBGP routing is enabled, NSX automatically plumbs an overlay segment between SRs similar to the transit segment and assigns an IP address from range 169.254.0.128/25. iBGP session gets created between SR and exchanges northbound routes, such as static, eBGP, and more. If physical routers do not have the same routing information, then instead of dropping the packet, the iBGP session is utilized to redirect the packet to the correct physical router.

It is important to note here is that inter-SR iBGP routing can only be configured with Active-Active Tier0 gateway.

Active-Active HA mode with OSPF

If OSPF is configured with Active-Active HA mode, then all OSPF adjacencies with physical routers are established, and they have the same cost assigned to them.

Traffic coming from DR is load-balanced across all SRs. Tier0 SR announces an OSPF cost of 20 for all paths northbound to the physical router. An important point to note here is that a maximum of two paths can be configured per Edge node with ECMP enabled.

Active-Standby HA Mode

In the Active-Standby Edge node, only one Edge node is active, and the other Edge node is set as standby, ready to take over in case of any failure within the Edge cluster. Active-Standby HA mode can be configured on either Tier1 or Tier0 gateway and supports stateful services such as stateful firewall or NAT services. *Figure* 5.42 shows the same topology covered earlier but with Tier0 gateway configured as Active-Standby HA mode:

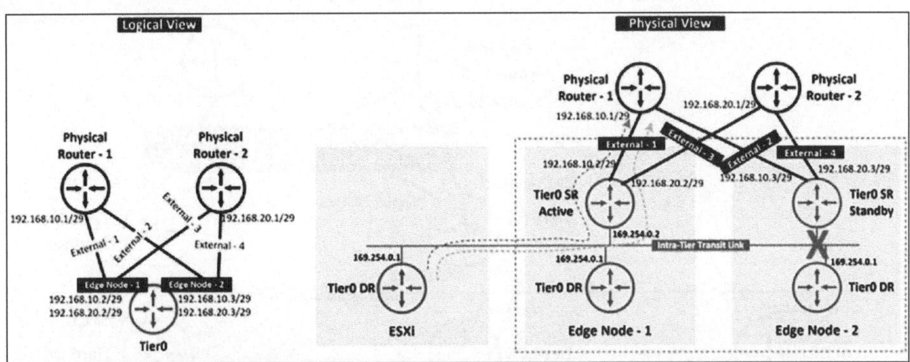

Figure 5.42: *Tier0 gateway configured in Active-Standby HA mode*

This time NSX Management plane configures single default routes on Tier0 DR with the next hop as active Tier0 SR hosted on Edge Node 1 with IP address 169.254.0.2 to forward overlay traffic coming from workload machines running on ESXi hosts. Only Tier0 SR running on Edge Node 1 is configured as Active forwarder and Tier0 SR running on Edge Node 2 remains in standby mode. As network traffic leaves and enters through the same Edge node hosting active Tier0 SR, this mode maintains a tracking table for maintaining states of connections and services providing stateful services.

In Active-Standby mode, Tier0 SR form dynamic routing peering with physical routers; however, standby Tier0 SR have a higher cost assigned to its path to influence routing decision on the physical router and ensure traffic is sent from the physical router to active Tier0 SR only.

Active-Standby HA mode with BGP

In Active-Standby HA mode with BGP as routing protocol, all Tier0 SR form a BGP neighborship with physical routers, but the standby Tier0 SR have AS_PATH prepended three times by the local ASN to make it less favorable. *Figure* 5.43 shows Tier0 SR running on Edge Node 1 and Edge Node 2, forming eBGP peering with physical routers. The Tier0 SR hosted on Edge Node 2 have AS_PATH prepended three times with the local ASN of Tier0 gateway. This ensures that physical router 1 or physical router 2 sends traffic to Tier0 SR running on Edge Node 1 only as long as it's up and running. This AS Path prepend is automatically taken care by the NSX Management plane, and no intervention is required from the user end. In addition, please note that there is no iBGP session configured between Tier0 SR running on different Edge nodes:

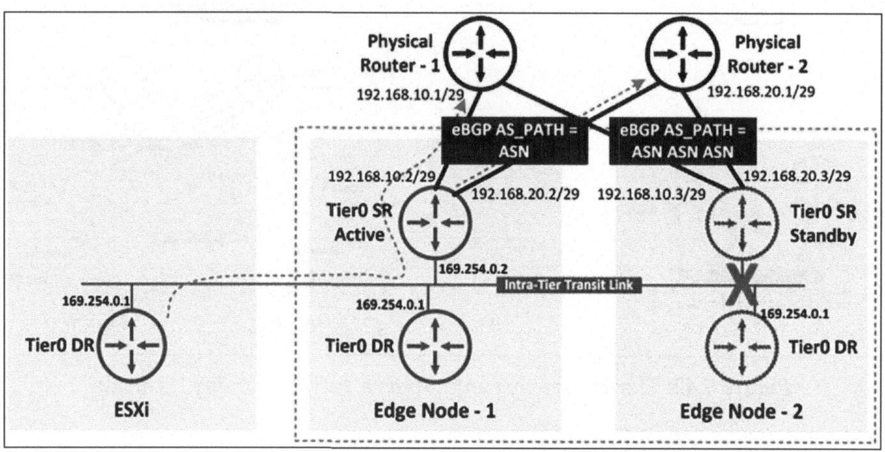

***Figure* 5.43**: *BGP configuration in Active-Standby HA mode*

Active-Standby HA mode with OSPF

If OSPF is configured with Active-Standby HA mode, then all OSPF adjacencies with physical routers are established, but the standby Tier0 SR sends an OSPF cost of 65534 to make it less favorable. This is a hard-coded value and cannot be overridden by the administrator. The physical router chooses the path with the lowest cost, which is Active Tier0 SR. DR sends traffic coming from workload machines running on ESXi hosts to active SR only.

High-Availability Failover Detection Mechanisms

There are two different types of failover events: the first where the entire Edge node is marked as down, causing all the SRs running on the Edge node to fail, and the second where failover affects only individual services or SRs. In the first type of failure event, SRs running on the peer Edge node will take over, whereas in the second type of failure event, the SR running on the peer Edge node for failed service will take over, but other SRs will keep on running on the original Edge node.

The following conditions will cause a failover event, causing all services and SRs to fail over to the peer Edge node:

- The dataplane service is not running on the Edge node.
- All TEP interfaces configured on Edge nodes go down. This is more specific to bare metal Edge node, as in the case of Edge VMs, technically vNICs never physically go down.
- The Edge node is put into maintenance mode.
- Edge nodes within the Edge cluster run Bidirectional Forwarding Detection (BFD) on management and overlay/TEP interfaces. Each Edge node monitors the status of its peer Edge node on both interfaces. If both are down, then the peer Edge node is considered down, and it will take over corresponding SRs.
- Edge node TEPs run BFD with other Edge nodes and compute hosts to monitor the health of TEP tunnels. If a Host Transport node is present and all overlay tunnels are down to both Edge nodes and Host Transport nodes, then all SRs on Edge nodes will be declared down. This condition doesn't apply if no Host Transport node is present.

The following conditions will cause a failover event, causing specific services and SRs to fail over to their peer Edge node:

- Northbound routing on Tier0 SR is down. It can be either dynamic routing running BGP or OSPF with/without BFD enabled or static routing with BFD.
- Services are configured on SR and the health score of the service is less than its peer SR.

Let us cover different failover scenarios in more detail.

Failover Scenario with BFD

Figure 5.44 shows the condition for the first type of failover event where an Edge node is marked down. BFD sessions on both management network and tunnel network are lost between Edge Node 1 and Edge Node 2; hence, standby Tier0 SR and Tier1 SR will become active on Edge Node 2. This condition addresses the issue where the Edge node becomes isolated on the network and loses all connectivity:

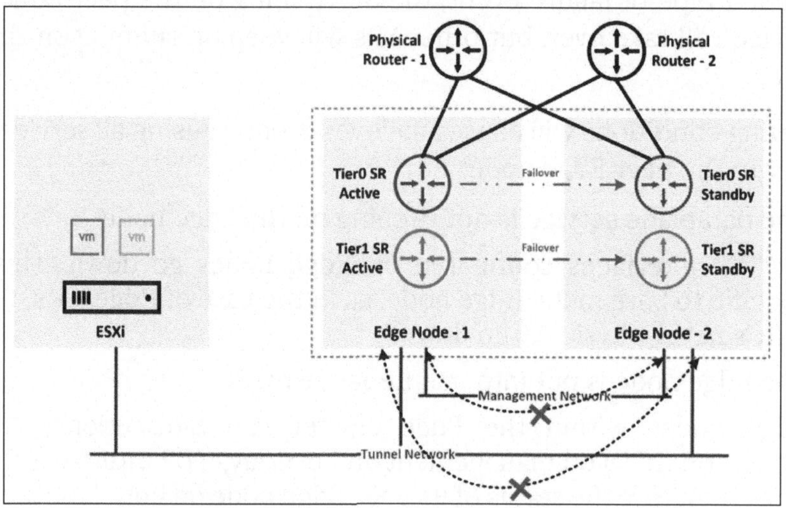

Figure 5.44: *Failover trigger with BFD*

Failover Scenario with Northbound Routing Loss

Figure 5.45 shows the condition for the second type of failover event where a specific SR is failed over to the peer Edge node. In this case, a northbound connectivity issue is detected on Tier0 SR running on Edge Node 1, as all paths configured in dynamic routing protocol BGP/OSPF are marked down, or if static routing is in use, then static routing BFD peer is marked down. Here only affected Tier0 SR will face failover event. Tier1 SR will keep running on Edge Node 1 and Tier0 SR on Edge Node 2 will become active:

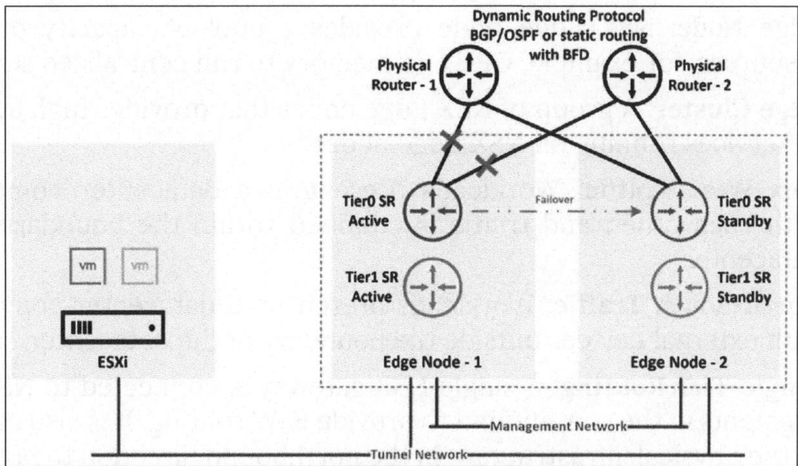

Figure 5.45: *Failover Trigger with northbound routing loss*

Apart from the aforementioned scenarios, if Active-Standby HA mode is configured, there can be two different failover modes as follows:

- **Pre-emptive**: In pre-emptive failover, if the preferred Edge node fails and eventually recovers, then it takes over from its peer post recovery and becomes the active node again. The peer node changes its status back to the standby node.
- **Non-Preemptive**: In this failover mode, if the preferred Edge node fails and recovers, then it checks the status of its peer node. If the peer node is active, then it changes its status to a standby node.

Conclusion

This concludes the logical routing features provided by NSX. In summary, this chapter started with different routing topologies supported by NSX and how to configure them, along with dynamic routing protocols BGP and OSPF. This chapter also covered high-availability options to ensure routing services are always available.

In the next chapter, we will cover VRF lite and EVPN to provide end-to-end isolation for different tenants in the network fabric.

Key Terms

- **Segment:** Segments are layer 2 subnets representing layer 2 broadcasting domain across transport nodes in NSX networking.

- **Edge Node:** NSX Edge node provides a pool of capacity or pool of resources, for example, CPU and memory to run centralized services.
- **Edge Cluster:** A group of NSX Edge nodes that provides high availability to services running on NSX Edge nodes.
- **East-West Traffic:** Workloads present in a datacenter communicate with each other, and traffic is confined within the boundaries of the datacenter.
- **North-South Traffic:** Workloads present in a datacenter communicate with external devices outside the boundary of the datacenter.
- **Single-Tier Routing:** A single NSX gateway is connected to NSX logical segments in the southbound to provide E-W routing. It is also connected to the physical infrastructure in the northbound direction to provide N-S connectivity.
- **Multi-Tier Routing:** Provides isolation between different gateways, with a provider gateway for N-S traffic and a different tenant gateway for E-W traffic.
- **Dynamic Routing:** Enables different gateways to exchange network information with each other and is used to obtain routes dynamically from each other.
- **VRF:** Virtual Routing Forwarding (VRF) is a routing virtualization method to create multiple virtual logical routing instances on a single physical router.
- **EVPN:** Ethernet VPN, or EVPN for short, is a standards-based BGP distributed control plane for network virtualization overlay (NVO) that provides Layer 2 and Layer 3 connectivity over IP and IP/MPLS underlay networks.

CHAPTER 6

Logical Routing – VRF and EVPN

Introduction

The last couple of chapters have covered Logical Routing in the NSX environment and how NSX provides fully distributed East-West routing so the hypervisor where the virtual machine is running is performing routing itself. Additionally, it offers extremely flexible and optimized North-South routing. However, does NSX allow for the use of VRFs to facilitate data and control plane isolation across various tenants? Can a network administrator extend a VRF fabric that was created on a physical network to the NSX Domain? The answer is, as you may have suspected, yes. Sounds fascinating! Yes, it is.

This chapter covers VRF lite and EVPN to provide end-to-end isolation for different tenants in the network fabric.

Structure

In this chapter, we will cover the following topics:

- VRF Lite
    - VRF Lite Requirements and Limitations
    - Configuring VRF Gateways
    - VRF Route Leaking

- Network Topology
- Ethernet VPN (EVPN)
    - EVPN Support in NSX
    - EVPN Requirements
    - Configuring EVPN in NSX

VRF Lite

Virtual Routing Forwarding (VRF) is a routing virtualization method to create multiple virtual logical routing instances on a single physical router. It is widely used in enterprise and service providers' networks to provide control plane and data plane isolation between different routing domains, allowing the following use cases:

- With the help of VRF, the same overlapping IP addressing scheme can be used simultaneously in different routing domains.
- Provide isolation between regulated workloads and normal workloads.
- Provide isolation between external and internal networks while consolidating hardware resources.

Also, VRF provides the main use case of multi-tenancy in physical network infrastructure. NSX introduced support for VRF in release v3.0 to extend VRF instances configured in physical network infrastructure to the NSX domain. Prior to NSX-T v3.0, it was required to deploy a dedicated Tier0 gateway for each VRF instance configured in physical network infrastructure, resulting in a higher amount of compute resources to extend VRF instances in the NSX environment. Starting with NSX-T v3.0, multiple VRF instances can be hosted on the same Tier0 gateway, allowing them to share compute resources and still providing control plane and data plane isolation from each other.

Figure 6.1 shows a multi-tenancy topology where three different tenants are configured on physical infrastructure. If a separate routing instance is required in the NSX environment for each tenant, then in case of without VRFs depicted on the left side, a separate Tier0 gateway is required. This will require deploying a minimum of six Edge nodes for high availability and redundancy. Whereas if VRF functionality is used provided by NSX shown on the right side in *Figure* 6.1, then three separate VRF instances can be created on the same Tier0-GW, hence reducing the number of Edge nodes to two.

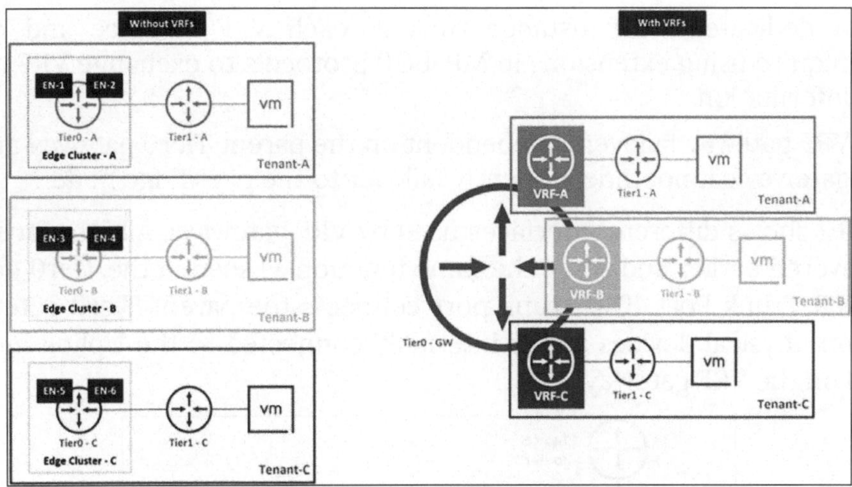

***Figure 6.1**: VRF gateway hosted on Tier0 gateway*

VRF Lite Requirements and Limitations

Before VRF Lite can be configured in the NSX environment, there are a few requirements that need to be fulfilled.

- A parent Tier0 gateway must be deployed or configured before creating Tier0 VRF gateways. An existing Tier0 can also be used to host VRF gateways.
- Multiple Tier0 gateways can be deployed in an environment with VRF gateways.
- Parent Tier0 gateway must have external interfaces configured on it before external interfaces on VRF gateways can be configured.
- VLAN Tagging is used to differentiate traffic between different VRFs. The external interface of the VRF gateway must be connected to a trunk segment with the corresponding VLAN ID defined in the segment VLAN range. A dedicated trunk segment with a single VLAN range (x-x) can be used to configure external interfaces on VRF gateways but as a best practice, VRF uplinks should be connected to the same uplink trunk interface as this reduces the number of resources required.
- OSPF and VPN are not supported on the VRF gateway however, a Tier1 gateway with VPN services can be connected to a VRF gateway.
- Static routes and BGP dynamic routing protocol are supported on the VRF gateway.
- VRF gateways are not supported on NSX Federation and VRF gateways cannot be configured from NSX Global Manager.

- A dedicated BGP instance runs in each VRF instance and doesn't require using extensions in MP-BGP protocols to exchange VRF routing information.
- VRF gateway failover is dependent on the parent Tier0 gateway and VRF gateway cannot independently failover to the peer Edge node.

Figure 6.2 shows different interfaces used by VRF gateways. All interfaces have been covered earlier and serve the same function as seen in the Tier0 gateway except LR Trunk Port. This trunk port connects the parent Tier0 gateway to upstream physical devices and is internally connected to the Uplink interface defined on the VRF gateway.

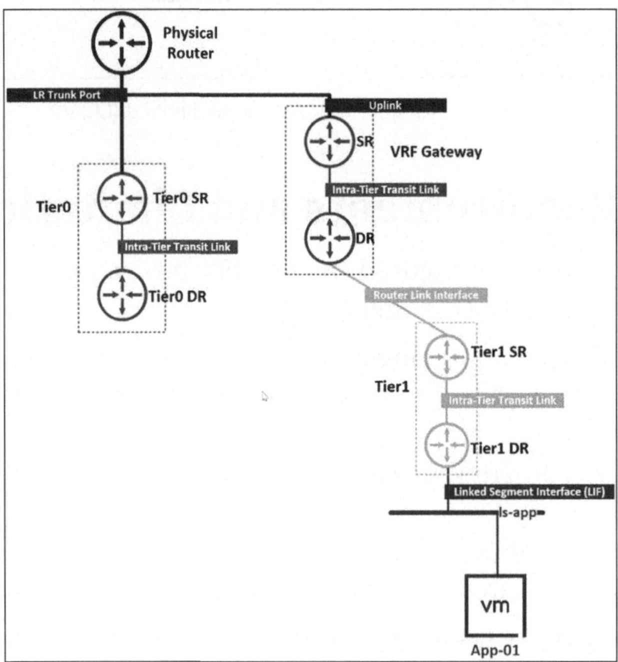

Figure 6.2: *Interfaces used by VRF gateway*

Configuring VRF Gateways

Alright! A lot of ground has been covered on VRF lite and it is now time to see how the VRF gateway is configured in the NSX environment. *Figure* 6.3 shows an example of topology from our previous multi-tier topology. But this time, there are two VRF instances configured on the physical router, namely VRF-A and VRF-B. To provide end-to-end isolation between tenants, VRF gateways need to be configured on the parent Tier0 gateway and move Tier1 gateways from the parent Tier0 gateway to their respective VRF gateways.

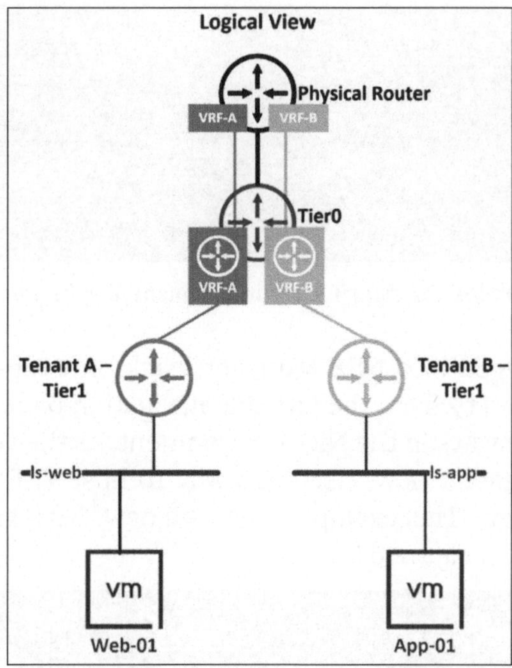

***Figure 6.3**: An example VRF topology*

Completing pre-requisites of a VRF gateway

The first step in order to configure the VRF gateway is to create a trunk segment for VRF gateway external interfaces and a parent Tier0 gateway.

Step 1: Login into NSX Manager with admin privileges and navigate to the `Networking` menu. Click on `Segments` from the left side navigation panel under `Connectivity` to view segments configured in the environment. Click on `Add Segment` to create a new segment and provide the following information.

a. `Name` : Provide an appropriate name for the segment for identification

b. `Transport Zone`: Select the VLAN Transport Zone configured on Edge nodes

c. `VLAN`: Provide the range of VLAN IDs that carry traffic for VRFs

Figure 6.4 shows an example segment VRF-Uplink-Trunk connected to VLAN Transport Zone TZ-VLAN-Edge and has a VLAN range defined as 1090-1210.

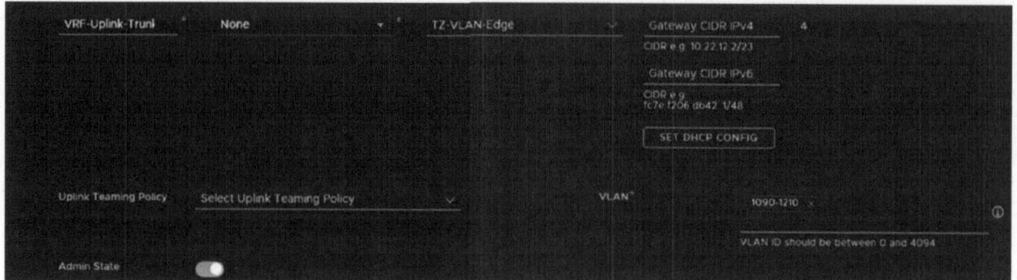

Figure 6.4: *Configuring a trunk segment for VRF gateway*

Step 2: While logged into NSX Manager, click on **`Tier-0 Gateways`** under **`Connectivity`** from the left side navigation panel to view configured Tier0 gateways in the NSX environment. As the steps covered earlier, either create a new Tier0 gateway to host VRF instances or use an existing one. This example creates a new Tier0 gateway LAB-T0-VRF as shown in *Figure* 6.5.

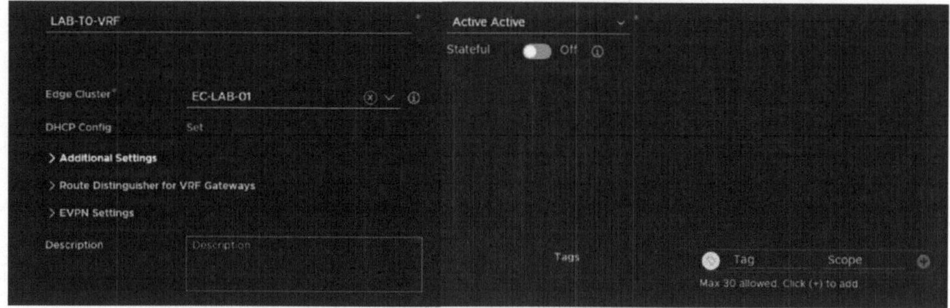

Figure 6.5: *Adding a new Tier0 gateway for VRF instances*

Step 3: If this is a new Tier0 gateway, then add External Interfaces by clicking on the **`Set`** in **`Interfaces`** field. This is a mandatory requirement to add an external interface on the Tier0 gateway before adding external interfaces on VRF gateways. *Figure* 6.6 shows two external interfaces configured on the newly created Tier0 gateway.

Figure 6.6: *Adding external interfaces on Tier0 gateway*

Step 4: No further configuration is required on the Tier0 gateway as BGP is by default enabled and starting NSX 4.1 BGP ASN can be set on individual VRF gateways.

Creating a VRF gateway

Creating a VRF gateway is very similar to creating a Tier0 gateway with similar options.

Step 1: While logged into the NSX Manager and on the **`Tier-0 Gateways`** screen, click on **`Add Gateway`** and select **`VRF`**. This will add a new VRF gateway. Provide the following information:

a. **`Name`**: Provide the name of the VRF gateway for identification.

b. **`Connect to Tier-0 Gateway`**: Select the parent Tier0 gateway on which this VRF gateway is hosted.

c. **`HA Mode`:** HA Mode is inherited from the Tier0 gateway and cannot be modified at the VRF gateway level.

Figure 6.7 shows a VRF gateway VRF-Tenant-A with parent Tier0 gateway LAB-T0-VRF created in the previous step. This VRF gateway will connect to VRF-A hosted on the physical router.

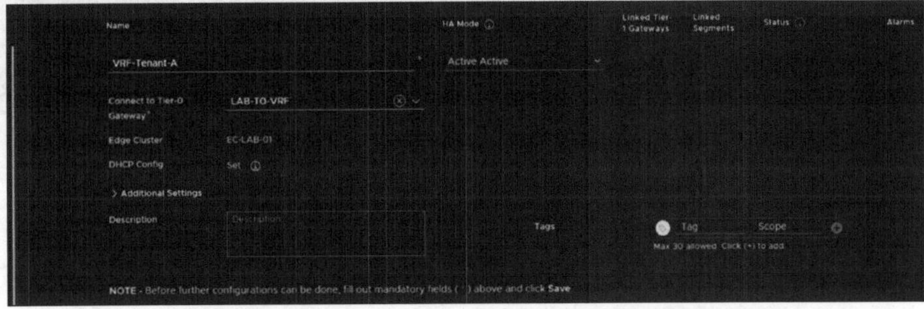

Figure 6.7: *Adding a VRF gateway in NSX Manager UI*

Step 2: Click on **`Save`** to finish adding the VRF gateway. Similar to the Tier0 gateway, select **`Yes`** to continue modifying the VRF gateway or **`No`** to finish the configuration.

Step 3: Similar to the Tier0 gateway, click on **`Set`** in **`Interfaces`** field to add External Interface on the VRF gateway. All the options remain the same as the Tier0 external interface, except for one field.

a. **`Access VLAN ID`**: This is a mandatory field to be provided while adding external interfaces on the VRF gateway. Provide the VLAN ID for a specific VRF.

Figure 6.8 shows an external interface **`tenant-A-up-1-edge-1`** being added on VRF gateway with IP address **`10.10.110.10/24`** connected to trunk segment VRF-Uplink-Trunk configured as part of pre-requisites with Access VLAN ID as 1100 which is used by VRF-A on the physical router.

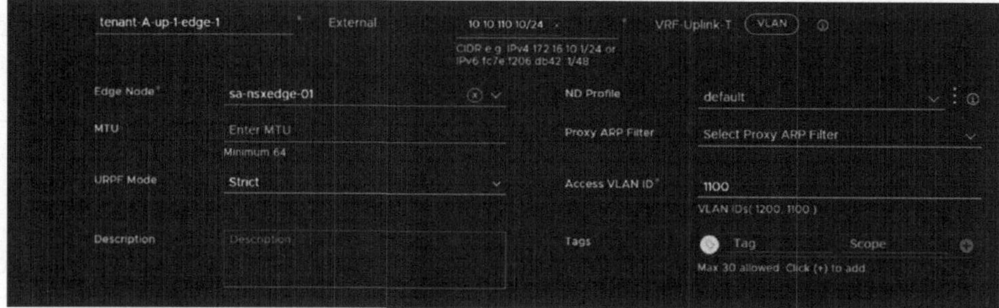

Figure 6.8: *Adding an external interface on the VRF gateway*

Step 4: *Figure* 6.9 shows external interfaces configured following step 3 on the VRF gateway successfully realized on Edge Node 1 and Edge Node 2.

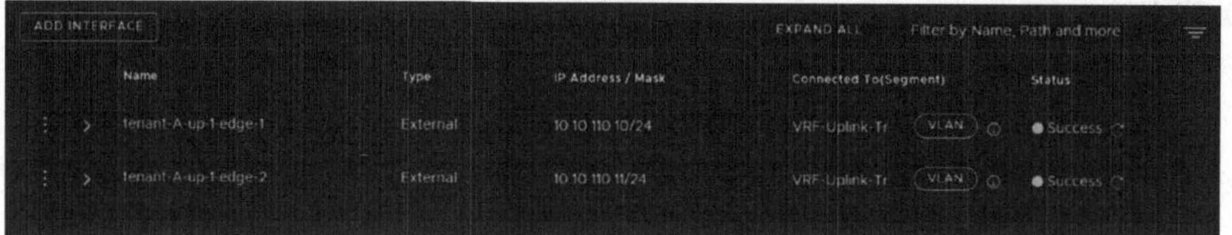

Figure 6.9: *Viewing configured external interfaces on the VRF gateway*

Step 5: The next step is to configure BGP. Similar to the Tier0 gateway, expand BGP to configure the following options.

a. **`BGP`**: By default, BGP is disabled on the VRF gateway. Toggle the button in front of BGP to enable or disable BGP protocol on the VRF gateway.

b. **`Local AS`**: Starting NSX 4.1, the Local AS number can be configured on a per VRF gateway basis. In prior releases, this value was inherited from the parent Tier0 gateway.

c. **`Inter SR iBGP`**: This option is not supported for VRF gateways hosted on the Tier0 gateway.

d. **`Graceful Restart`**: This cannot be modified at the VRF gateway level and value is inherited from the parent Tier0 gateway.

e. **`Multipath Relax`:** Again this is inherited from the parent Tier0 gateway.

Figure 6.10 shows an example BGP configuration with Local AS configured as 64110 whereas parent Tier0 BGP Local AS is configured as 65000.

Figure 6.10: *Configuring BGP on VRF gateway*

Step 6: Similar to the Tier0 gateway, click on **`Set`** in **`BGP Neighbors`** to add remote BGP peers for the VRF instance. While configuring the BGP neighbor, provide the same information as described while configuring the BGP neighbor on the Tier0 gateway (Refer to *Chapter* 5, *Logical Routing* – NSX *Gateways*, Section BGP steps 3–5)

Figure 6.11 shows a remote BGP peer with IP address **`10.10.110.1`** configured on VRF-A on the physical router with Remote ASN 110.

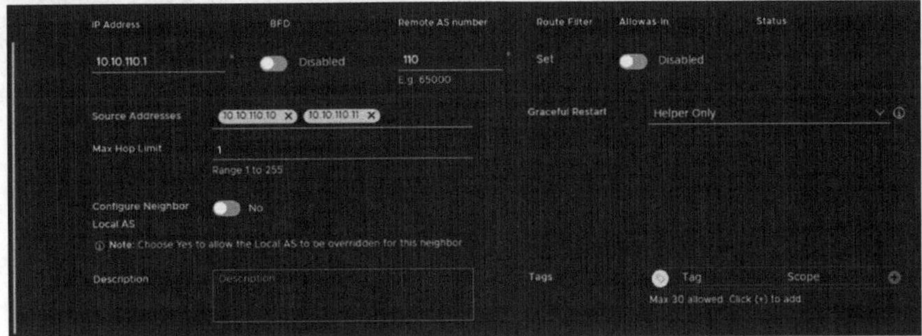

Figure 6.11: *Configuring BGP neighbor on VRF gateway*

Step 7: Click on **`Set`** in the **`Route Re-distribution`** field to configure route redistribution in BGP protocol similar to Tier0 route redistribution. (*Refer to section Route Redistribution in Dynamic Routing*). *Figure* 6.12 shows route redistribution configured for `tenant-A`.

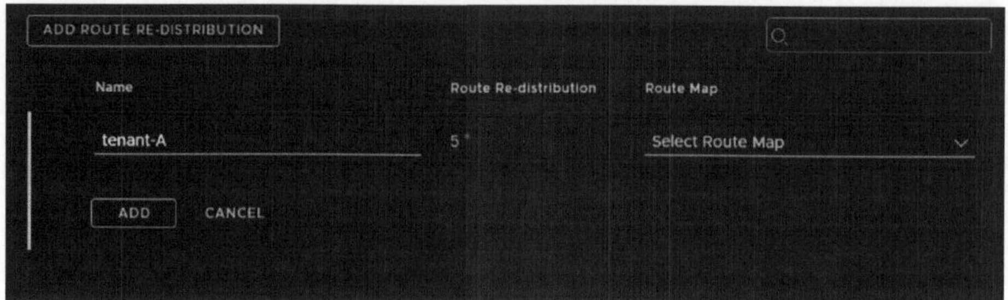

***Figure 6.12**: Configure route re-distribution on VRF gateway*

Step 8: Navigate to **`Tier-1 Gateway`** under **`Connectivity`** to view Tier1 gateways in NSX Manager UI. Click on three dots for the desired Tier1 gateway and select **`Edit.`** Change the **`Linked Tier-0 Gateway`** to the VRF gateway to connect the Tier1 gateway to the VRF gateway and provide end-to-end isolation. *Figure* 6.13 shows Tier1 gateway **`LAB-T1-A`** now connected to VRF-Tenant-A to complete our example topology.

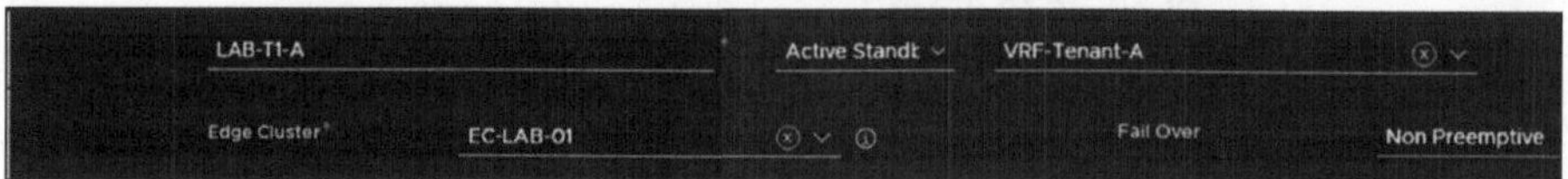

***Figure 6.13:** Changing next hop gateway for Tier1 gateway*

Step 9: Repeat Steps 1 to 8 to configure another VRF gateway `VRF-Tenant-B`, providing connectivity to VRF-B on the physical router as shown in *Figure* 6.14.

***Figure 6.14:** Viewing configured VRF gateways in NSX Manager UI*

Validating VRF Gateways

This section covers how to validate VRF gateways configured in the NSX environment. Follow these steps to validate configured VRF gateways:

Step 1: While in the Tier-0 Gateways menu, click on three dots against the desired VRF Gateway and select **`Generate BGP Summary`**. If all settings are configured correctly with upstream routers configuration complete, BGP Summary should show all sessions in the Established state as shown in *Figure* 6.15.

BGP Summary

Tier-0 Gateway VRF-Tenant-A

Edge Node All

Edge Node	Source Address	Neighbor Address	Remote AS	Connection Status	Connection Drop Count	Established Connection Count	Address Families
sa-nsxedge-02.lab.local	10.10.110.11	10.10.110.1	110	Established	0	1	IPv4 Unicast In 1 | Out 1
sa-nsxedge-01	10.10.110.10	10.10.110.1	110	Established	0	1	IPv4 Unicast In 1 | Out 1

Figure 6.15: *Validating BGP sessions on VRF gateway*

Step 2: Also, the upstream router should be learning routes from the VRF gateway via the BGP session. *Figure 6.16* shows an example snippet from the upstream router with VRF instance tenant-A successfully learning routes via BGP from the VRF gateway configured in previous steps.

```
vyos@vyos-1:~$ show ip route vrf tenant-A
Codes: K - kernel route, C - connected, S - static, R - RIP,
       O - OSPF, I - IS-IS, B - BGP, E - EIGRP, N - NHRP,
       T - Table, v - VNC, V - VNC-Direct, A - Babel, F - PBR,
       f - OpenFabric,
       > - selected route, * - FIB route, q - queued, r - rejected, b - backup
       t - trapped, o - offload failure

VRF tenant-A:
B   10.10.110.0/24 [20/0] via 10.10.110.10 inactive, weight 1, 00:04:10
                          via 10.10.110.11 inactive, weight 1, 00:04:10
C>* 10.10.110.0/24 is directly connected, eth0.1100, 00:28:19
B>* 172.16.51.0/24 [20/0] via 10.10.110.10, eth0.1100, weight 1, 00:01:41
  *                       via 10.10.110.11, eth0.1100, weight 1, 00:01:41
B>* 172.16.110.0/24 [20/0] via 10.10.110.10, eth0.1100, weight 1, 00:01:41
  *                        via 10.10.110.11, eth0.1100, weight 1, 00:01:41
```

Figure 6.16: *Successful validation of VRF route exchange on a physical router*

This successfully completes the configuration of the VRF gateway in the NSX environment. Next, let's see how NSX v4.1 introduced easier workflows to manage route leaking in VRF instances.

VRF Route Leaking

By default, data plane traffic is isolated between different VRF instances in NSX. However, by configuring Inter VRF routing, it is possible to exchange traffic between different VRF instances. This was possible prior to NSX v4.1, but it involves configuring static routes and was complex in nature. In NSX v4.1, the Inter VRF routing feature allows to import and export routes between VRFs. This can be achieved with the help of inter-VRF route advertisement or inter-VRF BGP route leaking instead of manually configuring static routes.

Figure 6.17 shows an example topology from the previous section where inter-VRF routing is configured to enable traffic exchange between different VRF instances.

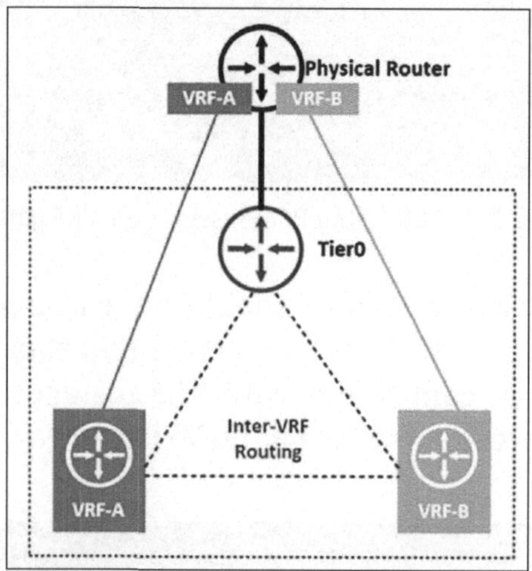

Figure 6.17: *Example topology with inter-VRF routing*

Let's see the steps to achieve this example topology in the NSX environment.

Step 1: If you try to reach the virtual machine connected to VRF instance B from the virtual machine in VRF instance A, traffic will get dropped as there is no routing configured between different VRF instances. *Figure* 6.18 shows a similar output when trying to reach IP address **`172.16.120.10/24`** present in VRF-Tenant-B from IP address **`172.16.110.10/24`** in VRF-Tenant-A.

```
lab@web-desktop-01:~$ ping 172.16.120.10
PING 172.16.120.10 (172.16.120.10) 56(84) bytes of data.
From 10.10.110.1 icmp_seq=1 Destination Net Unreachable
^C
--- 172.16.120.10 ping statistics ---
4 packets transmitted, 0 received, +1 errors, 100% packet loss, time 3030ms

lab@web-desktop-01:~$
```

Figure 6.18: *Example output of ping command when inter-VRF routing is not configured*

Step 2: While in the **`Tier-0 Gateways`** menu, click on three dots of the desired VRF gateway and select **`Edit`**. Expand the **`Routing`** section to view the option for **`Inter VRF Routing`** as shown in *Figure* 6.19.

***Figure 6.19**: Viewing inter-VRF routing in NSX Manager UI*

Step 3: Click on **`Set`** in **`Inter VRF Routing`** Field and a new screen will open to **`Set Inter VRF Routing.`** Click on **`Add Inter VRF Routing`** and provide the following information:

a. **`Connected Gateway`**: Select the gateway with which to enable inter-VRF routing from the drop-down menu. In this example, per *Figure* 6.20, we are on the **`VRF-Tenant-A`** gateway, so will add both **`LAB-T0-VRF`** and **`VRF-Tenant-B`** one by one.

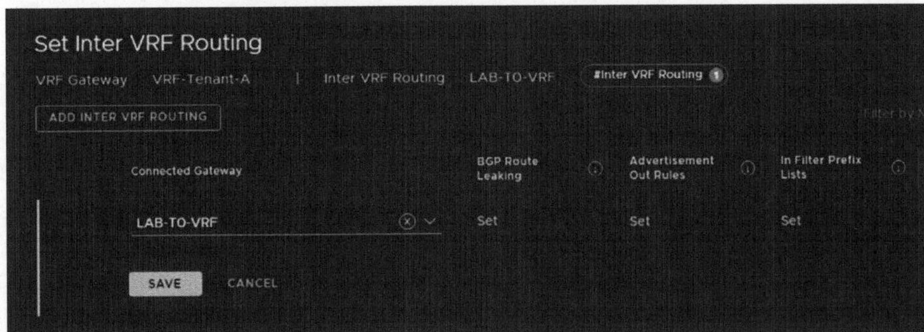

***Figure 6.20**: Adding Inter VRF Routing on gateway*

Here, you have two options to enable Inter VRF Routing.

Inter VRF Route Advertisement

Inter-VRF Route Advertisement is used to configure advertisement rules to advertise routes and prefixes on the connected gateway to create inter-VRF routing between different VRF instances.

Click on **`Set`** under **`Advertisement Out Rules`** to configure this option. This will open a new screen as shown in *Figure* 6.21. Provide the **`Name`** for Advertisement rule and select **`Advertisement Action`** as **`Allow`** to allow the exchange of routes and **`Deny`** to block the exchange of routes. **`Subnets`** are optional and if left blank, they will be selected as any. Additionally, select the type of routes to be filtered. Click on **`Add`** and then click on **`Apply`** to save this Advertise Rule and assign it to the gateway.

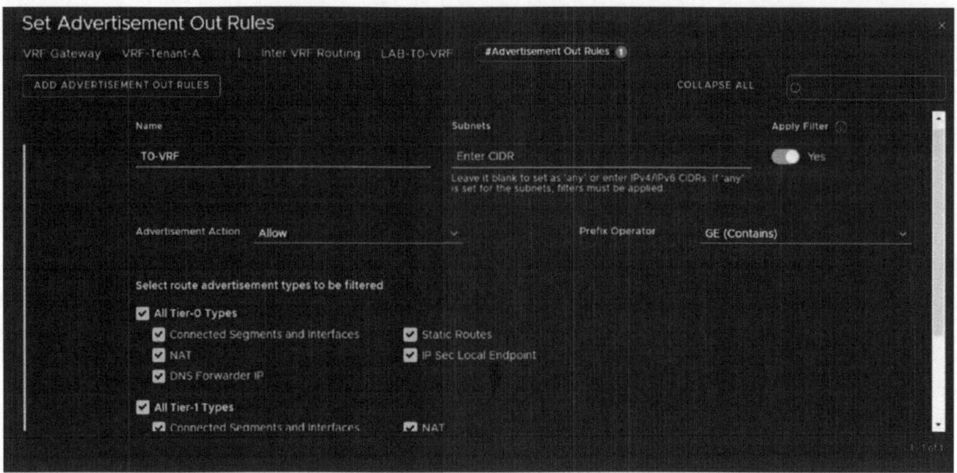

Figure 6.21: *Configuring Inter VRF Route advertisement*

Inter-VRF BGP Route Leaking

Inter-VRF BGP route leaking is used to configure BGP route leak for IPv4, IPv6 or both address families between VRF instances. Inter-VRF BGP route leaking uses BGP VPN to leak BGP routes and NSX internally configures RT(s) for route import and export. For this option to work, BGP must be enabled and local AS must be configured on both source and target VRF.

To configure this option, click on **`Set`** under **`BGP Route Leaking`**. This will open a new screen as shown in *Figure* 6.22. Click on three dots against the address family and toggle the button to enable or disable BGP route leaking. Optionally configure the **`In Filter`** and **`Out Filter`** to filter out the route leaking between VRF instances. Click on **`Add`** and then click on **`Apply`** to save the BGP Route leaking and assign it to the gateway.

Figure 6.22: *Configuring BGP route leaking in VRF gateway*

Step 4: Add the other gateways and select the desired method to leak routes between VRF instances. *Figure* 6.23 shows BGP Route Leaking configured on **`VRF-Tenant-B`** gateway and parent Tier0 gateway **`LAB-T0-VRF`**.

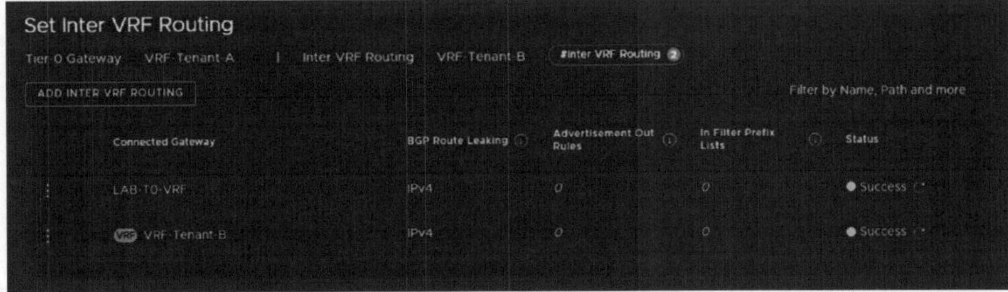

Figure 6.23: *Viewing Inter VRF Routing configured on gateways*

Step 5: Click on **`Close`** to finish configuring Inter VRF Routing. Click on **`Close Editing`** to finish configuring the gateway. Configure Inter VRF Routing similarly on remaining connected gateways to leak routes in VRF instances. If done correctly, a virtual machine in one VRF instance should be able to reach the virtual machine in another VRF instance as evident from *Figure* 6.24.

```
lab@web-desktop-01:~$ ping 172.16.120.10
PING 172.16.120.10 (172.16.120.10) 56(84) bytes of data.
64 bytes from 172.16.120.10: icmp_seq=1 ttl=60 time=2.81 ms
64 bytes from 172.16.120.10: icmp_seq=2 ttl=60 time=1.82 ms
64 bytes from 172.16.120.10: icmp_seq=3 ttl=60 time=1.46 ms
^C
--- 172.16.120.10 ping statistics ---
3 packets transmitted, 3 received, 0% packet loss, time 2003ms
rtt min/avg/max/mdev = 1.467/2.038/2.819/0.572 ms
```

Figure 6.24: *Example output of ping command when inter-VRF routing is configured*

Step 6: If you go back to VRF gateways after configuring Inter VRF routing and view the Interfaces, there will be a new interface automatically plumbed by NSX with the name INTERVRF to import and export routes between different VRF instances as *Figure* 6.25 illustrates.

Name	Type	IP Address / Mask	Connected To(Segment)	Status
INTERVRF	Inter VRF	169.254.2.2/23 View More	Not Set	Success
URPF Mode: Strict				
Description: Not Set				VIEW STATISTICS

Figure 6.25: *Viewing inter VRF configured interfaces in VRF gateway*

NSX still supports legacy workflow for inter-VRF routing for backward compatibility. It can be referenced on VMware Documentation (https://docs.vmware.com/en/VMware-NSX/4.1/administration/GUID-6DF4F3CC-17DC-4F44-ACEE-D8771D6675F1.html) if required. However, in both scenarios, stateful services such as firewalls and NAT cannot be applied to inter-VRF traffic.

Network Topology

NSX offers a visual representation of network topologies configured in the NSX environment. This can be viewed directly from NSX Manager UI by navigating to the **`Networking`** menu and clicking on **`Network Topology`** from the left side navigation panel. This view helps in verifying network configuration and troubleshooting errors. *Table* 6.1 lists the entities and corresponding services visible in Network Topology view courtesy VMware Documentation (https://docs.vmware.com/en/VMware-NSX/4.1/administration/GUID-A75B2553-7595-40B9-A902-854941BB06FD.html?hWord=N4IghgNiBcIHYFMAuB3A9gJwNYAIloAc0I0BzATxAF8g).

Entity	Service
Network Services	Load Balancer, NAT, and Distributed Firewall
Tier-0	L2 VPN service, IPSec VPN service, NAT rules, DNS forwarder, Gateway firewall rules, DHCP
Tier-1	Load Balancer, L2 VPN service, IPSec VPN service, NAT rules, DNS forwarder, Gateway firewall rules, DHCP
Segment	DHCP, Metadata proxy
Edge Transport Node	Switches, uplink interfaces, host configuration, uplinks, PortGroup connectivity
VirtualMachine	Underlying host cluster and host transport nodes
Pod	None
PhysicalServer	None
VRF	NAT rules, Gateway firewall rules, DHCP

Table 6.1: *Different entities and services present in Network Topology view*

Figure 6.26 shows a snippet from the lab environment with network topology configured during the writing of this chapter.

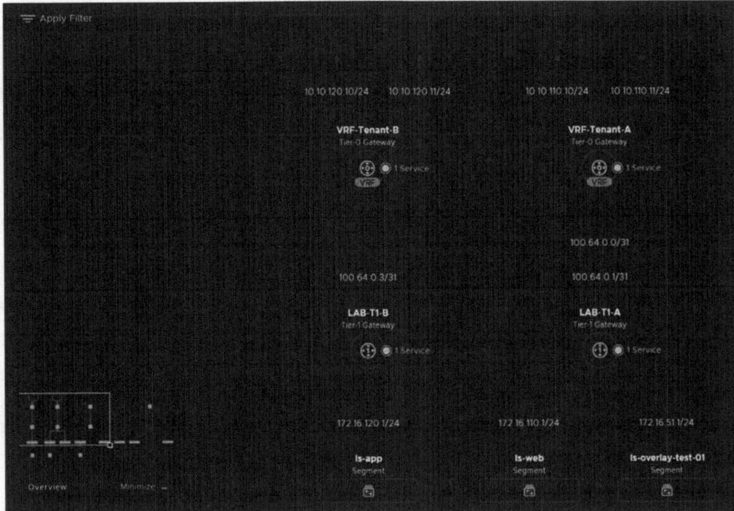

Figure 6.26: *Viewing Network Topology in NSX Manager UI*

This is a really nice feature provided by NSX Manager UI, which can help in easily identifying different services and gateways configured in the NSX environment for faster resolution of issues.

Ethernet VPN (EVPN)

In VRF lite, we covered each VRF instance needs to establish its own BGP peering session with an upstream router or physical router VRF. This required unique constructs to be created for each VRF instance, such as NSX Segment and VLANs, Subnets and IP address, BGP configuration and BFD timers. If the number of tenants is high, these constructs needed on both physical infrastructure and the NSX environment can quickly become an operational challenge for administrators. So, how this situation can be avoided? The answer is using EVPN VXLAN to advertise VRF prefixes over a single BGP session. So, what is EVPN? Ethernet VPN or EVPN for short is a standards-based BGP distributed control plane for network virtualization overlay (NVO) that provides Layer 2 and Layer 3 connectivity over IP and IP/MPLS underlay networks.

BGP is one of the most popular routing protocols due to its flexibility, granularity, and interoperability over the learned and advertised network layer information (NRLI). MP-BGP (Multi-Protocol BGP) is an extension of BGP that leverages multiple address families, such as IPv4/IPv6 unicast, and VPNv4/VPNv6 to distribute routing information. With the introduction of VXLAN in the datacenter, an additional sub address family was introduced in the MP-BGP protocol to replace native flood and learn the behavior of VXLAN. EVPN NRLI is the new addition to the MP-BGP protocol and is carried in Address Family Indicator L2VPN (25) and Subsequent Address Family Indicator EVPN (70). For BGP speakers to exchange L2VPN/EVPN NRLI, they must exchange EVPN BGP capability during the initial BGP OPEN message.

BGP EVPN uses the same options to provide multi-tenancy and uniqueness in the environment as other BGP VPN technologies. These are:

- **Route Distinguisher (RD)**: This is used in EVPN to create addresses unique in the environment globally and usually assigned in the format BGP_ASN:VRF. It uses the same encoding defined in RFC 4364.
- **Route Target (RT)**: These are used to import and export prefixes between VRFs.

Further EVPN NRLI is classified into six route types, as described in *Table 6.2* courtesy VMware Documentation.

Route Type	Description	Purpose	NSX Inline Mode	NSX Route Server Mode
Type 1 (RT-1)	Ethernet Auto-Discovery (A-D) route	Used in data centers to support EVPN active-active of multihoming.	No	Yes
Type 2 (RT-2)	MAC/IP Advertisement route	Advertises reachability of a specific MAC address, and optionally MAC and IP address binding.	No	Yes
Type 3 (RT-3)	Inclusive Multicast Ethernet Tag route	Advertises the reachability of a VNI associated with a particular VTEP in a virtual network. Type 3 routes are required for BUM traffic delivery across EVPN networks.	No	Yes
Type 4 (RT-4)	Ethernet Segment route	These are used with multihomed endpoints and used to Designate Forwarder Election, ensuring only one VTEP forwards BUM Traffic.	No	No

Type 5 (RT-5)	IP Prefix route	Advertises IPv4 and IPv6 prefixes reachability. This advertisement of prefixes into the EVPN domain provides the ability to build L3VPN similar services.	Yes	Yes
Type 6 (RT-6)	Selective Multicast Ethernet Tag route	Used to advertise the intent of the host or VM to receive multicast traffic for a certain Multicast Group (*,G) or Source-Group combination (S,G).	No	No

Table 6.2: *EVPN NRLI Route Types*

Figure 6.27 shows a comparison between VRF Lite mode and EVPN mode for multiple VRF instances configured on the Tier0 gateway. In EVPN mode, only a single BGP session with AF L2VPN/EVPN is required to exchange routes between the physical infrastructure and the NSX environment.

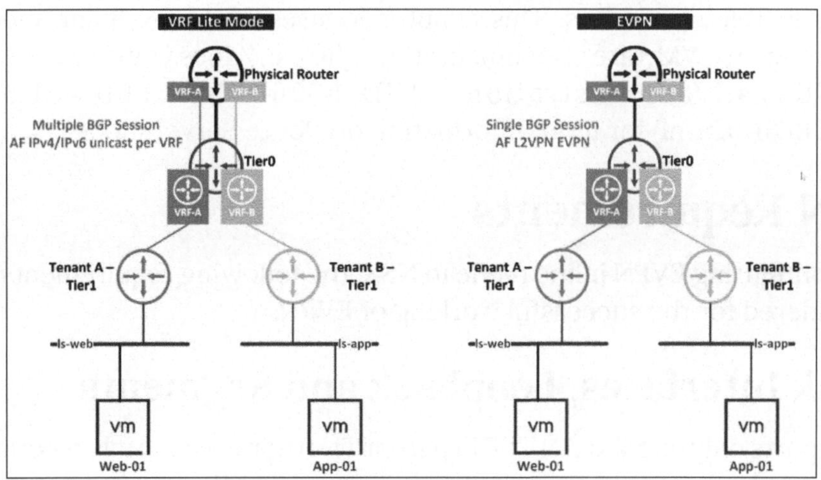

Figure 6.27: *VRF Lite vs. EVPN*

When EVPN is used to advertise IP prefixes reachability using Route Type 5 and VXLAN encapsulation, then VNI identifies the VRF instance.

EVPN Support in NSX

NSX supports two different connectivity modes for EVPN implementation in the datacenter.

Inline Mode

In Inline mode, the Tier0 gateway establishes MG-BGP EVPN control plane session with the physical router to exchange routing information. In the data plane, Edge nodes forward all the traffic existing NSX datacenter to the remote datacenter, receive all the incoming traffic from the remote datacenter and forward it to hypervisor hosts. Edge nodes sit in the data path hence, this model is called Inline mode. The inline mode supports EVPN Route Type 5 only. *Figure 6.27* shows EVPN inline mode on the right side.

Route Server Mode

In Route Server mode, the Tier0 gateway establishes MG-BGP EVPN control plane session with a physical router or route reflectors to exchange routing information. However, in the data plane, hypervisor hosts forward the traffic to the datacenter gateway or Top of Rack switches over VXLAN tunnels. TEPs used for VXLAN encapsulation are the same as those used by Geneve encapsulation.

Note: EVPN Route Server mode is beyond the writing of this book as its main use case is Telco providers. This chapter focuses on EVPN Inline mode only. Please refer to VMware Documentation (https://docs.vmware.com/en/VMware-NSX/4.1/administration/GUID-B796D6B0-5FB0-45D6-A7FA-F16CB3CBF6D9.html) for more information on Route Server mode.

EVPN Requirements

When configuring EVPN inline mode in NSX, the following requirements need to be considered for the successful working of EVPN.

Uplink Interfaces, Loopback and Segments

NSX supports only one VXLAN TEP in parent Tier0 gateway, so it is recommended to use a loopback interface. To successfully form an MP-BGP peering, there are two key requirements:

- TEP interfaces (loopbacks) must be reachable, i.e., Top of Rack loopbacks must have connectivity to Tier0 loopback hosted on Edge nodes.
- Address family L2VPN/EVPN is negotiated between the Top of Rack switch and Tier0 gateway during the start of the BGP session.

Connectivity between loopbacks can be achieved in two different ways. The first way is to form a BGP peering between Tier0 SR and Top of Rack Switch using external interfaces and redistribute loopbacks in BGP so the entire network fabric is aware of TEP IP to reach different VRF prefixes. It is recommended to follow the redistribution of loopbacks using BGP as it simplifies the architecture.

The second option is to form BGP multi-hop peering between Tier0 SR and ToR (Top of Rack) switch with loopback interfaces. In this case, connectivity between loopbacks is achieved by either static routing or OSPF.

Route Distinguishers

RDs (Route Distinguishers) allow VRF prefixes to be unique in network fabric even if different VRF instances have overlapping IP address subnets. It is an eight-byte identifier and can be configured manually by the administrator, or NSX can automatically assign RD. It is generally configured in the format `BGP_AS:VRF`.

VXLAN ID

Each VRF must be assigned a unique VNI (Virtual Network Identifier) to different traffic between VRF instances on the data plane. As NSX uses Geneve overlay internally to allow communication between TEPs and VXLAN overlay is used between Tier0 SR and ToR switch. To avoid conflict between the Geneve overlay and the VXLAN overlay, the VNI pool must have a unique range defined outside of the VNI range defined for Geneve.

Configuring EVPN in NSX

High-level workflow to configure EVPN involves the following steps:

1. Create a VXLAN VNI pool in NSX Manager for VNI assignment on VRF instances
2. Enable EVPN on a Tier0 gateway
3. Configure Tier0 BGP neighbors to advertise L2VPN EVPN Address family
4. Finally, configure L3 VRF settings on VRF gateways for inline EVPN

Creating a VXLAN VNI Pool

Step 1: Login into NSX Manager with admin privileges and navigate to the **`Networking`** menu. Click on **`Global Network Config`** from the left side navigation panel under **`Settings`**. Click on the `EVPN/VXLAN VNI Pool` option to view VXLAN pools configured in the NSX environment as shown in *Figure* 6.28.

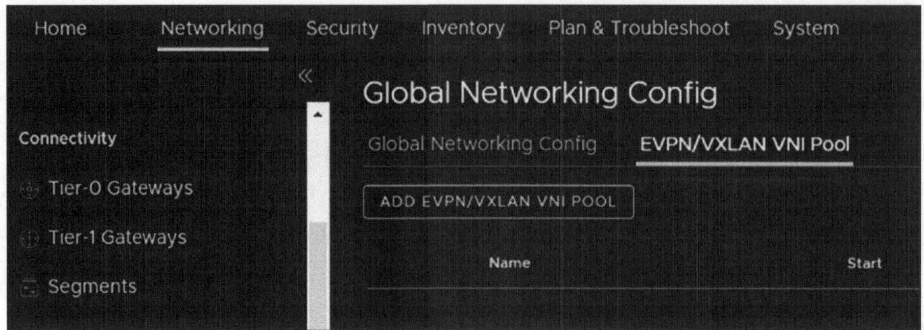

***Figure 6.28**: Viewing VXLAN VNI Pool in NSX Manager UI*

Step 2: Click on **ADD EVPN/VXLAN VNI POOL** to add a new pool and provide the following information:

a. **Name**: Provide an appropriate name for identification of the pool

b. **Start**: Provide the start value of the VNI pool range. By default, NSX uses up to VNI 75000 for the Geneve overlay. Ensure VXLAN VNI pool values are not overlapping with the Geneve VNI pool.

c. **End**: Provide the ending value of the VNI pool range depending on VRF instances.

Click **Save** to create the VNI pool. *Figure* 6.29 shows a configured VNI pool with the name **EVPN_VNI_Pool** with a VNI range defined as **85001** to **85010.**

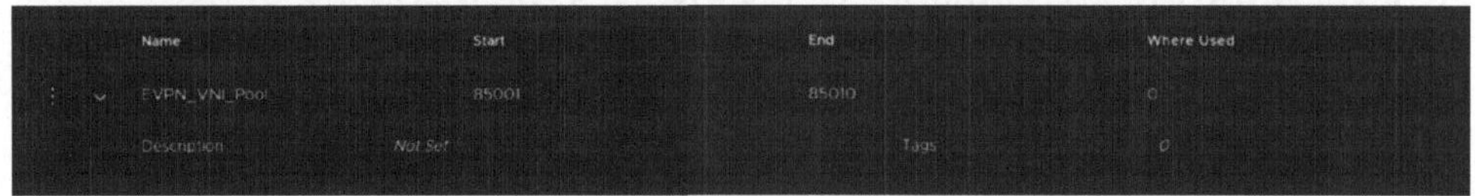

***Figure 6.29**: A configured VXLAN VNI Pool in NSX Manager UI*

Advertising L2VPN EVPN on Tier0 BGP Neighbors

The next step is to ensure BGP neighbors are advertising L2VPN EVPN address family to their peers. By default, it is not enabled but can be configured by following these steps:

Step 1: While logged into NSX Manager, navigate to **Networking** and click on **Tier-0 Gateways** under **Connectivity** to view configured Tier0 and VRF gateways in the environment. Expand the configuration of the desired Tier0 gateway by clicking on the triangle icon **>** and scroll down to view BGP settings. Click on the numerical value in the **`BGP Neighbors`** field to view configured neighbors on the Tier0 gateway. *Figure* 6.30 shows an example of a BGP neighbor configured on Tier0 gateway LAB-T0-VRF configured previously.

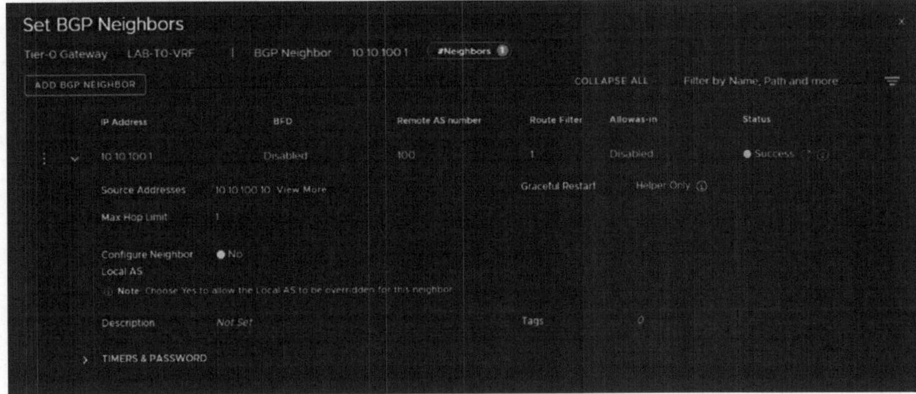

***Figure 6.30**: Viewing configured BGP neighbors on Tier0 gateway*

Step 2: Click on the numerical value under **`Route Filter`** to open another screen for **`Router Filters`** configured on Tier0 BGP neighbor. As *Figure* 6.31 shows, by default, only the IPv4 Address family is enabled. Click on **`Edit`** to add more address families.

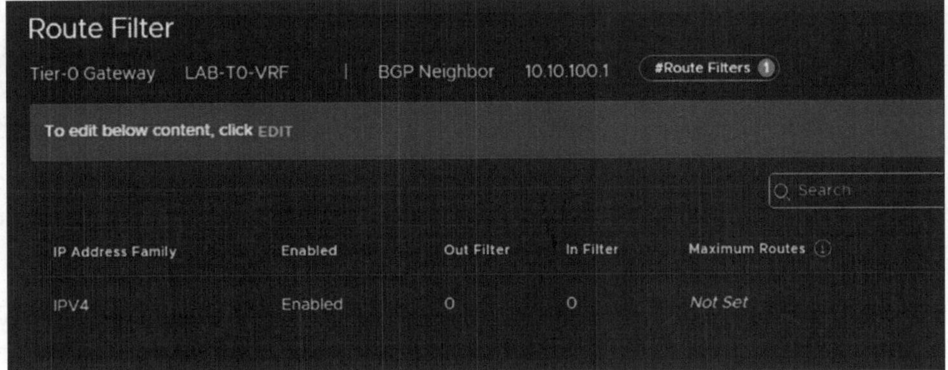

***Figure 6.31**: Viewing route filters configured on BGP neighbors*

Step 3: Clicking on **`Edit`** will change the view to a modifying view. Click on **`Add Route Filter`** to add additional address family. In this case, select **`L2VPN EVPN`** as the **`IP Address Family`** with the status **`Enabled`**. If required, add any **`IN`** or **`OUT`** filters and click on **ADD** and then **APPLY** to save the configuration similar to *Figure* 6.32.

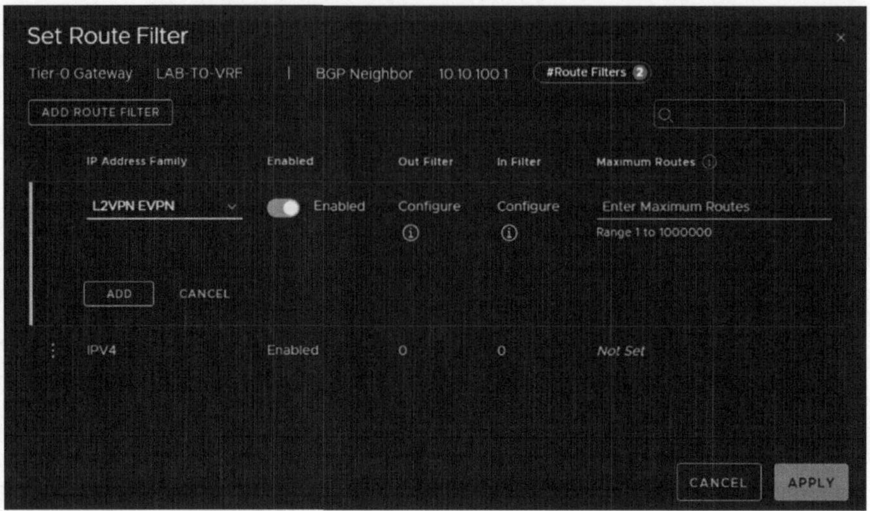

***Figure 6.32**: Adding additional address family on BGP neighbors*

Enabling EVPN on Tier0 Gateway

This step involves the configuration to enable Inline EVPN mode on the Tier0 gateway.

Step 4: Following up on previous steps, if still on the Tier0 gateway configuration screen, then scroll to **EVPN Settings**. Otherwise, click on three dots and select **Edit** to modify the desired Tier0 gateway. Optionally, configure **RD Admin Address** under **Route Distinguisher for VRF Gateway** to enable automatic assignment of RDs on VRF instances by Tier0 gateway. This RD Admin Address is just an ID and doesn't have to be configured or routable on the network.

Step 5: Expand **EVPN Settings** on the Tier0 gateway and provide the following configuration as shown in *Figure* 6.33.

a. **EVPN Mode**: Select **Inline** to configure EVPN Inline mode or **Route Server** to enable EVPN Route Server mode. Select **No EVPN** to disable EVPN on the Tier0 gateway.

b. **EVPN/VXLAN VNI Pool:** Select the VXLAN VNI pool configured earlier.

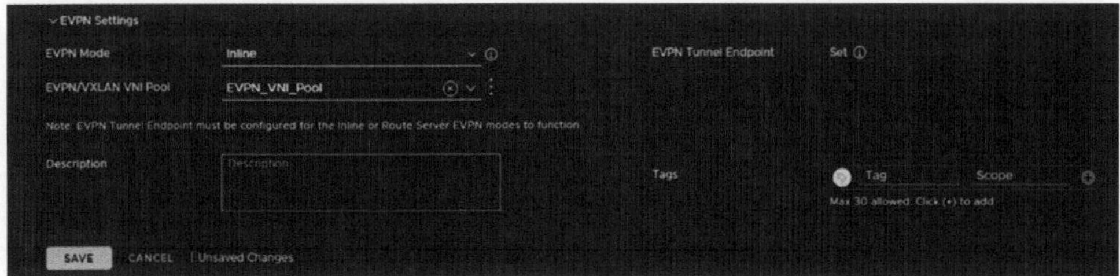

***Figure 6.33**: Configuring EVPN Inline mode on Tier0 gateway*

Step 6: Click on **`Set`** in front of **`EVPN Tunnel Endpoint`** to open a new screen to add EVPN TEPs. Click on **`Add EVPN Tunnel Endpoint`** to add a new TEP IP by providing the following information:

a. **`Name`**: Provide an appropriate name for the tunnel endpoint to easily identify it in the environment.

b. **`Edge Node`**: Select the Edge node where this TEP IP will be realized.

c. **`Local Address`**: Provide the unique IP Address of TEP.

d. **`MTU`**: Optionally configure MTU to match with the upstream switch.

Figure 6.34 shows an example configuration tunnel endpoint TEP **`TEP-1-Edge-1`** being configured on Tier0 gateway LAB-T0-VRF.

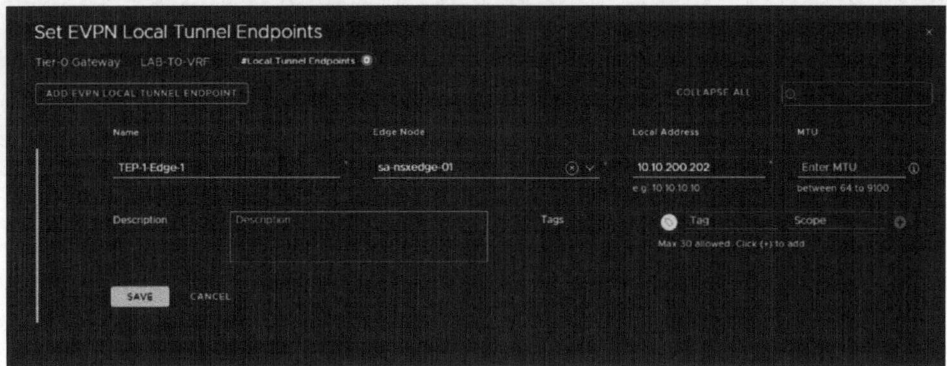

***Figure 6.34**: Configuring EVPN TEP on Tier0 gateway*

Click on **`Save`** to add a tunnel endpoint on the Tier0 gateway. Repeat this step to add a tunnel endpoint for other Edge nodes in the Edge cluster as well. Click on **`Close`** to return to the Tier0 gateway screen.

Step 7: As a final step, ensure **`EVPN TEP IP`** is selected in **`Route Redistribution`** for BGP to ensure TEP IP reachability in network fabric similar to *Figure* 6.35.

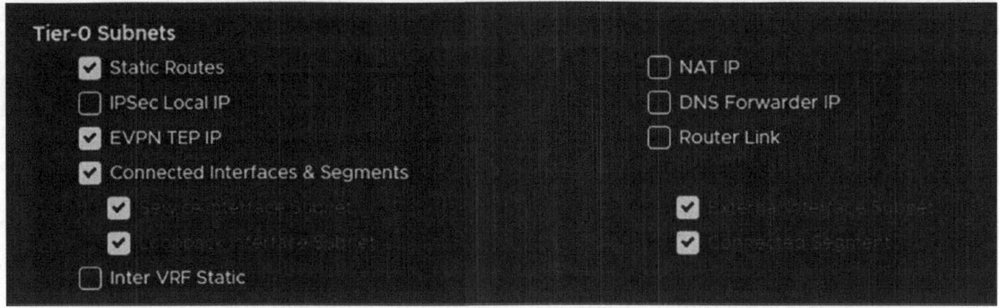

***Figure* 6.35**: *Enable* EVPN TEP *distribution in* BGP *route redistribution*

Configuring VRF Settings on VRF Gateway

This is the final step to enable EVPN inline on the Tier0 VRF gateway.

Step 1: While logged into the NSX Manager and on the **`Tier-0 Gateways screen`**, either add a new VRF gateway or edit an existing one to configure EVPN configuration. Scroll to the bottom and expand the **`BGP`** section to ensure **`BGP`** is disabled on the VRF gateway and the **`Local AS`** field is blank, as shown in *Figure* 6.36.

***Figure* 6.36**: *Ensuring* BGP *is disabled on the* VRF *gateway*

Step 2: Expand the **`VRF Settings`** section in the VRF gateway to configure EVPN settings. If RD Admin Address is configured on the Tier0 gateway, then Route Distinguisher and EVPN Tunnel VNI are automatically assigned by the Tier0 gateway. If no RD Admin Address is configured on the Tier0 gateway, then configure settings similar to *Figure* 6.37 on the VRF gateway.

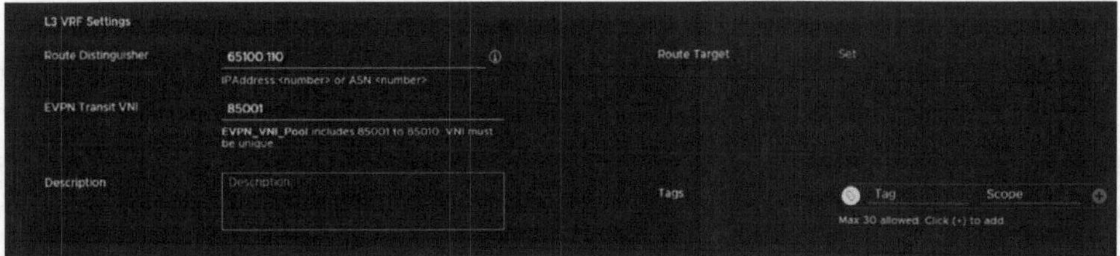

Figure 6.37: *Configuring EVPN settings on VRF gateway*

- **`Route Distinguisher`**: Provide an RD value to uniquely identify prefixes for different VRF instances. It is provided in format **`BGP_ASN:VRF`**. *Figure* 6.37 shows the value assigned as **`65100:110`** where 65100 is the BGP ASN assigned to Tier0 gateway and 110 is the VRF ID.
- **`EVPN Tunnel VNI`**: Enter the value of VNI from the pool range configured earlier. This value should be unique for each VRF.

Step 3: Click on **`Set`** in Route Target to add RT to import and export VRF prefixes. In the Set Route Target screen, click on Add Route Target to add a new RT. Select mode as **`Auto`** if **`RD Admin Address`** is configured on Tier0 gateway, else select **`Manual`**. Provide the value for Import and Export RTs where export RT is the value of RD configured on VRF gateway and import RT is the value of RD configured on ToR switch VRF. Click on **`Add`** to save the configuration for Route Target and click on **`Close`** to return to the VRF gateway screen.

Figure 6.38 shows the Route Target configuration where the Import RT value is **`100:110`** configured on the physical router VRF and Export RT is **`65100:110`** configured in the previous step.

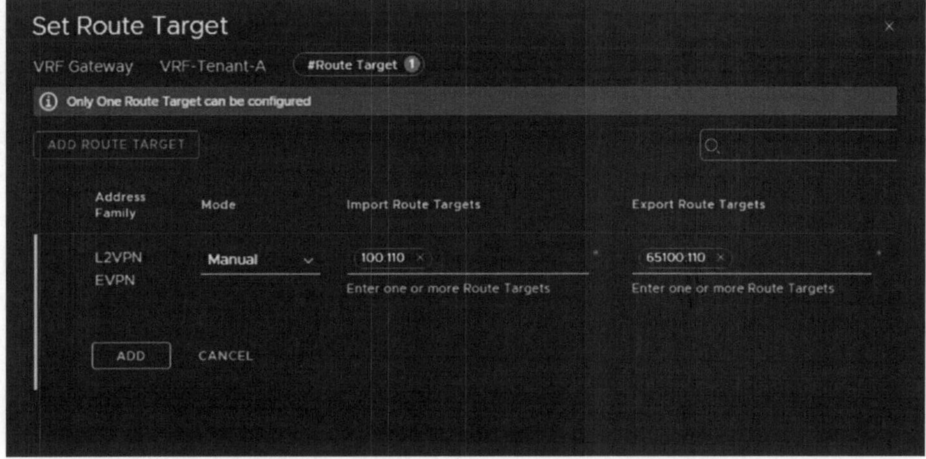

Figure 6.38: *Configuring Route Target in VRF gateway*

Step 4: Click on **Save** on the VRF gateway screen to finish configuring EVPN settings as shown in *Figure* 6.39. Click on **Close Editing** to exit from the editing view of the VRF gateway.

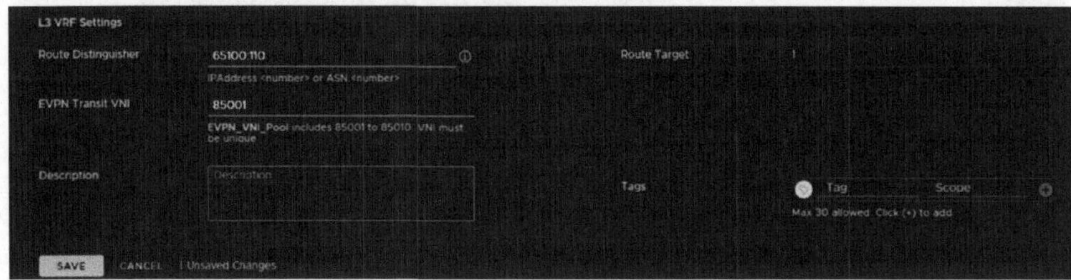

***Figure 6.39**: VPN configuration on VRF gateway*

Validating EVPN Configuration

EVPN configuration can be validated easily by checking if virtual machines connected to VRF-specific segments are able to reach their peers or not. If all configuration is correct, then Tier0 SR and ToR switch should be able to exchange routing information over MP-BGP with each other.

Figure 6.40 shows an example, where VRF for tenant-A is able to learn network **10.10.110.0/24** with the next hop as TEP of ToR switch **10.10.200.200** confirming successful route exchange.

```
sa-nsxedge-01(tier0_vrf_sr[21])> get route bgp

Flags: t0c - Tier0-Connected, t0s - Tier0-Static, b - BGP, o - OSPF
t0n - Tier0-NAT, t1s - Tier1-Static, t1c - Tier1-Connected,
t1n: Tier1-NAT, t1l: Tier1-LB VIP, t1ls: Tier1-LB SNAT,
t1d: Tier1-DNS FORWARDER, t1ipsec: Tier1-IPSec, isr: Inter-SR,
ivs: Inter-VRF-Static, > - selected route, * - FIB route

Total number of routes: 1

b  > * 10.10.110.0/24 [20/0] via 10.10.200.200, br-85001, 06:29:17
```

***Figure 6.40**: Viewing route learns in specific VRF gateway on NSX Edge node*

Similarly, if checked on the ToR switch, it should be able to see RDs and routes learned via L2VPN EVPN. *Figure* 6.41 shows an example output snippet from the ToR switch able to see RDs configured on VRF gateways in the NSX environment.

```
vyos@vyos-1:~$ show bgp l2vpn evpn
BGP table version is 6, local router ID is 192.168.0.251
Status codes: s suppressed, d damped, h history, * valid, > best, i - internal
Origin codes: i - IGP, e - EGP, ? - incomplete
EVPN type-1 prefix: [1]:[EthTag]:[ESI]:[IPlen]:[VTEP-IP]:[Frag-id]
EVPN type-2 prefix: [2]:[EthTag]:[MAClen]:[MAC]:[IPlen]:[IP]
EVPN type-3 prefix: [3]:[EthTag]:[IPlen]:[OrigIP]
EVPN type-4 prefix: [4]:[ESI]:[IPlen]:[OrigIP]
EVPN type-5 prefix: [5]:[EthTag]:[IPlen]:[IP]

   Network          Next Hop            Metric LocPrf Weight Path
Route Distinguisher: 65100:110
 *= [5]:[0]:[24]:[10.10.110.0]
                    10.10.200.203            0             0 65100 ?
                    RT:65100:110 ET:8 Rmac:02:50:56:00:70:00
 *>                  10.10.200.202            0             0 65100 ?
                    RT:65100:110 ET:8 Rmac:02:50:56:00:58:00
 *= [5]:[0]:[24]:[172.16.51.0]
                    10.10.200.203            0             0 65100 ?
                    RT:65100:110 ET:8 Rmac:02:50:56:00:70:00
 *>                  10.10.200.202            0             0 65100 ?
                    RT:65100:110 ET:8 Rmac:02:50:56:00:58:00
 *= [5]:[0]:[24]:[172.16.110.0]
                    10.10.200.203            0             0 65100 ?
                    RT:65100:110 ET:8 Rmac:02:50:56:00:70:00
 *>                  10.10.200.202            0             0 65100 ?
                    RT:65100:110 ET:8 Rmac:02:50:56:00:58:00
Route Distinguisher: 65100:120
 *= [5]:[0]:[24]:[172.16.120.0]
                    10.10.200.203            0             0 65100 ?
                    RT:65100:120 ET:8 Rmac:02:50:56:00:70:00
 *>                  10.10.200.202            0             0 65100 ?
                    RT:65100:120 ET:8 Rmac:02:50:56:00:58:00
```

Figure 6.41: *Viewing EVPN information on the ToR switch*

This completes the EVPN Inline mode configuration in the NSX environment. If you are following along, well done. Grab yourself a coffee, as the journey has just started with NSX.

Conclusion

This concludes the logical routing features provided by NSX. In summary, in the last few chapters, we covered Edge node architecture, different sizing options and options available to deploy Edge node in the datacenter. Then we dived a bit more into the world of NSX logical routers and covered different routing topologies supported by NSX and how to configure them along with dynamic routing protocols BGP and OSPF. This chapter also covered high-availability options to ensure routing services are always available. Last but not least, we covered VRF lite and EVPN to provide end-to-end isolation for different tenants in the network fabric.

In the next chapter, we will cover NSX bridges, which help to bridge traditional VLAN-backed networks with NSX overlay segments, allowing network administrator to use the same IP address subnet in overlay network used by VLAN.

Key Terms

- **Segment:** Segments are layer 2 subnets representing layer 2 broadcasting domain across transport nodes in NSX networking.
- **Edge Node:** NSX Edge node provides a pool of capacity or pool of resources, e.g., CPU and memory, to run centralized services.
- **Edge Cluster:** A group of NSX Edge nodes that provides high availability to services running on NSX Edge nodes.
- **East-West Traffic:** Workloads present in a datacenter communicating with each other and traffic is confined within the boundaries of the datacenter.
- **North-South Traffic:** Workloads present in a datacenter communicating with external devices outside the boundary of the datacenter.
- **Single Tier Routing:** A single NSX gateway is connected to NSX logical segments southbound to provide E-W routing, and is also connected to physical infrastructure in the northbound direction to provide N-S connectivity.
- **Multi-Tier Routing:** Provides isolation between different gateways with a provider gateway for N-S traffic and a different tenant gateway for E-W traffic.
- **Dynamic Routing:** Enables different gateways to exchange network information with each other and is used to obtain routes dynamically from each other.
- **VRF:** Virtual Routing Forwarding (VRF) is a routing virtualization method to create multiple virtual logical routing instances on a single physical router.
- **EVPN:** Ethernet VPN or EVPN for short is a standards-based BGP distributed control plane for network virtualization overlay (NVO) that provides Layer 2 and Layer 3 connectivity over IP and IP/MPLS underlay networks.

Chapter 7
Logical Bridging

Introduction

In the last couple of chapters, we covered how NSX overlay networking can help you achieve highly flexible and easy-to-use switching/routing services in the data center. But many times you will come across a workload that cannot be migrated to a virtualized environment due to license restrictions or other application-specific reasons or a virtual workload requires layer 2 connectivity with VLAN-backed workloads or migrating workloads from older NSX-V environment to NSX environment (NSX-V2T migrations) without changing IP address of workloads. In such cases, it is necessary to bridge NSX overlay layer 2 networks to VLAN-backed networks/NSX-V VXLAN logical switches to allow layer 2 communication between VMs and physical workloads/workloads running in NSX-V environment.

This chapter covers logical bridging, a network service provided by NSX which can help bridge the gap between overlay networks and VLAN-backed networks.

Structure

In this chapter, we will cover the following topics:

- Bridging Overlay to VLAN
    - NSX Bridging Use Cases
    - NSX Bridging Components
- Configuring Bridging in NSX
    - Configure NSX Edge Node for Bridging
    - Configure Edge Bridge Profile
    - Attaching Bridge Profile to NSX Segment

Bridging Overlay to VLAN

NSX logical bridging works by creating a logical bridge between two or more physical networks. This bridge acts as a layer 2 switch, allowing virtual machines to communicate with each other as if they were on the same broadcast domain. This allows for the creation of logical networks that span multiple physical networks, providing greater flexibility and agility for virtualized workloads. To set up NSX logical bridging, you will need to configure logical switches and bridge endpoints, as well as establish a transport zone to define the scope of the logical network. You will also need to configure the physical network to allow for the transmission of Layer 2 traffic between the physical networks that are being bridged. The configuration of logical bridging in NSX has been covered in detail in the subsequent section.

Some of the key benefits provided by NSX logical bridging are:

- NSX logical bridging allows for the creation of logical networks that can span multiple physical networks, providing greater flexibility and agility for virtualized workloads.
- NSX logical bridging allows for the seamless integration of virtual and physical workloads by bridging the gap between overlay network and VLAN-backed network making it easier to manage and optimize your network infrastructure.
- NSX Bridges are instantiated NSX Edge nodes providing data plane performance leveraging the Data Plane Development Kit (DPDK) which provides low latency, high bandwidth and scalable traffic forwarding performance

NSX Bridging Use Cases

We touched on two key points in the introduction of this chapter. Few customers require to migrate their physical workload to the virtual environment but need to keep the same IP addresses on workloads and sometimes due to certain restrictions physical workload cannot be migrated to a virtual environment, requiring them to communicate over the same layer 2 subnet. These are the typical use cases covered by NSX logical bridging.

Workload Migration

This is one of the most common use cases normally used as a temporary solution. In order to keep the IP address the same on workloads or applications, the VLAN network is virtualized to an overlay-backed network in NSX. It is normal for migrations to run for a longer period of time and in order to provide connectivity between overlay network and workloads running on VLAN-backed network, the NSX bridge is instantiated to provide layer 2 connectivity. *Figure* 7.1 shows such an example where workloads are being migrated to the NSX overlay network and the NSX Edge bridge is being used to provide connectivity between different workloads during migration on the same layer 2 domain.

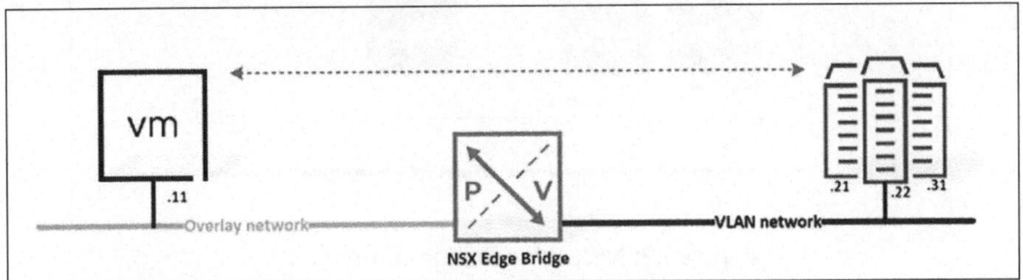

***Figure* 7.1:** *Workload migration with the help of NSX Edge bridge*

L2 connectivity between non-virtual and virtual workload

Sometimes it is not possible to migrate the physical workload to a virtual environment due to certain restrictions such as licenses or application restrictions. In such cases, it is required to provide layer 2 connectivity between the physical workload running on VLAN backed network and the workload running on NSX backed network. NSX bridge provides connectivity in such cases by creating a bridge between both overlay and VLAN networks. An important point to understand here is NSX Edge bridge should not be considered a replacement for NSX layer 3 services as utilizing the gateway on edges is always more efficient due to the use of ECMP (Equal Cost Multipathing) resulting in higher bandwidth and redundancy model. However, if necessary NSX Edge bridge can be used as a permanent solution to extend overlay networks in VLAN networks with proper design considerations such as dedicated resources and protection of bridged topologies.

NSX Bridging Components

Figure 7.2 shows key components involved in an NSX Bridge environment. Some of these are:

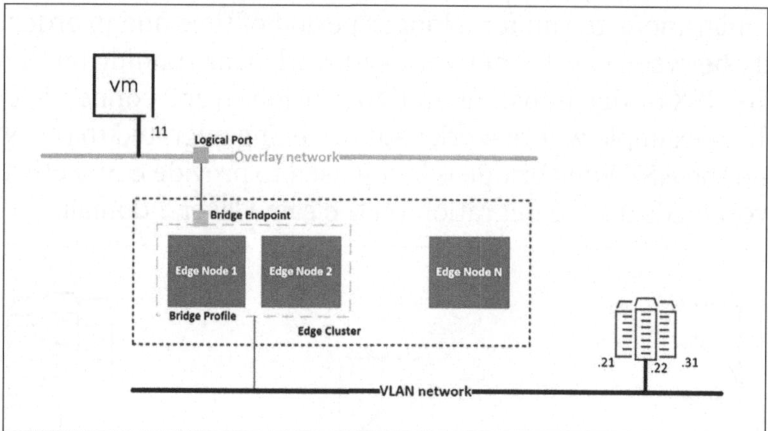

Figure 7.2: *NSX Edge Bridge components*

- **NSX Edge node VM**: Edge nodes are NSX Transport Nodes which provide compute resources to host NSX services. In this specific case, NSX Edge nodes are used to host bridges to forward traffic between the overlay network and the VLAN-backed network by connecting a fast path interface of the Edge node to both the overlay network and the VLAN-backed network. It is recommended to use a dedicated Edge node for bridging.
- **NSX Edge Cluster**: Edge cluster is a group of NSX Edge nodes to provide high availability of services hosted on Edge nodes. If more than one Edge nodes are part of the NSX Edge Cluster, then it can host active standby bridges to provide high-availability services in a bridging environment.
- **Bridge Profile**: Bridge profile is used as a configuration template to create new bridges in the NSX environment. This profile defines which Edge Cluster to utilize to host new bridges, which VLAN network to connect with and also define primary and standby Edge nodes to host active and backup bridge.
- **Bridge Endpoint**: When a segment is attached with a Bridge Profile, NSX create an object defined as Bridge Endpoint which represents pair of the active and backup bridge as a single bridge.
- **Logical Port**: This is the interface on the overlay segment which is attached to Bridge Endpoint.

Configuring Bridging in NSX

Bridging in NSX Manager is configured in three high-level steps:

- Configure Edge nodes to be used for bridging

- Configure Edge Bridge Profile
- Attach Bridge Profile to overlay segment

The deployment of edge nodes has been covered in detail in the previous chapter. However, there are a few important points to consider while deploying edge nodes for NSX bridges. *Figure* 7.3 displays the configuration of network adapters of an NSX Edge node post-configuration.

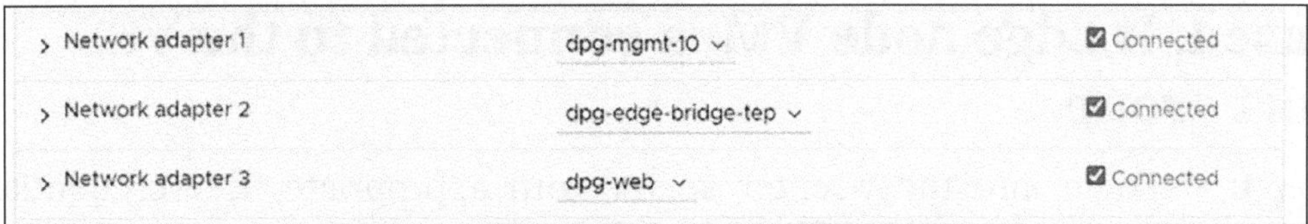

Figure 7.3: *NSX Edge node NIC configuration*

The first NIC of Edge node eth0 is connected to the management network which is reachable from NSX Manager. The first fast path NIC or fp-eth0 is connected to the TEP network to provide connectivity to overlay networking and the second fast path NIC or fp-eth1 is connected to the VLAN network which requires an extension to overlay networks.

Figure 7.4 shows the example, we will be working on to configure the NSX bridge.

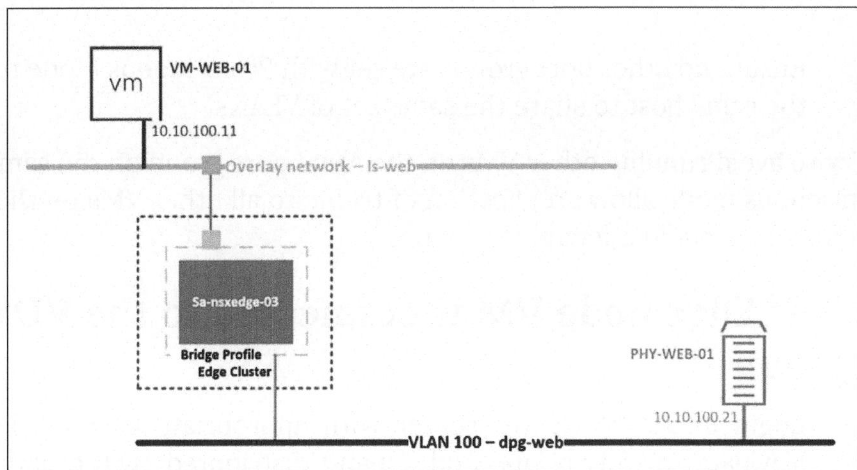

Figure 7.4: *Setting up NSX Edge bridge between overlay and VLAN network*

VM-WEB-01 is running on overlay network ls-web whereas workload **`PHY-WEB-01`** is running on VLAN-backed port group **`dpg-web`**. Both **`VM-WEB-01`** and **`PHY-WEB-01`** belong to the same broadcast domain and they need to communicate with each other on the same layer 2 domain. We will be taking this as an example in our sample configurations in the next section.

Configure NSX Edge Node for Bridging

There are a few settings that need to be enabled which are by default disabled in the vCenter server or ESXi host to make the NSX bridge function properly. These are dependent upon the network to be bridged or put simply where the fp-eth1 of Edge node VM is connected.

Case 1: If Edge node VM is connected to the VSS port group

Step 1: Login into the vCenter server with appropriate user credentials. Navigate to the ESXi host where Edge VM is running. Click on `Configure` and then `Virtual Switches` under `Networking.` Click on three dots against the port group and select `Edit.`

Step 2: Under `Securities,` set `Promiscuous Mode` and `Forged Transmit` to allow.

Step 3: Login into ESXi host using root credentials on which NSX Edge node VM is running and run the following command:

```
esxcli system settings advanced set -o /Net/ReversePathFwdCheckPromisc
-i 1
```

Step 4: Ensure no other port groups are set with Promiscuous Mode to allow the same host to share the same set of VLANs.

Note: Try to avoid running other VMs on the same port group on the same host as promiscuous mode allows replication of traffic to all other VMs on the same port group which could affect performance.

Case 2: If Edge node VM is connected to the VDS port group

Step 1: Login into the vCenter server with appropriate user credentials. Navigate to Networking and expand distributed switch and select desired port group on which Edge node VM is connected. Click on `Action` and select `Edit.`

Step 2: Under **`Security`**, set **`Promiscuous Mode`** and **`Forged Transmit`** to Accept. *Figure* 7.5 shows the required security policies set to Accept.

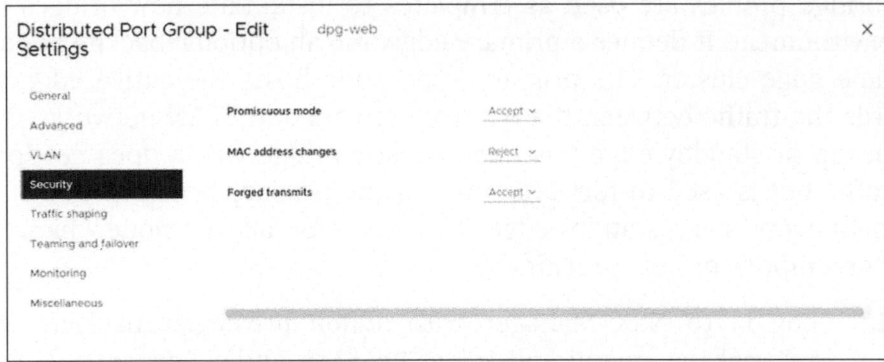

***Figure 7.5**: Configuring security policies on vSphere VDS*

Step 3: Login into ESXi host using root credentials on which NSX Edge node VM is running and run the following command:

```
esxcli system settings advanced set -o /Net/ReversePathFwdCheckPromisc
-i 1
```

Step 4: Ensure no other port groups are set with Promiscuous Mode to allow the same host to share the same set of VLANs.

Tip: If using VDS 6.6 or above, Enable **`MAC learning`** with the option allow unicast flooding on the distributed port group to avoid enabling Promiscuous Mode.

Case 3: If Edge node VM is connected to NSX Segment

Step 1: Login into NSX Manager with appropriate credentials and navigate to the **`Networking`** tab and select **`Profiles`** under the **`Segments`** menu.

Step 2: Click on **`Add Segment Profile`** and select **`MAC Discovery.`**

Step 3: Click on the checkbox to enable **`MAC Learning`** and also ensure **`Unknown Unicast Flooding`** is enabled.

Step 4: Navigate back to **`Segments`** under **`Networking,`** click on three dots against the segment to which Edge node VM is connected and select **`Edit`**.

Step 5: Expand the **`Segment Profiles`** section and then select the **`MAC Discovery profile`** created earlier from the drop-down menu.

Configure Edge Bridge Profile

Edge bridge profiles are used as templates to instantiate new bridges in the NSX environment. It defines a primary edge and an optional backup edge from the same edge cluster. The primary edge node hosts the active edge which forwards the traffic between the overlay network and VLAN network whereas the backup or standby edge hosts the backup bridge which does not forward any traffic but is used to forward traffic if the primary bridge is down. Apart from defining primary/standby edge, it also asks for failover mode which can be either preemptive or non-preemptive.

Step 1: Log in to NSX Manager with admin privileges, navigate to the **`Networking`** menu and select **`Profiles`** under **`Segments`**. *Figure* 7.6 displays Edge Bridge Profile view in NSX Manager. Currently, no bridge profile is configured hence screen is showing blank.

***Figure* 7.6**: *Edge Bridge Profile view in NSX Manager*

Step 2: Select the tab **`Edge Bridge Profiles`** and then click on **`Add Edge Bridge Profile.`** *Figure* 7.7 shows the inputs required during the creation of the Edge Bridge Profile.

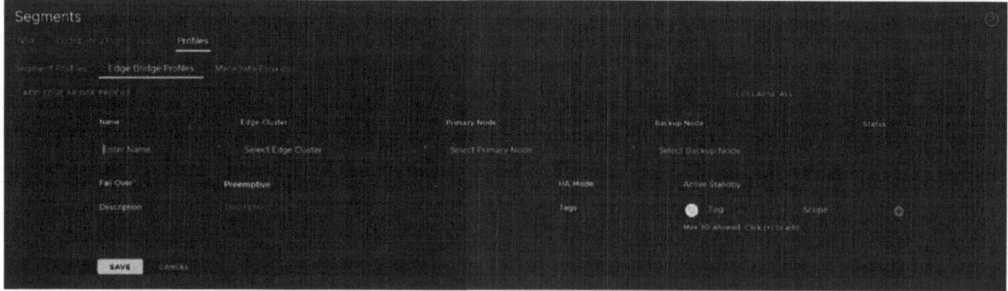

***Figure* 7.7**: *Create a new Edge Bridge Profile*

Step 3: Provide a **`name`** for the Edge bridge profile and a **`description`** (optional) of the Edge bridge profile.

Step 4: From the drop-down menu, select the appropriate **`NSX Edge cluster`**, and then select the **`primary node`** and **`backup node.`**

Step 5: Under the **`failover mode`** drop-down menu, select either **`Preemptive`** and **`Non-Preemptive`** mode. *Figure* 7.8 displays a completed view of the Edge Bridge Profile.

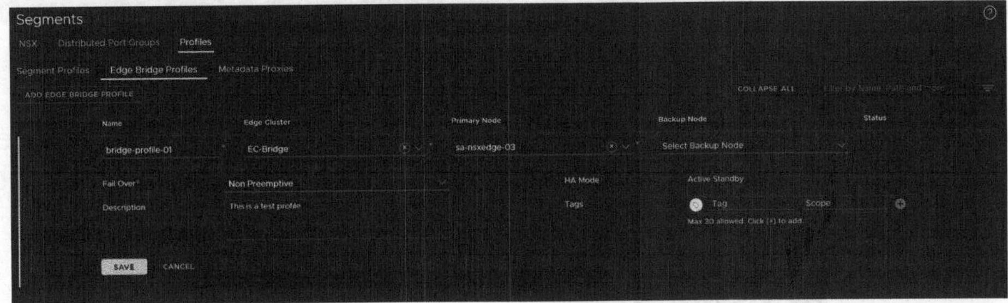

Figure 7.8: *Edge Bridge Profile with completed details*

Step 6: Click **`Save`** to create an Edge bridge profile. *Figure* 7.9 displays a successfully created Edge Bridge Profile. In order for bridging to work correctly, Edge Bridge Profile should have a success status.

Figure 7.9: *Edge Bridge Profile with a success status*

Attaching Bridge Profile to NSX Segment

As a last step, the Edge bridge profile needs to be attached to the desired NSX segment in order to extend overlay networks to the VLAN network. When an Edge bridge profile is attached to the NSX overlay segment, the VLAN ID option will become available to specify the VLAN ID of the network to bridge your segment. This step also creates one or two bridges on the edges identified in the edge bridge profile. When a bridge is configured with a single VLAN ID, a frame received on the overlay segment by the bridge gets decapsulated and forwarded on the VLAN uplink of the bridge with an added 802.1Q tag corresponding to the same VLAN ID.

Step 1: Login into NSX Manager with user credentials with admin privileges and go to **`Segments`** under the **`Networking`** menu. *Figure* 7.10 illustrates an NSX overlay segment ls-web which is getting bridged to VLAN backed network.

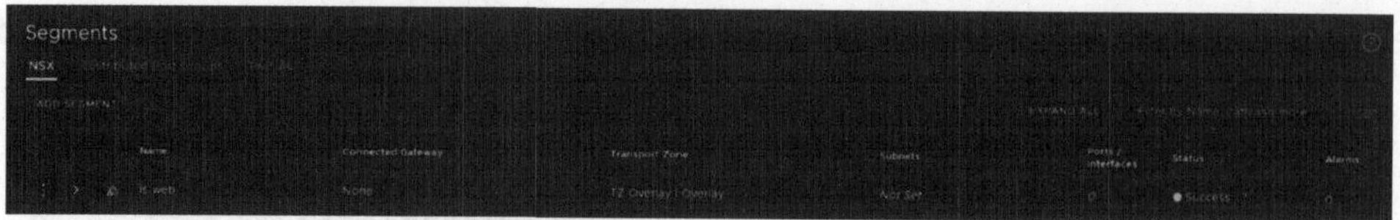

Figure 7.10*: NSX overlay segment ls-web*

Step 2: Click on the three dots icon of the desired overlay segment that needs to be bridged to VLAN-backed network and click on **`Edit`** as shown in *Figure* 7.11 for NSX segment **`ls-web`**.

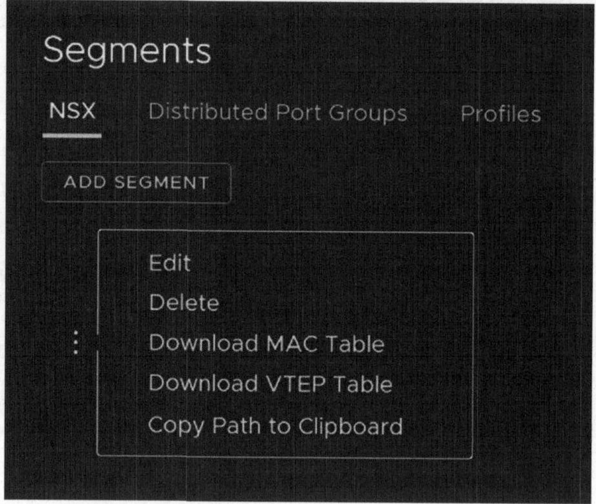

Figure 7.11*: Editing an NSX segment ls-web*

Step 3: Click on the little triangle icon (**>**) to expand **`Additional Settings`** and click on **`Set`** under the **`Edge Bridges`** field as shown in *Figure* 7.12.

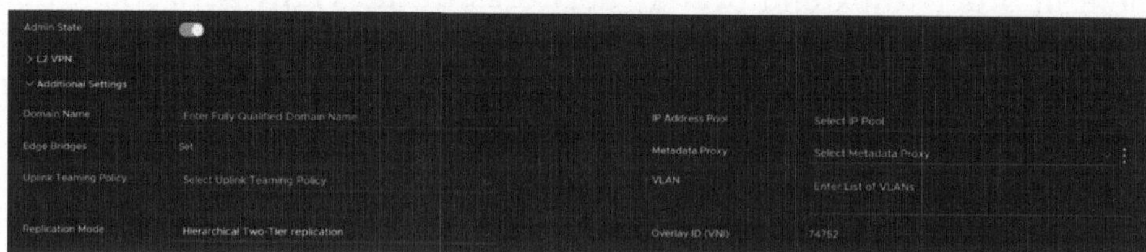

Figure 7.12*: Expanding additional details of segment ls-web*

Step 4: Click on **`Add Edge Bridge`** and select the Edge bridge profile created earlier. *Figure* 7.13 shows adding Edge Bridge Profile named **`bridge-profile-01`** created earlier to segment **`ls-web`**.

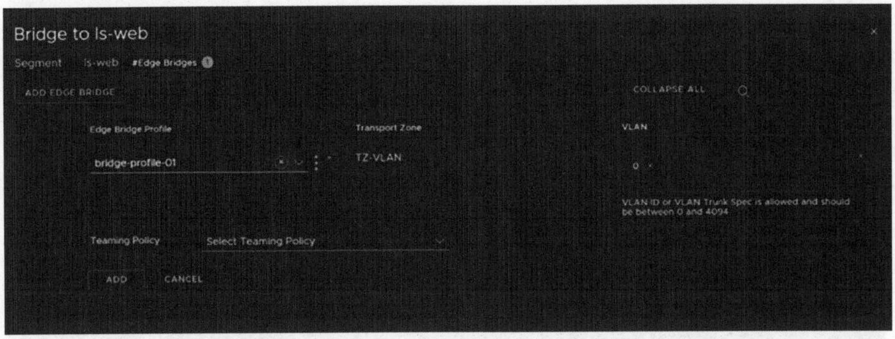

Figure 7.13: Adding an Edge Bridge Profile to segment

Step 5: Select a `VLAN transport zone` to identify the VLAN uplinks used by the bridge on Edge node VM and provide a **`VLAN ID`** or a **`VLAN ID range.`**

Step 6: Select a **teaming policy** if using named teaming policies. This is an optional field and not mandatory to provide. *Figure* 7.14 shows completed bridge details on segment `ls-web` with bridge profile attached and VLAN 0 tagged for bridging (the reason for using untagged VLAN ID is because VLAN 100 is already tagged at port group level).

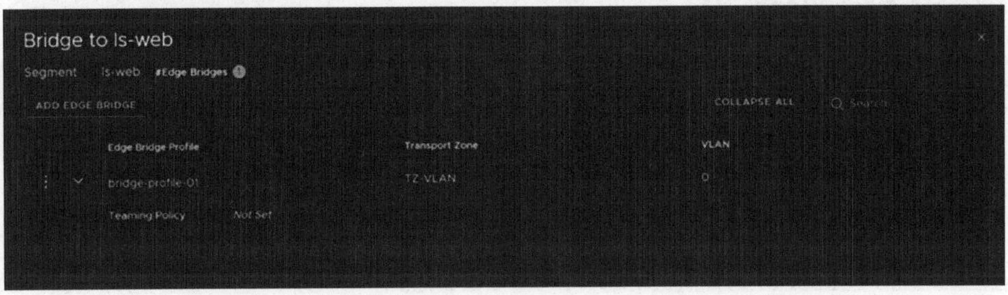

Figure 7.14: NSX Edge bridge added to segment ls-web

Step 7: Click on **`Add`** and then select **`Save`** `to` create Edge Bridge and extend the NSX overlay segment to the VLAN network.

Validate Edge Bridging

As illustrated in *Figure* 7.4, **`VM-WEB-01`** is running on overlay network ls-web configured with IP address 10.10.100.11 whereas workload **`PHY-WEB-01`** is running on VLAN-backed port group dpg-web configured with IP address 10.10.100.21. Both **`VM-WEB-01`** and **`PHY-WEB-01`** belong to the same network and they need to talk with each other on the same layer 2 domain. A bridge has been configured between overlay network ls-web and VLAN-backed port group **`dpg-web`** with help of the NSX Edge node, both VMs should be able to communicate with each other.

Figure 7.15 shows the console output of machine **`VM-WEB-01`**, trying to ping machine **`PHY-WEB-01`** and being able to reach it successfully.

```
root@VM-WEB-01 [ ~ ]# ping 10.10.100.21
PING 10.10.100.21 (10.10.100.21) 56(84) bytes of data.
64 bytes from 10.10.100.21: icmp_seq=1 ttl=64 time=1.44 ms
64 bytes from 10.10.100.21: icmp_seq=2 ttl=64 time=1.10 ms
64 bytes from 10.10.100.21: icmp_seq=3 ttl=64 time=1.01 ms
64 bytes from 10.10.100.21: icmp_seq=4 ttl=64 time=1.05 ms
^C
--- 10.10.100.21 ping statistics ---
4 packets transmitted, 4 received, 0% packet loss, time 3005ms
rtt min/avg/max/mdev = 1.011/1.149/1.440/0.170 ms
root@VM-WEB-01 [ ~ ]# _
```

Figure 7.15: *Console output of machine* VM-WEB-01

Figure 7.16 shows the console output of machine **`PHY-WEB-01`**, trying to ping machine **`VM-WEB-01`** and being able to reach it successfully.

```
root@PHY-WEB-01 [ ~ ]# ping 10.10.100.11
PING 10.10.100.11 (10.10.100.11) 56(84) bytes of data.
64 bytes from 10.10.100.11: icmp_seq=1 ttl=64 time=1.13 ms
64 bytes from 10.10.100.11: icmp_seq=2 ttl=64 time=1.06 ms
64 bytes from 10.10.100.11: icmp_seq=3 ttl=64 time=1.18 ms
64 bytes from 10.10.100.11: icmp_seq=4 ttl=64 time=1.32 ms
^C
--- 10.10.100.11 ping statistics ---
4 packets transmitted, 4 received, 0% packet loss, time 3005ms
rtt min/avg/max/mdev = 1.058/1.173/1.323/0.096 ms
root@PHY-WEB-01 [ ~ ]# _
```

Figure 7.16: *Console output of machine* PHY-WEB-01

Figure 7.17 shows the output of the NSX Edge node VM with an active bridge instantiated on it and forwarding traffic to the VLAN network.

```
sa-nsxedge-03> get bridge
Tue Mar 14 2023 UTC 19:22:09.603
Bridge Port UUID               : b3ea4cf7-d921-4f5b-83c7-2fffcfebce6b
Bridge Logical Switch UUID     : afbc91c9-a580-7371-a4e8-8fa84d7e5ede
Attached Logical Switch UUID   : 6e547e95-d04e-4f58-9490-e02e383e2d20
Attached Logical Switch Name   : ls-web
VLAN ID                        : untagged
State                          : Forwarding
Transport Zone                 : fc28fa49-831e-4da0-b9d6-84bae3b55b7e
Device                         : fp-eth1
Device State                   : Up
Rank                           : 0
HA Failover Mode               : Non-Preemptive
  State                        : Active
  Event                        : Node Up
  Time                         : 2023-03-14T19:00:05.657853
Last RARP                      : 2023-03-14 19:00:06.658
RARP Count                     : 1

sa-nsxedge-03>
```

Figure 7.17: *Verifying bridge details on NSX Edge node*

Similarly, the MAC table currently being synced on the bridge port can be viewed with the help of the command get bridge mac-sync-table. *Figure 7.18* shows the sample output of the aforementioned command in real-time where MAC address 00:05:56:93:58:e3 belongs to virtual machine **`VM-WEB-01`** connected to overlay network ls-web and MAC address 00:0c:2:38:a7:b4 belongs to workload **`PHY-WEB-01`** connected to VLAN-backed port group `dpg-web`.

```
sa-nsxedge-03> get bridge mac-sync-table
Tue Mar 14 2023 UTC 19:22:50.325
MAC-SYNC Table
MAC                  : 00:50:56:93:58:e3
TYPE                 : Local
VNI                  : 74752
Bridge Port UUID     : b3ea4cf7-d921-4f5b-83c7-2fffcfebce6b

MAC                  : 00:0c:29:38:a7:b4
TYPE                 : Local
VNI                  : 74752
Bridge Port UUID     : b3ea4cf7-d921-4f5b-83c7-2fffcfebce6b

sa-nsxedge-03>
```

Figure 7.18: *Viewing MAC table on NSX bridge in an Edge node*

Conclusion

This concludes the logical bridging in the NSX environment. In this chapter, we covered the creation of edge bridge profiles, configured edge nodes and how to extend the NSX segment to VLAN backed network with help of edge bridge profiles. We also covered different use cases of edge bridging and how it can help migrate workload from one environment to NSX with minimal downtime. This covers the layer 2 and layer 3 services provided by NSX-T in the data center.

In the next few chapters, we will cover different security features provided by NSX-T and how they can help achieve zero-trust models for applications. In the next chapter, we will see how NSX provides micro-segmentation with help of distributed firewall providing more security for east-west traffic and stopping lateral movements in the datacenter.

Key Terms

- **NSX Bridge:** A logical configuration instantiated on NSX Edge node to extend overlay segment to VLAN backed network.
- **NSX Edge node:** Edge nodes are NSX Transport Nodes which provide compute resources to host NSX services.
- **Bridge Profile:** Edge bridge profiles are used as templates to instantiate new bridges in the NSX environment.
- **Segment:** Segments are layer 2 subnets representing layer 2 broadcasting domain across transport nodes in NSX networking
- **Logical Port:** Logical port on the segment to which Bridge Endpoint is attached
- **VNI (Virtual Network Identifier):** Unique ID assigned to segments created in the NSX environment
- **TEP (Tunnel Endpoint):** IP address assigned to Transport Nodes that enables the creation of encapsulated Geneve tunnel between nodes to allow participation in overlay networking
- **VSS (vSphere Standard Switch):** Virtual switch default configured on ESXi host whose both management plane and I/O plane reside with ESXi host.
- **VDS (vSphere Distributed Switch):** Virtual switch provided by VMware whose management plane resides with the vCenter server allowing centralized management

Chapter 8
Security - Micro-segmentation

Introduction

In the last couple of chapters, we covered how NSX overlay networking can help you achieve highly flexible and easy-to-use switching/routing services in a datacenter. However, what about security? In today's highly dynamic and complex IT environments, traditional perimeter-based security measures are no longer sufficient to protect modern applications and data flowing inside a datacenter. NSX provides a plethora of security features that can help achieve zero trust security in a datacenter.

This chapter covers NSX Distributed Firewall, one of the most popular features of NSX - a security service that can help protect East-West traffic inside a datacenter and protect workloads from lateral attacks.

Structure

In this chapter, we will cover the following topics:

- Traditional Datacenter Security Challenges
- NSX Service Defined Firewall
  - Zero Trust Security – Micro-segmentation
- NSX Distributed Firewall
  - NSX DFW Architecture – ESXi
- Configuring NSX Distributed Firewall
  - NSX DFW Policy Structure

- NSX DFW Categories
- NSX DFW Applied To Field
- NSX Grouping
- Creating a Distributed Firewall Policy
- Creating a Layer 7 Context Profile
- Configuring FQDN Filtering
- Creating a Time Base Firewall Policy
- Configuring Identity Firewall

- NSX Distributed Security for VDS
    - Installing Distributed Security on VDS
- Conclusion

Traditional Datacenter Security Challenges

Traditionally, datacenter security has primarily been about the perimeter defense, that is, securing North-South traffic and assuming that East-West traffic in the datacenter is safe. However, in today's highly dynamic and complex IT environments, traditional perimeter-based security measures are no longer sufficient to protect modern applications and data. A few of the challenges with traditional perimeter defense appliances are as follows:

- **Hairpinning of Traffic:** Centrally hosted security appliances, such as a firewall or IDS/IPS appliances, require traffic to be routed through them, resulting in hairpinning of traffic, which can add to latency or poor performance in application and unnecessary use of network bandwidth.
- **Static Policies:** Traditionally, security policies are based on IP address or gateway interface, which can quickly become cumbersome to manage. It is difficult to change static security policies on the fly, especially in today's datacenter where workload rapidly scale out or scale in.
- **Macro Segmentation:** Traditional security solution provides the ability to perform very broad segmentation without an option to do either application level or micro-segmentation, which is required to protect an organization from East-West lateral attacks.
- **Inflexibility:** Another key disadvantage with traditional physical firewall appliances is their inability to scale as more applications or workloads are added. The only solution is to upgrade existing appliances or add newer appliances to accommodate increasing demand.

NSX Service Defined Firewall

We have discussed all these drawbacks of traditional perimeter-based security, but the question is how these can be controlled. Well, look no further than NSX. NSX provides a distributed scale-out internal firewall that can protect all East-West traffic across all workloads without any network changes, thereby simplifying the security deployment model. There are many security features supported by NSX, including:

- Distributed Firewall
- Gateway Firewall
- Advance Threat Protection (ATP), which includes IDS/IPS, Malware Prevention
- Network Traffic Analysis (NTA)
- Network Detection and Response (NDR)

Some of the advantages provided by NSX service-defined firewall are as follows:

- **Distributed and Granular Enforcement:** NSX provides distributed and granular enforcement of security policies down to the application level to protect workloads without the need to make any network changes on underlying devices.
- **Scalability:** Due to its distributed nature, the NSX service firewall is elastic and dynamic, which enables it to auto-scale as workloads increase or decrease.
- **Application Rule Recommendation:** The service-defined firewall automatically determines the communication patterns across all types of workloads and makes security policy recommendations based on those patterns.
- **Advanced Threat Prevention:** Apart from providing firewall capabilities, NSX also features distributed IDS/IPS services, network sandboxing, and Network traffic analysis capabilities, which the security team can leverage to protect against zero-day threats.

With these capabilities, organizations can deploy application workloads rapidly to get the speed and flexibility needed to quickly create and reconfigure virtual security zones by leveraging automation using declarative API. Another uniqueness of NSX service-defined firewall architecture is its intrinsic built right into hypervisor at the vNIC level, eliminating the need to manage additional appliances or other third-party agents and reducing administrative overhead. This allows NSX security policies to be enforced for every flow at the vNIC level in a network-agnostic manner.

Zero Trust Security - Micro-segmentation

Zero Trust security is a security model with a view of trusting nothing and verifying everything. It is not a day-one job but more of a journey to enhance enterprise security posture. This requires understanding and handling the complexity of environments and accessing the right security technology and platform to achieve a zero trust security model. This is where NSX comes in, helping with the segmentation. Segmentation is the process of dividing infrastructure into small zones, allowing granular control and inspection of network traffic between these zones. There are different types of segmentation coexisting together:

- **Zone Segmentation:** It is a general segmentation achieved by defining zones such as Production, Non-production, DMZ, Non-DMZ, and more, which is independent of segments, VLANs, or other constructs.
- **VLAN Segmentation:** As the name suggests, its IP segment-based and IP segment defines the source and destination of security policy.
- **Application Segmentation:** This defines a logical security ring around an application. Intra-application components do not have restricted traffic flows and provides more security than zone segmentation, which may have multiple applications.
- **Micro-segmentation:** This is the security model where network communication between different elements is defined as explicitly as possible. For example, a single application can consist of different components, such as a Web frontend, a middleware application, and a backend database. Network communication between these different components or tiers is restricted with security policies clearly defining what flows are allowed between different components, such as anyone would be able to access the web frontend but direct access to middleware applications and databases will be blocked. Similarly, the Web frontend can access middleware applications but access from the Web frontend to the database will be blocked.

Figure 8.1 illustrates the preceding different segmentations in an environment:

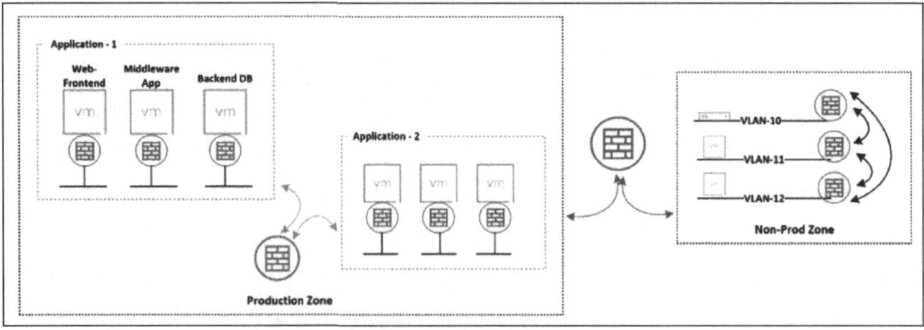

***Figure 8.1**: Security segmentation*

NSX Distributed Firewall

NSX distributed firewall (DFW) is used for network and micro-segmentation for NSX-managed virtual machines and/or physical servers. Instead of redirecting traffic to a central appliance, NSX utilizes hypervisor kernel modules on ESXi hosts for vCenter-managed virtual machines and NSX agents installed on supported Windows and Linux OS physical servers to implement firewall policies. Essentially, in NSX DFW, each network interface of workloads has a firewall attached to it, which is responsible for allowing or blocking the network traffic.

Figure 8.2 illustrates a different type of workload, including both virtual machines and physical servers, with NSX distributed firewall applied to their interfaces. This makes NSX DFW truly distributed in nature without needing to forward traffic to any central appliance:

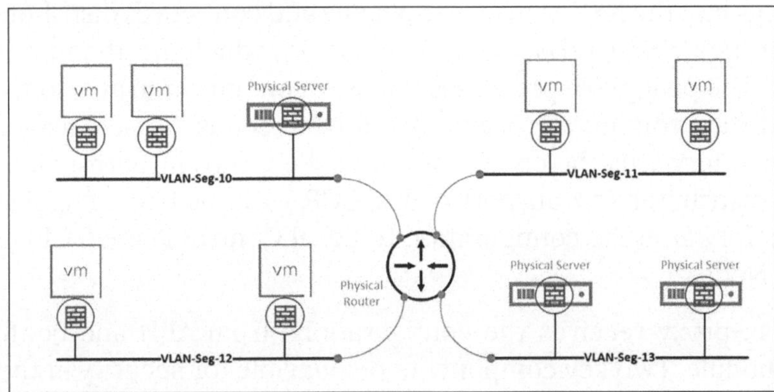

Figure 8.2: *NSX distributed firewall applied to workloads*

NSX DFW Architecture - ESXi

In previous chapters, we understand about three different planes, namely Management Plane, Control Plane, and Data Plane. NSX Distributed Firewall (DFW) is implemented in the data plane in transport nodes, making it distributed in nature without the need to forward traffic to any central appliance. It has a common communication path similar to logical network services. *Figure* 8.3 depicts the NSX distributed firewall architecture implemented in the ESXi data plane:

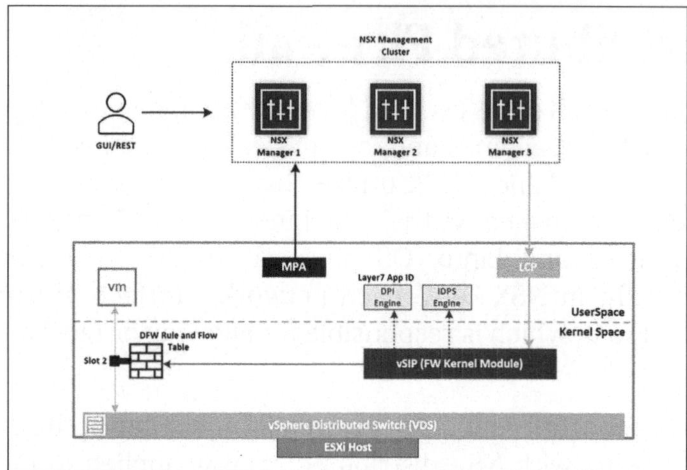

Figure 8.3: *NSX DFW Architecture for ESXi host*

The user logs into the NSX Manager appliance and configures distributed firewall policies through NSX UI (User Interface) or API, which are then pushed to the policy role. The policy role processes the user configuration and converts it into the desired state configuration, and then further sends it to a Manager role. The Manager role forwards the configuration to the Central Control Plane (CCP) to be further distributed to transport nodes. CCP, with the help of Appliance Proxy Hub (APH), forwards the configuration to Local Control Plane (LCP) running on Transport Nodes.

In ESXi, nsx-proxy receives the configurations from APH and configures the datapath module. Two key components responsible for security in the datapath module are VMware Deep Packet Inspection Engine (VDPI) and VMware Internetworking Services Insertion Protocol (VSIP). VDPI is responsible for Layer 7 packet inspection, whereas VSIP receives the context data and applies firewall rules on vNIC. Also, VSIP maintains statistics such as flows, hit counts, and more, which are forwarded by nsx-proxy service back to the NSX Manager with the help of the stats exporter.

Distributed firewall rule processing is taken care of with the help of two tables, namely the rule table and the connection table. These tables are maintained by vmware-sfw, which is a software construct where firewall rules are stored and enforced. Whenever a DFW rule is configured, its entry is created in the rule table, and the connection table stores the previously allowed flows. Now, when a packet is received by DFW, it is looked upon in the connection table if the entry of connection exists in the connection table. If an entry is found in the connection table, then a packet is allowed. However, if a connection entry does not exist in the connection table, then the packet is matched against the rule table. If the packet is allowed and the traffic type is stateful, then a corresponding connection entry is created in the connection table, and subsequent packets for the same connection are allowed directly from the connection table. However, if the traffic type is stateless, then it is always matched against the rule table.

Configuring NSX Distributed Firewall

While it is possible to configure NSX firewall rules in the same way that legacy or traditional firewall policies are configured, it is best to start fresh and configure NSX firewall policies from the ground up while learning from past challenges. It is possible to recreate legacy firewall policies (from physical appliances) in the NSX environment, but it should be done with translations and optimizations provided by NSX. One may ask what are those optimizations that you speak of? Well, you have come to the right place. Before we deep dive into configuring distributed firewall policies in the NSX environment, let's talk about certain key elements of an NSX distributed firewall.

NSX DFW Policy Structure

Figure 8.4 shows a high-level depiction of NSX distributed firewall policy structure with some key elements, such as Security Policy, Rule, Service, Context Profile, and Groups:

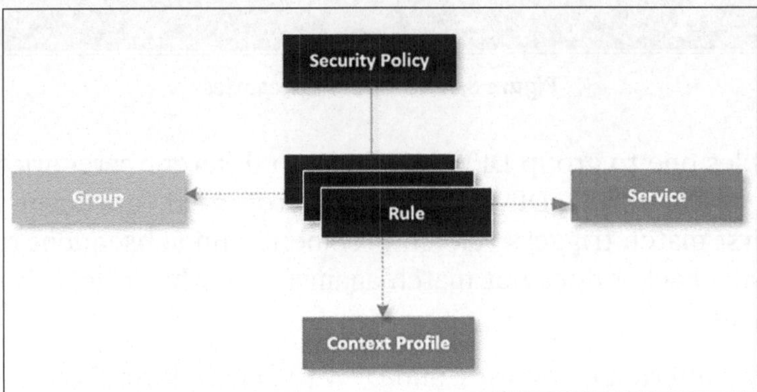

Figure 8.4: *NSX DFW policy structure*

- **Security Policy:** When we talk about NSX distributed firewall, the first thing we talk about is Policies. NSX DFW Security Policy is a group of firewall rules and service configurations that are used to organize NSX DFW rules. Before creating a distributed firewall rule, a security policy needs to be created.

- **Firewall Rule:** The firewall rule is a 5-tuple-based configuration, which based on the instruction given in different fields, such as Source, Destination, Service or Action, and more, calculates whether a packet should be allowed or blocked.
- **Service:** Services are a logical construct combination of port and protocol, defined in a firewall rule to specify the type of traffic that is allowed or blocked.
- **Context Profile:** To enable Layer 7 inspection, context profiles are applied in a firewall rule.
- **Group:** A group is a logical construct that pools multiple objects together, such as Virtual Machine, IP Sets, Active Directory groups, and more, either statically or dynamically. This is covered in more detail in the later section "NSX *Grouping*".

NSX DFW Categories

When you first log in to NSX Manager UI, you will see **`Security`** as a menu, and within it, you will find **`Distributed Firewall`**. Within the Distributed Firewall menu, the first thing you will notice is **`Category-Specific Rules`**. *Figure* 8.5 shows a sample screenshot of DFW categories from NSX UI:

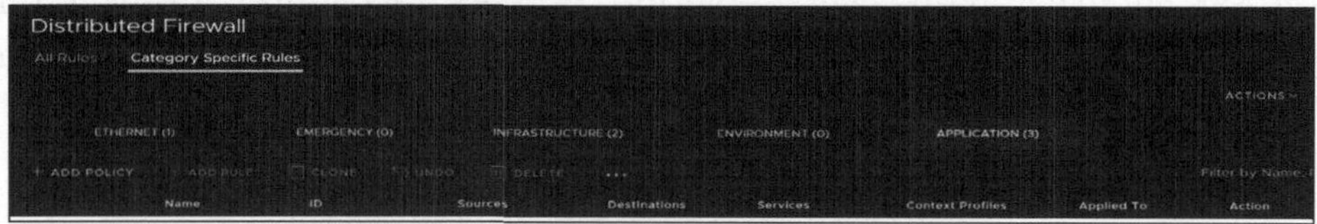

***Figure* 8.5**: *NSX DFW Categories*

NSX UI enables one to group DFW policies into different categories, which are laid out left to right. NSX DFW policies are processed top-down and left-to-right. The first match triggers rule enforcement, and subsequent rules are not checked. If any packet does not match against any other rule, it is matched by the default rule.

There are five different categories, and DFW policies within them are processed from top-down and left-to-right. In order of policy processing, different categories are listed as follows:

- **`Ethernet`:** This category holds Layer 2 rules based on MAC addresses.
- **`Emergency`:** This category is specifically created to put any emergency rules that are processed first before any other rules. Examples could include

isolating or blocking traffic to/from specific sources/destinations to limit the spread of malware. Another example could be troubleshooting.

- `Infrastructure`: This category is used to define rules for shared services such as AD, DNS, NTP, Backup, Patching services, Management access, and more.
- `Environment`: These are the rules between zones. Examples include Prod to Non-Prod, DMZ to Non-DMZ, and more.
- `Application`: These are the most granular rules that are created between different applications, within application tiers, or for micro-services. These rules help in achieving zero trust security within an organization.

NSX DFW Applied To Field

One of the most important optimizations in NSX DFW policies is the use of the Applied To field. You might ask about the purpose of the Applied To field and why it's so important. Well, this is the field that governs which vNICs are going to receive the firewall rules in question. By default, the Applied To field is set to DFW, which means every vNIC is going to receive every rule. So, how is this a problem? Imagine, there are 1000 virtual machines running in an environment with NSX DFW enabled. You configure 10 rules for traffic control between VM A and VM B. Now, those 10 rules will be applied to all 1000 VMs, quickly making a count of total firewall rules to 10,000, even if the other 998 VMs do not need those rules. This can quickly become an issue in environments with a large number of rules. However, with the help of the Applied To field, one can govern which vNICs will receive the desired rules and which do not.

A few best practices while configuring the Applied To field are as follows:

- If the source is Any and external to the NSX environment, then apply the rule to destinations only.
- If the source is Any and can include sources from the NSX environment, then apply the rule to everything by setting the Applied To field to DFW.
- If the source and destination are known and within the NSX environment, then apply the rule to both the source and destination.

Another key thing while configuring the Applied To field is that one can set Applied To at both the Policy level and Rule level. The following rules govern the precedence order in which the Applied To field is honored:

- If the Applied To field is set to default (DFW) on a Policy level and the Applied To field is set to default (DFW) on a Rule level, then all rules are pushed to everyone.

- If the Applied To field is set to a specific group on the Policy level and the Applied To field is set to default (DFW) on the Rule level, then all rules are pushed to the group specified at the Policy level.
- If the Applied To field is set to default (DFW) on the Policy level and the Applied To field is set to a specific group on the Rule level, then rules are pushed to specific groups as per Rule specification.
- If the Applied To field is set to a specific group on the Policy level and the Applied To field is also set to specific groups on the Rule level, then the Policy level Applied To will override the Rule level Applied To groups.

Note: Groups consisting of only IP addresses, MAC Addresses, or Active Directory groups should not be used in the Applied To field. If used, the rule/policy will be ignored and not be applied to any of the workloads, as that group doesn't have any segment-port members.

NSX Grouping

NSX groups are a collection of different objects that can be defined either statically or dynamically and can be used as either source or destination in firewall rules. Different members who can be a part of NSX groups are as follows:

- **Groups:** Other NSX groups can be members of one NSX group to create nested groups. It is generally advisable not to go more than three layers deep in nested groups, although it is supported in the NSX environment. This advised is for better manageability, resource optimization, avoiding unintentional policy results, and easier troubleshooting.
- NSX Segments
- Segment Ports
- Distributed Port Groups
- VIFs
- Virtual Machines
- Physical Servers
- Cloud Native Service Instances

Apart from these static members, dynamic membership of a group can be defined on different criteria, such as Tags, Machine Name, OS Name, or Computer Name.

NSX Tags

Tags in an NSX environment are labels that can be applied to different NSX objects, which helps quickly search or filter NSX objects or use them to define the dynamic criteria of a group. There are two attributes for each tag as follows:

- **Tag Name**: This is a required value and must be unique. It is case-sensitive. In a key-value pair, it can be viewed as a value.
- **Scope**: This is an optional attribute and is analogous to the key in a key-value pair.

An example of a Tag Name and Scope: in an NSX environment, it is required to label all database virtual machines based on their type of database. So, here, the Scope could be **Database**, and the Tag Name could be different values of the database, such as **MSSQL**, **Oracle**, **MySQL**, and more.

Creating an NSX Group

Perform the following steps to create an NSX group:

Step 1: Log in to NSX Manager with admin privileges and navigate to **`Inventory`**. Click **`Groups`** in the left panel menu.

Step 2: Click **`Add Group`**, which will ask for a group name. Provide an appropriate name and then click **`Set`** to add members.

Step 3: In the **`Set Members`** dialogue box, select the Group Type:

a. **`Generic`**: This is the default selection while adding members to a group. A generic group can have dynamic membership criteria, static members, IP addresses, or Active Directory groups.

b. **`IP Addresses Only`**: If this option is selected, then the group will only contain IP addresses (IPv4 or IPv6).

c. **`Antrea`**: This group type is only available if Antrea container clusters are registered with NSX Manager.

Step 4: If **`Group Type`** is selected as **`Generic`**, then add members based on **`Membership Criteria`**, **`Members`** (Static), **`IP/Mac Addresses`**, or **`AD Groups`**:

a. **`Membership Criteria`**: Click **`Add Criterion`** to add one or more conditions to dynamically add members to the group. *Figure* 8.6 shows the use of a condition to add any virtual machine whose name starts with web to be added to the group:

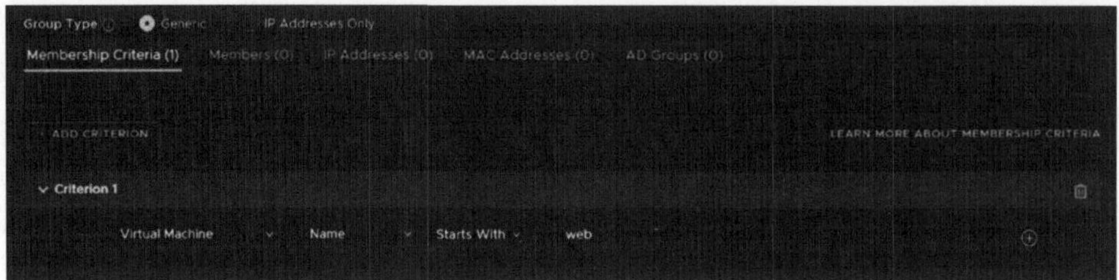

Figure 8.6: Setting Membership Criteria in NSX Group

b. **Members:** Click **`Members`** if group members need to be defined statically. Different types of members that can be added as members of the group are shown in *Figure* 8.7:

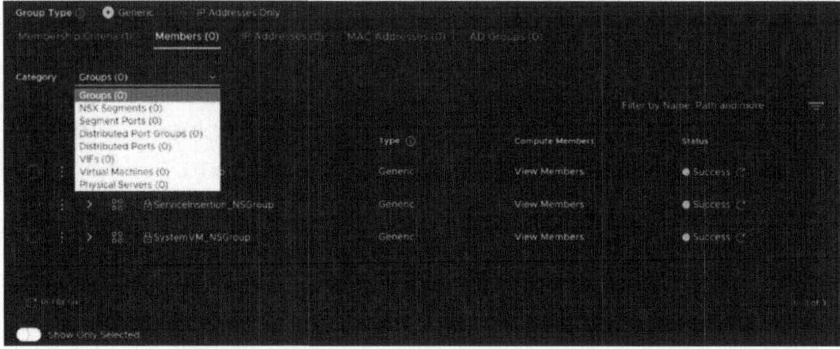

Figure 8.7: Static members types in NSX Group

c. **`IP Addresses`:** Click **`IP Addresses`** to add IP and MAC addresses as group members. IP Addresses can be imported from TXT or CSV files as well.

d. **`AD Group`:** Click **`AD Groups`** to add Active Directory groups. These are used for Identity firewall rules.

Step 5: Provide a **`Description`** and **`Tag`** to identify the group and click **`Apply`** to create the group.

Creating a Distributed Firewall Policy

We have gone through all the components of a distributed firewall. Now is the time to create a distributed firewall policy and start protecting workloads. There are different options to configure, which make a distributed firewall policy different from one another, and each has its own use case, such as Identity Firewall, time base firewall, or Layer 7 context firewall. All of these options are covered in subsequent sections going from the normal 5-tuple rule to more advanced Identity firewall rules. In this section, we will cover how to create a simple distributed firewall rule. Here are the steps:

Step 1: Log in to NSX Manager with admin privileges. Navigate to **`Security`** and click **`Distributed Firewall`** from the left navigation panel.

Step 2: Click **`Actions`** and select **`Exclusion List`**. NSX has two types of exclusion lists: System excluded VM and User excluded VMs. Under **`User Excluded Groups`**, click **`Add Group`** to add an NSX group containing virtual machines to be excluded from the distributed firewall. This will ensure no distributed firewall policies are applied to virtual machines added under the Exclusion List. Click **`Save`** to commit the exclusion list. *Figure* 8.8 illustrates a group with the name User-Excluded-VMs being added to the DFW Exclusion List:

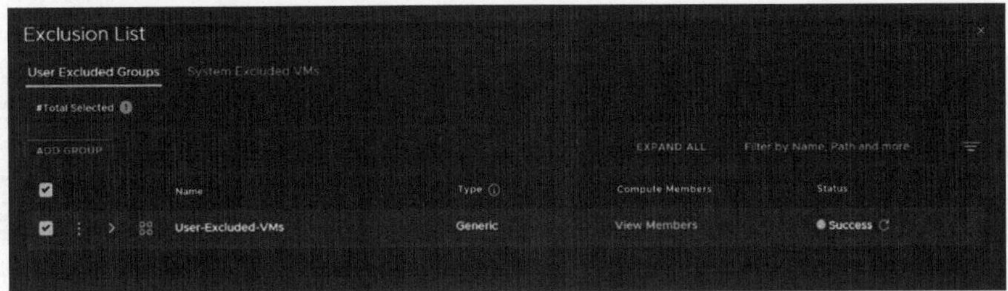

Figure 8.8: DFW Exclusion List

Step 3: Under **`Actions,`** there is an option to **`Export FW Configuration`**, which exports all the firewall rules published in the distributed firewall. However, an important point is that it does not export group definitions used in a firewall rule. *Figure* 8.9 shows the **`Export Firewall Configuration`** window in action:

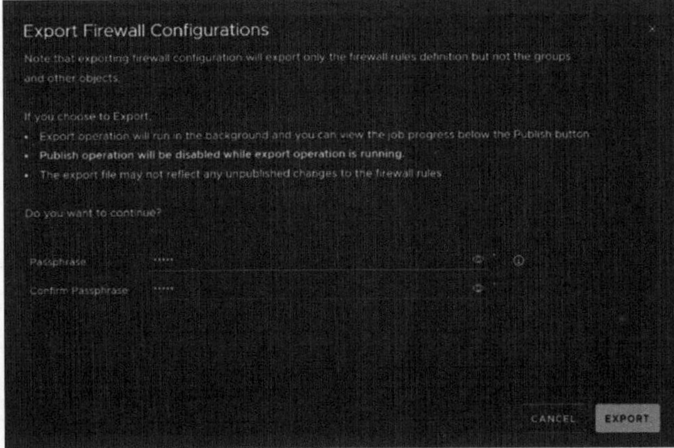

Figure 8.9: Export DFW Configuration

Step 4: Ensure that **`Category Specific Rules`** is selected and click on the desired category under which to configure a firewall policy. The **`Add Rule`** option will be greyed out unless a firewall policy is selected. *Figure* 8.10 illustrates that an Add Rule is greyed out, and the only option highlighted is Add Policy:

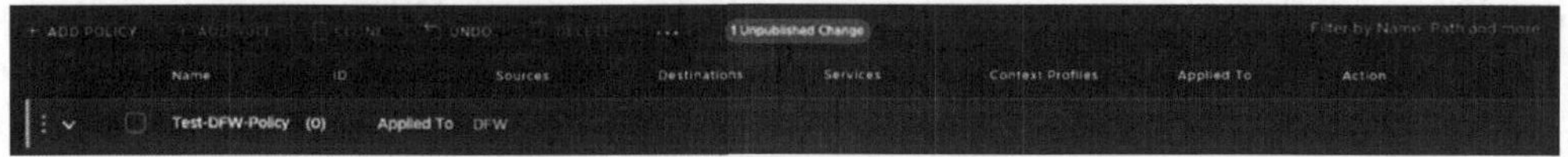

***Figure* 8.10**: NSX DFW *Categories*

Step 5: Click **`Add Policy.`** This will create a new section above the existing policy. It can be dragged up and down to move its position between different policies. Click the **`Name`** field and edit it to a descriptive meaningful name.

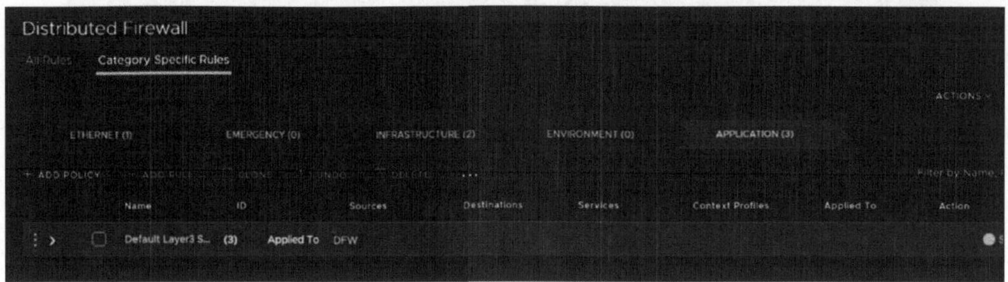

***Figure* 8.11**: *Adding a policy in* NSX DFW

Step 6: Click the gear icon at the far right on policy to access policy settings:

a. **`TCP Strict:`** Move the slider to enable or disable TCP strict mode.

b. **`Stateful:`** Enable or disable the stateful nature of the distributed firewall.

c. **`Locked:`** Lock the policy to prevent multiple users from editing the same section.

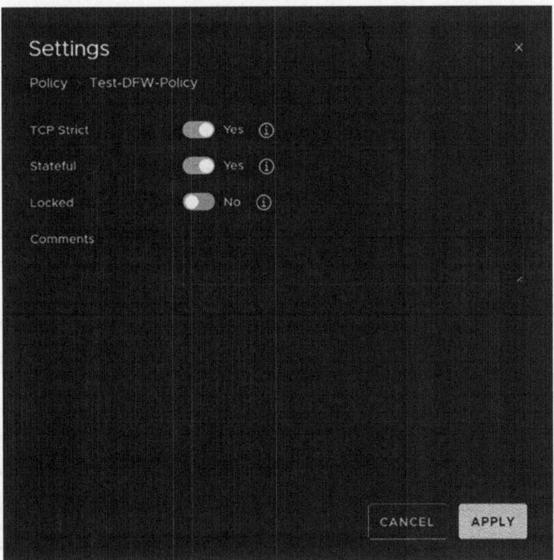

***Figure 8.12**: NSX DFW Policy Settings*

Step 7: Click the checkbox against policy and the **`Add Rule`** option will be highlighted. Click **`Add Rule`** to add a new firewall rule under Policy. Click the **`Name`** field to change the name of the rule to a more meaningful name.

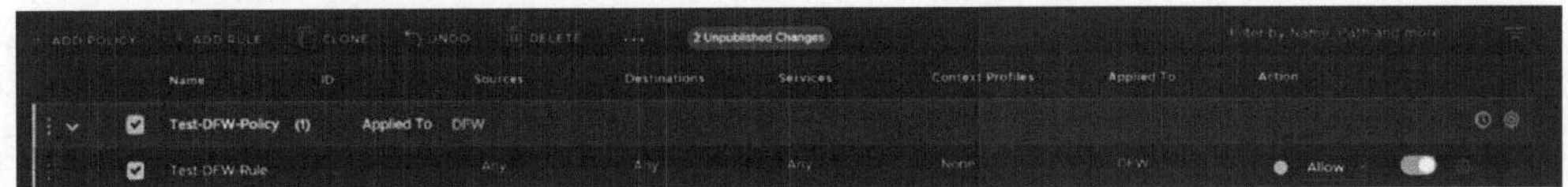

***Figure 8.13**: Adding a rule in NSX DFW*

Step 8: There are a few more fields to be configured to make the rule more effective and to avoid any unintentional behavior:

a. **`Sources:`** Click the Pencil icon to edit the sources field. The default option is any, which can be replaced with an NSX group or IP address.

b. **`Destinations:`** Click the Pencil icon to edit the sources field. The default option is any, which can be replaced with NSX group or IP address.

c. **`Services:`** Specify the ports and protocols to be allowed or disallowed between source and destination.

d. **`Applied To:`** Default is DFW, but as discussed earlier, it can be made more specific to avoid firewall rule sprawl in the

NSX environment. It can be applied at both the Policy level and Rule level.

e. **`Action:`** Specify if the traffic is to be allowed, rejected, or dropped entirely. If the Environment category is selected, then there is a fourth option available **`Jump To`**, which redirects rule processing to the Application category.

Figure 8.14 shows a test rule with the name Test-DFW-Rule, which blocks ICMP communication from member of group SG-Source-VMs to member of group SG-Destination-VMs:

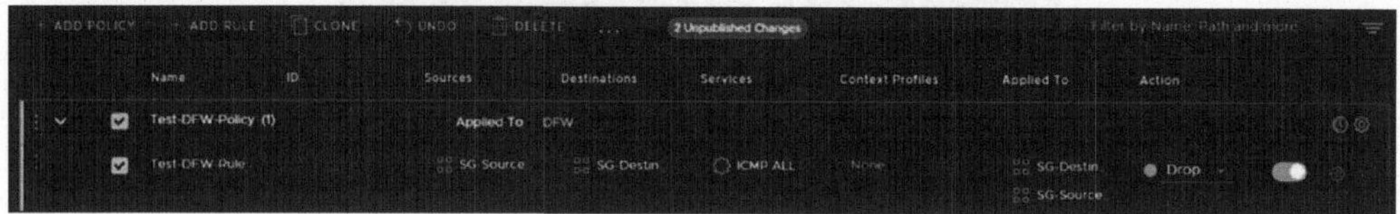

***Figure 8.14**: Sample NSX DFW Rule*

Step 9: Click the gear icon after the green slider to access a few settings, which are illustrated in *Figure* 8.15:

a. **`Logging:`** Move the slider to enable or disable rule logging. Logs are stored locally on ESXi host at location **`/var/log/`** in a file named **`dfwpktlogs.log`**. Syslog can be configured on the ESXi host to forward these logs to the central syslog location.

b. **`Direction:`** Specify the rule direction to be more specific, that is, in, out, or in-out.

c. **`IP Protocol:`** Specify whether the rule applies to a specific IP protocol or both.

d. **`Log Label:`** This option is helpful to identify rules in logs with the use of the provided label.

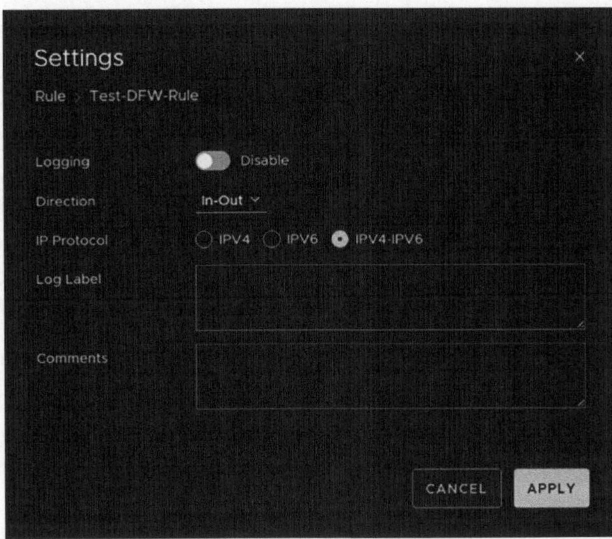

***Figure 8.15**: NSX DFW Firewall rule settings*

Step 10: Currently, the firewall policy is in a Draft state and changes haven't been committed yet. Click **`Revert`** to discard any unpublished changes or click **`Publish`** to commit changes and push the changes to the data plane.

Step 11: After changes are pushed successfully, the firewall policy status is changed to **`Success`**, as shown in *Figure 8.16*:

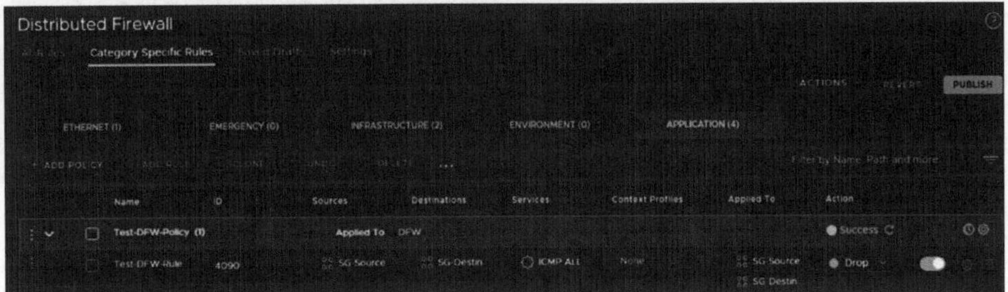

***Figure 8.16**: NSX DFW security policy post Publish*

Creating a Layer 7 Context Profile

The Layer 7 context profile is used to enable Layer 7 inspection of traffic. Layer 7 context profile consists of one or more App IDs and their sub-attributes. Distributed firewall supports including FQDN or URL as part of context profile to enable FQDN whitelisting and blacklisting. If a packet is matched against a rule specifying a Layer 7 context profile, then the packet is redirected to the vDPI engine. When a packet enters the distributed firewall, it is first matched against a flow table or connection table based on a 5-tuple. If the packet does not matched against the flow table, then it is matched against the rule table based on a 5-tuple, and an entry is created in the flow table. If the packet is matched against a rule with Layer 7 context profile, then the flow table status is marked as DPI In Progress. The packet is then pushed to the vDPI engine, which determines the App ID. Once the App ID is determined by the vDPI engine, it forwards the attributes to be inserted in the context table for this particular flow. The previously set flag of DPI In Progress flag is removed from the flow table, and the packet is re-evaluated against all rules that match the App ID. Once a rule is matched and action is taken to either allow or block the traffic, its entry is created in the flow table for subsequent packets. To enable Layer 7 inspection of traffic, a context profile needs to be created first in NSX Manager.

Step 1: Log in to NSX Manager with admin privileges. Navigate to `Inventory` and click `Profiles` in the left navigation panel, as illustrated in *Figure* 8.17:

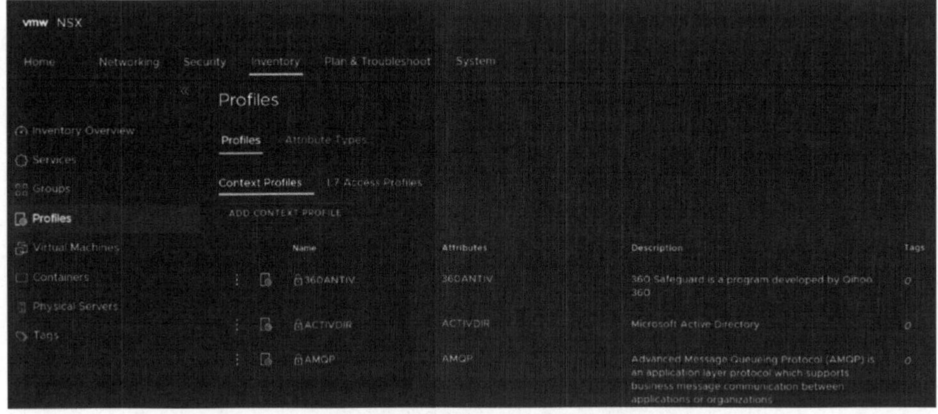

***Figure 8.17**: NSX Context Profiles*

Step 2: There are multiple predefined Context Profiles already present, which can be used in distributed firewall rules or one can create a custom profile as per requirements. Click `Add Context Profile` and provide an appropriate name. *Figure* 8.18 shows a context profile with the name CP-DFW-TLS-v1:

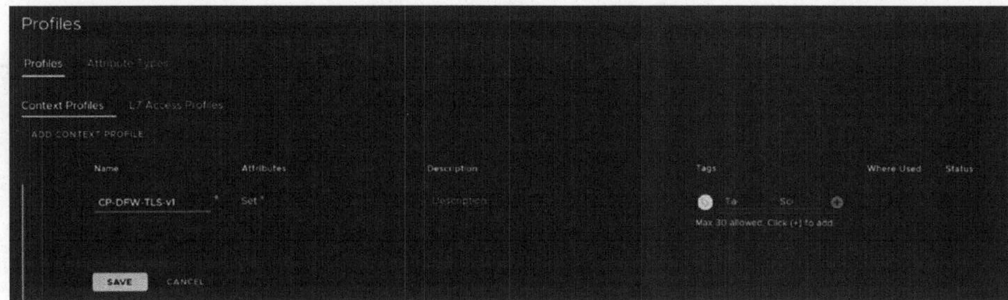

***Figure 8.18**: Adding a new context profile*

Step 3: Click **`Set`** to open a new window for **`Set Attributes.`** Click **`Add Attribute`** and select the desired attribute that needs to be added to the context profile. These options are illustrated in *Figure* 8.19:

a. **`App ID:`** Advance App IDs to be used in firewall rules.

b. **`Custom URL:`** Add a partial or full domain/URL name with special characters.

c. **`Domain (FQDN) Name:`** Add a Fully Qualified Domain Name URL or partial regex with * at the beginning.

d. **`URL Category:`** Select different URL categories to whitelist or blacklist.

e. **`URL Reputation:`** Select different risk values of the URL.

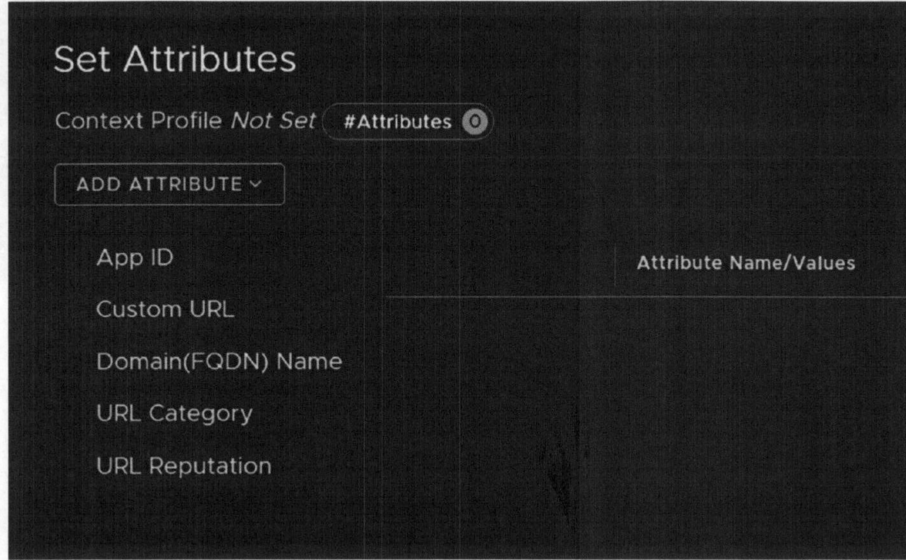

***Figure 8.19**: Different attribute options available in context profile*

In this example, we are trying to set up a context profile for TLS versions 1.0 and 1.1. *Figure* 8.20 shows the Attribute type selected as **`App ID`** with the **`Attribute Name`** as **`SSL`**:

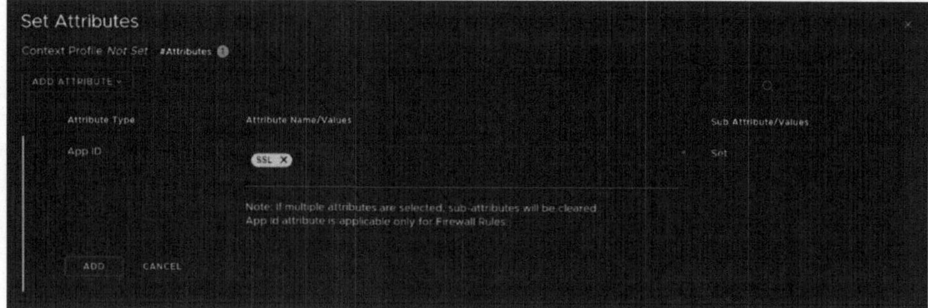

***Figure* 8.20**: *Sample context profile with attribute name* SSL

Step 4: Click **`Set`** under **`Sub Attribute/Values`** if required. Continuing with the previous example, in *Figure* 8.21, a new window named **`Set Sub Attributes`** is illustrated. This window opens when clicking **`Set`**, and post clicking **`Add Sub Attribute`**, it provides the option to select TLS Version, where TLS versions 1.0 and 1.1 have been selected. Click **`Add`** and then click **`Apply`** to save changes:

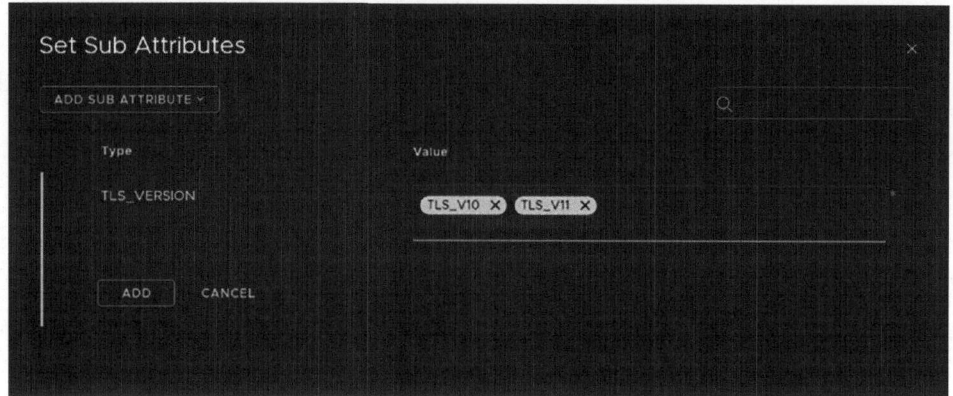

***Figure* 8.21**: *Adding sub-attribute in context profile*

Step 5: Click **`Add`** and then click **`Apply`** to save Attributes values. Again, click **`Save`** to successfully create a Context Profile.

***Figure 8.22**: Newly created NSX Context Profile*

Step 6: This context profile can now be used in DFW firewall policy to enable Layer 7 inspection. Navigate to **`Security`** and click **`Distributed Firewall.`** Either create a new rule or modify an existing rule, and click the Pencil icon under the context profile to add the newly created profile. *Figure* 8.23 shows a firewall rule with the name Layer7-Test, which states that any traffic using TLSv1 or TLSv1.1 for SSL originating from source SG-Source-VMs to destination SG-Destination-VMs will be blocked by the firewall:

***Figure 8.23**: NSX DFW rule with Layer 7 context profile*

Step 7: Click **`Publish`** to commit changes and push configuration to transport nodes.

***Figure 8.24**: Publishing changes to NSX DFW*

This concludes Layer 7 distributed firewall rule creation in an NSX environment.

Configuring FQDN Filtering

FQDN filtering is creating a distributed firewall rule that filters specific domains to whitelist or blacklist FQDN. The way it works is that NSX snoops DNS responses coming from DNS servers to virtual machines to map DNS names to IP addresses. For NSX to snoop DNS responses, a Layer 7 DNS rule must be created before configuring the FQDN filtering rule.

Step 1: Log in to NSX Manager UI with admin privileges. Navigate to **Security** and click **Distributed Firewall** from the left navigation panel. Click **Infrastructure** category.

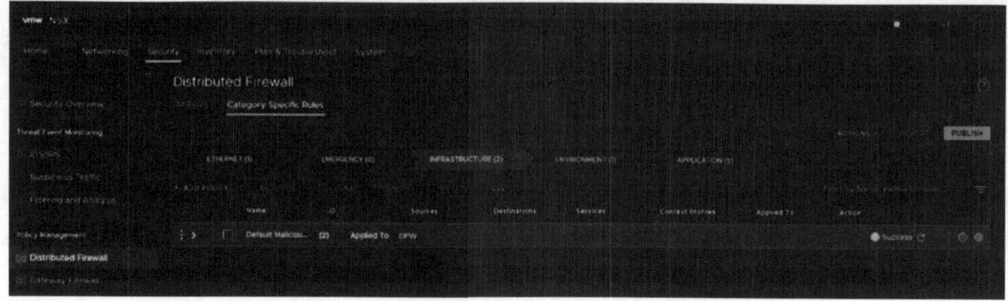

Figure 8.25: *NSX DFW Infrastructure Category*

Step 2: Add a new policy or select an existing policy to add a new rule. Click **Add Rule** to create a new firewall rule. Give it an appropriate name for easier management.

Figure 8.26: *A DNS firewall rule for FQDN filtering*

Step 3: Configure the DNS Layer 7 Rule, as illustrated in *Figure* 8.27:

a. **Sources:** Any

b. **Destination:** Any

c. **Services:** Click the Pencil icon and search for dns in the Set Services Window. Select both DNS-TCP and **Action** DNS-UDP services. Click **Apply** to set the required services.

d. **Context Profile:** Click the Pencil icon and search for dns in the **Set Context** Profile Window. Select predefined context profile DNS. Click **Apply** to set the required context profile.

e. **Applied To:** Set is appropriate to either DFW or NSX group.

f. It should be set to **Allow.**

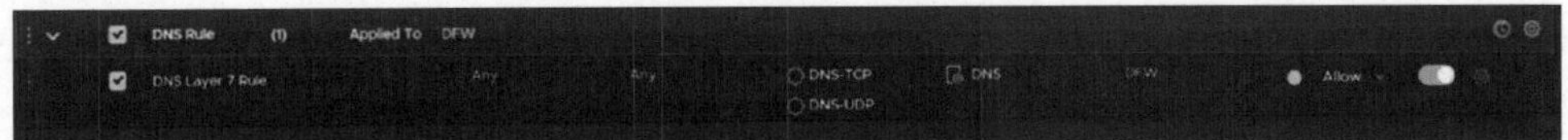

***Figure 8.27**: Configured DNS firewall rule for FQDN filtering*

Step 4: Click **`Publish`** to commit changes and push configuration to transport nodes.

Step 5: Once the DNS rule has been created, the next rule to set up is the FQDN Filtering rule. This example uses the Environment category to create this rule, but other categories can also be used for FQDN filtering. Click **`Environment`** Category, add a new policy, or select an existing policy to add a new rule. Click **`Add Rule`** to create a new firewall rule, and give it a meaningful name, such as FQDN Filtering Rule.

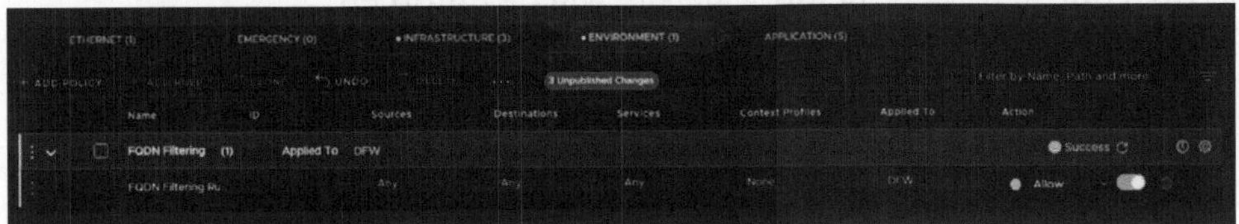

***Figure 8.28**: A new rule for FQDN filtering*

Step 6: Configure the FQDN Filtering Rule, as shown in *Figure* 8.29:

a. **`Services:`** Set the desired services such as HTTP and HTTPS for web traffic.

b. **`Context Profile:`** Click the Pencil icon to set the desired context profile. If the profile has not been created earlier, then click **`Add Context Profile`**, provide a name, and click **`Set`** to add an attribute with FQDN. Click **`Apply`** to add the desired context profile.

c. **Applied To:** Set is appropriate to either DFW or NSX group.

d. **Action:** Set the action to **`Drop/Reject`** to block the traffic or **`Allow`** to allow the traffic.

***Figure 8.29**: Configured firewall rule for FQDN filtering*

Step 7: Click **`Publish`** to commit changes and enable the FQDN filtering rule in the NSX environment.

Creating a Time Base Firewall Policy

NSX allows an additional option to configure a time base firewall policy in the distributed firewall. This ensures that the rule is only enforced during the time span configured on the firewall policy, and outside the configured time span, it is automatically deactivated. To enable time base firewall policy, NTP service must be running on each and every transport node, and the time should be synchronized. Navigate to any firewall policy within NSX DFW and click **`small clock icon`** on the far right, just beside the gear icon. This opens a new Time Window, click **`Add New Time Window`** to set a new time window during which the rule will be enforced. *Figure* 8.30 shows the Time Window in action to set up the time span during which the firewall rule will be enforced.

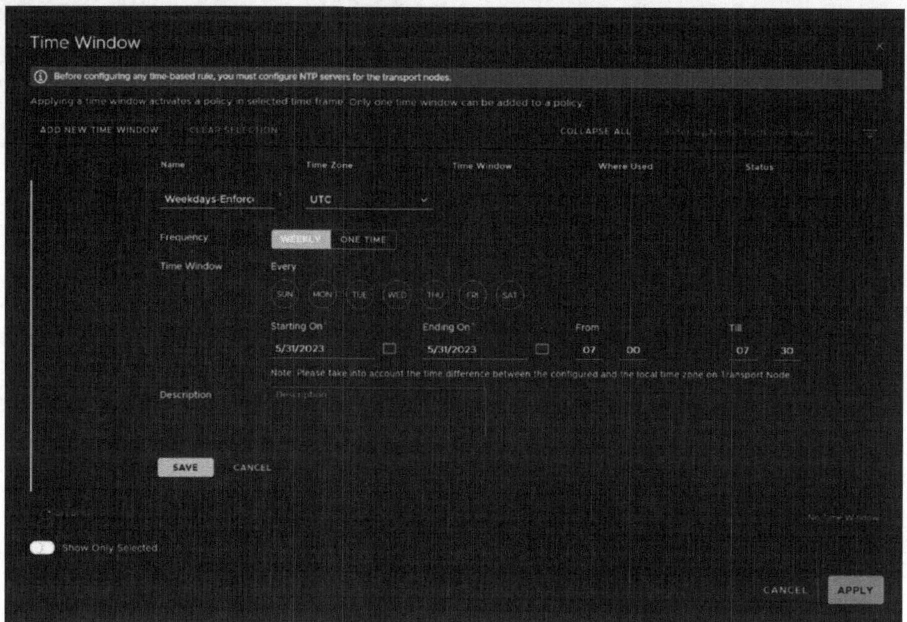

Figure 8.30: *Time Window in NSX DFW*

Configuring Identity Firewall

Identity firewall (IDFW) allows the creation of firewall rules based on user identity. Instead of using a virtual machine or IP set as a source, the security administrator can configure the Active Directory group as a source for an identity firewall rule, which enables the security administrator to control access to the same destinations based on different user groups. For example, there are HR and Finance users who can connect to the same RDSH server and have access to different applications from that server.

For IDFW to work, it must know about the desktop on which the user logs in to apply firewall rules, and there are two different methods supported by NSX for logon detection as follows:

- **Guest Introspection**: It uses a guest agent installed inside the virtual machine to forward the logon event generated to NSX Manager.
- **Event Log Scrapping**: This option is used for physical devices where Active Directory log events are forwarded to the NSX Manager. If both Guest Introspection and Event log scrapping is enabled, then Guest Introspection will take precedence.

As of version NSX 4.x, IDFW is supported on the following operating systems listed in *Table* 8.1 and AD Domain Controllers:

Guest Operating Systems	Enforcement Type
Windows 8	Desktop - supports desktop users use case
Windows 10	Desktop - supports desktop users use case
Windows 2012	Server - supports server users use case
Windows 2012R2	Server - supports server users use case
Windows 2016	Server - supports server users use case
Windows 2019	Server - supports server users use case
Windows 2012R2	RDSH - supports Remote Desktop Session Host
Windows 2016	RDSH - supports Remote Desktop Session Host
Windows 2019	RDSH - supports Remote Desktop Session Host

Table 8.1: *Supported Guest OS in NSX IDFW*

- Active Directory Domain Controllers:
  - Windows Server 2012
  - Windows Server 2012R2
  - Windows Server 2016
  - Windows Server 2019

Note: IDFW processes the user identity at the source only in firewall rules. Identity-based groups cannot be used as the destination in firewall rules.

To configure IDFW firewall rules, the following is the high-level workflow, which has been covered in detail later on:

- Ensure NSX File Introspection driver and NSX Network Introspection drivers are installed on destination virtual machines.
- Configure Active Directory for Identity Firewall in NSX Manager and optionally configure event log scrapping.
- Enable Identity Firewall on distributed firewall and gateway firewall.
- Configure NSX group with members as Active Directory Groups.
- Create a distributed firewall rule with AD Group members as the source and target virtual machines as destinations, with the Applied To field set to the destination group.

Let us now take a closer look at the configuration inside the NSX environment for IDFW:

Step 1: Log in to NSX Manager with admin privileges. Navigate to **`System`** and click **`Identity Firewall AD`** in the left navigation panel, as depicted in *Figure* 8.31. This is required to sync AD groups with NSX Manager for identity firewall:

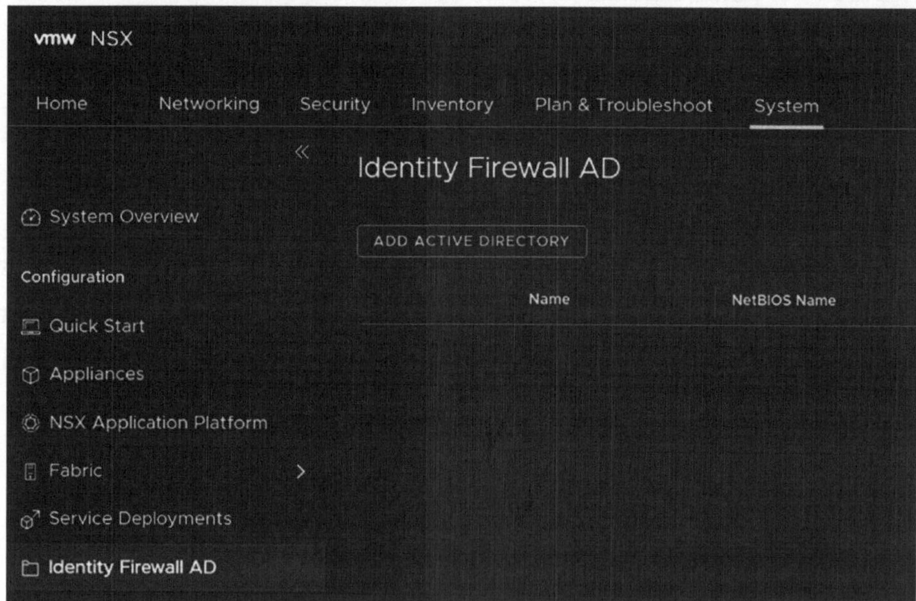

Figure 8.31: *Identity Firewall AD Configuration*

Step 2: Click **`Add Active Directory`** to add a domain. Provide the following inputs, as shown in *Figure* 8.32:

a. **`Domain FQDN`:** Enter the FQDN URL of the AD domain, for example, lab.local.

b. **`NetBIOS Name`:** Enter the short name of the AD domain, for example, LAB.

c. **`Base Distinguished Name`:** Enter the DN value of the AD domain, for example, dc=lab,dc=local.

d. **`LDAP Server`**: Click **`Set`** to add an AD domain controller.

e. Optionally select OU to be synced with NSX Manager. Default All is selected for sync.

f. Optionally configure Event Log Server by clicking Set and providing the event log server address, username, and password.

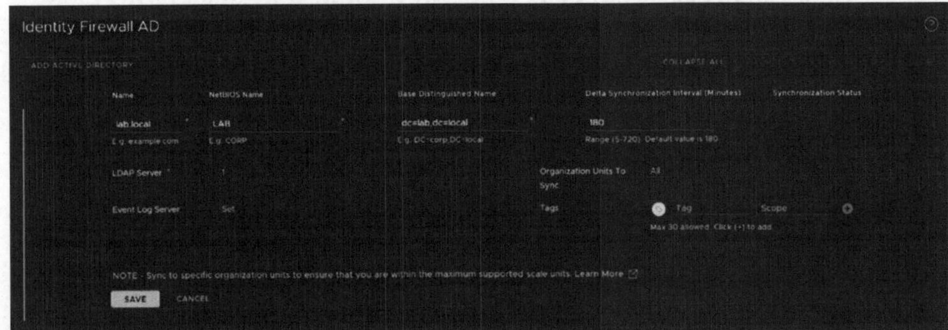

Figure 8.32: *Configuring Active Directory domain for IDFW*

Step 3: Click **Save** to configure Active Directory in NSX for Identity Firewall.

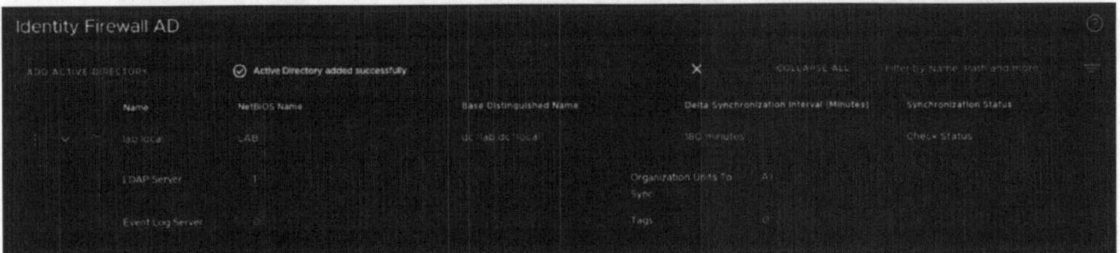

Figure 8.33: *Successful integration of AD domain*

Step 4: Next, navigate to **`Security`** and select **`Distributed Firewall`** from the left navigation panel. Click **`Action`** and select **`General Settings`**. Move the slider in front of Identity Firewall Status to turn on Identity Firewall for distributed firewall, as shown in *Figure* 8.34:

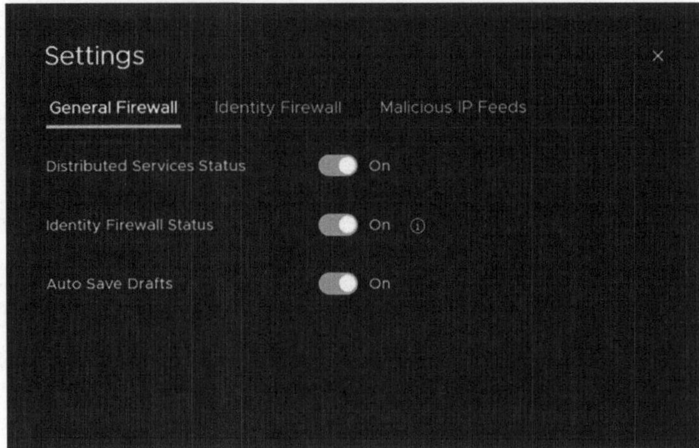

Figure 8.34: *Enabling Identity firewall in NSX DFW*

Step 5: Click `Identity Firewall` in the middle and select the cluster on which to enable Identity Firewall. Optionally, if standalone hosts are present in the NSX environment, then move the slider to enable IDFW on standalone hosts.

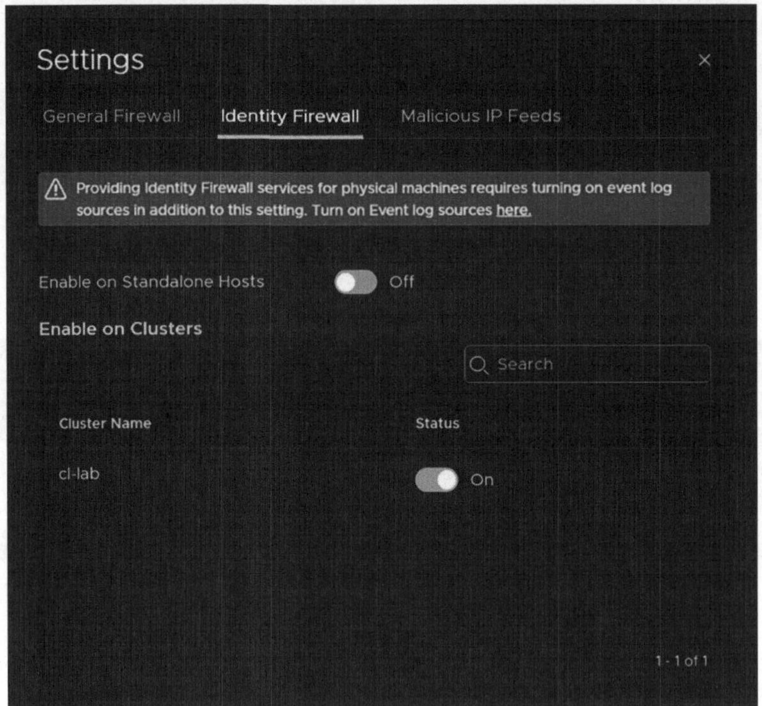

Figure 8.35: *Enabling Identity firewall on vSphere cluster*

Step 6: Click **`Save`** to commit changes and enable Identity Firewall in NSX DFW.

Step 7: Next, navigate to **`Inventory`** and select **`Groups.`** Click **`Add Group`** to create a new group with AD group members. In **`Set Members`** window, click **`AD Groups`** and select the desired AD group to make it a member of the NSX group.

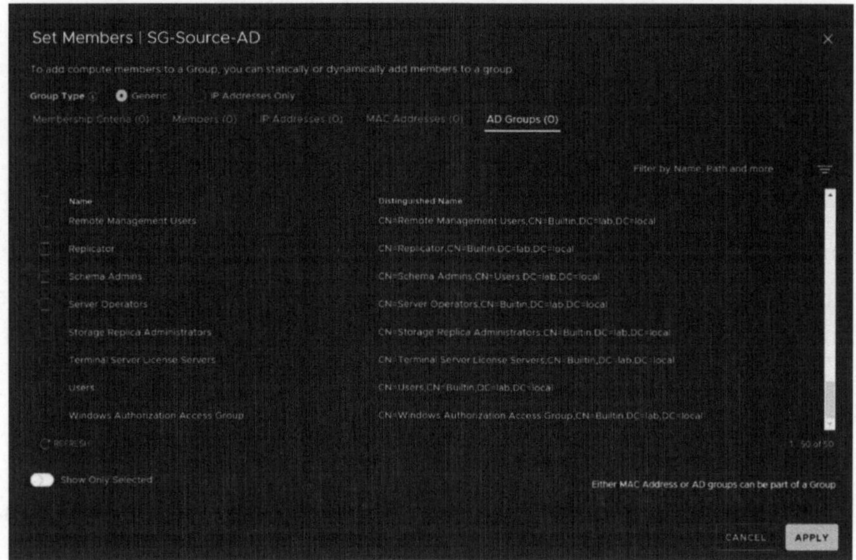

***Figure 8.36**: Adding AD group in an NSX group*

Step 8: As a last step, configure the DFW firewall policy with the source as a newly created NSX group with AD group members, and the destination as a virtual machine with services either allowed or disallowed as per business requirements.

NSX Distributed Security for VDS

Traditionally, with an earlier release of NSX-T, distributed firewall rules could only have been applied on NSX-managed segments, either VLAN-backed or Overlay-backed. Now, consider a use case where only distributed security is required without the need to use any network services provided by NSX. In such cases, NSX-T Manager needs to be deployed to prepare hosts for the NSX environment and create VLAN-backed segments within the NSX environment. The most tedious task is to migrate all workload from the existing vSphere distributed port group to NSX segments, which increases operational overhead and administrative efforts.

However, starting NSX-T 3.2 release with vSphere distributed switch to version 6.6 and later, distributed security features can be directly enabled on VDS without the need to modify anything in the vSphere environment. Different security capabilities that can be utilized in this model are as follows:

- Distributed Firewall (DFW)
- Distributed IDS/IPS
- Identity Firewall
- L7 App ID
- Fully Qualified Domain Name (FQDN) Filtering
- NSX Intelligence
- NSX Malware Prevention
- NSX Guest Introspection

In order to enable distributed security on the vSphere distributed switch, certain requirements need to be met such as:

- vSphere version should be at least 6.7 or later
- vSphere cluster should have at least one VDS with a distributed switch version of at least 6.6 or later
- vCenter as a compute manager must be registered with NSX Manager
- VDS configuration should be in sync across all hosts in a cluster

Note: If a virtual machine is vMotion (hot migration) from the cluster with distributed security to the cluster without distributed security, then all the security policies applied to the VM are removed. Conversely, if a VM is vMotion from a cluster without distributed security to a cluster with distributed security, then the security policies of the cluster with distributed security are applied to the VM.

Installing Distributed Security on VDS

In NSX Manager, there is an option introduced with NSX-T release 3.2 termed Security Only in the quick start menu. When a vSphere cluster is prepared with security-only option, then the following objects are automatically created in NSX; however, there are no changes performed in the vCenter server:

- A transport node profile for each cluster.
- A host switch for each VDS.
- A VLAN transport zone for each VDS.

All of these objects are system-generated and cannot be edited by users.

Step 1: Log in to NSX Manager with admin privileges. Navigate to **`System`** and click **`Quick Start.`** This will provide a quick start to Prepare Clusters for Networking and Security. Click **`Get Started`** as shown in *Figure 8.37*:

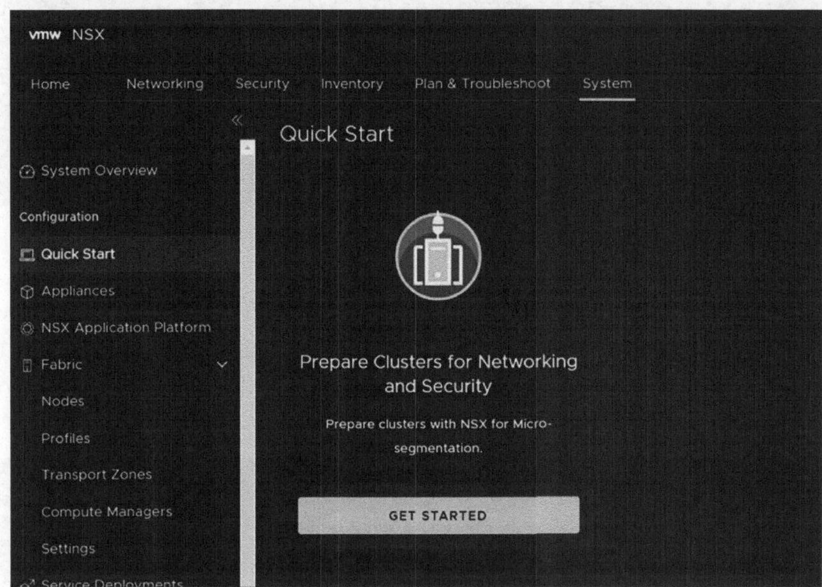

***Figure 8.37**: NSX Quick Start Window*

Step 2: The next screen will show the available clusters, which haven't been prepared for the NSX environment. Select the cluster using the checkbox and click on **`Install NSX.`** A drop-down menu will pop out, here select **`Security Only`** in order to enable distributed security on vSphere distributed switch.

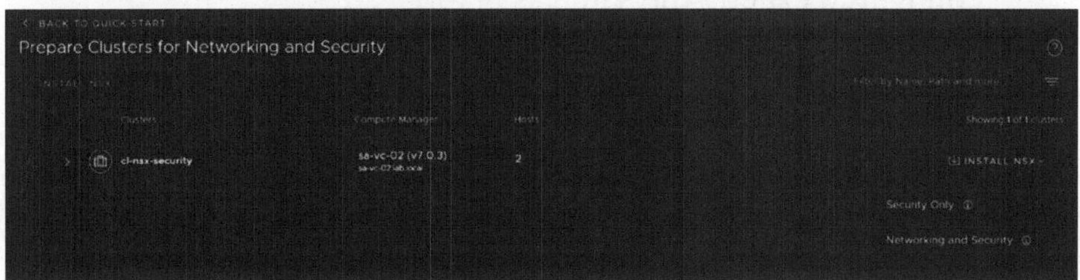

***Figure 8.38**: Security Only option to prepare vSphere Cluster*

Step 3: Click **`Install`** to start configuring hosts for the NSX environment.

Step 4: This results in an automated creation of a Transport Node Profile, Transport Zone specific for distributed security on VDS. *Figure* 8.39 illustrates cluster **`cl-nsx-security`** prepared for Security only, which is identifiable by tag **`Security`** and has a system-created Transport Node Profile attached to it.

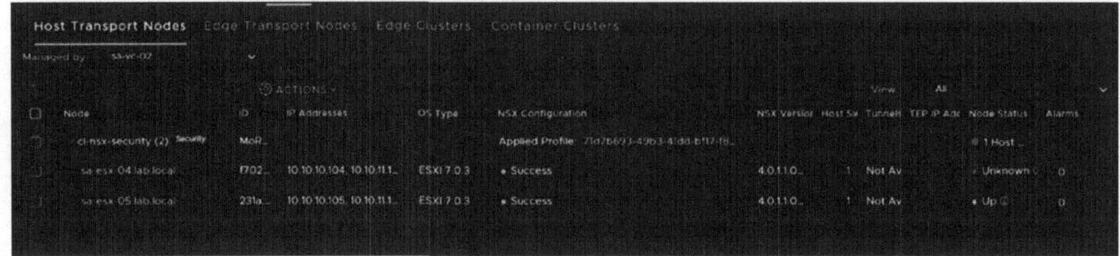

***Figure 8.39**: vSphere cluster prepared for* NSX *distributed security on* VDS

Step 5: Navigate to **`Networking`** and click **`Segments`**. There is a new option **`Distributed Port Groups`** has been created and all distributed port groups are automatically discovered in NSX Manager, as evident in *Figure* 8.40:

***Figure 8.40**: Distributed Port Groups discovered in* NSX *Manager*

Step 6: The next step is to configure distributed firewall policies, which are configured exactly the same as before.

Conclusion

This concludes the NSX Distributed Firewall configuration in the NSX environment. In this chapter, we covered the architecture of NSX DFW and how policies are pushed from NSX Manager to transport nodes. Also, we covered different features provided by NSX DFW, such as Identity Firewall, Time Base firewall, FQDN filtering, Layer 7 context profile, and how to configure them. One of the most requested features to enable distributed security on the vSphere distributed switch was also introduced with NSX release 3.2, which we covered in detail.

In the next few chapters, we will cover more advanced security features, including ATP and NTA/NDR provided by NSX, and how they can help achieve a zero-trust model for applications and protect from zero-day vulnerabilities.

Key Terms

- **Segment:** Segments are layer 2 subnets representing layer 2 broadcasting domain across transport nodes in NSX networking
- **VNI (Virtual Network Identifier):** Unique ID assigned to segments created in the NSX environment.
- **VSS (vSphere Standard Switch):** Virtual switch default configured on ESXi host, where both management plane and I/O plane reside with ESXi host.
- **VDS (vSphere Distributed Switch):** Virtual switch provided by Vmware, where management plane resides with the vCenter server, allowing centralized management.
- **Distributed Firewall:** A stateful firewall runs in the kernel as a VIB package on all ESXi hosts in a cluster.
- **Context Profile:** Layer 7 App IDs configured as part of Context profile to enable Layer 7 inspection in distributed firewall.
- **Identity Firewall:** Security policies based on Active Directory groups as a source to enforce rules on users logged into the machine.
- **vSIP:** VMware kernel module responsible for configuring security policies on virtual machines.
- **VDPI:** VMware Deep Packet Inspection engine, which performs Layer 7 inspection based on context profile in network packet.

CHAPTER 9

Security – Advanced Threat Prevention

Introduction

In the last chapter, we discussed micro-segmentation and how NSX with the help of Distributed Firewall can help protect applications. But if you feel that's all that NSX has to offer, you are in for a surprise. No doubt, NSX DFW is one of the most powerful features offered by NSX in the security space, but there are other equally powerful security features provided by NSX. We had just scratched the surface of the security features NSX provides and there are more advanced threat prevention services on the counter.

This chapter covers NSX Gateway Firewall along with two of ATP features, IDS/IPS and Malware Prevention. Both can be used to protect East-West traffic as well as North-South traffic. Now that's what I call as interesting.

Structure

In this chapter, we will cover the following topics:

- NSX Gateway Firewall
    - NSX Gateway Firewall Categories
    - NSX Gateway Firewall Architecture
    - Configuring NSX Gateway Firewall
- NSX Intrusion Detection and Prevention Service
    - NSX IDPS Architecture

- Configuring NSX IDS/IPS
  - Activate NSX IDS/IPS
  - Configuring NSX IDS/IPS Security Profile
  - Configuring NSX IDS/IPS Rules
  - Monitoring and Validating NSX IDS/IPS
- NSX Malware Prevention
  - Requirements for NSX Malware Prevention
  - NSX Malware Prevention Architecture
- Configuring NSX Malware Prevention
  - Activate Malware Prevention on NAPP
  - Activating NSX Distributed Malware Prevention
  - Activating NSX Gateway Malware Prevention
  - Configuring NSX Malware Prevention Profile
  - Configuring NSX Malware Prevention Rule
  - Monitoring NSX Malware Prevention

NSX Gateway Firewall

In the last chapter, we covered NSX Distributed Firewall in detail along with the different functions provided by it. Aside from providing a Distributed Firewall, NSX also supports a gateway firewall which is enforced on the northbound interface of NSX gateway, i.e., Tier1 and Tier0. NSX gateway firewalling is usually consumed to provide network segmentation between physical workload and NSX managed workload, act as perimeter firewall between NSX managed environment and non-NSX environment, or act as a tenant firewall. NSX gateway firewall is independent of distributed firewall and is realized at gateway northbound interface level instead of virtual machine vNIC level. NSX supports both stateful and stateless gateway firewalls and requires SR (Service Router) to be instantiated meaning the gateway should have an edge cluster assigned to it, especially in the case of Tier1 where it is possible to create Tier1 in Distributed Routing form factor without needing an edge cluster. *Figure* 9.1 illustrates a warning thrown by NSX Manager as no edge cluster is associated with the Tier1 gateway resulting in no realization of security policies on the Tier1 gateway LAB-Tier1-01 unless an edge cluster is associated with it.

***Figure 9.1**: Gateway Firewall warning for Tier1 without Edge Cluster*

Note: In prior releases of NSX, before 4.0.1. Active-Active Tier0 gateway supported stateless firewall only. However, starting release NSX 4.0.1 Active-Active Tier0 now supports a stateful firewall as well. Not all features are supported in Active-Active Tier0 stateful configuration. Please consult docs.vmware.com for a comprehensive list of features supported.

Figure 9.2 displays a good example of how a gateway firewall is enforced at the uplink interface of either Tier0 or Tier1 gateway.

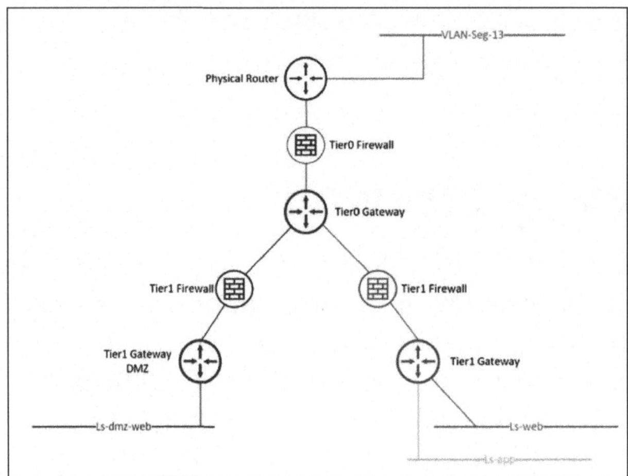

***Figure 9.2**: Gateway firewall enforcement in NSX*

In the preceding example, if virtual machines connected to Ls-web and Ls-app segments need to communicate with each other both segments connected to the same Tier1 gateway will have no gateway firewall in their path as both segments Ls-web and Ls-app are downlink interface to Tier1 Gateway and no traffic is passing through an uplink interface. In the same example, if VMs connected to Ls-dmz-web and Ls-web needs to communicate with each other, then Tier1 Firewall will come into play however, Tier0 Firewall will not be enforced as both Tier1 Gateway DMZ and Tier1 Gateway are downlink interface of Tier0 Gateway.

Tier0 Firewall plays a key role when a server or machine connected to segment VLAN-Seg-13 tries to communicate with any VMs connected to either Ls-dmz-web, Ls-web or Ls-app segments as traffic will be passing through an uplink interface of Tier0 Gateway.

NSX Gateway Firewall Categories

Similar to NSX Distributed Firewall, there are different categories under which gateway firewall policies can be configured. These categories are visible by navigating to **`Security`**, selecting **`Gateway Firewall`** and then clicking on **`All Shared Rules`**. *Figure* 9.3 shows different categories available in the NSX gateway firewall. Also, similar to NSX Distributed Firewall, gateway firewall rules processing occurs from left to right in between categories and top to bottom within categories.

***Figure* 9.3:** NSX *Gateway Firewall Categories*

Different categories available in the NSX gateway firewall are:

- **Emergency:** As the name suggests, this category is used to create quarantine rules to isolate traffic or allow rules for any troubleshooting.
- **System:** This category contains rules which are automatically generated by NSX and specific to internal control plane traffic for services such as VPN, BFD, etc. One cannot add any rules in this category as an option to add policy and rules are greyed out and any rules created by NSX should not be modified as modifying rules here can result in unexpected behavior.
- **Pre-Rules:** This is a global policy that applies across all gateways present in the NSX environment.
- **Local Gateway:** As the name suggests, this category contains gateway-specific rules which are applied to specified gateway only.
- **Auto Service:** Again, rules in this category are automatically generated by NSX for other NSX services. One cannot add any rules in this category as an option to add policy and rules are greyed out. However, rules can be modified based on requirement.
- **Default:** This category contains a default policy which acts as a catch-all rule for any traffic which does not match any previous rules.

Another tip, if required, category names can be changed through API.

NSX Gateway Firewall Architecture

NSX gateway firewall architecture is very similar to NSX Distributed Firewall (DFW) architecture with subtle differences. As the gateway firewall requires SR to be instantiated for the gateway, all rules tables and flow tables are managed by Edge Node. *Figure* 9.4 shows the NSX gateway firewall architecture implemented in an Edge Node.

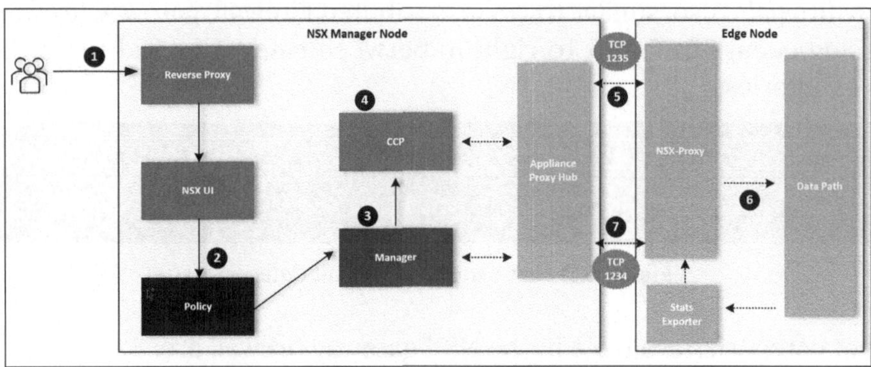

***Figure 9.4**: NSX Gateway Firewall Architecture*

The user logs into the NSX Manager appliance and configures gateway firewall policies through NSX UI (User Interface) or API which are pushed to the policy role. The policy role processes the user configuration, converts it into the desired state configuration and further sends it to a Manager role. The Manager role forwards the configuration to CCP (Central Control Plane) to be further distributed to transport nodes. CCP, with the help of APH (Appliance Proxy Hub) forwards the configuration to nsx-proxy running on Edge Node and configures the datapath module. Also, statistics such as flows, hit counts, etc. are forwarded by the nsx-proxy service back to the NSX Manager with the help of the stats exporter.

Gateway firewall rule processing is taken care of with the help of two tables, namely rule classifier and flow table. Whenever a gateway firewall rule is configured, its entry is created in the rule table in the rule classifier module and the flow table stores the previously allowed flows to track stateful connections. Now, when a packet is received by the gateway firewall, it is looked upon in the flow table if the entry of connection exists. If an entry is found in the flow table, then a packet is processed. However, if a connection entry does not exist in the flow table, then the packet is matched against the rule table. If the packet is allowed and the traffic type is stateful, then a corresponding connection entry is created in the flow table and subsequent packets for the same connection are allowed directly from the flow table. However, if the traffic type is stateless, then it is always matched against the rule table.

Configuring NSX Gateway Firewall

Although the NSX gateway firewall is completely independent of NSX DFW still objects such as Groups, Tags, Context Profiles, Services, etc. are globally available in the NSX environment. So, managing a gateway firewall is very similar to managing an NSX Distributed firewall. The same concept and configuration, such as time-based firewall policies, and Layer 7 context profile, also apply to the gateway firewall. These topics have been covered in great detail in *Chapter 8, Security – Micro-segmentation.*

Step 1: Login into NSX Manager with admin privileges and navigate to **`Security`**. Select **`Gateway Firewall`** from the left navigation panel to view gateway firewall policies, as shown in *Figure* 9.5.

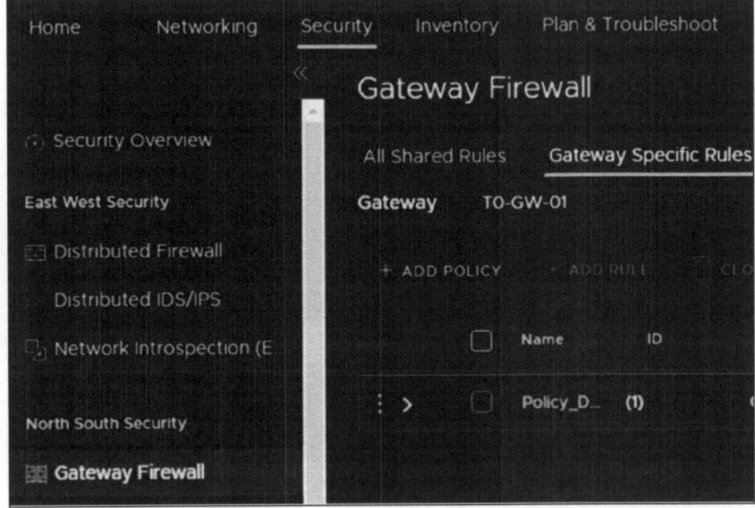

***Figure* 9.5:** *Gateway Firewall Policies in NSX UI*

Step 2: Select the appropriate gateway from the drop-down menu in front of **`Gateway`** on which firewall policies need to be configured. *Figure* 9.5 shows Tier0 gateway **`T0-GW-01`** selected.

Step 3: Click on **`Add Policy`** to create a new firewall policy and provide an appropriate name. *Figure* 9.6 illustrates a firewall policy with the name **`LAB-Tier0-Policy`** created with the help of Add Policy. Here category is automatically selected as **`Local Gateway`** as this policy is specific to Tier0 gateway.

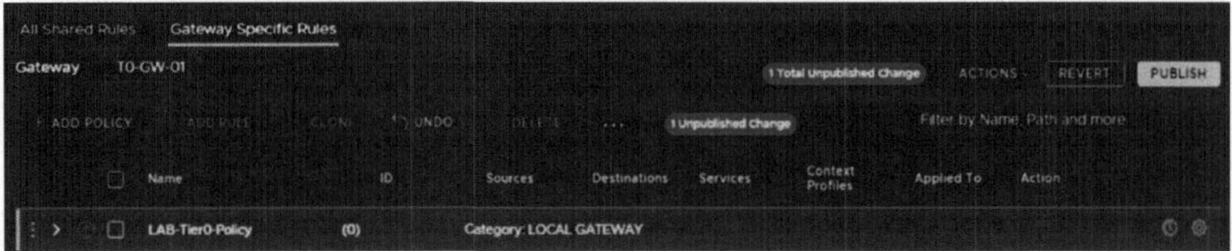

***Figure 9.6:** Creating a new policy in a gateway firewall*

Step 4: Click on the gear icon in the far-right corner of the newly created policy to configure policy settings which are exactly the same as distributed firewall policy.

Figure 9.7 shows different policy configuration settings available in the gateway firewall.

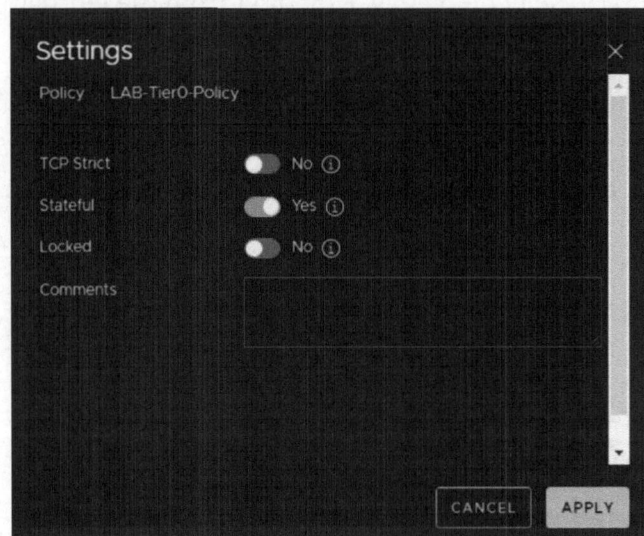

***Figure 9.7**: NSX Gateway Firewall policy configuration settings*

a. **TCP Strict:** Move the slider to enable or disable the TCP strict mode.

b. **Stateful:** Enable or disable the stateful nature of the distributed firewall.

c. **Locked:** Lock the policy to prevent multiple users from editing the same section.

Step 5: Click on the checkbox against policy and the `Add Rule` option will be highlighted. Click on `Add Rule` to add a new firewall rule under Policy. Click on the `Name` field to change the name of the rule to a more meaningful name. *Figure* 9.8 illustrates a firewall rule `LAB-Tier0-Rule-Ping-Block` created under policy `LAB-Tier0-Policy`.

***Figure 9.8**: Adding a rule in NSX DFW*

Step 6: There are a few more fields to be configured to make the rule more effective and avoid any unintentional behavior.

a. **Sources:** Click on the pencil icon to edit the sources field. The default option is any which can be replaced with an NSX group or IP address.

b. **Destinations:** Click on the pencil icon to edit the sources field. The default option is any which can be replaced with an NSX group or IP address.

c. **Services:** Specify the ports and protocols to be allowed or disallowed between source and destination.

d. **Applied To:** Default is Gateway, but if the rule needs to be applied to a specific uplink interface, then it can be selected here.

e. **Action:** Specify if the traffic is to be allowed, rejected, or dropped entirely.

Figure 9.9 shows a test rule with the name `LAB-Tier0-Rule-Ping-Block`, which blocks ICMP communication from any source to any destination.

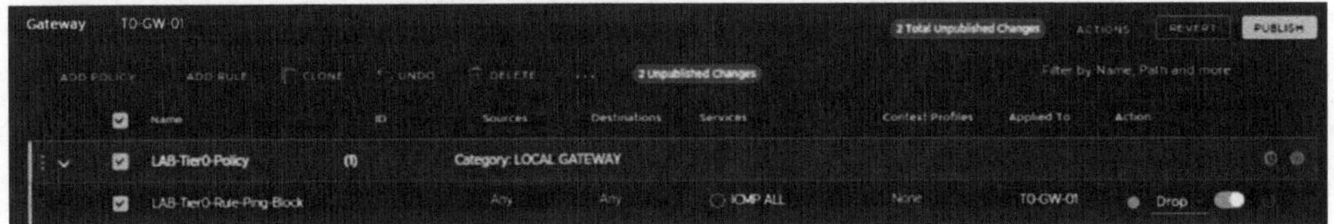

***Figure 9.9**: A fully configured NSX gateway firewall rule*

Step 7: Click on the gear icon after the green slider to access a few settings specific to the firewall rule, which are illustrated in *Figure* 9.10:

a. **Logging:** Move the slider to enable or disable rule logging. Gateway firewall logs are stored in the /var/log directory in a file named firewallpkt.log.

b. **Direction:** Specify the rule direction to be more specific, i.e., in, out, or in-out.

c. **IP Protocol:** Specify whether the rule applies to a specific IP protocol or both.

d. **Comments:** Optional, provide any extra remarks related to the firewall rule.

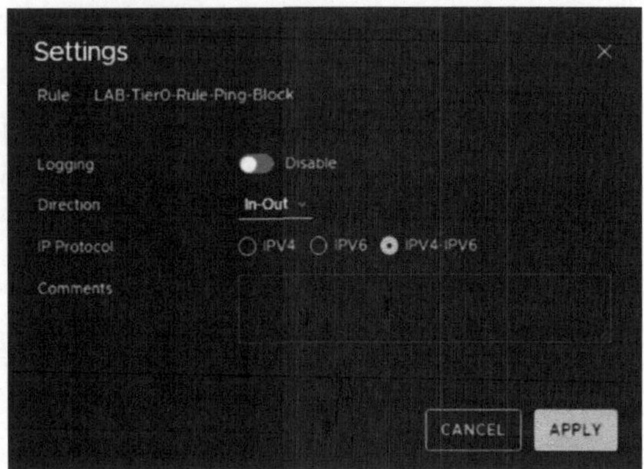

Figure 9.10: *NSX Gateway Firewall rule settings*

Step 8: Currently, the firewall policy is in a draft state and changes haven't been committed yet. Click on **`Revert`** to discard any unpublished changes or click on **`Publish`** to commit changes and push the changes to the data plane.

Step 9: After changes are pushed successfully, the firewall policy status is changed to **`Success`** as shown in *Figure* 9.11.

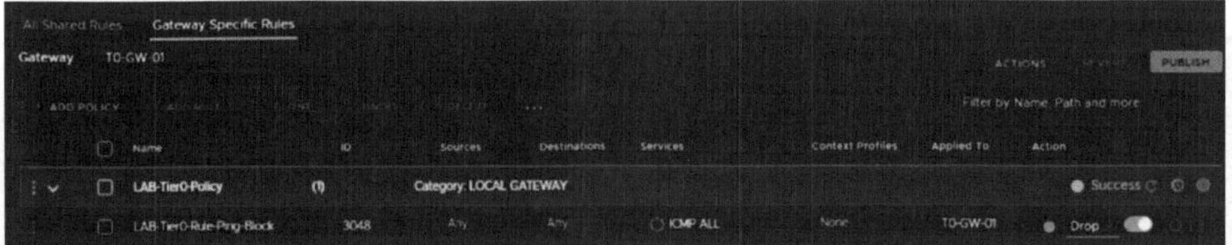

Figure 9.11: *NSX Gateway Firewall policy after publishing*

One important point for gateway firewall is the form factor of Edge Node. As a gateway firewall is implemented inside Edge Node, the form factor of Edge

Node plays an important part in determining what features can be enabled on a gateway firewall. *Table* 9.1 (courtesy VMware Documentation) provides a summarized view of different features which can be enabled or not based on different form factor sizes of Edge Node. A few of the features have already been covered and a few such as IDPS, Malware Prevention, etc. will be covered later in the chapter.

Features/NSX Edge Form Factor	**Small (2 vCPU, 4GB RAM) (POC only)**	**Medium (4 vCPU, 8 GB RAM)**	**Large (8 vCPU, 32 GB RAM)**	**Extra Large (16 vCPU, 64 GB RAM)**	**Bare Metal**
L3-L4 Firewall	Yes	Yes	Yes	Yes	Yes
User ID-based Access Control	Yes	Yes	Yes	Yes	Yes
Application Access Control	No	Yes	Yes	Yes	Yes
URL Filtering	No	Yes	Yes	Yes	Yes
FQDN Analysis	No	Yes	Yes	Yes	Yes
IDPS	No	No	Yes	Yes	Yes
Malware Detection	No	No	No	Yes	No
Sandboxing for unknown Threats	No	No	No	Yes	No
TLS Inspection	No	No	Yes	Yes	Yes
L2 and L3 VPN	Yes	Yes	Yes	Yes	Yes
Static, Dynamic Routing	Yes	Yes	Yes	Yes	Yes

Table 9.1: *Gateway Firewall features supported on NSX Edge form factor*

NSX Intrusion Detection and Prevention Service

Apart from providing firewall capabilities, NSX also provides other advanced security features which can protect organizations from zero-day vulnerabilities. As of the current release v4.1, different advanced security features supported by NSX are:

- IDPS (Intrusion Detection and Prevention Service)
- Malware Prevention

- Network Traffic Analysis
- NDR (Network Detection and Response)

Going a step further from firewalling, IDS/IPS (Intrusion Detection Service/ Intrusion Prevention Service) looks out for suspicious activities in the network even if the traffic is allowed through firewall rules to protect against application or guest OS vulnerabilities. IDS/IPS achieve this with the help of signatures. Signatures define a pattern for intrusion-type traffic that needs to be detected and prevented. Starting with NSX 4.x, NSX goes beyond a signature-based approach and provides Behavior-based detection as well. NSX IDPS protects against intrusion based on the following two methods:

- **Knowledge-based Signatures**: This approach utilizes signatures for a known type of attack to detect intrusion in the network. One drawback of this approach is its limitation in detecting new types of attacks, as their knowledge is not yet known and signatures of such attacks are not available.
- **Behavior-based Detection**: This approach looks out for anomalous behavior in the network with the help of events that are different or unusual compared to normal baseline network traffic. These events are termed as informational or info in nature and may not always point to malicious traffic, but can be used as valuable information. IDPS combines these custom logic events with signatures to detect intrusion in the environment.

NSX IDS/IPS services can be enabled on both the Distributed firewall and Gateway firewall independently, however, there are a few requirements that need to be fulfilled before enabling IDS/IPS in the NSX environment, which is:

- **License Requirements**: In order to enable NSX IDS/IPS services, an additional add-on license Threat Prevention or Advanced Threat Prevention is required.
- **Edge Node Size Requirements**: If NSX IDS/IPS is to be enabled on the Gateway firewall, then the edge node VM size must be at least large or above as covered earlier in *Table 9.1*.
- **Internet Connectivity**: This is optional, as one can download the IDS/ IPS signatures manually from the Threat Intelligence Cloud and upload them from NSX Manager UI.

Note: NSX IDS/IPS services on the Gateway firewall are supported only on Tier1 gateways backed by Edge Cluster.

NSX IDPS Architecture

Figure 9.12 shows the overall architecture of NSX IDS/IPS services for both distributed firewalls and gateway firewalls. There are three sections in an NSX IDPS environment:

1. NSX IDS/IPS Signatures
2. NSX Distributed IDS/IPS
3. NSX Gateway (North-South) IDS/IPS

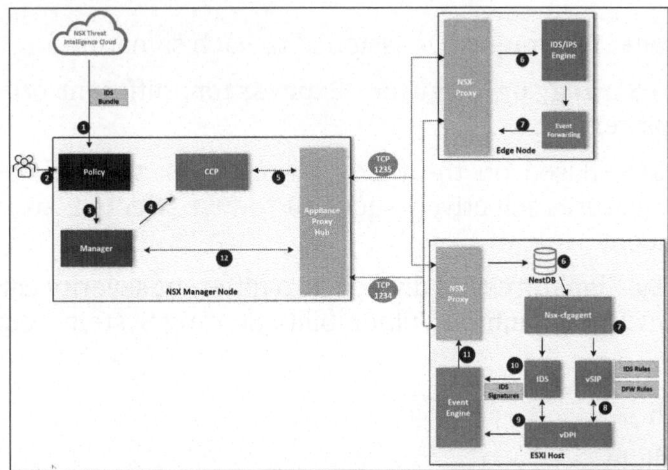

***Figure* 9.12**: NSX IDS/IPS *Architecture*

***Figure* 9.12** covers IDS signatures, gateway firewall IDS and distributed firewall IDS components. Let's cover these different sections in detail.

NSX IDS/IPS Signatures

NSX IDS/IPS signature contains metadata that helps in the identification of intrusion attempts by exploiting known application or operating system vulnerabilities. As shown in *Figure* 9.12, Step 1, these signatures are downloaded from NSX Threat Intelligence Cloud whose curator engine provides combined signatures from Trustwave, Secureworks, and Lastline into a single signature set as an IDS Bundle. NSX Manager downloads IDS/IPS signatures daily from Threat Intelligence Cloud. However, if the NSX Manager has no internet connectivity, then these signatures need to be manually downloaded from Threat Intelligence Cloud and uploaded on the NSX Manager, which further distributes these signatures to transport nodes for consumption.

Figure 9.13 illustrates the different components a signature has.

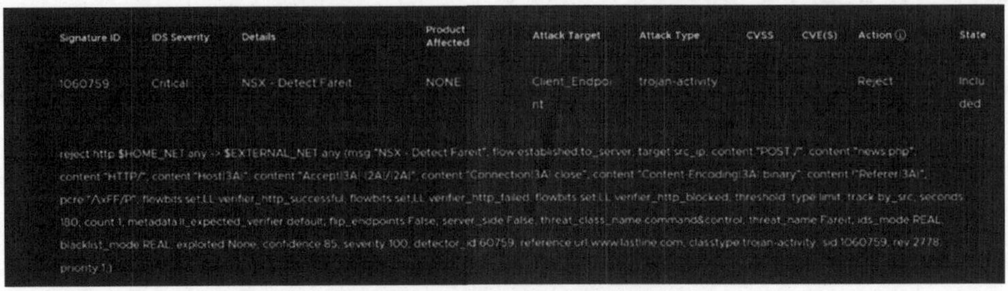

Signature ID	IDS Severity	Details	Product Affected	Attack Target	Attack Type	CVSS	CVE(S)	Action	State
1060759	Critical	NSX - Detect Fareit	NONE	Client_Endpoint	trojan-activity			Reject	Included

reject http $HOME_NET any -> $EXTERNAL_NET any (msg "NSX - Detect Fareit", flow established,to_server, target src_ip, content "POST /", content "news.php", content "HTTP/", content "Host|3A|", content "Accept|3A| |2A|/|2A|", content "Connection|3A| close", content "Content-Encoding|3A| binary", content !"Referer|3A|", pcre "/\xFF/P", flowbits set,LL verifier_http_successful, flowbits set,LL verifier_http_failed, flowbits set,LL verifier_http_blocked, threshold type limit, track by_src, seconds 180, count 1, metadata ll_expected_verifier default, flip_endpoints False, server_side False, threat_class_name command&control, threat_name Fareit, ids_mode REAL, blacklist_mode REAL, exploited None, confidence 85, severity 100, detector_id 60759, reference url www.lastline.com, classtype trojan-activity, sid 1060759, rev 2778, priority 1;)

***Figure* 9.13:** A NSX IDS/IPS *Signature*

- **`Signature ID`**: Unique IDs assigned to each signature.
- **`Simple String or Regular Expression`**: different criteria to match traffic patterns.
- **`Meta-Data`**: Based on the type of workloads, these fields are used to apply signatures selectively such as Product Affected, Attack Target, and Deployment.
- **`Severity`**: Signatures are divided into different severity categories based on their CVSS (Common Vulnerability Scoring System) score, which are:
  - Critical
  - High
  - Medium
  - Low
  - Suspicious

NSX Distributed IDS/IPS Architecture

NSX Distributed IDS/IPS components are the same as NSX DFW components as both are collocated in the vSphere hypervisor kernel. *Figure* 9.12 covers the entire flow of NSX Distributed IDS/IPS services and the different components involved.

1. NSX Manager downloads the curated signatures from NSX Threat Intelligence Cloud either with the help of internet access or through manual upload by the administrator.

2. As an end user, the administrator configures the NSX IDS/IPS profiles and rules with the help of API or UI.

3. In the management plane, the Policy role stores the configuration and passes it to the Manager role for realization with the help of the controller role.

4. The Manager role computes the realized configuration and pushes it to the CCP (Central Control Plane).
5. CCP pushes the stateless configuration to ESXi host LCP with the help of APH (Appliance Proxy Host) service running on NSX Manager. NSX-proxy running on the ESXi host receives the configuration from APH over TCP port 1235.
6. NSX-proxy post receiving the configuration from APH writes the configuration in NestDB and NestDB stores IDPS signatures and rules locally on the ESXi host.
7. Nsx-cfgagent receives the configuration from NestDB and pushes IDPS signatures to the IDS engine and IDPS rules to the vSIP module.
8. As covered in NSX DFW, the vSIP module falls in the traffic dataplane and it compares the traffic against the IDPS rule. If a match is found then it forwards the traffic to the vDPI engine for deep packet inspection.
9. vDPI creates a copy of the packet and forwards the copy to the IDS engine to compare it against IDS signatures. It releases the packet after inspection is completed by the IDS engine.
10. Events generated by the IDS engine are forwarded to the Event Engine.
11. Event Engine collects the metadata of flow, generates alerts and forwards these to the NSX-proxy service to further send it to the NSX Manager via APH.
12. APH receives the IDPS alerts generated and forwards them to the Manager role which parses the data and displays these events in NSX Manager UI.

One important point here to remember is that NSX DFW rules are always processed before Distributed IDS/IPS rules. So, if a traffic flow is blocked by the NSX DFW rule then it will never be processed by Distributed IDS/IPS even if the rule has been created for the same.

NSX Gateway IDS/IPS Architecture

Figure 9.12 also displays an Edge Node which hosts components for NSX Gateway IDS/IPS services. Similar to NSX Distributed IDS/IPS, the initial flow remains the same i.e., NSX IDPS signatures are downloaded on NSX Manager and the user configures IDPS rules through UI or API which are pushed to Policy to Manager to CCP. However, the difference between Distributed IDS/IPS and Gateway

IDS/IPS comes to which LCP node CCP pushes configuration. In Gateway IDS/IPS, as a Step 5, CCP pushes the configuration via APH to NSX-proxy service running on NSX Edge Node instead of ESXi host.

Similar to the ESXi host, the Edge node also stores the signatures and IDPS rules locally and configures the datapath. The event forwarding engine collects the metadata about traffic and events generated by the IDS engine on the NSX Edge node and forwards it to NSX Manager with the help of the APH service running on NSX Manager. NSX Manager role parses the data and displays events on UI.

Configuring NSX IDS/IPS

On a high level, the following steps need to be followed to configure NSX IDS/IPS services in the environment:

1. Activate and configure NSX IDS/IPS
2. Add NSX IDS/IPS Security Profile
3. Add NSX IDS/IPS Rule and publish rules
4. Validate/Monitor NSX IDS/IPS

These steps are covered in detail in subsequent sections.

Activate NSX IDS/IPS

By default, NSX IDS/IPS services are in a disabled state. These need to be enabled or activated before NSX IDS/IPS rules can be enforced. If you configure a security profile and add rules but do not activate NSX IDS/IPS services, then these rules will not be realized or pushed to transport nodes. Also, another important point, is before activity NSX IDS/IPS service, ensure the appropriate license has been added under Settings to avoid any unexpected behavior.

Step 1: Login into NSX Manager with admin privileges. Navigate to **`Security`** and click on **`IDS/IPS and Malware Prevention`** under **`Policy Management`**. This will open a window with warnings that NSX IDS/IPS or Malware Prevention services have not been configured and rules will not be enforced as shown in *Figure* 9.14.

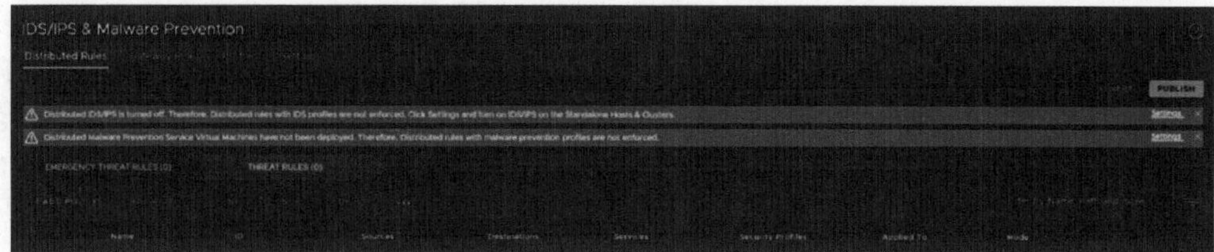

Figure 9.14: NSX IDS/IPS *Configuration Window*

This is the key screen, where all configurations for NSX IDS/IPS or Malware Prevention (covered in section NSX Malware Prevention) is done. There are four tabs present which are:

- **`Distributed Rule`**:This tab lists all the IDS/IPS or Malware Prevention rules used to inspect East-West traffic.
- **`Gateway Rule`**: This tab is used to configure rules for North-South Traffic and these rules are enforced in the Tier1 gateway.
- **`Profile`**: Different security profiles as per requirements are configured under Profile.
- **`Settings`**: Key settings such as activating services, uploading signatures, or managing signatures.

Step 2: Click on **`Settings`** and click on **`Shared`**. This window provides options to configure NSX IDS/IPS or Malware Prevention services for both East-West traffic (on standalone hosts, clusters, or gateways) and North-South traffic (on Tier1 gateways). *Figure* 9.15 shows one cluster with the name CL-LAB and one tier1 gateway with the name LAB-Tier1-01 with IDS/IPS services in a disabled state. By default, both NSX IDS/IPS and Malware Prevention services are in the disabled state.

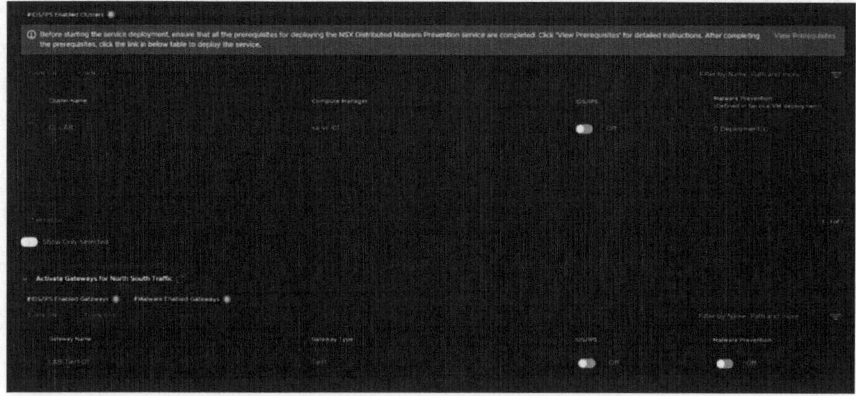

Figure 9.15: NSX IDS/IPS *or Malware Prevention Service in the disabled state*

Step 3: Move the slider to under **`IDS/IPS`** to **`On`** state in the East-West traffic section for standalone or Clusters to enable Distributed IDS/IPS services or in the North-South traffic section against Tier1 gateway to enable Gateway IDS/IPS services. A dialogue box will pop up for confirmation, as shown in *Figure* 9.16. Click **`Yes`** to enable IDS/IPS services on the selected cluster or gateway.

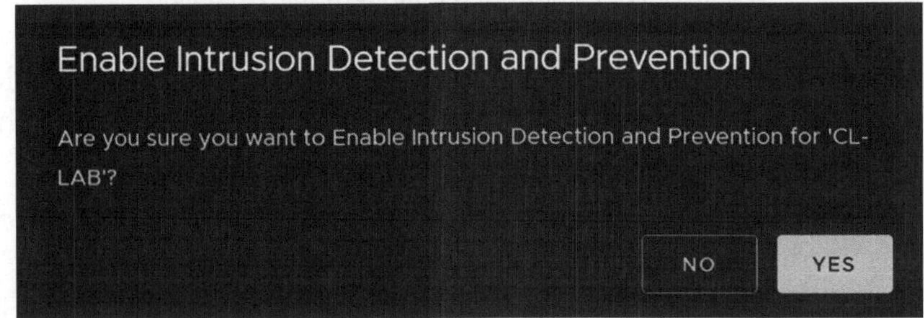

Figure 9.16: *Confirmation dialogue box to enable IDS/IPS services*

Figure 9.17 shows cluster CL-LAB with NSX Distributed IDS/IPS services enabled.

Figure 9.17: *Enabling NSX Distributed IDS/IPS*

Step 4: Click on **`IDS/IPS`** under **`Settings`** to manage IDS signatures. *Figure* 9.18 illustrates different signature management options.

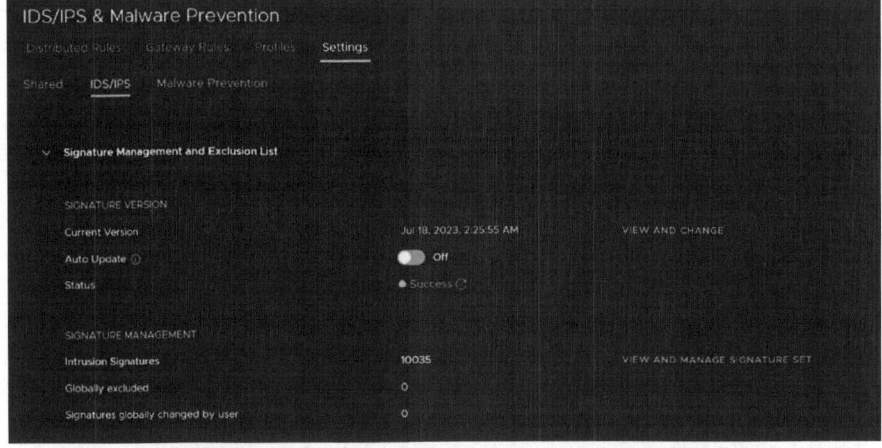

Figure 9.18: NSX IDS *Signature Management*

a. **Auto Update**: Toggle this button to the **On** position to automatically download IDS signatures from Threat Intelligence Cloud and apply them to ESXi host and Edge nodes.

b. **View and Manage Signature Set**: Use this option to manage IDS signatures.

c. **Advanced Settings**: Expand **Advanced Settings** as shown In *Figure* 9.19, to configure **Syslog Settings** and **Oversubscription Settings**.

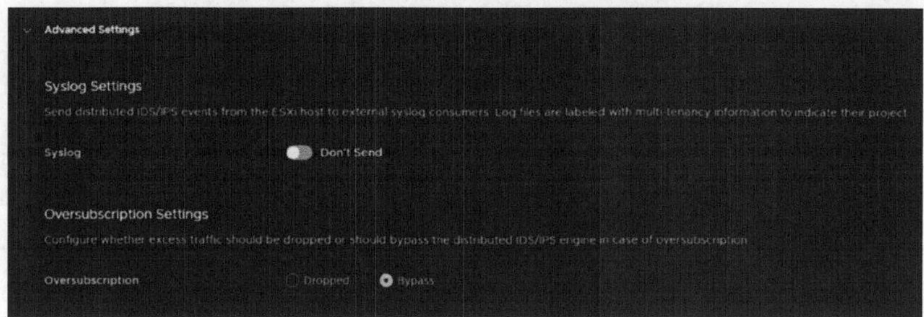

***Figure 9.19**: Configuring oversubscription settings for IDS/IPS rules*

i. **Syslog**: Toggle the button to enable or disable Syslog.

ii. **Oversubscription**: In the case of oversubscription, If **Bypass** Is selected, then traffic will be bypassed. However, If **Dropped** Is selected, then traffic will be dropped.

NSX IDS Signature Management

Step 5: Click on **View and Manage Signature Set** to open a new window that lists all the signatures currently present in the NSX Manager as shown in *Figure* 9.20.

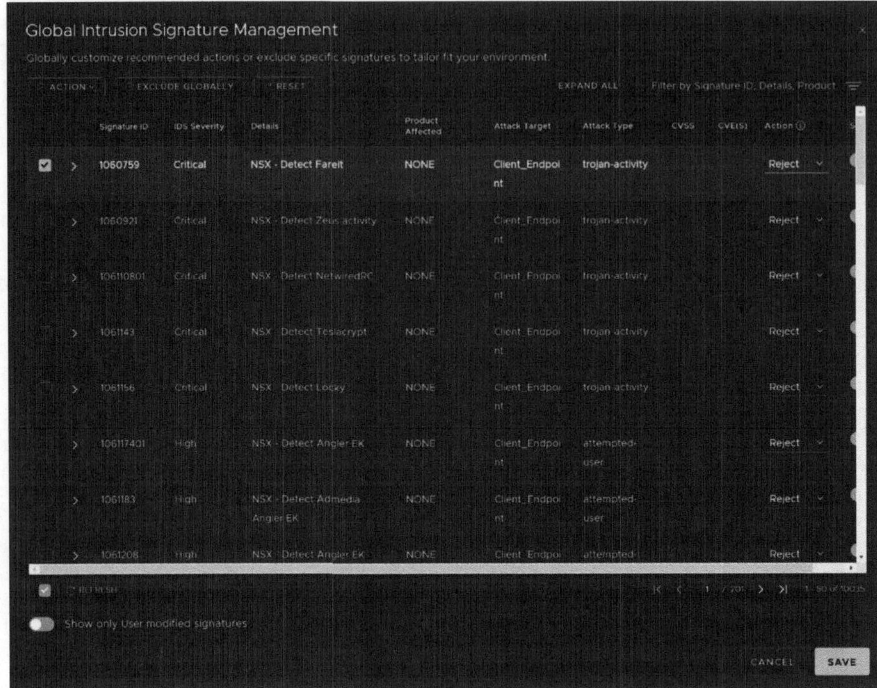

Figure 9.20: Managing NSX IDS Signatures

Step 6: Select the desired signature and click on **`Action`** to override its default Action.

a. **`Allow`**: An alert is generated and traffic is allowed.

b. **`Drop`**: An alert is generated and traffic is dropped.

c. **`Reject`**: An alert is generated and traffic is dropped. A TCP RST packet is generated by IDS and is sent to the source and destination of the packet.

Step 7: Click **`Save`** `to` commit changes and move out of signature management.

Configuring NSX IDS/IPS Security Profile

NSX IDS/IPS security profile groups signatures as per requirements which can then be either included or excluded from intrusion detection. There is a default IDS profile already present in NSX Manager, which includes all IDS signatures labelled as critical as illustrated in *Figure* 9.21.

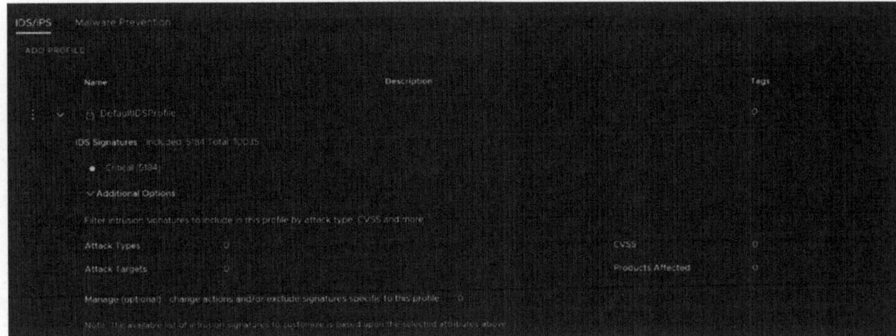

Figure 9.21: *NSX IDS Default Security Profile*

Note: A maximum of 100 custom IDS profiles can be configured in NSX Manager alongside default IDS security profiles.

To create a custom IDS security profile, perform the following steps:

Step 1: Login into NSX Manager with admin privileges. Navigate to **`Security`** and select **`IDS/IPS & Malware Prevention`** under **`Policy Management`**. Click on **`Profile`** and ensure **`IDS/IPS`** is selected.

Step 2: It will show the default IDS profile already created and present. Click on **`Add Profile`** to create a new IDS profile. There are multiple criteria that can be selected to exclude or include signatures from intrusion detection. As you put more filters, the IDS Signature Included count will change as more and more signatures are excluded. By default, all signatures are included when a new profile is created as shown in *Figure 9.22*.

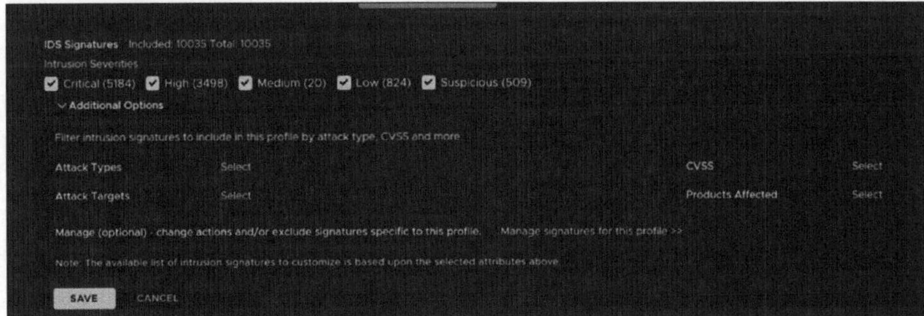

Figure 9.22: *IDS Signatures included in Security Profile*

Step 3: Different options to tune the IDS profile are:

a. **`Name:`** Provide a relevant name for the IDS security profile.

b. **`Intrusion Severities`:** Check or Uncheck the box to include or exclude signatures based on their CVSS severity score.

c. Expand **`Additional options`** to select different metadata to further include or exclude signatures such as:

   i. Attack Types

   ii. Attack Targets

   iii. CVSS

   iv. Products Affected

d. **`Manage Signatures for this profile`:** This option provides the capability to include or exclude individual signatures.

Step 4: Click on **Save** to create the custom IDS profile. *Figure* 9.23 shows the IDS profile with the name LAB-IDS-Profile01 with High and Critical Severity signatures only included.

***Figure 9.23**: Custom IDS Security Profile*

Configuring NSX IDS/IPS Rules

Similar to NSX Firewall policies, NSX IDS/IPS policy is a collection of IDS/IPS rules and an IDS/IPS rule defines the instructions which determine from which source to destination, types of services the traffic will be analyzed against the selected IDS security profile and based on action either the traffic will be allowed with alerts or blocked with alerts.

NSX IDS/IPS policies are configured independently for Distributed IDS/IPS and Gateway IDS/IPS. As shown in *Figure* 9.24, navigate to Distributed Rules to configure Distributed IDS/IPS policies and rules whereas navigate to Gateway Rules to configure IDS/IPS policies and rules for Tier1 gateway in the NSX environment. However, different attributes for the configuration of rules remain the same for both Distributed (East-West) and Gateway (North-South) IDS/IPS services.

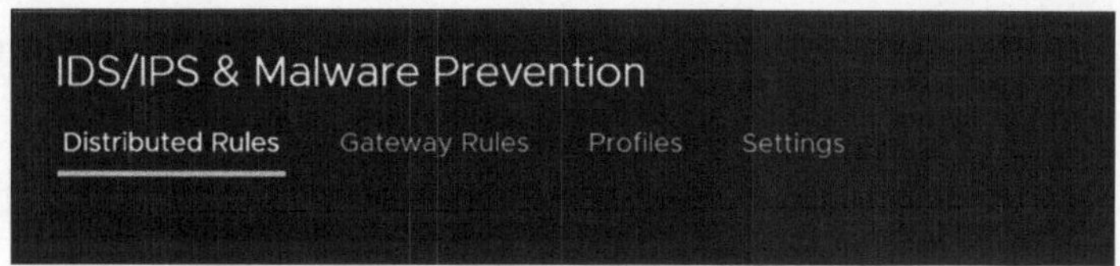

***Figure 9.24:** Configuring rules for IDS/IPS*

Step 1: Login into NSX Manager with admin privileges. Navigate to **`Security`** and select **`IDS/IPS & Malware Prevention`** under **`Policy Management.`** Click on either the **`Distribute Rule`** or **`Gateway Rule`** to add the IDS/IPS rule. These steps are using screenshots from the Distribute Rule, but the same can be used to configure the Gateway rule as well.

Step 2: Click on **`Add Policy`** to create a new IDS/IPS policy and add a relevant name for the policy.

Step 3: Click on the checkbox to select the newly created policy and click on **`Add Rule`** to add a new rule or click on three dots beside the policy and then click **on `Add Rule`** to add a rule under the policy as shown in *Figure* 9.25.

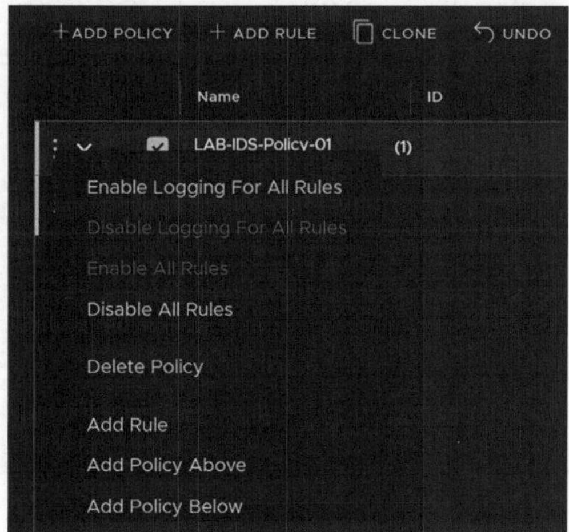

***Figure 9.25**: Adding an IDS/IPS rule in the policy*

Step 4: Provide the following details to add the IDS/IPS rule:

a. **`Name`**: Provide an appropriate for the rule.

b. **Sources**: Select the group for the source of traffic. The default is Any.

c. **Destinations**: Select the group for the destination of the traffic. The default is Any.

d. **Services**: Select the services against which traffic will be analyzed.

e. **Security Profile**: Select the IDS Profile to define IDS signatures against which traffic will be analyzed for intrusion detection.

f. **Applied To**: Default is DFW for Distributed Rule and Gateway for Gateway Rule. It is a best practice to select the NSX group here to limit the scope of the Distributed IDS/IPS rule.

g. **Mode**: Define whether the IDS/IPS rule runs in detect mode only or detect and prevent mode. In Detect Only, only alerts are generated but traffic is still allowed. However, in Detect and Prevent, both alerts are generated and traffic is blocked.

Step 5: Click on **Publish** to commit changes and push the configuration to transport nodes. *Figure* 9.26 shows an IDS/IPS rule LAB-IDS-Rule-01 under Policy LAB-IDS-Policy-01 which analyses traffic being sent to members of group SG-WEB-VM for any services against security profile LAB-IDS-Profile01.

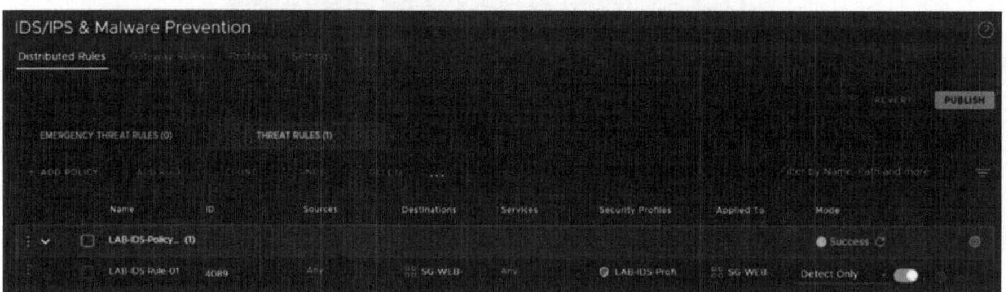

***Figure* 9.26**: *An example of IDS/IPS Rule*

Congratulations! You have successfully configured IDS/IPS in the NSX environment. Let's see how we can monitor events generated by NSX IDS/IPS and validate IDS/IPS rules being applied to VM (Virtual Machine).

Monitoring and Validating NSX IDS/IPS

The concrete way to identify if NSX ISD/IPS rules are being applied on the VM or Gateway is to log into transport nodes and get the list of rules being applied on the vNIC of the virtual machine or interface of the gateway.

Validate NSX IDS/IPS rule on Virtual Machine

Login via SSH into the ESXi host on which the virtual machine is running. After successful login into the ESXi host, run the following command to list the dvfilter applied on the vNIC of the virtual machine.

```
summarize-dvfilter | grep -A 3 vmm
```

Figure 9.27 shows the output of the command listed earlier with dvfilter of VM sa-web-03-victim.

```
--
world 21338136 vmm0:sa-web-03 vcUuid:'50 18 b8 bc b3 89 fc 4c-c8 7b 72 60 47 8e 2f ae'
 port 67108894 sa-web-03.eth0
  vNic slot 2
   name: nic-21338136-eth0-vmware-sfw.2
```

Figure 9.27: *Output of command summarize-dvfilter*

After finding out the name of the dvfilter assigned to vNIC, run the following command to list all rules assigned to it.

```
vsipioctl getrules -f <dvfiltername>
```

Figure 9.28 shows the output with the IDS rule applied to it created earlier in the chapter.

```
vsipioctl getrules -f nic-21338136-eth0-vmware-sfw.2
ruleset mainrs {
  # generation number: 0
  # realization time : 2023-09-04T17:06:49
  # PRE_FILTER rules
  rule 5 at 1 inout protocol any from malicious to any drop tag 'MALICIOUS IP AT SOURCE RULE';
  rule 6 at 2 inout protocol any from any to malicious drop tag 'MALICIOUS IP AT DESTINATION RULE';
  # FILTER (APP Category) rules
  rule 3 at 1 inout inet6 protocol ipv6-icmp icmptype 136 from any to any accept;
  rule 3 at 2 inout inet6 protocol ipv6-icmp icmptype 135 from any to any accept;
  rule 4 at 3 inout protocol udp from any to any port {67, 68} accept;
  rule 2 at 4 inout protocol any from any to any accept;
  # IDP rules
  rule 4089 at 1 inout protocol any from any to addrset 345cf525-9548-46ae-b730-a4ad02aaafbf with ids profile a3fffdf4-5ad3
-442d-b799-f33116013525 idp_detect oversubscription inherit;
}

ruleset mainrs_L2 {
  # generation number: 0
  # realization time : 2023-09-04T17:06:49
  # FILTER rules
  rule 1 at 1 inout ethertype any stateless from any to any accept;
}
```

Figure 9.28: *Listing IDS rules applied on VM*

This output confirms the rules successfully pushed to the ESXi host from the NSX Manager and applied to the desired virtual machine.

Validate NSX IDS/IPS rule on Tier1 Gateway

Login via SSH into Edge Node on which the active instance of Tier1 gateway is running. After successful login into Edge Node, run the following command to list the UUID of the Tier1 gateway.

```
get logical-router
```

Next, after identifying the UUID of the Tier1 gateway, list all interfaces assigned to the Tier1 gateway with the following command.

```
get logical-router <UUID of Tier1 SR> interfaces
```

From the output of the preceding command, find the interface with Port-Type as Uplink and note down its interface ID. Run the following command to list all rules being applied on the interface.

```
get firewall <interface ID> ruleset type idp rules
```

Figure 9.29 shows the output of the command, which lists the IDS rule being applied on the NSX Tier1 gateway uplink interface.

```
sa-nsxedge-01> get firewall bd7e94fa-bd71-432b-871f-c222849d5122 ruleset type idp rules
Sat Jul 29 2023 UTC 19:24:36.750
Rule count: 1
    Rule ID   : 3049
    Rule      : inout protocol any from any to any with idsprofile 8d46466c-091a-4209-b459-9877419fdad1 idp_detect
```

Figure 9.29: *Example output of IDS/IPS rule on Tier1*

Monitoring NSX IDS/IPS Events

All the IDS/IPS generated by the ESXi host or Tier1 gateway are received by the NSX Manager, which is further parsed and displayed to the user in NSX Manager UI itself. In order to access IDS/IPS events, navigate to **Security** and click on **IDS/IPS** under **Threat Event Monitoring**.

It will provide a list of events on a timescale according to their severity, as shown in *Figure* 9.30.

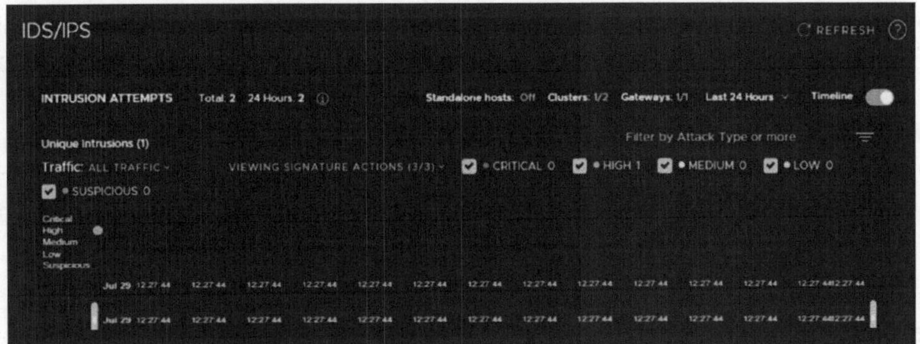

Figure 9.30: *Monitoring NSX IDS/IPS events*

Click on individual dots to select the interesting event and view details of the intrusion event in the environment. It provides in-depth details such as source, destination, type of vulnerability used, and risk score, as illustrated in *Figure* 9.31.

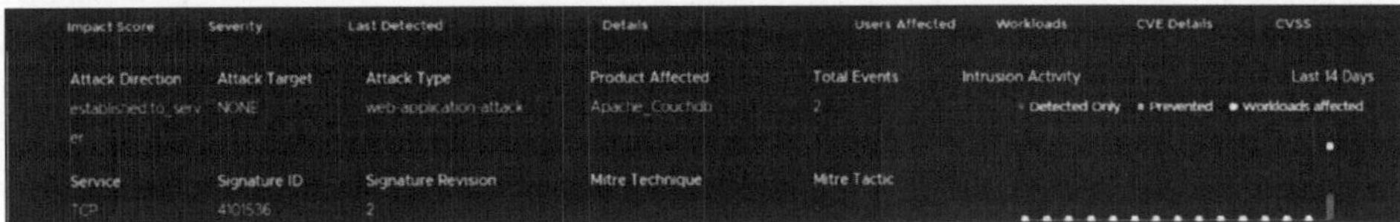

Figure 9.31: *Viewing details of the IDS event*

Tip: NSX IDS/IPS is located in location /var/log/nsx-idps/nsx-idps-events.log which is helpful in troubleshooting.

This concludes the implementation of NSX IDS/IPS services in the environment. NSX IDS/IPS is a powerful security feature, which helps protect against application or operating system vulnerabilities in the environment.

NSX Malware Prevention

NSX Malware Prevention helps protect the environment from malware such as viruses, worms, trojans, spyware, and ransomware, and so on, by detecting and preventing known or unknown malicious files. These unknown files are also known as zero-day threats and NSX Malware Prevention Service (MPS) helps protect using a combination of the following techniques:

- **Signature-based detection:** This approach uses databases of known malware patterns similar to IDS/IPS signatures. It scans the file and memory of a system to match against known patterns.

- **Local analysis of unknown file:** This approach extracts unique characteristics of the file and uses a machine learning algorithm to identify any malware patterns.
- **Cloud analysis of unknown file:** This approach sends the unknown files to VMware Threat Analyzer Cloud to execute the file in a sandbox environment and record its behavior and further classify its behavior as malware or safe. Currently supported regions are the US, EU and Australia.

Note: As of the current release of NSX v4.1, the maximum file size supported by the NSX Malware Prevention service is 64 MB.

Malware Prevention is supported for both East-West traffic and North-South traffic. *Figure* 9.32 illustrates different locations where NSX Malware Prevention can be enabled.

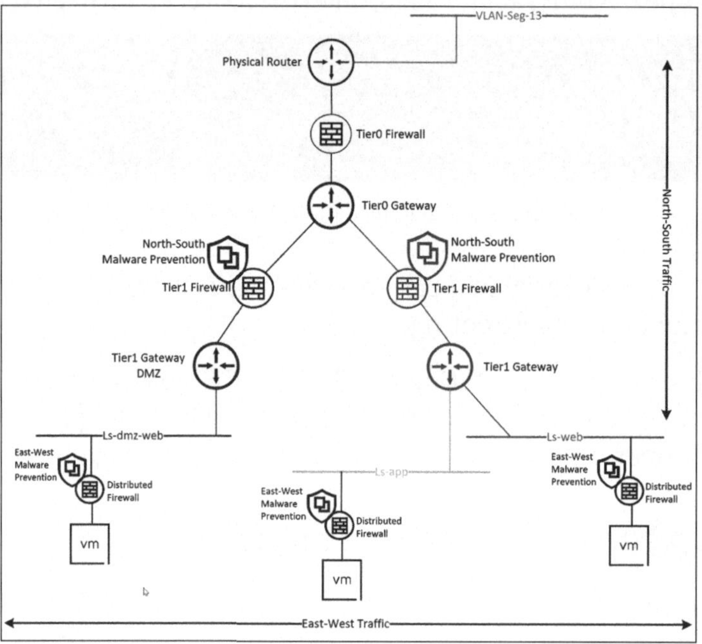

***Figure 9.32**: Malware Prevention in NSX environment*

- **NSX Distributed Malware Prevention**: NSX supports both the detection and prevention of malware on the distributed firewall for both Windows and Linux guest endpoints running on the vSphere cluster prepared for NSX. It supports both local analysis as well as cloud analysis of unknown files. Starting NSX release v4.0, all file types are supported for Distributed Malware Prevention whereas previously with NSX-T 3.2 only execution file types were supported for NSX Distributed MPS.

- **NSX Gateway Malware Prevention**: On Gateway Malware Prevention, only detection is supported as of the current release of NSX v4.1 and is enabled on the Tier1 gateway attached to the edge cluster. It also supports both local and cloud analysis of unknown files with all file supports.

Requirements for NSX Malware Prevention

There are multiple requirements to enable and consume NSX Malware Prevention services in the NSX environment. These requirements must be fulfilled to use MPS. Following are the high-level requirements and a more exhaustive list can be accessed on official VMware documentation.

- **License**: NSX Malware Prevention requires Advanced Threat Prevention licenses to be applied in addition to base NSX Advanced or NSX Enterprise Plus licenses.
- **NSX Application Platform (NAPP)**: The NSX Application Platform must be deployed and configured before activating Malware Prevention services. Deployment of the NAPP platform is covered in the next chapter.
- **Internet Access**: Internet access is mandatory to consume Malware Prevention services even if cloud analysis of unknown files is disabled.
- **NSX Edge Node Size**: NSX Edge Nodes must be deployed with an Extra Large form factor or utilize a bare metal server to enable Gateway Malware Prevention services.
- **NSX File Introspection Driver**: For Distributed Malware Prevention, Windows and Linux Guest endpoints must have a File introspection driver installed as part of VMware Tools. This is not installed by default hence administrator needs to ensure NSX File Introspection drivers are installed.
- **Web Server**: A web server is required to host NSX Malware Prevention SVM (Service Virtual Machines) OVA.

NSX Malware Prevention Architecture

NSX Malware Prevention includes components on multiple platforms such as NSX Application Platform, ESXi host, Edge Nodes, and VMware Threat Cloud. *Figure* 9.33 displays the overall architecture of NSX Malware Prevention services. It can feel overwhelming to look at so many components involved in a single service but if we divide architecture into different sections, it becomes very easy to understand the architecture behind NSX Malware Prevention services.

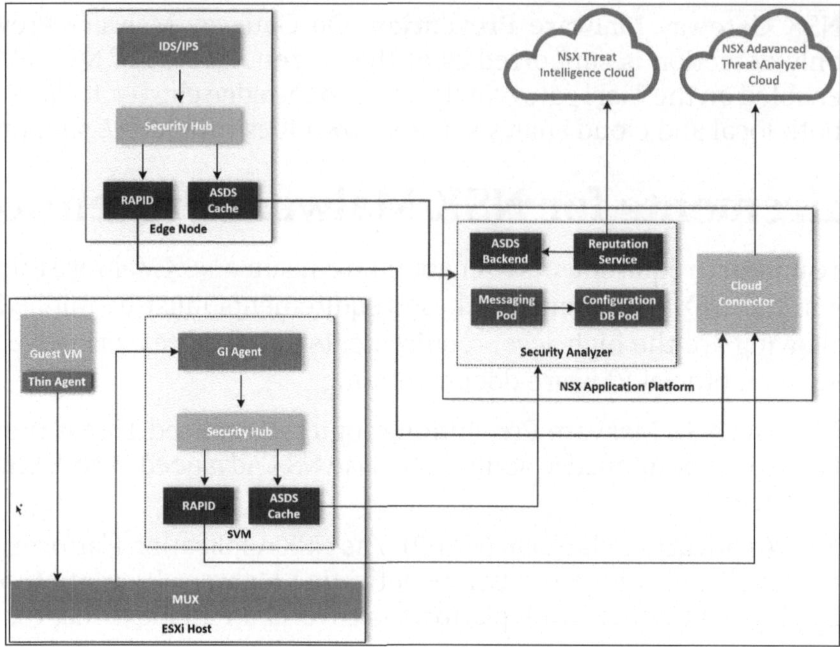

***Figure* 9.33:** NSX *Malware Prevention Architecture*

Cloud Services

NSX Malware Prevention uses the following Cloud services visible in the top-right corner of *Figure 9.32*:

- **NSX Threat Intelligence Cloud**: This obtains file reputation scores from VMware Carbon Black cloud and caches them to provide reputation scores to files in the NSX environment.
- **NSX Advanced Threat Analyzer Cloud**: It provides a sandbox environment to perform dynamic analysis of unknown files.

NSX Application Platform

NSX Application Platform (NAPP) includes the following components used by Malware Prevention services:

- **Security Analyzer**: It maintains two databases namely Configuration DB which saves all the file events and ASDS (NSX Advanced Signature Distribution Service) backend which saves the reputation of all known file types with the help of Reputation Service in turn receives the score from NSX Threat Intelligence Cloud. A messaging pod is used to communicate with the transport node to gather all information.

- **Cloud Connector**: Cloud connector is responsible for sending unknown files to NSX Advanced Threat Analyzer cloud for dynamic analysis. It acts as a gateway between the on-premise environment and cloud services.

ESXi Host Components

ESXi host enables East-West Malware Prevention services or NSX Distributed Malware Prevention and involves the following components for same:

- **Guest VM**: These are either Windows or Linux guest endpoints running the File Introspection driver. In Windows OS, the guest introspection driver is installed as part of VMware Tools however it needs to be manually enabled during installation whereas Linux thing agent comes as part of OSPs (Operating System Specific package) provided by VMware and can be downloaded from the VMware portal. These thin agent offloads the scanning of files to NSX Malware Prevention SVM (Service Virtual Machine) to avoid high resource usage on guest OS.
- **MUX**: Also termed as Content Multiplexer. It acts as a relay between guest VMs and SVMs. It also saves SVM configuration and processes distributed malware prevention policies.
- **SVM (Service Virtual Machine)**: SVM is a special appliance deployed on each ESXi host part of the vSphere cluster and scans files offloaded from guest VMs. It consists of the following sub-components:
    - **GI (Guest Introspection) Agent**: It acts as a messenger between guest VMs and the security hub to relay data and events.
    - **Security Hub**: It collects file events, receives verdicts for known file types and sends unknown files for local or cloud-based analysis.
    - **RAPID (Rapid API for Detection)**: It helps in performing a local analysis of unknown files and, if enabled, sends files for cloud analysis.
    - **ASDS Cache**: This maintains a local database of known file verdicts and reputation received from the ASDS backend in the NSX Application Platform.

Edge Components

Edge nodes enable North-South Malware Prevention services or Gateway Malware Prevention by hosting components for the same. All components are the same as of SVM except GI Agent, whose functionality is taken over by the IDS/IPS engine in Edge node.

- **IDS/IPS**: NSX Edge node utilized the file extraction feature of the IDS engine already running on it and sent data/events to the security hub.

Rest other components such as Security Hub, RAPID, and ASDS Cache perform the same function as SVM to help protect against malware in the environment.

Wow, that's a lot of components involved in NSX Malware Prevention services but each performs a unique function, and in the end, all stitches together to perform a singular function i.e., protect the NSX environment from different malware.

Configuring NSX Malware Prevention

On a high level, the following steps need to be followed to configure NSX IDS/IPS services in the environment:

1. Activate NSX Malware Prevention on the NSX Application Platform.
2. For Distributed Malware Prevention, register NSX Distributed Malware Prevention Service.
3. For Distributed Malware Prevention, deploy NSX Malware Prevention SVM (Service Virtual Machine).
4. For Gateway Malware Prevention, activate Malware Prevention on the Tier1 gateway.
5. Add Malware Prevention security profile.
6. Add Malware Prevention rules and publish rules.
7. Monitor Malware Prevention events.

These steps are covered in detail in subsequent sections.

Activate Malware Prevention on NAPP

To utilize NSX Malware Prevention services, first Malware Prevention needs to be activated on NAPP (NSX Application Platform) to connect to cloud services. Perform the following steps to achieve the same:

Step 1: Login into NSX Manager with admin privileges and navigate to **`Settings`**. Click on the **`NSX Application Platform`** under **`Configuration`** and go **`to NSX Malware Prevention`** tile card as *Figure 9.34* displays.

Figure 9.34: *NSX Malware Prevention tile card in NAPP*

Step 2: Click on **`Activate`** and a new screen will pop up to configure the cloud region. Select the nearest cloud region and click on **`Run Prechecks`** as shown in *Figure* 9.35. One important point to remember is that once the NSX cloud region is selected the same will be used for other services as well, such as NSX NDR.

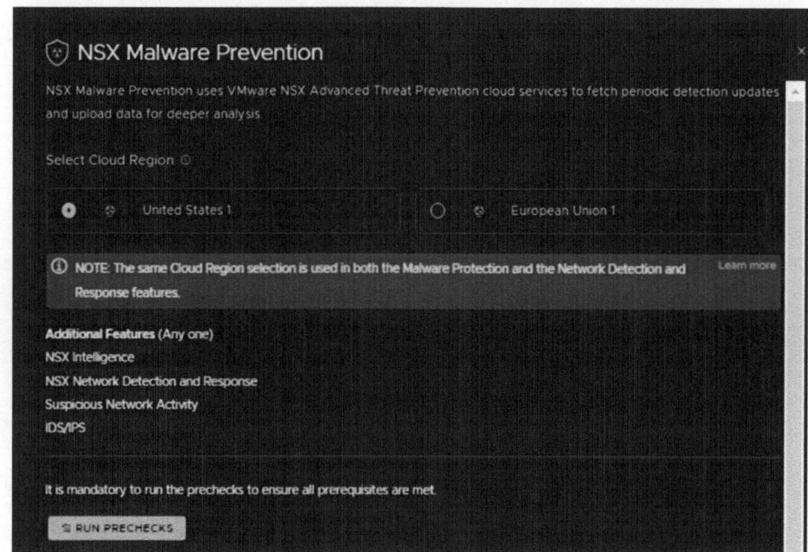

Figure 9.35: *Selecting cloud region for NSX Malware Prevention*

Step 3: After prechecks are successful, click on **`Activate`** to start activation of the feature on NAPP similar to *Figure* 9.36.

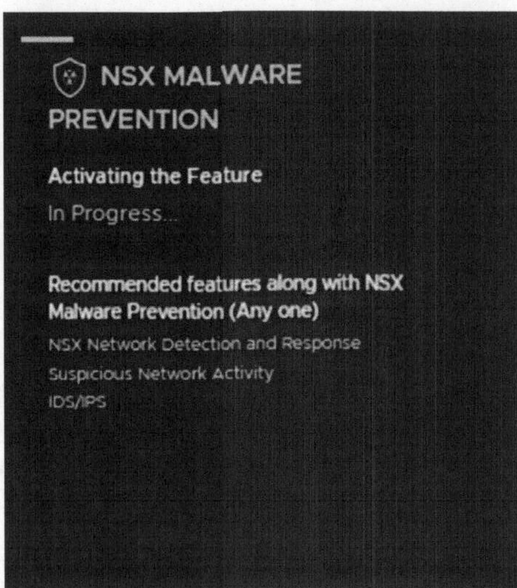

Figure 9.36: *Activating NSX Malware Prevention on NAPP*

Step 4: Successful activation of the feature will result in a screen similar to *Figure 9.37.*

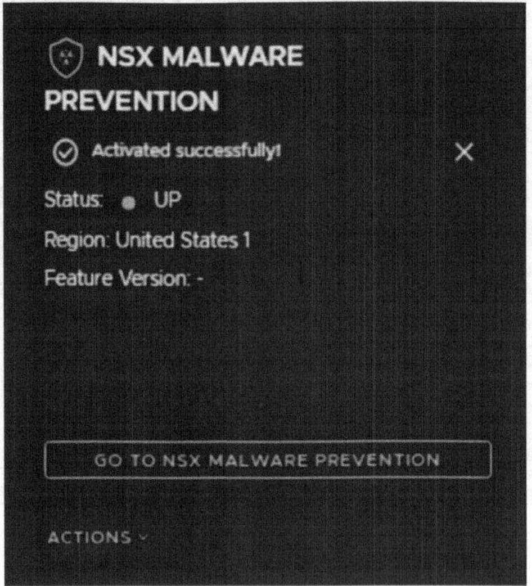

Figure 9.37: *Successful active of Malware Prevention on NAPP*

Step 5: Login into your Kubernetes platform hosting NAPP and run the following command to validate pods successfully created and running for NSX Malware Prevention service.

```
kubectl get pods -n nsxi-platform | grep "(cloud-connector|
malware-prevention|sa|reputation-service)"
```

Figure 9.38 shows an example output of the preceding command showing pods in either a running state or a completed state.

```
cloud-connector-check-license-status-754c855696-bpbcd           2/2   Running     0   5m55s
cloud-connector-proxy-798b5f4d9f-r9k55                          2/2   Running     0   5m55s
cloud-connector-register-js8jw                                  0/2   Completed   0   6m6s
cloud-connector-update-license-status-6dff57569d-tq2wc          2/2   Running     0   5m55s
malware-prevention-create-kafka-topic-bhrb9                     0/1   Completed   0   5m25s
malware-prevention-feature-switch-watcher-notifier-ndr-b862vfnq 1/1   Running     0   5m26s
malware-prevention-ui-6d89bcd777-sz654                          1/1   Running     0   5m26s
reputation-service-fcf9d9f4f-ng6c4                              1/1   Running     0   5m24s
reputation-service-feature-switch-watcher-notifier-depende62vv8 1/1   Running     1   6m6s
sa-asds-86f7967699-jtv95                                        1/1   Running     0   5m26s
sa-events-processor-6f589cc467-tj55j                            1/1   Running     0   5m26s
sa-scheduler-services-5cb7757b6f-b6p7x                          1/1   Running     0   5m26s
sa-web-services-6cf5fdcc77-z4kp4                                1/1   Running     0   5m24s
```

Figure 9.38: *Validating* NSX *Malware Prevention pods in* NAPP

Activating NSX Distributed Malware Prevention

Contrary to NSX IDS/IPS services, NSX Malware Prevention are activated very differently for distributed firewall (East-West traffic) and Tier1 gateways (North-South traffic). But, after activating respective Malware Prevention services, their security profile and rules are configured very similarly to NSX IDS/IPS rules. This section covers the details on how to activate and configure NSX Distributed Malware Prevention services to consume them.

Step 1: As a first step, register the NSX Distributed Malware Prevention service using API. There are different API clients that can be used to achieve this. For example, Postman.

a. **API URI**: POST https://{nsx-manager-ip}/napp/api/v1/malware-prevention/svm-spec

b. **API BODY**:

```
{
    "ovf_url" : "http://{webserver-ip}/{path-to-ovf-file}/{filename}.ovf",
    "deployment_spec_name" : "NSX_Distributed_MPS",
    "svm_version" : "4.1"
}
```

Here, **`ovf_url`** is the path of the web server hosting the SVM OVA as covered in the requirements section and **`svm_version`** is the SVM version downloaded from the VMware portal.

Figure 9.39 shows the example execution of API from the Postman client.

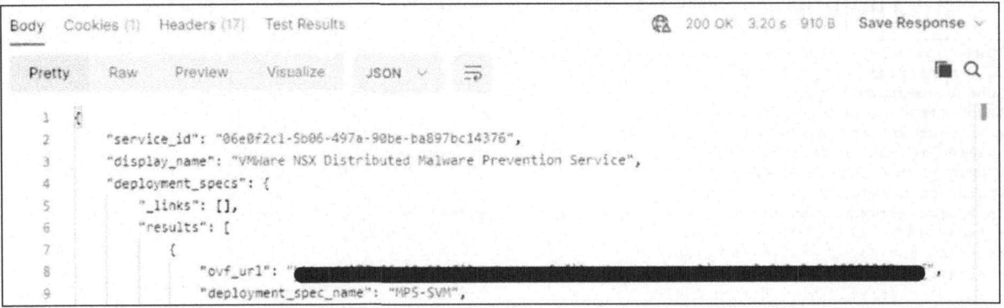

Figure 9.39: *Registering NSX Distributed Malware Prevention Service*

Step 2: Login into NSX Manager with admin privileges and navigate to **Settings**. Click on **Service Deployments** under **Configuration** and select **Catalog.** Newly registered VMware NSX Distributed Malware Prevention Service should be visible now.

Step 3: Click on **Deployments** under **Service Deployments** and ensure **VMware NSX Distributed Malware Prevention Service** is selected in the drop-down menu against **Partner Service**. The next step to activate the Distributed Malware Prevention service is to deploy SVMs. SVMs will be deployed on each ESXi host in a vSphere cluster. For example, if there are ten hosts in a cluster, then ten SVMs will be deployed on each ESXi host.

Step 4: Click on **Deploy Service** which will require the following inputs:

a. **Name**: Provide a name for service deployment.

b. **Compute Manager**: Select the registered vCenter server with NSX Manager in which SVMs to be deployed.

c. **Cluster**: Select the cluster in which SVMs will be deployed and the Malware Prevention service will be enabled.

d. **Datastore**: Select the datastore to be used for SVM storage requirements.

e. **Networks**: SVMs require a management interface to communicate with the NSX manager and other components. Click on **Edit Details** to provide network information such as VDS Portgroup and Network Pool to allocate IP addresses. DHCP allocation is also supported for the SVM management interface. Control NIC is auto-configured by NSX Manager and no inputs are required for the same. *Figure* 9.40 shows the completed network configuration for SVM deployment utilizing the NSX IP Pool to allocate IP addresses.

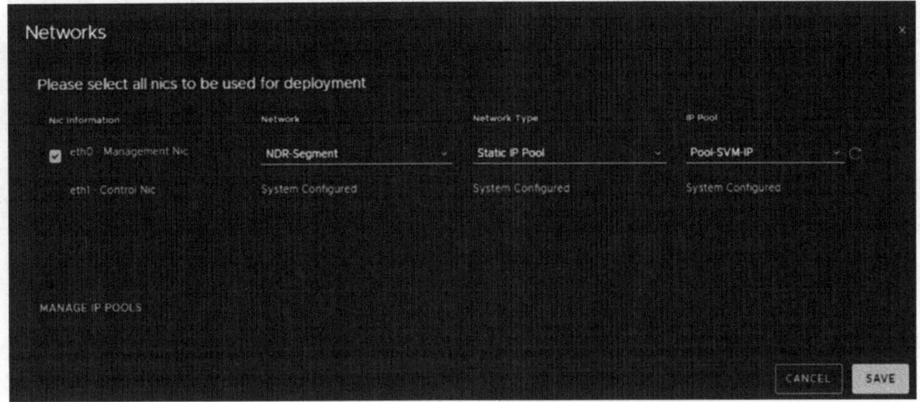

Figure 9.40: *Configuring networks for SVM*

f. **`Configure Attributes`**: Click on **`Configure Attributes`** to provide SSH public key for SVM password less authentication. Appliance Public Key provides the public key of key-pair generated as part of requirements, as shown in *Figure* 9.41.

Figure 9.41: *Providing public key to SVM appliances*

Figure 9.42 shows an example configuration for Distributed Malware Prevention Service deployment.

Figure 9.42: *Example configuration of NSX Distributed Malware Prevention Service*

Step 5: Click on **`Save`** to start the deployment of SVMs. After successful deployment of SVMs, navigate to **`Security`** and click on **`NSX IDS/IPS & Malware Prevention`** under **`Policy Management`**. Click on **`Setting`** and then click on **`Shared`**. The cluster will be now enabled for the Distributed Malware Prevention service, as shown in *Figure* 9.43.

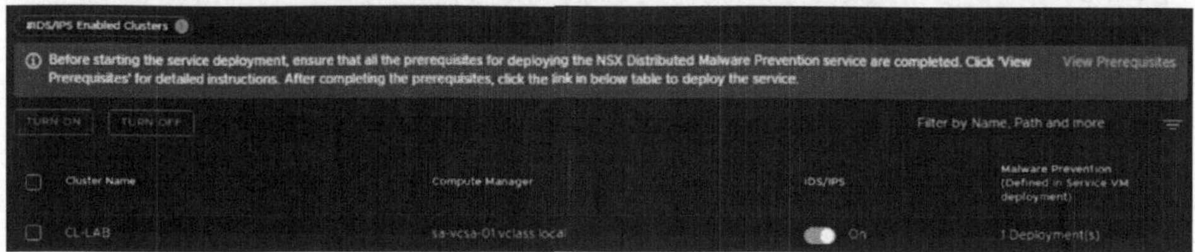

***Figure 9.43:** NSX Distributed Malware Prevention service activated for cluster* CL-LAB

Step 6: To validate successful SVM deployment, go back to **`Service Deployment`** in **`Settings`**. SVM deployment should be in a success state. Click on **`Service Instances`** and it will list all instances of SVMs. Ensure their health status is showing up as shown in *Figure* 9.44.

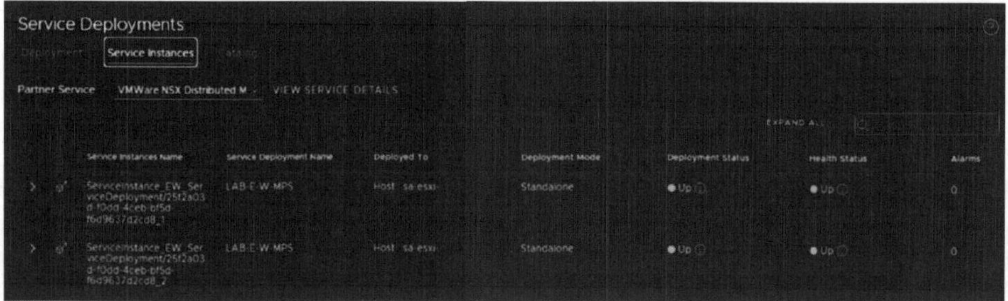

***Figure 9.44:** Validating* NSX MPS SVMs

Activating NSX Gateway Malware Prevention

Compared to NSX Distributed Malware Prevention service activation, Gateway Malware Prevention service activation is a walk in the park as you will see in the following steps:

Step 1: Login into NSX Manager with admin privileges. Navigate to **`Security`** and select **`IDS/IPS & Malware Prevention`** under **`Policy Management`**. Click on **`Settings`** and then click on **`Shared.`**

Step 2: Scroll down to the section **`Activate Gateway for North South Traffic`**. Change the toggle button from Off to On position under

Malware Prevention for the desired Tier1 gateway. *Figure* 9.45 shows Malware Prevention turned on for Tier1 gateway LAB-Tier1-01.

***Figure* 9.45:** *Activate Gateway Malware Prevention service*

That's it! NSX Gateway Malware Prevention service is now successfully activated on the Tier1 gateway.

Configuring NSX Malware Prevention Profile

NSX Malware Prevention profile defines the types of files that will be analyzed for malware and if it is an unknown file defines whether NSX should send the file to the cloud for in-depth analysis or not. A default NSX Malware Prevention profile is already predefined in the NSX Manager and can be used in Malware Prevention rules. However, if required custom Malware Prevention profiles can be created based on requirements.

Note: Prior to NSX 4.x, NSX-T 3.2 supported only executable file type for Distributed Malware Prevention service, hence separate Malware Prevention profile was required for Distributed MPS services. Starting NSX 4.x, Distributed MPS also supports all file types as of Gateway Malware Prevention Service.

Step 1: Login into NSX Manager with admin privileges. Navigate to **Security** and select **IDS/IPS & Malware Prevention** under **Policy Management**. Click on **Profiles** and then click on **Malware Prevention**.

Step 2: A default Malware Prevention file is already present in the UI. Click on **Add Profile** to create a new profile. Provide an appropriate name to profile and select the **File Types** to be analyzed for malware. Optionally, check or uncheck the option **Cloud File Analysis** to select if an unknown file type needs to be forwarded to the VMware Threat Analyzer Cloud or not.

Figure 9.46 shows a custom MPS profile with the name LAB-Profile-MPS-01 which will analyze Executable, Scripts, and Archive file types and in case of unknown files, it will send it to VMware Threat Analyzer Cloud for analysis.

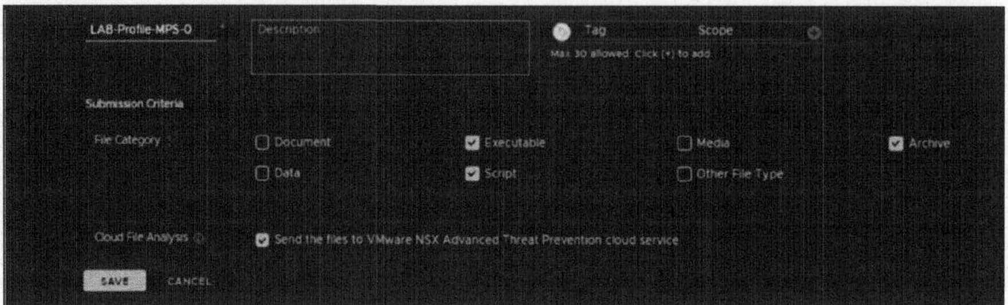

Figure 9.46: *A custom* NSX MPS *Profile*

Step 3: Click on **`Save`** to configure the profile and use it later on for NSX MPS rules.

Configuring NSX Malware Prevention Rule

Similarly, to NSX IDS/IPS rules, NSX Malware Prevention rules are configured in the same manner for both Distributed and Gateway Malware Prevention services. It depends on the tab that is selected for rule creation.

One key difference between NSX Distributed Malware Prevention and NSX Gateway Malware Prevention rule is that in gateway MPS Mode there is only one option i.e., Detect Only. Detect and Prevent Mode is only available for Distributed Malware Prevention Services.

Step 1: Login into NSX Manager with admin privileges. Navigate to **`Security`** and select **`IDS/IPS & Malware Prevention`** under **`Policy Management`**. Click on either **`Distribute Rule`** or **`Gateway Rule`** to add the MPS rule. These steps are using screenshots from the Distribute Rule but the same can be used to configure the Gateway rule as well.

Step 2: Click on **`Add Policy`** to create a new MPS policy and add a relevant name for the policy.

Step 3: Click on the checkbox to select the newly created policy and click on **`Add Rule`** to add a new rule or click on three dots beside the policy and then click on **`Add Rule`** to add a rule under the policy.

Step 4: Provide the following details to add the MPS rule –

a. **`Name`**: Provide an appropriate for the rule.

b. **`Sources:`** Select the group for the source of traffic. The default is Any.

c. **Destinations**: Select the group for the destination of the traffic. The default is Any.

d. **Services** : Select the services against which traffic will be analyzed.

e. **Security Profile**: Select the MPS Profile to define the types of files to be analyzed for malware.

f. **Applied To**: For MPS-only rules, DFW cannot be selected and NSX Group must be selected.

g. **Mode**: Define whether the MPS rule runs in detect mode only or detect and prevent mode. In Detect Only, only alerts are generated but traffic is still allowed. However, in Detect and Prevent, both alerts are generated and traffic is blocked. Detect and Prevent Mode is only available for the Distributed MPS rule.

Step 5: Click on **Publish** to commit changes and push the configuration to transport nodes. *Figure* 9.47 shows an MPS rule **LAB-MPS-Rule-01** under Policy **LAB-MPS-Policy-01** which is analyzing traffic being sent to members of group SG-Windows for any services against security profile **LAB-MPS-Profile-01**.

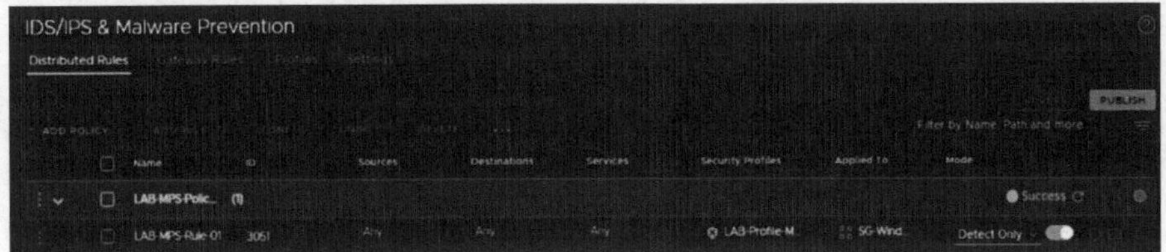

***Figure 9.47:** An example of MPS Rule*

This completes the configuration for NSX Malware Prevention services in the environment. As a next step, let's see how to monitor alerts generated by NSX Malware Prevention.

Monitoring NSX Malware Prevention

To monitor alerts generated by NSX Malware Prevention services, follow these steps:

Step 1: Login into NSX Manager with admin privileges. Navigate to **Security** and select **Security Overview**. Click on **Threat Detection Response**

and then select **Malware Prevention** to view the NSX Malware Prevention Dashboard, as shown in *Figure* 9.48. The first section of the dashboard provides a quick summary of how many files have been inspected and out of which how many are malicious/suspicious. If Mode is set to Detect and Prevent, then File Blocked count will also get updated.

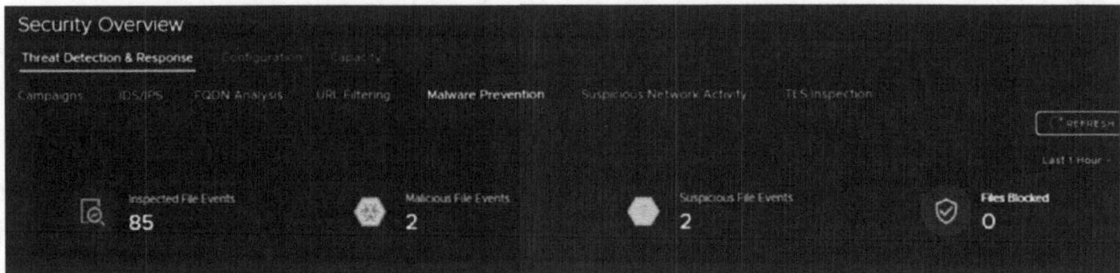

***Figure* 9.48**: *NSX Malware Prevention Dashboard*

Step 2: Scrolling down, it shows the number of files inspected divided by their threat score and going further detected malware on a timescale to correlate events.

Figure 9.49 illustrates potential malware on a timescale chart in more detail.

***Figure* 9.49**: *Potential Malware Trends*

These file events are further fed to NSX Network Detection and Response (NDR) if enabled to create campaigns and the same can be analyzed from NDR UI as well. NSX NDR has been covered in detail in *Chapter 10, Security – Network Detection and Response.*

Conclusion

This concludes the NSX IDS/IPS and Malware Prevention services configuration in the NSX environment. In this chapter, we covered NSX Gateway Firewall and NSX Advanced security features NSX IDS/IPS and NSX Malware Prevention, their architecture, configuration, and packet flows. NSX ATP features help protect an organization from various vulnerabilities not limited to the network only but also from application or operating system vulnerabilities and cover from day zero.

In the next chapter, we will cover a few more advanced security features which are NTA and NDR provided by NSX and are part of ATP suite only. We will also cover the NSX Application Platform, which is required to enable NTA, NDR, and Malware Prevention with its deployment.

Key Terms

- **Gateway Firewall:** A stateful firewall runs on a Tier1 gateway or Tier0 gateway.
- **IDS/IPS (Intrusion Detection Service/Intrusion Prevention Service):** Looks for suspicious activities in the network even if the traffic is allowed through firewall rules to protect against application or guest OS vulnerabilities.
- **IDS Signatures:** Contains metadata that helps in the identification of intrusion attempts in the network by matching traffic against known patterns.
- **NSX Threat Intelligence Cloud**: This obtains file reputation scores from VMware Carbon Black cloud and caches them to provide reputation scores to files in the NSX environment.
- **NSX Advanced Threat Analyzer Cloud:** It provides a sandbox environment to perform a dynamic analysis of unknown files.
- **NSX Malware Prevention:** Helps protect against different malware in the NSX environment.
- **NSX Application Platform:** A distributed platform that provides hosting resources for different services such as NDR, Intelligence, and Malware Prevention.
- **SVM (Service Virtual Machine):** A special VMware appliance that offloads scanning of files from guest VMs to itself.
- **Security Hub:** It collects file events, receives verdicts for known file types and sends unknown files for local or cloud-based analysis.
- **RAPID (Rapid API for Detection)**: It helps in performing a local analysis of unknown files and, if enabled, sends files for cloud analysis.

- **ASDS Cache:** This maintains a local database of known file verdicts and reputation received from the ASDS backend in the NSX Application Platform.
- **vSIP:** VMware kernel module responsible for configuring security policies on virtual machines.
- **VDPI:** VMware Deep Packet Inspection engine which performs Layer 7 inspection based on the context profile in the network packet.

Chapter 10

Security - Network Detection and Response

Introduction

In the last couple of chapters, we covered various security features such as NSX Distributed firewall, NSX Gateway Firewall, IDS/IPS, and Malware Prevention services. However, there is still a lot more that NSX has to offer. Can I have an analytics engine that can provide rules for micro-segmentation for different applications based on traffic flows between different components, detect abnormal behavior in the network, or which can ingest all the security events generated by different NSX components and provide a consolidated timeline of attack? If it were any other solution, you might have received an answer - aren't you becoming greedy? Jokes aside, with NSX, achieving all these different tasks is possible.

This chapter covers the NSX Application platform, which is a distributed platform hosting all these analytics engines. NSX Intelligence provides recommendations for NSX DFW and detects anomalies in the network using its suspicious detectors. Additionally, we will cover NSX Network Detection and Response, which creates campaigns by taking all events from Malware Prevention, Intelligence, IDS, and analyzing them, thereby reducing the burden on security administrators.

Structure

In this chapter, we will cover the following topics:

- NSX Application Platform
  - NAPP Requirements
  - NAPP Form Factor
  - Deploying NAPP
  - Validate NAPP Deployment
- NSX Intelligence
  - NSX Intelligence Requirements
  - Activating NSX Intelligence
  - Configuring NSX Intelligence
  - Traffic Visualization and Policy Recommendation
  - Suspicious Traffic Detection
- NSX Network Detection and Response
  - NSX NDR Architecture
  - NSX NDR Requirements
  - Activating NSX NDR
  - Working with NSX NDR
- Conclusion

NSX Application Platform

NSX Application Platform, or NAPP for short, is a distributed microservices platform deployed on an existing Kubernetes cluster. This is an infrastructure component that must be deployed in the NSX environment before enabling the following NSX security features:

- NSX Malware Prevention
- NSX Intelligence including Network Traffic Analysis (NTA)
- NSX Network Detection and Response (NDR)
- NSX Metrics

As evident from the list, NAPP is required to be deployed in the environment if NSX advanced security features are needed to be enabled in the NSX environment. Since NAPP is a container-based solution, it can be easily scaled out based on traffic flow in the environment. Before NAPP can be deployed in the environment, there are a few requirements or prerequisites that need to be fulfilled.

NAPP Requirements

To successfully install the NAPP platform, the environment must meet the following requirements. Please note that this list is not exhaustive; it covers the most important prerequisites. For the full list, please refer to docs.vmware.com (https://docs.vmware.com/en/VMware-NSX/4.1/nsx-application-platform/GUID-42EDE0AD-CD65-41AC-9694-AD0CCEC35969.html).

NSX Version Compatibility

NAPP is available for deployment from NSX-T release v3.2 onwards only. The NAPP version is independent of the NSX version; however, both should be compatible with each other as per the VMware Interoperability list. *Table 10.1* lists the compatible version of NSX with the NSX Application Platform as of writing this book.

NSX version	Compatible NSX Application Platform version
3.2.x	3.2.0, 3.2.1, 4.0.1
4.0.0.1	3.2.1, 4.0.1
4.0.1.1, 4.1.0	4.0.1

***Table 10.1**: Compatible NSX version with NAPP versions*

NSX also supports the upgrade of the old NSX Intelligence appliance 3.1 to NAPP 3.2, which is covered in the official VMware documentation and is outside the scope of this book.

NSX Licenses

NAPP requires a valid NSX license or additional add-on licenses. If the NSX base license is either one of NSX Data Center Evaluation, NSX-T Evaluation, NSX-T Enterprise Plus, or NSX Data Center Enterprise Plus, then no additional add-on licenses are required. However, if the base license is either one of NSX Data Center Advanced, NSX Firewall, or NSX-T Advanced, then additional add-on licenses such as the NSX Advanced Threat Prevention license are required. Please validate the entitlement of licenses received before deploying NAPP to ensure it is included with licenses.

NSX Privileges

NAPP requires NSX Enterprise Admin privileges to deploy.

Kubernetes Cluster

NAPP requires a specific version of the Kubernetes cluster to run successfully. As a best practice, it is recommended to utilize a VMware Tanzu Kubernetes cluster to run NAPP deployments; however, upstream Kubernetes clusters can also be used to run NAPP.

Table 10.2 lists the supported upstream Tanzu Kubernetes cluster and upstream Kubernetes cluster version that are compatible with different NAPP versions.

NAPP version	Tanzu Kubernetes cluster version	Upstream Kubernetes cluster version
3.2.0, 3.2.1	1.17 - 1.21	1.17 - 1.21
4.0.1	1.20 - 1.22	1.20 - 1.24

***Table* 10.2**: *Upstream Kubernetes Cluster requirements*

Please note that the upstream Kubernetes cluster must be prepared in advance before deploying NAPP. This needs to be completed by the infrastructure administrator. Another important point to remember is the size of the Kubernetes cluster nodes, that is, Controller and Worker nodes. Their size must comply with the system requirements of NAPP as per the form factor. Additionally, apart from setting up the Kubernetes cluster, they must set up Container Network Interface (CNI), such as Calico or Antrea, and the Container Storage Interface (CSI) as well.

Internet Access

NSX System requires internet access to a public VMware-hosted registry and repository to obtain NAPP Helm charts and Docker images. This outbound internet access is required on port 443 from both NSX Appliances and Kubernetes worker nodes during installation and upgrade operations. While NSX manager can be configured with a proxy to access the internet; however, as of writing, proxy access to the internet is not supported for NAPP deployment.

Table 10.3 lists the internet access requirements for NAPP deployment.

Source System	TCP Ports	Target URL
NSX Appliances	HTTPS 443	https://projects.registry.vmware.com
Kubernetes Worker Nodes	HTTPS 443	https://projects.registry.vmware.com

***Table* 10.3**: *Outbound Internet Access requirements*

If NAPP needs to be deployed in an air-gapped environment or direct internet access cannot be allowed, then infrastructure administrator may optionally needs to build a private container registry with a chart repository service. This private registry can then be used to upload NSX Application Platform Helm charts and Docker images for use during deployments. Setting up a private registry is outside the scope of this book; however, as a reference, one can follow the documentation on Harbor (https://goharbor.io/docs/2.1.0/install-config/).

Kubeconfig File

During NAPP deployment, setup will require a kubeconfig file to authenticate with the upstream Kubernetes cluster. This is usually provided by the administrator managing the Kubernetes cluster and should include all privileges to access all resources of the Kubernetes cluster.

The NSX documentation provides a script to generate a non-expiring Kubeconfig as the default **kubeconfig** expires after 10 hours, which results in warning messages on NSX UI. To avoid these warning messages, use the following script to generate a non-expiring **kubeconfig** file, as listed in *Table* 10.4:

Step 1: Login to the vSphere Tanzu Guest Kubernetes cluster using the following command:

```
kubectl vsphere login --server <supervisor-cluster_ip> -u <user>
--tanzu-kubernetes-cluster-name <tk-cluster-name> --tanzu-kubernetes
-cluster-namespace <namespace>
```

Here:

- **`<supervisor-cluster_ip>`** is the Control Plane node address visible under Workload Manager in the vCenter server.
- **`<user>`** is the account name with administrator access to TKGs.
- **`<tk-cluster-name>`** is the guest cluster name created in vSphere Tanzu.
- **`<namespace>`** is the namespace under which the guest cluster has been created.

Figure 10.1 shows the output of a command to connect successfully to the vSphere Tanzu Guest cluster and lists different contexts available to connect.

Figure 10.1: *Connecting to vSphere Tanzu Guest Cluster*

Step 2: After connecting successfully to the Tanzu Kubernetes Guest cluster, use the following command to use the Tanzu Kubernetes guest cluster context by default:

```
kubectl config use-context <context>
```

Here, **<context>** is the name of the Tanzu Kubernetes Guest cluster, as shown in *Figure* 10.2.

```
~# kubectl config use-context napp-advanced-01
Switched to context "napp-advanced-01".
```

Figure 10.2: *Using Tanzu Guest cluster as the default context*

Step 3: Run the following script to generate a non-expiring `kubeconfig` file and save it:

```
kubectl create serviceaccount napp-admin -n kube-system

kubectl create clusterrolebinding napp-admin --serviceac-
count=kube-system:napp-admin --clusterrole=cluster-admin

SECRET=$(kubectl get serviceaccount napp-admin -n kube-system
-ojsonpath=’{.secrets[].name}’)

TOKEN=$(kubectl get secret $SECRET -n kube-system -ojsonpath=’{.
data.token}’ | base64 -d)

kubectl get secrets $SECRET -n kube-system -o jsonpath=’{.data.ca\.
crt}’ | base64 -d > ./ca.crt

CONTEXT=$(kubectl config view -o jsonpath=’{.current-context}’)

CLUSTER=$(kubectl config view -o jsonpath=’{.contexts[?(@.name ==
“’”$CONTEXT”’”)].context.cluster}’)

URL=$(kubectl config view -o jsonpath=’{.clusters[?(@.name ==
“’”$CLUSTER”’”)].cluster.server}’)
```

```
TO_BE_CREATED_KUBECONFIG_FILE="<file-name>"
kubectl config --kubeconfig=$TO_BE_CREATED_KUBECONFIG_FILE set-cluster $CLUSTER --server=$URL --certificate-authority=./ca.crt --embed-certs=true
kubectl config --kubeconfig=$TO_BE_CREATED_KUBECONFIG_FILE set-credentials napp-admin --token=$TOKEN
kubectl config --kubeconfig=$TO_BE_CREATED_KUBECONFIG_FILE set-context $CONTEXT --cluster=$CLUSTER --user=napp-admin
kubectl config --kubeconfig=$TO_BE_CREATED_KUBECONFIG_FILE use-context $CONTEXT
```

Figure 10.3 shows the execution of the script in the console to generate a **kubeconfig** file.

TO_BE_CREATED_KUBECONFIG_FILE in the output has been modified to **NON_EXPIRING_KUBECONFIG_FILE.**

<file-name> in the output has been modified to **kubeconfig.**

***Figure 10.3**: Sample output of the execution of script*

DNS Name

NAPP deployment requires two DNS records to be created as part of preparations for the NAPP service interface and NAPP messaging service. These are used as HTTPS endpoints to connect to the NAPP platform by different components such as ESXi host, Edge nodes, or NSX Manager.

Other Requirements

Other than these, there are standard requirements as follows:

- Communication must be allowed between different components, such as NSX Manager, worker nodes, controller nodes, and more, listed in details on ports.vmware.com.
- Time must be synchronized between NSX Manager and Kubernetes cluster.

NAPP Form Factor

NSX Application Platform supports three different form factors based on feature requirements. *Table* 10.4 lists these different form factors along with worker node system requirements.

NAPP Form Factor	Features Supported	System Requirements for Worker Node
Standard	NSX NDR NSX Malware Prevention NSX Metrics	1 Controller and 3 Worker Each worker node with 4 vCPU, 16 GB RAM, and 200 GB Storage Each controller node with 2 vCPU, 4 GB RAM, and 200 GB Storage
Advanced	NSX NDR NSX Malware Prevention NSX Intelligence NSX Metrics	1 Controller and 3 Worker Each worker node with 16 vCPU, 64 GB RAM, and 1 TB Storage Each controller node with 2 vCPU, 4 GB RAM, and 200 GB Storage
Evaluation	NSX NDR NSX Malware Prevention NSX Intelligence NSX Metrics **Note**: This is only for PoC or evaluation as the name suggests and is not supported for the production environment	1 Controller and 1 Worker Each worker node with 16 vCPU, 64 GB RAM, and 1 TB Storage Each controller node with 2 vCPU, 4 GB RAM, and 200 GB Storage

***Table* 10.4**: *Different form factors for NAPP deployment*

NAPP deployment can then be further scaled out to accommodate additional traffic flow requirements if needed.

Deploying NAPP

After meeting all the requirements described in the previous section, the deployment of the NAPP platform becomes very easy and is a matter of providing the requested information in the NSX Manager UI. This section outlines the steps to deploy NAPP in the environment.

Step 1: Login to NSX Manager with admin privileges, navigate to **System**, and click **NSX Application Platform**, as shown in *Figure 10.4*.

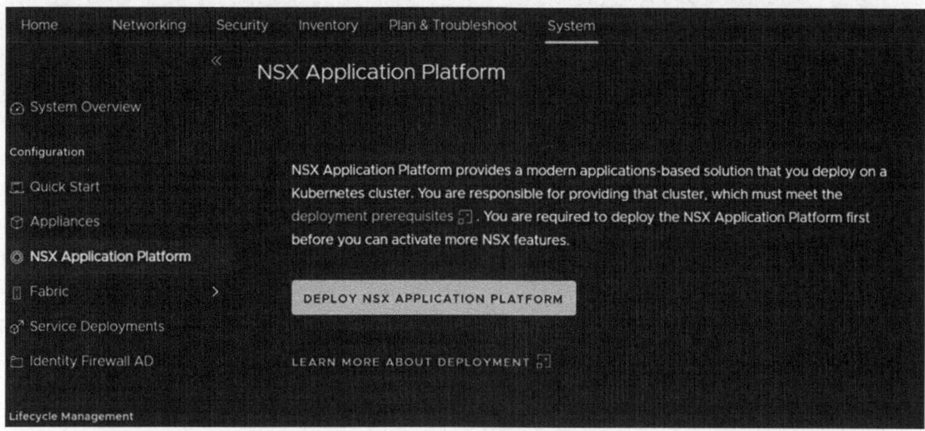

***Figure 10.4**: Accessing the NAPP deployment option in NSX Manager UI*

Step 2: Click **Deploy NSX Application Platform** to start the deployment of NAPP. By default, it uses the VMware public Harbor registry to download Docker images required for NAPP. If you are using a private registry, then provide the URL of the private registry and click **Save URL**, as shown in *Figure 10.5*, where it uses a public VMware-hosted registry.

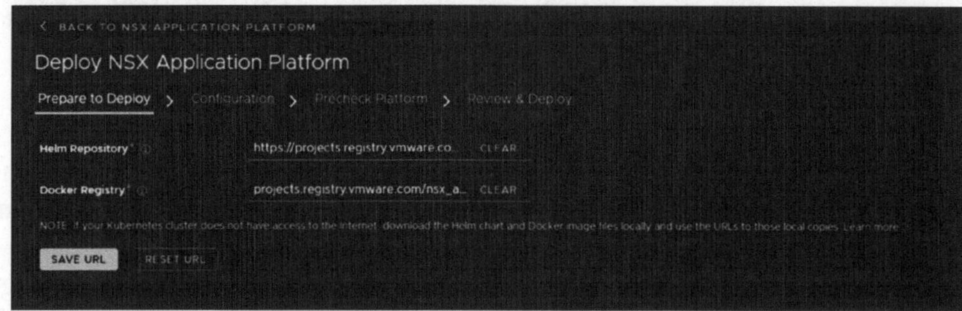

***Figure 10.5**: Setting up registry and repository URL*

Step 3: Select the target platform version compatible with NSX Manager. As shown in *Figure* 10.6, only NAPP 4.0.1 is compatible with NSX 4.1.0. Ignore **`Chart Name`** as it cannot be modified and click **`Next`** to continue deployment.

Deploy NSX Application Platform
Prepare to Deploy > Configuration > Precheck Platform > Review & Deploy
Helm Repository https://projects.registry.vmware.co... CLEAR
Docker Registry projects.registry.vmware.com/nsx_a... CLEAR
Platform Target Version 4.0.1-0.0-2060
Chart Name NSX Application Platform

***Figure* 10.6**: *Selecting version of the NAPP Platform*

Step 4: Provide the **`kubeconfig`** file to authenticate with the Kubernetes cluster created as part of the requirements and click **`Upload`** to validate connectivity with the K8S cluster. If there is a version difference between the K8S server and NSX Manager K8S client, then download the appropriate Kubernetes tools from VMware downloads and upload them, as shown in *Figure* 10.7.

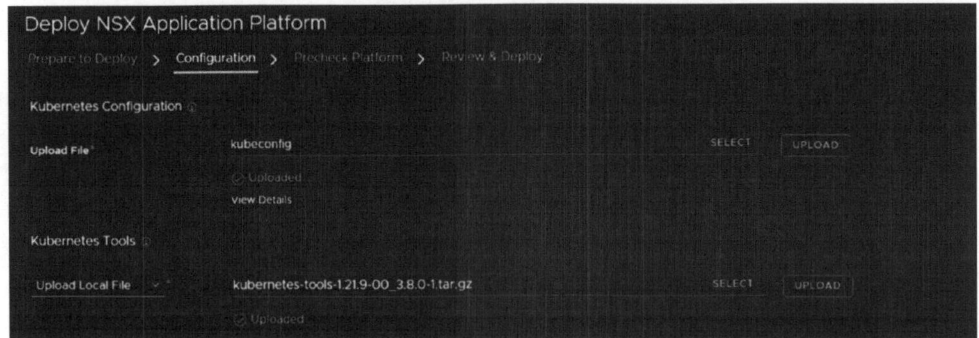

***Figure* 10.7**: *Uploading kubeconfig file and Kubernetes tools*

Step 5: Ignore the **`Cluster Type`** as it cannot be modified and is fixed as standard. Select the desired **`Storage Class`**, which, in turn, defines datastores to be used for NAPP pods. Provide the DNS resolvable name for **`Interface Service Name`** and **`Messaging Service Name`**, which will be used by the NAPP platform to communicate with NSX Manager and other components. Select the desired form factor based on the features to be enabled on NAPP. Select **`Advanced`** if NSX Intelligence will be required; otherwise, the **`Standard`** form factor can be used.

Figure 10.8 shows NAPP deployment with vSAN Default Storage Policy and Advanced form factor.

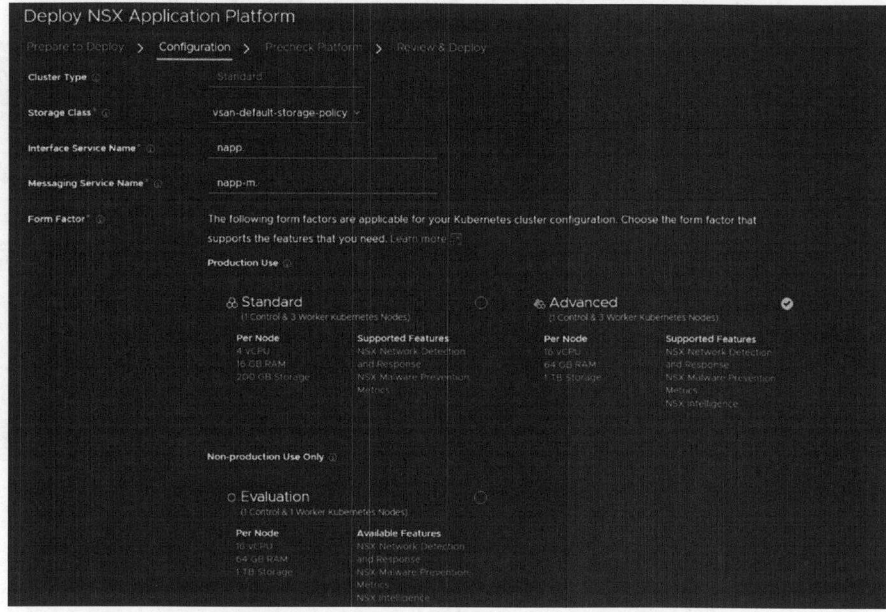

Figure 10.8: *Selecting deployment options for* NAPP

Step 6: Click **`Next`** to continue to prechecks. Click **`Run Prechecks`** and ensure the **`Status`** is **`Completed`** for all prechecks, as shown in *Figure* 10.9. If there are any errors, then check the error and fix them first before continuing.

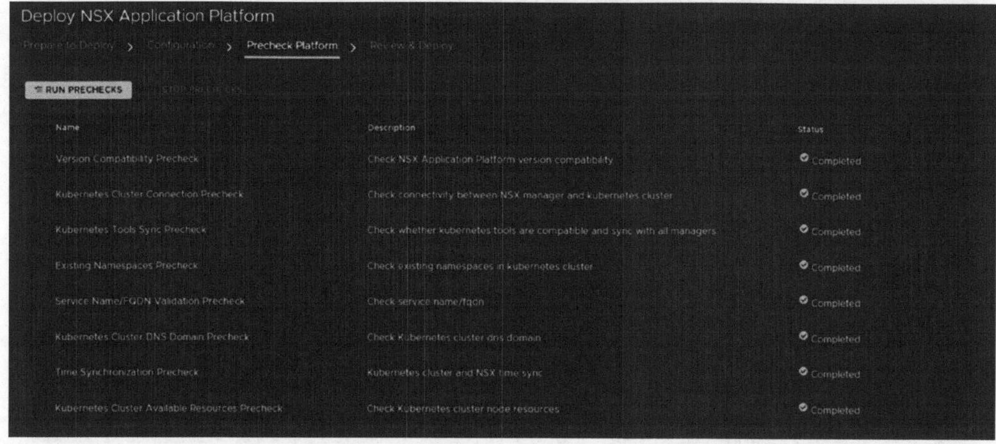

Figure 10.9: *Running precheck for* NAPP *deployment*

Step 7: Click `Next` to review the final configuration. If all configurations look correct, then click `Deploy` to start the NAPP deployment. There are multiple stages to NAPP deployment, as listed in *Figure* 10.10.

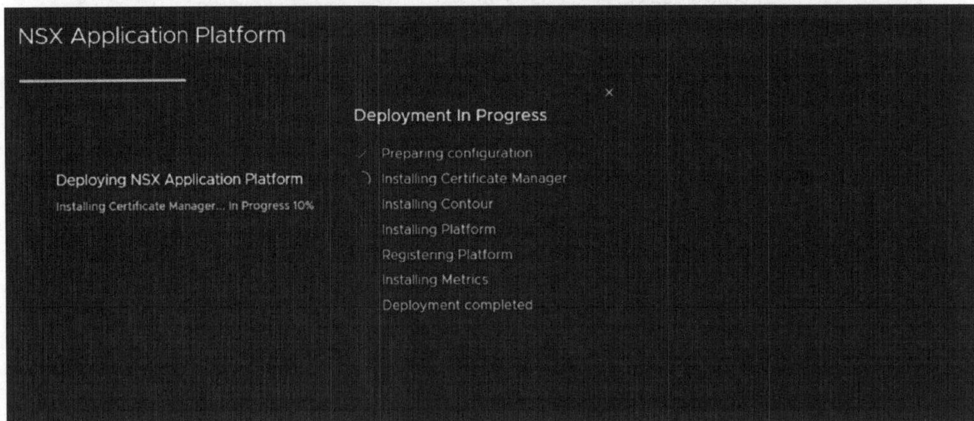

Figure 10.10: *Different steps involved in NAPP deployment*

Step 8: If you are logged into the K8S cluster, then run the following command to monitor NAPP pods deployment in near real-time in the K8S cluster:

```
watch -n 5 kubectl get pods -A
```

Figure 10.11 shows a sample output of the preceding command with NAPP container images being deployed in the Kubernetes cluster.

Figure 10.11: *Monitoring NAPP deployment from Kubernetes cluster*

Step 9: As NAPP deployment completes, it will reload the NSX Manager UI and show a successful deployment message with K8S cluster details, similar to *Figure* 10.12.

***Figure* 10.12**: *Successful deployment of* NAPP *in* NSX *Manager* UI

Validate NAPP Deployment

After NAPP deployment has been completed, the following steps can be used to validate that the NAPP deployment is successful and to see the behind-the-scene actions:

- While on the **`NSX Application Platform`** screen, click **`Core Services`** to view all core services such as **`ANALYTICS`**, **`MESSAGING`**, **`PLATFORM`**, and more. They should be in an **`Up`** state, similar to *Figure* 10.13.

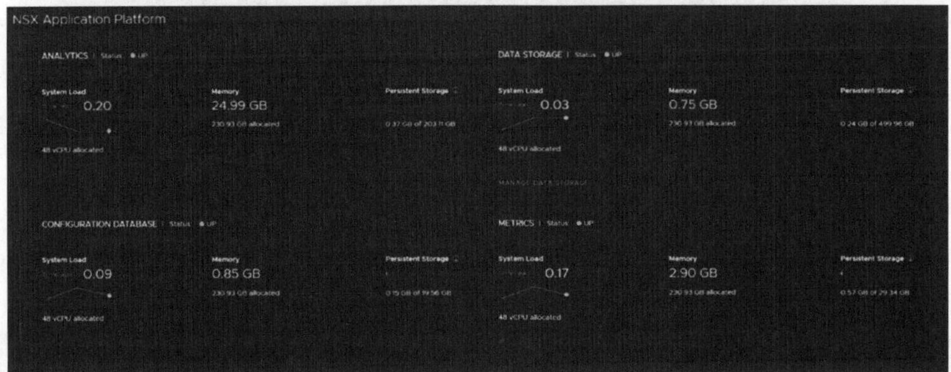

***Figure* 10.13**: *Validating services running in* NAPP *platform*

- Login to your Kubernetes controller server and run the following command:

```
kubectl get pods -n nsxi-platform
```

This command lists all the pods running in the namespace **`nsxi-platform`**. NAPP platform pods are deployed in the above-listed namespace. The status of all pods should be either running or completed. There should not be any pod in **`Error`** or **`crashloopedbackoff`** state. *Figure* 10.14 shows the expected output of the preceding command.

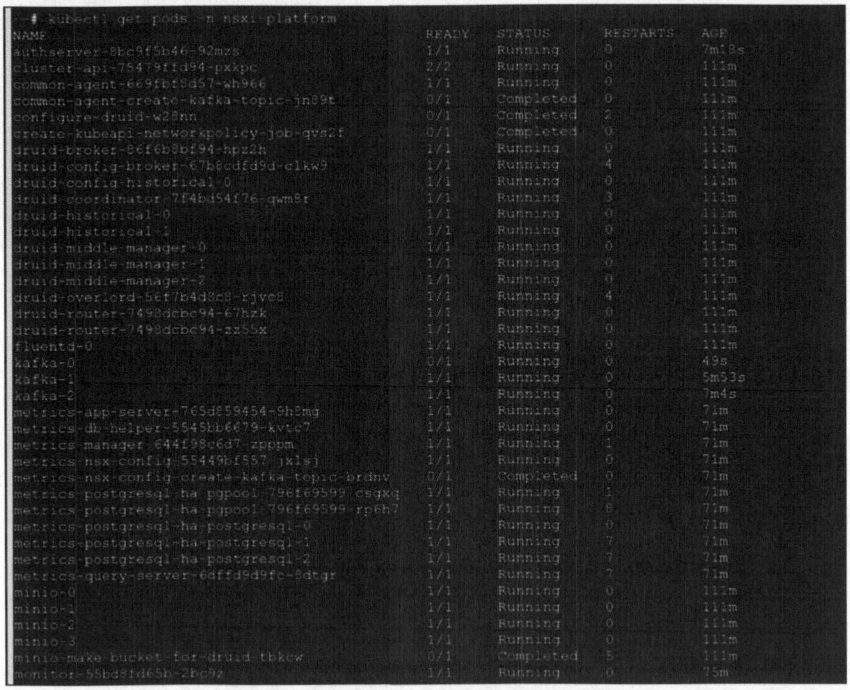

```
~# kubectl get pods -n nsxi-platform
NAME                                              READY   STATUS      RESTARTS   AGE
authserver-8bc9f5b46-92mzs                        1/1     Running     0          7m18s
cluster-api-75479ffd94-pxkpc                      2/2     Running     0          111m
common-agent-669fbf8d57-wh966                     1/1     Running     0          111m
common-agent-create-kafka-topic-jn89t             0/1     Completed   0          111m
configure-druid-w28nn                             0/1     Completed   2          111m
create-kubeapi-networkpolicy-job-qvs2f            0/1     Completed   0          111m
druid-broker-86f6b8bf94-hpz2h                     1/1     Running     0          111m
druid-config-broker-67b8cdfd9d-clkw9              1/1     Running     4          111m
druid-config-historical-0                         1/1     Running     0          111m
druid-coordinator-7f4bd54f76-qwm8r                1/1     Running     3          111m
druid-historical-0                                1/1     Running     0          111m
druid-historical-1                                1/1     Running     0          111m
druid-middle-manager-0                            1/1     Running     0          111m
druid-middle-manager-1                            1/1     Running     0          111m
druid-middle-manager-2                            1/1     Running     0          111m
druid-overlord-56f7b4d8c8-rjvc8                   1/1     Running     4          111m
druid-router-7498dcbc94-67hzk                     1/1     Running     0          111m
druid-router-7498dcbc94-zz55x                     1/1     Running     0          111m
fluentd-0                                         1/1     Running     0          111m
kafka-0                                           0/1     Running     0          49s
kafka-1                                           1/1     Running     0          5m53s
kafka-2                                           1/1     Running     0          7m4s
metrics-app-server-765d859454-9h8mg               1/1     Running     0          71m
metrics-db-helper-5545bb6679-kvtc7                1/1     Running     0          71m
metrics-manager-644f98c6d7-zpppm                  1/1     Running     1          71m
metrics-nsx-config-55449bf557-jxlsj               1/1     Running     0          71m
metrics-nsx-config-create-kafka-topic-brdnv       0/1     Completed   0          71m
metrics-postgresql-ha-pgpool-796f69599-csgxq      1/1     Running     1          71m
metrics-postgresql-ha-pgpool-796f69599-rp6h7      1/1     Running     8          71m
metrics-postgresql-ha-postgresql-0                1/1     Running     0          71m
metrics-postgresql-ha-postgresql-1                1/1     Running     7          71m
metrics-postgresql-ha-postgresql-2                1/1     Running     7          71m
metrics-query-server-6dffd9d9fc-8dtgr             1/1     Running     7          71m
minio-0                                           1/1     Running     0          111m
minio-1                                           1/1     Running     0          111m
minio-2                                           1/1     Running     0          111m
minio-3                                           1/1     Running     0          111m
minio-make-bucket-for-druid-tbkcw                 0/1     Completed   5          111m
monitor-55bd8fd65b-2bc9z                          1/1     Running     0          75m
```

Figure 10.14: *Validating pods running in Kubernetes cluster for* NAPP

- Run the following command to view services configured in K8S for the NAPP platform in the **`projectcontour`** namespace:

```
kubectl get svc -n projectcontour
```

Figure 10.15 displays an example output of the preceding command with services exposed on External-IP.

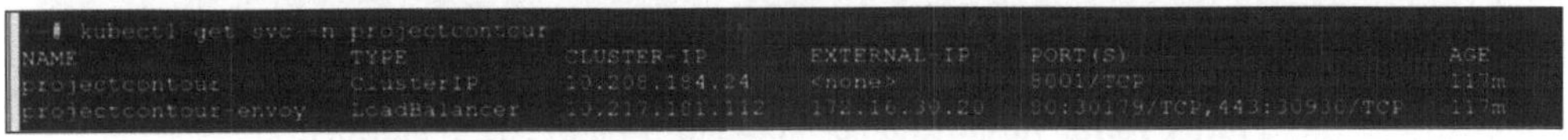

```
~# kubectl get svc -n projectcontour
NAME                    TYPE           CLUSTER-IP       EXTERNAL-IP    PORT(S)                       AGE
projectcontour          ClusterIP      10.208.184.24    <none>         8001/TCP                      117m
projectcontour-envoy    LoadBalancer   10.217.181.112   172.16.30.20   80:30179/TCP,443:30930/TCP    117m
```

Figure 10.15: *Viewing* NAPP *service interface configured*

This completes the deployment of the NAPP platform and based on the licenses installed, different features on NAPP can be activated. For example, if an Advanced Threat Prevention license is installed, then NTA, NDR, and Malware Prevention can be enabled. However, if only NSX Enterprise Plus license is installed, then, in such a case, only NSX Intelligence can be enabled.

NSX Intelligence

NSX Intelligence is a distributed analytics platform hosted in NSX Application Platform, starting from NSX release 3.2 and later. Previously, it was deployed as an OVA appliance in prior releases that provides a graphical interface to visualize the security posture and network traffic flows in the NSX environment.

It provides the following capabilities in the environment if enabled:

- **Visibility**: It provides insight into network traffic flows aggregated over a period of time by visualizing different NSX objects such as groups, virtual machines, IPs, and more, and the traffic paths between them.
- **Recommendation**: It provides recommendations for security policies, groups, and services for applications and assists with micro-segmentation using DFW at the application level.
- **Suspicious Traffic Detection**: It can detect suspicious or anomalies in the network traffic with the help of NSX suspicious traffic detection feature, which uses different threat detectors to filter out interesting events from a security perspective. These interesting events can then be further fed to NSX NDR if activated in the NSX environment for further analysis.

NSX Intelligence Requirements

There are a few requirements that need to be fulfilled before activating NSX Intelligence and consuming its services in the NSX environment. These requirements are as follows:

License Requirements

NSX Intelligence requires a valid NSX license or additional add-on licenses. If the NSX base license is either one of NSX Data Center Evaluation, NSX-T Evaluation, NSX-T Enterprise Plus, or NSX Data Center Enterprise Plus, then no additional add-on licenses are required. However, if the base license is either one of NSX Data Center Advanced, NSX Firewall, or NSX-T Advanced, then additional add-on licenses such as the NSX Advanced Threat Prevention license are required.

If the NSX Suspicious Traffic detection feature needs to be used, then any one of the following licenses is also required:

- NSX Distributed Firewall with Advanced Threat Prevention
- NSX Advanced with Advanced Threat Prevention
- NSX Enterprise Plus with Advanced Threat Prevention

NSX Application Platform

NSX-T version 3.2 or later, NSX 4.x is required to activate NSX Intelligence on NSX Application Platform. Also, the NAPP platform form factor should be one of the following:

- **Advanced**: This form factor is required for a production-supported environment.
- **Evaluation**: This form factor can be used for evaluation or proof of concept deployments.

In addition to the aforementioned points, users must have Enterprise Admin privileges to activate, backup, restore, or upgrade NSX Intelligence.

Activating NSX Intelligence

As a first step to use NSX Intelligence, it needs to be activated on the NAPP platform through the NSX Manager UI. Perform the following step to activate NSX Intelligence in the environment:

Step 1: Login to NSX Manager with Enterprise Admin privileges. Navigate to `System` and click `NSX Application Platform` in the left navigation panel. Scroll to the very bottom, and under the `Features` section, there is `NSX INTELLIGENCE` tile card, as shown in *Figure* 10.16.

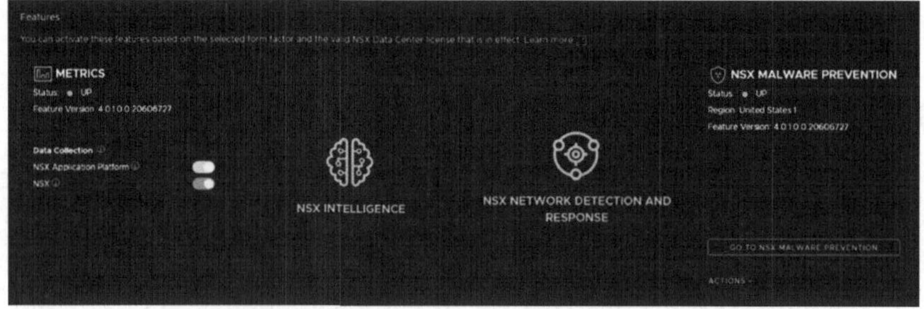

Figure 10.16: NSX *Intelligence under Features in* NAPP

Step 2: Hover the mouse over the **`NSX Intelligence`** tile card, and it will show the **`Activate`** button. Click **`Activate`** to prompt a new screen titled **`NSX Intelligence`**, as shown in *Figure* 10.17. Click **`RUN PRECHECKS`** to perform mandatory prechecks for NSX Intelligence.

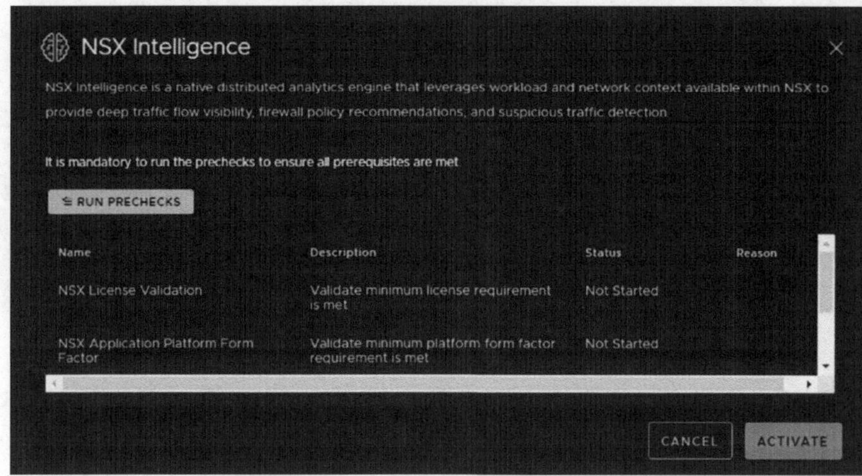

***Figure 10.17**: Running prechecks for NSX Intelligence*

Step 3: After the prechecks are completed successfully, click **`Activate`** to start the NSX Intelligence pods deployment in the Kubernetes cluster, as shown in *Figure* 10.18.

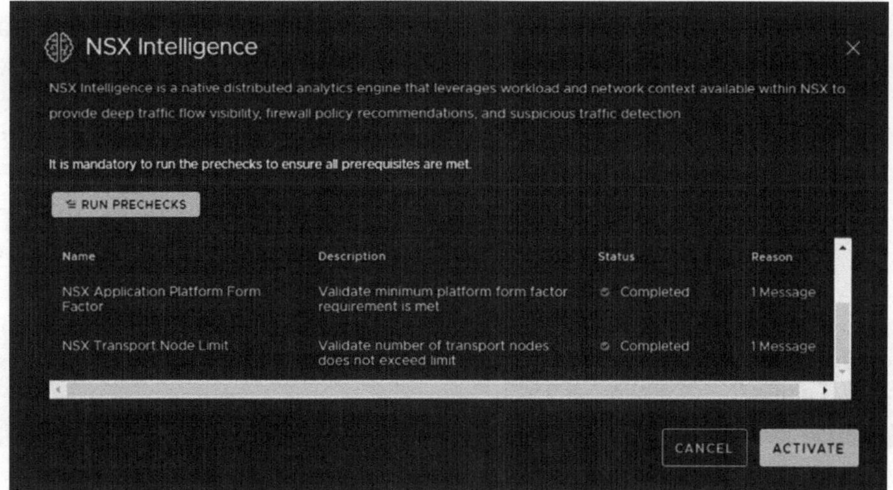

***Figure 10.18**: Activating NSX Intelligence in NAPP*

Step 4: This will start the deployment of pods required for NSX Intelligence in the Kubernetes cluster. Once all the pods have been deployed and are running successfully, the NSX Manager UI will display NSX Intelligence activated successfully, as shown in *Figure* 10.19.

***Figure 10.19**: NSX Intelligence successful deployment in NAPP*

These steps are simply activating the NSX Intelligence feature in the NSX environment. There are a few more configurations required to consume NSX Intelligence services.

Configuring NSX Intelligence

These steps are not mandatory to follow, but performing them can help provide more relevant security policy recommendations from NSX Intelligence.

Step 1: While logging into NSX Manager with admin privileges, navigate to **`System`** and then click **`NSX Intelligence`** under **`Settings`**. This screen provides an option to activate or deactivate **`standalone ESXi host`** or **`vSphere clusters`** for network flow collection by NSX Intelligence. As shown in *Figure* 10.20, cluster CL-LAB has been activated to allow NSX Intelligence to collect network flows to provide security policy recommendations or detect suspicious traffic. One can move the slider another way to deactivate the same.

***Figure 10.20**: Activating cluster for NSX Intelligence network flow collection*

Step 2: Next is setting up Private IP Ranges for NSX Intelligence. This helps in identifying private traffic from public traffic. Navigate to **`Security`**

and click **General Settings** under **Settings.** Select **Private IP Ranges** and enter the appropriate IPv4 range and IPv6 range. As illustrated in *Figure* 10.21, IPv4 range has been set as 172.17.0.0/16, as we will be using this as a private range, whereas other 10.x.x.x and 192.168.x.x as public networks. Similarly, organizations might be using public ranges within data centers, so it is a good practice to configure all those private IP ranges here. This is used by both NSX Intelligence and NSX NDR.

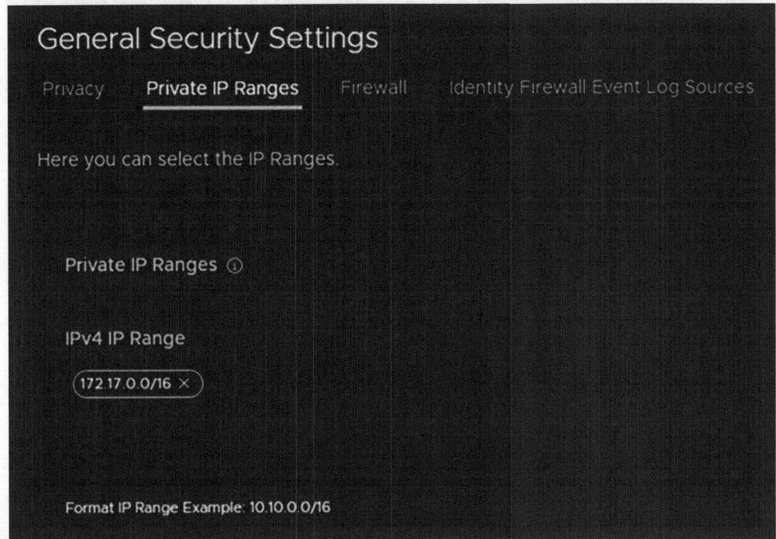

***Figure 10.21**: Setting Private IP ranges in NSX Manager*

Step 3: Next are **Privacy** settings. This is used to enable or disable if file hashes need to be sent to NSX Threat Intelligence Cloud or not. To configure this setting, NSX Malware Prevention must be enabled.

Step 4: NSX Intelligence 4.0 introduces a new feature, that is, Classifications. If an entity has network flows of more than 30 days, then NSX Intelligence tries to classify whether the compute entity is an Infrastructure service or a non-Infrastructure service. Infrastructure services include different services such as DNS, DHCP, LDAP, and Active Directory. Navigate to **Plan & Troubleshoot** and select **Configurations** under **Discover & Plan.** Click **Modify** after selecting an entity to override these classifications. *Figure* 10.22 shows whether to modify the classification for entity App-01 or not.

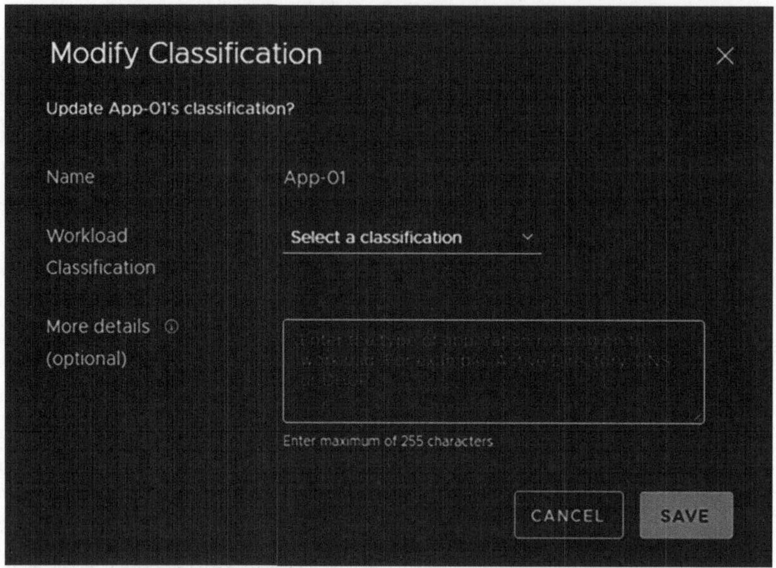

***Figure 10.22**: Modifying classification of an entity*

Traffic Visualization and Policy Recommendation

NSX Intelligence provides insights into traffic flows between virtual machines running in an enabled cluster and can help provide recommendations for micro-segmentation as well. Let's take a sample topology and try to understand NSX Intelligence Discovery and Recommendations. *Figure* 10.23 illustrates a three-tier application with VMs Web-01, Web-02, DB-01, App-01, and App-02.

VMs Web-01 and Web-02 are connected to overlay segment ls-overlay-web with tags applied to them with the value demo-app-WEB and scope App-Tier. Similarly, App-01 and App-02 are connected to the overlay segment ls-overlay-app with a tag applied to them with the value demo-app-APP and scope App-Tier. Lastly, there is a DB VM db-01 connected to the segment ls-overlay-db with the tag demo-app-DB with the same scope. All three segments are connected to Tier1 gateway LAB-Tier1-01, which is further connected to Tier0 gateway LAB-Tier0-01 exchanging routes with the Physical Router through BGP. The user, as a client, is trying to access this three-tier application from outside the NSX environment. Currently, there are no firewall rules configured, and we would like NSX Intelligence to provide DFW recommendations to secure our three-tier application.

We will be using this topology throughout this section to understand how NSX Intelligence provides visualization of network flows between different tiers and how it can be used to provide recommendations for NSX DFW policies.

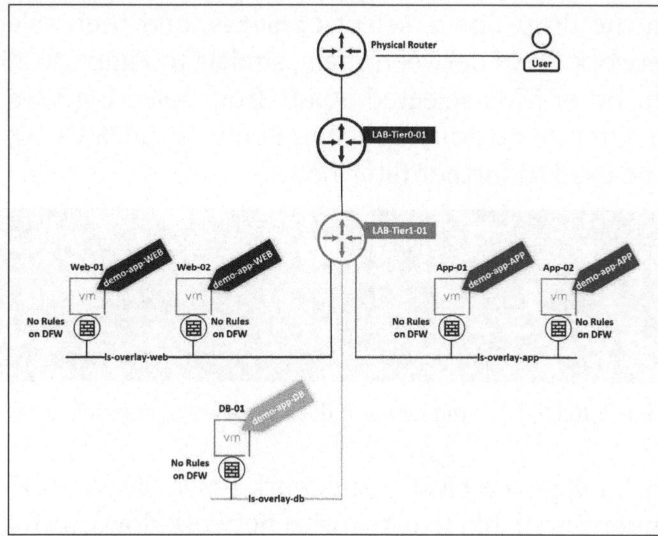

***Figure 10.23**: Sample topology for NSX Intelligence*

Navigate to **`Plan & Troubleshoot`** and click **`Discover & Take Action`**. This is the initial landing screen to view the network flow being collected by NSX Intelligence. *Figure* 10.24 illustrates the network flows categorized by NSX Groups. As there are no NSX groups created in the environment, all compute entities fall under Uncategorized Computes.

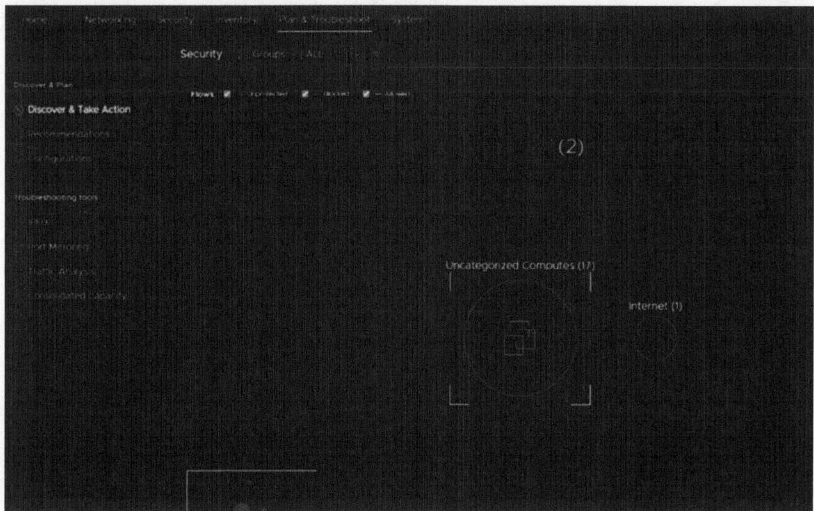

***Figure 10.24**: Viewing network flows in NSX Intelligence*

If groups are not present, then flows can be filtered based on compute entities as well.

In our example, we are interested in our three-Tier application. So, besides **Security**, from the drop-down, select **Computes**, and then select the desired VMs to view network flows between them, similar to *Figure* 10.25, which shows App-01 and four other VMs selected. Apart from selecting VMs, several other filters based on different attributes such as Public IP, BIOS UUID, OS Name, and more, can also be used to further filter flows.

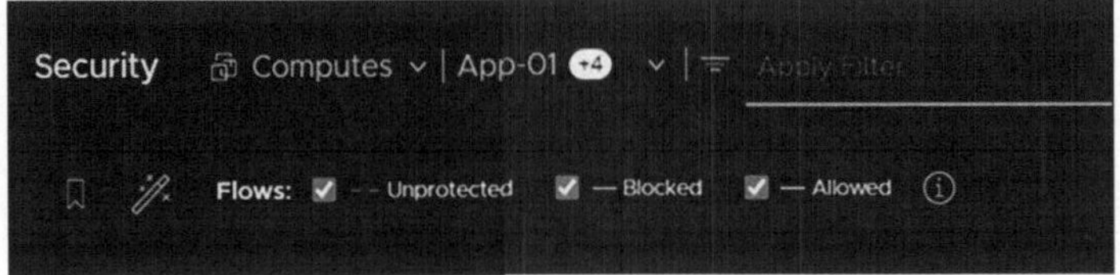

Figure 10.25: *Filtering network flows based on compute entities*

By default, NSX Intelligence clusters network flows based on Flows, but there are different options available to categorize network flows, as follows:

- Flows
- Labels
- Names
- Tags

These different options can be selected by the **Clustering** option in the bottom-right corner of the screen, highlighted in the red box, and selecting the desired option, as shown in *Figure* 10.26, where we are using Tags with scope App-Tier to cluster our network flows.

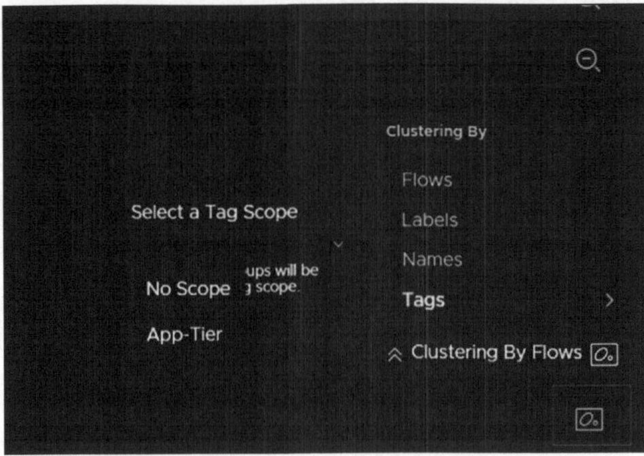

Figure 10.26: *Changing clustering of network flow in NSX Intelligence*

This provides a clear understanding of flows between different compute entities, indicating the type of traffic, direction of traffic, and whether traffic is protected, unprotected, allowed, or blocked, as shown in *Figure* 10.27.

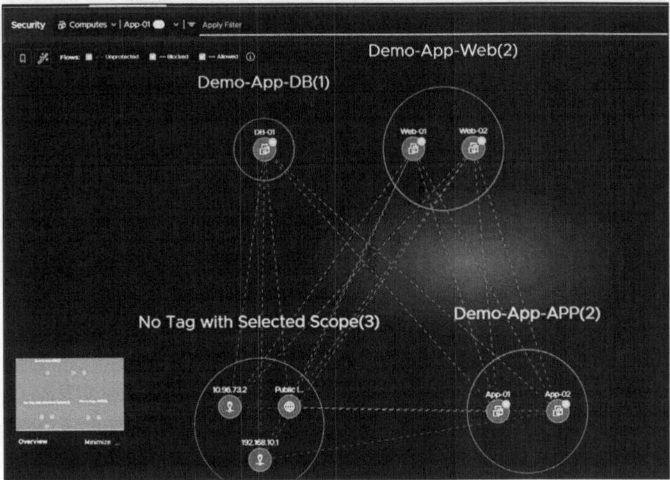

Figure 10.27: *Clustering of network flow by Tags*

This network visualization provides a deep insight into traffic flowing between different entities. You can perform different operations, including but not limited to the following:

- Zoom in and zoom out of network visualization to view different services along the traffic paths, as shown in *Figure* 10.28.

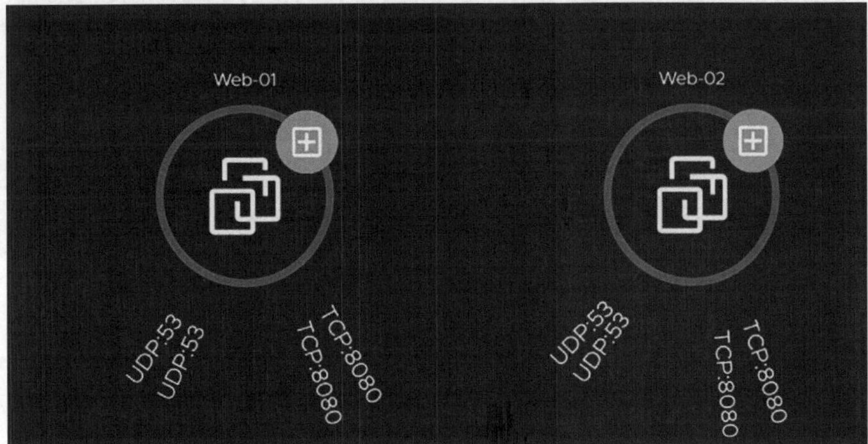

Figure 10.28: *Viewing more information about traffic paths*

- Select any compute entity to view its communication with other compute entities by highlighting only specific entities.

- Select any traffic path to view in-depth information about source, destination, services, and more, as shown in *Figure 10.29*.

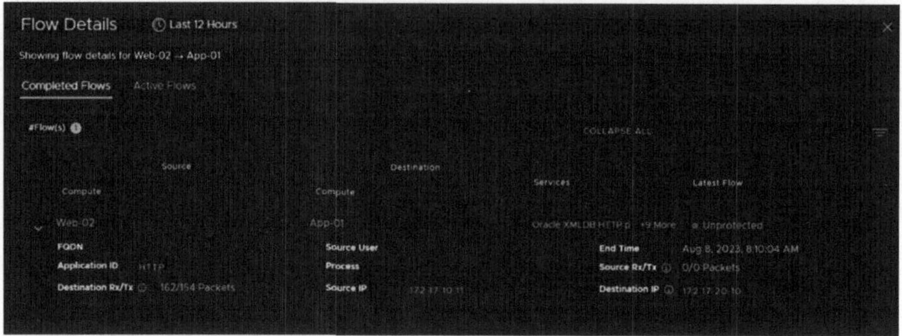

Figure 10.29: *Viewing more details of a specific traffic path*

Once you are satisfied with the selection of applications and traffic flows, the next step is to start Recommendations. Click **`little wizard`** icon, as highlighted in the red box in *Figure* 10.30, and then select **`Start Recommendation for the Filtered Components`**. Another way to go to the same menu is by clicking **`Recommendations`** just under **`Discover & Take Action`**. However, you will need to start from ground zero and filter the desired compute entities again.

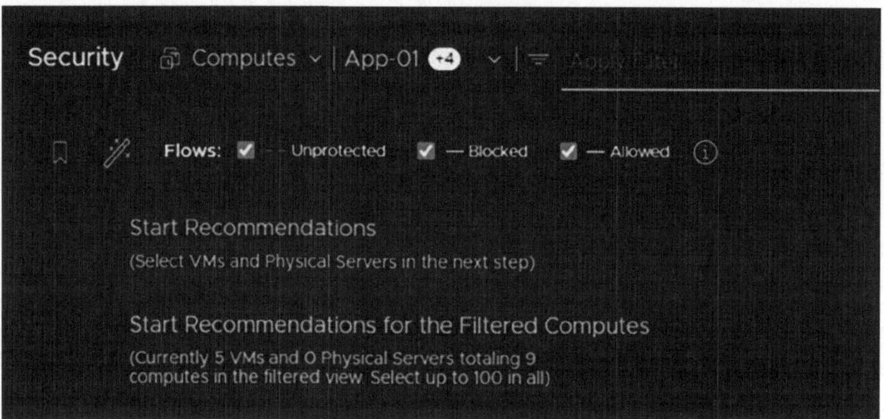

Figure 10.30: *Starting Recommendations in NSX Intelligence*

This will pop up a new screen with the name **`Start New Recommendation`** with selected entities as the filtered-out VMs from flows. Provide the following inputs as shown in *Figure* 10.31:

- **`Recommendation Name`**: Provide an appropriate to identify the recommendation.
- **`Time Range`**: Select the time range to analyze for network traffic.

Figure 10.31: *Starting a new Recommendation in NSX Intelligence*

Click **`Advanced Options`** to open advanced settings for Recommendations, as shown in *Figure* 10.32. Here are a few settings that can be tweaked to influence rule recommendations by NSX Intelligence:

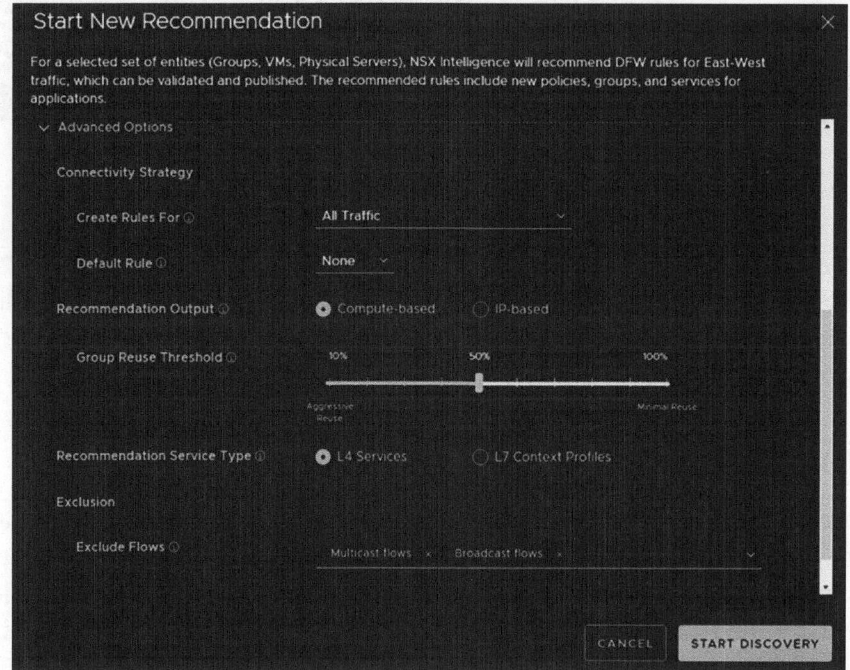

Figure 10.32: *Advance Settings in NSX Intelligence Recommendations*

- **`Default Rule`**: Select whether to create a default allow or block rule.

- **`Recommendation Output`**: Select either Compute-based, which uses Virtual Machine as group members, or IP-based, which, as the name suggests, uses IP addresses.
- **`Group Reuse Threshold`**: This slider influences how many or how less groups to be created for DFW rules.
- **`Recommendation Service Type`**: This influences whether to create simply L4 type rules or L7 Context Profile rules.
- **`Exclusions`**: Define exclusion for either broadcast traffic, multicast traffic, or both.

Click **`Start Discovery`** to save Recommendations, and NSX Intelligence will start analyzing network traffic to provide NSX DFW rules based on network flows captured. *Figure* 10.33 shows our recommendation 3-Tier-Demo-App-DFW in the Waiting state with NSX Intelligence working in the background to generate rules for VMs in scope. This process can take some time before it provides recommendations.

***Figure* 10.33**: *Viewing recommendations in NSX Manager*

As a last step, after the Recommendation status changes to **`Ready to Publish`**, click three dots against the Recommendation, then click **`Review and Publish`** to automatically create DFW rules for the application by NSX Intelligence. Alternatively, click **`Export to JSON`** `or` **`CSV`** options to export the output of rules to review and then implement them in the NSX environment.

Suspicious Traffic Detection

NSX Intelligence Suspicious Traffic Detection feature detects anomalies in the network traffic behaviors with the help of different threat detectors. This works only for East-West traffic, as NSX Intelligence collects network flows from Standalone ESXi hosts or vSphere clusters only. It shows all these different detected events under Suspicious Traffic under Security. If NSX NDR is enabled, then it also forwards these events to NDR for correlation with other security events in the environment.

Table 10.5 lists the supported Threat detectors supported by NSX Intelligence courtesy of VMware documentation.

Detector Name	**Detector Definition**
Data Upload/Download	It detects unusual amounts of data transfer either uploads or downloads for a host
Destination IP Profiler	This is for East-West traffic where it detects unusual connection attempts by internal hosts towards other internal hosts
DNS Tunneling	It detects attempts by an internal device to communicate covertly with an external server by abusing DNS traffic
Domain Generation Algorithm (DGA)	It detects DNS lookup anomalies caused by DGA malware
Horizontal Port Scan	It looks for attempts to scan one or more ports or services across multiple systems (sweeping)
LLMNR/NBT-NS Poisoning and Relay	Detect if a VM shows an unusual response pattern to LLMNR/NBT-NS requests
Netflow Beaconing	Detect beaconing behavior from an internal host
Network Traffic Drop	Detect if an unusually high amount of traffic is dropped by a distributed firewall rule
Port Profiler	It looks out for attempts by the internal host to the external host over unusual ports
Server Port Profiler	It detects when an internal host is connected to another internal host on an unusual port
Remote Services	Detect suspicious behavior for remote connections, such as telnet, SSH, and VNC
Uncommonly Used Port	Detect L7 Application ID Traffic mismatch with the standard assigned port/protocol. For example, SSH traffic runs on a non-standard port instead of the standard Port 22
Unusual Network Traffic Pattern	Detect anomalies in the time series profile of a host
Vertical Port Scan	It looks for attempts to open multiple ports or services on a single system (scanning)

Table 10.5: *Suspicious Detectors in NSX Intelligence*

Configuring Suspicious Traffic Detectors

By default, all the suspicious detectors are in off state and need to be enabled manually. The steps outlined here can be used to enable these detectors:

Step 1: Login to NSX Manager with admin privileges and navigate to the **`Security`** menu. Click **`Suspicious Traffic`** under **`Threat Event Monitoring`** in the left navigation panel, and then click **`Detector Definitions`** to view all the suspicious detectors, as shown in *Figure 10.34*.

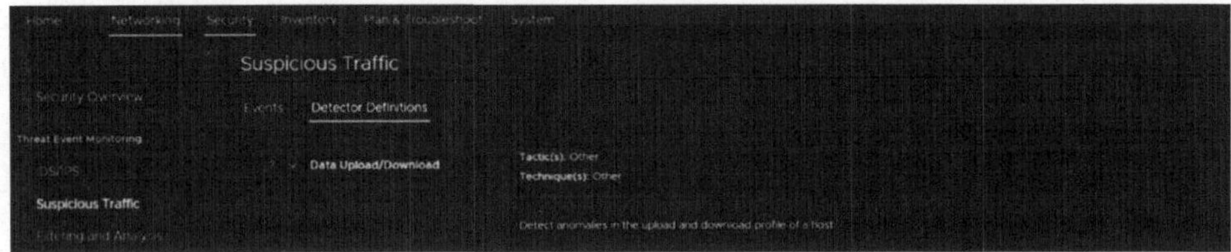

***Figure 10.34**: Viewing Suspicious Detectors in NSX Manager*

Step 2: Click pencil icon to edit the Suspicious detector definition. Under **`Exclusions`**, provide the VMs that need to be excluded from network traffic detection. Alternatively, in some detector definitions, NSX group can be selected to exclude from detection. Move the slider to the on position to enable the suspicious detector. Click **`Save`** to finish editing the suspicious detector and enable it. *Figure* 10.35 shows the suspicious detector definition for Data Upload/Download enabled with an exclusion set for virtual machine External-VM.

***Figure 10.35**: Editing a suspicious detector definition*

Step 3: Repeat step 2 to enable the rest of the suspicious detectors as per requirements.

Remember that there is a learning time for a few of the Suspicious Detector definitions, which are different for different detectors. NSX Intelligence will only provide suspicious traffic events after the learning time is complete.

Viewing Suspicious Traffic Events

Suspicious Traffic events are visible under the same menu where Suspicious Detectors definitions are configured. Navigate to **Suspicious Traffic** under **Threat Event Monitoring** in the **Security** menu. Click **Events** to view detected security events in the NSX environment. *Figure* 10.36 shows a graph with one low suspicious event detected in the last hour.

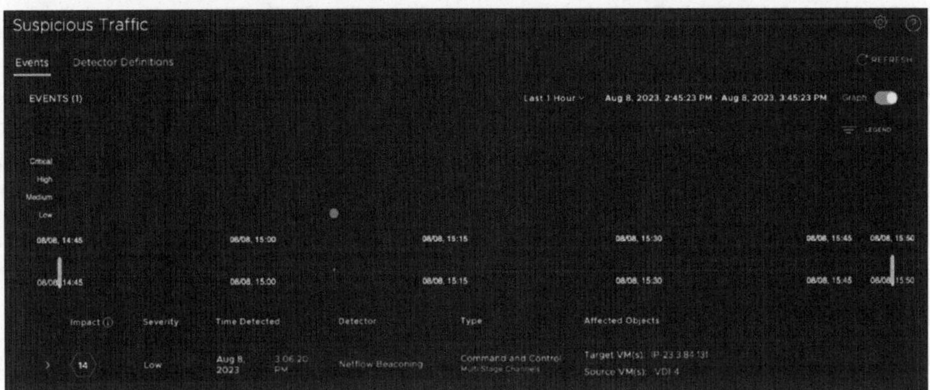

Figure 10.36: *Viewing suspicious traffic events in NSX environment*

The time span menu can be changed from 1 hour to different options such as 12 hours, 24 hours, 1 week, 2 weeks, or the last 1 month to view events over a span of time. Graph option can be disabled to view only events and hide graphical representation of events. Also, events can be expanded to view more details such as Target VMs, Source VMs, duration, and more, as shown in *Figure* 10.37. Clicking **View affected VMs and their current traffic** will take you to the Discover & Take Option to analyze traffic flows to validate different traffic flows and block the traffic if required.

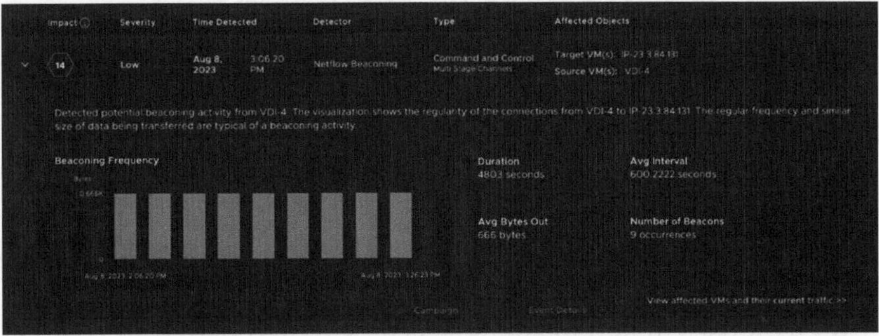

Figure 10.37: *Expanding details of a specific event*

Alright! This completes the NSX Intelligence feature walkthrough in the NSX environment. As you might be wondering about all these different security features provided by NSX and their different dashboards, is there a way where we can intelligently correlate all these different event sources such as IDS/IPS, Malware Prevention, and Suspicious Traffic (NTA) together and see the bigger picture? Well, you do not need any additional appliances or external systems to be deployed. NSX provides this functionality out of the box, that is, NSX NDR, that performs exactly, which is covered in the next section.

NSX Network Detection and Response

NSX Network Detection and Response, or NDR in short form, is an advanced threat prevention feature provided by NSX, whose main function is to collect abnormal activity or malicious event from all the activated sources in the NSX environment and provides complete network visibility and detect/prevent threats to the environment.

As of writing, NSX NDR collects events from different sources listed in *Table* 10.6.

Event Type	Events Source
Malicious File Events	North-South Malware Prevention if activated on NSX Edge node
IDS/IPS Events	East-West Distributed IDS events if activated in the environment
Network Traffic Anomaly Events	NSX Intelligence Suspicious Traffic detector events if activated in the environment

Table 10.6: *Different event sources for NDR ingestion*

Different features provided by NSX NDR are as follows:

- NSX NDR can help in the detection of threats entering the NSX environment from North-South traffic and East-West lateral attacks as well in NSX environment.
- NSX NDR collects events from all activated different sources and correlates them to create a campaign blueprint and provides a detailed timeline of threats across the network to quickly assess the impact of the attack.
- NSX NDR uses AI and Machine Learning to detect and stop threats.
- NSX NDR helps in reducing false positives in the environment.

NSX NDR Architecture

Figure 10.38 illustrates the architecture and components involved in NSX Network Detection and Response services. NSX NDR, at a high level, contains three different tiers, each serving a distinct function. These three different tiers are as follows:

- Scalable Analytics Tier
- Management Tier
- Sensor Tier

Figure 10.38 also shows different NSX components already configured in the environment as part of these different tiers. Let's cover these different tiers in more detail.

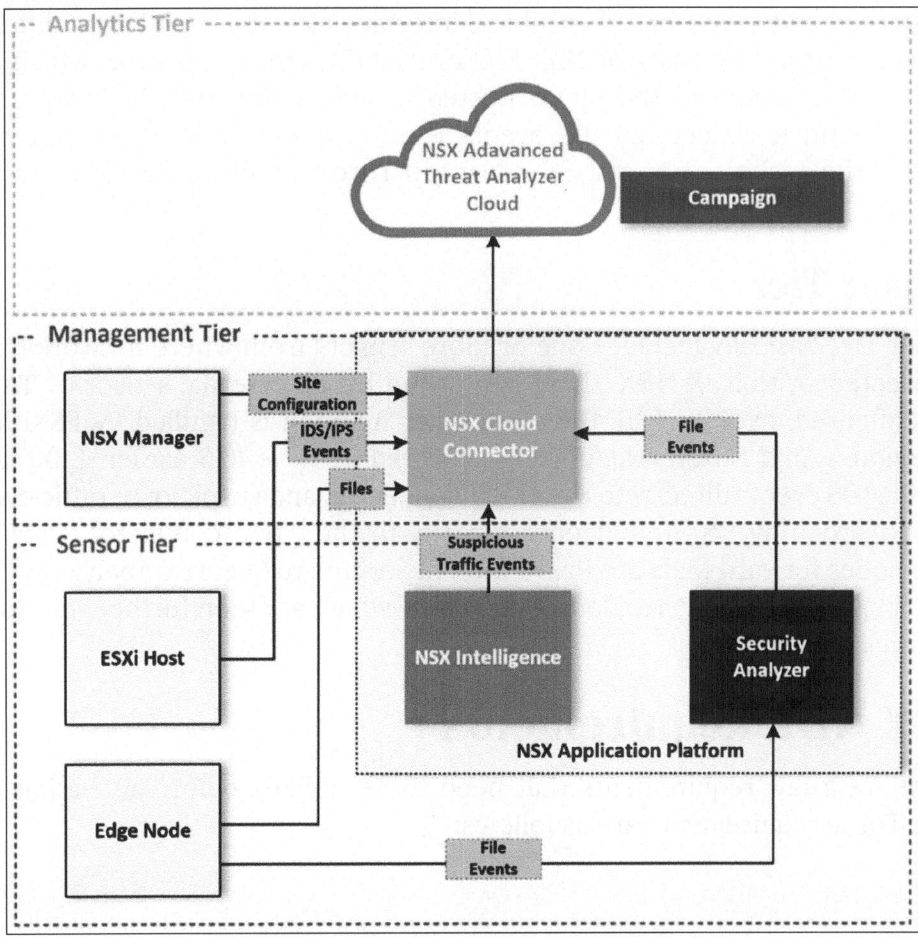

Figure 10.38: *Architecture of NSX NDR*

Analytics Tier

This is similar to the brain of the entire operations and consists of a distributed analytics platform that performs deep content inspection, network traffic analysis, and anomaly detection. It is hosted in NSX Advanced Threat Analyzer Cloud and receives data from NSX Cloud Connector hosted on-premise on the NSX Application Platform. It correlates different events received from IDS, Malware Prevention, and suspicious traffic to create a campaign and send it to the Cloud Connector for the visibility of users through a graphical interface hosted by Management Tier.

Management Tier

Management Tier, as the name suggests, provides an entry point for users in the form of API and a web-based graphical interface to manage and view different configurations. It consists of NSX Manager and Cloud Connector, which acts as a gateway between the cloud-hosted analytics tier and the on-premise environment. It collects all the events from different sources and forwards them to the analytics tier or NSX Advanced Threat Analyzer Cloud for further analysis.

Sensor Tier

Sensor Tier basically includes one or more sensors from where network traffic is collected. With NSX NDR, there is no need for an external sensor or TAP to be configured. In NSX NDR, the sensor tier function is handled by ESXi host, Edge nodes, and NSX Intelligence. As covered in *Table* 10.6 earlier, ESXi hosts provide IDS events directly to the cloud connector, and suspicious traffic events are forwarded by NSX Intelligence directly to the cloud connector. However, Edge nodes forward Malware Prevention file events to Security Analyzer, which then forwards the same to Cloud Connector, which are then further sent to the analytics tier for analysis.

NSX NDR Requirements

There are a few requirements that need to be fulfilled before activating NSX NDR. These requirements are as follows:

License Requirements

NSX NDR requires either one of the following licenses installed in the NSX Manager before it can be activated:

- NSX Advanced Threat Prevention
- NSX Distributed Firewall with Advanced Threat Prevention
- NSX Gateway Firewall with Advanced Threat Prevention
- NSX Advanced with Advanced Threat Prevention
- NSX Enterprise Plus with Advanced Threat Prevention

If either one of NSX Enterprise Plus, NSX Advanced license, NSX Distributed Firewall with Threat Prevention, or NSX Distributed Firewall license is installed, then an additional add-on license NSX Advanced Threat Prevention for Distributed Firewall needs to be installed with it.

Software Requirements

NSX NDR is available on the NSX Application Platform only starting from NSX-T release v3.2. Hence, it requires a minimum NSX Application Platform to be deployed in NSX Manager and NSX Manager v3.2 and above.

NSX NDR can be activated on either form factor of the NSX Application Platform, that is, it can be deployed on both Standard or Advanced form factor.

Internet Access

NSX NDR requires access to the internet to connect to NSX Advanced Threat Analyzer Cloud and forward events for analysis and correlation.

Activating NSX NDR

The process to activate NSX NDR in the environment is the same as other features such as Malware Prevention or NSX Intelligence.

Note: If NSX Malware Prevention was previously enabled, NSX NDR will use the same cloud as configured in NSX Malware Prevention. Similarly, NSX Malware Prevention will use the cloud region configured in NSX NDR. Both features cannot use different cloud regions.

Here are the steps to activate NSX NDR:

Step 1: Login to NSX Manager with Enterprise Admin privileges. Navigate to **`System`** and click **`NSX Application Platform`** in the left navigation panel. Scroll to the very bottom, and under the Features section, there is **`NSX Network Detection and Response`** tile card, as shown in *Figure* 10.39, and click **`Activate.`**

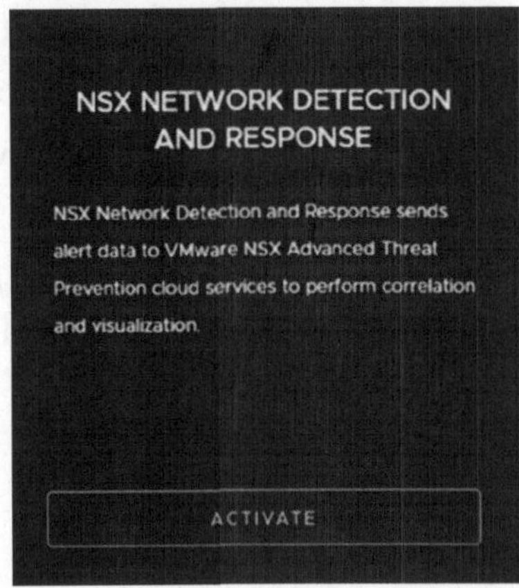

***Figure* 10.39**: *Activating* NSX NDR *in* NAPP *Platform*

Step 2: Select the Cloud Region nearest to the data center. If Malware Prevention was previously enabled, then this option will be greyed out, as shown in *Figure* 10.40. Click **`Run Prechecks`** to start the mandatory prechecks for the NSX NDR feature.

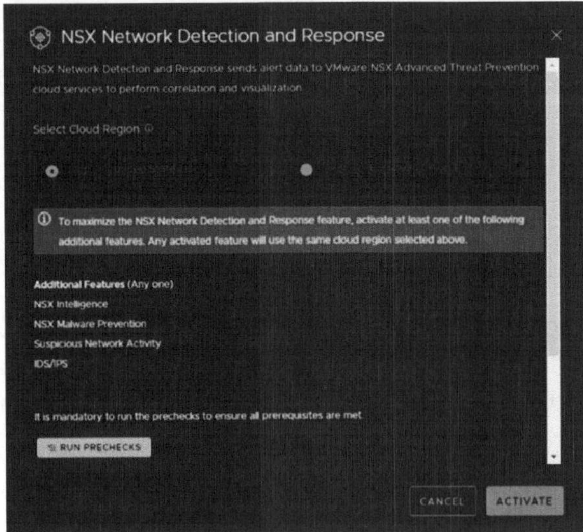

***Figure* 10.40**: *Selecting Cloud Region for* NSX NDR

Step 3: After prechecks are completed successfully, the **`Activate`** button will become available. Click **`Activate`** to start the deployment of NSX NDR pods in the Kubernetes cluster, similar to *Figure* 10.41.

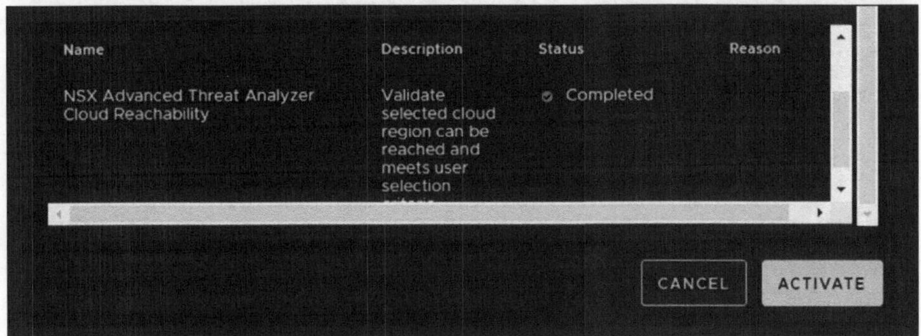

***Figure* 10.41:** *Prechecks with completed status for* NSX NDR

Figure 10.42 shows the NSX NDR feature in the deploying state on the NSX Manager UI. In the backend, NSX Application Platform is deploying pods on the Kubernetes cluster required for NSX NDR.

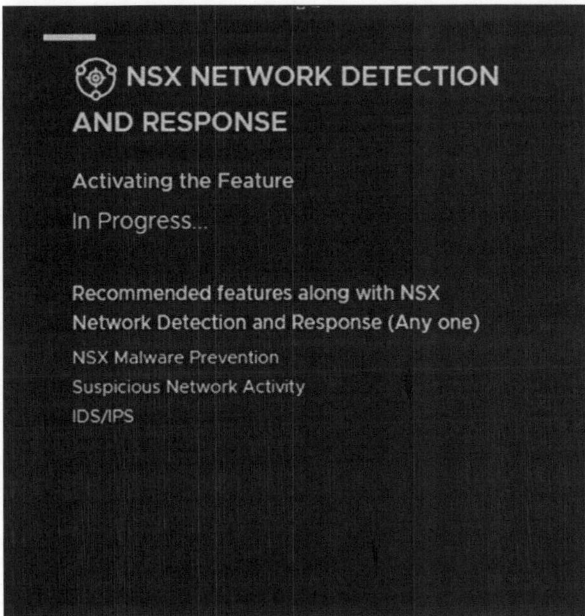

***Figure* 10.42:** *Deploying* NSX NDR *on* NAPP

Step 4: After NSX NDR pods have been deployed successfully, it will show the status as UP in the NSX Manager UI with the cloud region selected earlier during configuration, as illustrated in *Figure* 10.43.

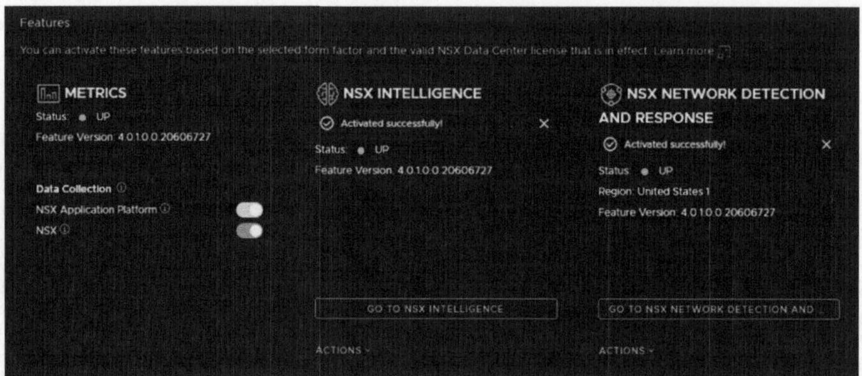

***Figure 10.43**: NSX NDR activated successfully in NSX environment*

There are no configurations required for NSX NDR. As soon as NSX NDR is activated, it starts receiving events from different sources described earlier. Usually, there might be a delay of 10–15 minutes between events forwarded to NSX NDR and them being visible on the NDR dashboard because NDR forwards these events to NSX Advanced Threat Prevention Cloud for analysis.

Working with NSX NDR

NSX NDR UI is the single pane of glass for managing the threat events and viewing campaigns in the NSX environment. There are two different ways to access the NSX NDR user interface. Additionally, the user should have either one of the following roles assigned to them to access the NDR user interface: Enterprise Admin, Security Admin, Security Operator, or Auditor (Read Only) .

The first way is to utilize the Application Launcher Icon to access the NDR user interface, which opens a new web browser tab with NSX NDR UI loaded. Simply, log into NSX Manager with the appropriate role assigned and look for nine dots in the top-right corner of NSX Manager UI, similar to those shown in *Figure* 10.44. Click the dots and then click **`NSX NETWORK DETECTION AND RESPONSE`** to open NDR UI in a separate tab.

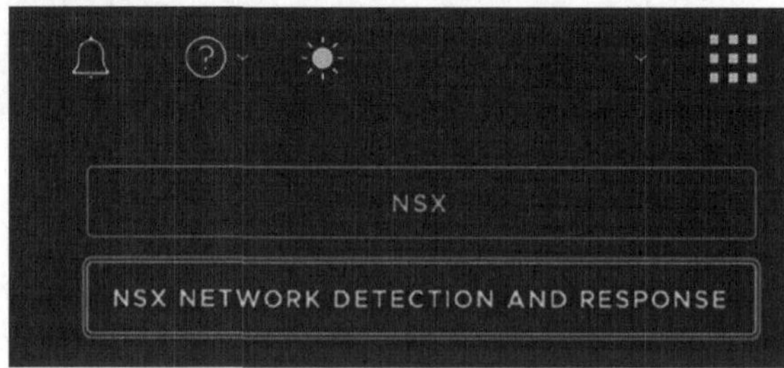

***Figure 10.44**: Accessing NSX NDR UI*

Another way to access NSX NDR UI is to go to the **`Security`** tab and click **`Security Overview.`** Ensure **`Threat Event Monitoring`** is selected, and under this, click **`Campaigns`** to view a summary of campaigns currently in the environment. Click **Go to `Campaigns`**, as shown in *Figure* 10.45, to access the NSX NDR user interface in a separate tab of the same web browser.

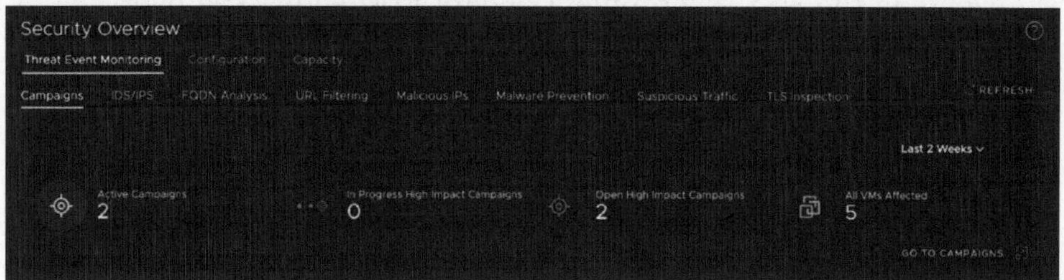

***Figure 10.45**: Accessing NSX NDR UI through security campaigns*

After accessing the NSX NDR user interface, there is a primary navigation menu on the left-hand side with different options, as listed in *Figure* 10.46, to explore and work with NSX NDR. Subsequent sections cover each of these different menus in detail.

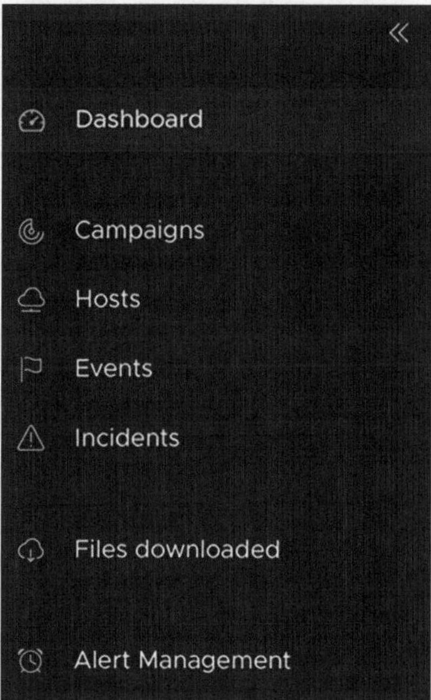

***Figure 10.46**: Accessing primary menu in NSX NDR UI*

Dashboard

This is the first menu item in the NSX NDR user interface. The page provides a quick overview of active campaigns correlated by NSX Advanced Threat Analyzer Cloud, detected incidents and threats, and the most recent observed threat events in the NSX environment. *Figure* 10.47 shows the overview of the Dashboard page with different widgets.

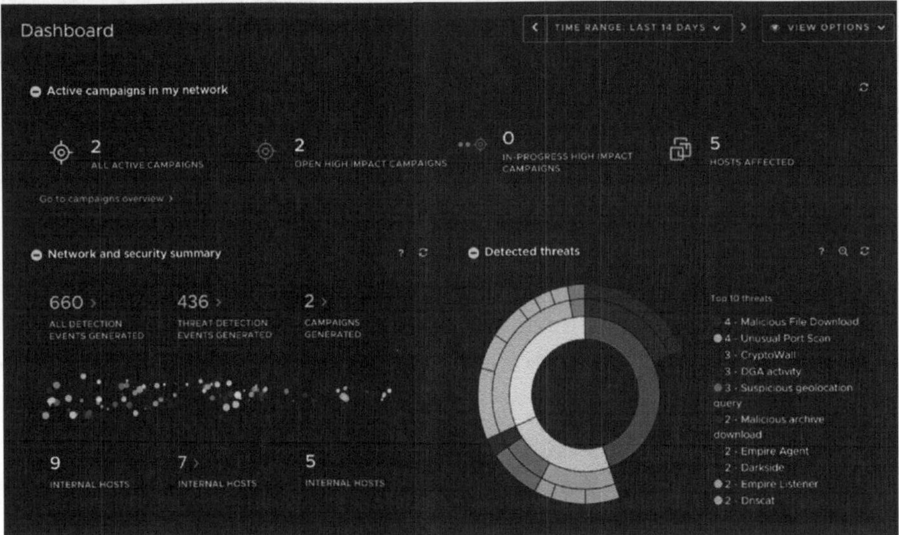

Figure 10.47: *Viewing Dashboard in NDR UI*

It provides a quick summary of the threats detected by NDR with the help of the following widgets:

- `Active Campaign in my network`: This widget provides an overview of active campaigns in the environment. These can be further drilled down in Campaigns.
- `Network and Security Summary`: This provides a quick summary of how NSX NDR handles and processes the traffic flow data.
- `Detected Threats`: This widget provides a quick summary of different threats detected in the environment.
- `Global Event Map`: This widget provides a map of events over different geographies.
- `New Unique Detections`: It lists different events that have been detected for the first time in the NSX environment.
- `Downloaded Files List`: This widget shows data received from the NSX Malware Prevention service.

Campaigns

Campaigns is the main page in the NSX NDR user interface, which shows all the campaigns detected and correlated by NDR in the network. There are mainly two widgets here, as shown in *Figure 10.48*:

- First lists all the campaigns detected in the environment in a list format alongside a summary, such as score, campaign ID, status, and how many hosts are impacted, along with different threats related to it.
- Second shows all the interesting events, which may not be malicious but are suspicious and can point to an issue or anomaly in the network.

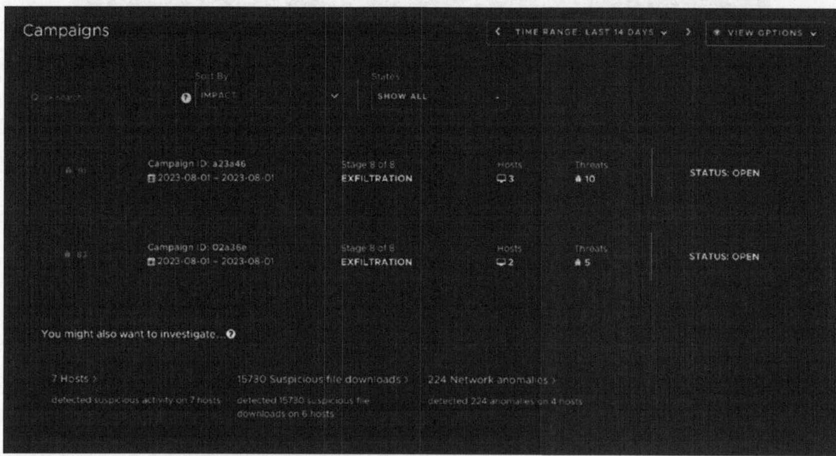

Figure 10.48: *Viewing Campaigns in the* NSX NDR *UI*

Click any one of the campaign IDs to view in-depth details of the campaign. A few of the important details captured as part of the campaign are as follows:

- **Threats and Hosts**: This provides different threats detected against hosts. It provides the unique IP of the host on which type of threat corresponding to the MITRE attack framework is detected.
- **Campaign Blueprint**: This provides the entire visualization of the attack of how it has been carried out in the environment. It lists all the hosts, types of attacks, and flows between them. *Figure* 10.49 shows such a blueprint of a campaign.

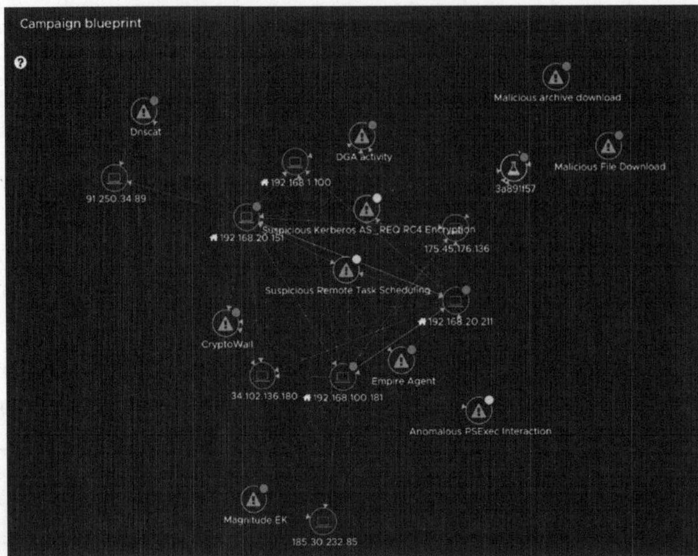

Figure 10.49: *View Campaign blueprint in* NSX NDR UI

- **Timeline**: This provides the complete timeline of the attack with timestamps indicating what happens and when. This provides a type of attack and the stage at which it was performed.
- **Evidence**: This tab displays a list of evidence detected for the currently selected campaign.

Hosts

The Hosts page provides the list of hosts currently being monitored in the NSX environment. There are filters that you can apply on different attributes such as Host IP, Threat, and more, to quickly filter out specific hosts from the entire list of hosts.

Events

This page provides information on individual events detected by NSX NDR in the environment. There are different widgets available on this page that can be used to view more details about individual events, as follows:

- **Global Event Map**: This widget provides a map of events over different geographies.
- **Detected Threats**: This widget provides a visualization of different threats by their class detected in the NSX environment.

- **Filters**: This provides an option to filter specific threats and view their details from a list of all threats.
- **Detection Events**: This widget provides a list of all the individual events that have been detected by NDR in the environment.
- **Event Profile**: This page provides in-depth details of the detected event. This is accessed by clicking `Details` on the `Event Summary` view, which can be accessed by clicking `Detection Events` widget.

Incidents

The Incidents page provides details about incidents and their different threat ratings. This page is used to inspect, manage, and prioritize the incidents reported by NDR. *Figure* 10.50 shows a snippet of the Incidents page from the NSX NDR user interface.

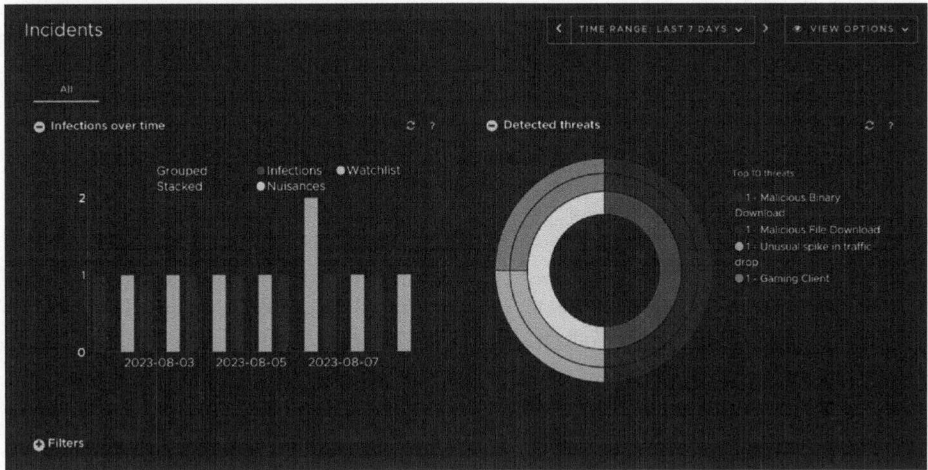

Figure 10.50: *Viewing incidents details from* NSX NDR UI

Different tasks that can be performed on this page are as follows:

- Keeping track of all the incidents being received from NDR
- Viewing the list of affected hosts against an incident
- View the score of incidents and prioritize their handling
- Mark or clear affected hosts as being cleaned
- Filter reported threats for specific hosts, and more

This completes the NSX Network Detection and Response walkthrough. This is a great tool for security administrators to monitor threats and campaigns in the NSX environment and promptly take action to minimize the impact.

Conclusion

This concludes the various security features provided by NSX. Over the last three chapters, we covered a lot about security, starting from NSX Distributed Firewall, followed by NSX Gateway firewall, and then deep diving into advanced threat prevention techniques provided by NSX. In continuation of this series, we covered NSX Intelligence and how it can help administrators to achieve micro-segmentation by providing recommendations on DFW policies after analyzing network traffic flows. We also explored its suspicious traffic detection to find anomalies in the network. Additionally, we covered NSX Network Detection and Response, which collects all these security events from different sources and helps security administrators by correlating these events together to create campaigns that can then be further utilized to detect and prevent different sophisticated threats.

In the next few chapters, we will cover some additional networking capabilities provided by NSX. We will be discussing NAT, VPN, DNS, and DHCP services provided by the NSX Manager without the need to deploy any additional appliances.

Key Terms

- **Segment:** Segments are layer 2 subnets representing layer 2 broadcasting domain across transport nodes in NSX networking.
- **Kubernetes:** Also known as K8S, it is an open-source platform for managing the lifecycle of containerized applications.
- **NSX Application Platform:** NAPP, in short, is a distributed microservices platform that is deployed on the Kubernetes cluster. It is used to host different NSX features such as NSX NDR, Intelligence, and Malware Prevention.
- **Recommendations:** Created in NSX Intelligence to provide NSX Distributed firewall policies for compute entities based on analyzed traffic flows.
- **Campaigns:** A campaign is a set of correlated events that affect one or more workloads over some time.
- **Event:** A security-relevant activity or an abnormal behavior that occurred in the network.
- **Nuisance:** This is a low-risk incident that corresponds to an activity that doesn't necessarily indicate an infection in the environment.

- **NSX Cloud Connector**: Acts as a gateway between on-premise sensor tier to collect data from them and then forward it to NSX Advanced Threat Analyzer Cloud.

Chapter 11

NSX DataCenter Services – 1

Introduction

Well, NSX is all configured, up and running. You have configured NSX networking services and impressed your peers with the advanced security features NSX has to offer. But what if, say you can take it up a notch and impress more by enabling additional datacenter services in NSX? You need a NAT solution to enable overlapping IP address space for multiple tenants, or a VPN to securely connect your HQ or corporate location to offsite locations, or how about distributing IP addresses to VDIs running on NSX segments using DHCP, how about configuring all these services within NSX without any additional resources.

This chapter covers all these different features that we just talked about, i.e., NAT, DHCP, DNS, IPSec VPN, and Layer 2 VPN, and how to configure them in an NSX environment. Also, we will see a new feature introduced in NSX which enables stateful services on Active-Active gateways.

Structure

In this chapter, we will cover the following topics:

- Active-Active Stateful Services
    - Stateful Services Architecture
    - Active-Active Stateful Supported Topologies
    - Configuring Active-Active Stateful Gateway
- Network Address Translation
    - Configuring NAT in NSX

- DHCP
  - DHCP Support in NSX
  - Configuring DHCP Services in NSX
  - Validating DHCP Services
- DNS
- Virtual Private Network
  - IPSec VPN
  - Configuring IPSec VPN Services
  - Layer 2 VPN
  - Configuring Layer 2 VPN
  - Configuring Autonomous Edge as L2VPN Client

Active-Active Stateful Services

NSX supports other stateful services such as NAT, VPN, Gateway Firewall, DNS, and DHCP, which can be enabled in the environment with the help of NSX Edge nodes on Tier1 or Tier0 gateway depending on the services. In the previous release, it was only possible to run stateful services in Active-Standby configuration which possesses scalability issues for bandwidth or throughput in the NSX environment. However, starting NSX release v4.0.1, VMware introduced support from stateful services on Tier1 and Tier0 gateway running in Active-Active configuration. This is possible due to the introduction of new features, such as routing methodology based on IP hashing and traffic punting in NSX. Before we dive into different networking services supported by NSX, let's take a look at this newly released feature, as it can be a game changer for a few when migrating from traditional networking to NSX networking. However, not all stateful services are supported in Active-Active configuration. *Table 11.1* summarizes the list of services that are supported and not supported in Active-Active configuration.

Supported Stateful Gateway Services	**Unsupported Stateful Gateway Services**
Gateway Firewall L3-L4	FQDN Analysis
APP-ID (L7)	L2VPN
User-ID	IPSecVPN
URL Filtering	Gateway Network Introspection

TLS Inspection	Local DHCP Server
IDS/IPS	Service Interface
Malware Detection and Sandboxing	FQDN Analysis
NAT	L2VPN
DHCP Relay Server	
DHCP Server	

Table 11.1: *Different stateful services supported on Active-Active gateway*

Note: In a brownfield environment or existing environment, if the current Tier0 is configured as Active-Standby, it cannot be reconfigured to Active-Active high availability mode. Also, the same Edge cluster cannot be used to host another Active-Active stateful Tier0 gateways.

Stateful Services Architecture

With the introduction of stateful services on Active-Active gateways, there are a couple of new concepts introduced in NSX that should be well understood before configuring stateful services. *Figure* 11.1 illustrates different components that work together to implement stateful services on Active-Active gateways. It shows two views with a logical view depicting an overlay segment connected to a Tier0 gateway named LAB-Tier0-01 which is further connected to the Physical router via an external interface. Another view is an internal view which shows Tier0 realized on Edge cluster consisting of four Edge nodes and internal connectivity. *Figure* 11.1 only shows components for Active-Active Tier 0 in stateful configuration, but the same components will be created for Tier1 gateway in Active-Active stateful configuration.

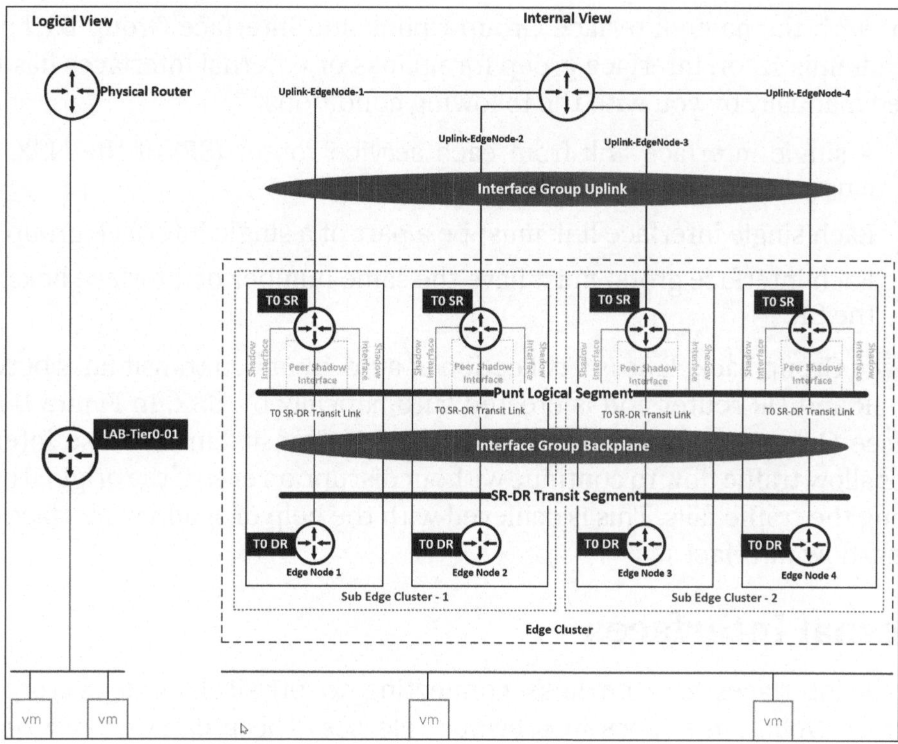

***Figure 11.1**: Active-Active Tier0 Stateful architecture*

Edge Sub Cluster

NSX automatically creates a sub-cluster within the Edge Cluster when stateful services are enabled in the Active-Active gateway. As illustrated in *Figure* 11.1, NSX has automatically created two sub-cluster namely **Sub Edge Cluster -1** and **Sub Edge Cluster -2** within an Edge cluster. **Edge Node 1** and **Edge Node 2** are part of sub-Edge cluster 1 whereas **Edge Node 3** and **Edge Node 4** are part of Sub Edge cluster 2. Edge nodes within a Sub Edge cluster act as peers and sync state with each other. So, if traffic is flowing through Edge Node 1 and it fails, all ingress/egress traffic gets switched over to Edge Node 2. Essentially, within a sub-Edge cluster, Edge nodes act originally with one Edge node running as active and another Edge node running as standby.

Interface Groups

As the name suggests, an interface group is the collection of equivalent interfaces where equivalent interface means interfaces which have the same inbound policies such as NAT or firewall policies. *Figure* 11.1 shows two interface groups with the name Interface Group Uplink and Interface Group Backplane. As an administrator, interface group for uplinks or external interfaces has to be created manually by you with the following conditions:

- A single interface link from each service router (SR) of the NSX Edge cluster must participate in the interface group.
- Each single interface link must be a part of a single interface group.
- Each interface group must have the same number of interface links from the SR.

Interface Group Backplane is a collection of auto-plumbed transit links between Tier0 SR and DR router and is created automatically by NSX. In *Figure* 11.1, the Interface Group Backplane contains T0 SR-DR Transit Links. These interface groups allow traffic flow to continue without disruption even if the original uplink carrying the traffic fails. This is achieved with the help of shadow interfaces and peer shadow interfaces.

External Interfaces

External interfaces are the links connecting to physical infrastructure also known as Uplink interfaces in previous releases. These carry ingress/egress traffic from the physical network. These are denoted as **Uplink-EdgeNode-1, Uplink-EdgeNode-2, Uplink-EdgeNode3**, and **Uplink-EdgeNode-4** in *Figure* 11.1 connecting Tier0 SR to Physical router. Both static routing and BGP are supported on external interfaces.

Shadow and Peer Shadow Interfaces

This is the interesting bit here. For every interface added in the interface group such as the External Interface connecting to a physical network or Backplane interface i.e., SR-DR transit link connecting Tier0 service router and distributed router, will have a shadow port created. In *Figure* 11.1, there are two shadow interfaces and two peer shadow interfaces created on each Tier0 SR, one pair of shadow/peer shadow interface for T0 SR-DR Transit Link member of Interface Group Backplane and a second pair for external interface member of Interface Group Uplink. So, if another external interface link is added to T0 SR then another pair of shadow/peer shadow interfaces will be realized on the Edge node. These interfaces are connected to the system to generate VNI punt logical segment which spans across are Edge nodes and carries traffic across Edge nodes.

These shadow interfaces have unique MAC addresses assigned to them and synced across all Edge nodes. For each shadow interface, there is a peer shadow interface which acts as a backup of the peer Edge node and remains in a down state. This interface is used to punt traffic if the peer Edge node goes down.

Punt Logical Segment

Punt logical segment is a system-generated VNI that carries the punted traffic across Edge nodes. This segment is realized only if stateful services are enabled on the Active-Active gateway and are present only on edge nodes. All shadow interfaces and peer shadow interfaces connect to punt logical segments to forward traffic across Edge nodes.

Active-Active Stateful Supported Topologies

While configuring stateful services on the Active-Active HA NSX gateway, there are a few considerations to follow. For a new deployment, these considerations are:

- Tier1 stateful Active-Active gateway running stateful services must be connected to a stateful enabled Active-Active Tier0 gateway hosted in the same Edge cluster.
- Tier1 running in Active-Standby configuration can be connected to a Stateful Active-Active Tier0 gateway, but Tier1 must be hosted in a different Edge cluster from Tier0.

For an existing deployment, these are:

- Any existing Tier1 configured as Active-Standby cannot be converted to an Active-Active Tier1. A new Tier1 must be created in Active-Active HA and migrate services from the existing Tier1 to the new Tier1 gateway.
- Any Tier0 gateway running in Active-Standby HA configuration cannot be converted to an Active-Active HA mode.
- A stateless Tier1 Active-Active gateway can be converted to a stateful Active-Active gateway if there are no Tier1 gateways attached to the Tier0 gateway.

Note: If there are an odd number of nodes in an Edge cluster, then enabling stateful services in Active-Active HA mode will result in the creation of a Sub Edge cluster with no standby Edge node. If the Edge node fails in this Sub Edge cluster, then traffic will be disrupted. NSX will raise an alarm about incorrect configuration, so it is a best practice to ensure the Edge cluster is running with an even number of Edge nodes before configuring the Active-Active stateful gateway.

Configuring Active-Active Stateful Gateway

This section covers steps to enable stateful services on the Active-Active HA Tier0 gateway. High-level steps to enable stateful services on Tier1 or Tier0 gateway are:

- Validate NSX Edge cluster has an even number of Edge nodes
- Create a new Tier0 gateway with a Stateful option enabled
- Create an interface group and add external interfaces to it
- Create a new Tier1 gateway with Active-Active HA and connect to the Tier0 gateway
- Validate configuration
- Enable stateful services such as NAT, and gateway firewall on an interface group

The detailed steps are as follows:

Step 1: Login into NSX Manager with admin privileges. Navigate to **`System`** and click on **`Nodes`** from the left navigation panel under **`Fabric.`** Click on the **`Edge Clusters`** menu and edit the existing Edge cluster to view the Edge nodes present in it. *Figure* 11.2 shows an Edge cluster EC-LAB-01 created with four Edge nodes.

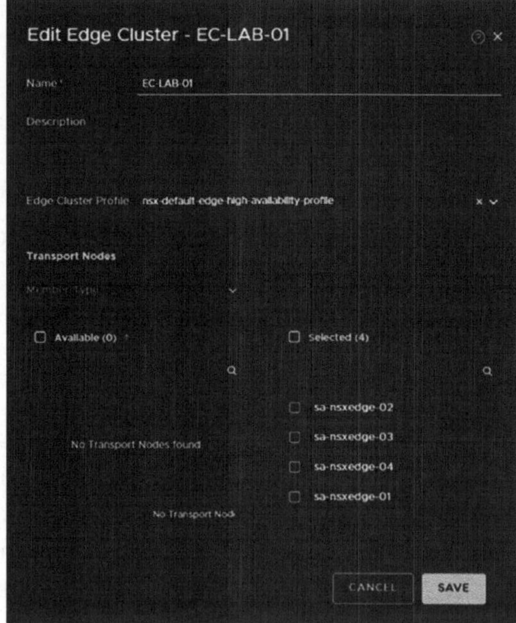

Figure 11.2: *Validating Edge nodes in an Edge cluster*

Step 2: Navigate to the **`Networking`** menu and click on **`Tier-0 Gateways`** under **`Connectivity.`** Click on **`Add Gateway`** and select **`Tier-0.`** Provide an appropriate name with **`HA Mode`** as **`Active-Active`** and enable the **`Stateful`** option by moving the slider to the right as shown in *Figure* 11.3.

Figure 11.3: *Create a new Tier0 gateway with Stateful enabled*

Step 3: NSX Manager will prompt a **`Confirm`** dialogue box shown in *Figure* 11.4 advising if stateful services are enabled then you cannot modify HA mode later on. Click on **`Yes`** to continue.

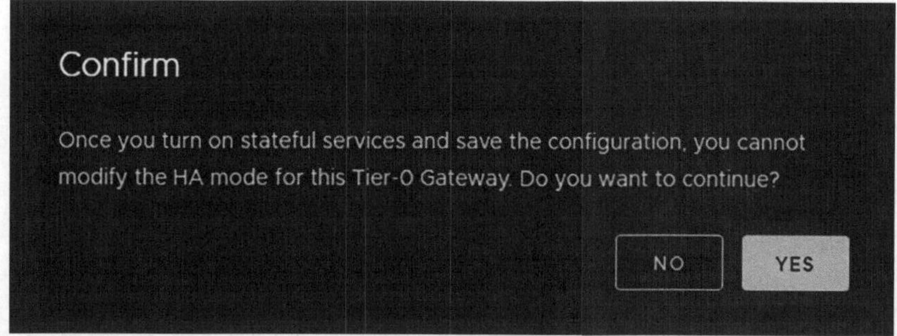

Figure 11.4: *Confirm enabling stateful services on Active-Active Tier0*

Step 4: Click on **`Save`** to create a Tier0 gateway. NSX Manager will prompt another dialogue box similar to *Figure* 11.5 suggesting creating Interface Groups to complete configuration for stateful services.

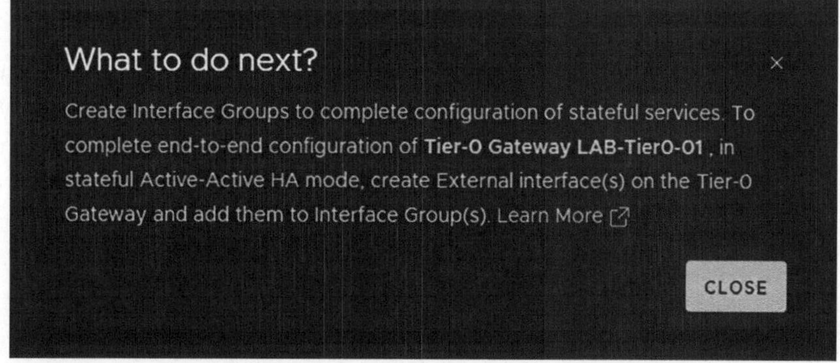

Figure 11.5: *Next steps prompted by NSX Manager for stateful services*

Step 5: As covered in *Chapter* 5, *Logical Routing – NSX Gateways*, configure external interfaces to provide North-South to the physical network. *Figure* 11.6 displays four external interfaces configured with the upstream physical router. Also, note the **`Interface Groups`** option, which is not available unless stateful services are enabled.

***Figure 11.6:** Configuring external interfaces on Tier0 gateway*

Step 6: Click on **`Set`** in front of **`Interface Groups`** to create a new interface group. Provide an appropriate name and add the external interfaces under Interfaces to add them to the interface group. *Figure* 11.7 shows an interface group with the name LAB-IG-01 created with four external interfaces. Click on **`Save`** to create an interface group.

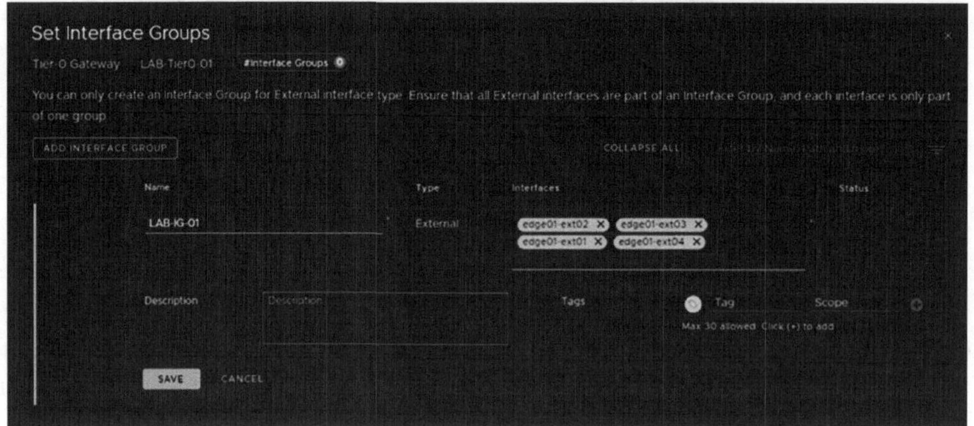

***Figure 11.7**: Creating a new interface group*

Step 7: Click on **`Close Editing`** to finish modifying the Tier0 gateway and save the configuration. *Figure* 11.8 shows the Tier0 gateway named LAB-Tier0-01 running in Active-Active stateful configuration. This is evident with the tag **`Stateful`** under **`HA Mode.`** Similarly, to create a Tier1 Active-Active stateful, select its **`HA Mode`** as **`Active-Active`**.

***Figure 11.8**: Viewing a Tier0 gateway running in stateful Active-Active HA*

Validate Active-Active Stateful Configuration

This completes the creation of an NSX gateway in Active-Active stateful HA mode. But how can we validate the configuration and different components that we have covered in the stateful Active-Active architecture? Follow these steps to validate the configuration in the NSX environment.

Step 1: While logged into NSX Manager and in the **`Tier-0 Gateways`** section under **`Networking.`** Click on **`Active-Active stateful`** under **`HA Mode`** to open a new dialogue box. This dialogue box shows sub-Edge cluster UUID and their member edge nodes. *Figure* 11.9 shows HA Mode for LAB-Tier0-01 with two sub-Edge clusters configured each with two NSX Edge nodes. NSX automatically creates this sub-cluster within the Edge cluster.

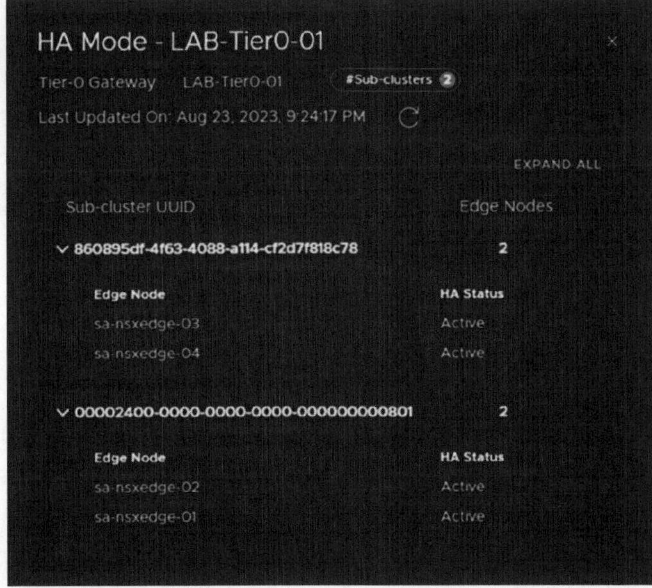

***Figure 11.9**: View sub-Edge cluster configuration in NSX*

Step 2: Click on the numeral in front of **`Interface Groups`** and then click on **`View Statistics`** to open Interface Group Statistics which shows different metrics such as **`Data, Total Packets`**, and **`Dropped Packets`** as *Figure* 11.10 shows.

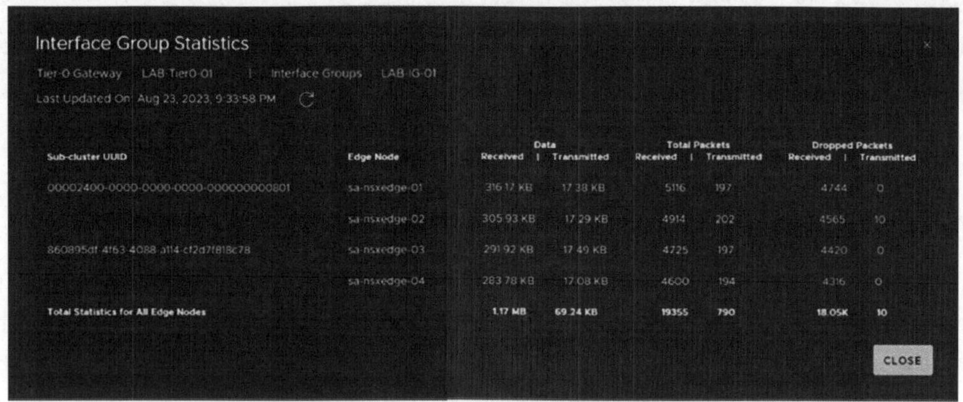

Interface Group Statistics

Tier-0 Gateway LAB-Tier0-01 | Interface Groups LAB-IG-01

Last Updated On Aug 23, 2023, 9:33:58 PM

Sub-cluster UUID	Edge Node	Data Received	Data Transmitted	Total Packets Received	Total Packets Transmitted	Dropped Packets Received	Dropped Packets Transmitted
00002400-0000-0000-0000-000000000801	sa-nsxedge-01	316.17 KB	17.38 KB	5116	197	4744	0
	sa-nsxedge-02	305.93 KB	17.29 KB	4914	202	4565	10
860895df-4f63-4088-a114-cf2d7f818c78	sa-nsxedge-03	291.92 KB	17.49 KB	4725	197	4420	0
	sa-nsxedge-04	283.78 KB	17.08 KB	4600	194	4316	0
Total Statistics for All Edge Nodes		**1.17 MB**	**69.24 KB**	**19355**	**790**	**18.05K**	**10**

CLOSE

Figure 11.10: *View statistics of Interface Group*

Step 3: Login into the NSX Edge node via SSH session using admin credentials and run the following command to view MACs of shadow interfaces. Shadow MACs will be synced on all Edge nodes in the Edge cluster.

```
get logical-router interface <interface-UUID> shadow-macs
```

Figure 11.11 shows the sample output of running the preceding command.

```
sa-nsxedge-01> get logical-router  interface 210ca992-2309-4224-b732-3cd38bf07aa0 shadow-macs
Wed Aug 23 2023 UTC 18:43:41.045
Logical Router Interface
UUID          : 210ca992-2309-4224-b732-3cd38bf07aa0
Shadow MACs:
    02:50:56:56:00:04
    02:50:56:56:01:04
    02:50:56:56:02:04
    02:50:56:56:03:04

sa-nsxedge-01>
```

Figure 11.11: *View shadow interfaces MAC in Edge node*

Step 4: Run command get logical-switch to view punt segment created by NSX automatically. Then run the command get logical-switch <punt-segment-UUID> mac-address-table to view MACs synced across Edge nodes. *Figure* 11.12 shows the sample output of these two commands.

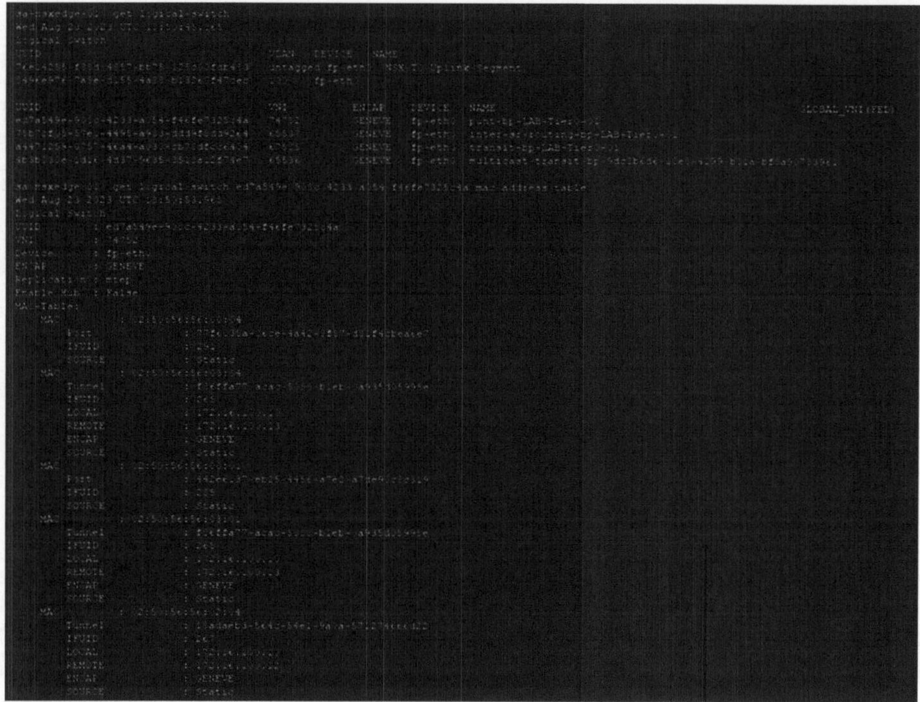

Figure 11.12: *Viewing the punt segment and its MAC table*

To configure stateful services such as gateway firewall or NAT, ensure service is enabled on Interface Group instead of individual interface or gateway, else, NSX will generate an alarm for inconsistent configuration.

Figure 11.13 shows gateway firewall rules being applied to Interface Group LAB-IG-01 created earlier.

Figure 11.13: *Configure stateful firewall on Active-Active Tier0 gateway*

This completes the configuration of stateful services on the NSX gateway running in Active-Active HA mode. In subsequent sections, we will cover different NSX services.

Network Address Translation

Network Address Translation or NAT is a service that maps one IP address space to a different IP address. NSX supports configuring NAT services on both Tier 0 and Tier 1 gateways. There are different NAT rules configurable on both Tier1 and Tier0 gateways listed in *Table* 11.2.

NAT Rule Types	NSX Gateway	NSX Edge HA
SNAT, DNAT, No SNAT, No DNAT, NAT64	Tier0, Tier1	Active - Standby
Reflexive NAT	Tier0	Stateless Active-Active
Stateful Active-Active SNAT, DNAT	Tier0, Tier1	Stateful Active-Active

Table 11.2: *Different NAT configurations supported on NSX gateways*

Originally, NAT was designed to reduce the usage of public address space. It helped by translating private IP address space to public IP address space by Internet Providers to reduce the allocation of public IP addresses to converse over the Internet. In the NSX environment, the main use case of NAT is to allow sharing of the same IP address space across multiple tenants and still be able to communicate with physical networks. Different types of NAT rules supported by NSX are:

- **SNAT**: Source NAT translates the source IP address of outbound packets to a different IP address defined as translated IP. It is supported on both Tier0 and Tier1 gateway. In NSX, SNAT is applied to traffic egressing from the NSX environment.
- **DNAT**: Destination NAT enables access to internal IP addresses from the outside world by translating the destination IP address of the inbound packet to an internal IP address. DNAT is supported on both Tier0 and Tier1 gateway. Both SNAT and DNAT maintain a connection table to track replies.
- **Reflexive NAT**: This is also known as stateless NAT, and it is configured on a Tier0 gateway running in Active-Active configuration without stateful services enabled. This does not maintain a connection table and needs to be defined in both directions.
- **NAT64**: NAT64 provides a mechanism for translating IPv6 packets to IPv4 packets and vice versa. With the help of NAT64, IPv6 clients can communicate with IPv4 servers using unicast TCP or UDP. NAT64 is

only supported for external IPv6 traffic ingress through the Edge node external interface to the IPv4 server running in the overlay. NAT64 is stateful and supported on both Tier 0 and Tier 1 gateways.

While configuring NAT rules, a few of the fields are optional, whereas a few fields are mandatory to be provided. *Table* 11.3 covers the configuration of different NAT rules and marks the fields necessary to be provided while creating them.

NAT Rule Type	Source Address	Destination Address	Translated Address	Translated Port	Match Service
SNAT	optional	optional	Required	No	optional
DNAT	optional	Required	Required	optional	optional
NO_SNAT	Required	optional	No	No	optional
NO_DNAT	optional	Required	No	No	optional
REFLEXIVE	Required	No	Required	No	No
NAT64	optional	Required	Required	optional	optional

Table 11.3: *Required fields for different NAT rules*

Note: If the gateway firewall is disabled, then it will cause NAT rules to drop the traffic. If the gateway firewall needs to be disabled, then create an ANY-ANY ALLOW rule.

Configuring NAT in NSX

Before configuring NAT rules on the Tier1 gateway, ensure that the Tier1 gateway is hosted on an Edge cluster. If the Tier1 gateway is running as a Distributed Only configuration, NAT rules realization will be failed as there is no SR hosted on the Edge node for DR only Tier1 gateway, which is a requirement to enable stateful services. Follow these steps to configure NAT rules in the NSX environment:

Step 1: Login into NSX Manager with admin privileges. Navigate to the **`Networking`** menu and click on **`NAT`** under **`Network Services`** from the left-side navigation panel. This will open the configuration screen for **`NAT`** in UI. There are two options, namely **`Gateway`** and **`View`**. Click on the drop-down menu for **`Gateway`** to select NSX gateway on which NAT rule is to be configured and select either **`NAT`** or **`NAT64`** as per the requirement to view corresponding NAT rules. *Figure* 11.14 shows an example where Gateway is selected as LAB-Tier1-01 to view NAT rules configured on it.

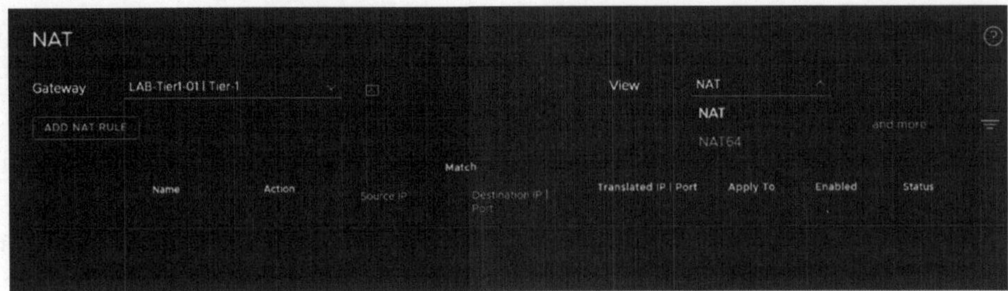

***Figure 11.14**: View NAT rules configured on the NSX gateway*

Step 2: Click on **`Add NAT Rule`** to start creating a new NAT rule on the selected gateway. If **`NAT64`** is selected in **`View`**, then the option will change to **`Add NAT64 Rule`**, however remaining configuration will remain similar. In the first section of the configuration, provide the values for the following attributes –

a. **`Name:`** Provide an appropriate to identify the NAT rule in the environment.

b. **`Action:`** Select the Type of NAT rule. Different options are SNAT, DNAT, No SNAT, No DNAT, and Reflexive NAT, and for NAT64 there will be only one option i.e., NAT64.

c. **`Source IP`**: Provide the source IP address of the packet or IP address range in CIDR format. Please refer to *Table* 11.3 to identify if this is a required field according to the type of NAT rule.

d. **`Destination IP`**: Provide the destination IP address of the packet or IP address range in CIDR format. Please refer to *Table* 11.3 to identify if this is a required field according to the type of NAT rule.

e. **`Destination Port`**: This is an optional field to provide a destination port if required.

f. **`Translated IP`**: Provide an IP address or IP address range in CIDR format to which either source IP or destination IP will be translated. Please refer to *Table* 11.3 to identify if this is a required field according to the type of NAT rule.

g. **`Service`**: Use this option to set the services.

h. **`Apply To`**: Select the specific Interface on which to apply the NAT rule for ingress/egress traffic. If this is a stateful Active-Active gateway, ensure to set it to Interface Group.

i. **`Enabled`**: Toggle the button to either enable or disable the NAT rule.

Figure 11.15 shows an example NAT rule with the name DNAT-Rule-01 configured to translate destination IP 180.80.80.80 with port 90980 of inbound packets to internal IP address 172.16.110.11 on port 80.

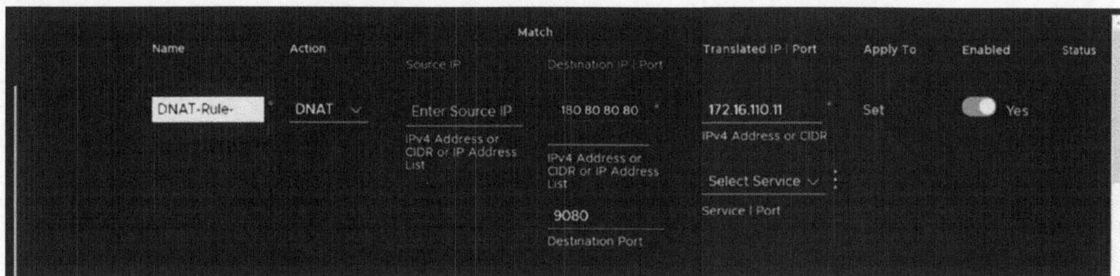

Figure 11.15: *Configuring a NAT rule*

Step 3: In the second section of the configuration, select the following attributes as per requirements as shown in *Figure* 11.16.

a. **`Firewall`**: Select the different option from the dropdown menu to select different firewall settings. These are:

   i. **`Match Internal Address`**: This is the default option. Selecting this option will apply the firewall rules to the internal address of the NAT rule.

   ii. **`Match External Address`**: If this option is selected, then firewall rules are applied to the external address of the NAT rule.

   iii. **`Bypass`**: If this option is selected, firewall rules are not applied to NAT packets.

b. **`Logging`**: Toggle the button to enable or disable logging for the NAT rule.

c. **`Priority`**: This option is used to define priority between NAT rules. A lower value means a higher priority to the NAT rule. The default is 0.

d. **`Apply to Policy-based VPN`**: This option is only applicable for DNAT or No DNAT rules. Use the drop-down menu to select different options:

i. **`Bypass`**: This is the default option. Setting this option will bypass the traffic decrypted from a policy-based IPSec VPN tunnel.

ii. **`Match`**: If this option is selected, then the NAT rule will match only traffic decrypted from the policy-based IPSec VPN tunnel.

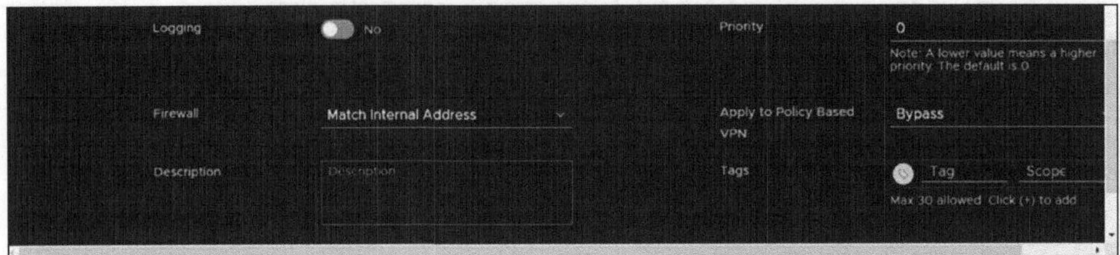

Figure 11.16: *Configuring optional settings of a NAT rule*

Step 4: Click on **`Save`** to finish configuring the NAT rule. After the NAT rule has been successfully realized, its Status will be shown as Success as shown in *Figure 11.17.*

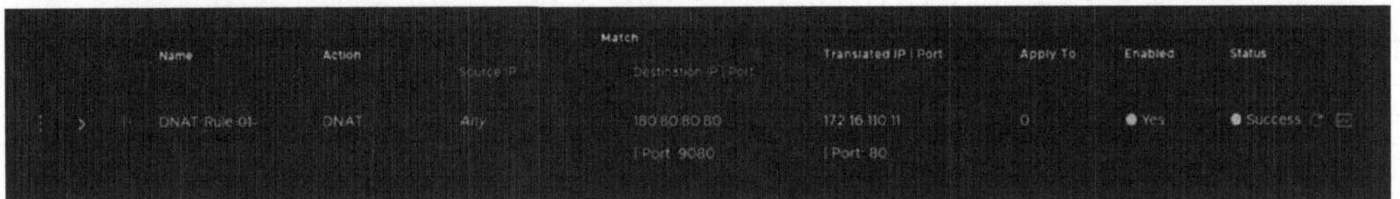

Figure 11.17: *A successful realized NAT rule on Tier1 gateway*

Step 5: This is an optional step. However, ensure that the Tier0 gateway is redistributing **`NAT IP`** from **`Tier-0 Subnets`** and **`NAT IP`** from **`Advertised Tier-1 Subnets`** to a physical network. If NAT IPs are not redistributed, then it results in improper configuration and NAT traffic drops. *Figure* 11.18 shows NAT IP enabled for redistribution in the LAB-Tier0-01 gateway.

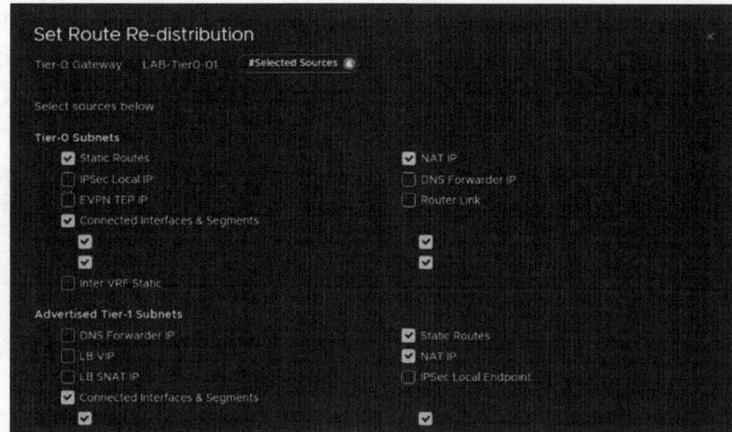

Figure 11.18: *Enabling NAT IP redistribution on Tier0 gateway*

Step 6: Similarly, ensure Route Advertisement is enabled for All NAT IPs on the Tier1 gateway if NAT rules are configured on the Tier1 gateway as shown in *Figure* 11.19.

Figure 11.19: *Advertising NAT IPs to Tier0 gateway from Tier1 gateway*

This completes the configuration of NAT rules in the NSX environment. There are different ways to validate NAT rules. The easiest one is to access the service through NAT IP. In this example, we have a virtual machine hosting a website on port 80 configured with IP address 172.16.110.11. But we want this website to access via public IP i.e., 180.80.80.80 over port 9080, and accordingly, we have created a DNAT rule. So, let's try to access this website through the web browser and see if NAT is working or not. As illustrated in *Figure* 11.20, we can access the website using IP 180.80.80.80 over port 9080 validating NAT configuration.

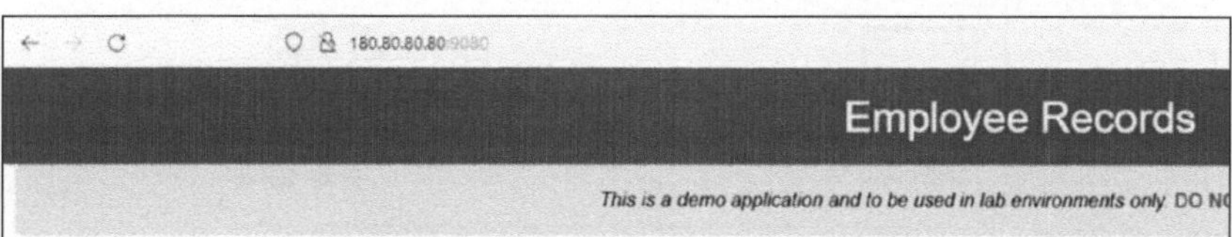

Figure 11.20: *Access services via NAT*

Also, there is a statistics button in the far-right corner of a NAT rule under Status. Click on it to view NAT rule Statistics as shown in *Figure 11.21* displaying the total number of active sessions, count of packets, and total data passed through the NAT rule.

Figure 11.21: *Viewing statistics of a NAT rule*

DHCP

DHCP or Dynamic Host Configuration Protocol allows a server to automatically assign network configurations such as IP addresses, subnet mask, gateway, NTP, and DNS configuration to a DHCP client in the network. DHCP works on a client-server model and uses the DORA (Discover, Offer, Request, Acknowledge) process. *Figure* 11.22 shows the process of network configuration assignment by DHCP.

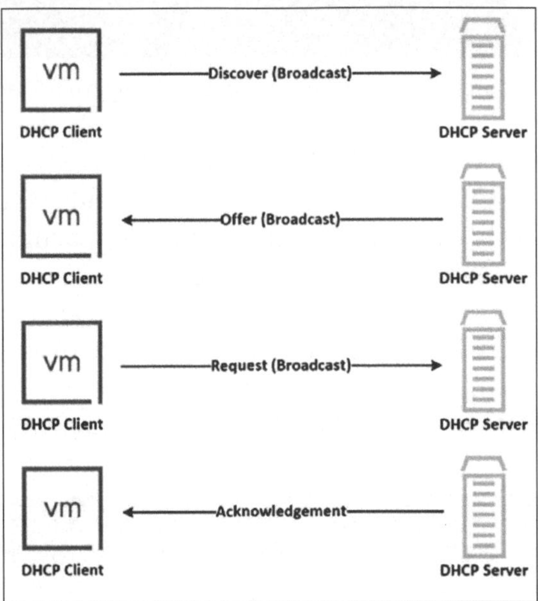

Figure 11.22: *DHCP process to assign network configuration to DHCP client*

In summary, when the DHCP client first comes online on the network with the configuration to obtain an IP address automatically, it sends a broadcast with a DHCP discover message to locate the available DHCP server on the subnet. DHCP server receives the broadcast and sends a DHCP offer message informing its availability and proposing networking configuration such as IP address, subnet mask, gateway, DNS, lease time, and DHCP Server IP address. DHCP client again sends a DHCP request message to the server requesting for proposed configuration. The DHCP server received the request message from the client and sent an acknowledgment message for the requested IP.

DHCP works on broadcast traffic, however, the broadcast is limited to a subnet. So, what if the DHCP server is present in a different subnet from the DHCP client subnets? This is where the DHCP relay agent comes in handy which helps in providing centralized DHCP services across multiple subnets. DHCP relay agent achieves this by converting a local DHCP broadcast message into a unicast message and sending that unicast message to a DHCP server hosted in a different subnet. *Figure* 11.23 shows two different DHCP clients present in two different subnets with a DHCP relay agent configured for the subnet. DHCP relay agent facilitates DHCP client-server communication by converting broadcast messages to unicast messages and sending them to DHCP servers hosted outside of DHCP client subnets.

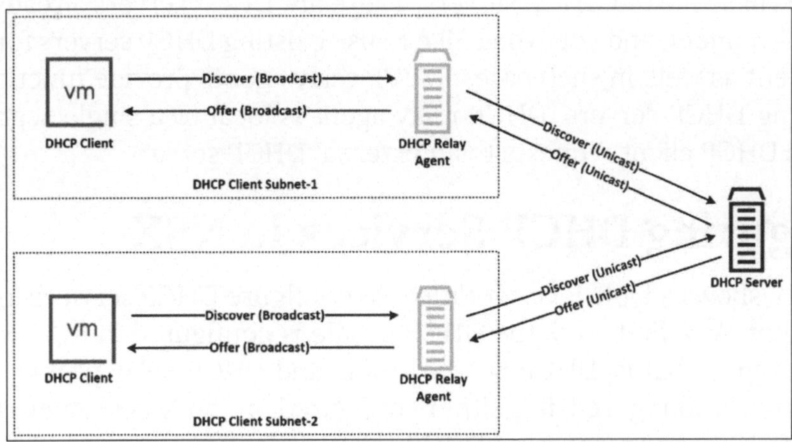

Figure 11.23: *DHCP relay agent configured in client subnets*

DHCP Support in NSX

NSX supports three different types of DHCP services in the environment, local to segment, gateway DHCP, and DHCP relay agent. NSX supports both IPv4 and IPv6 DHCP servers. Let's cover these different services in a bit more detail.

Segment DHCP Server

Segment DHCP server is local to a segment and can assign IP addresses only to clients connected in the same segment. If IP assignment is required for DHCP clients present in different segments, then a separate DHCP server needs to be configured for each segment. Segment DHCP server supports any segment connected to Tier0 or Tier1 gateway or segments not connected to any gateway and can provide DHCP services to both VLAN backed, and Overlay backed segments.

Gateway DHCP Server

As the name suggests, the gateway DHCP server is a centralized DHCP server managed by NSX and configured on an NSX gateway. It can provide DHCP services to all segments connected to the DHCP-configured gateway. It is supported on both Tier0 and Tier1 gateway and, by default, segments connected to the gateway use the gateway DHCP server.

DHCP Relay

DHCP relay agent is used to provide DHCP services in the NSX environment using externally hosted DHCP servers. There are DHCP servers already present in the environment, and you would like to use existing DHCP servers for the NSX environment as well. In such cases, DHCP relay agents provide functionality to use existing DHCP servers. DHCP relay agent is local to a single segment and relays the DHCP client requests to an external DHCP server.

Configuring DHCP Services in NSX

Figure 11.24 shows a high-level workflow to configure DHCP services in the NSX environment. As a first step, the DHCP profile is configured in NSX, which can be of two types, that is, DHCP Server profile and DHCP Relay profile. After the DHCP profile is configured, it is either configured on the NSX segment to enable segment DHCP server/segment DHCP relay or configured on the NSX Tier0/ Tier1 gateway to enable the gateway DHCP server.

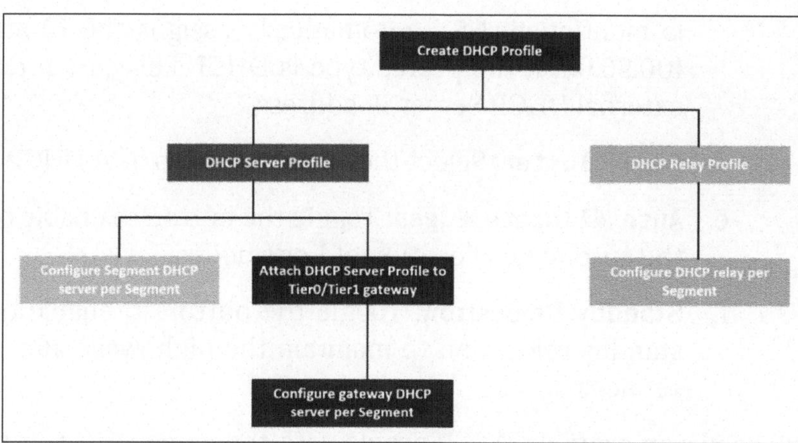

***Figure 11.24**: DHCP Configuration workflow in NSX*

Creating DHCP Profile

As a first step, create a DHCP profile following these steps.

Step 1: Login into NSX Manager with admin privileges. Navigate to **`Networking`** and then click on **`Networking Profiles`** under **`Settings`** in the left navigation panel. Click on **`DHCP`** to configure the DHCP profile as shown in *Figure 11.25.*

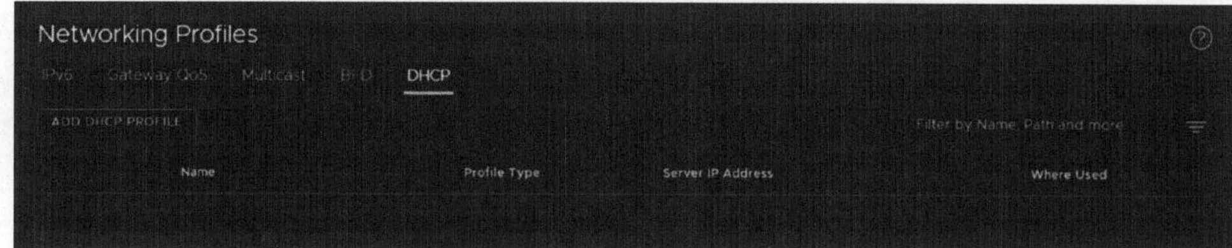

***Figure 11.25**: Viewing DHCP profile in NSX UI*

Step 2: Click on **`Add DHCP Profile`** to create a new profile and provide values for different attributes –

a. **`Name:`** Provide an appropriate name to identify the DHCP profile in the NSX environment

b. **`Profile Type`**: Select either DHCP Server to host the DHCP server within the NSX environment or DHCP Relay to configure the external DHCP server.

c. **`Server IP Address:`** Provide an IP address for the DHCP server. If the profile type is DHCP server and no IP address is mentioned, NSX automatically assigns the IP address as 100.96.0.1. If the profile type is DHCP Relay, then provide an external DHCP Server IP address.

d. `Edge Cluster`: Select the Edge cluster to host DHCP services.

e. `Auto Allocate Edges`: Toggle the button to enable or disable the automatic allocation of Edge nodes.

f. **Standby Relocation**: Toggle the button to enable or disable standby relocation to maintain the high availability of DHCP services.

Figure 11.26 shows an example DHCP profile with the name DHCP-Profile-01 of type DHCP Server.

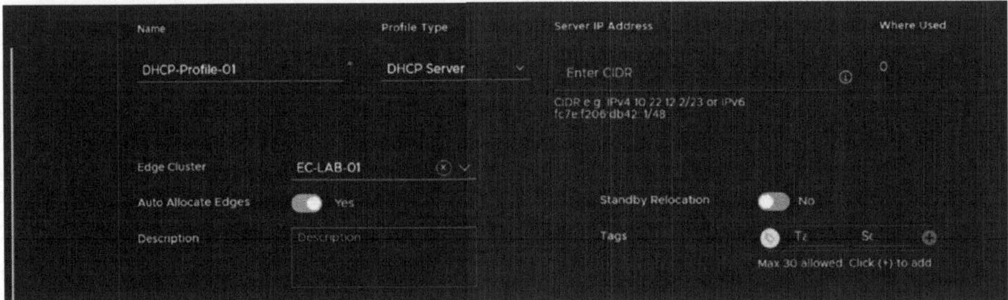

Figure 11.26: *Creating a DHCP server profile*

Step 3: Click on `Save` to finish creating a DHCP profile. *Figure* 11.27 shows the DHCP server profile configured in NSX and the Server IP address assigned as 100.96.0.1/30 automatically assigned by NSX.

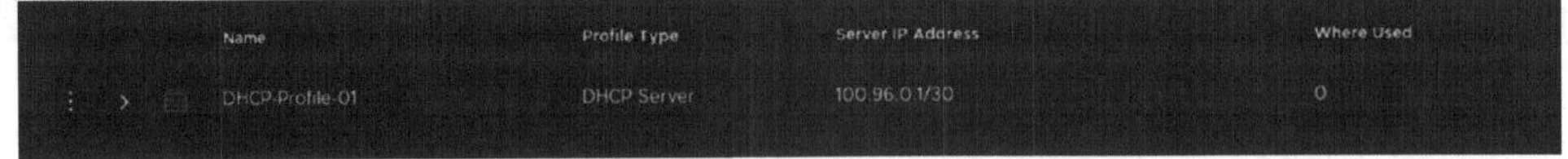

Figure 11.27: *Viewing newly configured DHCP Server profile in* NSX UI

Attaching DHCP Server Profile on NSX Gateway

The next step is to attach the DHPC Server profile to the Tier 0/Tier 1 gateway. DHCP profile can be directly attached to the segment as well, which is covered in the next section.

Step 4: While logged into NSX Manager, Navigate to `Networking` and click on either `Tier-0 Gateway` or `Tier-1 Gateway` to select the desired gateway to configure the gateway DHCP server. `Edit` the desired gateway and click on **Set** in front of DHCP Config as shown in *Figure* 11.28.

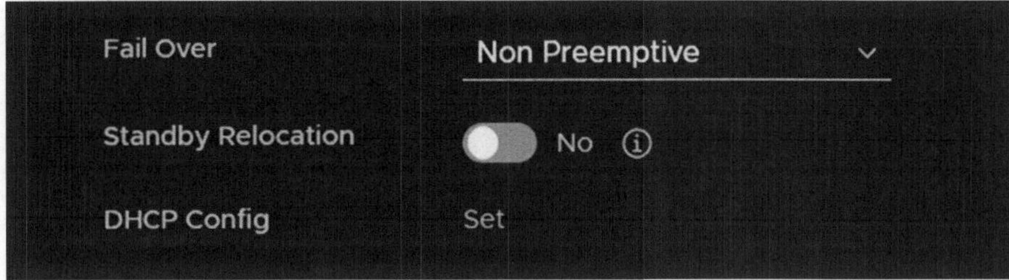

***Figure 11.28**: Edit DHCP Config on Tier0/Tier1 gateway*

Step 5: This opens a new dialogue box with the name **Set DHCP Configuration.** Change the type to **DHCP Server** and select the **DHCP Server Profile** as created earlier. *Figure* 11.29 shows an example where a profile created earlier with the name DHCP-Profile-01 is selected to configure the gateway DHCP server.

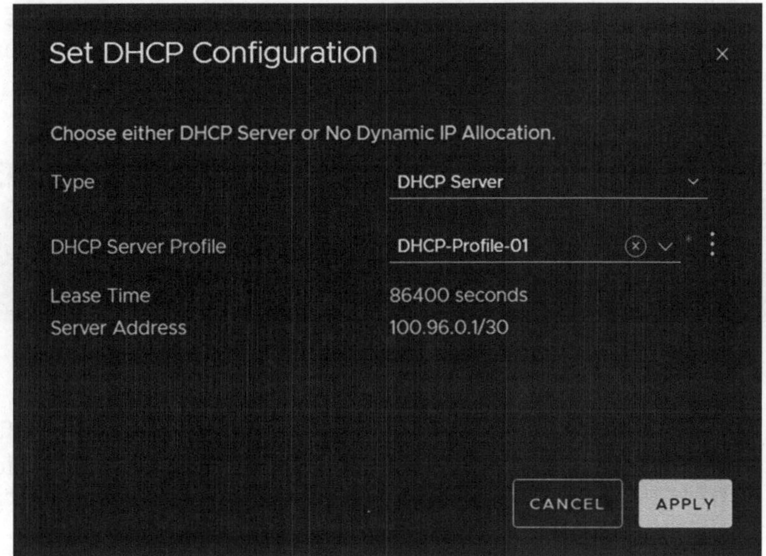

***Figure 11.29**: Configuring gateway DHCP server*

Step 6: Click on **Apply** to save configuration. Also, the status of DHCP Config will change to 1 Server as shown in *Figure* 11.30. Click on **Close Editing** to finish configuring DHCP services on the gateway.

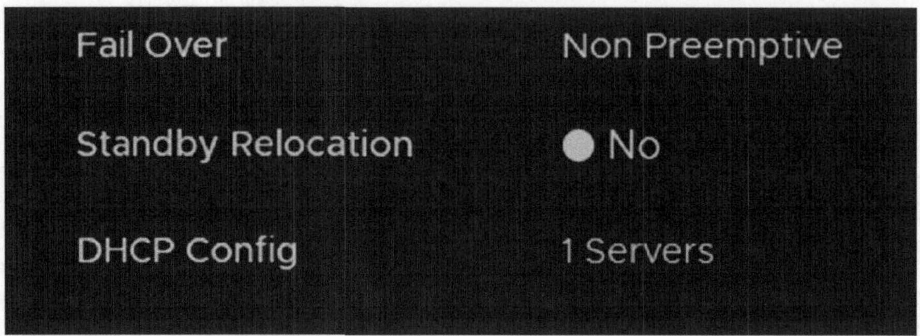

Figure 11.30: *Viewing DHCP Config on NSX gateway*

Configuring DHCP services on Segment

As a last step, the DHCP profile is attached to the NSX segment to enable clients connected on the segment to receive network configuration from the DHCP server. Let's see the steps to configure DHCP services in the NSX segment.

Step 1: While logged into NSX Manager, navigate to **Networking** and click on **Segments** under **Connectivity** in the left navigation panel. **Edit** the desired segment and click on **Set DHCP Config** as shown in *Figure* 11.31.

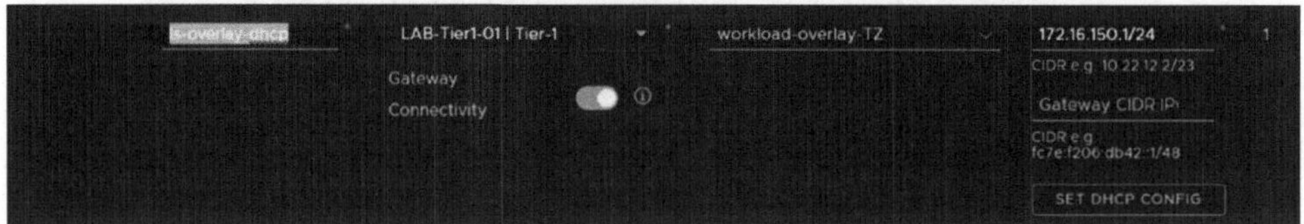

Figure 11.31: *Configuring DHCP on NSX segment*

Step 2: This opens a new dialogue box with the name **Set DHCP Config**. The first thing to select here is **DHCP Type,** which defines which type of DHCP services need to be enabled on the segment. As *Figure* 11.32 shows, there are three different options covered earlier.

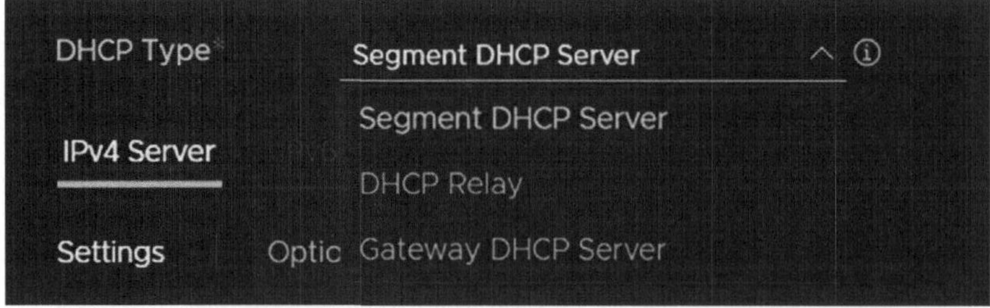

Figure 11.32: *Different types of DHCP services on NSX segment*

a. If the **DHCP Type** is **Segment DHCP Server**, then the DHCP Server Address needs to be provided mandatory which should be a local address from the same subnet as *Figure* 11.33 reflects.

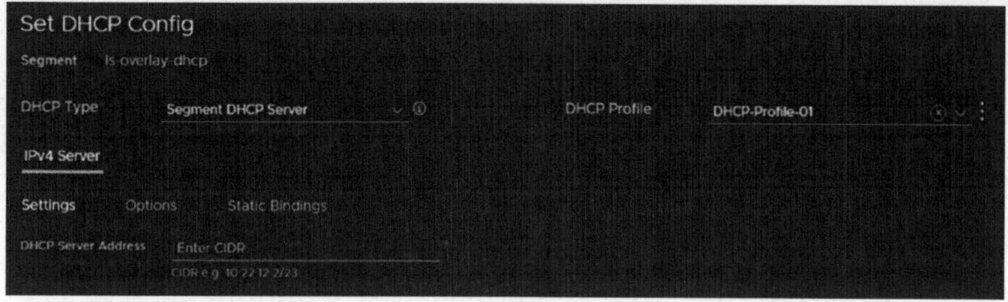

***Figure 11.33**: Configuring DHCP Type as Segment DHCP Server*

b. If the **DHCP Type** is **DHCP Relay**, then no further configuration is required. Only the DHCP Relay profile needs to be selected as shown in *Figure* 11.34.

***Figure 11.34**: Configuring DHCP Type as DHCP Relay*

c. If the **DHCP Type** is **Gateway DHCP Server**, then the **DHCP Server Address** is taken automatically from the DHCP Server profile configured while creating the DHCP Server profile.

Step 3: After selecting the desired DHCP Type, depending upon selection, it may require you to input a few more details. In the case of the Gateway DHCP server and Segment DHCP server, provide the following details as shown in *Figure* 11.35.

a. **DHCP Ranges**: Provide the range of IP addresses to be allocated by DHCP service

b. **Lease Time (seconds)**: Set the IP address lease time in seconds

c. **DNS Servers**: Provide the DNS Servers IP addresses up to three to set nameserver for DHCP clients

Figure 11.35: Configuring additional settings for DHCP service

Step 4: Click on **`Options`** to set additional DHCP options such as NIS Server, NTP Servers, NBT etc. *Figure* 11.36 shows the option to add additional DHCP options by clicking on **`Add Generic Option`** and selecting the desired **`code`**.

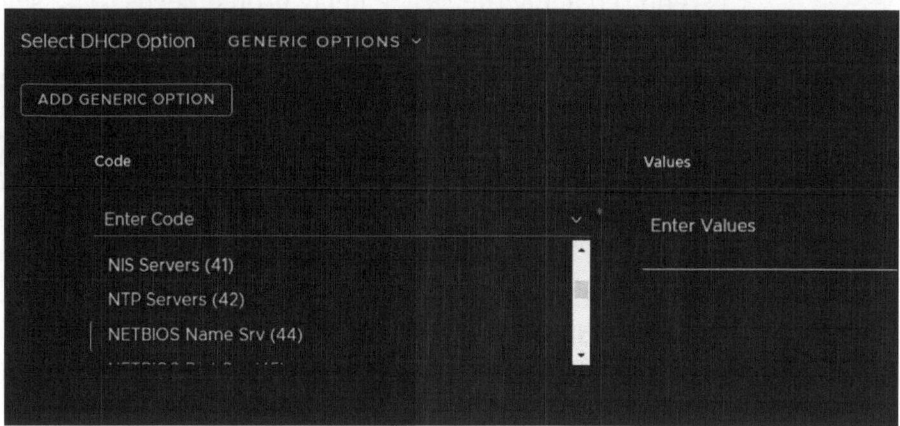

Figure 11.36: Setting additional DHCP options

Step 5: Click on **`Static Bindings`** to add DHCP reservations based on the MAC address of DHCP clients. Click on **`Add IPV4 Static Binding`** to create a new binding by providing the following details as shown in *Figure* 11.37.

a. **`Name`**: Provide an appropriate name for the DHCP binding

b. **`MAC Address`**: Provide the MAC address of the DHCP client

c. **`IP Address`**: Provide the IP address to be reserved for DHCP client

d. **`Gateway Address`**: Optionally provide gateway address

e. **`Host Name`**: Optionally provide the hostname of the DHCP client

Click on **Add** to finish setting up a static binding and save the configuration.

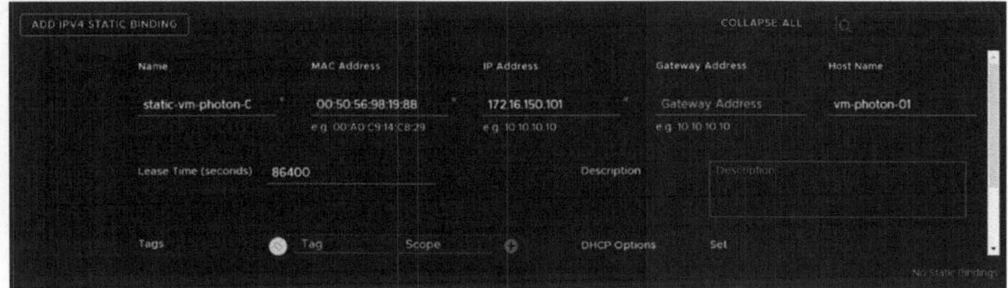

Figure 11.37: *Adding a static binding in DHCP*

Step 6: Click on **`Apply`** to save DHCP configuration on a segment and enable DHCP services on the segment. As illustrated in *Figure* 11.38, a DHCP-configured segment will show subnets in highlighted status which can be clicked to view DHCP configuration.

ls-overlay-db	LAB-Tier1-01	workload-overlay-TZ | Overlay	172.16.130.1/24	1
ls-overlay-dhcp	LAB-Tier1-01	workload-overlay-TZ | Overlay	172.16.150.1/24	1
ls-overlay-web	LAB-Tier1-01	workload-overlay-TZ | Overlay	172.16.110.1/24	2

Figure 11.38: *Viewing DHCP configured segment in NSX*

This completes the configuration of DHCP in the NSX environment. Clients connected to the DHCP-enabled segment will be able to automatically receive network configuration from the DHCP server.

Validating DHCP Services

Connect the virtual machine to the NSX segment and set it to obtain IP automatically from DHCP. If DHCP services are configured properly, the virtual machine will be able to receive an IP address from the DHCP server and become reachable on the network. *Figure* 11.39 shows a Linux virtual machine connected to NSX segment ls-overlay-dhcp configured for DHCP received IP address 172.16.150.101 for which we had created a static binding in DHCP shown in *Figure* 11.39.

```
       valid_lft forever preferred_lft forever
2: eth0: <BROADCAST,MULTICAST,UP,LOWER_UP> mtu 1500 qdisc fq_codel state UP group default qlen 1000
    link/ether 00:50:56:98:19:88 brd ff:ff:ff:ff:ff:ff
    altname eno1
    altname enp11s0
    altname ens192
    inet 172.16.150.101/24 metric 1024 brd 172.16.150.255 scope global dynamic eth0
       valid_lft 86355sec preferred_lft 86355sec
    inet6 fe80::250:56ff:fe98:1988/64 scope link
       valid_lft forever preferred_lft forever
```

Figure 11.39: *VM receiving IP address from DHCP server in NSX*

To view DHCP statistics, if configured gateway DHCP server, navigate to the gateway and click on **DHCP Config** which opens the DHCP Configuration screen shown in *Figure* 11.40.

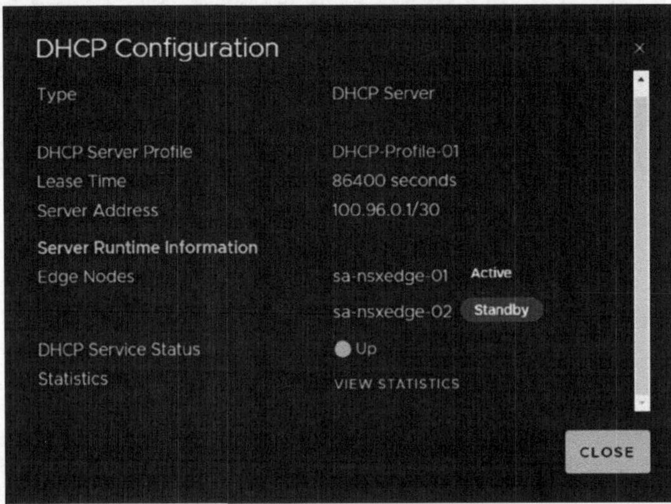

Figure 11.40: *Viewing DHCP Configuration on NSX gateway*

Click on **`View Statistics`** to view DHCP Statistics shown in *Figure* 11.41, providing insights into how many requests were received by the DHCP server and how many were rejected. What is the pool size, allocated number, and percentage to track DHCP pool usage?

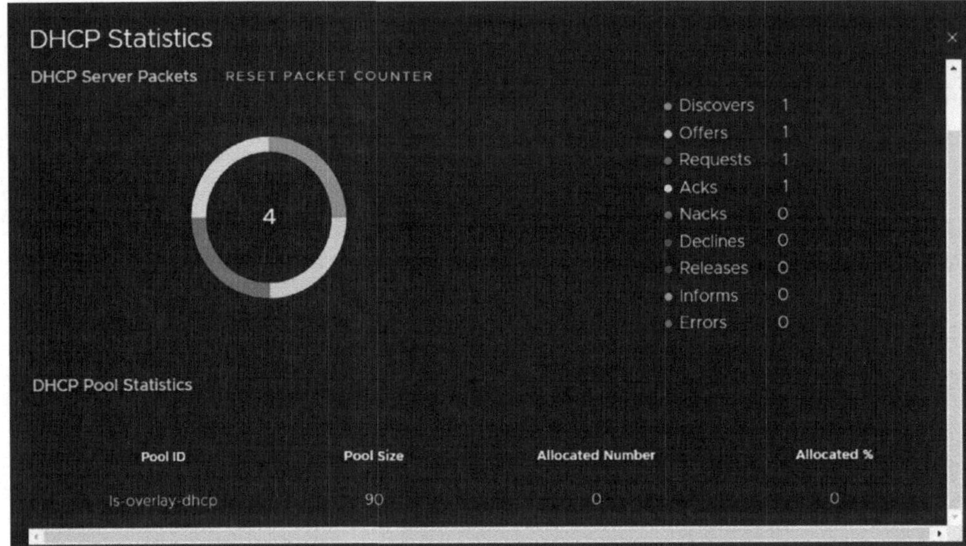

Figure 11.41: *Viewing Statistics of gateway DHCP server*

If configured segment DHCP server, then click on the **View Statistics** option present in a segment which opens **Segment Statistics**. Click on **DHCP Statistics** to view DHCP statistics for specific segments DHCP server.

Note: If both DHCP IPv4 and DHCP IPv6 servers are configured on a segment, the DHCP Statistics page will display only DHCPv4 packet counts and pool usage. DHCPv6 packet counts and pool usage statistics are not supported as of writing.

DNS

In NSX, DNS services are supported as a cache DNS forwarder only. This means any DNS requests from clients will be forwarded by NSX to an external DNS server. NSX DNS forwarder then caches the responses received from the external DNS server and next time provides the name resolution to DNS clients based on cached responses. This can reduce system load on external DNS servers and provide improved performance for DNS clients. Below are the high-level steps to configure the DNS forwarder in the NSX environment:

- Configure a default DNS Zone
- Optionally configure one or more FQDN Zone
- Create a DNS forwarder service
- Validate DNS forwarder connectivity
- Optionally, configure DHCP to allocate DNS server IP

Let's cover these steps in detail.

Step 1: Log into NSX Manager with admin privileges. Navigate to **Networking** and click on **DNS** under **IP Management** from the left navigation panel. This opens the DNS configuration screen. Click on **DNS Zones** to configure either the default DNS zone or FQDN DNS zone as shown in *Figure 11.42*.

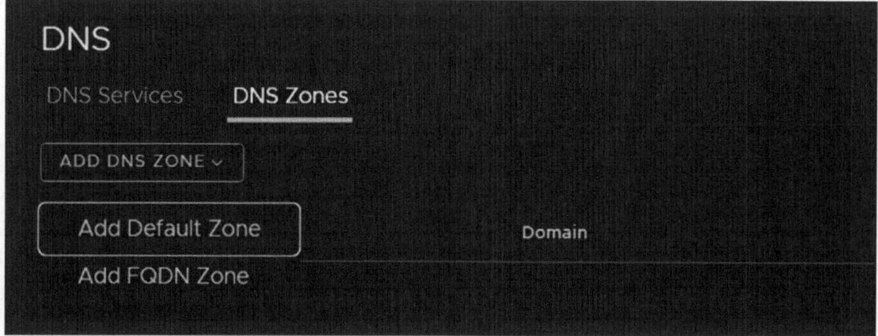

Figure 11.42: *Adding a DNS Zone in NSX*

Step 2: Click on either **`Add Default Zone`** or **`Add FQDN Zone`** to add a DNS zone. The only difference between the two options is **`Domain`**. In the default zone, the domain is set to **`Any`** and cannot be modified whereas in the FQDN zone, the domain can be modified, and a different domain name can be provided. This is helpful where the DNS server is different for a specific FQDN. Additionally, provide a name to identify different DNS zones in NSX and the IP address of DNS Servers. Source IP is optional. *Figure* 11.43 shows an example configuration of the default zone.

***Figure 11.43:** Configuring DNS zone in NSX*

Step 3: Click on **`DNS Services`** after adding DNS zones. Click on **`Add DNS Service`** to add DNS forwarder. Provide the following details as shown in *Figure* 11.44:

a. **`Name`**: Provide an appropriate name for DNS forwarder service.

b. **`Gateway`**: Select the desired gateway on which to enable DNS forwarder service.

c. **`DNS Service IP`**: Provide a DNS forwarder service IP which will be used by the DNS client as a DNS server.

d. **`Default DNS Zone`**: Select the default DNS zone.

e. **`FQDN Zones`**: Optionally, add FQDN zones created earlier.

f. **`Admin Status:`** Toggle the button to enable or disable DNS forwarder service.

g. **`Log Level`**: If required, change the log level, the default is set to Info.

h. **`Cache Size`**: The default value is 1024. This defines the number of responses to be cached by the DNS forwarder.

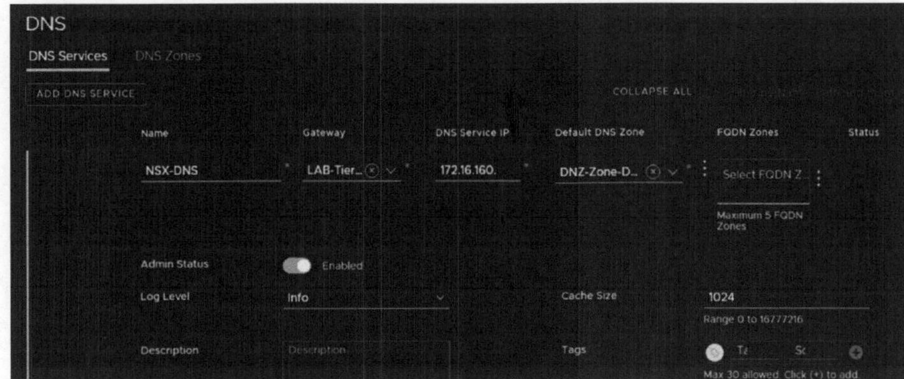

Figure 11.44: Adding a DNS forwarder service in NSX

Step 4: Click on **Save** to finish creating the DNS forwarder service. After the successful realization of the DNS forwarder on the gateway, its status will change to Success as shown in *Figure 11.45*.

Figure 11.45: Successful realized DNS forwarder service

This completes the DNS forwarder service in the NSX Manager. Optionally, DNS Service IP can be configured in DHCP configuration if enabled on the segment to distribute DNS service IP automatically via DHCP or it can be configured manually on clients.

Validating DNS Forwarder Service

There are multiple tools to validate DNS forwarder services such as dig, nslookup, and so on. While using nslookup, use command server `<DNS Service IP>` to change the name server to NSX DNS forwarder IP. *Figure* 11.46 shows an example, where nslookup is set to use the DNS server as 172.16.160.10 which is the NSX DNS forwarder IP configured earlier. When performing name resolution, the request is sent to 172.16.160.10 which forwards the request to the DNS server on behalf of the client and receives the response from the DNS server and provides it to the client.

```
PS C:\Users\Administrator> nslookup
Default Server:
Address:

> server 172.16.160.10
Default Server:  [172.16.160.10]
Address:  172.16.160.10

> esx-01a.corp.local
Server:  [172.16.160.10]
Address:  172.16.160.10

Name:    esx-01a.corp.local
Address:  192.168.20.1

> _
```

Figure 11.46: *Performing NSX DNS forwarder validation using nslookup*

Another way to validate the DNS forwarder service on NSX is to log into the NSX Edge node as an admin using SSH running an active instance of gateway configured for DNS service. Jump into the Service Router of gateway using command **`vrf <number>`** which can be obtained by **`get logical-router`** command. Run the following to validate the status of the DNS forwarder service:

```
get dns-forwarder table

get dns-forwarder stats

get dns-forwarder cache
```

Figure 11.47 shows the sample output of the previous command.

```
sa-nsxedge-01(tier1_sr[7])> get dns-forwarder table
Thu Aug 24 2023 UTC 07:58:29.126
    ERR_MSG:
    TABLE:

        DNS_SERVER_ADDRESS: 192.168.0.253
        DOMAIN_NAME:
        FORWARDER_SOURCE_ADDRESS: 172.16.160.10
        QUERIES_FAILED: 0
        QUERIES_FORWARDED: 138
        QUERIES_TIMEOUT: 96
        RESPONSE_DETAILS:
            FORMERR: 0
            HEADERERR: 0
            NOERROR: 20
            NONLOCAL: 0
            NOTIMP: 0
            NXDOMAIN: 2
            RECVERR: 0
            REFUSED: 0
            SERVFAIL: 0
            UNTRUSTIF: 0
            ZROSRCPORT: 0
        TOTAL_QUERY_NUMBER: 138
        TOTAL_RESPONSE_NUMBER: 22
    UUID: d91351cf-2434-43bf-928d-e48e3e492cee
```

Figure 11.47: *Example output of DNS forwarder command on Edge node*

These commands show various metrics such as in-depth response details. Cache responses stored by DNS forwarder service and its current status whether any queries are getting timed out in the last 10 minutes, 1-minute intervals which help in troubleshooting.

Virtual Private Networks

Virtual Private Networks or VPNs for short provide a mechanism to create a secure connection between the computing device and a network or between two networks over an unsecured communication channel such as the public internet. This helps in extending access to a private network of an organization securely over the internet to other offsite locations or users working remotely. NSX supports two different VPN services, IPSec VPN and L2VPN (Layer 2 VPN) on Edge nodes.

IPSec VPN provides site-to-site connectivity and extends IP networks to remote locations. It uses a routing-based connection between different nonoverlapping IP subnets and connects over the public network through an IPSec gateway termed as an endpoint. Whereas L2VPN enables to extend L2 network across datacenters using L2 tunnels established between L2 VPN endpoints which are connected over L3 networks. Both IPSec VPN and L2VPN are supported on Tier0 and Tier1 gateway, however, Tier0 must be running in Active-Standby HA mode.

IPSec VPN

IPSec (Internet Protocol Security) VPN secures traffic communication between two networks connected through public internet. It uses different protocols and algorithms to provide confidentiality, integrity, and authentication for VPN. These different protocols are:

- IKE (Internet Key Exchange) for Key Management
- Preshared key certificates for Authentication
- AES (Advanced Encryption Standard) for Encryption
- SHA (Secure Hash Algorithm) for Data Integrity

IPSec VPN supports two different modes for security traffic which are:

- **Transport Mode**: This mode preserves the original IP header and is typically used for remote access clients. This mode is not supported by NSX.
- **Tunnel Mode**: This mode encapsulates the entire IP datagram into a new header essentially rewriting the IP header. This is typically used for site-to-site VPN connectivity and is used by NSX.

NSX supports configuring IPSec VPN services on both Tier 0 and Tier 1 gateways. As of writing, IPSec VPN is only supported on Tier 0/Tier 1 gateways running in Active-Standby HA mode and is not supported on Active-Active stateful gateways. NSX uses the gateway-level failover functionality to provide support for the high availability of IPSec VPN services. IPSec VPN configuration data is synchronized between Active and Standby Edge nodes and in case of Edge node failure, tunnels are re-established. An important point to note here is that before NSX-T release v3.0, the IPSec VPN state is not synchronized as tunnels are being re-established. However, starting with NSX-T release v3.0, the IPSec VPN state is synchronized to the standby Edge node when the active Edge node fails and the standby Edge node becomes the new active Edge node without renegotiating the tunnels.

NSX Edge supports two different types of IPSec VPN namely Policy-Based IPSec VPN and Route-Based IPSec VPN.

Policy-Based IPSec VPN

Policy-Based IPSec VPN uses a VPN policy to determine which traffic is to be protected by IPSec and passes through a VPN tunnel. This IPSec VPN type is static as any change in local network topology or configuration requires the VPN policy to be updated as well to accommodate changes. IPSec tunnels are used to connect one or more local subnets behind the NSX Edge node to remote peer networks on remote VPN sites. *Table* 11.4 (courtesy VMware Documentation) provides a summary of the maximum number of IPSec tunnels supported by the NSX Edge node based on its form factor.

Edge Node Form Factor	**Number of IPSec Tunnels Per VPN Session (Policy-Based)**	**Number of Sessions Per VPN Service**	**Number of IPSec Tunnels Per VPN Service (16 tunnels per session)**
Small	Not Applicable	Not Applicable	Not Applicable
Medium	128	128	2048
Large	128 (soft limit)	256	4096
Bare Metal	128 (soft limit)	512	6000

Table 11.4: *Configuration limitation of Policy-based IPSec tunnels based on Edge node*

Route-based IPSec VPN

Route-based IPSec VPN uses a special interface called VTI (Virtual Tunnel Interface) to learn routes dynamically using BGP protocol and tunnel traffic based on static routes or dynamically learned routes. IPSec secures all traffic flowing through VTI. OSPF protocol is not supported for dynamic routing in IPSec VPN and BGP is the sole protocol supported for route-based VPNs that are learned over VTI in Tier0 logical routers. As dynamic routing for VTI is not supported on the Tier 1 gateway, the Tier 1 gateway can only offer policy-based VPN connections. Also, multiple tunnels can be set up between two sites to provide VPN tunnel redundancy with Route-Based IPSec VPN.

Configuring IPSec VPN

Figure 11.48 shows the high-level workflow to configure IPSec VPN services in the NSX environment. In summary, the first step is configuring the IPSec VPN service, which is to enable IPSec VPN services on the selected NSX gateway. NSX provides system default profiles for IKE, DPD, and IPSec but if required to configure custom profiles as per organization requirements, then optionally configure these profiles. After profiles have been created, create a local IPSec endpoint which will be used to configure either a Policy-Based IPSec VPN session or a Route-based IPSec VPN session.

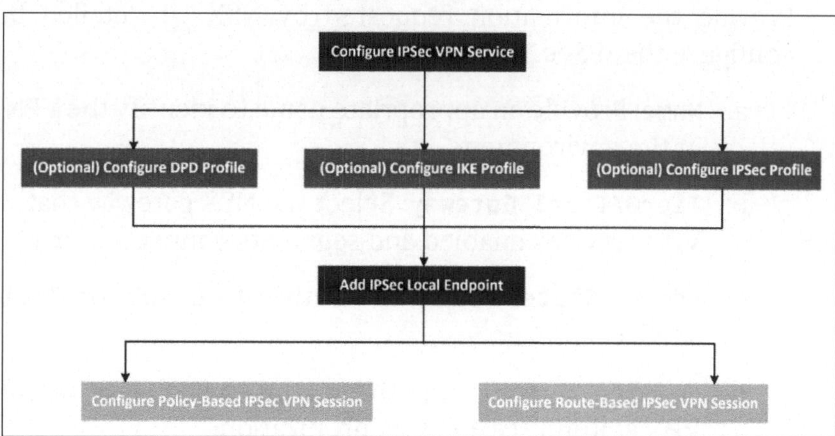

Figure 11.48: *High-level workflow to configure IPSec VPN*

Configuring IPSec VPN

The first step in configuring the IPSec VPN service is to create a VPN service that is attached to either Tier0 or Tier1 gateway.

Step 1: Login into NSX Manager with admin privileges. Navigate to **`Networking`** and click on **`VPN`** under **`Network Services`** in the left navigation panel. This will open the VPN configuration screen. Click on **`VPN Services`** and then click on **`Add Service`** and select **`IPSec`** to add an IPSec VPN service shown in *Figure* 11.49.

***Figure 11.49**: Adding an IPSec VPN service in NSX UI*

Step 2: Provide the information requested by NSX UI detailed below to configure the IPSec VPN service.

a. **`Name`**: Provide an appropriate name to identify the VPN service in the environment.

b. **`Tier0/Tier1 Gateway`**: Select the NSX gateway that will have VPN services enabled and segments connected to it.

c. **`Admin State`**: Toggle the button to enable or disable VPN service.

d. **`Session Sync`**: Toggle the button to enable or disable IPSec VPN stateful session synchronization.

e. **`IKE Log Level`**: The default value is Info, but can be changed to log only errors or warnings.

f. **Global Bypass `Rules`**: Provide subnet information in **`Local Networks`** and **`Remote Networks`** if data packets between needs to be exchanged without IPSec VPN.

Figure 11.50 shows an example IPSec VPN service with the name SVC-IPSec-VPN configured on a dedicated Tier0 gateway named LAB-Tier0-VPN.

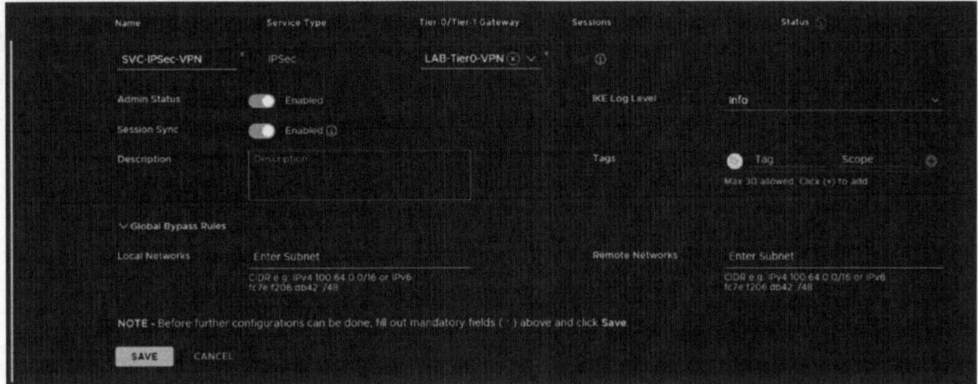

Figure 11.50: *Configuring IPSec VPN service in NSX UI*

Step 3: Click on **Save** to finish configuring the IPSec VPN service and commit the configuration. *Figure* 11.51 shows VPN service SVC-IPSec-VPN configured successfully and realized on Tier0 gateway LAB-Tier0-VPN with its status as success.

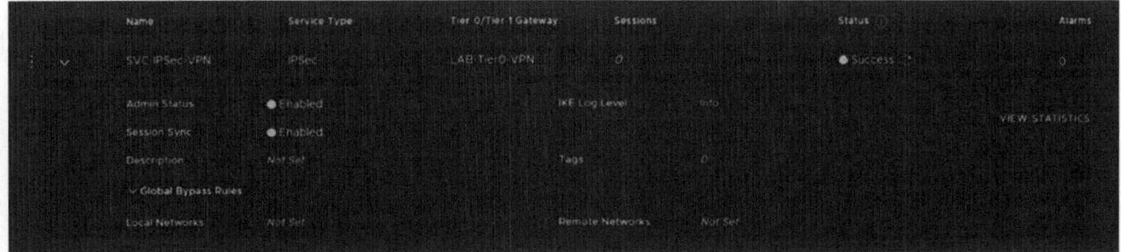

Figure 11.51: *Viewing configured IPSec VPN service*

Configuring VPN Profiles

NSX provides system default profiles for IKE, DPD, and IPSec to use with VPN sessions but it may be required by an organization to change the default configuration to satisfy organization requirements. This is an optional step to configure custom profiles for IKE, DPD, and IPSec, so let's take a look.

Adding a new IKE Profile

IKE profiles provide information about algorithms that are used to authenticate, encrypt, and establish a shared secret between network sites when an IKE tunnel is established.

Step 4: While logged into NSX Manager and on the VPN configuration screen, click on **Profiles** under **VPN** to view system-configured profiles. By default, **IKE Profiles** are selected as **Profile Type** which can be changed to different options using the drop-down menu. While **IKE Profiles** is selected, click on **Add IKE Profile** to add a new IKE profile shown in *Figure* 11.52.

***Figure* 11.52:** *Adding a new IKE Profile*

Step 5: Provide information requested by NSX UI detailed below to configure the IKE Profile.

a. **Name:** Provide an appropriate name to distinguish the IKE profile

b. **IKE Version**: Use the drop-down menu to select one of the below options:

   i. **IKE V1**: When IKE V1 is selected, IPSec VPN uses only the IKE V1 protocol

   ii. **IKE V2**: When IKE V2 is selected, IPSec VPN uses only the IKE V2 protocol

   iii. **IKE-Flex**: As the name suggests, it is flexible, if IKE V2 is failed then it falls back to IKE V1.

c. **Encryption Algorithm**: Select the appropriate encryption algorithm as per requirement. Please note that AES128 and AES256 use CBC mode of operation.

d. **Digest Algorithm**: Select the appropriate algorithm for secure hash to be used during IKE negotiation.

e. **Diffie-Hellman Group**: Group 14 is selected by default, but if required can be changed to a different value used for establishing a shared secret.

Figure 11.53 displays a custom IKE profile with different encryption and digest algorithms selected as per requirements from the peer site. Click on **`Save`** to finish configuring and save the IKE profile.

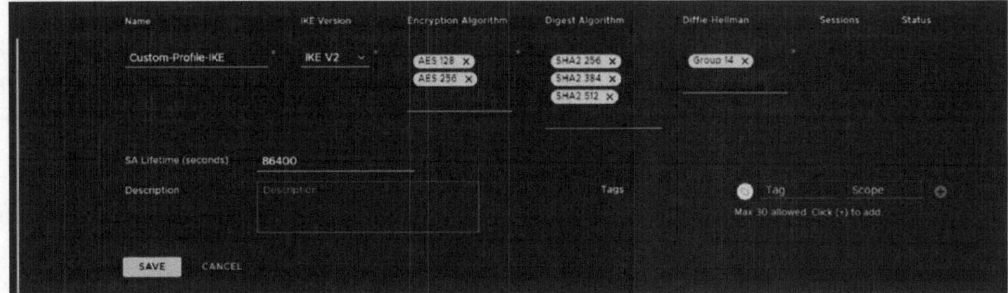

***Figure 11.53:** Configuring an IKE profile*

Adding a new IPSec Profile

IPSec profiles provide information about algorithms that are used to authenticate, encrypt, and establish a shared secret between network sites when an IPSec tunnel is established.

Step 6: While logged into NSX Manager and on the VPN configuration screen, click on **`Profiles`** under **`VPN`** to view system-configured profiles. Using the drop-down menu for **`Select Profile Type`** select **`IPSec Profiles,`** and click on **`Add IPSec Profile`** to add a new IPSec profile shown in *Figure* 11.54.

***Figure 11.54**: Adding a new IPSec profile*

Step 7: Provide the information requested by NSX UI detailed below to configure the IPSec Profile.

a. **`Name`**: Provide an appropriate name to distinguish the IPSec profile.

b. **`Encryption Algorithm`**: Select the appropriate encryption algorithm as per requirement. Please note that AES128 and

AES256 use CBC mode of operation.

c. **Digest Algorithm**: Select the appropriate algorithm for secure hash to be used during IPSec negotiation.

d. **PFS Group**: Group 14 is selected by default, but if required can be changed to a different value used for establishing a shared secret.

e. **PFS**: Toggle the button to enable or disable the usage of the PFS Group protocol in the IPSec tunnel. It is enabled by default.

f. **SA Lifetime**: Provide the default number of seconds before the IPSec tunnel is re-established.

g. **DF Bit**: This value determines how to handle the Do not Fragment (DF) bit included in the data packet. It can be one of two options –

    i. **Copy:** If the copy is selected, the value of the DF bit is copied from the received data packet to the forwarded packet. This means that if the received data packet has a DF set, then after encryption, the packet will have also a DF bit set.

    ii. **Clear**: If clear is selected, after encryption, the DF bit of the packet is always set to 0.

Figure 11.55 displays a custom IPSec profile with different encryption and digest algorithms selected as per requirements from the peer site. Click on **Save** to finish configuring and save the IPSec profile.

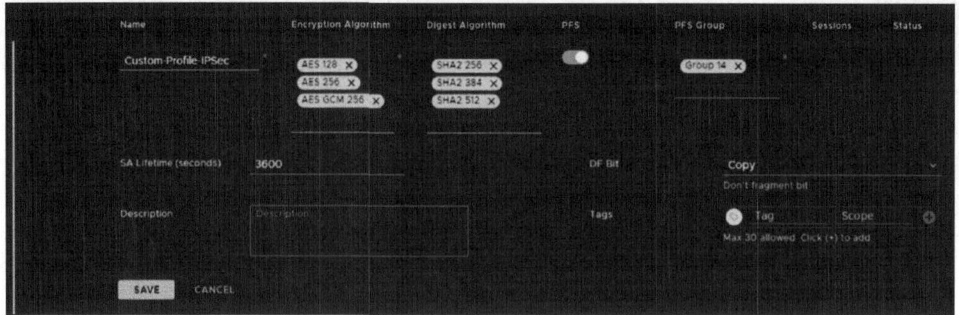

Figure 11.55: *Adding a new IPSec Profile*

Adding a new DPD Profile

DPD (Dead Peer Detection) profiles provide information about the number of seconds to wait, and the total retry count for the probes to determine if a peer is alive or down.

Step 8: While logged into NSX Manager and on the VPN configuration screen, click on **`Profiles`** under **`VPN`** to view system-configured profiles. Using the drop-down menu for **`Select Profile Type`**, select **`DPD Profiles,`** and click on **`Add DPD Profile`** to add a new IPSec profile shown in *Figure* 11.56.

Figure 11.56: *Adding a new DPD profile*

Step 9: Provide an appropriate **`Name`** to the DPD profile to identify in the NSX environment. Under the **`DPD Probe Interval`**, provide the value in seconds for the Edge node to wait before sending the next probe. Provide the total number of **`Retry Count`** to tell the Edge node to send a number of probes before declaring a peer down. **`DPD Probe`** mode is set to **`Periodic`** by default, which sends probes on regular interval but can be changed to **`On Demand`** to send probe if no IPSec packets are received and the session is idle. *Figure* 11.57 shows a custom DPD profile with the name **`Custom-Profile-DPD`** configured in NSX.

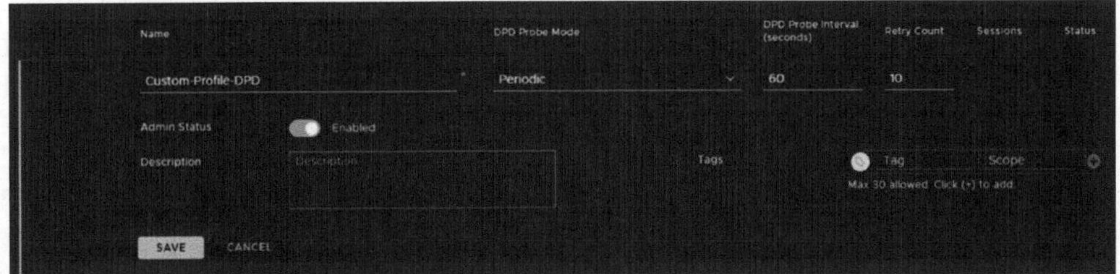

Figure 11.57: *Configuring a DPD profile in NSX UI*

Adding IPSec Local Endpoint

This is a mandatory step to configure the local endpoint before configuring

IPSec VPN sessions. It provides the IP address and ID of the endpoint that is used in the IPSec VPN session. Also, ensure that Tier0 gateway is redistributing Local IPSec IP in route advertisement to an external network and similarly Tier0 gateway is advertising Local IPSec Endpoint to Tier0 gateway to ensure IP address of endpoint is being learned by the physical network.

Step 1: While logged into NSX Manager and on the VPN configuration screen, click on `Local Endpoints` under `VPN` to view configured endpoints. Click on `Add Local Endpoint` to add a new IPSec endpoint, as shown in *Figure* 11.58.

***Figure 11.58**: Adding a new IPSec local endpoint*

Step 2: Provide the information requested by NSX UI detailed here to configure the IPSec endpoint.

a. `Name`: Provide an appropriate name to identify the IPSec endpoint.

b. `VPN Service`: Select the IPSec VPN service created earlier.

c. `IP Address`: Provide an IP address of the local endpoint. If the VPN Service is configured on Tier 0, then the IP address of the local endpoint must be different from the Tier 0 uplink interface IP address.

d. `Site Certificate`: If certificate-based authentication is being used, then select the appropriate certificate to be used by the local endpoint.

e. `Local ID`: Provide a unique string to identify the endpoint. This local ID is a peer ID on a remote site. If this is left blank, then the IP address is used as the local ID and if certificate-based authentication is being used then the Local ID is calculated from the certificate.

f. **`Trusted CA/Self Signed Certificates`**: Provide root certificate for site certificate being used by local endpoint if the certificate is not issued by a well-known CA.

Figure 11.59 shows an example configuration of the IPSec local endpoint.

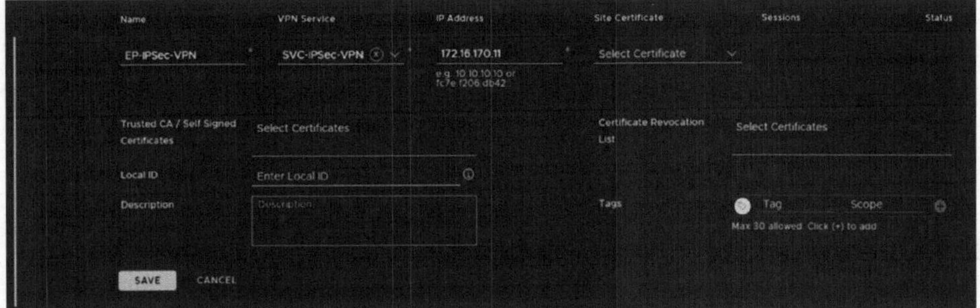

Figure 11.59: *Configuring an IPSec local endpoint*

Step 3: Click on **`Save`** to finish configuring the IPSec endpoint and commit the configuration as shown in *Figure* 11.60. Also, in the example configuration, no Local ID was provided and NSX has automatically set the IP address as Local ID as visible in *Figure* 11.60.

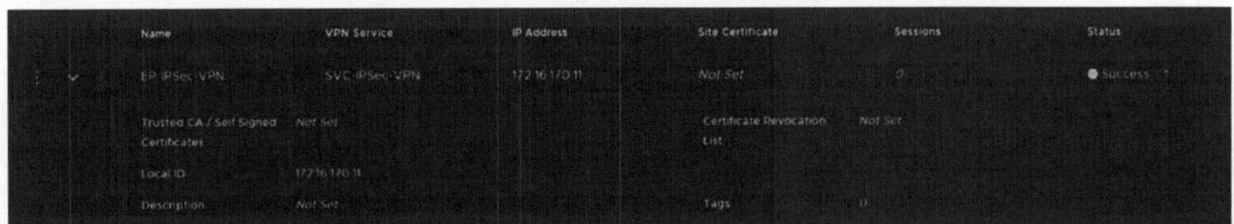

Figure 11.60: *Viewing configured IPSec endpoint in NSX*

Configuring IPSec VPN Session

This is the final step to complete the IPSec VPN configuration.

Step 1: While logged into NSX Manager and on the VPN configuration screen, click on **`IPSec Sessions`** under **`VPN`** to view configured VPN Sessions. Click on **`Add IPSec Session`** to add a new IPSec VPN Session as shown in *Figure* 11.61.

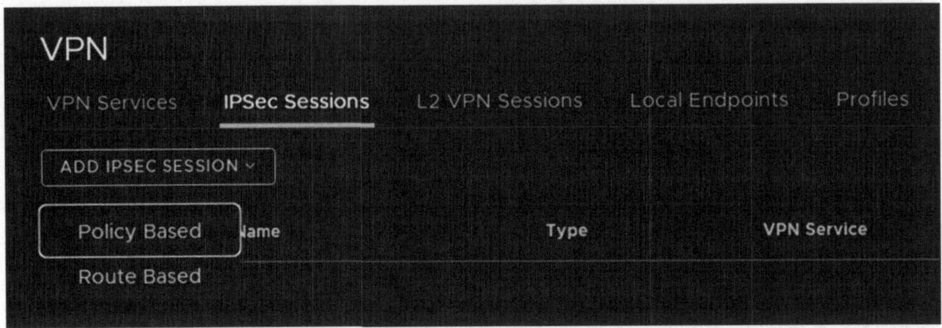

Figure 11.61: *Adding a new* IPSec VPN Session

Adding a Policy-based IPSec VPN Session

Step 2: Click on **`Policy Based`** under **`Add IPSec Session`** to start configuring a policy-based IPSec VPN session. Provide the following details to configure a policy-based IPSec session:

a. **`Name`**: Provide an appropriate to identify IPSec session in the NSX environment.

b. **`VPN Service`**: Select the desired VPN service created earlier.

c. **`Local Endpoint`**: Select the desired local endpoint configured earlier.

d. **`Remote IP`**: Provide the IP address of the remote site VPN.

e. **`Compliance Suite`**: This is an optional configuration and the default value is set as **`None.`** If the compliance suite is changed, then authentication is changed to **`certificate`** and VPN profiles under **`Advanced Settings`** are changed to system defaults and cannot be modified.

f. **`Authentication Mode`**: Select **`PSK`** to enable Pre-shared Key authentication or **`Certificate`** to enable certification-based authentication.

g. **`Pre-Shared Key`**: Provide the key value.

h. **`Remote ID`**: Provide the ID of the remote VPN peer.

i. **`Admin State`**: Toggle the button to enable or disable the VPN Session.

j. **`Local Networks/Remote Networks`**: Provide at least one IP subnet in CIDR format for both the local site and remote peer site whose traffic will be passed through the IPSec tunnel.

Figure 11.62 shows an example configuration of Policy-Based IPSec VPN with the name LAB-IPSec-VPN-Policy configured to use SVC-IPSec-VPN service and local endpoint EP-IPSec-VPN configured earlier. The remote site VPN peer is configured with IP address 10.16.170.10 and the same for ID. Hence, 10.16.170.10 has been configured as Remote IP and Remote ID. This configuration will allow traffic between the local subnet 172.16.110.0/24 and the remote subnet 10.16.110.0/24 to pass through the IPSec tunnel.

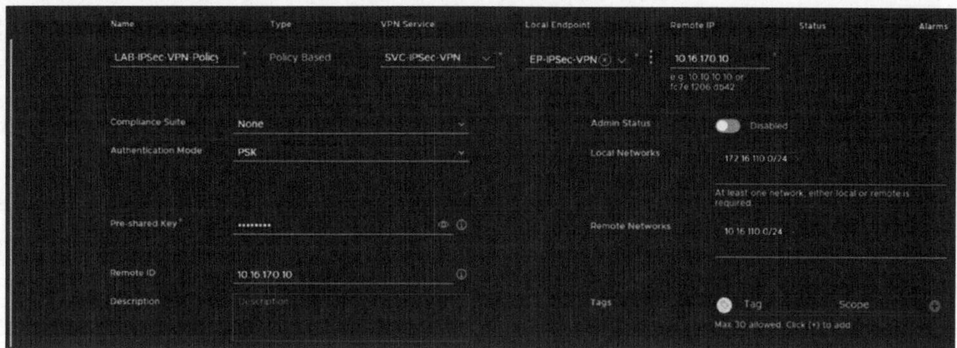

Figure 11.62: *Configuring Policy-Based IPSec VPN session*

Click on **`Save`** to finish configuring the IPSec session and commit the configuration. If the remote peer is also configured correctly, the IPSec VPN session will show **`Status`** as **`Success`** else it will show as **`Down.`**

Adding a Route-Based IPSec VPN Session

Step 3: Click on **`Route Based`** under **`Add IPSec Session`** to start configuring a route-based IPSec VPN session. Provide the following details to configure a route-based IPSec session:

a. **`Name`**: Provide an appropriate to identify IPSec session in the NSX environment.

b. **`VPN Service`**: Select the desired VPN service created earlier.

c. **`Local Endpoint`**: Select the desired local endpoint configured earlier.

d. **`Remote IP`**: Provide the IP address of the remote site VPN.

e. **`Compliance Suite`**: This is an optional configuration and the default value is set as **None**. If the compliance suite is changed then authentication is changed to **certificate** and VPN profiles under **Advanced Settings** are changed to system defaults and cannot be modified.

f. **Authentication Mode**: Select **PSK** to enable Pre-shared Key authentication or **Certificate** to enable certification-based authentication.

g. **Pre-Shared Key**: Provide the key value.

h. **Remote ID**: Provide the ID of the remote VPN peer.

i. **Admin State**: Toggle the button to enable or disable the VPN Session.

j. **Tunnel Interface**: Provide IP address in CIDR format for the tunnel interface.

Figure 11.63 shows an example configuration of Policy-Based IPSec VPN with the name LAB-IPSec-VPN-Route configured to use SVC-IPSec-VPN service and local endpoint EP-IPSec-VPN configured earlier. The remote site VPN peer is configured with IP address 10.16.170.10 and the same for ID. Please note the previous policy-based IPSec VPN session was deleted before configuring the route-based IPSec VPN session to capture configuration. Notice, there is no need to provide local networks and remote networks as that information is learned via BGP over tunnel interface by IPSec VPN.

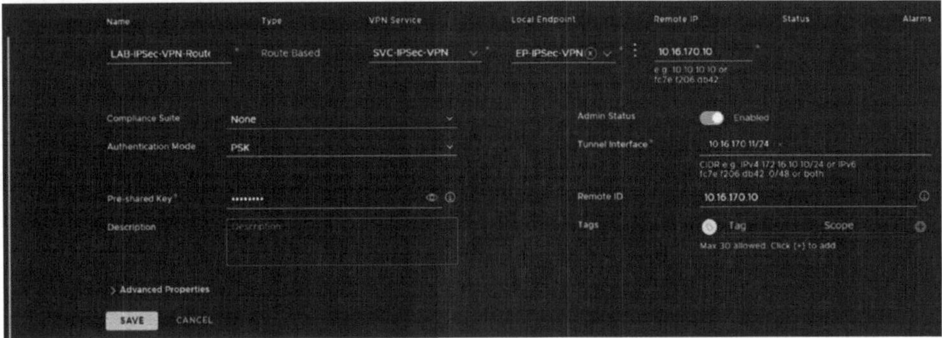

Figure 11.63: *Configuring route-based IPSec VPN session*

Click on **Save** to finish configuring the IPSec session and commit the configuration. If the remote peer is also configured correctly, the IPSec VPN session will show **Status** as **Success** else it will show as **Down**.

Additionally, for both Policy-Based and Route-Based IPSec VPN sessions, there are **`Advanced Properties`** that can be expanded to change IKE, IPSec and DPD profiles from system defaults to custom-created profiles.

Woah! That was a long read on IPSec VPN and a lot of settings to be configured. However, this completes the IPSec VPN configuration in the NSX environment. But what if there is a requirement to extend Layer 2 subnets between two sites? IPSec VPN cannot be used as it doesn't allow overlapping subnets. To tackle this problem, NSX provides another type of VPN service, that is, L2VPN. So, let's see how L2VPN can be used in the NSX environment to extend overlay or VLAN segments to another site.

Layer 2 VPN

Layer 2 VPN or L2VPN for short allows to extend Layer 2 networks whether it overlay backed segments or VLAN-backed segments across multiple sites sharing the same broadcast domain. L2VPN includes an L2VPN server which clients connect to and an L2VPN client which is the source imitating communication with the destination L2VPN server. This connection between the L2VPN server and the L2VPN client is secured by a route-based IPSec VPN tunnel. Also, an inner GRE (Generic Routing Encapsulation) tunnel is used to support multicast traffic across sites. L2VPN enables VM mobility across datacenters as the extended network shares the broadcast domain and the virtual machine IP address doesn't need to be changed enabling easy migration strategies. Also, apart from supporting migration, L2VPN can be used to enable hybrid cloud solutions where the workload can scale on the public cloud in case of increased demands.

L2VPN is supported on both Tier0 and Tier1 gateways. However, only one L2VPN service can be configured for either Tier0 or Tier1 gateway.

Note: L2VPN feature is supported only on NSX and does not have third-party interoperability. However, L2 VPN configuration is possible from an NSX-managed environment to a non-NSX environment with the help of NSX Autonomous Edge.

L2VPN service is supported in the following different deployments:

- The L2VPN server is hosted on NSX Edge and the L2VPN client is hosted on Edge managed by NSX for vSphere. In this deployment, both overlay-backed segments and VLAN-backed segments are supported.
- The L2VPN server is hosted on NSX Edge and the L2VPN client is hosted on unmanaged Edge or standalone Edge. An unmanaged client supports only VLANs.

- The L2VPN server is hosted on the NSX Edge and the L2VPN client is hosted on autonomous Edge. An autonomous client supports only VLANs.
- Starting with NSX-T release v2.4, the L2VPN server hosted on NSX Edge and the L2VPN client hosted on NSX Edge are supported. A managed Edge node supports both overlay-backed and VLAN segments.

Table 11.5 provides a summary of supported and validated versions of different L2VPN Server and L2VPN clients (courtesy VMware documentation). Please refer VMware documentation link https://docs.vmware.com/en/VMware-NSX/4.1/administration/GUID-86C8D6BB-F185-46DC-828C-1E1876B854E8.html for a complete and updated list of L2VPN clients including non-validated but supported.

L2 VPN Server Version (NSX)	L2 VPN Client Version (NSX) Validated	L2 VPN Client Version (NSX-V) Validated
4.0.1.1	4.0.1.1, 4.0.0.1, 3.2.1.2	-
3.2.0	3.2.0, 3.1.3, 3.1.2	6.4.12
3.1.3	3.1.3, 3.1.2, 3.1.1	6.4.8
3.1.2	3.1.2, 3.1.1, 2.5.3	6.4.8
3.1.1	3.1.1, 3.1.0, 3.0.1	6.4.8
3.1.0	3.1.0, 3.0.1, 3.0.0	6.4.8
3.0.3	3.0.3, 3.0.2, 3.0.1	-
3.0.2	3.0.2, 3.0.1, 2.5.2	-
3.0.0	3.0.0, 2.5.0, 2.5.1	-

Table 11.5: *Supported and Validated L2VPN clients*

Configuring Layer 2 VPN

Figure 11.64 illustrates a high-level workflow used to configure the L2VPN server in the NSX environment. We have already covered adding IPSec VPN service and IPSec local endpoint as part of the IPSec VPN configuration. After these, it is required to add an L2VPN server service similar to the IPSec VPN service and then use the service to create an L2VPN server session. Once the server session is created, attach different segments to L2VPN to extend them to different sites.

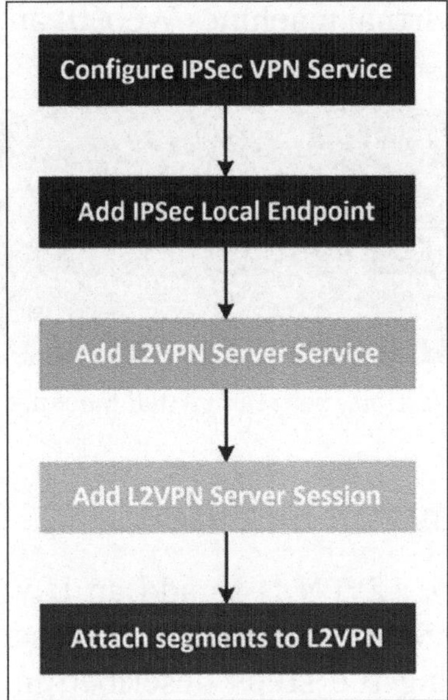

Figure 11.64: *High-level workflow to configure* L2VPN

It will be easier to understand L2VPN configuration with the help of a topology. *Figure* 11.65 shows a sample network topology for L2VPN.

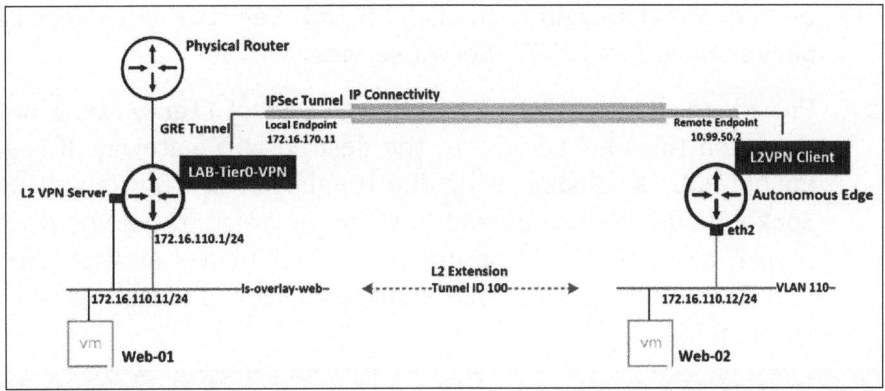

Figure 11.65: *An example network topology to understand L2VPN configuration*

As illustrated in *Figure* 11.65, it utilizes an L2VPN server and an autonomous Edge node as an L2VPN client to establish communication between two web servers sharing the same IP subnet. This topology doesn't utilize a local egress gateway to send traffic to the gateway configured locally but instead sends all traffic to the LAB-Tier0-VPN gateway. Two virtual machines Web-01 and Web-02 are running configured with IP addresses `172.16.110.11` and `172.16.110.12`, respectively, from the same subnet but are running in different locations. Currently, there is no connectivity between virtual machines Web-01 and Web-02 as evident from *Figure 11.66*.

```
web-01:~# ping 172.16.110.12
PING 172.16.110.12 (172.16.110.12): 56 data bytes
^C
--- 172.16.110.12 ping statistics ---
4 packets transmitted, 0 packets received, 100% packet loss
web-01:~#
```

Figure 11.66*: No connectivity between virtual machine Web-01 and Web-02*

Adding L2VPN Server Service

The first step to configure L2VPN is to add an L2VPN Server service. Before configuring the L2VPN service, ensure IPSec VPN service and a local endpoint have been configured using the steps described in the section "Configuring IPSec VPN".

Step 1: Login into NSX Manager with admin privileges. Navigate to `Networking` and click on `VPN` under `Network Services` in the left navigation panel. This will open the VPN configuration screen. Click on `VPN Services` and then click on `Add Service` and select `L2 VPN Server` to add an L2VPN Server service.

Step 2: Provide the `Name` of the VPN service and select `Tier0/Tier1 Gateway` to attach the VPN service to the desired NSX gateway. If required, enable `Hub & Spoke` using the toggle button. By default, `Hub & Spoke` is disabled. Considering the network topology described earlier, our L2VPN will be hosted on Tier0 gateway with the name LAB-Tier0-VPN, hence the same has been selected as shown in *Figure 11.67*.

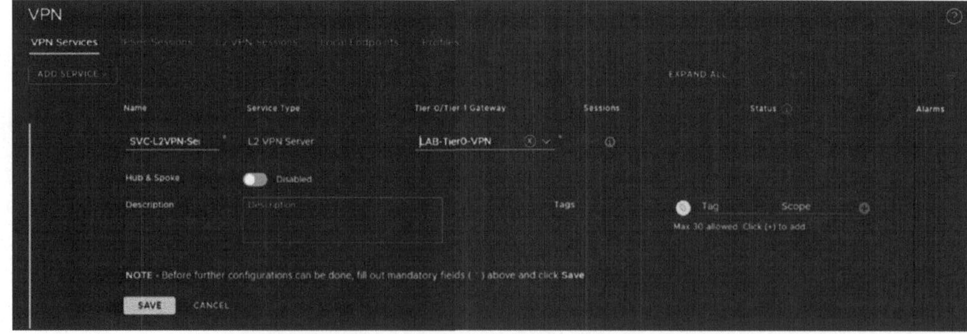

Figure 11.67*: Adding an L2VPN Server service*

Step 3: Click on **`Save`** to finish configuring the L2 VPN Server service and commit the configuration.

Adding L2VPN Server Session

After adding an L2VPN Server service, the next step is to add an L2VPN session. It can be either an L2VPN server or an L2VPN client session. For our topology, the L2VPN server session is hosted on NSX Edge, so let's take a look to configure the L2VPN server session.

Step 1: While logged into NSX Manager and on the VPN configuration screen, click on **`L2 VPN Sessions`** under **`VPN`** to view configured VPN Sessions. Click on **`Add L2 VPN Session`** and select **`L2 VPN Server`** to add a new L2VPN Session as shown in *Figure* 11.68.

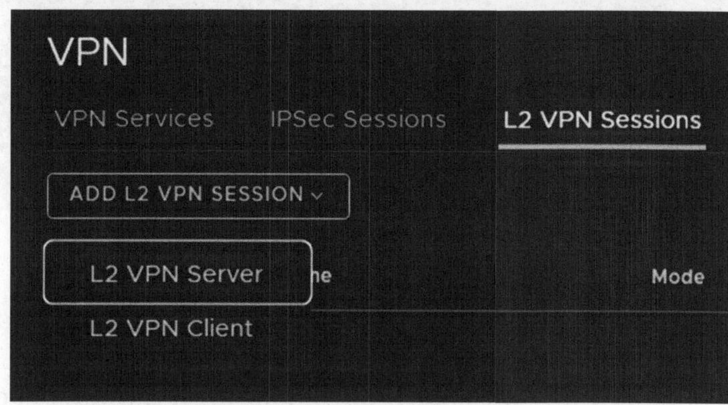

***Figure 11.68**: Adding a new L2 VPN Server session*

Step 2: Provide the following information to successfully configure an L2VPN server session.

a. **`Name`**: Provide an appropriate for L2VPN server session.

b. **`VPN Service:`** Select the L2VPN service configured earlier.

c. **`Local Endpoint/IP:`** Select the Local Endpoint configured earlier or click on three dots to create a new local endpoint for the session.

d. **`Remote IP`**: Provide the IP address of the remote VPN client.

e. **`Pre-shared Key`**: Provide a key to authenticate the client.

f. **`Admin Status`**: Toggle the button to enable or disable L2VPN session.

g. **`Tunnel Interface`**: Provide tunnel interface IP address in CIDR format.

h. **`Additional Properties`**: These settings are used to reduce the MSS (Maximum Segment Size) payload of the TCP session. By default, **`TCP MSS Clamping`** is enabled and **`TCP MSS Direction`** is set to **`Both.`**

Figure 11.69, shows an example configuration of an L2VPN server session. In our topology, the remote VPN client IP address is 10.99.50.2, and the tunnel interface is 172.16.180.2/24, and the same has been configured.

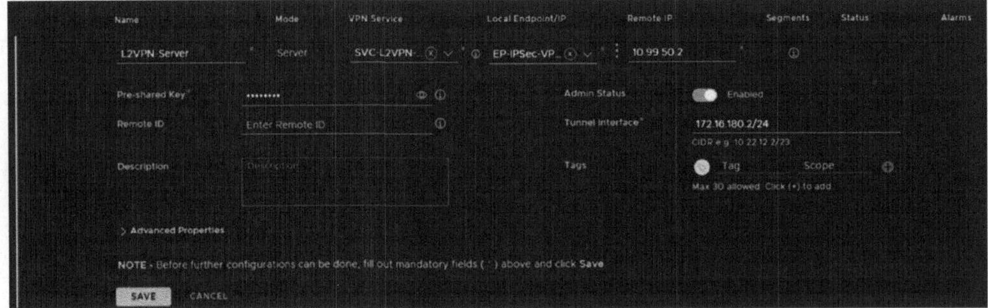

Figure 11.69: *Configuring L2VPN server session*

Step 3: Click on **`Save`** to finish setting up the L2VPN server session. Initially, its Status might show as down as the L2VPN client configuration is pending. Click on **`Download Config`** to fetch peer_code which is required for L2VPN client configuration, as *Figure* 11.70 shows.

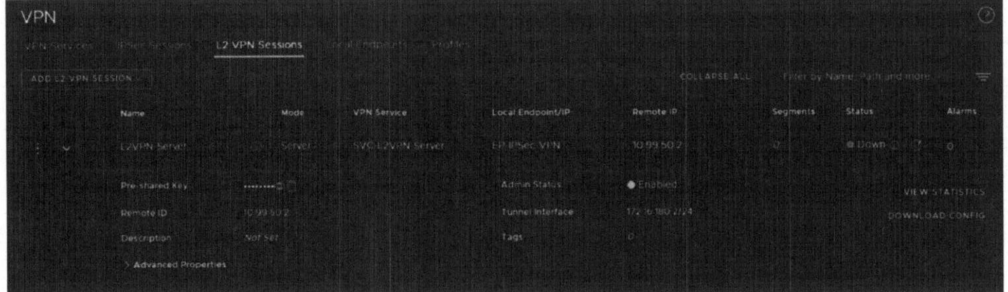

Figure 11.70: *Downloading L2VPN session configuration for L2VPN client*

Step 4: After the L2VPN client session has been configured with peer_code retrieved from the L2VPN server session, the L2VPN tunnel will come online and the **`Status`** will change to **`success`** as shown in *Figure* 11.71.

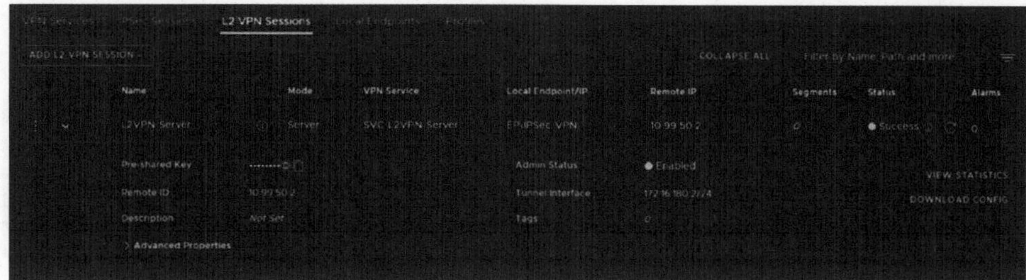

Figure 11.71: *L2VPN server session setup successfully with L2VPN client*

Step 5: Click on **`IPSec Sessions`** under VPN and there is a Route-Based IPSec VPN session that has automatically been created by NSX to carry traffic securely over the IPSec tunnel, as illustrated in *Figure* 11.72.

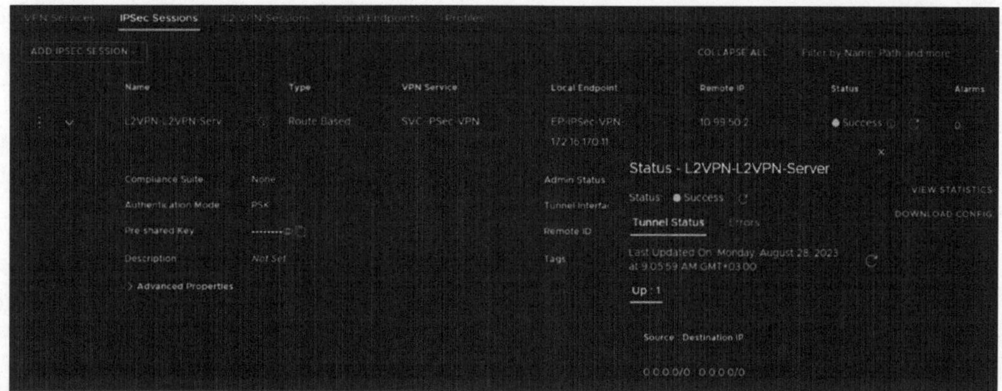

Figure 11.72: *Viewing IPSec session created by NSX for L2VPN*

Here, we have set up an L2VPN server session. However, NSX also supports L2VPN client sessions. To configure an L2VPN client session instead of an L2VPN server session, select **`L2 VPN Client`** and then provide the **`Name`** of the session, the **`VPN service`** configured earlier, the local endpoint IP address, the IP address of the remote L2VPN server and peer_code retrieved from L2VPN server.

Adding L2VPN to Segment

Once the L2VPN session has been configured, it can be added to an NSX segment to extend it. To attach an L2VPN with a segment, Navigate to **`Segments`** under **`Connectivity`** in the **`Networking`** menu and edit the desired segment. Under **`L2 VPN`**, select the L2VPN session and provide a **`VPN Tunnel ID`**. Optionally, if local egress traffic needs to be routed through the local gateway, provide a **`Local Egress Gateway IP`**. *Figure* 11.73 shows an overlay segment ls-overlay-web from our network topology, configured with L2VPN session L2VPN-Server configured earlier with VPN Tunnel ID set to 100.

Figure 11.73: *Attaching an L2VPN to a segment*

Configuring Autonomous Edge as L2VPN Client

Autonomous Edge is generally deployed on sites where NSX is not configured or present in the environment. It supports only VLANs and can be configured as an L2VPN client only. There are a few pre-requisites before deploying and configuring Autonomous Edge listed below:

- A port group is configured with security policy promiscuous mode and forged transmit set to accept. By default, in the vSphere distributed switch, these policies are set to reject.
- Download the **`peer_code`** from L2VPN server.
- Obtain the remote IP address and local IP address to be used with the L2VPN client.
- Download the Edge OVA file from the VMware Customer Connect portal.
- Autonomous Edge OVA needs to be deployed manually on the vCenter server or ESXi host. Either access to deploy OVA is required or work with the vSphere administrator.

During the deployment of Autonomous Edge OVA, ensure the **`External Port`** and **`External Gateway`** have been configured. Referencing back to the same network topology, our autonomous Edge has local IP 10.99.50.2/29 belonging to VLAN 300. *Figure* 11.74 shows the configuration of the External Port according to these inputs. Also, ensure the option **`Is Autonomous Edge`** is checked during OVA deployment.

External	2 settings
External Port	PORT (Vlan Id[0-4091], Exit Interface, Ip, PrefixLength), example: 20,eth2,192.168.5.1,24 300,eth2,10.99.50.2,29
External Gateway	The default gateway of external router port 10.99.50.1

Figure 11.74: *Configuring external port during OVA deployment*

After OVA deployment is complete, power on autonomous Edge and wait for it to become accessible over the network. After autonomous Edge is accessible over the network, open a tab in the web browser and type the management IP address of autonomous Edge. Log in using the username as admin and password set during deployment. Click on **`Port`** in the left navigation panel and click on **`Add Port`** to add a new port. Provide the **`Port Name`** to identify different ports configured, subnet information (optional), and the **`VLAN ID`** of the subnet to be stretched. Select the **`Exit Interface`** as the network adapter connected to the correct port group in the vCenter server. *Figure* 11.75 shows an example configuration, where VLAN 110 on site 2 will be stretched to the overlay segment in site 1.

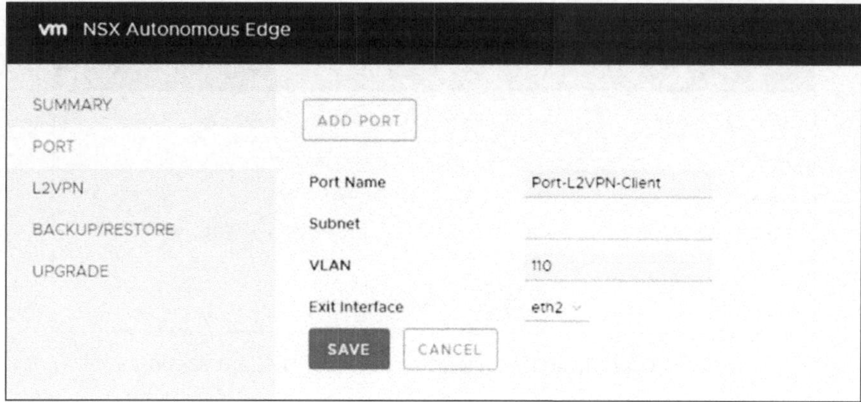

Figure 11.75: *Adding a port in autonomous Edge*

Click on **`L2VPN`** to add an L2VPN client session. Click on **`Add Session`** and provide **`Session Name`** for the L2VPN client session, **`Admin Status`** whether to Enable or Disable the L2VPN, **`Local IP`** as the IP address of the VPN client and **`Remote IP`** as the IP address of the remote L2VPN server. Paste the peer_code fetched from the L2VPN server in **`Peer code`** and click on **`Save`** to create the L2VPN client session as shown in *Figure* 11.76.

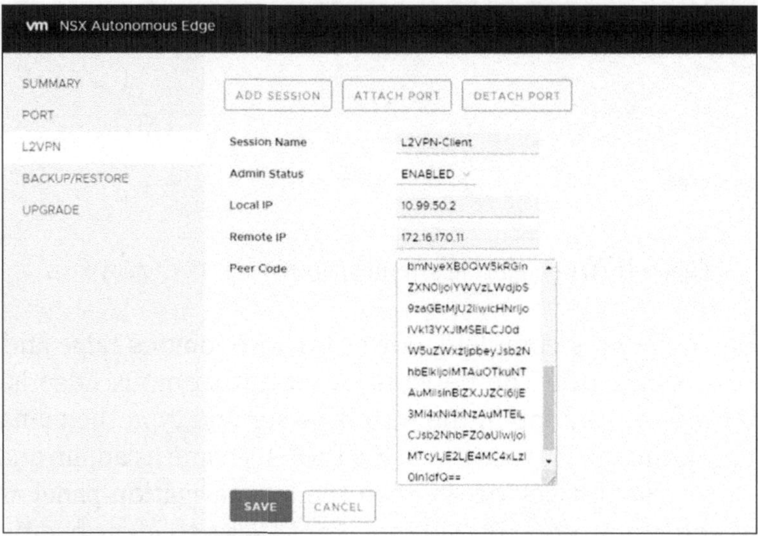

Figure 11.76: *Adding an L2VPN client session in autonomous Edge*

Click on **Attach Port** and select the **L2VPN** session and **Port** configured earlier with **Tunnel ID** same as set on the NSX segment and click on **Save.** *Figure* 11.77 shows the Tunnel ID set to 100 as we have configured the same Tunnel ID in the NSX overlay segment.

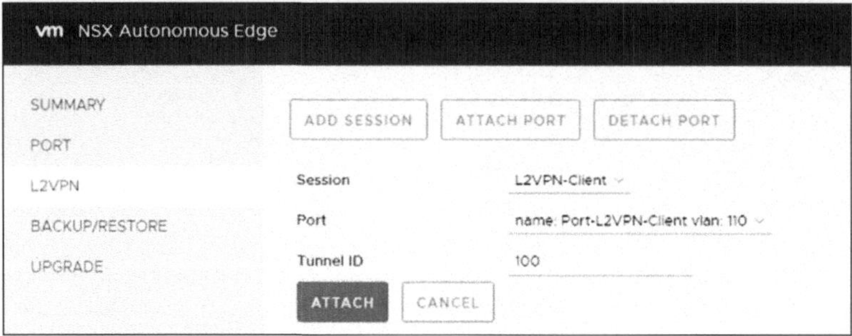

Figure 11.77: *Attaching a port to the L2VPN client session*

If the L2VPN server and L2VPN client are configured correctly, the L2VPN tunnel status will come online and show status as UP as shown in *Figure* 11.78.

Figure 11.78: *Viewing L2VPN status in autonomous Edge*

This completes the configuration of L2VPN in the NSX environment. Now, if we try to ping the IP address of Web-02 from the virtual machine Web-01, it should be reachable which was previously unreachable and it is as evident from *Figure 11.79*.

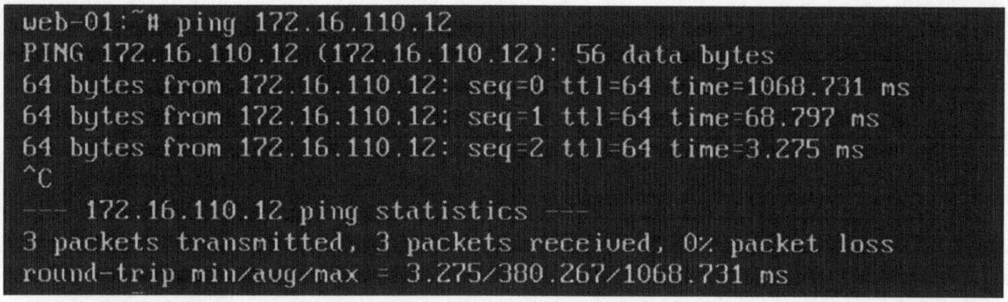

```
web-01:~# ping 172.16.110.12
PING 172.16.110.12 (172.16.110.12): 56 data bytes
64 bytes from 172.16.110.12: seq=0 ttl=64 time=1068.731 ms
64 bytes from 172.16.110.12: seq=1 ttl=64 time=68.797 ms
64 bytes from 172.16.110.12: seq=2 ttl=64 time=3.275 ms
^C
--- 172.16.110.12 ping statistics ---
3 packets transmitted, 3 packets received, 0% packet loss
round-trip min/avg/max = 3.275/380.267/1068.731 ms
```

Figure 11.79: *Network connectivity established between Web-01 and Web-02*

Also, if navigate back to the L2 VPN Session and click on View Statistics, NSX provides a complete traffic statistic for the specified segment as illustrated in *Figure 11.80*.

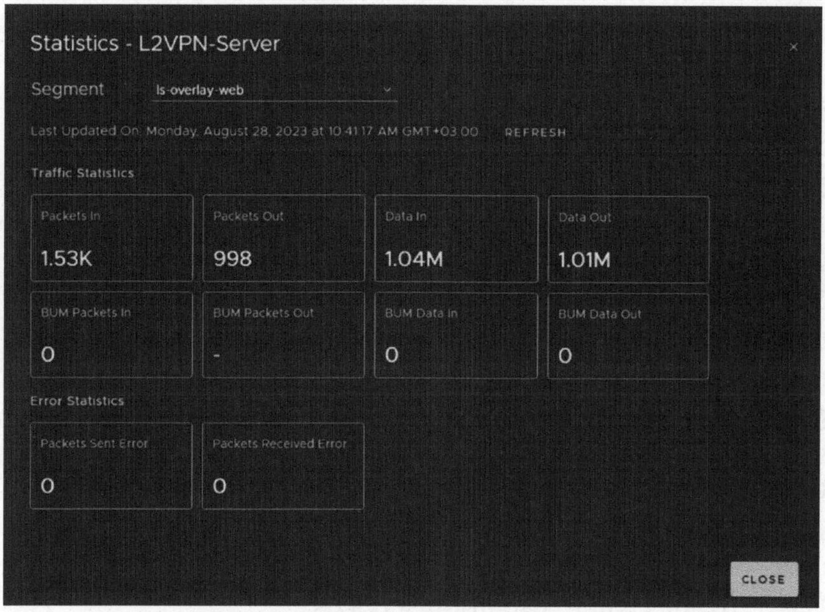

Statistics - L2VPN-Server
Segment ls-overlay-web
Last Updated On: Monday, August 28, 2023 at 10:41:17 AM GMT+03:00 REFRESH
Traffic Statistics
Packets In 1.53K | Packets Out 998 | Data In 1.04M | Data Out 1.01M
BUM Packets In 0 | BUM Packets Out - | BUM Data In 0 | BUM Data Out 0
Error Statistics
Packets Sent Error 0 | Packets Received Error 0
CLOSE

Figure 11.80: *Viewing traffic statistics of L2VPN*

This brings us closure to VPN services in the NSX environment. In summary, NSX supports IPSec VPN for site-to-site connectivity for non-overlapping subnets and also L2VPN for extending NSX segments across datacenters with shared broadcast domains.

Conclusion

Woah! That's a lot of information to digest. We discussed how NSX enables stateful services on Active-Active Tier0/Tier1 gateways with the help of the new routing architecture. Also, we covered different datacenter services like NAT, DHCP, DNS, IPSec VPN, and Layer 2 VPN and how to configure them in an NSX environment. But that's not all. We are still missing one more service.

In the next chapter, we will cover load balancing and how with the help of NSX Advanced Load Balancer we can provide load-balancing capabilities in datacenter.

Key Terms

- **Edge Sub-Cluster:** An NSX automatically creates a sub-cluster within the Edge Cluster when stateful services are enabled in the Active-Active gateway.
- **Interface Group:** A collection or group of equivalent configured external interfaces on the Tier 0 gateway to enable stateful services.
- **Punt logical segment:** A system-generated VNI which carries the punted traffic across Edge nodes.
- **SNAT:** Source NAT translates the source IP address of outbound packets to a different IP address.
- **DNAT: Destination** NAT enables access to internal IP addresses from the outside world by translating the destination IP address of the inbound packet to an internal IP address.
- **Reflexive NAT:** Also known as stateless NAT.
- **NAT64:** NAT64 provides a mechanism for translating IPv6 packets to IPv4 packets and vice versa.
- **DHCP:** Allows a server to automatically assign network configurations such as IP addresses, subnet mask, gateway, NTP, and DNS configuration to a DHCP client in the network.
- **DHCP relay agent:** Used to provide DHCP services in the NSX environment using externally hosted DHCP servers.
- **DNS:** Provides name resolution services.
- **IPSec (Internet Protocol Security) VPN:** Secures traffic communication between two networks connected through public networks such as the Internet.
- **L2VPN:** Allows to extend Layer 2 networks whether it is overlay-backed segments or VLAN-backed segments across multiple sites sharing the same broadcast domain.

CHAPTER 12

NSX Datacenter Services - 2

In the last chapter, we covered different datacenter services provided by NSX such as NAT, VPN, DNS, and DHCP in an environment. But one major service is used in one form or another – Load Balancing. In previous releases, NSX provided load-balancing services with the help of Tier-1 gateway and Edge Nodes. But with the introduction of NSX Advanced Load Balancer, this has been changed. VMware is moving away from NSX native load balancing to a more feature-rich platform, i.e., NSX ALB.

This chapter covers the NSX Advanced Load Balancer, its features, architecture, and how it is integrated with the NSX environment.

Structure

In this chapter, we will cover the following topics:

- NSX Advance Load Balancer
  - NSX ALB Architecture
  - NSX ALB Service Components
  - NSX ALB Topologies with NSX
- Deploying NSX Advanced Load Balancer
  - Deploying NSX ALB Control Plane
  - Performing Initial Configuration of NSX ALB
  - Configuring Service Engine Group in NSX ALB

- Configuring Virtual Services in NSX ALB
  - Creating a Virtual Service VIP
  - Creating a Server Pool
  - Creating a Virtual Service
  - Validating Virtual Service

NSX Advanced Load Balancer

NSX ALB (Advanced Load Balancer) (formerly Avi Networks) is VMware's enterprise load balancing solution. It is available as a standalone product providing numerous features such as load balancing, web application firewall, advanced analytics, and container ingress to any application in any datacenter and cloud. VMware is providing a basic edition of NSX ALB with Advance or Enterprise Plus license of NSX. NSX ALB will be the only solution for load balancing moving forward, hence this chapter focuses on NSX ALB instead of NSX Native load balancing solution due to the following reasons:

- No new features are being added to the NSX native load balancing solution, starting with the release NSX-T 3.2.
- VMware recommends migrating NSX native load balancing services to NSX ALB.

Note: The enterprise edition of NSX ALB provides a vast number of features such as GSLB, WAF, Advanced Analytics and Container Ingress services. Such enterprise edition features are out of the scope of this book. For more information on these features please visit https://avinetworks.com/docs/.

NSX ALB offers several advantages, some of which are:

- **Multi-Cloud Consistency**: It simplifies administration with the help of centralized policies and operational consistency.
- **End-to-End Automation**: It simplifies deployment and lifecycle management of load-balancing components.
- **Performance**: NSX ALB is distributed in nature, providing optimal traffic flows and avoiding hair pinning of traffic.
- **Easy Troubleshooting**: With the help of inbuilt log analysis and application analytics, one can easily troubleshoot issues with applications.
- **On-Demand Scalability**: It can automatically scale up or down based on traffic needs.

Starting with NSX ALB (AVI Vantage) release 20.1.2, it is now available in three different editions for tight integration with other VMware products:

- **VMware NSX ALB Enterprise Edition**: Most feature-rich edition and offers all features of NSX ALB
- **VMware NSX ALB Basic Edition**: Included with NSX license to help migrate from NSX native load balancing to NSX ALB
- **VMware NSX ALB Essentials Edition:** Included with Tanzu to enable basic container services

Table 12.1 summarizes the feature differences between different editions of NSX ALB.

Categories	**Feature**	**Essentials**	**Basic**	**Enterprise**
Local Traffic Management	L4 LB	TCP and UDP Fast Path No SSL/TLS	TCP and UDP Fast Path and Proxy No L4 SSL/TLS	TCP, UDP, DNS, SIP, RADIUS DSR, TLS support, PROXY protocol support
	L7 LB	X	Limited to basic L7 features; no HTTP/2	HTTP/2, content rewrite, compression, caching
	L3/4 Policies	X	Policies limited to connection drops No DataScript support	Full-featured, including DataScripts and live IP Reputation
	L7 Policies	X	Basic match and actions	Match on: IP Reputation DB, string groups, and much more Actions to: Rate-limit, ICAP, and much more
Global Traffic Management	Global Server Load Balancing	X	X	Enterprise grade GSLB

Application Security	SSL/TLS	X	Very limited feature-set	Dynamic CRLs, OCSP stapling, TLSv1.3, HSM, and cert management
	Application Rate Limiting	X	X	Rate limiters can be applied for L4, L7, DNS and WAF
	DDoS Protection	X	X	L3, L4 and L7 DDos protection
	Intelligent WAF	X	X	CRS, learning/ PSM, IP Reputation, application signatures, bot detection
Container Ingress	Service Type LB	Yes	Yes	Yes
	Container Ingress	X	Available in Future (Limited)	Full Ingress DNS and GSLB integration Multi K8s cluster and multi-AZ support

Software Defined Platform	Administration	Basic LB administration	Basic LB administration	Fully multi-tenant and granular RBAC Rich alerts and events Various 3rd part integrations Integrations with various IDPs
	Scale and HA	Active/ Standby only	Active/Standby only	Active/ Active, N+M deployments BGP and ECMP support Autoscale of load balancers
	Flexible upgrades	X	X	Flexible LCM across tenants/ clouds/ se-groups
	Ecosystem automation	No Access Cloud vCenter	No Access Cloud NSX-T Cloud	Native integrations with all major public and private clouds and container orchestration platforms
	Pulse	X	X	Enhanced case management Live Security Threat Updates
Advanced Analytics	Application Visibility/ Analytics	X	X	Advanced application telemetry Log insights

***Table 12.1**: Available* NSX ALB *editions*

NSX ALB Architecture

Similar to NSX, NSX ALB is also built on software-defined principles, distributed in nature with its Control Plane and Data Plane separated to provide elasticity and flexibility. It delivers different services such as application analytics, predictive autoscaling, and micro-segmentation apart from providing load balancing capabilities. *Figure* 12.1 illustrates a high-level architecture view of NSX ALB in a multi-cloud environment.

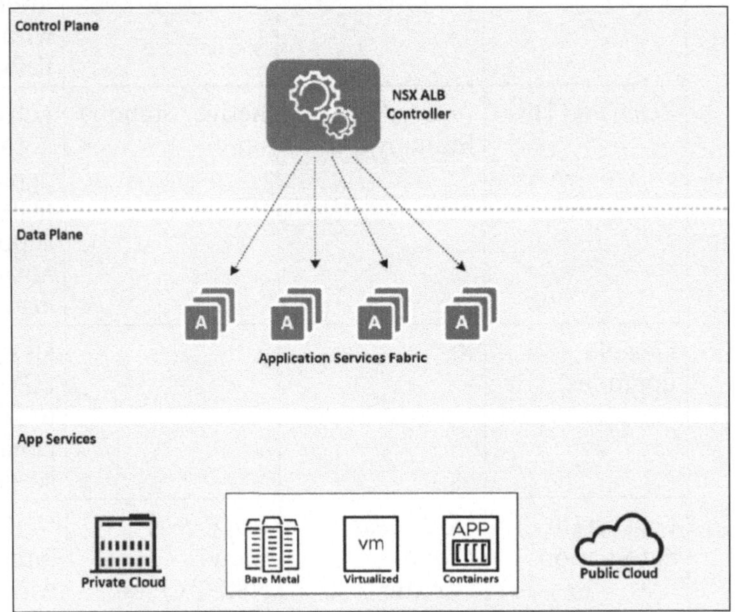

Figure 12.1: NSX ALB *environment Architecture*

Avi Controller makes up the Control Plane whereas Service Engine, denoted as Application Services Fabric, makes up the Data Plane. To deliver application services, close to individual applications, Avi Controller provides a centrally managed dynamic pool of resources that can be deployed on bare metal servers, virtualized machines or containers hosted on-premise or in the public cloud.

Key components of the NSX ALB environment are shown in *Figure* 12.2:

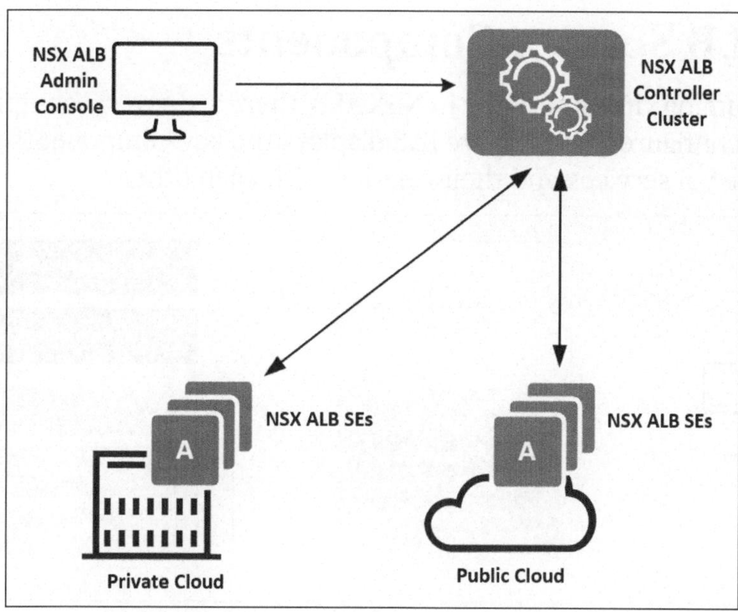

Figure 12.2: *Core Components of NSX ALB environment*

- **NSX ALB Controller Cluster**: The NSX ALB Controller cluster is responsible for providing a central management console and control policies. It acts as a brain of the NSX ALB environment and is deployed as a three-node cluster to provide high availability and load sharing. It also provides application analytics with the use of big data analytics and automates the configuration and deployment of data planes.
- **NSX ALB Service Engines**: NSX ALB Service Engines (SEs) make up the data plane of the NSX ALB environment. It handles all the data plane operations by instructions received from the NSX ALB Controller Cluster and executes them. SEs are the point where actual load balancing is performed and all client/server end interactions happen. Apart from performing load balancing these also collect real-time application telemetry data from application traffic flows and forward them to NSX ALB Controller Cluster for analytics.
- **NSX ALB Admin Console**: NSX ALB Admin Console is a web-based user interface (UI) that provides role-based access control (RBAC) to configure, manage and monitor application services. NSX ALB Admin Console runs on the NSX ALB Controller Cluster and there are no additional components that need to be deployed. Also, all application services configuration can be performed with the help of REST API fully supported by NSX ALB Controller Cluster.

NSX ALB Service Components

While consuming virtual services in NSX ALB, there are several components that need to be configured first. *Figure* 12.3 displays the key components required to consume virtual services and their relation with each other.

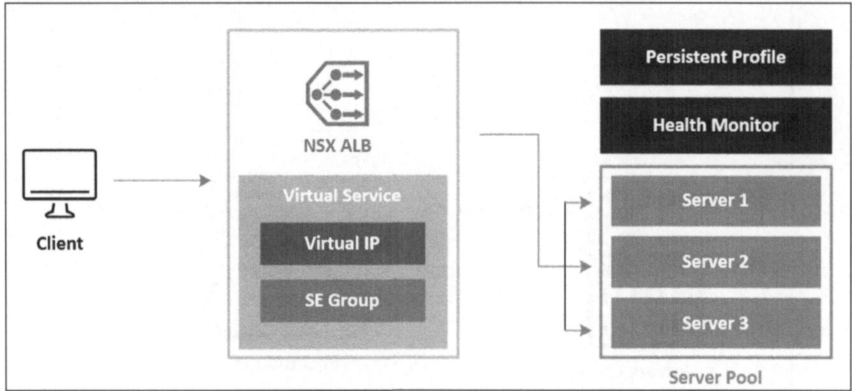

***Figure* 12.3**: NSX ALB *Service Components*

- **Virtual Service**: It is a logical construct that contains an IP address, port, and protocol. Virtual service is associated with an SE group and its scope is limited to assigned SE groups only, for example, if SE group A failed and there is another SE group B available then virtual service will not fail over to SE group B.
- **Server Pool**: It is a collection of servers associated with virtual service and responsible for responding to client requests. A server pool is not mandatory to be attached to a virtual service. For example, an http to https redirection request can be handled without a server pool. However, any request by the client will be forwarded to a specific server in the server pool based on the load balancing algorithm configured.
- **Health Monitor**: The health monitor gets assigned to the server pool and it validates the status of servers within the server pool. If a server does not respond to a request sent by Health Monitor, then it is marked as down/degraded, and no/less further requests are sent to it.
- **Persistent Profile**: Persistent Profile is again assigned to the server pool and it maintains connection from a client to the same pool member.

NSX ALB Topologies with NSX

NSX ALB only supports one arm deployment of Service Engine (SE) in the NSX environment which means for a virtual service, the client to VIP traffic and SE to backend server pool traffic both use the same SE data interface. Based on this, two different types of deployment are possible for NSX ALB in the NSX environment.

- **SE on Dedicated Segment:** In this deployment, Service Engines are placed on a dedicated segment which enables separate IP address management for SEs and server pools. As of the writing of this book, this dedicated overlay segment needs to be created manually in NSX Manager before creating the NSX-T cloud connector in the NSX ALB Controller cluster.
- **SE on Shared Segment:** In this deployment, Service Engines are placed alongside server pool members and they share the same IP address space as server pool members.

In both deployments, Service Engines require a management interface to communicate with NSX ALB controllers. In the NSX-T cloud, it can be implemented with the help of a dedicated management overlay segment connected to a dedicated Tier1 gateway. The management interface of Service Engines connects to a dedicated management segment. Another option is to utilize a VLAN-backed segment to connect the management interface of SE.

Figure 12.4 illustrates both the supported topologies in the NSX environment. SE1 and SE2 are placed on a dedicated segment connected to Tier-1A, whereas SE3 and SE4 are placed on a shared segment connected to Tier-1B.

There is one particular topology that is unsupported, that is, Service Engine placed on a segment directly connected to Tier-0.

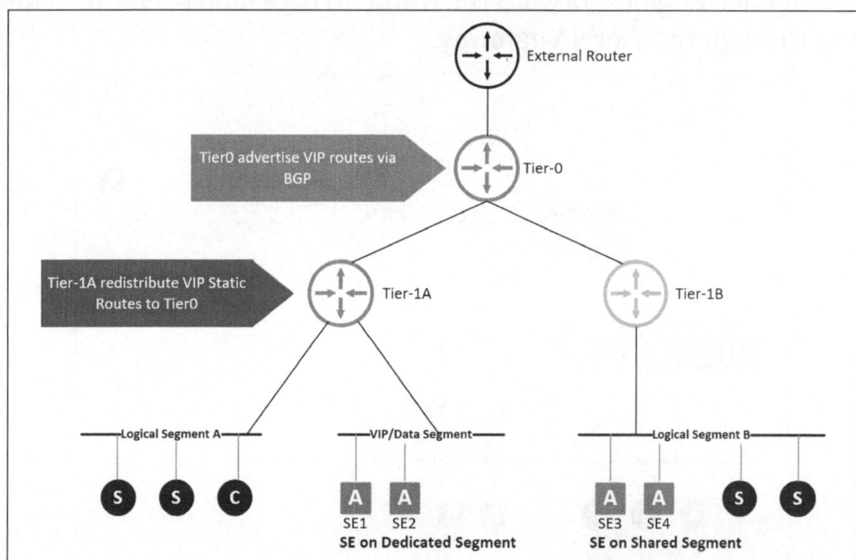

Figure 12.4: NSX ALB *Supported Topologies in* NSX

In both placements, after a virtual service is placed on a Service Engine, the NSX ALB Controller updates the VIP static routes on the Tier1 router associated with the logical segment selected for virtual service placement. These static routes are redistributed from Tier1 to Tier0 and for North-South connectivity of the VIP, Tier0 is configured to advertise the VIP routes to the external router via BGP.

North-South Traffic Walk

In the case of North-South traffic, when the client is external to the NSX environment and tries to access a virtual service hosted on the NSX ALB environment, the network traffic flows as shown in *Figure* 12.5.

Step 1: The client tries to access the VIP of virtual service hosted in the NSX ALB environment. Client reach their default gateway and through routing, their request is forwarded to the uplink of the Tier-0 gateway.

Step 2: Tier-0 gateway receives the traffic from the external router.

Step 3: Tier-0 gateway identifies the VIP network connected to the Tier-1A gateway and forwards the traffic to the Tier-1A gateway.

Step 4: Using the static VIP routes configured on the Tier-1A gateway, it forwards the request to VIP hosted on service engines.

Step 5: Service Engines forward the traffic to back-end server pool members through the Tier-1A gateway.

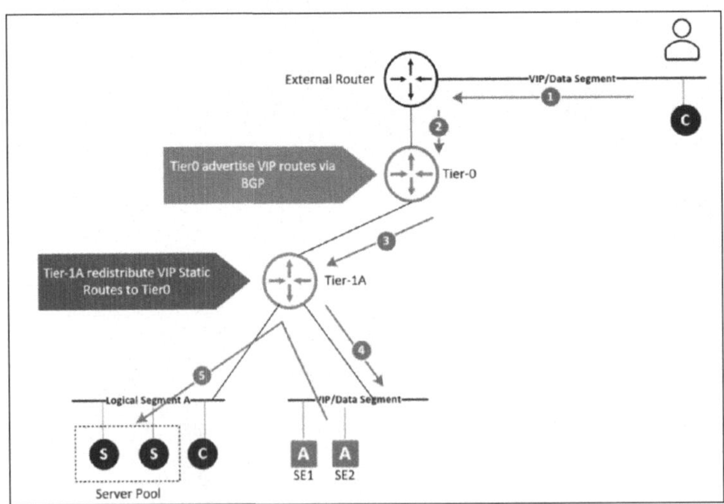

Figure 12.5: *North-South Traffic Walk*

East-West Traffic Walk

In the case of East-West traffic, when the client is connected to a segment within the NSX environment and tries to access a virtual service hosted on NSX ALB then network traffic is routed internally by Tier1 and Tier0 if required as illustrated in *Figure* 12.6.

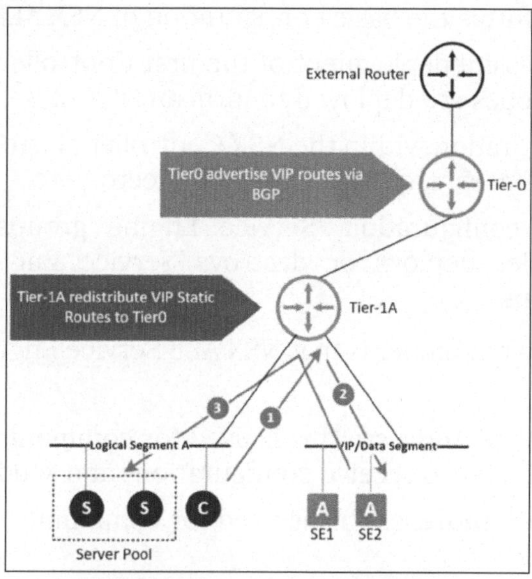

Figure 12.6: *East-West Traffic Walk*

Step 1: The client tries to access the VIP of virtual service hosted in the NSX ALB environment. A client request is sent to the Tier-1A gateway, where the client network is connected.

Step 2: Using the static VIP routes configured on the Tier-1A gateway, it forwards the request to VIP hosted on service engines.

Step 3: Service Engines forward the traffic to back-end server pool members through the Tier-1A gateway.

Deploying NSX Advanced Load Balancer

Deploying NSX Advanced Load Balancer (ALB) is very simple and follows a step-by-step approach. On a high level, the following activities are performed during the deployment of the NSX ALB environment:

- Download the NSX ALB Controller OVA file from the VMware Customer Connect portal and upload the OVA file in NSX Manager UI along with deployment information such as vCenter server, IP address, hostname, etc.

- NSX Manager invokes deployment of NSX ALB Controller OVA in target vCenter server and vCenter server deploys OVA file.
- During initial boot, NSX ALB Controller registers with NSX Manager with the help of Avi LCM (Lifecycle Manager) service, and post-registration Avi LCM performs the basic configuration of NSX ALB.
- After a successful deployment of the first Controller node, 2nd and 3rd Controller nodes are deployed to form an NSX ALB Controller cluster.
- Initial configuration within the NSX Controller cluster is performed such as adding licenses, creating a cloud connector, etc.
- Post initial configuration, Service Engine groups are created and the Controller deploys or destroys Service Engine VMs based on configurations.

Another key point to remember is that NSX ALB Service Engine VMs require two IP addresses:

- **Management IP Address**: This is used for communication with the NSX Controller cluster to receive configurations and send telemetry data.
- **Data Plane IP Address**: This is used for communication with the server pool network.

Deploying NSX ALB Control Plane

As covered earlier, the NSX ALB Control Plane consist of three controller nodes. These can be deployed directly from the vCenter server or leveraging NSX Manager UI. However, NSX Manager UI is the preferred way to deploy the NSX ALB basic edition packaged with NSX Advance or Enterprise Plus edition. As this book focuses on the NSX ALB basic edition, the following process covers a step-by-step guide to deploying NSX ALB Controller nodes from NSX Manager UI.

Note: This book covers NSX ALB controller deployment from NSX Manager, however, this method soon will be deprecated and it is advised to deploy the NSX ALB Controller directly in the vCenter server with the help of OVA.

Step 1: Login into NSX Manager UI with admin privileges. Navigate to **`System`** and click on **`Appliances`** from the left navigation panel. Ensure **`NSX Manager`** is selected under Appliances. As a pre-requisite to deploy NSX ALB from NSX Manager, ensure **`Virtual IP`** is set for the NSX Management cluster, as shown in *Figure 12.7*.

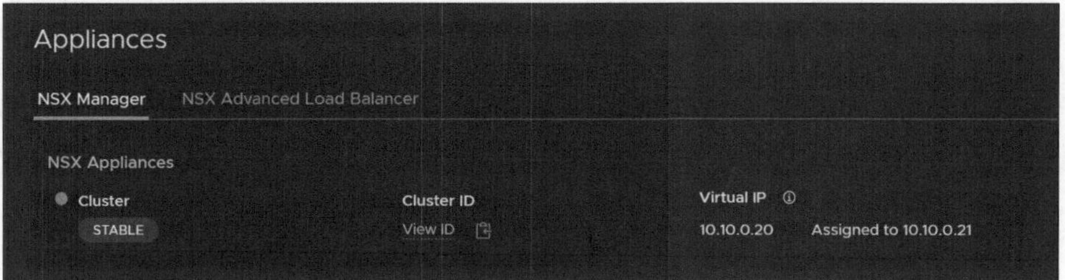

***Figure 12.7**: Virtual IP assigned to NSX Management Cluster*

Step 2: Scroll down to view **`NSX Advance Load Balancer`** with a recommendation to set another **`Virtual IP.`** This virtual IP is assigned NSX ALB Controller cluster, which is used by the NSX Manager appliance for API communication between the NSX ALB Controller and NSX Manager. Also, it provides a built-in high availability feature for NSX ALB controller and spread load across controller nodes. Click on **`Set Virtual IP`** and provide an IPv4 address to be used as VIP for the NSX ALB Controller cluster as shown in *Figure* 12.8.

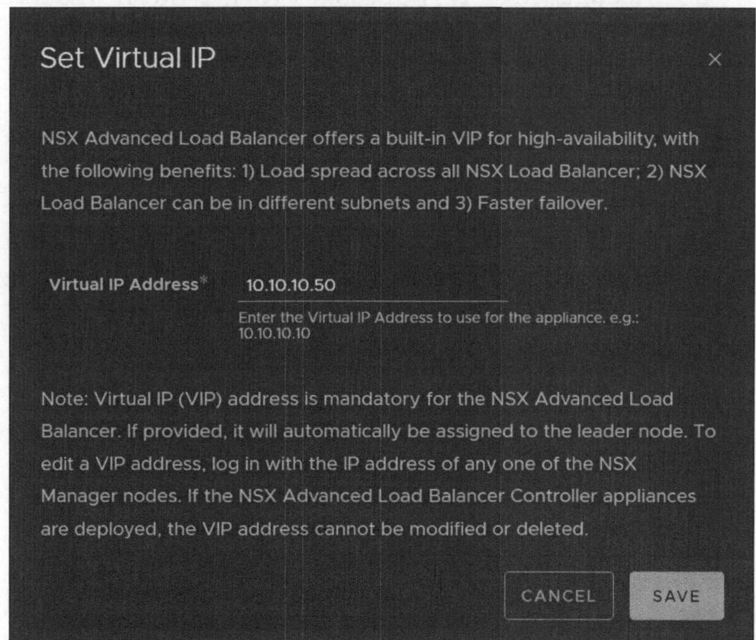

***Figure 12.8**: Set Virtual IP for NSX ALB Controller Cluster*

Step 3: Click on **`Add NSX Advance Load Balancer`**, which opens a new window for **`Add Appliance`**. Enter the requested information as illustrated in Figure 12.10 and click **`Next`** to continue:

a. **`Upload OVA File:`** Either provide the location to the local controller OVA file downloaded or a weblink hosting controller OVA file and click on Upload to start uploading OVA file to NSX Manager as shown in *Figure* 12.9.

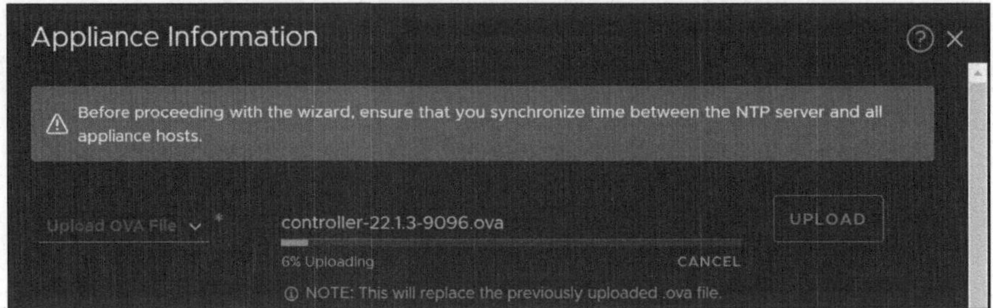

Figure 12.9: *Upload NSX ALB Controller OVA file*

b. **`Hostname:`** Provide the FQDN for the first NSX ALB Controller reserved in DNS.

c. **`Management IP/Netmask`**: Provide the IP reserved for NSX ALB Controller in CIDR format.

d. **`DNS Server`**: This is automatically filled from NSX Manager but can be modified if required.

e. **`NTP Server`**: This is automatically filled from NSX Manager but can be modified if required.

f. **`Node Size`**: Select the appropriate size for the NSX ALB Controller node as per the size of the environment.

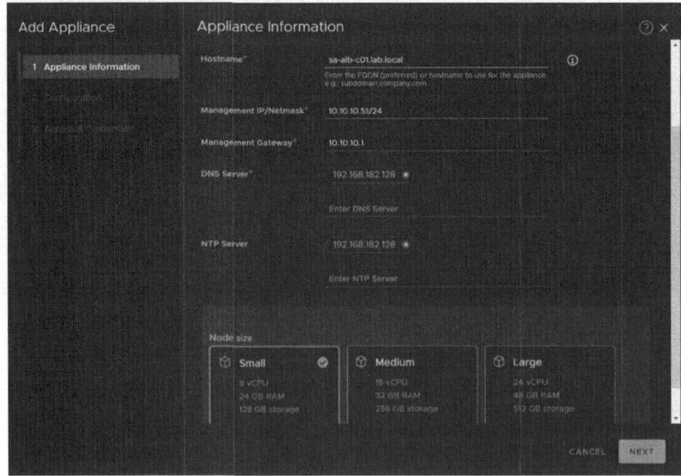

Figure 12.10: *Adding an NSX ALB Controller node*

Step 4: In the next window, select the compute and storage resources where the NSX ALB controller node will be deployed which is similar to deploying NSX Manager appliances and also select the network to which the management interface of the ALB Controller will be connected. A sample screenshot with resources selected is illustrated in *Figure 12.11* and click **`Next`** to continue.

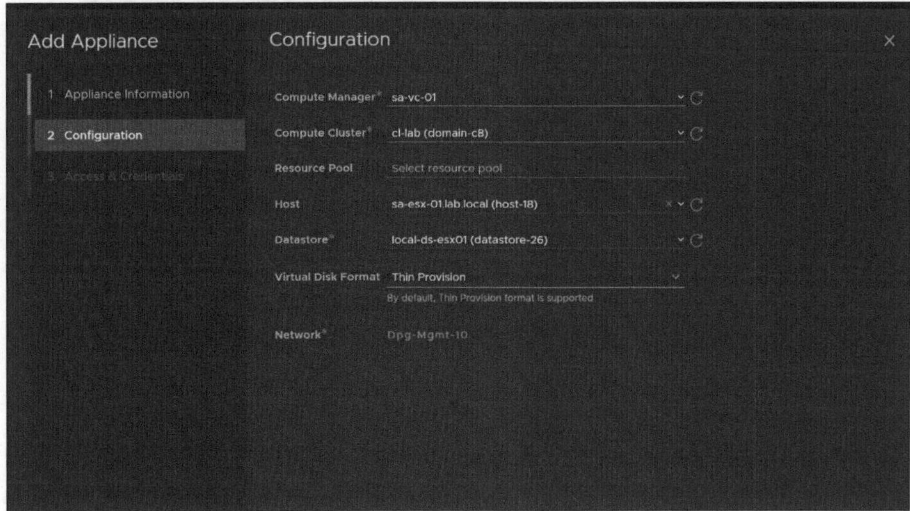

Figure 12.11: *NSX ALB Controller node placement in vCenter server*

Step 5: As a last step, provide the admin credentials and public SSH key (optional but cannot be modified later on) for password less authentication. Hit **`Install Appliance`** to start deploying the first NSX ALB Controller node.

Access & Credentials
System Admin Credentials
System Username admin
Admin Password
Confirm Admin Password
SSH Public Key
Note: This cannot be added later
- 12 characters min
- 1 lower case
- 1 upper case
- 1 number
- At least 5 different characters
- No palindromes
- 1 special character

Figure 12.12: *Credential options in NSX ALB Controller*

Step 6: This will start the deployment of NSX ALB Controller OVA in the vCenter server. Its progress can be tracked from the same screen in NSX Manager UI as *Figure* 12.13 shows.

Figure 12.13: *Tracking the progress of NSX ALB Controller deployment*

Step 7: After the first NSX ALB Controller is deployed successfully, repeat the same process to deploy the second and third controller nodes and form a controller cluster to enable high availability in the NSX ALB Control plane.

Step 8: To continue deployment of the NSX ALB environment, after cluster formation is complete from NSX Manager and it is showing stable in UI; open a new web browser tab and enter FQDN of NSX ALB Controller VIP. It will prompt for credentials, here provide admin credentials set earlier during deployment. This will show a welcome with information to be provided as captured in *Figure* 12.14 and click **`Next`** to continue:

a. **`Passphrase:`** Provide a passphrase to protect configuration exports and backups. It is recommended to configure a backup schedule post-configuration and configure a SCP/SFTP server to securely save a copy of the backup on a remote location.

b. **`Confirm Passphrase`**: Provide the same passphrase entered earlier to avoid any mistakes in typing.

c. **`DNS Resolver(s):`** It will be pre-filled from deployment however can be modified if required.

d. **DNS Search Domain**: Enter the search domains for single hostname resolutions.

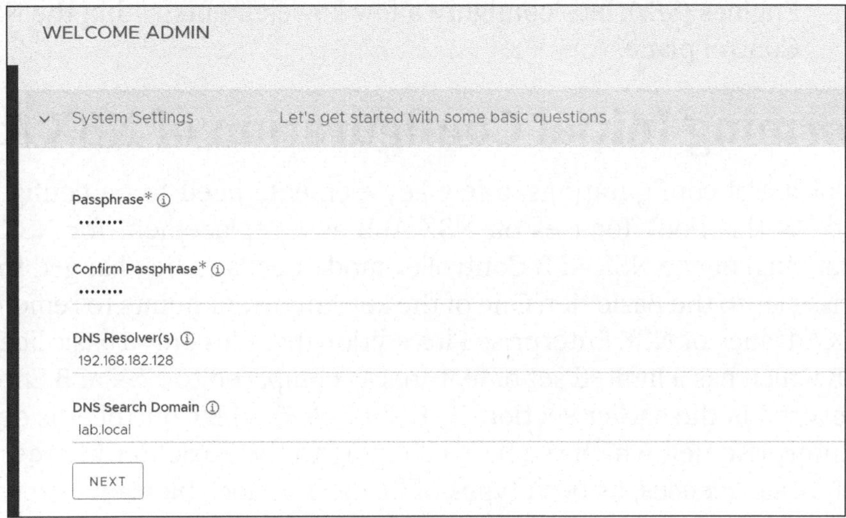

Figure 12.14: *Welcome Screen of NSX ALB Controller*

Step 9: If required, set up an SMTP server and from Email Address to receive notifications from the NSX ALB Controller.

Step 10: Next, set up the multi-tenant properties as per the requirement, as shown in *Figure* 12.15, and click **Save** to continue.

a. **IP Route Domain**: This option lets you choose whether different tenants will share a common routing domain and each will have their own IP routing domains.

b. **Service Engines are managed within the**: Select if all tenants will share the SEs or each tenant will have their dedicated SEs.

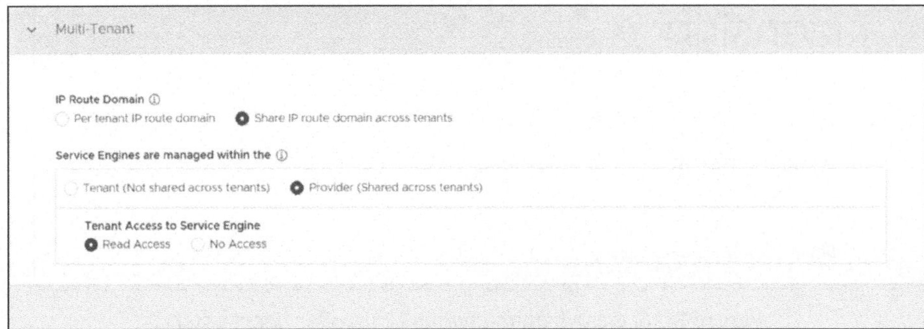

Figure 12.15: *Multi-tenant setup in NSX ALB*

Step 11: Congratulations! You have successfully deployed the NSX ALB Control plane. But how about the Data plane? Before deploying Service Engines (SEs), let's configure a few key elements within the NSX ALB Control plane.

Performing Initial Configuration of NSX ALB

As part of initial configurations, a few key elements need to be configured or modified. As this book focuses on NSX ALB as a replacement for NSX native load balancing, hence NSX ALB Controller mode needs to be changed from the Enterprise tier to the Basic tier. One of the key important points to remember is, that NSX Advance or NSX Enterprise Plus edition includes only a basic license for NSX ALB which has a limited set of features as compared to NSX ALB Enterprise as we covered in the earlier section. By default, NSX ALB Controller is deployed in the Enterprise tier, which requires changing to the Basic tier in order to use NSX ALB Basic licenses, as both types of licenses cannot be used concurrently. Also, NSX ALB Basic only support NSX-T cloud or No Access cloud with Service Engine in Active/Standby deployments. To configure NSX-T cloud NSX ALB, there are some pre-requisites to be completed in NSX Manager manually as listed here:

- NSX Transport Zone
- NSX Segment
- Tier-1 gateway used as a default gateway

Step 1: Login into NSX ALB Controller with admin privileges. Navigate to **`Administration`** and click on **`Licensing`**. It will show evaluation licenses with the **`Enterprise`** tier already installed on the controller. Click on the little gear icon beside **`Licensing`** to open a new window as shown in *Figure 12.16*.

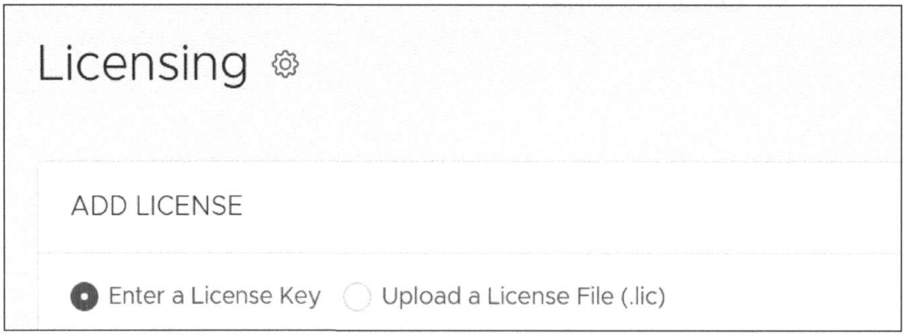

Licensing

ADD LICENSE

Enter a License Key   Upload a License File (.lic)

***Figure 12.16**: Gear icon to change Controller license tier*

Step 2: Select Basic Tier as shown in *Figure* 12.17, and click on **Save** to continue.

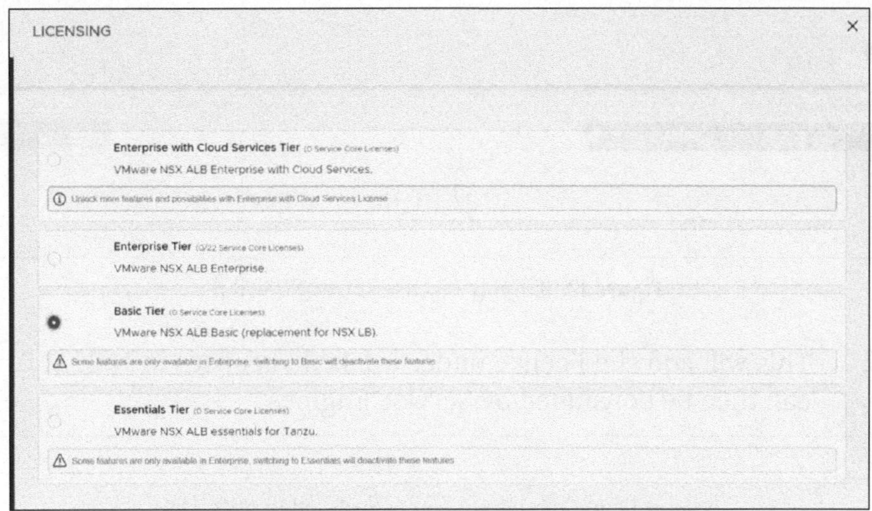

Figure 12.17: *Selecting Tier in NSX ALB Controller*

Step 3: It will take a few seconds and now the License will show as Basic confirming the tier change in NSX ALB.

Figure 12.18: *Basic Tier License in NSX ALB*

Step 4: Copy the NSX Advance/Enterprise Plus License key and paste it under the **`Add License`** window with the **`License Key*`** field similar to *Figure* 12.19 and click **`Apply Key`**.

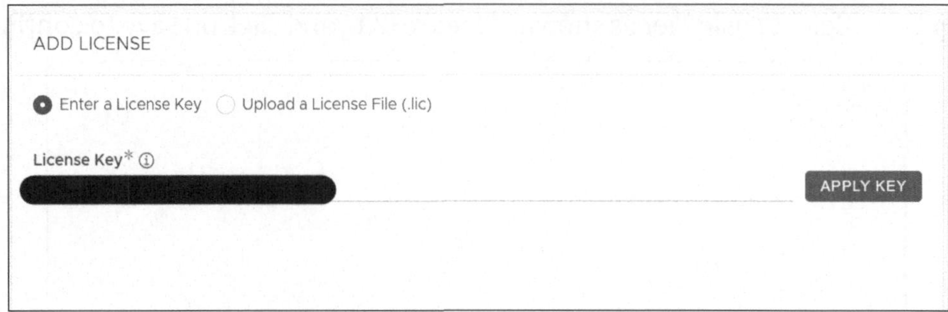

Figure 12.19: *Apply License key in NSX ALB*

Step 5: This will add the license under available licenses in NSX ALB, which can then be consumed by Service Engines.

Figure 12.20: *Available licenses installed in NSX ALB*

Step 6: The next step is to add an NSX-T cloud in NSX ALB. Click on the **`Infrastructure`** tab from the main menu and then select **`Clouds`** in the left navigation panel. Click on **`Create`** and select **`NSX-T Cloud`** as shown in *Figure* 12.21.

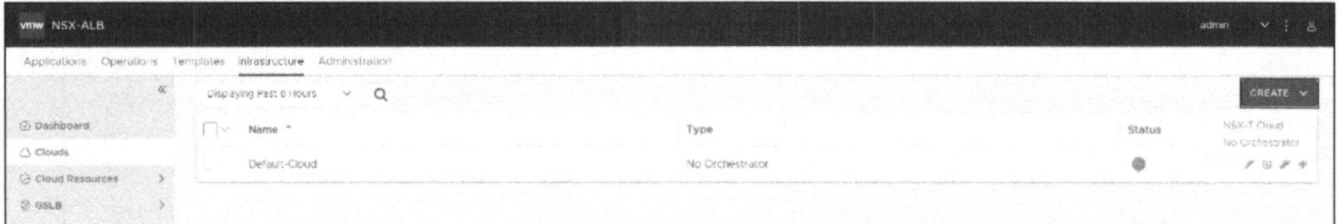

Figure 12.21: *Adding an NSX-T Cloud in NSX ALB*

Step 7: This opens a new window for **`New Cloud`** divided into three sections, **General**, **`NSX-T`**, and **`IPAM/DNS`**. Let's cover these sections one by one.

a. **`General`**: This section covers the general properties such as name and default prefix to be used for objects automatically created by NSX ALB Controller such as Service Engines. Provide suitable names for both fields as per *Figure* 12.22. Optionally, select if DHCP is to be used for IP addressing.

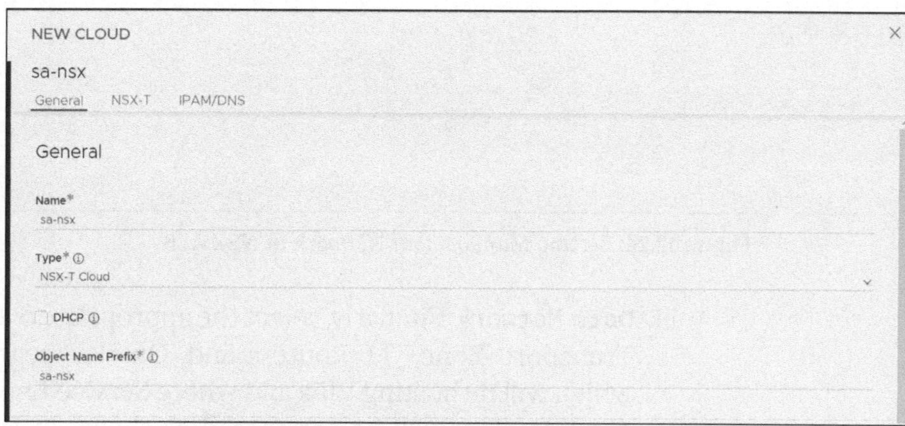

Figure 12.22: *General properties of New NSX-T Cloud*

b. **`NSX-T`**: This section defines the NSX Manager to be connected with and then selects transport zones, T1, etc. for management and data network of Service Engines.

   i. Click on **`Change Credentials`** and set **`NSX Manager Cluster VIP`** and click on **three dots** to create a new entry for NSX Manager credentials. *Figure* 12.23 shows the entered VIP address and NSX credentials. Click on **`Connect`** to continue and discover NSX objects in NSX ALB.

Figure 12.23: *Set* NSX-T *Credentials in* NSX ALB

   ii. **`Management Network`**: Select the appropriate Transport Zone either VLAN or Overlay backed and NSX segment to which the management network of Service Engine will be connected. A sample screenshot is captured in *Figure* 12.24.

Figure 12.24: *Setting Management Network in* NSX ALB

iii. **Data Network**: Similarly, select the appropriate overlay Transport Zone, T1 Router, and Overlay segment which will be hosting VIPs and where Service Engines' data interface will be connected as shown in *Figure* 12.25.

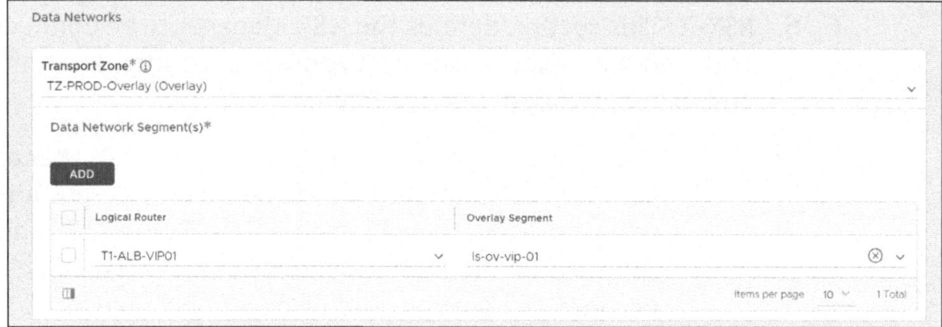

Figure 12.25*: Setting up Data Network in* NSX ALB

iv. **vCenter**: Click on **Add** to add a new vCenter server connection which will be used for the automated deployment of Service Engines. Provide an appropriate **Name** for connection and click on **Change Credentials** to select the vCenter server paired with the connected NSX Manager and appropriate credentials. Last but not least, select **Content Library** to host Service Engine OVA files. *Figure* 12.26 shows a sample screenshot with all the requested information provided. Click **Done** to save the configuration.

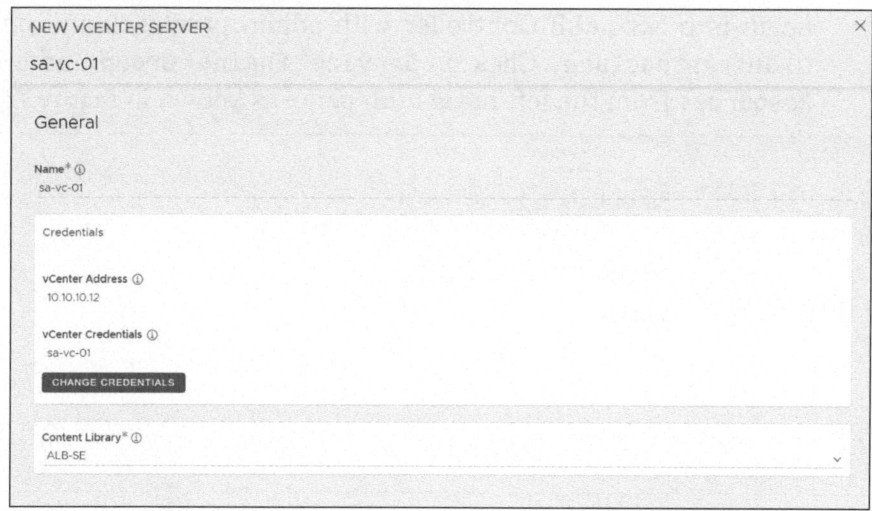

Figure 12.26: *Setting up vCenter server in NSX-T Cloud*

c. **`IPAM/DNS Profile`**: As a last step in NSX-T Cloud, Optionally, provide the desired IPAM and DNS profiles for SE deployments. The basic tier, however, will not let you set DNS resolvers or DNS profile.

Step 8: This completes the initial configuration to be performed before Service Engines can be deployed. *Figure* 12.27 shows a successfully created NSX-T cloud within NSX ALB.

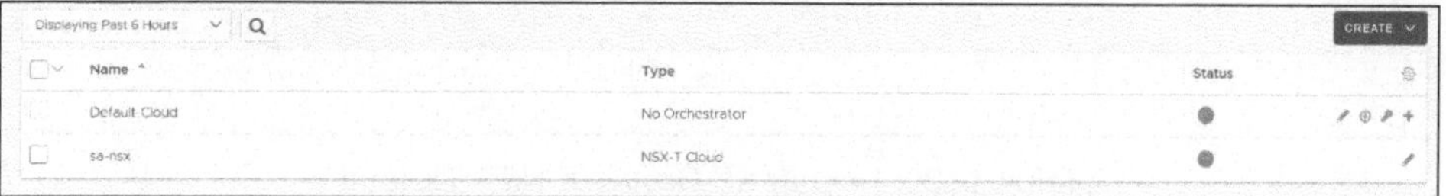

Figure 12.27: *NSX-T Cloud in NSX ALB*

Configuring Service Engine Group in NSX ALB

The next step is to deploy Service Engines however, deploying SEs can be automated thanks to NSX-T Cloud integration with the vCenter server content library which hosts Service Engines OVA files. But this requires a template to be defined that tells the NSX ALB Controller to deploy Service Engine with desired configurations, who in turn instructs the vCenter server to deploy OVA files.

Step 1: Login into NSX ALB Controller with admin privileges and navigate to **Infrastructure.** Click on **Service Engine Group** under **Cloud Resources** from the left navigation panel as shown in *Figure* 12.28.

***Figure* 12.28**: *SE Group in NSX ALB*

Step 2: Click on the drop-down menu next to **Select Cloud** and select the **NSX Cloud**. A Default-Group is created by the NSX ALB Controller when a new NSX-T Cloud is created. Either Edit the Default-Group by clicking on the Pencil icon or click on **Create** to add a new SE Group.

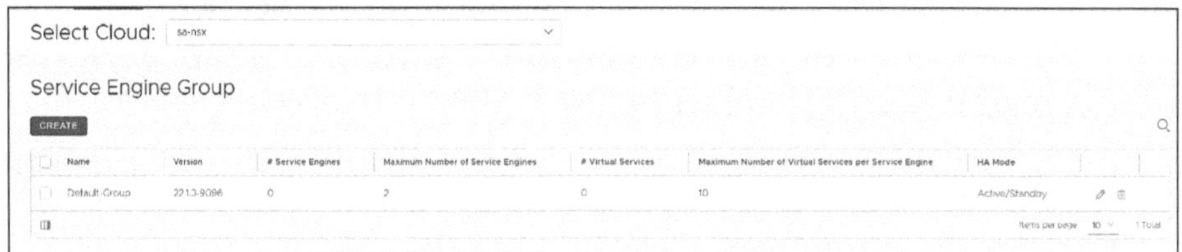

***Figure* 12.29:** *Default SE Group in NSX-T Cloud*

Step 3: This opens a new window similar to *Figure* 12.30. Click on **Save** to change any modifications in configurations. A few key configuration items which can be set here are:

a. **High Availability Mode**: This defines the mode in which the Service Engine operates. A basic license only supports Active/Standby which is the least efficient model.

b. **Virtual Services per Service Engine**: Maximum number of Virtual Services which can be placed on a single Service Engine. This can range from 1 to 1000 and will depend upon SE sizing.

c. **`Service Engine Name Prefix`**: Prefix for a virtual machine in the vCenter server to easily identify Service Engines.

d. **`Delete Unused Service Engines After`**: Automatically deletes a Service Engine if it is not being used after the threshold timer defined in SE Group.

e. **`Memory per Service Engine`**: Memory to be allocated to the Service Engine.

f. **`vCPU per Service Engine`**: vCPU cores to be assigned to Service Engine, this will consume licenses from NSX ALB.

g. **`Disk per Service Engine`**: Size of the disk to be assigned to the Service Engine in GB.

h. **`Scope`**: Define the placement criteria within the vCenter server to place Service Engines. This can be used to include or exclude specific hosts or clusters and datastores (can be local or shared) from Service Engine placement.

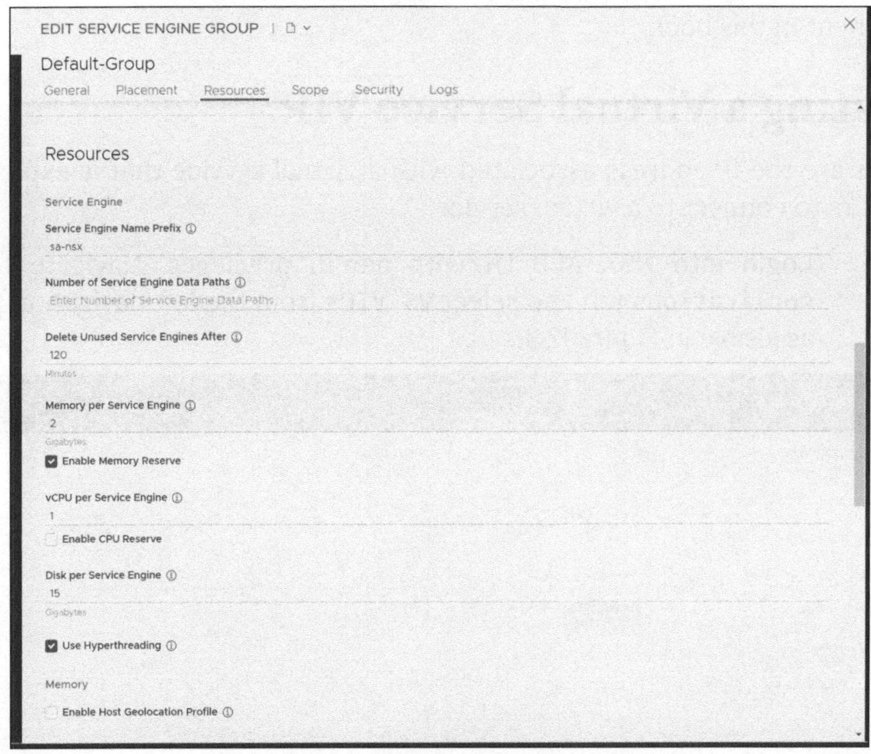

Figure 12.30: *Modifying SE Group in NSX ALB*

This covers the deployment of NSX Advance Load Balancer which comes packaged with NSX to replace its native load balancing capabilities. Next is to configure and set up virtual services within NSX ALB to which users can connect and which load balance the users' requests to backend servers.

Configuring Virtual Services in NSX ALB

This is the interesting part where we configure Virtual Services, which will be consumed by end users. When you log into NSX ALB User Interface (UI), the first screen you will see is Applications. Applications are the main window in UI where you will be spending most of your time, as this is where all different service components such as Virtual Service, Virtual Service IP, Server Pools, etc. are configured. Now, before we create a Virtual Service, there are different components that need to be created first. Either you can create them beforehand and select during the creation of Virtual Service or while creating Virtual Service you can create all these components as Virtual Service is a collection of different components and will not function in the desired manner if any of these are missing. We will take the first approach and configure component by component in this book.

Creating a Virtual Service VIP

VS VIPs are the IP address associated with a virtual service that is exposed to end users to connect to a virtual service.

Step 1: Login into NSX ALB UI with admin privileges. Navigate to the **`Applications`** tab and select **`VS VIPs`** from the left navigation panel, as visible in *Figure* 12.31.

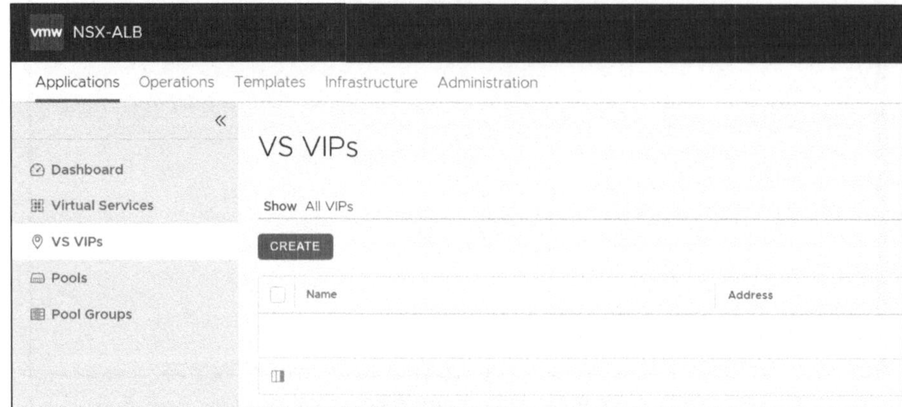

***Figure* 12.31:** VS VIPs *in* NSX ALB

Step 2: Click on **`Create`** to add a new VS VIP. This will open a new window titled **`Create VS VIP`** and provide the required information shown in *Figure* 12.32 and click on **`Save`** to create the VIP.

a. **`Name`**: Provide a descriptive name for the VIP.

b. **`Cloud, VRF Context`**: Click on **`Set`** to select the NSX cloud created earlier, in NSX-T cloud, VRF Context is the Tier-1 gateway to which the data segment is connected.

c. **`Tier1 Logical Router`**: Select the Tier-1 gateway.

d. **`VIPs`**: Click on **`Add`** to create an IP address entry for VIP. It supports both Auto Allocation or Static entry.

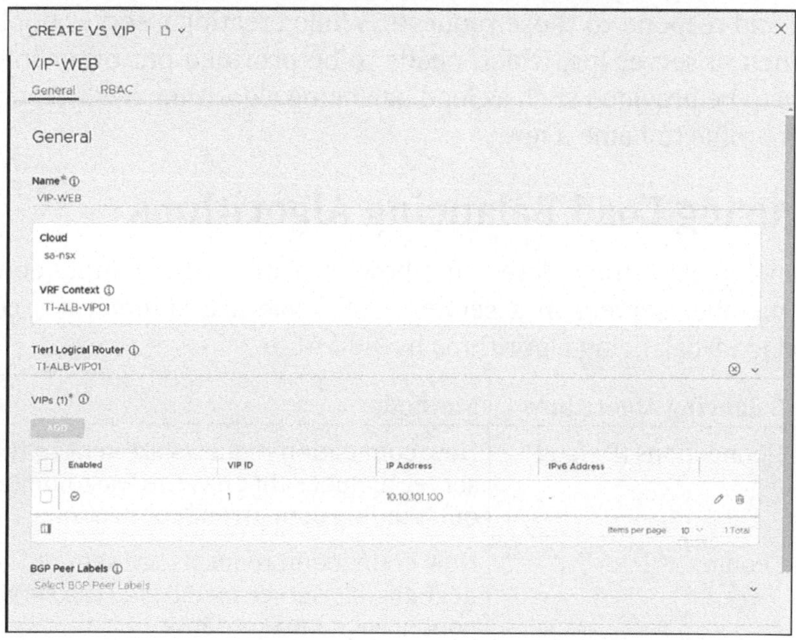

***Figure* 12.32:** *Creating a new* VIP *in* NSX ALB

Step 3: Newly created VIP will be visible in the main UI similar to *Figure* 12.33. It will have a minus in a circle sign stating that VIP has not been assigned yet. It will show a green check within the circle if VIP is assigned and successfully configured.

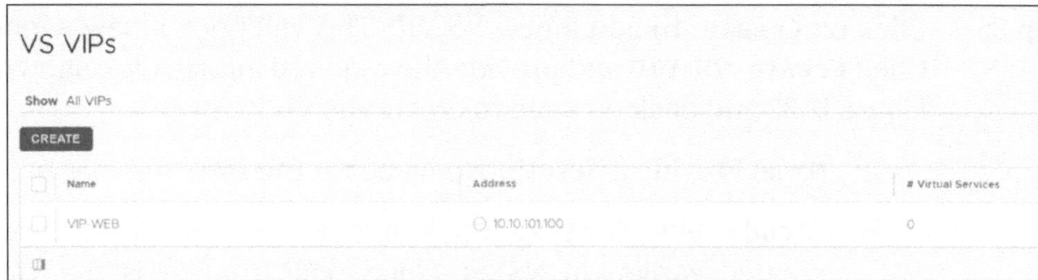

Figure 12.33: *Newly created VIP in NSX ALB UI*

Creating a Server Pool

A server pool is a group of servers that load balance the requests coming from the client and respond to those requests. While creating a server pool, it is not only a bunch of server Ips, which needs to be provided but other information also needs to be provided such as load balancing algorithm, health monitor, and persistent profile to name a few.

Configuring Load Balancing Algorithms

Load balancing algorithms determine how to distribute incoming connections between member servers in a server pool. *Table* 12.2 summarizes commonly supported load-balancing algorithms by NSX ALB.

Load-Balancing Algorithms	**Methods**
Least Connections (Default)	New connection requests are sent to the server member that has the least number of outstanding concurrent connections.
Round Robin	New connection requests are sent to the next eligible server member in the server pool in sequential order.
Fastest Response	New connection requests are sent to the server that is currently providing the fastest response to new connections or requests.
Consistent Hash	New connections are distributed across the servers using a hash key.
Least Load	New connections are sent to the server with the lightest load, regardless of the number of connections that the server has.

Fewest Servers	Instead of trying to distribute all connections or requests across all servers, NSX ALB determines the fewest number of servers required to satisfy the current client load.

Table 12.2: NSX ALB *Load Balancing Algorithms*

The following process covers the step-by-step approach to creating a server pool and configuring important parameters such as Health Monitor and Persistent Profile.

Step 1: Login into NSX ALB with admin privileges and navigate to the **Applications** tab. Click on **Pools** from the left navigation pool to view server pools present in the environment. *Figure* 12.34 shows blank, as there are no server pools currently configured.

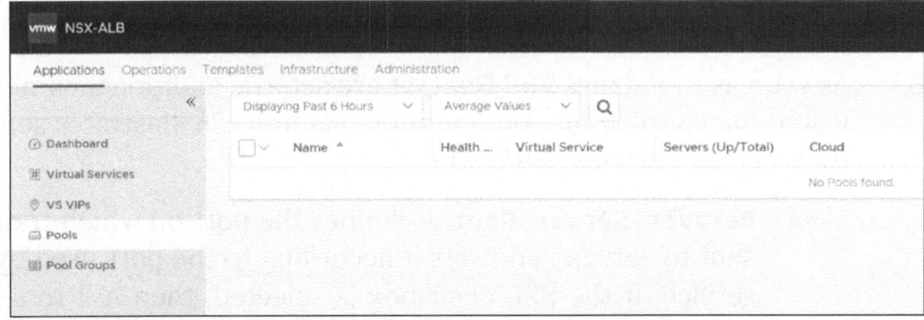

Figure 12.34: *Viewing Server Pools in NSX ALB*

Step 2: Click on **Create Pool** to start creating a new server pool. This opens a new window titled **Create Pool** requesting information to be filled as shown in *Figure* 12.35.

a. **Name**: Provide a unique name for the Server Pool.

b. **Type**: Select if it is a generic application or an oAuth application.

c. **Cloud, VRF Context**: Click on **Set** to select the NSX cloud created earlier, in NSX cloud, VRF Context is the Tier-1 gateway to which the data segment is connected.

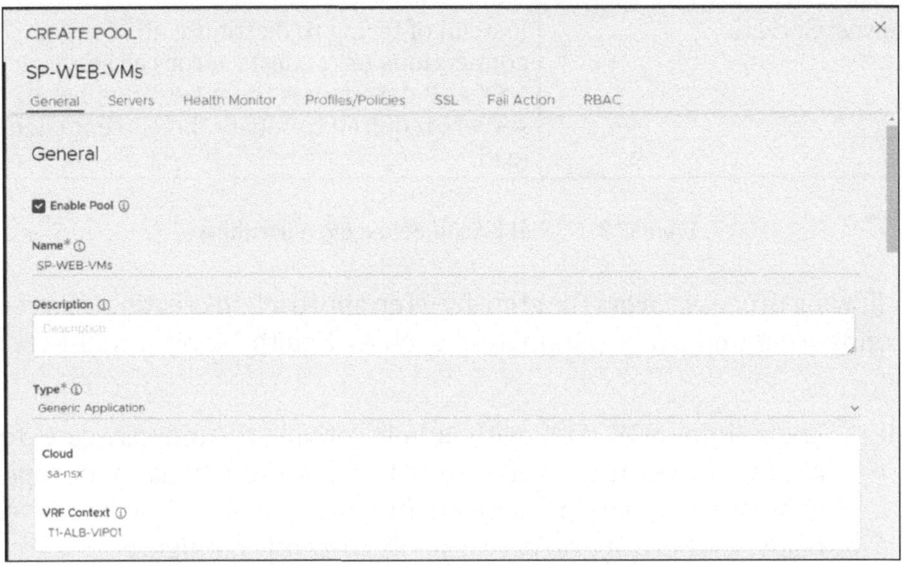

Figure 12.35: *Initial configuration of Server Pool in* NSX ALB

Step 3: As soon as Cloud and VRF Context are set, the additional parameter will become visible for configuration. *Figure* 12.36 illustrates some of the key parameters to set next are:

a. **`Default Server Port`**: It defines the port on which traffic is sent to servers, and sets it according to the port used by the service. If the SSL checkbox is selected, then AVI to server traffic is encrypted else it is a clear text communication.

b. **`oad Balance Algorithm`**: Select the desired load balancing algorithm as per application requirements.

c. **`Tier1 Logical Router`**: Select the Tier-1 gateway as selected for virtual service.

Figure 12.36: *Configuring Load Balance Algorithm in* NSX ALB

Step 4: The next step is to select servers that will become members of this server pool. There are three different ways to add servers to a pool:

a. IP Address, Range, or DNS Name: Provide a specific FQDN, IP address to add a server in the pool.

b. IP Group: Select the IP Group created in NSX Manager to add servers in the pool.

c. Security Group: Select the Group created in NSX Manager to add its members as servers in the pool.

Figure 12.37 shows a security group with the name SG-WEB-Pool configured in NSX Manager to add its two members as servers in the server pool.

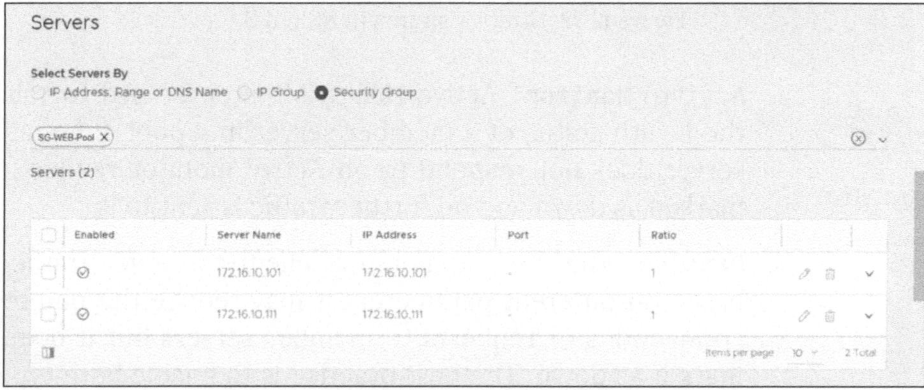

Figure 12.37: *Adding a server in the Server Pool*

Step 5: This brings us to configuring the Health Monitor for the server pool. As discussed earlier, the Health Monitor validates the member servers of a pool and marks them up or down. There are different pre-defined Health Monitors which can be used with the server pool. *Figure* 12.38 shows such Health Monitors in the NSX ALB environment. Another key point here is whether to enable Passive Monitor or not. There are two monitors in NSX ALB, namely Active and Passive, and they serve different functions.

***Figure 12.38**: Health Monitors in NSX ALB*

a. **`Active Monitor:`** Active Health Monitor is used to validate the health status of a member server in a pool. If a member server does not respond to an Active monitor request, it is marked as down and no further traffic is sent to it.

b. **`Passive Monitor:`** It monitors client-to-server traffic and based on different parameters it may reduce the number of connections or requests to member servers but it does not mark it as down. The best practice is to enable both types of monitors in the environment.

Step 6: Under **`Profiles/Policies,`** select if any persistent profile needs to be used. Persistence profiles are used mainly with stateful applications to direct all related connections to the same back-end member server. NSX ALB supports the following types of persistence profiles based on cookies apart from standard Source IP based persistence:

a. **`HTTP Cookie`**: In this type, SEs insert an HTTP cookie into a server's first response to a client, and no configuration changes are required on the back-end servers.

b. **`App Cookie:`** In this type, instead of SEs inserting cookies into the HTTP header, persistence relied on an existing cookie inserted by the back-end server.

Step 7: Click on **`Save`** to create a server pool and it becomes visible in the Pools UI as shown in *Figure* 12.39.

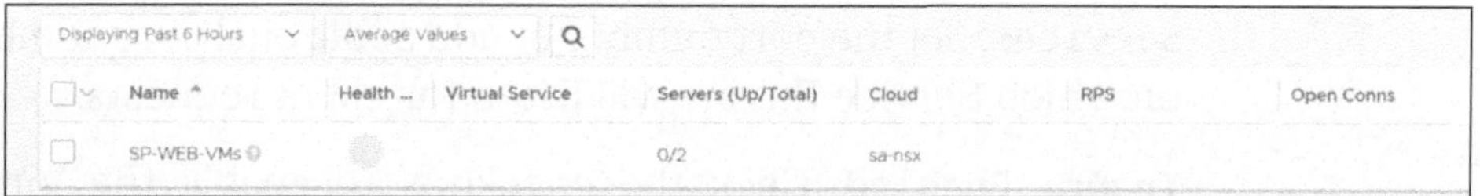

Figure 12.39*: Newly created Server Pool in NSX ALB*

Creating a Virtual Service

Now that all the different components have been created, it is time to create a Virtual Service.

Step 1: Login into NSX ALB with admin privileges and navigate to the **`Applications`** tab. Click on **`Virtual Services`** from the left navigation pool to view all configured Virtual Services in the environment.

Step 2: Click on **`Create Virtual Service`** to add a new Virtual Service. *Figure* 12.40 shows two modes available to create a Virtual Service:

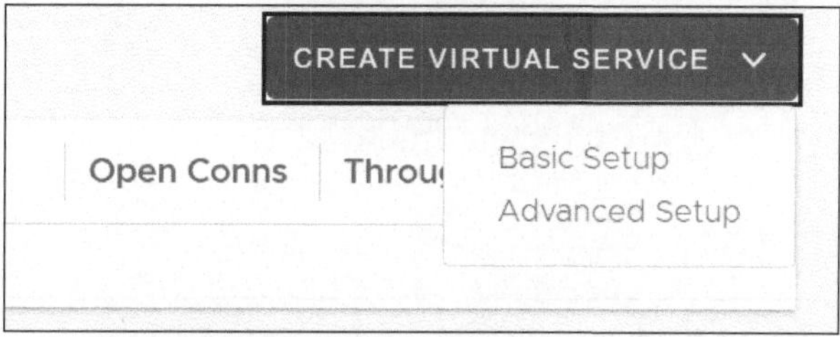

Figure 12.40: *Different modes to create a VS*

a. **`Basic Setup`**: Basic setup creates a simple virtual service with port 80, server pool, and VIP.

b. **`Advanced Setup`**: This mode gives full control over the creation of a Virtual Service.

Step 3: Click on **`Set`** to select the NSX cloud created earlier, and VRF Context is the Tier-1 gateway to which the data segment is connected.

Step 4: Next, select the different components created earlier as shown in *Figure* 12.41.

a. **`Name`**: A unique name of Virtual Service.

b. **`VS VIP`**: Virtual IP Address to be associated with service.

c. **`Pool`**: Select the server pool which will serve the function of back-end.

d. **`Services`**: Set the port number or add additional port numbers on which Service Engine will listen for client requests.

e. **`Traffic Enabled`**: Click the checkbox to enable the Virtual Service traffic to Service Engines or uncheck to disable it. It is only effective if the Enabled flag is true.

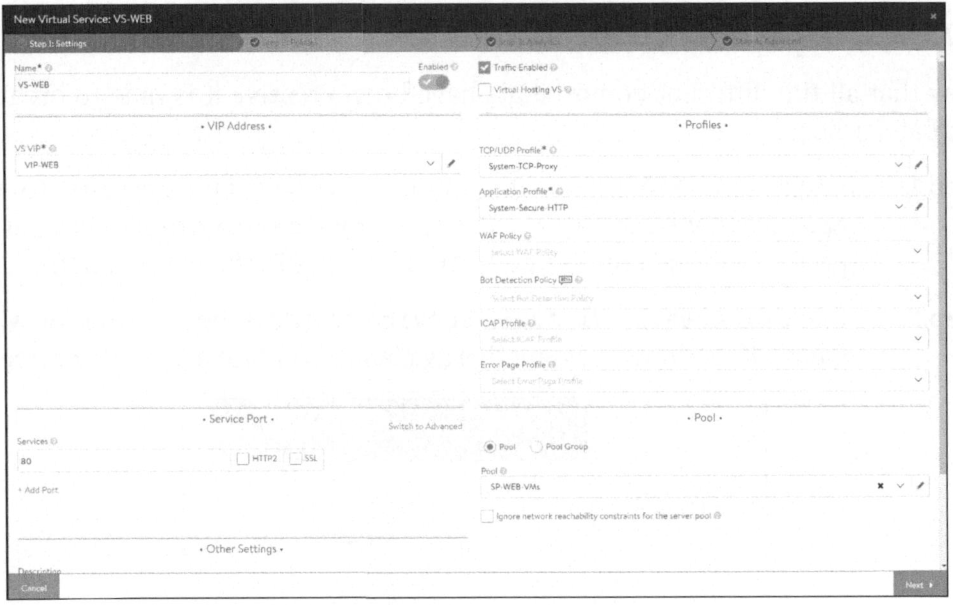

***Figure 12.41**: Initial Configuration of Virtual Service*

Step 5: Next, select the desired application profile or create a new one as per application requirement as it determines the behavior of the virtual services, based on application type. Different types of profiles pre-defined in NSX ALB as visible in *Figure* 12.42 are:

a. **`System-HTTP`**: It is the default for processing nonsecure layer 7 HTTP traffic and uses port 80.

b. **`System-L4-Application`**: The virtual service listens for layer 4 requests on the port that you specify in the Service Port field.

c. **`System-Secure-HTTP`**: It is the default for processing secure layer 7 HTTPS traffic and uses port 443.

d. **`System-Secure-HTTP-VDI`**: It is the default for processing virtual desktop HTTP traffic.

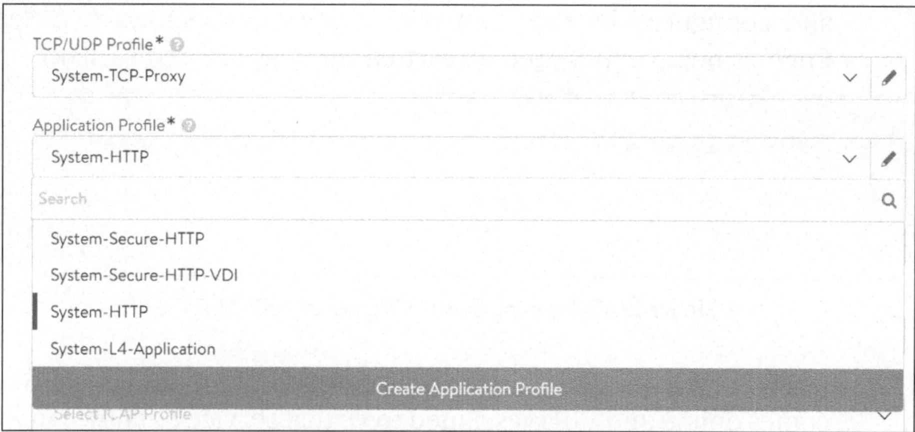

***Figure 12.42**: Different types of Application Profile*

Step 6: Click on **Advanced** and then click on **Save** to finish creating Virtual Service.

Step 7: As soon as the Virtual service is created, the NSX ALB Controller invokes deployment of the OVA file of the Service Engine in vCenter, and the vCenter server starts deploying OVA files. *Figure* 12.43 shows different tasks being carried out in the vCenter server to deploy SEs OVA files.

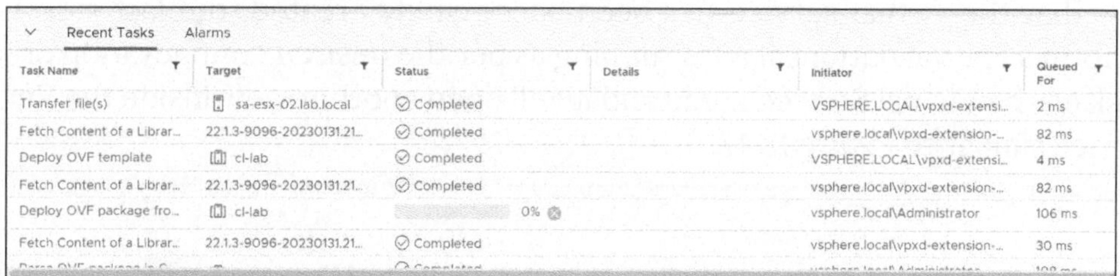

***Figure 12.43**: Service Engine automatic deployment in vCenter server*

Step 8: Newly created Virtual Service will show red status as Service Engine deployment is in progress and virtual service has not been realized yet as illustrated in *Figure* 12.44.

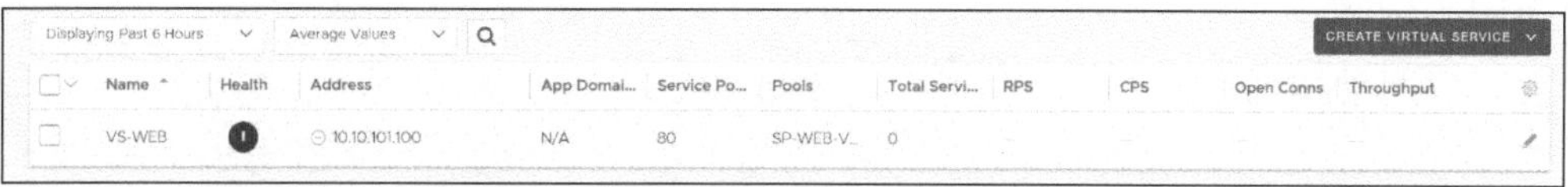

***Figure 12.44**: Virtual Service in Red Status*

Step 9: Navigate to **`Infrastructure`** and select **`Service Engines`** under **`Cloud Resources`**. It will show new Service Engines being deployed and configured by the Controller. *Figure* 12.45 shows two Service Engines being configured for virtual services created earlier.

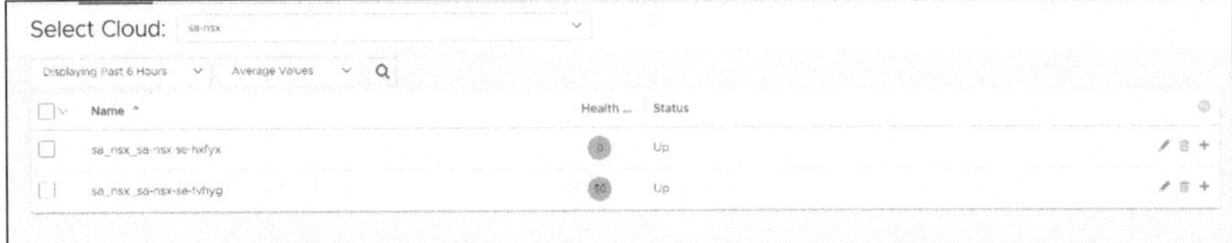

Figure 12.45: *Viewing Service Engine in NSX ALB*

Step 10: After Service Engines are successfully configured, Virtual Service comes online and VIP is assigned to virtual service as shown in *Figure* 12.46.

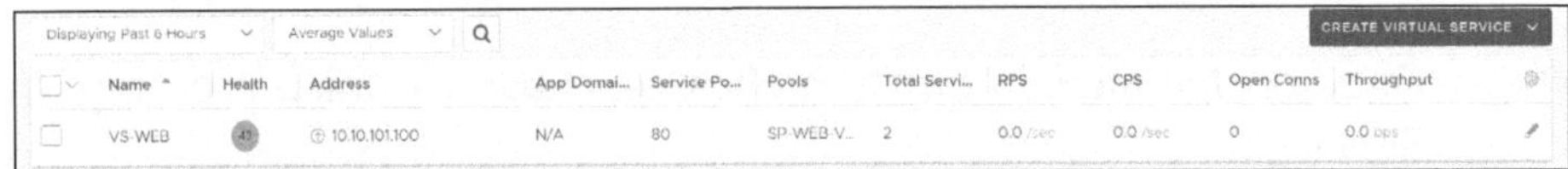

Figure 12.46: *A successfully configured Virtual Service*

Validating Virtual Service

Now that the virtual service has been successfully created, the last step is to perform a few validations if all is running as per the desired configuration or not. Click on the Virtual Service name and it will open another view inside the Virtual Service similar to *Figure* 12.47.

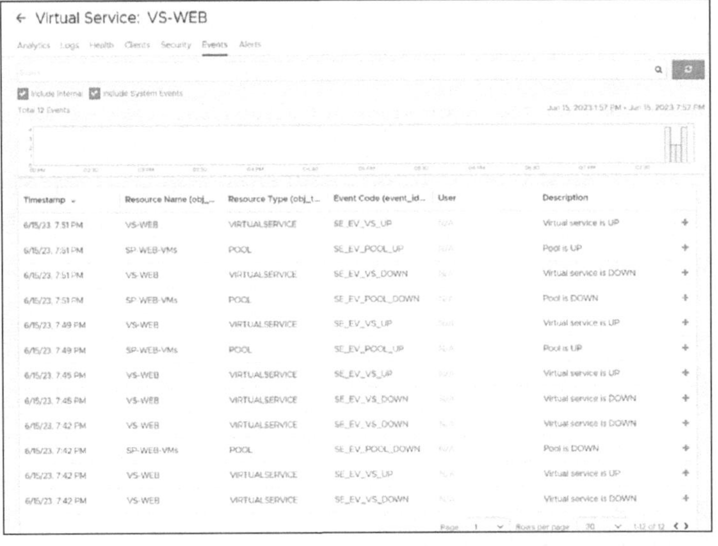

Figure 12.47: Validating Virtual Service

Different options available here to troubleshoot or view deep inside Virtual Service are:

- `Analytics`: This tab provides insights into performance through the real-time analysis of key performance indicators however it is only available in the Enterprise edition license.
- `Logs`: NSX ALB UI provides a central place to view all logs which can be filtered, indexed, or viewed locally. One key point, insignificant logs can only be enabled with an Enterprise edition license.
- `Health`: This score denotes both the responsiveness of the virtual service or pool and any vulnerabilities.
- `Security`: This provides detailed security information for SSL and DDoS, along with other parameters.
- `Events`: This tab provides a history of changes that have occurred in a virtual service.
- `Alerts`: As the name suggests, this informs the administrator of any significant events happening in the environment.

Conclusion

This concludes the NSX Advanced Load Balancer configuration in the NSX environment. In this chapter, we covered different editions, features, and architecture of NSX ALB, and different load-balancing topologies supported by NSX ALB in an NSX environment. Also, we covered the deployment of NSX ALB and the configuration of virtual services in detail.

In the next few chapters, we will cover how to monitor and manage an NSX environment. Also, what are multisite options available in NSX to stretch network services from one location to another? Interested? I bet you are.

Key Terms

- **Segment:** Segments are layer 2 subnets representing layer 2 broadcasting domain across transport nodes in NSX networking.
- **NSX ALB Controller Cluster**: The NSX ALB Controller cluster is responsible for providing a central management console and control policies.
- **NSX ALB Service Engines:** NSX ALB Service Engines (SEs) make up the data plane of the NSX ALB environment and handle all the data plane operations in accordance with instructions received from the NSX ALB Controller Cluster and execute them.

- **NSX ALB Admin Console:** NSX ALB Admin Console is a web-based user interface (UI) that provides role-based access control (RBAC) to configure, manage and monitor application services.
- **Virtual Service**: It is a logical construct that contains an IP address, port, and protocol.
- **Server Pool**: It is a collection of servers associated with virtual service and responsible for responding to client requests.
- **Health Monitor:** It validates the status of servers within the server pool.
- **Persistent Profile**: Persistent Profile maintains a connection from a client to the same pool member.
- **Load Balancing Algorithms:** Load balancing algorithms determine how to distribute incoming connections between member servers in a server pool.

CHAPTER 13

NSX Multisite Deployment

Introduction

The last few chapters have discussed configuring different networking and security services. Until now, it's always been from the viewpoint of a single location. However, in today's world, organizations are interested in running workloads across multiple locations to provide easy Disaster Recovery solutions or have a backup location to run workloads in case the primary location becomes unavailable. This requires network as well as security services to be stretched across multiple locations and has a centralized system to manage these stretched services. Can NSX be of help with this scenario? I bet you, it can. Introducing the NSX Multisite solution.

This chapter covers different NSX Multisite solutions, NSX Federation, its architecture, and how it is onboarded and managed in the NSX environment.

Structure

In this chapter, we will cover the following topics:

- NSX Multisite and Federation
    - o NSX Multisite
    - o NSX Federation
- NSX Federation Architecture
    - o NSX Global Manager
    - o NSX Local Manager

    - Edge RTEP
    - Federation Regions
- Onboarding NSX Federation
    - Deploying NSX Global Manager
    - Configuring NSX Global Manager
    - Pre-Configuring RTEP
    - Onboarding NSX Local Manager
    - Importing Configuration from Local Managers
- NSX Federation Networking
    - Stretched Layer 2 Deployment
    - Multilocation Routing Deployment
    - Configuring Tier0 Gateway
    - Configuring Tier1 Gateway
    - Configuring Segments
    - Validating NSX Federation Networking
    - Multilocation Traceflow
- NSX Federation Security
    - Regions
    - Global Manager Groups
    - Configuring Distributed Firewall Policies
- Conclusion

NSX Multisite and Federation

NSX provides support for managing the NSX environment across multiple locations. For understanding, a location in this chapter can refer to a site (datacenter in different cities), a building (datacenter in different buildings but in the same campus), or racks (different racks within a datacenter). Organizations use multiple locations to enable different use cases, such as:

- A location doesn't have enough resources to host all applications and additional locations are required to host all applications or distribute load across multiple locations.
- To provide mobility of workload or application deployed in different locations for maintenance, disaster recovery test, or datacenter migration.

- To provide disaster avoidance or disaster recovery services, so if one location is down, then applications can be recovered easily in another location.

All these use cases require network services to be configured and managed across multiple locations. NSX provides two distinct approaches to manage the NSX environment across multiple locations.

NSX Multisite

This is the first solution introduced way back in NSX-T release v2.3 and enhanced further with newer releases. In high-level architecture, this solution consists of a single NSX Management cluster that manages different vSphere clusters and Edge nodes spanning across multiple locations. User login into NSX Management cluster either using UI or API to configure and manage network/ security services across multiple locations. The upside with this solution is a small footprint of infrastructure resources required, that is, only one set of NSX Management cluster and a large set of networking and security features available for configuration. However, there are a few downsides as well such as the large MTU requirements across locations over WAN for East-West data plane communication that can be a challenge, and the scale of the environment is limited to the configuration maximums of a single set of NSX Management clusters.

Figure 13.1 illustrates the NSX Multisite solution on a high level. There are three different locations, namely A, B, and C, with workloads running on each location. NSX Manager Cluster is running in Location A where the User can log in via UI/API to manage the NSX environment. Distributed networking and security services (Firewall and IDS/IPS) can be provided across locations along with other security and network services such as NAT, Firewall, Load Balancing, and more on each location.

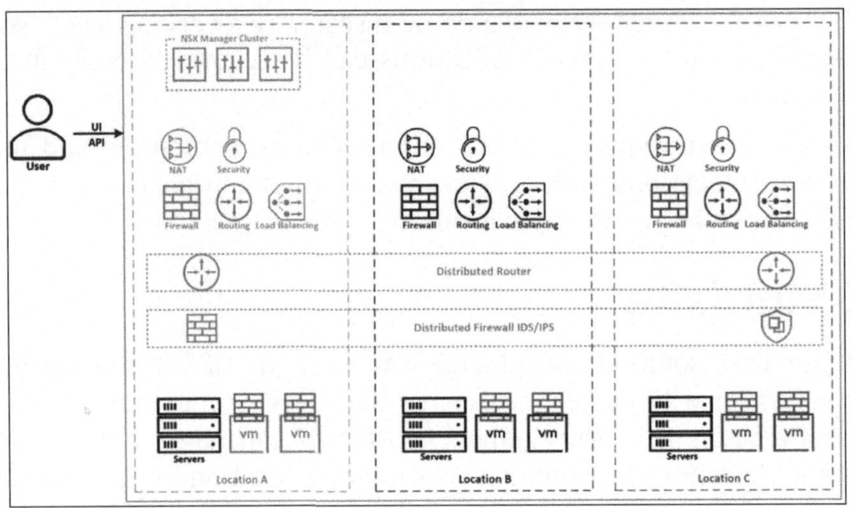

Figure 13.1: NSX *Multisite Logical Topology*

NSX Federation

The second solution is NSX Federation introduced in NSX-T release v3.0; however, production deployment is recommended to use at least NSX-T v3.1. Instead of managing multiple locations through a single NSX Management cluster, a new central entity is introduced in the NSX Federation named as **Global Manager**. Global Manager cluster provides centralized networking and security services for multiple locations and NSX Manager cluster running locally on each location is added as Location Manager in Global Manager, which in turn manages hypervisor hosts and Edge nodes locally. User login into Global Manager either using UI or API to manage network or security policies spanning across multiple locations. Global Manager pushes each policy to the Local Manager on each location, which implements them locally. The big advantage with this solution is that there is no requirement of a large MTU for East-West traffic communication, a local Management plane to comply with policy requirements such as GDPR, and a single console to manage the entire NSX environment. However, there are a few downsides as well, such as a limited set of networking and security features supported by Global Manager and a large footprint of infrastructure resources.

Figure 13.2 illustrates an NSX Federation solution at a high level with three different locations A, B, and C. Each location has an NSX Location Manager (cluster of three nodes) running, which is added to NSX Global Manager (another cluster of three) running in Active-Standby mode, providing distributed networking and distributed firewall services along with NAT services on each location.

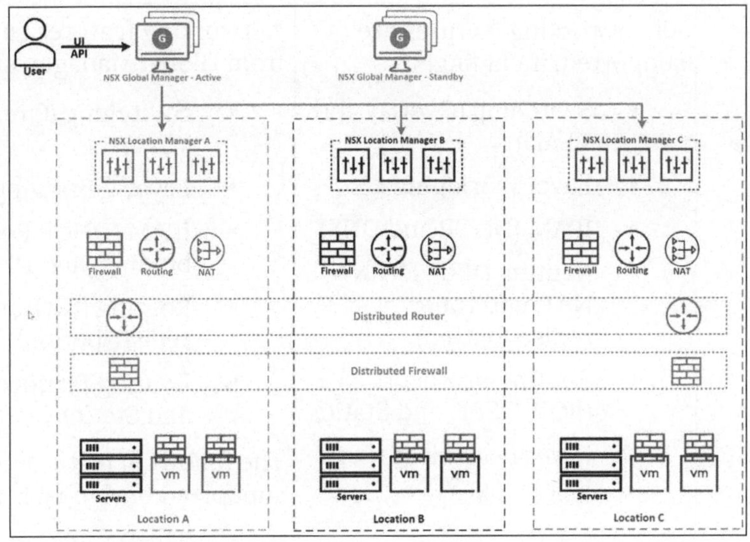

Figure 13.2: *NSX Federation Logical Topology*

NSX provides two different solutions for multi-location management, which raises another question – what solution should be used? Well, each solution has its own advantages and disadvantages, and comparing both will answer this question. *Table* 13.1 provides a summarized comparison between NSX Multisite and NSX Federation with regards to their requirements and features supported by each solution, which can help you decide which solution will best fit your requirements.

Features	**NSX Multisite**	**NSX Federation**
Availability	NSX release v2.3 and later	NSX release v3.0 and later
Underlay Network	• Two datacenters in metro location with <10ms RTT latency and stretched VLANs • Require jumbo frame support	• Maximum RTT between locations should be <150ms • Recommended jumbo frame support but 1500 MTU is also supported
NSX Manager Clusters	One NSX Manager Cluster	Two Global Manager Cluster and one NSX Manager Cluster at each location

<table>
<tr><td>Network Services</td><td>All networking features are supported, including:<ul><li>Switching (Overlay and VLAN)</li><li>Layer 2 Bridging</li><li>IPAM (DHCP and DNS)</li><li>Routing (VRF, EVPN, NAT, and route redistribution)</li><li>Routing Protocols (BGP, OSPF, and Static)</li><li>Layer4+ services (Load Balancing, VPN)</li></ul></td><td>Networking features supported from Global Manager, such as:<ul><li>Switching (Overlay and VLAN)</li><li>Layer 2 Bridging</li><li>IPAM (DHCP Relay, static binding, and DNS)</li><li>Routing (NAT and route redistribution)</li><li>Routing Protocols (BGP and Static)</li></ul>The following features are not supported on Global Manager:<ul><li>Tier0 VRF Gateways</li><li>Layer4+ services (Load Balancing, VPN)</li><li>DHCP Dynamic binding</li><li>EVPN</li><li>Routing Protocol OSPF</li></ul></td></tr>
<tr><td>Security Services</td><td>All security features are supported, such as:<ul><li>Distributed Firewall</li><li>Gateway Firewall</li><li>FQDN Filtering</li><li>L7 APP ID Context Profile support</li><li>Identity Firewall</li><li>Distributed IDS/IPS</li><li>Malware Prevention</li><li>Network Introspection</li><li>Endpoint Protection</li><li>Time-based Firewall</li></ul></td><td>Security features supported from Global Manager, such as:<ul><li>Distributed Firewall</li><li>Gateway Firewall</li><li>FQDN Filtering</li><li>L7 APP ID Context Profile support</li><li>Time-Based Firewall</li></ul>The following features are not supported on Global Manager:<ul><li>Identity Firewall</li><li>Distributed IDS/IPS</li><li>Malware Prevention</li><li>Network Introspection and Endpoint Protection</li></ul></td></tr>
</table>

Recovery	NSX Manager VMs can be recovered either with the help of SRM, vSphere HA, or backups	NSX recovery through Standby Global Manager and NSX Manager recovery with the help of SRM

***Table 13.1**: Comparison between NSX Multisite and NSX Federation*

Note: This chapter focuses on NSX Federation and further topics cover NSX Federation concept only. For more information on NSX Multisite, please refer to NSX Multi-Location Design Guide (Federation + Multisite) (https://communities.vmware.com/t5/VMware-NSX-Documents/NSX-T-Multi-Location-Design-Guide-Federation-Multisite/ta-p/2810327).

NSX Federation Architecture

NSX Federation introduces a few extra architectural components apart from using traditional NSX components to enable centralized management and visibility across multiple locations. These components are as follows:

- NSX Global Manager
- Edge RTEP (Remote Tunnel End Point)
- Regions

Figure 13.3 illustrates these components and how they communicate with each other with the help of an example topology. There are three locations, namely A, B, and C, managed through NSX Global Manager with an active instance running in location A and a standby instance running in location B. User is pushing configuration consisting of stretched Tier0, Tier1, and segment across all three locations and a group consisting of virtual machines running in all three locations through Global Manager.

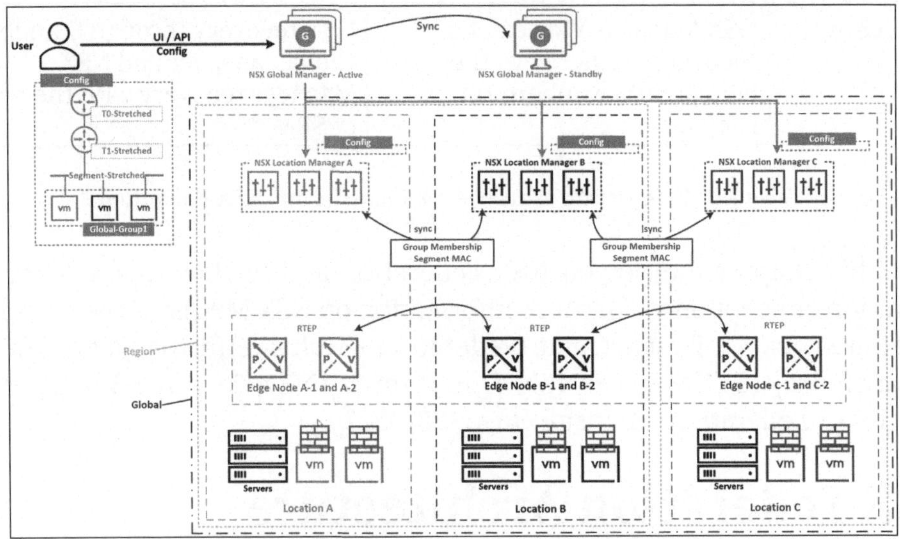

Figure 13.3: *NSX Federation Architecture*

So, let's break this architecture into different sections for easier understanding. As a first step, the user creates Tier0/Tier1 gateway, segments, and groups on Global Manager either through UI or API deployed in Active-Standby mode.

NSX Global Manager

NSX Global Manager (GM) Cluster consists of three NSX nodes deployed as Global Manager (GM) in a cluster. There are two Global Manager clusters with one acting as active and the other as standby. In case of any failure, the standby Global Manager can be made active to restore management plane functionality. The maximum latency requirement between GM-Active and GM-Standby is 500 ms. Any configuration is carried out on GM-Active, which synchronizes the configuration to GM-Standby, as shown in *Figure* 13.3. Also, GM-Active synchronizes other configurations such as security, vIDM users, and principal identity users on GM-Standby as well. However, it does not synchronize vIDM/LDAP configuration to GM-Standby.

NSX Local Manager

NSX Local Manager (LM) cluster consists of three NSX nodes deployed on NSX Manager nodes in a cluster on each location. These Local Managers are onboarded to Global Manager so they receive any configuration being done on Global Manager. Global Manager pushes the configuration to Local Manager, which in turn realizes the configuration on Transport nodes. In *Figure* 13.3, the user is pushing configuration from Global Manager to all three locations, so GM-Active pushes the config to all three Local Managers on locations A, B, and C. If a configuration is spanned across a single location or subset of locations, then GM-Active pushes the configuration to specific LMs running on those locations only instead of pushing the configurations to all LMs. The maximum latency requirement between GM-Active and LM is 500ms. Async Replicator (AR) is responsible for synchronizing these configurations between GM-Active to GM-Standby and GM-Active to LM and LM to LM. AR service runs on port 1236 opened by APH (Appliance Proxy Host) service running on GM/LM. A maximum of eight Local Managers can be added to the NSX Federation.

In two specific use cases, The Local Manager will synchronize information with other Local Managers, as follows:

- **Stretched NSX Group**: In *Figure* 13.3, Group 1 has been defined to span across all three locations. In this case, each Local Manager will synchronize its local group membership with other Local Managers so all LMs will have information about remote group memberships.
- **Stretched Segments**: In *Figure* 13.3, The NSX segment segment-stretched is spanned across all three locations, each Local Manager receives segment-stretched and fills its local segment table with the location, MAC, and IP address of the VM. Also, LMs sync this information with other LMs, so at the end, each LM has information about the remote segment table as well.

Another important point to note here is any configuration changes done directly on NSX Local Manager will not be pushed to Global Manager. Configuration is always pushed from NSX Global Manager to Local Manager and no other way around. Also, any configuration done directly on the Local Manager will not be synchronized with other Local Managers except for the two cases explained earlier.

Edge RTEP

NSX Federation introduces one more tunnel interface, that is, Remote Tunnel End Point (RTEP). This RTEP is configured only on Edge nodes and forms tunnels with other Edge nodes running in different locations, as shown in *Figure* 13.3. North-South traffic in each location is processed by Edge nodes and East-West traffic is processed by hypervisor hosts. However, East-West traffic across locations is processed by Edge nodes and travels through RTEP interfaces. Unlike TEP interfaces, fragmentation of packets is supported on RTEP interfaces, but it is recommended to use jumbo frames to minimize fragmentation and improve performance so the Edge node can fragment packets traveling across locations if client-server MTU is larger than RTEP MTU. However, Edge Node RTEP traffic is set with the DNF (Do not Fragment) flag so physical devices cannot fragment packets if their MTU is lower than RTEP MTU. Hence, it becomes really important to ensure RTEP MTU is set correctly so it is supported by physical devices.

Federation Regions

Regions in NSX Federation is a logical construct that defines the scope of the boundary of security services (Groups and DFW) across different locations. Region does not apply to network services and only applies to the security section. By default, NSX Federation creates a Global region that includes all LMs onboarded to NSX Federation and one region specific to LM containing only individual LM of location. It is possible to create additional regions with individual LM or multiple LMs. *Figure* 13.3 shows one Global region spanning across all three locations and two additional regions with one spanning across locations A, B, and another region with location C only. Group and DFW policies are tied to specific regions and pushed to locations part of the configured region only.

Onboarding NSX Federation

The last section discussed different communication flows between components across multiple locations, so how these communication channels are established? This is where NSX Federation onboarding comes into play. On a high level, the onboarding process involves multiple steps as follows:

1. Deploy the NSX Global Manager appliance and configure the NSX Global Manager cluster.
2. Make the Global Manager active on the primary location.
3. (Optional) Add a standby Global Manager to sync configuration on a secondary location for high availability.
4. (Optional) Create RTEP Pool and configure RTEP MTU.
5. Add locations by onboarding the NSX Manager.
6. (Optional) Configure networking on the Edge cluster if stretch network services are required. This step is not required for security-only management.

7. (Optional) Import objects from the Local Manager (NSX Manager) to the Global Manager.

Let's cover these steps in more detail.

Deploying NSX Global Manager

NSX Global Manager deployment is mostly the same as NSX Manager deployment with differences in roles selected during OVA deployment. There is no different OVA file for NSX Global Manager and the same OVA file downloaded earlier for NSX Manager deployment is used to deploy NSX Global Manager.

Step 1: Login into the vCenter server with privileges to deploy the OVA template or ask help from a vSphere administrator. Select the desired cluster/host/resource pool in the vCenter server and use the option **`Deploy OVF Template`** by clicking **`Action`** to begin deployment. This will open a dialogue box to **`Deploy OVF Template`**, as shown in *Figure 13.4*. Click **`Local File`** and use **`Upload Files`** option to provide the location of the OVF template stored on the local desktop. Click **`Next`** to continue.

***Figure 13.4**: Deploy Global Manager OVF file*

Step 2: Provide the **`name`** of the Global Manager virtual machine and select the VM folder location in vCenter Inventory. *Figure* 13.5 shows an example of Global Manager getting deployed with the same name **`sa-gmgr-01`** in the VM folder Discovered virtual machine (default created in vCenter server). Click **`Next`** to select compute resources, for example, ESXi host/Cluster/Resource Pool, and click **`Next`** to continue. Review the OVF template information and click **`Next`** again.

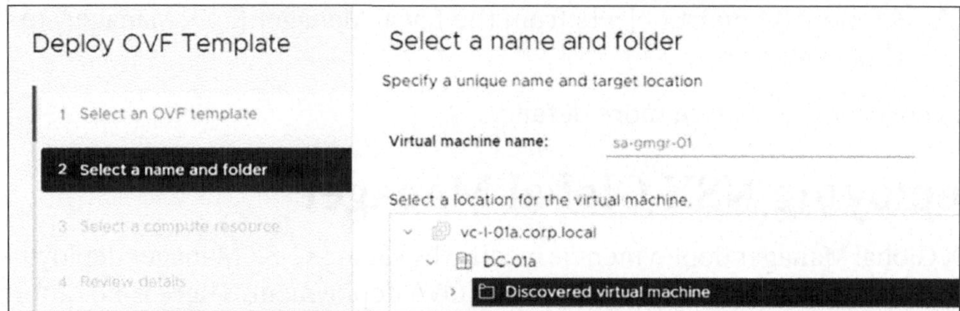

Figure 13.5: *Providing virtual machine name for vCenter server inventory*

Step 3: Under the **`Configuration`** page, select the size of the Global Manager appliance based on the environment scale and click **`Next.`** The small size of the Global Manager appliance is supported for the production use case, as shown in *Figure* 13.6.

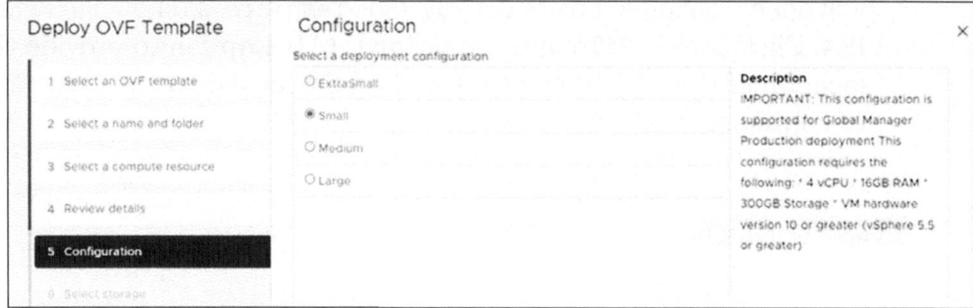

Figure 13.6: *Selecting size of Global Manager appliance*

Step 4: Select the management network port group in **`Network 1`** field using the drop-down menu and **`IP Protocol`** and then click **`Next`** to select datastore to store virtual machine files. Click **`Next`** to customize a template and ensure **`Rolename`** is selected as **`NSX Global Manager`**, as shown in *Figure* 13.7. Provide credentials and appropriate hostname, IP Address, Gateway, and subnet mask to continue.

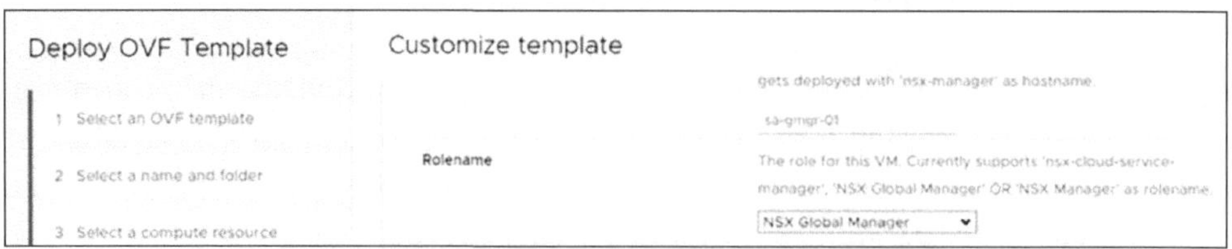

Figure 13.7: *Selecting role as NSX Global Manager*

Step 5: Click **`Next`** to review the configuration and click **`Finish`** to deploy the NSX Global Manager appliance. *Figure* 13.8 shows deployment in progress in vCenter server Tasks. After deployment is complete, power on the VM.

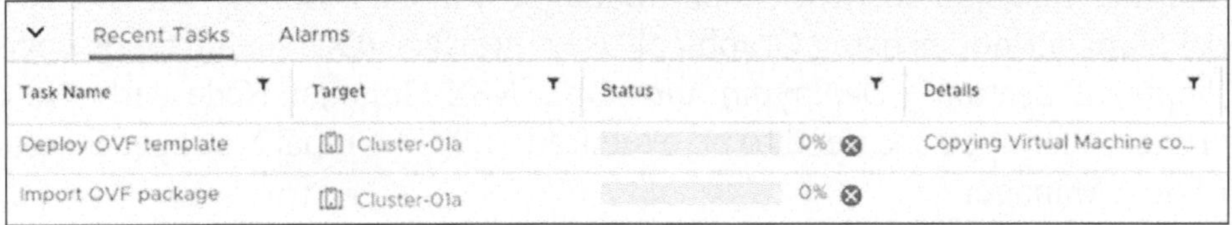

Figure 13.8: *NSX Global Manager deployment progress in vCenter server*

Step 6: Logging into NSX Global Manager using admin as username and password set during deployment. Navigate to **`System`** and the first tab opens up is **`System Overview`** with the warning **`Global Manager is not available`**, as shown in *Figure* 13.9. This is expected as this is the first appliance and no configuration has been carried out yet.

Figure 13.9: *NSX Global Manager UI*

Step 7: Click **`Global Manager Appliances`** and setup cluster virtual IP using the **`Set Virtual IP`** option, as shown in *Figure* 13.10.

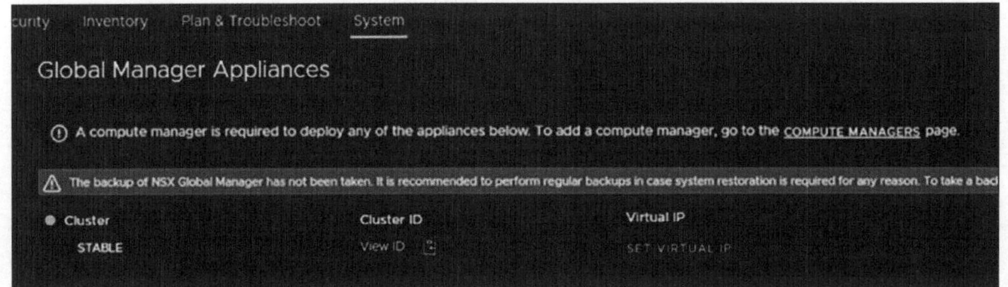

Figure 13.10: *Setting Virtual IP on NSX Global Manager*

Additional NSX Global Manager appliances can be deployed similar to the steps covered earlier using the OVA file and then joined to form a three-node cluster with the help of the join command covered earlier in *Chapter 2, Section - Creating* NSX *Management Cluster using* CLI. Another option is to register vCenter server as compute manager in NSX Global Manager and then deploy additional NSX Global Manager nodes using Graphical User Interface (GUI) using steps covered in *Chapter 2, Section - Deploying Additional* NSX *Manager Node* with the only difference, these actions need to be executed on NSX Global Manager instead of NSX Local Manager.

Configuring NSX Global Manager

Before NSX Managers can be onboarded to NSX Federation, NSX Global Manager needs to be enabled for NSX Federation with the following steps:

Step 1: Login into NSX **Global Manager** deployed on the primary location that needs to be set as active using admin credentials. Navigate to **System** and click **Location Manager**. Click **Make Active**, similar to *Figure* 13.11, to configure this Global Manager as active.

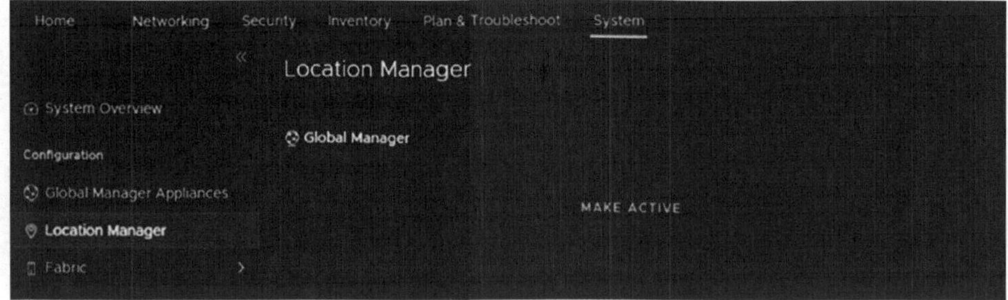

Figure 13.11: *Configuring Global Manage as active*

Step 2: Provide the Global Manage Name to identify GM-Active in the NSX Federation environment and click **Save.** *Figure* 13.12 shows **GM-Site-A** being made active in the NSX Federation.

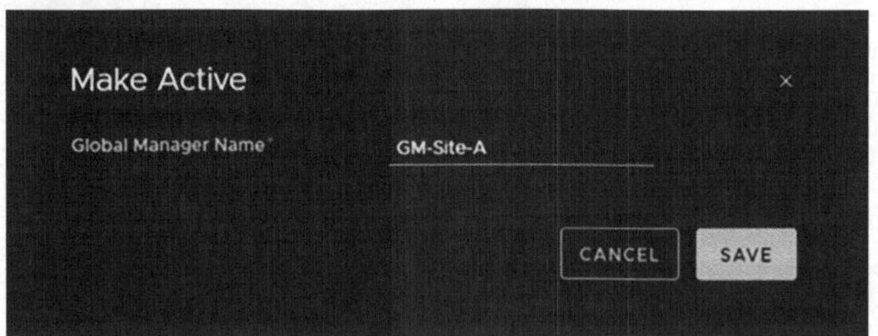

Figure 13.12: *Configuring NSX Global Manager name*

Step 3: After NSX **`Global Manager`** successfully becomes Active, additional options are visible in the Location Manager menu. These additional options are to **`ADD STANDBY GLOBAL MANAGER`** and onboard **new locations**, as shown in *Figure* 13.13.

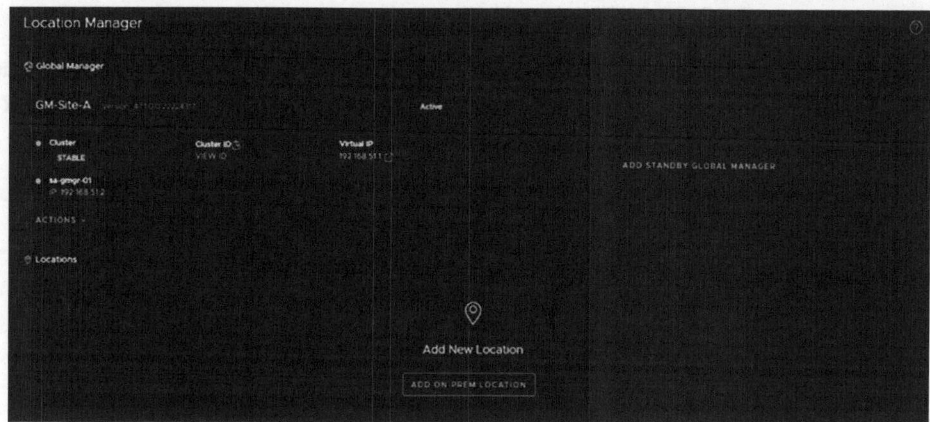

Figure 13.13: *Additional options to configure NSX Federation*

Step 4: Before adding a standby Global Manager or any Local Manager, it is required to retrieve SHA256 Thumbprint of the cluster being added into the Active Global Manager. Login into standby Global Manager VIP via SSH session and run the command **`get certificate cluster thumbprint`** to retrieve thumbprint. *Figure* 13.14 shows an example output of said command on GM.

```
sb-sgmgr-01> get certificate cluster thumbprint
Wed Oct 11 2023 UTC 14:48:45.935
478d17f42fa6c77acf86c44bf83415e9d39af47ff0714198823044032c5f8756
```

Figure 13.14: *Retrieving cluster thumbprint using SSH session*

Step 5: While logged into Active NSX Global Manager, click **`Add Standby Global Manager`** in the **`Location Manager`** view to add additional GM-Standby by providing the following information:

a. **`Global Manager Name`**: Provide an appropriate name to identify the standby Global Manager in NSX Federation.

b. **`FQDN/IP`**: Provide the IP address or fully qualified domain name of NSX Global Manager. It is recommended to use cluster VIP here.

c. **Username**: Provide admin username.

d. **Password**: Provide admin password.

e. **SHA-256 Thumbprint**: Provide the output of the command from the previous step.

Click **Check Version Compatibility** to validate the connection to the standby Global Manager. *Figure* 13.15 shows an example configuration of standby Global Manager GM-Site-B being added to active Global Manager.

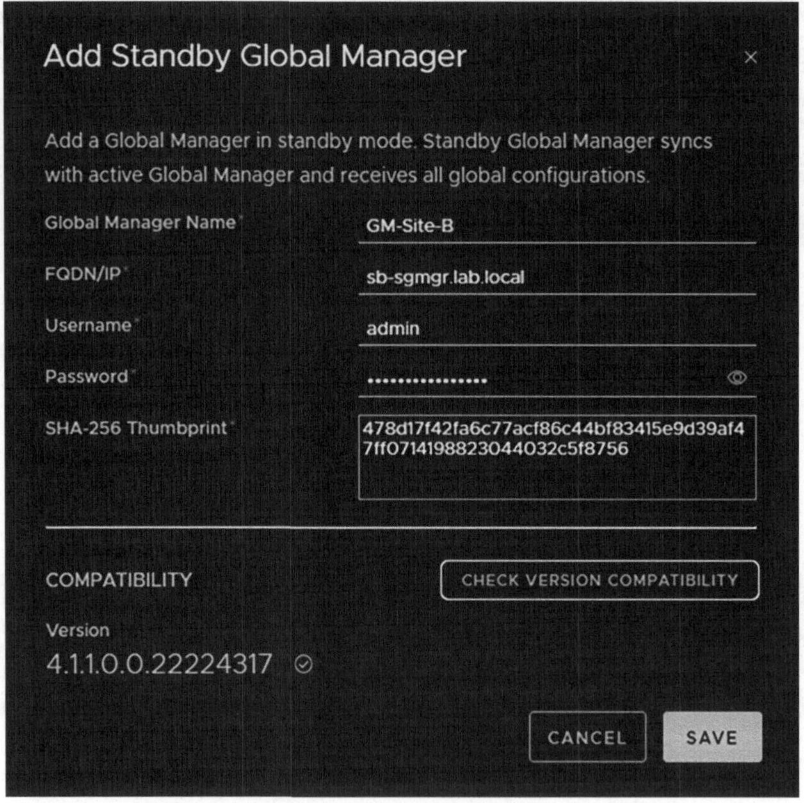

Figure 13.15: *Adding a standby Global Manager*

Step 6: Post successful version compatibility check, the **Save** button will become available. Click **Save** to add standby Global Manager. Allow one to two minutes to synchronize configurations between GM-Active and GM-Standby and the connection to become stable. *Figure* 13.16 shows a standby Global Manager **GM-Site-B** added successfully to active Global Manager **GM-Site-A**.

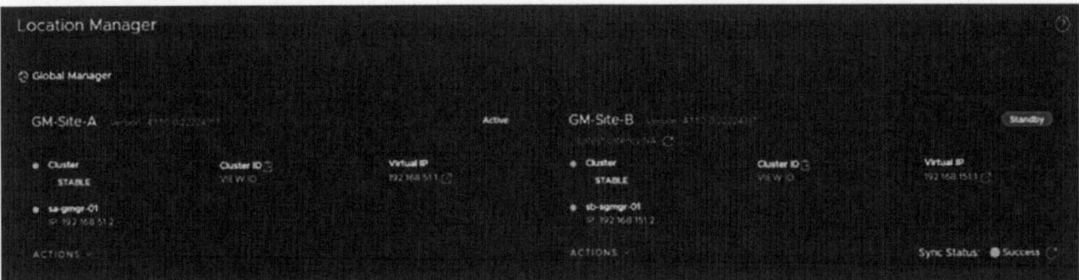

Figure 13.16: *Viewing configured Global Managers in UI*

After Global Manager has been added as Standby to active Global Manager, all options to configure any setting on standby Global Manager become greyed out and it goes into read-only mode. All the changes from GM-Active will be synced to GM-Standby, except vIDM/LDAP configuration. While logged into GM-Active, configure additional settings such as User Management or Backups similar to the configuration on NSX Manager.

Pre-Configuring RTEP

Another important step is to configure RTEP Pool and MTU on Local Managers if network services require to be spanned across multiple locations. This step needs to be performed on each individual NSX Manager responsible for a specific location.

Login into NSX Manager with admin privileges. Navigate to **`Networking`** menu and click **`IP Address Pools`** in the left-side navigation panel. Click **`Add IP Address`** Pool to add a new IP Pool for RTEP IP allocations similar to *Figure* 13.17.

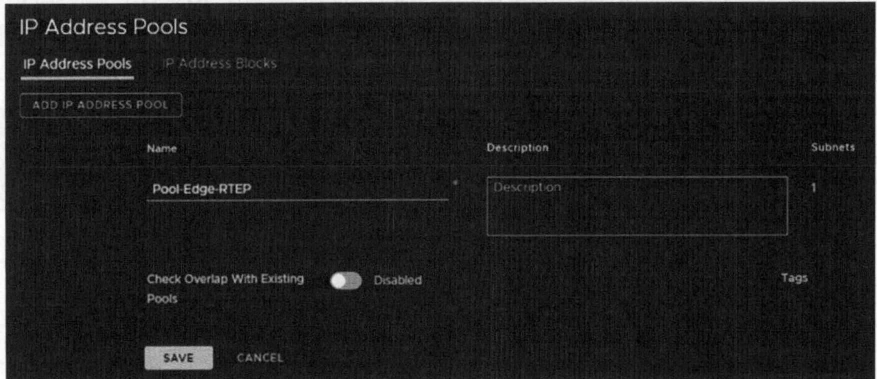

Figure 13.17: *Adding a RTEP IP Pool in NSX Manager*

While logged into NSX Manager, navigate to **`System`** and click **`Settings`** under **`Fabric`** to view **`Global Fabric Settings`**. By default, NSX configures **`RTEP MTU`** as 1700, as shown in *Figure* 13.18. This MTU value can be changed by clicking Edit and setting it to an appropriate value supported by physical devices such as 1500.

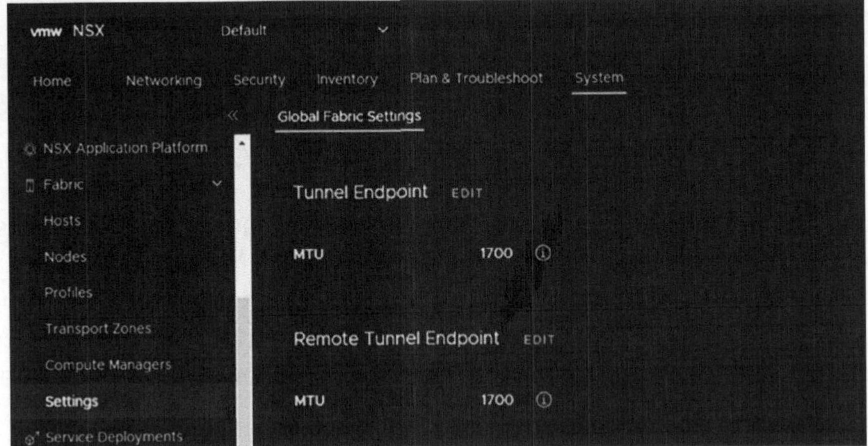

Figure 13.18: *Configuring RTEP MTU value*

Perform these steps on all NSX Managers that need to be onboarded to NSX Federation.

Onboarding NSX Local Manager

The final step in NSX Federation onboarding is to add locations in it by onboarding NSX Managers in Active Global Manager. Here are the steps:

Step 1: Login into NSX Manager VIP via SSH session and run the command **get certificate cluster thumbprint** to retrieve thumbprint. *Figure* 13.19 shows an example output of the said command on NSX Manager.

```
sa-nsxmgr-01> get certificate cluster thumbprint
Wed Oct 11 2023 UTC 14:52:25.863
7464d52609f2ac717fa5858e502a269ad7e5d3c9e85e7be850e2346a6396362e
```

Figure 13.19: *Retrieving thumbprint from NSX Manager*

Step 2: While logged into Active NSX Global Manager, click **`Add On-Prem Location`** in the Location Manager view, as shown in *Figure* 13.20, to add Local Managers.

Figure 13.20: *Adding Local Manager in NSX Federation*

Step 3: Provide the following information to add NSX Manager as Local Manager in NSX Federation:

a. **`Location Name`**: Provide an appropriate name to identify the NSX Manager in the NSX Federation.
b. **`FQDN/IP`**: Provide the IP address or fully qualified domain name of NSX Manager. It is recommended to use cluster VIP here.
c. **`Username`**: Provide admin username.
d. **`Password`**: Provide admin password.
e. **`SHA-256 Thumbprint`**: Provide the output of the command from step 1.

Click **`Check Version Compatibility`** to validate the connection to NSX Manager. *Figure* 13.21 shows an example configuration of NSX Manager **`LM-Site-A`** being added to the active Global Manager.

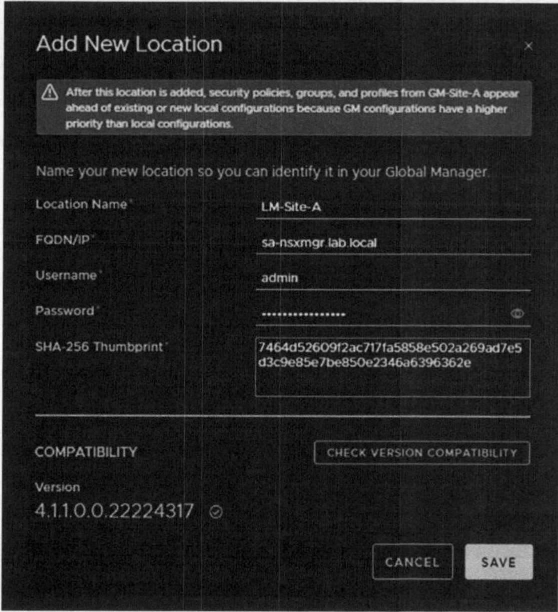

Figure 13.21: *Example configuration for adding Local Manager*

Step 4: Click **`Save`** to add NSX Local Manager. It will take a couple of minutes of sync configuration between NSX Global Manager and NSX Local Manager. You can safely acknowledge the warning about Transport Zone not visible on NSX Manager, as shown in *Figure* 13.22.

Figure 13.22: *Viewing configured NSX Local Manager on GM-Active*

Step 5: Click **`Networking`** to configure RTEP on Edge cluster for specific Local Manager. It may give an **`Error`** that **`No Edge Clusters found`** and search indexes are being re-created similar to *Figure* 13.23. If such is the case, give it a minute or two for NSX to finish processing changes.

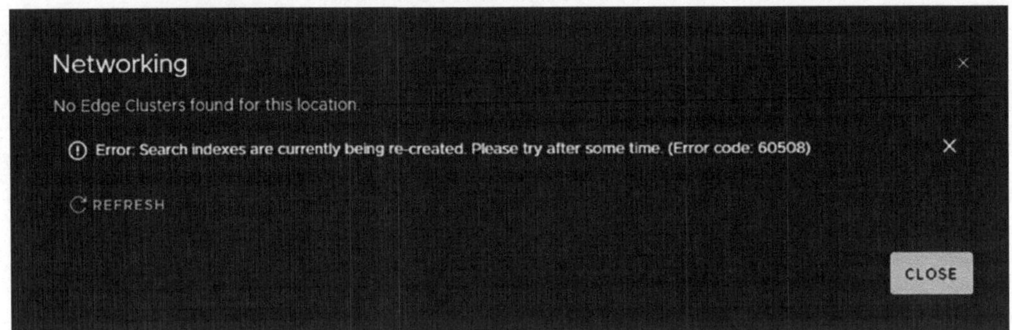

Figure 13.23: *Error while configuring RTEP on Edge Cluster*

Step 6: Click **`Refresh`** to reload the **`Networking`** view. If NSX Manager is properly configured, it will show the Edge Cluster currently configured in NSX Manager. *Figure* 13.24 shows Edge Cluster **`LAB-EC-A-01`** available in Local Manager LM-Site-A for RTEP configuration. Click **`CONFIGURE`**, which takes you to the QuickStart menu for RTEP configuration.

***Figure 13.24:** Viewing Edge Clusters available for RTEP configuration*

Step 7: It will bring to **`Configure Edge Nodes for Stretch Networking`** view in Local Manager. Select the **`Edge Cluster`** using the drop-down menu and select **`Edge nodes`** to be configured with RTEPs. Select the **`Edge Switch`** using the drop-down menu, provide **`RTEP VLAN`**, and select **`IP Pool for RTEP`** configured earlier. Click **`Save`** to configure RTEPs on Edge nodes.

Figure 13.25 shows an example configuration for RTEP configuration on Edge Cluster **`LAB-EC-A-01`** with Edge Switch as default **`nsxHostSwitch`**, **`RTEP VLAN 102`**, and IP **`Pool Pool-Edge-RTEP`** created earlier in the previous section.

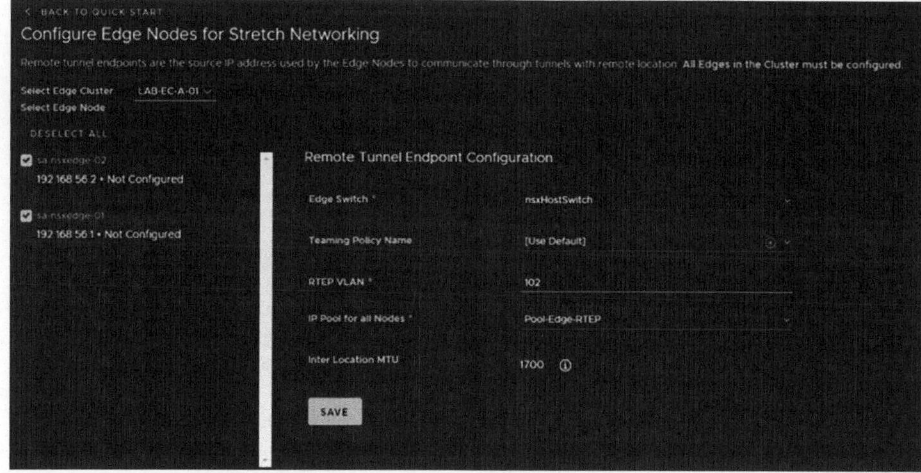

***Figure 13.25:** Configuring RTEP on Edge nodes*

Step 8: NSX UI displays a green message with information that Edge nodes are successfully configured for stretch networking similar to *Figure* 13.26.

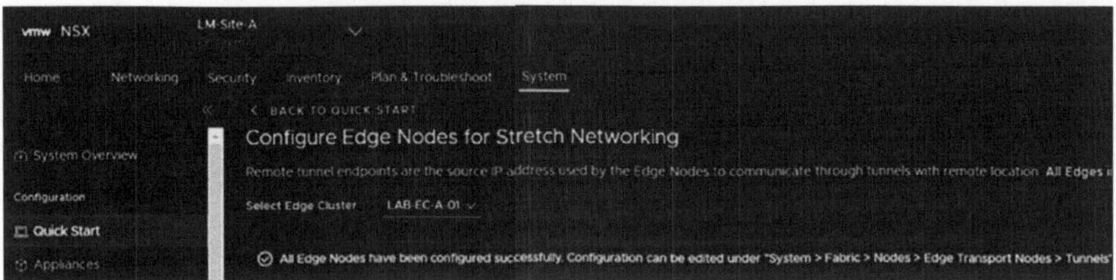

Figure 13.26: *Viewing configured RTEPs on Edge nodes*

In order to view RTEP tunnels created on Edge nodes, navigate to **`Nodes`** under **`Fabric`** and select the **`Edge node`**. It will show the Remote TEP configuration as well as tunnels established with remote Edge nodes.

Importing Configuration from Local Managers

This is an optional step to promote objects configured on Local Manager to Global Manager so that they can be managed through Global Manager only. One important point to remember here is Import option is available one time only. If you opt to Not Import objects from NSX Local Manager, NSX Global Manager asks for confirmation, as shown in *Figure* 13.27, and saves your decision. After this, no more import can be performed from a specific Local Manager.

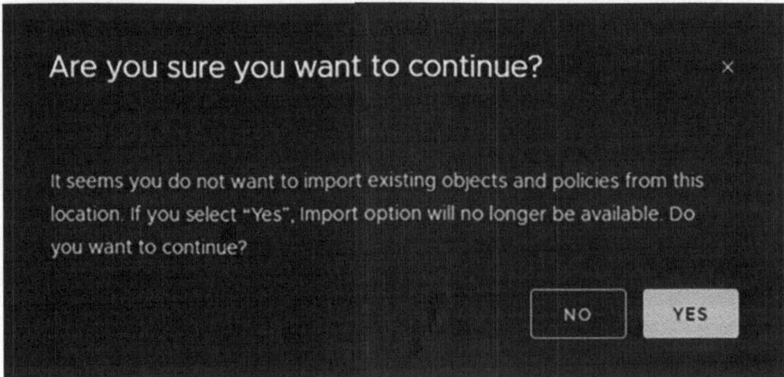

Figure 13.27: *Providing confirmation to not import objects from LM*

Step 1: Ensure you are logged into Active Global Manager with admin privileges. If continuing from the previous section, ensure to change the view to Global Manager instead of On-Prem view as post onboarding of LMs it is possible to manage multiple NSX environments from a single window, as shown in *Figure* 13.28.

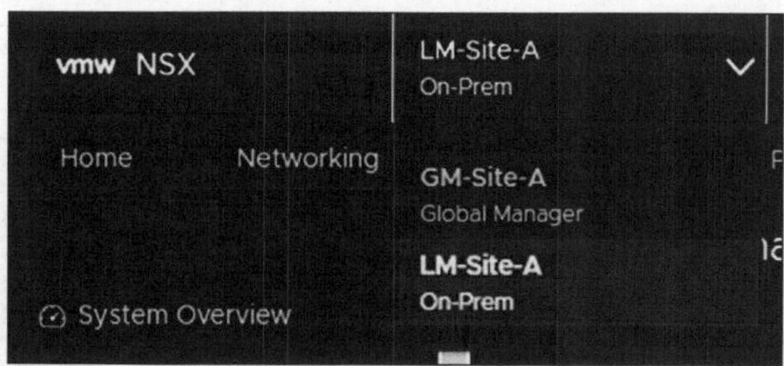

Figure 13.28: *Navigating between Global Manager and On-Prem view*

Step 2: Navigate to `System` view and click `Location Manager`. Under `Locations`, the newly onboarded NSX Manager will show a prompt to import objects with options `No, Thanks`, or `Import`, as shown in *Figure* 13.29. As described before, this is a one-time option, and if selected `No, Thanks`, future import cannot be performed.

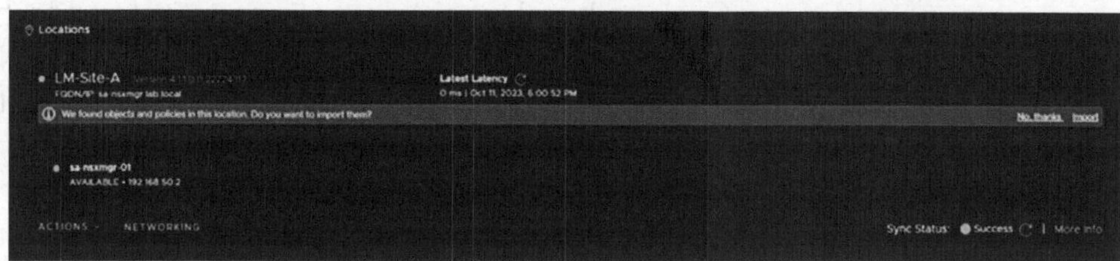

Figure 13.29: *Importing objects from NSX Local Manager*

Step 3: NSX Global Manager query for the last backup status on NSX Local Manager before doing an import operation. If the last backup status is `failed` or `not available`, then `PROCEED TO IMPORT` option will be greyed out and the Global Manager will deny to progress further with the import operation, as shown in *Figure* 13.30.

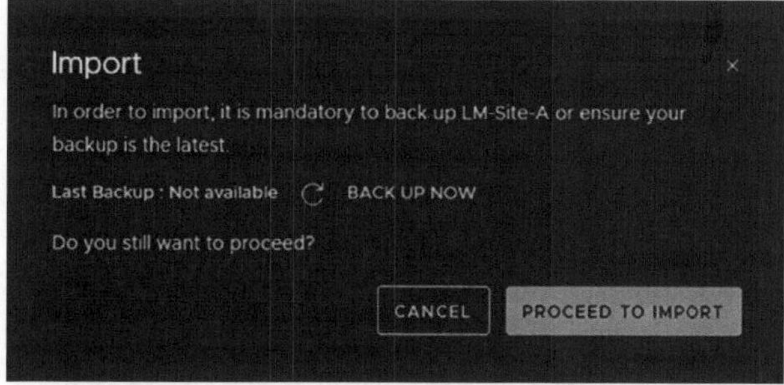

Figure 13.30: *Import option greyed out due to failed/no backup status*

Step 4: After backup is successfully taken on NSX Local Manager, click `Refresh` button and `PROCEED TO IMPORT` will be available. *Figure* 13.31

shows that after taking a successful backup on NSX Local Manager, **PROCEED TO IMPORT** is available to click.

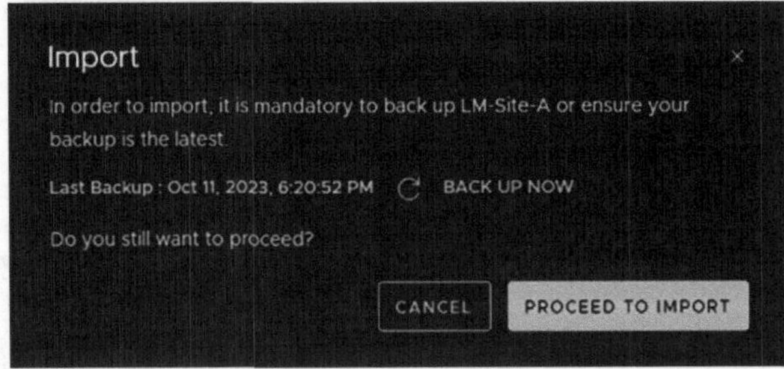

Figure 13.31: *View after successful backup of NSX Local Manager*

Step 5: The next window displays different objects that can be imported into NSX Global Managers, such as Tier0/Tier1 gateways, segments, groups, and more. Optionally, select either **Prefix** or **Suffix** to add while importing objects in Global Manager to uniquely identify them in NSX Federation, as shown in *Figure* 13.32. Also, if any object not supported in NSX Global Manager will be skipped during import operation, for example, VRF gateways are not supported in NSX Global Manager so they will not be imported if configured on NSX Local Manager. *Figure* 13.32 shows no entities found as Local Manger is a newly deployed appliance with no networking configured on it.

Figure 13.32: *Viewing objects being imported in* NSX GM

Step 6: Click **`NEXT`** to continue and NSX GM will show a final summary of the total objects being imported from NSX Local Manager. Click **`IMPORT`** to start importing from LM to GM, as shown in *Figure* 13.33.

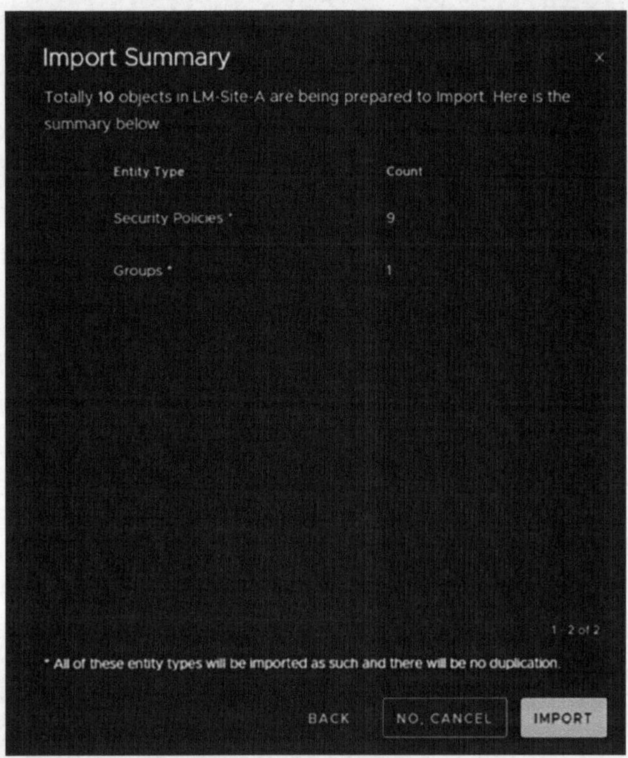

***Figure* 13.33:** *Viewing summary of objects imported into GM*

Step 7: After successful import of objects, NSX GM shows the status as successful, as shown in *Figure* 13.34.

***Figure* 13.34:** *Successful import of objects in NSX Global Manager*

These steps can be repeated to add multiple locations in the NSX Federation by onboarding multiple NSX Local Managers up to a maximum of eight. *Figure* 13.35 shows an example where an additional NSX Local Manager **`LM-Site-B`** has been added to span network and security services across two locations.

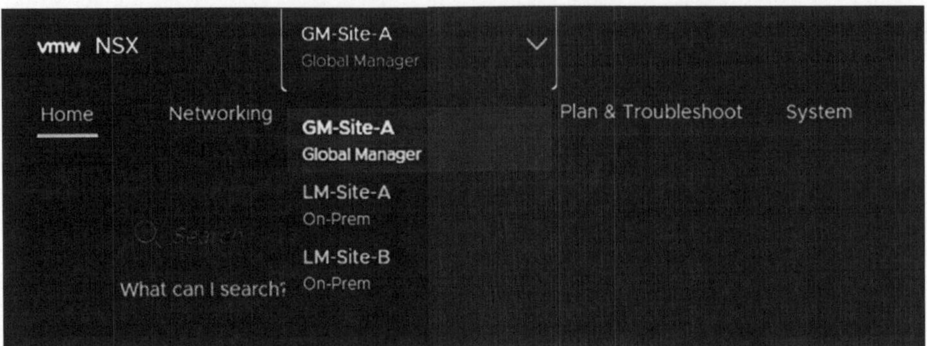

Figure 13.35: *Viewing and managing multiple locations from single console*

If logged into NSX Manager for a specific location and viewed configured **`User Role Assignment`** by navigating to **`User Management`** in **`System`** view, you will notice additional Principal Identity Users configured after onboarding NSX Manager to Global Managers. These Identity users are responsible for synchronizing configuration from the Global Manager to the Local Manager. Also, there will be an additional principal identity with Auditor access for NSX Local Manager in different locations to synchronize group membership and segment tables by reading the NSX Manager database, as shown in *Figure* 13.36.

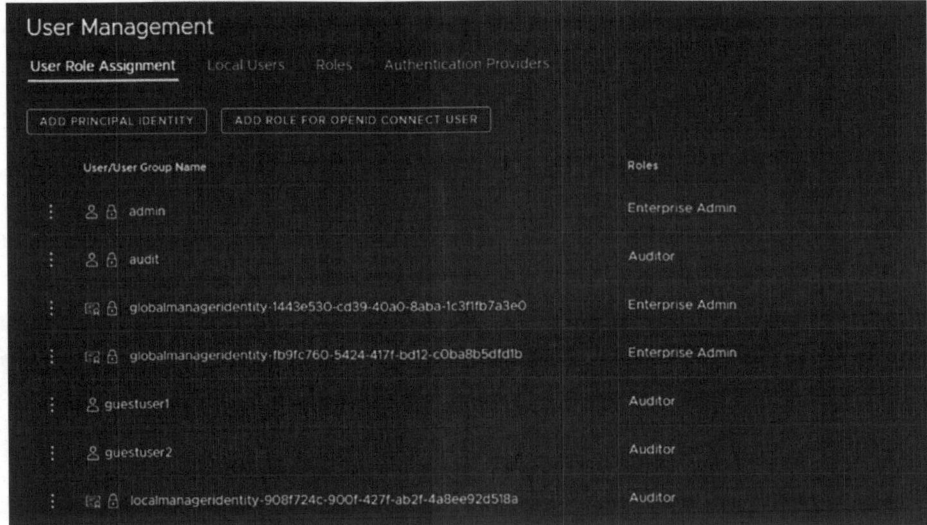

Figure 13.36: *Different principal identities configured by NSX Global Manager*

This completes the NSX Federation onboarding and the environment is now ready to consume different network and security services. Let's explore, different networking options available for consumption in the NSX Federation environment.

NSX Federation Networking

NSX Federation supports stretching networking constructs Tier0 gateway, Tier1 gateway, and Segments across locations. These constructs can be defined as stretched (spanned across multiple locations) or not stretched (present in a single location). In NSX Federation, the following services are supported on the Tier1 gateway:

- NAT
- Gateway Firewall
- IPv6
- DHCP
- DNS

NSX Federation supports different network topologies that can be configured to meet organization requirements. However, certain rules need to be followed while deploying network topology, as follows:

- GM Tier1 gateway in DR (Distributed Routing) only mode should have a span equal to the span of the attached Tier0 gateway.
- GM Tier1 gateway in SR (with services) should have a span equal to or is a subset of the span of the attached Tier0 gateway.
- GM overlay-backed segment should have a span equal to the span of the attached Tier0 or Tier1 gateway.
- GM overlay-backed segment is realized when it is connected to Tier0 or Tier1 gateway.

Based on the aforementioned rules, *Figure* 13.37 shows a variety of possible network topologies configured in the NSX Federation environment. At the top, the Tier0 gateway is stretched across all three locations and can have attachments from Tier1 running in a single location, across multiple locations, or Tier1 DR only. For Tier1 with SR, their span is defined by locations added to them during configuration, whereas Tier1-DR will span across all locations equal to the span of Tier0. If Tier0 is not stretched, then it can have attachments from Tier1 with SR and Tier1-DR only, but their span needs to be limited to the span of Tier0, that is, specific to location. A Tier1 spanned across multiple locations cannot have an attachment to Tier0 whose span is less than the Tier1 gateway.

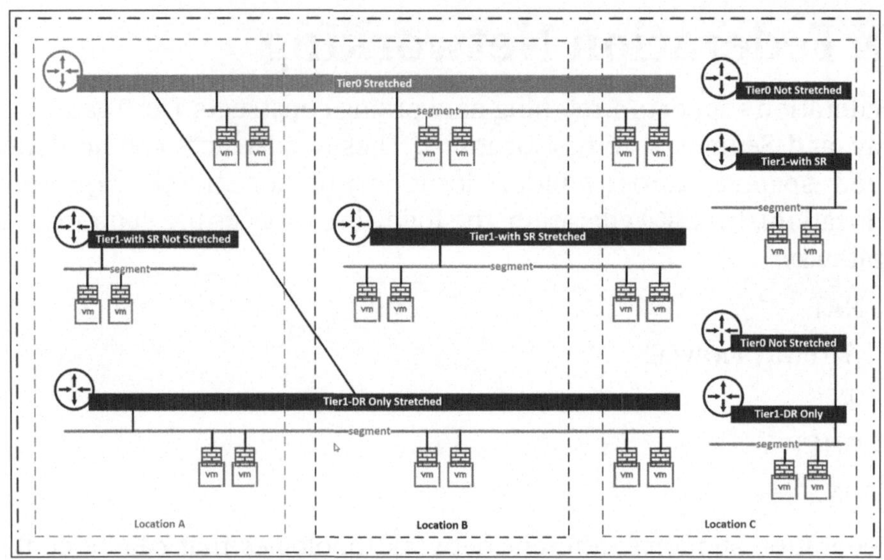

Figure 13.37: *Different network topologies in NSX Federation*

Also, as covered earlier, the span of a segment is always equal to the span of the Tier0 or Tier1 gateway to which it is attached and does not have individual location configuration.

Stretched Layer 2 Deployment

In NSX Federation, layer 2 communication across locations is handled by Edge nodes using RTEPs instead of creating tunnels between hypervisor hosts. This aims to avoid the management of multiple tunnels and BFD sessions between all hypervisor hosts across locations. The Edge node pair is selected based on the segment attached to the next hop gateway. If the segment is attached to the Tier1 gateway in DR-only mode, then two Edge nodes from the Edge cluster hosting the Tier0 gateway to which Tier1 DR is connected are used. If the segment is connected to Tier1 with SR gateway, then the same two Edge nodes that host Tier1 SR are used to handle cross-location traffic on the stretched layer 2 segment. And, if the segment is directly connected to Tier0 running in Active-Active or Active-Standby, then the same Edge nodes hosting Tier0 gateway are used for cross -location traffic communication.

Figure 13.38 shows an example of a stretched-segment spanning across Location A and B. The stretched segment is created from the Global Manager, which, in turn, sends the request to the Local Manager to create a local segment. the Local Manager creates a local segment and assigns a VNI. This VNI can be different on locations, as *Figure* 13.38 shows the VNI used at Location A is 5001, whereas at

Location B is 6001. In addition, the Global Manager selects the VNI for RTEP; in *Figure* 13.38, this is 5002. The Local Manager then performs the VNI mapping in the form of TEP-VNI:RTEP:VNI on Edge nodes to send traffic between locations.

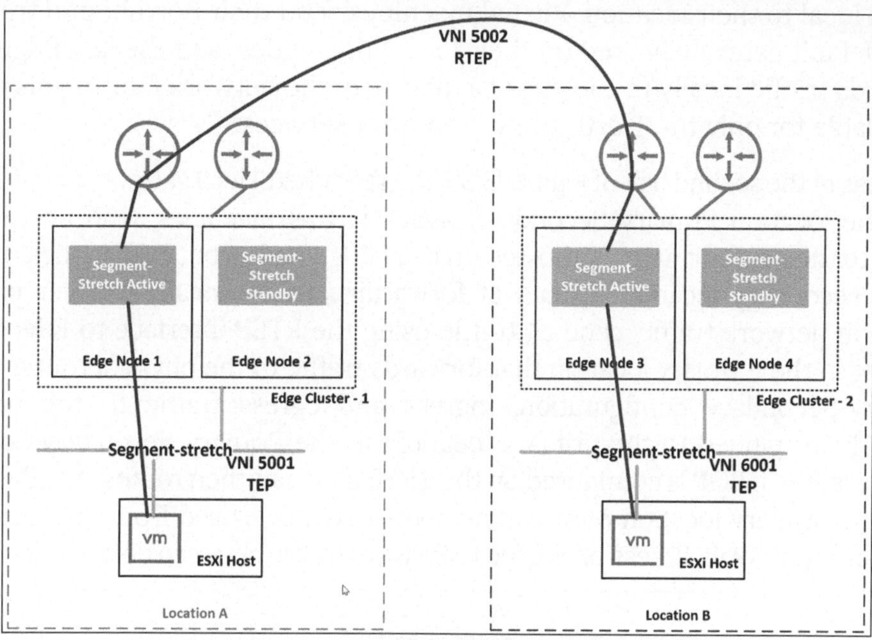

Figure 13.38: *VNI Mapping for stretched segment*

Multilocation Routing Deployment

In stretch networking, a location can be defined as either the Primary location or the Secondary location. This is applicable for both Tier0 and Tier1 (with SR) gateways. This results in different combinations of Tier0 running in Active-Active or Active-Standby HA mode with Primary or Secondary location configuration. *Table* 13.2 summarizes these different combinations and their supportability with NSX Federation.

Gateway	Location All Primary	Location Primary/Secondary
Tier0 Active-Active	Supported	Supported
Tier0 Active-Standby	Not Supported	Supported
Tier1 DR Only	Supported	Not Supported
Tier1 with SR	Not Supported	Supported

Table 13.2: *Multilocation routing supported configurations*

Figure 13.39 shows a stretched Tier0 gateway with locations configured as All Primary and Primary-Secondary. In the first half of *Figure* 13.39, the Tier0 gateway configured in the All Primary location will have traffic ingress and egress local to their location. Virtual machines send their northbound traffic to their default gateway hosted on their local Edge nodes, and the last Edge node forwards traffic locally to the physical device in the network fabric. This option is available for only the Tier0 gateway without services.

Whereas in the second half of *Figure* 13.39, the stretched Tier0 gateway is configured with the location Primary-Secondary. Again, virtual machines send northbound traffic to their default gateway hosted on local Edge nodes, but Edge nodes running in the secondary location instead of forwarding traffic locally to their physical device in network traffic, send all traffic using the RTEP interface to Edge nodes running in the Primary location that forwards traffic to the physical router. In the Primary-Secondary configuration, ingress and egress traffic to the physical network are pinned to the primary location. In the Primary-Secondary Location configuration, if BGP is configured on the Tier0 gateway, then routes are advertised from the primary location only, and no routes are advertised from the secondary location. Inter-SR iBGP session is used to forward traffic between different locations.

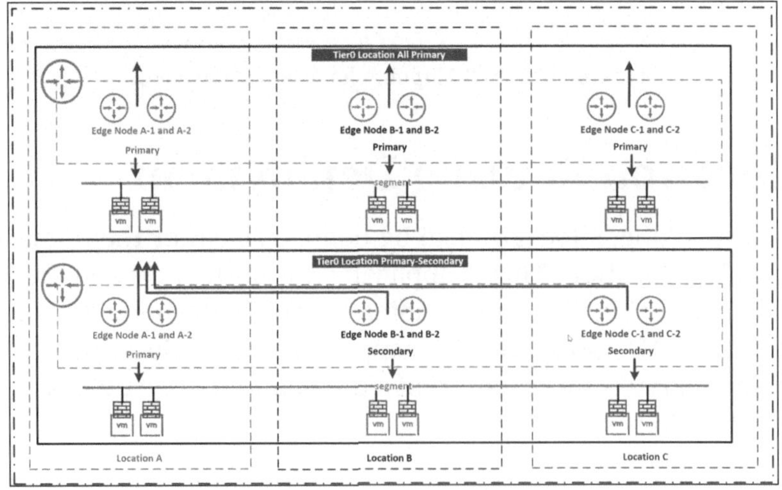

Figure 13.39: *Multilocation stretched Tier0 location configurations*

Figure 13.40 illustrates different configurations for a stretched Tier1 gateway. The first half of *Figure* 13.40 shows a Tier1 gateway running in DR-only configuration. This option is only available for the Tier1 gateway with no services configured on it. In this mode, there is no option to select configure locations as primary or secondary, and the span of the Tier1 gateway is equal to the span of the Tier0 gateway to which it connects. Virtual Machines send their northbound traffic to the default gateway hosted on the hypervisor, and the hypervisor sends traffic to the local Tier0 gateway.

The second half of *Figure* 13.40 shows a Tier1 configured with services. There is only one option for Tier1 with SR+DR, that is, locations in Primary-Secondary. There is no Location All Primary option for Tier1 with SR+DR. In this configuration, virtual machines send northbound traffic to their default gateway; however, secondary location hosting Tier1 sends traffic to primary location Edge nodes using RTEP interfaces to further forward it to Tier0 gateway.

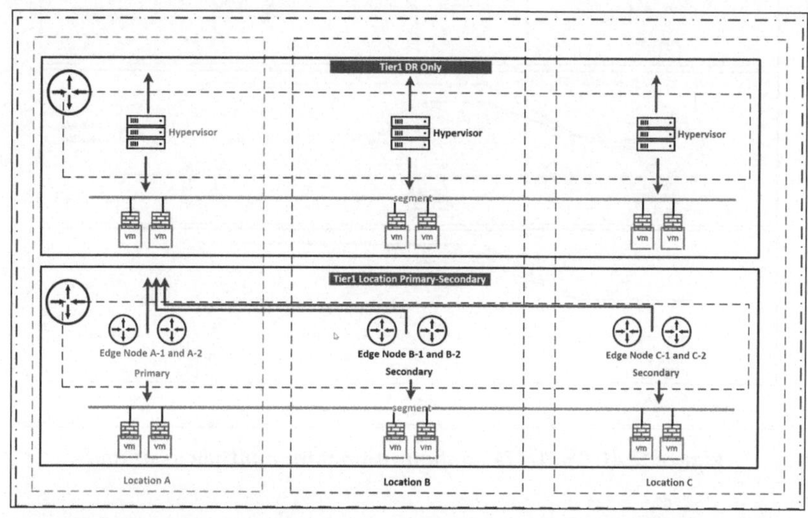

Figure 13.40: *Multilocation stretched Tier1 location configuration*

Now, within a location, Tier0 or Tier1 gateway can be configured in Active-Active or Active-Standby high availability mode, or Tier1 gateway in Distributed Routing only configuration. These topologies have been covered in great detail in *Chapter* 5, *Logical Routing – NSX Gateways*, and the same HA modes are supported in NSX Federation as well, along with different location configuration options. *Table* 13.2 provides this summary view of different HA modes supported with different location configurations.

Figure 13.41 illustrates a combined view of supported Tier0 HA configuration with location configurations. The first configuration in *Figure* 13.41 shows Tier0 configured in Active/Active HA with the Location marked as All Primary. Tier0 gateway is active on both Edge nodes, and northbound and southbound traffic is sent and received by respective Tier0 gateway in their locations. One important point to remember here is that this configuration can lead to asymmetric routing, and traffic manipulation is required to avoid asymmetric routing on physical devices.

The second and third configurations in *Figure* 13.41 are Tier0 configured as Active/Active or Active/Standby, but the location is marked as Primary/Secondary. In this configuration, all northbound and southbound is sent and received by the Tier0 gateway in the primary location, and the Tier0 gateway running in the secondary location sends traffic using RTEP interface to Tier0 in the primary location.

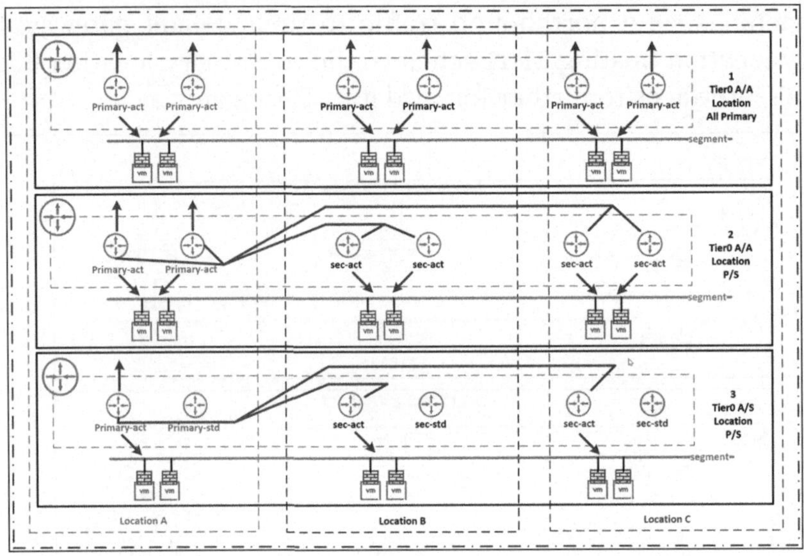

Figure 13.41: *Tier0 HA configuration with multiple locations*

Similarly, *Figure* 13.42 illustrates Tier1 HA configuration with multiple locations. There is no support for Tier1 Active-Standby with All Primary locations. Only Tier1 SR+DR is supported with a Primary/Secondary location, in which all traffic is sent to the primary location. In Tier1 DR-only configuration, traffic is forwarded locally to the Tier0 gateway.

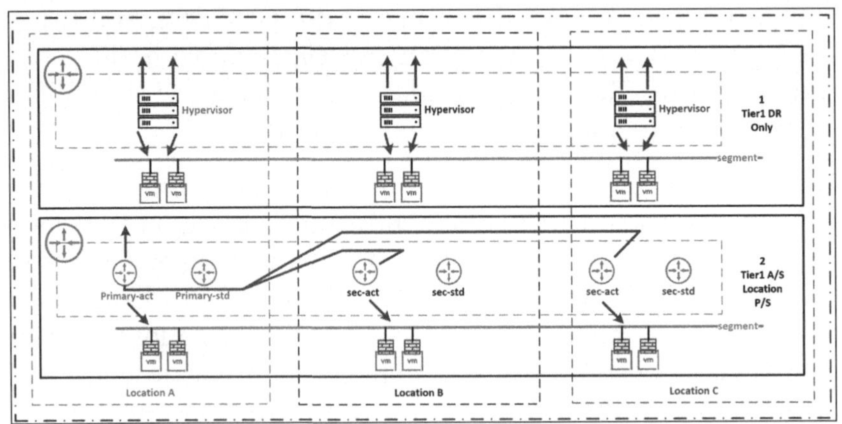

Figure 13.42: *Tier1 HA configuration with multiple locations*

Note: Coverage of detailed packet flow between different locations is beyond the scope of this book. For more information on route exchange and packet flow, please refer to the NSX Multi-Location Design Guide (Federation + Multisite) (https://communities.vmware.com/t5/VMware-NSX-Documents/NSX-T-Multi-Location-Design-Guide-Federation-Multisite/ta-p/2810327).

Configuring Tier0 Gateway

Creating and configuring networking objects such as Tier0, Tier1 gateway, and segment in NSX Federation is the same as configuring them on NSX Manager. The only difference is these objects are now created from the Global Manager to be able to be visible across locations, and they have a new section named Locations in settings. Configuration of Tier0 gateway has been discussed in great detail in *Chapter* 5, *Logical Routing – NSX Gateways*. Hence, this section covers only the differences and configurations required to successfully create the Tier0 gateway in NSX Federation.

Step 1: Login into NSX Global Manager with admin privileges and ensure you are in **Global Manager** view. Navigate to **Segments** under **Connectivity** in the **Networking** menu. Click **Add Segments** to add a new segment for uplinks of the Tier0 gateway. Notice the difference in *Figure* 13.43; there is an additional section called **Locations**. Select the Local Manager for the specific location using the drop-down menu, and then select the VLAN Transport Zone for the specific location. Provide the VLAN ID in **VLAN** and click **Save** to create the desired segment. *Figure* 13.43 shows an example configuration for segment sitea-t0-uplink in location LM-Site-A with VLAN ID 1000.

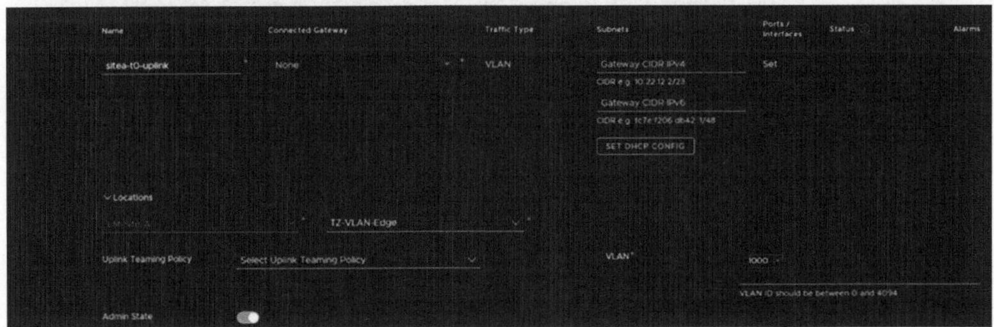

Figure 13.43: *Adding a new segment in Global Manager for Tier0 gateway*

Step 2: Similarly, create additional segments for different locations. *Figure* 13.44 shows two segments created for Tier0 uplink in Locations A and B.

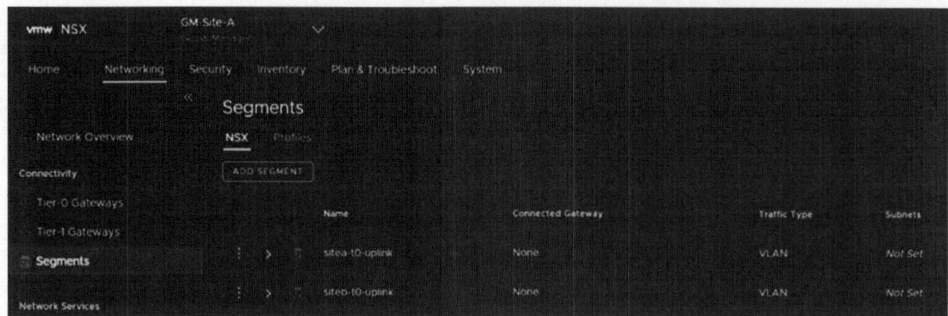

Figure 13.44: *Tier0 uplinks segments for multiple locations*

Step 3: Navigate to **`Tier-0 Gateways`** under **`Connectivity`** to create a new Tier0 gateway. Click **`Add Tier-0 Gateway`** to add a new Tier0 gateway. Under the **`Locations`** section, click **`Add Location`** to add Local Manager and RTEP configured Edge cluster using the drop-down menu.

Configuring All Location Primary

In order to create Tier0 gateway with all locations marked as Primary, ensure the toggle button in front of **`Mark all locations as Primary`** is enabled. This will ensure that locations have their mode set as Primary, as visible in *Figure* 13.45.

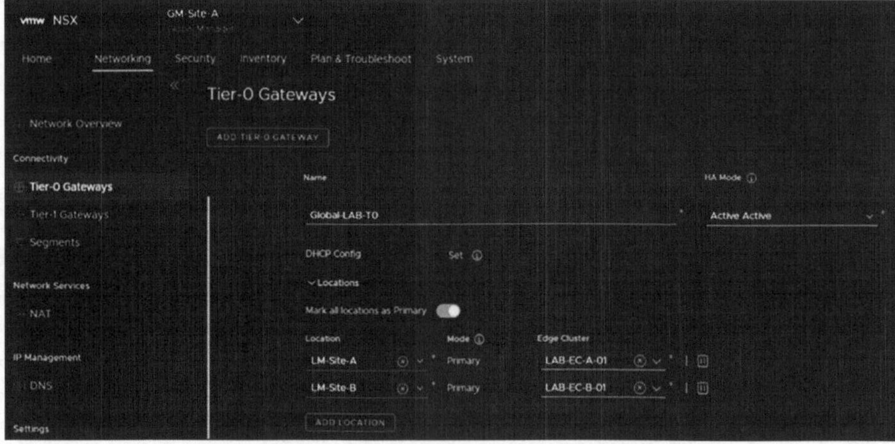

Figure 13.45: *Configure Tier0 with all location primary*

Configuring Location Primary Secondary

To configure the Tier0 gateway in a Primary-Secondary location configuration, move the toggle button **`Mark all Locations as Primary`** to the off position.

This will change the mode of locations to Primary and Secondary, as shown in *Figure* 13.46. Also, there is a **fallback preference** to set different priorities to locations, so in the event of a primary location failure, it helps NSX decide which location will become primary.

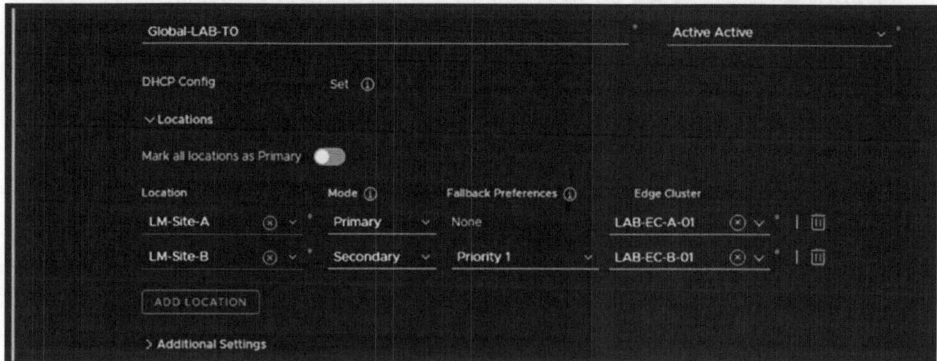

Figure 13.46: *Configuring Tier0 with Location Primary-Secondary*

Click **Save** to create the Tier0 gateway. Similar to Tier0 gateway on NSX Manager, select **Yes** to continue modifying Tier0 gateway or **No** to finish editing.

Step 4: Continuing Tier0 configuration, another important step is to add external interfaces. Click **Set** under **Interfaces** to add new interfaces similar to Tier0 on NSX Manager. An important point to remember here is if uplink segments of Tier0 gateway have been created on Local Manager, then they will not be visible while adding interfaces on Tier0 in Global Manager, as shown in *Figure* 13.47.

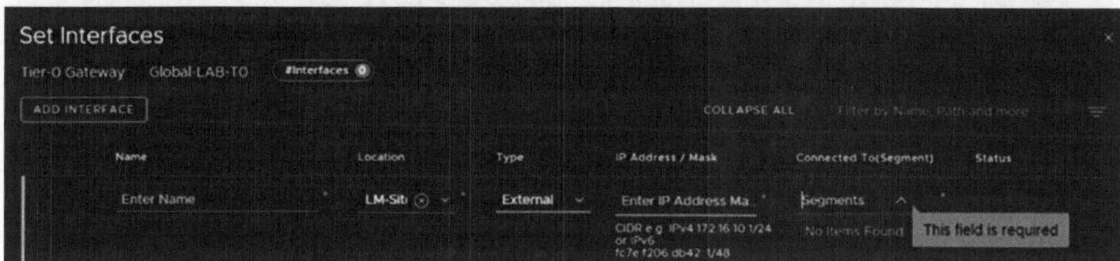

Figure 13.47: *Segments not visible to add on Tier0 gateway*

Ensure to create segments on Global Manager as covered in Step 1. *Figure* 13.48 shows an example configuration of the external interface on Tier0 gateway Global-LAB-T0. All settings are the same as Tier0 interface on NSX Manager, except now it provides an option to select **Location** using the drop-down menu to attach the Tier0 gateway interface to a specific location hosting Edge node and segment.

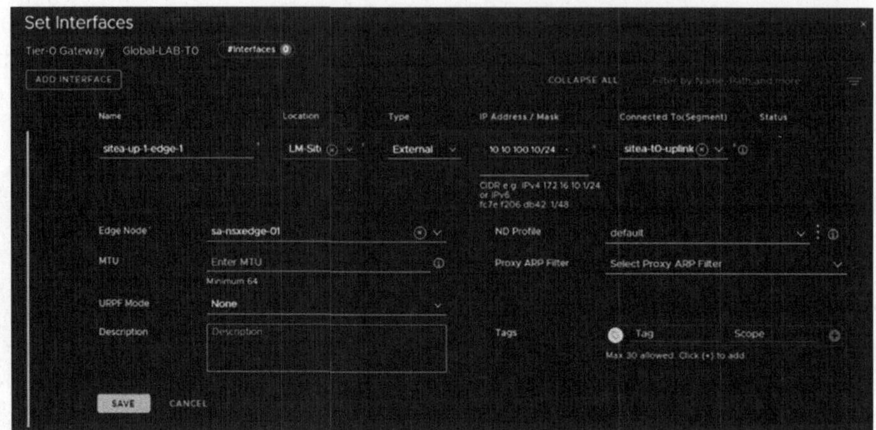

Figure 13.48: *Adding an interface on Tier0 gateway in Global Manager*

Use the **ADD INTERFACE** option to add additional external interfaces and use the **Location** option to create interfaces for all locations on a single Tier0 gateway. *Figure* 13.49 shows external interfaces created on the Tier0 gateway from both Location A and Location B.

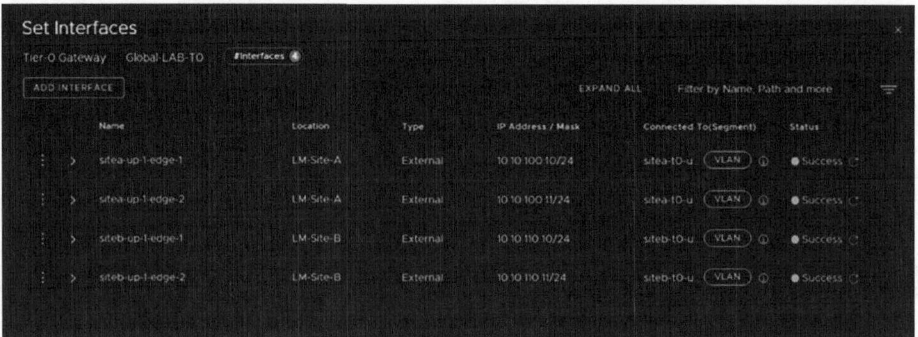

Figure 13.49: *Viewing interfaces on Tier0 gateway for multiple locations*

Step 5: Similar to Tier0 gateway configuration on NSX Manager, dynamic routing can be configured on Global Manager Tier0 gateway. However, only BGP is supported, and OSPF is not supported in NSX Federation. Expand the **BGP** section to configure BGP with all settings the same as before. The only difference is that now the Tier0 gateway on Global Manager shows **BGP Neighbors** and **Route Aggregation** for multiple locations instead of a single location. *Figure* 13.50 shows an example configuration of BGP on the Tier0 gateway.

Figure 13.50: *Configuring BGP on Tier0 gateway*

Also, BGP Neighbors configuration is the same as covered in *Chapter* 5, *Logical Routing – NSX Gateways.* with the only difference being the addition of the **`Location`** field. This field is used to select the IP address on interfaces configured earlier for a specific location. Starting NSX 4.1, it is possible to configure a different **`Neighbor Local AS`** from Tier0 Local AS; previously, it had to be the same. *Figure* 13.51 shows Neighbor Local AS is set to Yes with ASN 61646 configured, whereas Tier0 ASN is 60646.

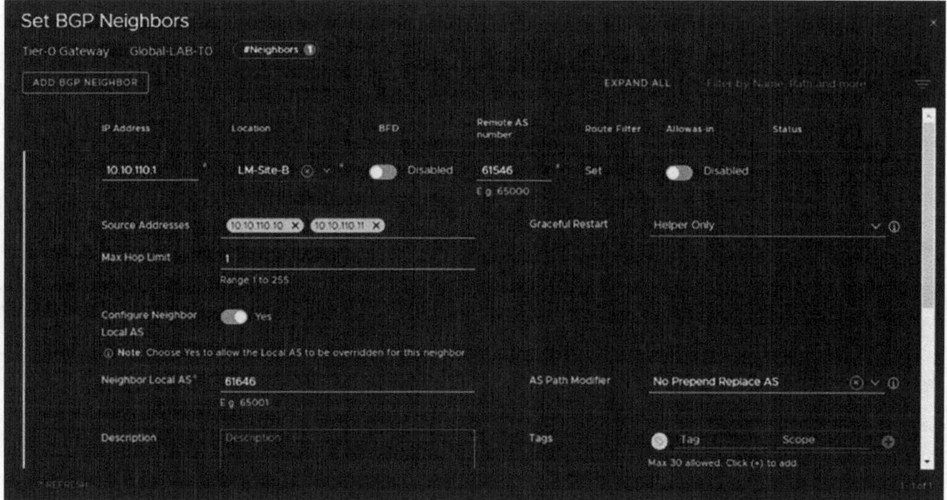

Figure 13.51: *Configuring BGP neighbor on Tier0 gateway*

Figure 13.52 shows an example snippet with BGP neighbors configured on the same Tier0 gateway for different locations A and B.

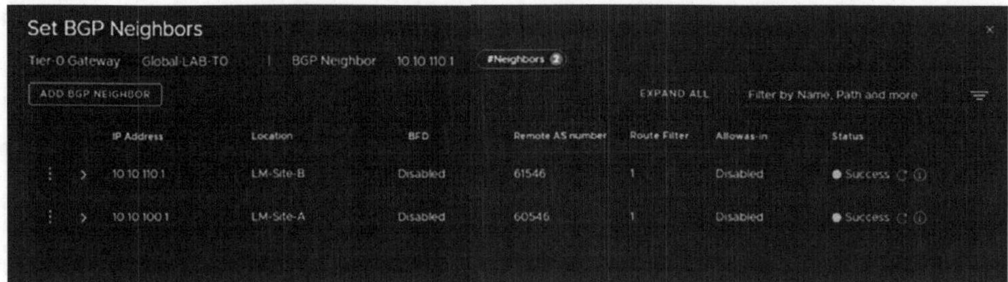

***Figure* 13.52:** *Viewing BGP Neighbors for multiple locations*

Step 6: Expand **`Route Re-Distribution`** to distribute routes learned by Tier0 gateway back into the BGP protocol. As *Figure* 13.53 shows, Route Re-Distribution needs to be configured separately for each location.

***Figure* 13.53:** *Configuring Route Re-Distribution on Tier0 gateway*

Step 7: Click **`Close Editing`** to finish modifying the Tier0 gateway. As a quick validation, click three dots and then click **`Generate BGP Summary`** to view all BGP sessions established by Tier0 SR. *Figure* 13.54 shows multiple eBGP sessions established with the physical router, as well as inter-SR iBGP sessions established with Tier0 SR hosted on other Edge nodes.

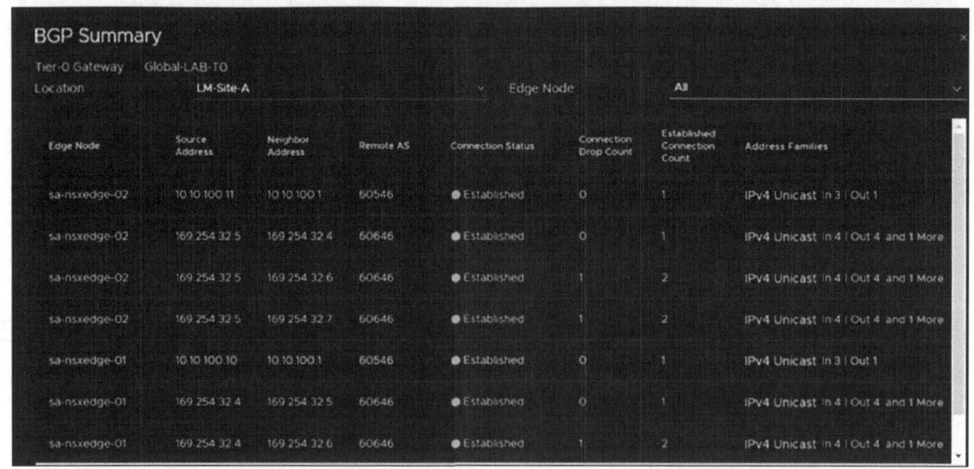

***Figure* 13.54:** *Viewing BGP session summary on Tier0 gateway*

Configuring Tier1 Gateway

Similar to Tier0 gateway, Tier1 gateways are configured very much the same as on NSX Manager with minor differences regarding the configuration of Location.

While logged into Global Manager with admin privileges, go to **`Tier-1 Gateways`** under **`Connectivity`** in the **`Networking`** Menu. Click **`ADD TIER-1 GATEWAY`** to add a new gateway, similar to *Figure* 13.55.

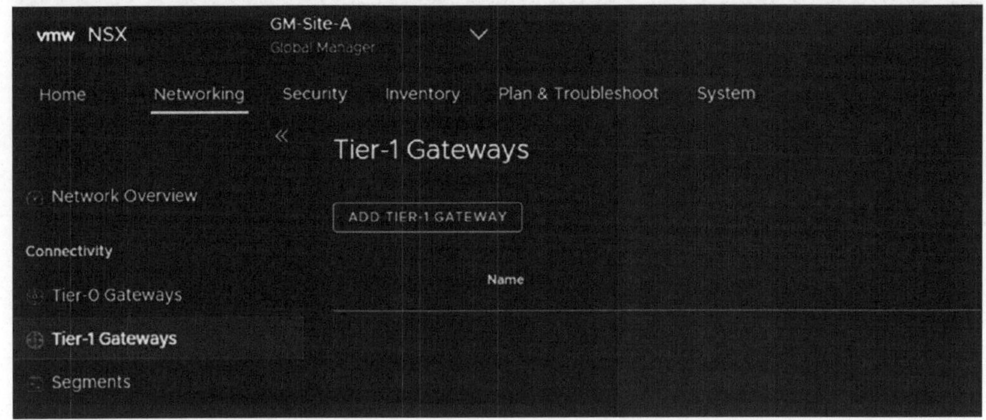

Figure 13.55: *Adding a Tier1 gateway in Global Manager*

Configuring Tier1 Distributed Only

Under **`HA Mode`**, select **`Distributed Only`**, and under **`Linked Tier-0 Gateway`**, select the Tier0 gateway configured earlier. Notice the **`Location`** section, it automatically populates all locations added in the Tier0 gateway with no option to modify them, as shown in *Figure* 13.56. Also, the **`Add Location`** option is greyed out. As covered earlier, Tier1 in DR-only configuration spans to all locations added in the Tier0 gateway to which it connects.

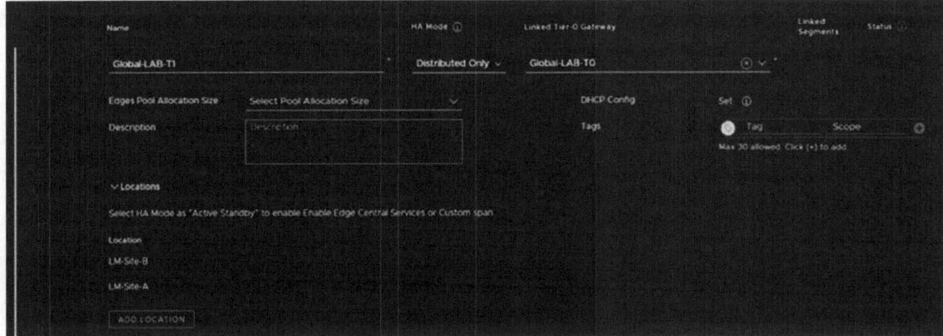

Figure 13.56: *Tier1 DR-only configuration*

Configuring Tier1 with Location Primary Secondary

Under **HA Mode**, select **Active Standby**, and under **Linked Tier-0 Gateway**, select the Tier0 gateway configured earlier. Notice the **Location** section in this scenario. Similar to the Tier0 gateway, we have the option to **Delete a Location**, **add a location,** and select which Location is Primary and which location is secondary, as shown in *Figure* 13.57 highlighted in red boxes.

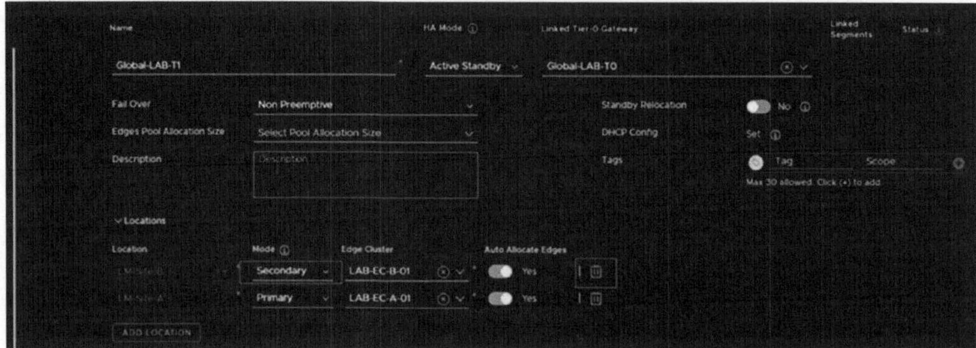

Figure 13.57: *Configuring Tier1 with Location Primary Secondary*

Expand the **Route Advertisement** section to set route advertisement to Tier0 gateway from Tier1 gateway. This is done by NSX automatically, but as an administrator, you need to toggle enable or disable which routes to be plumbed, as shown in *Figure* 13.58, which instructs NSX to plumb routes for Static, Connected Segments, Service Ports, and IPSec Local Endpoints to Tier0.

Figure 13.58: *Configuring route advertisement on Tier1 gateway*

Click **Save** to create the desired Tier1 gateway. *Figure* 13.59 shows a Tier1 gateway in a distributed-only configuration connected to the Global-LAB-T0 Tier0 gateway.

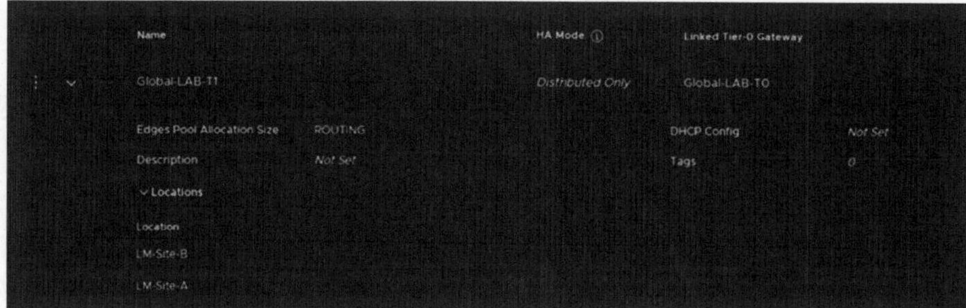

***Figure 13.59:** Viewing configured Tier1 gateway in GM*

Configuring Segments

While logged into Global Manager with admin privileges, go to **`Segments`** under **`Connectivity`** in the **`Networking`** Menu. Click **`Add Segments`** to add a new segment, as shown in *Figure* 13.60. Provide the **`name`** of the segment, select the **`next hop gateway`,** and enter the gateway IP in CIDR format. **`Locations`** are populated automatically, equal to the span of the connected gateway. Click **`Save`** to add the segment in NSX Federation and select No to deny any further modification.

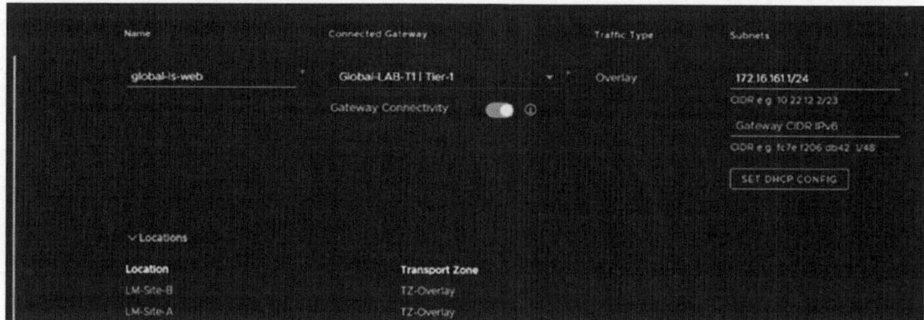

***Figure 13.60:** Adding a segment in NSX Federation*

Click **`ADD SEGMENT`** to add additional segments as per requirements. *Figure* 13.61 shows three different overlay segments configured in NSX Federation.

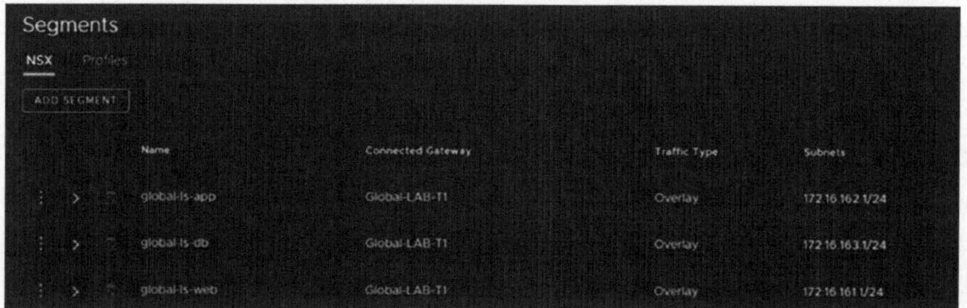

***Figure 13.61:** Viewing configured segment in NSX Federation*

Validating NSX Federation Networking

There are multiple ways to validate if NSX Federation networking is configured properly and working as expected.

One way to validate is to check if the same NSX port group is present on the vSphere distributed switch in vCenter for all locations where the said segment is spanned. For example, in the earlier example configuration, three overlay segments (**global-ls-web**, **global-ls-app**, and **global-ls-db**) were connected to **Global-LAB-T1** spanning across Locations A and B. *Figure* 13.62 shows these three segments present as port group on the vSphere distributed switch **vds-lab-a**.

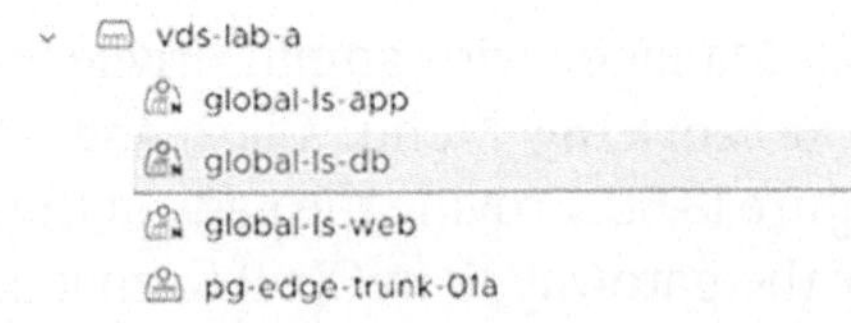

***Figure* 13.62:** NSX *port group present in Location A vCenter server*

Similarly, *Figure* 13.63 shows segments present in the vSphere distributed switch **vds-lab-b** in Location B, allowing the vSphere administrator to connect virtual machines to the same NSX segment in both locations.

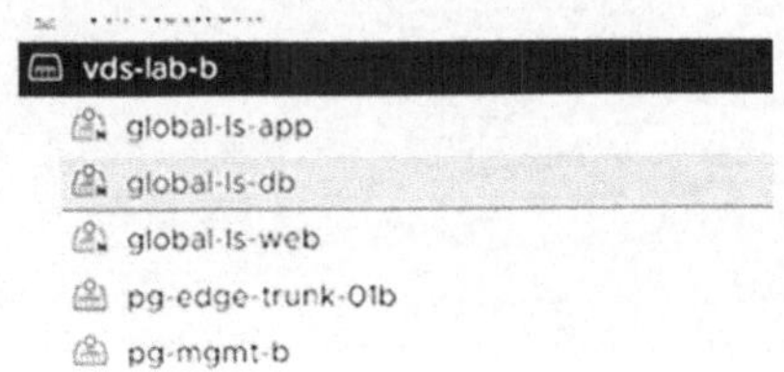

***Figure* 13.63:** NSX *port group present in Location B in vCenter server*

Another way to validate is to check if the upstream router or physical router is receiving routes from the Tier0 gateway or not. In the example configuration, the Tier0 gateway was configured as Active-Active with Location All Primary configuration. This configuration will result in learning routes in both locations A and B. If the Tier0 gateway was configured as Primary-Secondary location, then routes would have learned in the Primary location only by the physical router. *Figure* 13.64 shows an example snippet of routes being learned from the Tier0 gateway in Location A, showing three subnets configured in the NSX environment. In the location Site A, the Tier0 gateway is connected to the upstream router with IP address 10.10.100.1, and in Site B, it is connected to the upstream router with IP address 10.10.110.1. The three-tier overlay segments, App (172.16.162.0/24), DB (172.16.163.0/24), and Web (172.16.116.161.0/24), are connected to the Tier1 gateway running in DR-only configuration connected to Tier0 gateway. The physical router in Site A is learning routes from the Tier0 gateway and updated in its BGP table.

```
BGP table version is 11, local router ID is 10.10.100.1, vrf id 0
Default local pref 100, local AS 60546
Status codes:  s suppressed, d damped, h history, * valid, > best, = multipath,
               i internal, r RIB-failure, S Stale, R Removed
Nexthop codes: @NNN nexthop's vrf id, < announce-nh-self
Origin codes:  i - IGP, e - EGP, ? - incomplete

   Network          Next Hop            Metric LocPrf Weight Path
*> 0.0.0.0/0        192.168.0.253            0         32768 ?
*  10.10.100.0/24   10.10.100.10             0             0 60646 ?
*                   10.10.100.11             0             0 60646 ?
*>                  0.0.0.0                  1         32768 ?
*= 100.64.0.0/31    10.10.100.10             0             0 60646 ?
*>                  10.10.100.11             0             0 60646 ?
*= 172.16.161.0/24  10.10.100.10             0             0 60646 ?
*>                  10.10.100.11             0             0 60646 ?
*= 172.16.162.0/24  10.10.100.11             0             0 60646 ?
*>                  10.10.100.10             0             0 60646 ?
*= 172.16.163.0/24  10.10.100.11             0             0 60646 ?
*>                  10.10.100.10             0             0 60646 ?
*> 192.168.0.0/16   0.0.0.0                  1         32768 ?
```

Figure 13.64: *Route learning on Location A physical router from Tier0 gateway*

Similarly, *Figure* 13.65 shows routes learned by the physical router in Location B from Tier0 gateway, and you should be able to see the three subnets being learned with different next-hop IP addresses 10.10.110.10 and 10.10.110.11 (External Interfaces of Tier0 gateway in Site B).

```
BGP table version is 11, local router ID is 10.10.110.1, vrf id 0
Default local pref 100, local AS 61546
Status codes:  s suppressed, d damped, h history, * valid, > best, = multipath,
               i internal, r RIB-failure, S Stale, R Removed
Nexthop codes: @NNN nexthop's vrf id, < announce-nh-self
Origin codes:  i - IGP, e - EGP, ? - incomplete

   Network          Next Hop            Metric LocPrf Weight Path
*> 0.0.0.0/0        192.168.0.253            0         32768 ?
*  10.10.110.0/24   10.10.110.10             0             0 61646 ?
*                   10.10.110.11             0             0 61646 ?
*>                  0.0.0.0                  1         32768 ?
*= 100.64.0.0/31    10.10.110.10             0             0 61646 ?
*>                  10.10.110.11             0             0 61646 ?
*= 172.16.161.0/24  10.10.110.10             0             0 61646 ?
*>                  10.10.110.11             0             0 61646 ?
*= 172.16.162.0/24  10.10.110.11             0             0 61646 ?
*>                  10.10.110.10             0             0 61646 ?
*= 172.16.163.0/24  10.10.110.11             0             0 61646 ?
*>                  10.10.110.10             0             0 61646 ?
*> 192.168.0.0/16   0.0.0.0                  1         32768 ?
```

Figure 13.65: *Route learning on Location B physical router from Tier0 gateway*

One more way to validate NSX Federation networking is to validate RTEP tunnel status. Navigate to **`Local Manager`** and go to the **`System`** Menu. Click **`Nodes`,** and it will show the **`Edge Transport Nodes`** present in the NSX environment. It should be a **`green up arrow`** with a number under the Remote Tunnels column denoting tunnels in an up status, similar to *Figure* 13.66. If a red down arrow is present, it denotes that the tunnel status is down.

Edge Transport Nodes   Edge Clusters   Container Clusters

+ ADD EDGE NODE   EDIT   DELETE   ACTIONS   View All

Edge	ID	Deployment	Management IP	Host	Configuration St	NSX Version	N-VDS	Tunnels	Remote Tunnels	TEP IP Address	Edge Cluster	Logical Rout	Node Status
sa-nsxedge...	6cd0...d...	Virtual ...	192.168.56.1		Success	4.1.1.0.0.222...	1	5	2	172.16.101.10	LAB-EC-A-01	2	Up
sa-nsxedge...	e8ab...8...	Virtual ...	192.168.56.2		Success	4.1.1.0.0.222...	1	5	2	172.16.101.11	LAB-EC-A-01	2	Up

Figure 13.66: *Viewing status of remote tunnels on Edge nodes*

Click the number under the **`Remote Tunnels`** column to view the status of Remote Tunnels. It opens a new screen with **`Remote Tunnel Endpoint (RTEP)`** configuration and shows the tunnel status with RTEPs on remote Edge nodes, as illustrated in *Figure* 13.67.

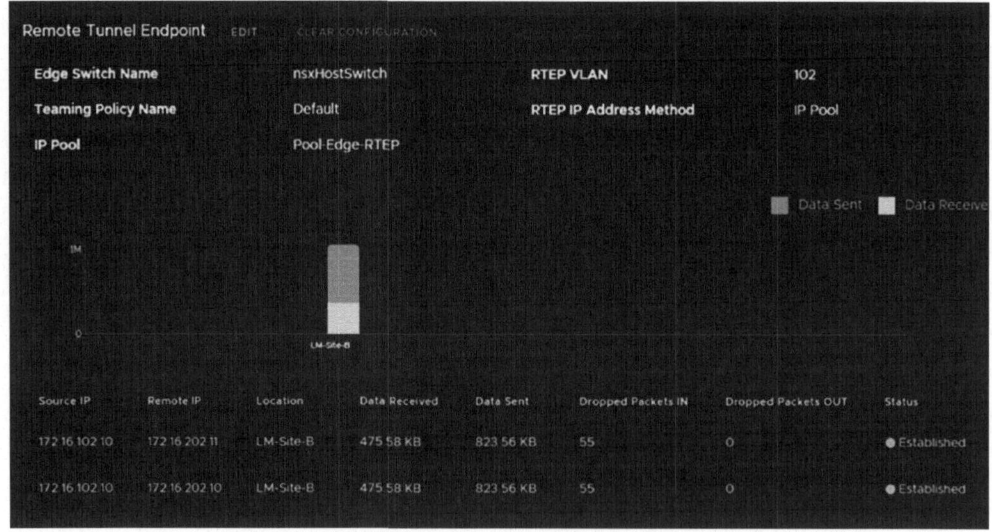

Figure 13.67: *Viewing RTEP and tunnel configuration on Edge node*

Multilocation Traceflow

NSX Global Manager provides functionality to trace packets between two workloads running in different locations. This is helpful in troubleshooting when working with issues affecting workloads connected to stretched networking across multiple locations. Instead of logging into Local Manager and using the destination as an IP address, Global Manager provides the option to select both the source as well as the destination as virtual machines, which can help in identifying where the packet is dropping. Click **`Plan & Troubleshoot`** while logged into Global Manager, and it will take you to **`Traceflow`**. Provide information such as source, destination, packet type, and more, similar to Traceflow on NSX Manager, and click **`Start Trace`**. This will provide an end-to-end packet flow with detailed network topology and hops it has gone through. *Figure 13.68* shows an example trace between virtual machine Web-01 connected to global-ls-web running on Location A and the virtual machine App-01 connected to global-ls-app running on Location B, clearly showing the packet traveling through the RTEP tunnel between locations.

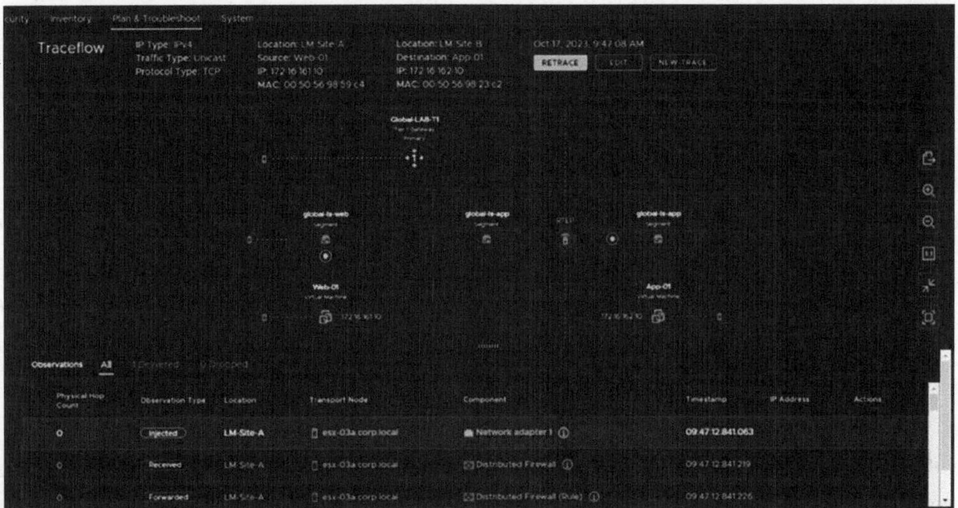

Figure 13.68: *Running Traceflow from NSX Global Manager*

NSX Federation Security

The last section covered Federation networking in great detail. But apart from providing stretched networking services, NSX Federation also provides stretched security services. It supports stretching the following security constructs across multiple locations for centralized management of policies:

- Distributed Firewall
- Gateway Firewall
- FQDN Filtering
- L7 APP ID Context Profile

However, the following security features are not supported by NSX Federation:

- Identity Firewall
- NSX Distributed IDS/IPS
- Network Introspection
- Endpoint Protection
- Malware Prevention
- Network Detection and Response

NSX Federation provides consistent policies across multiple locations, and in case of disaster recovery, it ensures security posture is maintained while workloads are recovered on the recovery site.

Regions

This topic was covered earlier while discussing NSX Federation Architecture. A quick recap: a region in the NSX federation is a collection of locations that can be used to create a focused group for security policies. A region can be of three types:

- **Global:** This is automatically created by NSX and contains all locations. Any group with a global scope will be propagated to all Local Managers.
- **Regional:** This is a user-created region, and different locations can be added to it as per requirements. Any group with a regional scope will be propagated to all Local Managers added to it.
- **Local:** This is also automatically created by NSX and has a single location in it. Any group with a local scope will be propagated to only specific Local Manager added to the local region.

To configure or view Regions in NSX Federation, log into the Active Global Manager. Navigate to **Inventory** and click **Regions** from the left-side navigation panel. *Figure* 13.69 shows multiple regions already created by NSX in the environment. There is a global region containing locations **LM-Site-A** and **LM-Site-B,** and there is a local region for each location.

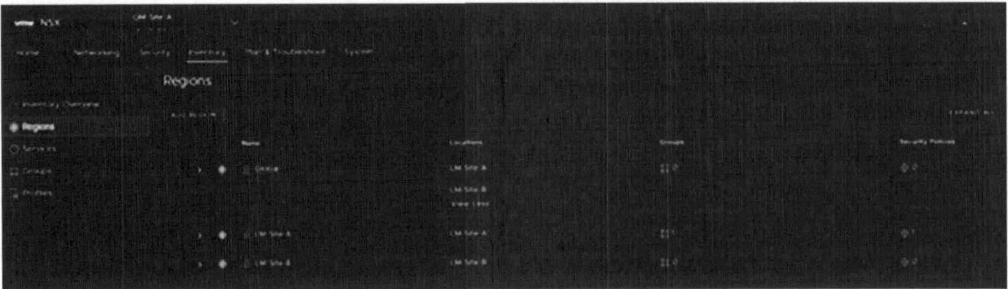

Figure 13.69: *Viewing regions in NSX Federation*

To create a new region, click **ADD REGION** and provide the following information, as shown in *Figure 13.70*:

a. **Name**: Provide an appropriate name to identify the region.

b. **Locations**: Use the drop-down menu to select locations that will be part of this region.

Click **Save** to create the region in the NSX Federation environment.

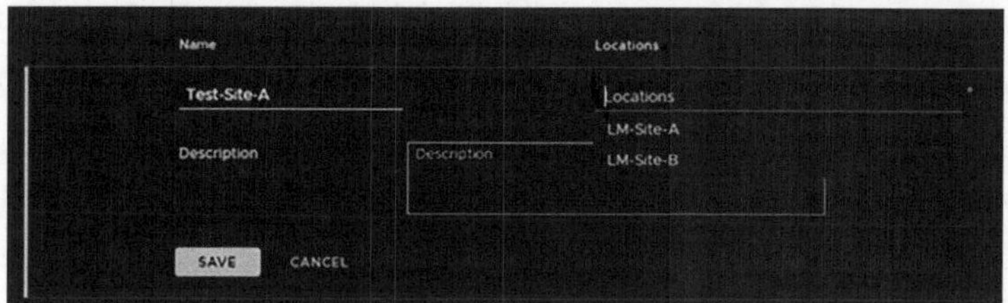

Figure 13.70: *Adding a new region in NSX Federation*

Global Manager Groups

NSX Federation Groups are configured very similarly to groups configuration in Local Manager, as covered in *Chapter 8, Security – Micro-Segmentation*. NSX Federation introduces one more concept to groups, that is, Regions. A group in Global Manager can be defined as Global, Regional, or Local, as covered in the previous section. Groups created from Global Manager can only be added, updated, or deleted from Global Manager, and no edit operation is allowed on them through Local Manager. *Figure 13.71* illustrates an example of groups and their span across multiple locations.

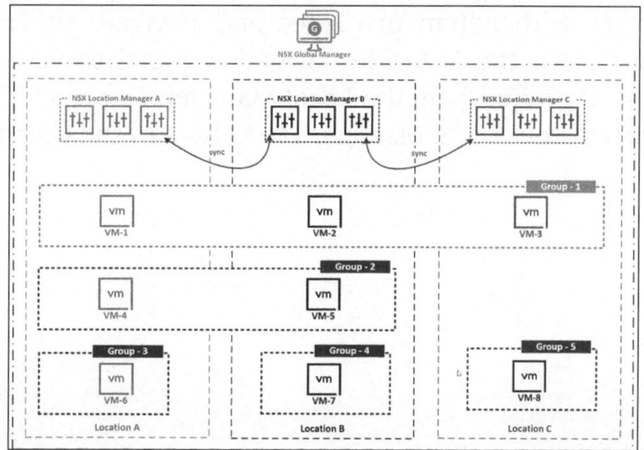

Figure 13.71: *Example group configuration in NSX Federation*

In this example, there are a total of five groups. Group-1 is global, with its span across locations A, B, and C. Group-2 is a regional group, with its span stretched to locations A and B only. Group-3, Group-4, and Group-5 are local groups, with their span local to a single location only. Local Manager synchronizes its local group memberships with other Local Managers for both global and regional groups. *Table* 13.3 summarizes group memberships on different locations based on the preceding example.

Group	**Local Manager - A**	**Local Manager - B**	**Local Manager - C**
Group-1 (Location A, B, C)	VM-1, VM-2, VM-3	VM-1, VM-2, VM-3	VM-1, VM-2, VM-3
Group-2 (Location A, B,)	VM-4, VM-5	VM-4, VM-5	Group not present
Group-3 (Location A)	VM-6	Group not present	Group not present
Group-4 (Location B)	Group not present	VM-7	Group not present
Group-5 (Location C)	Group not present	Group not present	VM-8

***Table* 13.3:** *Group memberships on Local Managers*

As mentioned earlier, the configuration of groups on Global Manager is very similar to groups on Local Manager. Let's see the steps to configure groups on Global Manager.

Step 1: To create a group on NSX Global Manager, log in to the Active Global Manager with admin privileges and navigate to **`Inventory`**. Click **`Groups`** from the left-side navigation panel to view configured or imported groups from the Local Manager. *Figure* 13.72 shows a group imported from Local Manager **`LM-Site-A`** in the Global Manager.

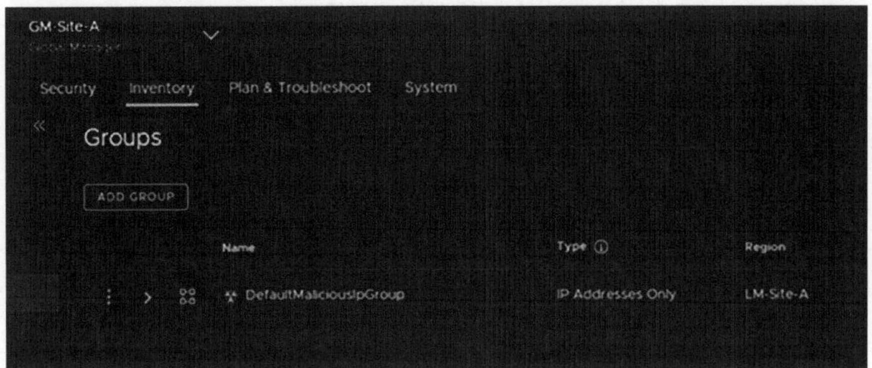

***Figure 13.72:** Viewing group in Global Manager*

Step 2: Click **`Add Group`** to add a new group and provide the following information:

a. **`Name`:** Provide an appropriate name for the group to identify it in the NSX environment.

b. **`Region`**: Select the region from the drop-down menu to define the scope of the group.

Figure 13.73 shows an example configuration of the group **`Global-VM-Web`** with the region to be selected from a drop-down list.

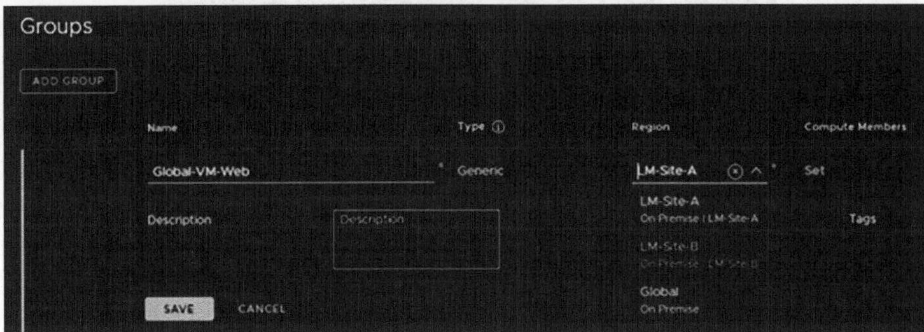

***Figure 13.73:** Creating a group in Global Manager*

Step 3: Click **`Set`** under the **`Compute Members`** column to set the membership criteria of the group. It can be dynamic or static in nature. One important point to remember here is the span of the member should not be greater than the span of the group; otherwise, it could result in incorrect security policies being applied. *Figure* 13.74 shows an example where dynamic criteria have been set to include member type **`Virtual Machine`** whose name contains the keyword **`Web.`**

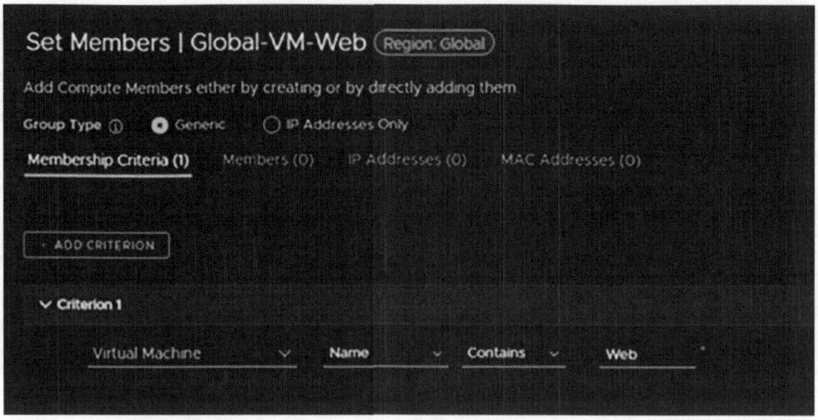

Figure 13.74: *Setting membership criteria on a group*

Step 4: Click `Save` to finish adding the group. Click `View Members` to see effective members of a group, as shown in *Figure* 13.75.

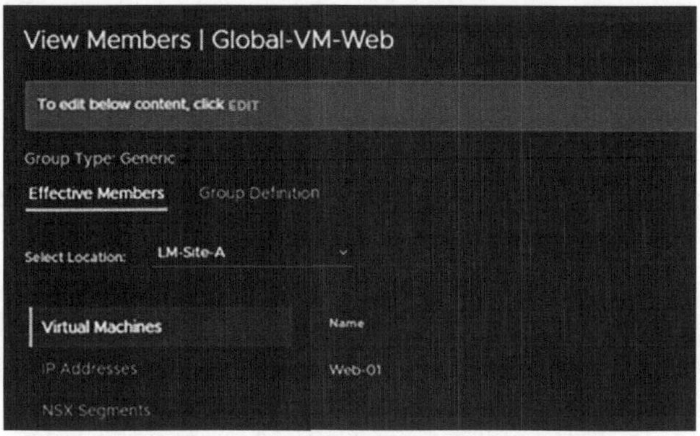

Figure 13.75: *Viewing effective members of a group*

Configuring Distributed Firewall Policies

Firewall policies for both Gateway Firewall and Distributed Firewall are configured in Global Manager very similarly to Local Manager, with very few differences. Gateway Firewall and Distributed Firewall configuration have been covered in great detail in *Chapter* 8, *Security – Micro-Segmentation*, and *Chapter* 9, *Security - Advanced Threat Prevention*. This section covers enhancement and differences brought by NSX Federation in Distributed Firewall (DFW) policies.

Starting NSX release v4.0.1, it is possible to manage the DFW Exclusion list and enable or disable DFW on registered Local Managers centrally from the Global Manager. If DFW is enabled or disabled on Global Manager, it is not possible to override the configuration from Local Manager. For the DFW exclusion list,

Local Manager maintains two exclusion lists, that is, one for Global Manager and one for locally configured exclusions. All excluded members are sent as a unified list to the Management Plane to be applied on Local Manager.

To configure these settings from Global Manager, navigate to **Security**. Click **Distributed Firewall**, and then click **Settings**, as shown in *Figure* 13.76. Move the toggle button under **Activation Status** to enable or disable DFW. Similarly, click **User Excluded Groups** to add globally excluded groups from DFW.

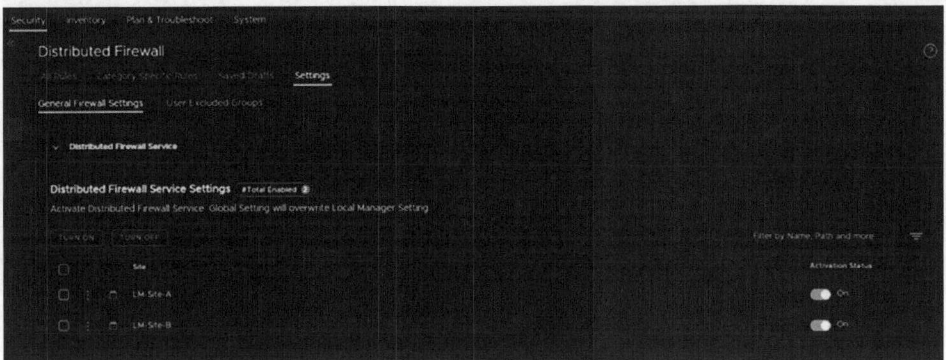

***Figure* 13.76:** *Managing DFW settings centrally from Global Manager*

It is possible to configure gateway or distributed firewall policies under the same category on Global Manager and Local Manager. In such cases, policies created by the Global Manager will always be on top of policies created from Local Manager. The only exception to this rule is the Emergency and Ethernet categories, as these two DFW categories are not available on Global Manager.

To configure firewall policies on the gateway, click **Gateway Firewall** in the **Security** menu. Click **Gateway Specific Rules** and select the desired gateway from the drop-down list in front of **Gateway** on which to apply the firewall policy, similar to *Figure* 13.77. The rest of the configuration is exactly the same as that of Local Manager.

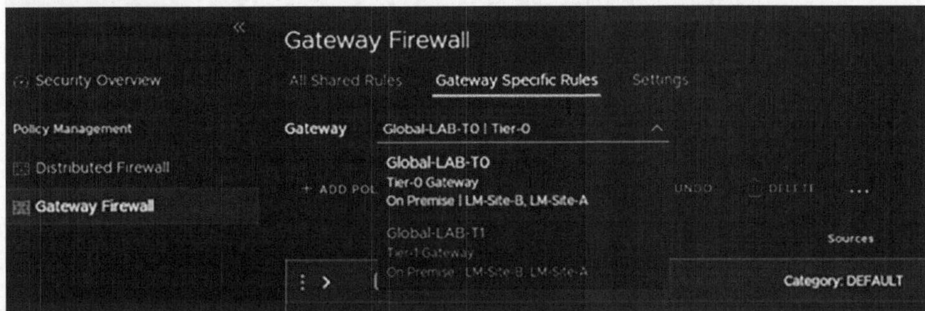

***Figure* 13.77:** *Configuring gateway firewall policies*

To configure DFW policies on Global Manager, click **`Distributed Firewall`** in the **`Security`** menu and then click **`Category Specific Rules`**. Select one of the three categories, as shown in *Figure* 13.78, to add firewall policies.

Figure 13.78: *Adding a DFW policy in Global Manager*

Click **`ADD POLICY`** to add a new policy. Click the **pencil icon** to modify the **`Applied To`** field. It will open a new screen, **`Set Applied To`**, similar to the one on Local Manager, as shown in *Figure* 13.79. There is one additional option, **`Region`**, to select the federation regions configured earlier to define the scope of the firewall policy. By default, the span of the security policy is set to **`Global`**, but it can be modified to a different region as well.

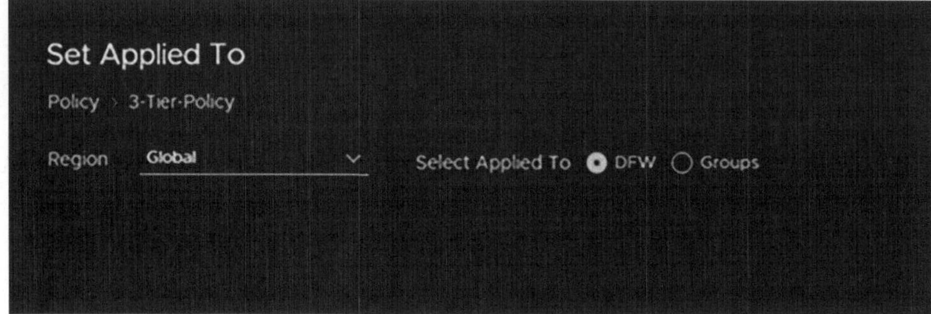

Figure 13.79: *Defining scope of DFW policy*

Figure 13.80 shows an example DFW policy with the name 3-Tier-Policy with the scope set as Global and is applied to DFW, meaning it will be applied to all virtual machines within a location if no **`Applied to`** field is set on the firewall rule.

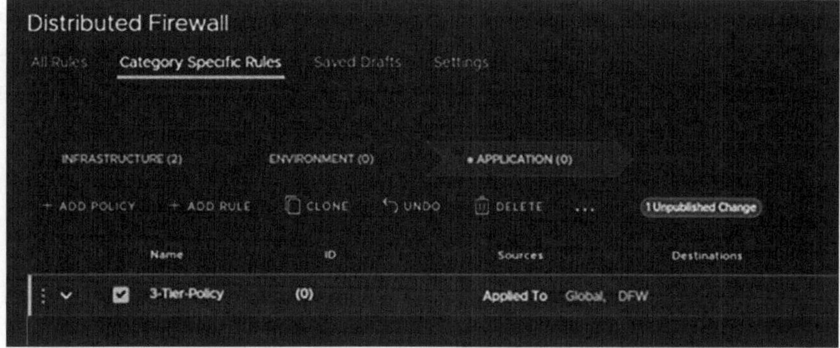

Figure 13.80: *An example DFW policy in Global Manager*

The remaining options to add firewall rules in a DFW policy and configuring different options such as **`Applied To`**, logging, directions, and TCP strict are exactly the same as configuring them on Local Manager, already covered in detail in *Chapter 8, Security – Micro-Segmentation*. *Figure* 13.81 shows an example DFW policy with multiple rules configured for a demo 3-Tier application with virtual machines running across locations A and B.

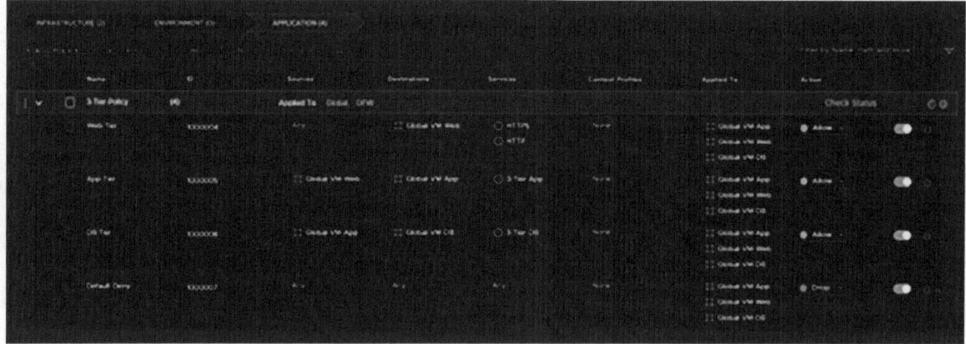

Figure 13.81: *An example DFW firewall rules for a demo application*

This completes the different networking and security features provided by NSX Federation to centrally manage multiple locations.

Conclusion

This concludes the NSX Federation configuration in the NSX environment. In this chapter, we covered two different solutions supported by NSX to manage multiple locations and discussed different features and constraints for each solution. Continuing, we discussed the NSX Federation architecture, a new component, Global Manager, introduced by NSX Federation, and how Global

Manager is configured to onboard multiple locations in NSX Federation. In addition, this chapter covers different networking and security services supported by NSX Federation, and how these can be configured and managed through Global Manager.

The next chapter covers different features provided by NSX to monitor and manage the NSX environment effectively and efficiently. It explains how you can enable different authentication providers in the NSX environment to provide secure access to the environment along with RBAC to control the level of access.

Key Terms

- **NSX Multisite:** Introduced way back in NSX-T release v2.3, this solution consists of a single NSX Management cluster that manages different vSphere clusters and Edge nodes spanning across multiple locations.
- **NSX Federation**: Introduced in NSX-T release v3.0, instead of managing multiple locations through a single NSX Management cluster, a new central entity is introduced in NSX Federation named Global Manager.
- **NSX Global Manager:** The NSX Global Manager (GM) Cluster consists of three NSX nodes deployed as Global Manager (GM) in a cluster. There are two Global Manager clusters, with one acting as active and the other acting as standby, centrally managing multiple locations.
- **NSX Local Manager:** The NSX Local Manager (LM) cluster consists of three NSX nodes deployed on NSX Manager nodes in a cluster on each location onboarded to Global Manager, so they receive any configuration being done on Global Manager.
- **RTEP (Remote Tunnel Endpoint)**: RTEP is configured only on Edge nodes and forms tunnels with other Edge nodes running in different locations to enable East-West communication for stretched networking services.
- **Region**: Regions in NSX Federation are a logical construct that defines the scope of the boundary of security services (Groups and DFW) across different locations.
- **Global Group:** This is automatically created by NSX and contains all locations. Any group with global scope will be propagated to all Local Managers.
- **Regional Group**: Any group with regional scope will be propagated to all Local Managers added in the user-configured region in NSX Federation.
- **Local Group:** A group local to a specific location only.

CHAPTER 14

Monitoring and Managing NSX

Introduction

In the previous chapters, we covered deployment, configuration, and consuming different NSX networking and security services. We explored how different features of NSX can make a datacenter environment more agile and secure at the same time. However, as with any other IT equipment, NSX also requires regular monitoring to ensure it functions as expected and complies with different governance policies an organization may have.

This chapter covers different features provided by NSX to monitor and manage the NSX environment effectively and efficiently. It explains how you can enable different authentication providers in the NSX environment to provide secure access to the environment along with RBAC to control the level of access. Different tools are provided by NSX Manager to monitor, identify, and remediate issues in the environment.

Structure

In this chapter, we will cover the following topics:

- Managing NSX Environment
    - Authentication and Authorization
    - Managing NSX Backups
    - Certificate Management
    - NSX Multi-Tenancy

- Monitoring NSX Environment
    - Configuring SNMP for Alarms
    - Configuring Syslog in NSX
    - VMware Aria Operations for Logs
- Conclusion

Managing NSX Environment

It is not always ideal to log in using local admin credentials, as this requires sharing credentials among team members, which can result in difficult tracing in case of troubleshooting and loss of ownership. Similarly, up until NSX-T 3.2, multi-tenancy was achieved using different Tier0 or Tier1 gateways. However, starting from NSX 4.x, specifically 4.1, multi-tenancy can be configured in the NSX environment, providing true isolation for networking and security services between different tenants. There are other Day 1 operations that an administrator needs to perform, such as replacing self-signed certificates with CA-signed certificates to meet with organizational compliance policies and configuring backups for NSX environment so that it can be recovered in case of any failure. This section covers all these different tasks in details and enables administrators to effectively manage NSX environment.

Authentication and Authorization

NSX Manager supports different types of authentication platforms to provide secure access to NSX Manager for any configuration changes. These different platforms are as follows:

- **Local Users**: These are system default local account managed by NSX Manager, which can be used as a backup if other authentication mechanisms are not working. Starting from NSX release v4.1, users with Enterprise Admin can add additional local user accounts, which was not possible in earlier releases.
- **LDAP (Lightweight Directory Access Protocol)**: NSX supports integration with directory services to use existing directory user accounts to provide access to NSX Manager. One of the most widely used directory services is Microsoft Active Directory, which can be integrated via LDAP or the openLDAP service.
- **WS1 or VMware Identity Manager**: Workspace One or VMware Identity Manager is an Identity as a Service solution offered by VMware. NSX Manager can be integrated with WS1/vIDM to provide access to users authenticated via VMware Identity services.

- **Principal Identity Users**: Principal Identity refers to a third-party application that can use certificate-based authentication to connect to NSX Manager. With the help of Principal Identity, users can create objects in NSX Manager, and modifications or deletions of the objects can only be done with the same identity.

In addition to different authentication mechanisms, NSX Manager also supports RBAC (Role-Based Access Control) to control the level of access to the environment with the help of different roles. There are four levels of access or permissions that can be assigned in NSX Manager as follows:

- Full Access: Includes Create, Read, Update, Delete
- Execute: Includes Read and Update
- Read: Read-only access
- None: No access

To effectively manage permissions on different objects in NSX Manager, these are clubbed into roles. There are multiple built-in roles already present in NSX Manager, as listed in *Table* 14.1. However, it also supports the capability to clone an existing role, add a new role, and edit or delete newly created roles. Users cannot modify or delete system built-in roles.

Role Name	**Role Description**
Auditor	Read-only access to both networking and security features
Enterprise Admin	Full Access to both networking and security features
GI Partner Admin (Guest Introspection)	Provide Full Access to Service Instances for third-party service registrations with limited Read-only access to corresponding features
LB Admin (Load Balancer)	Provide Full Access to NSX native Load Balancing feature with Read-only access to networking and no access to security or user management
LB Operator	Provide Read-only access to NSX native Load Balancing feature with Read-only access to networking and no access to security or user management

Network Admin	Full Access to networking with read-only access to security and no access to user management
Network Operator	Execute Access to networking with read-only access to security and no access to user management
Next Partner Admin (Network Introspection)	Provide Full Access to Network Introspection with limited read-only access to required networking features
Project Admin	A newer role in NSX v4.1 to provide multi-tenancy management
Security Admin	Full Access to security with read-only access to networking and no access to user management
Security Operator	Execute Access to security with read-only access to networking and no access to user management
Support Bundle Collector	Provide just enough access to collect the Support Bundle with no access to the rest of the environment
VPN Admin	Provide Full Access to NSX VPN features with limited Read-only access to Networking and no access to security or user management

Table 14.1: *NSX System Built-in Roles*

More information about these roles can be found in the official VMware documentation.

Managing Local Users

This section covers steps to manage local users in the NSX environment. The steps are as follows:

Step 1: Login into NSX Manager with enterprise admin privileges and navigate to `System`. Select `User Management` under `Settings` from the left navigation panel to view different user controls in NSX Manager. Click on `Local Users` to access local user control, as shown in *Figure 14.1*.

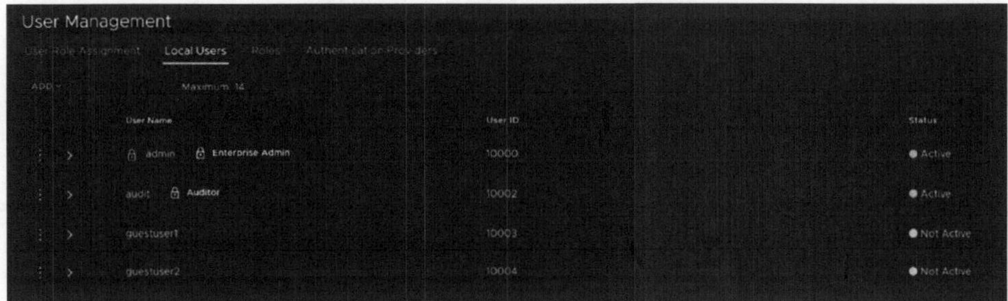

Figure 14.1: *Local user management in NSX Manager*

Step 2: Click on the three dots against guestuser1 or guestuser2 to expand additional actions, as shown in *Figure* 14.2. Click on **`Activate User`** to activate the guestuser account by setting a desired password. Click on **`Edit`** to change the name from guestuser1 to the desired account name. These guestusers were helpful in earlier releases of NSX when additional local user accounts couldn't have been created.

Figure 14.2: *Managing guestuser account in NSX Manager*

Figure 14.3 shows guestuser1 after it has been activated by setting a password and changing its name to new-name-01. Note the User ID to ensure that it is guestuser1 only.

Figure 14.3: *Modifying guest account properties*

Step 3: Click on **`ADD`**, and then select **`Local User`** to add a new local user account. Provide an appropriate name and click **`Save`** to create the user in NSX Manager. *Figure* 14.4 shows a user account named `new-local-01` created in Manager. All newly created accounts are disabled by default.

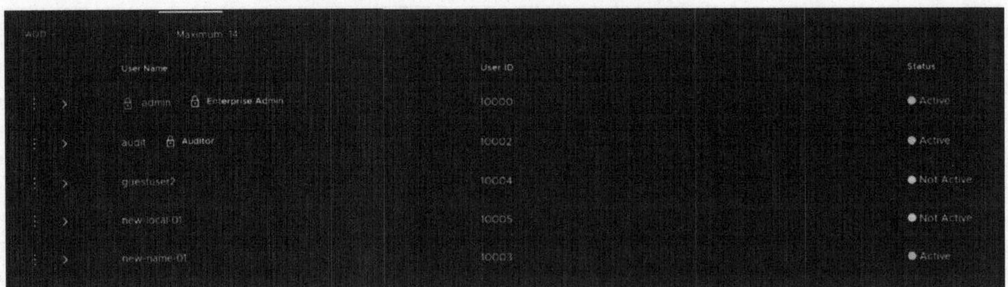

***Figure 14.4**: Adding a new local user account in NSX Manager*

Step 4: Follow the same steps as mentioned in Step 2 for the **`guestuser`** account to activate the newly added user account, set a password, or change the username.

Integrating Active Directory as LDAP

NSX Manager supports integrating with directory services over LDAP or openLDAP protocol. This section provides steps to configure Microsoft AD over LDAP as follows:

Step 1: While present in **`User Management`** with enterprise admin privileges from the previous section **`Local Users`** Management, click on **`Authentication Providers`** and select **`LDAP`,** as shown in *Figure* 14.5.

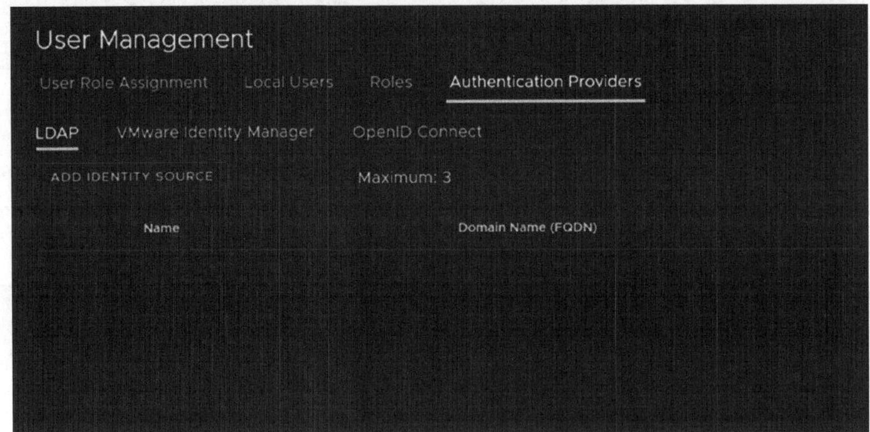

***Figure 14.5**: LDAP Identity Source in NSX Manager*

Step 2: Click on **`ADD IDENTITY SOURCE`** to add a new LDAP Directory and provide the required details:

a. **`Name`:** Provide an appropriate name for the LDAP directory source.

b. **`Domain Name (FQDN)`**: Provide the DNS name of the domain to be integrated.

c. **`Type`**: Select the type of directory, either Active Directory over LDAP or openLDAP.

d. **`LDAP Server`**: Click on **`Set`** to add domain controllers for directory service. Please keep in mind, at most only three LDAP domains can be added in NSX. Provide server details as follows:

   i. **`Hostname/IP`**: IP address or FQDN of the domain controller.

   ii. **`LDAP Protocol`**: Choose whether to use LDAPS (LDAP over SSL) or LDAP.

   iii. **`Port`**: 389 for LDAP and 636 for LDAPS.

   iv. **`Certificate`**: Required if using LDAPS, provide the certificate of the domain controller.

   v. **`Bind Identity`**: Username to connect to directory services.

   vi. **`Password`**: Password of Bind Identity.

Figure 14.6 shows an example of the configuration for the lab.com directory to use an LDAP server.

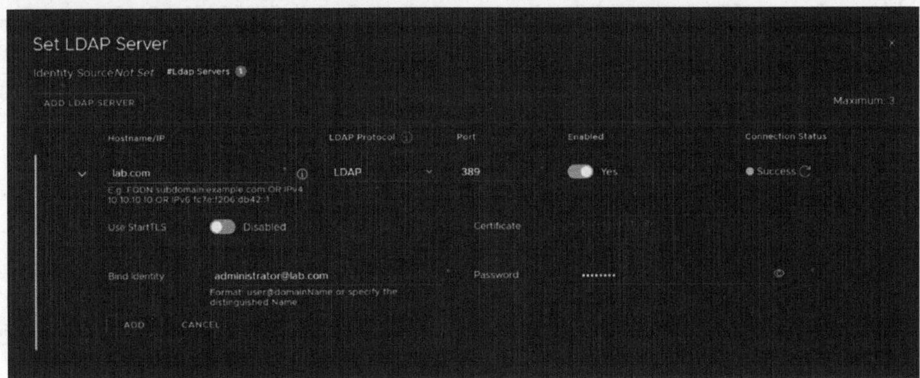

Figure 14.6: *Setting an LDAP server for directory services*

e. **`Alternative Domain Name`**: Optional, enter any domain aliases if in use.

f. **Base DN**: Provide the distinguished name of the root of the directory or OU from which users are synced to NSX Manager.

Figure 14.7 illustrates an example for the directory lab.com with completed configurations.

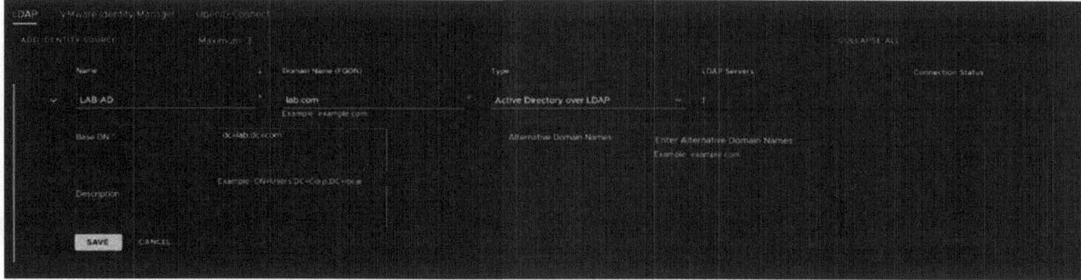

Figure 14.7*: Adding a Directory in NSX Manager*

Step 3: Click on **Save** to commit the configuration. Click on **Check Status** to ensure that directory integration is successful. It should be green, as shown in *Figure* 14.8, if not, correct the issue and save the configuration again.

Figure 14.8*: Successful integration of Active Directory with NSX Manager*

After Active Directory or openLDAP directory is successfully integrated with NSX Manager, users present in directories can be directly assigned roles in NSX. To log in with a directory account, provide the username in the format **<user-name>@<domain-name>** and the directory account password when logging into NSX Manager.

Integrating VMware Identity Manager

VMware Identity Manager (vIDM) or WS1 provides identity services in the environment. NSX Manager can be integrated with the existing vIDM in the environment, and no dedicated appliance is required for the same. However, before integrating NSX Manager with vIDM, there are certain requirements that need to be completed at the vIDM end. These are as follows:

- Obtain certificate thumbprint of vIDM. This can be provided by the vIDM administrator or can be obtained with the help of the following command:

```
openssl s_client -connect <FQDN of vIDM host>:443 < /dev/null 2> /dev/
null | openssl x509 -sha256 -fingerprint -noout -in /dev/stdin
```

Figure 14.9 shows a sample output of the preceding command run against the vIDM host vidm.lab.com.

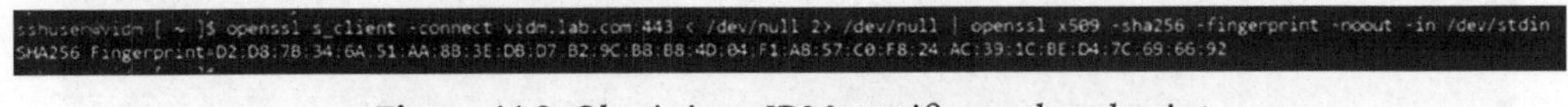

Figure 14.9: *Obtaining vIDM certificate thumbprint*

- vIDM administrator needs to configure Remote App Access in vIDM as a service client token or Oauth2 client for NSX Manager and share Client ID/Shared Secret. *Figure* 14.10 shows an example of such remote app access in vIDM for NSX Manager **`sa-nsxmgr-01`.**

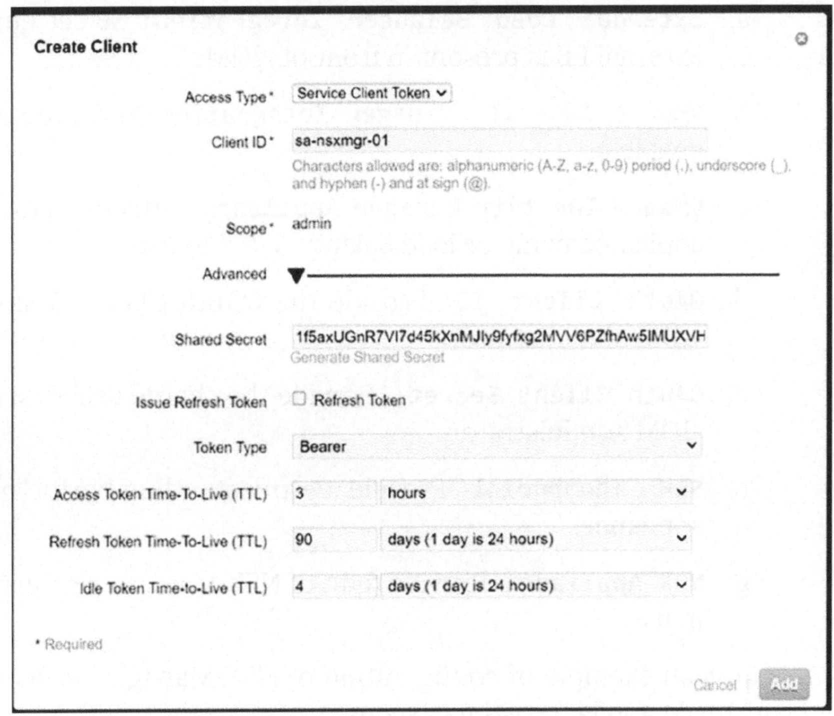

Figure 14.10: *Oauth2 client configuration in vIDM*

After these requirements are fulfilled, follow the following steps to integrate vIDM with NSX Manager:

Step 1: While present in **`User Management`** with enterprise admin privileges from the previous section **`Local Users`** Management, click on **`Authentication Providers`** and select **`VMware Identity Manager`**, as shown in *Figure* 14.11.

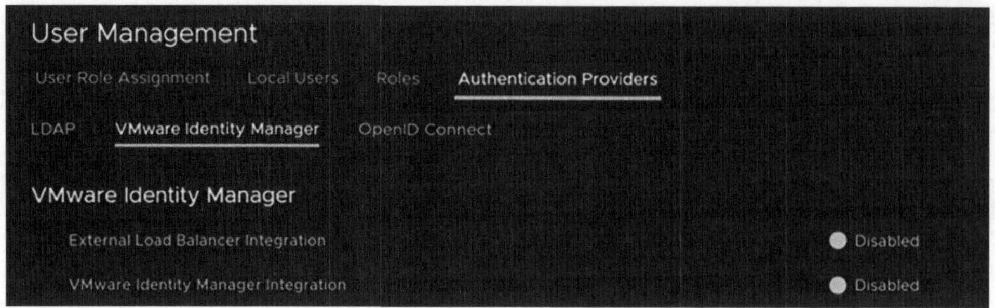

***Figure 14.11**: vIDM as an Authentication Provider in NSX*

Step 2: Click on `Edit` and provide the following information:

a. **`External Load Balancer Integration:`** Select enabled if external LB is present in front of vIDM.

b. **`VMware Identity Manager Integration`**: Move the slider to enable it.

c. **`VMware Identity Manager Appliance:`** Provide fqdn of vIDM appliance name or load balance VIP if in use.

d. **`OAuth Client ID:`** Provide the OAuth Client ID shared by vIDM administrator.

e. **`OAuth Client Secret:`** Provide the shared secret shared by vIDM administrator.

f. **`SSH Thumbprint`**: Provide certificate thumbprint of vIDM appliance.

g. **`NSX Appliance`**: Provide fqdn of NSX Manager or Cluster IP if in use.

Figure 14.12 shows an example of configuration of NSX Manager `sa-nsxmgr-01` integrated with vIDM appliance vidm.lab.com.

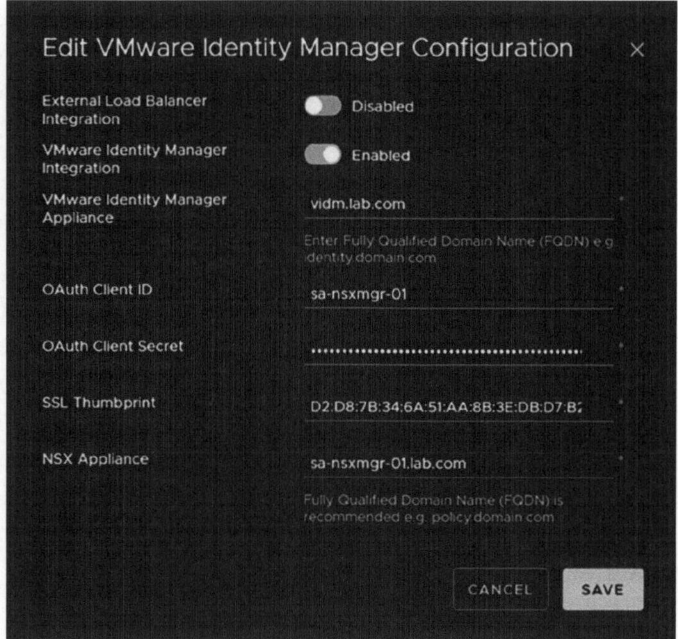

Figure 14.12: *Integrating vIDM with NSX Manager*

Step 3: Click on **Save** to commit the configuration. Log out of NSX Manager and try to log in again. If integration is successful, then NSX Manager will redirect the authentication request back to vIDM, as illustrated in *Figure 14.13*.

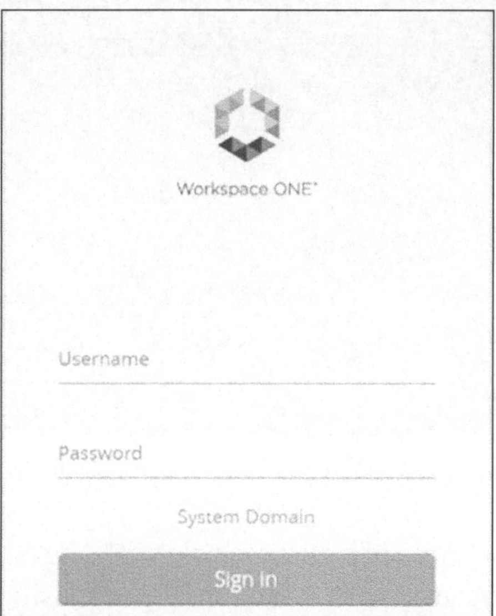

Figure 14.13: *Login into NSX Manager through vIDM*

Note: After vIDM integration, all authentication requests are redirected to vIDM appliance only. If AD authentication or local authentication is required, then use the following URL to force local authentication: https://<nsx-manager IP/FQDN>/login.jsp?idp=local

NSX Role Management

In the previous section, we covered how NSX can use different authentication providers to control access to NSX Manager. However, after getting access to NSX Manager, users must be authorized or have some level of access to navigate around NSX Manager. This is where RBAC or role assignment comes in handy, as no two different users may require the same level of access. NSX Manager already includes a wide number of system built-in roles defined with different levels of access, as listed in *Table* 14.1. If further customization to the level of access is required, then NSX Manager also supports creating a custom role as per requirements.

To create a custom role, while being present in **`User Management`** with enterprise admin privileges from the previous section **`Local Users`** Management, click on **`Roles`** and then select **`Add Role`** to create a new role. Here, define the different permissions for each individual component as per requirement under **`Set Permissions`** to control the level of access, as displayed in *Figure* 14.14.

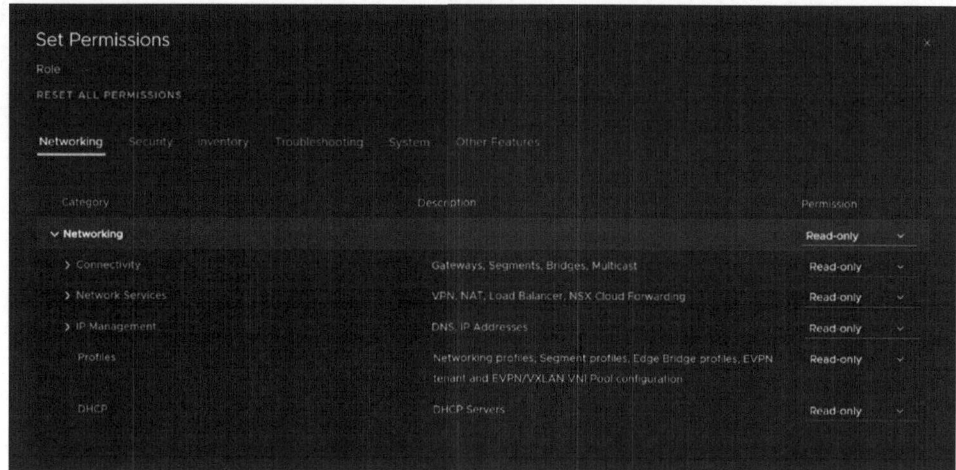

Figure 14.14: *Setting permissions for a custom role*

Figure 14.15 shows an example of a custom role with the name **`Custom-Read-Only`**, created by the administrator with **`Read-only`** permissions to all components in NSX manager.

Figure 14.15: *Adding a new role in NSX Manager*

The final step left in user management is the assignment of role to users. The following steps provide a step-by-step guide on how to assign roles to user accounts:

Step 1: While present in **`User Management`** with enterprise admin privileges from the previous section **`Local Users`** Management, click on **`User Role Assignment`** and it will provide options to assign roles to all different types of user accounts that is, Local, LDAP, vIDM, and Principal Identity.

Step 2: To change the role assigned to the local user, click on three dots against the user account name and click on **`Edit`**. It will show a numeric number under the column **`Roles`**, which can be clicked on to assign additional roles, as shown in *Figure* 14.16.

Figure 14.16: *Assign role to local user account*

Step 3: Click on the numeric number to open another window for **`Set Roles/ Scope.`** Click on **`ADD ROLE`** to add the required role to the user. Click **`Apply`** and then click **`Save`** to commit the changes.

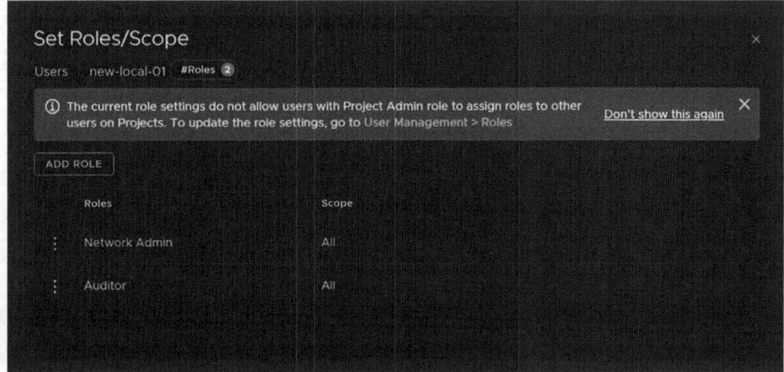

Figure 14.17: *Setting a role to user account*

Figure 14.18 shows a local user `new-local-01` with Network Admin and Auditor roles assigned to them.

Figure 14.18: *Local user with different roles assigned to it*

Step 4: To assign roles to **`VIDM`** or **`LDAP`** users, click on **`Add Role for Providers`** and select desired provider, i.e., **`VIDM`** or **`LDAP.`** It will ask for the user account name. As you start typing, it will search for the user account in the provider and show it in the drop-down menu. Select the desired user, and it will be added under the **`User/User Group name.`** Click on **`Set`** under **`Roles`** to assign the desired role to the user account. Finally, click **`SAVE`** to confirm the changes. *Figure* 14.19 shows a VIDM user admin assigned the Security Operator Role.

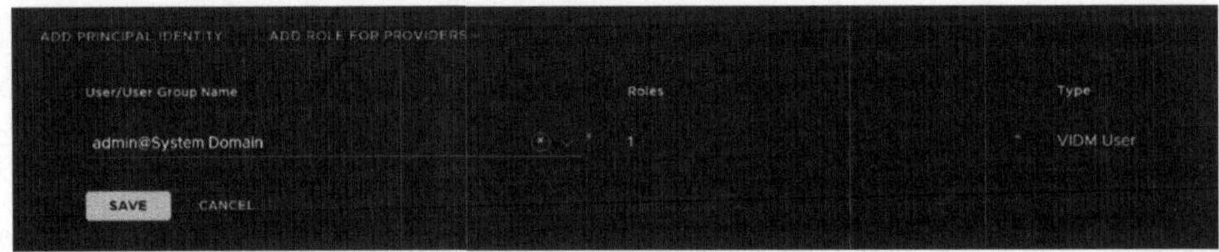

Figure 14.19: *Assigning a role to the VIDM user account*

Step 5: To create a principal Identity, simply click on **`ADD PRINCIPAL IDENTITY`** and provide **`Name`**, **`NodeID`**, **`Role`**, and **`Certificate`** to create a new principal identity.

Managing NSX Backups

As with any IT infrastructure component, backup is an integral part of NSX configuration. If things go wrong - and I mean really wrong - previous state backups can help you recover configurations back to a healthy state. NSX Manager requires an SFTP server to be configured beforehand with hashed ECDSA host key required to be present on server, where backups are saved and can be authenticated either through SSH username/password or SSH keys. Also, one important point to remember here is that NSX backups must be restored on the same version of NSX Manager only. To configure backups in NSX Manager, follow the steps as follows:

Step 1: Login into NSX Manager with enterprise admin privileges and navigate to **`System.`** Select **`Backup & Restore`** under **`Lifecycle Management`** from the left navigation panel to view the backup configuration.

Step 2: Click on **Edit** and a new screen will pop up with the name **Backup Configuration**. Provide the following details to successfully configure backups:

a. **`FQDN or IP Address:`** Provide the DNS FQDN or IP address of the SFTP server.

b. **`Port:`** The default port is 22, if any custom port is in use for SFTP, enter it here.

c. **`Directory Path:`** Complete path to the directory in which to store backups.

d. **`Username`**: SFTP username to authenticate with the SFTP server.

e. **`Password`**: SFTP password to authenticate with the SFTP server.

f. **`SSH Fingerprint:`** If it is known, add it here; otherwise, when you click on Save, NSX Manager will retrieve the fingerprint and save it here.

g. **`Passphrase`**: Provide a key to encrypt NSX backups.

Figure 14.20 shows an example of backup configuration in NSX Manager.

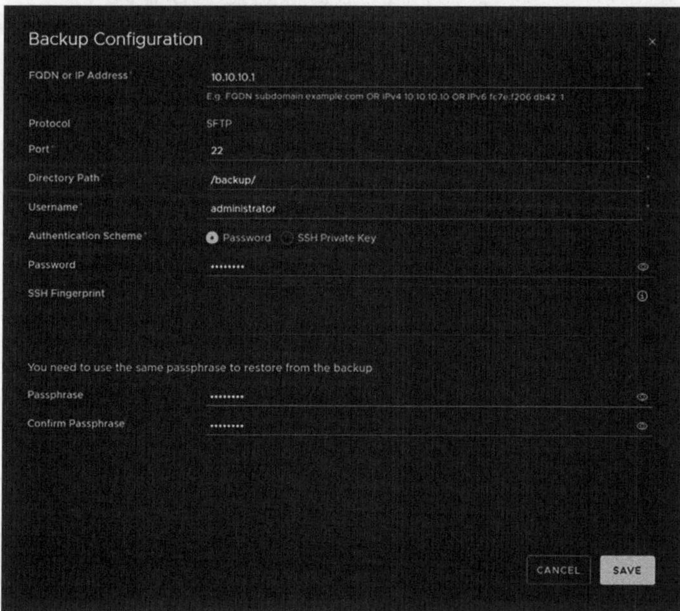

Figure 14.20: *NSX Manager Backup Configuration*

Step 3: Click on **SAVE** and a warning message will pop up to confirm Fingerprint. Click on Add to save the fingerprint and click on **SAVE** again to confirm the backup configuration.

Step 4: By default, the Backup Schedule is in a disabled state, so Backups have to be taken manually. Before enabling the Backup Schedule, it is a good practice to click on **START BACKUP** to initiate a manual backup. This will ensure that the backup configuration is correct and there are no errors occurring while taking backups, as shown in *Figure 14.21*.

Figure 14.21: *Taking a manual backup in NSX Manager*

Step 5: Click on **Edit** below **Schedule** to enable Automatic Backup schedules. It provides an option to configure Interval or Weekly-based backups. Also, there is an option for **Detect NSX Configuration Change,** which automatically takes a backup when NSX Manager detects an update in the configuration, as shown in *Figure 14.22*.

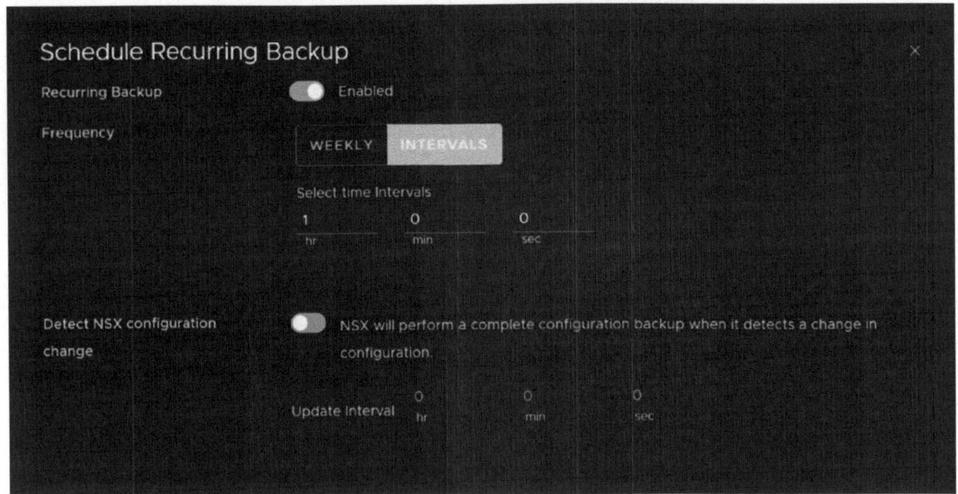

Figure 14.22: *Configuring Automatic Backup Schedule*

Post-successful backups, it will be presented under Backup History. There is one more tab for Last Successful Backup, which provides a bit more details about the most recent last successful backup, as shown in *Figure 14.23*.

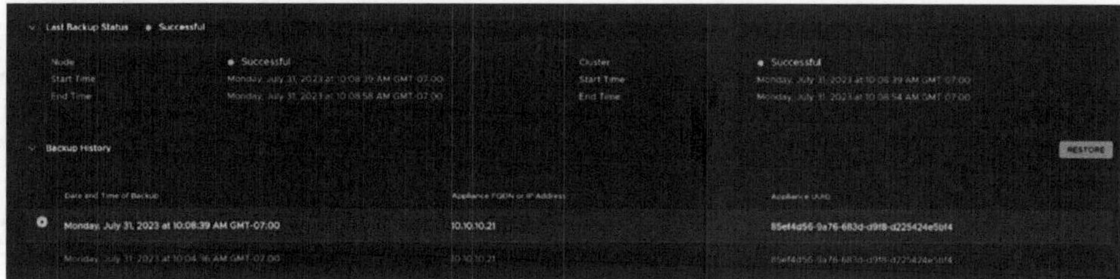

Figure 14.23: *Viewing backup history in NSX Manager*

In case of serious issues where restoration is required, deploy a new appliance with the same NSX Manager version as a backup with the same IP address and FQDN. Point the backup configuration on the newly deployed appliance to the old backup directory where previous backups are saved. Select the desired backup entry and click on restore to start the restoration of the backup on the new NSX Manager appliance.

Old NSX backups on SFTP backup file server can accumulate over time consuming storage space over time. There is no automatic cleanup of old backups performed by NSX manager and requires administrator to manually cleanup old files or scheduled scripts to perform this task. A Python script with name **nsx_backup_cleaner.py** is saved in the directory `/var/vmware/nsx/file-store` on NSX Manager that administrator can schedule on backup file server to perform automatic cleanup of old NSX backups.

Certificate Management

NSX installation uses self-signed certificates, which may not be ideal for organizations to use in order to comply with governance policies. NSX Manager supports replacing some of these users facing self-signed certificates. Also, there are certificates required for services hosted in an NSX environment, such as load balancing, VPN, and so on, as well as for principal identity users. There are three different types of certificates managed in the NSX environment as follows:

- **Platform Certificate**: These are the certificates created by the system during installation and used for internal communication between different services or for external communication when users connect to NSX Manager through UI or API. Internal communication certificates cannot be viewed or edited but external certificates that are API and Cluster certificates can be replaced.
- **Service Certificate**: These are certificates used by different NSX services, such as Load Balancing, VPN, or TLS Inspection, and are managed via policy API.

- **Principal Identity (PI) Certificate**: As covered earlier, principal identity is a third-party application that uses certificates to authenticate with NSX Manager. This certificate needs to be provided when creating a principal identity in NSX Manager.

The following section describes the process of replacing platform certificates for external communication, as a Day 1 operation for an administrator.

Generating a Certificate Signing Request (CSR)

The first step in replacing a certificate is to generate a CSR, which is then provided to Certificate Authority (CA) for generating a signed certificate that is trusted by the organization. Usually, organizations have a private CA such as Microsoft CA to provide signed certificates internally and root CA certificates are delivered through group policies to trust the signed certificate.

Step 1: Log in to NSX Manager with enterprise admin privileges and navigate to **`System.`** Select **`Certificates`** under **`Settings`** from the left navigation panel to view the different certificates present in NSX Manager.

Step 2: Click on the tab **`CSRs`** and then click on **`Generate CSR.`** Select **`Generate CSR`** to create a CSR for the signed certificate or **`Generate CA CSR`** to create a CSR for CA.

Step 3: Provide the following details to successfully create a CSR:

a. **`Common Name:`** Provide FQDN of NSX Manager.

b. **`Name:`** Provide a meaningful name to the certificate.

c. **`Organization Unit:`** Provide the department name of the organization.

d. **`Organization Name:`** Provide the organization name.

e. **`Locality:`** Provide the city name of the organization.

f. **`State:`** Provide the state in which the organization is located.

g. **`Country/Region:`** Provide the country information here.

h. **`Algorithm:`** Set the appropriate algorithm to use such as RSA or ECDSA.

i. **`Key Size:`** Enter the bits size of the encryption algorithm.

j. **`Description:`** *Optional, for remarks about the certificate.*

Figure 14.24 shows a completed configuration for a CSR.

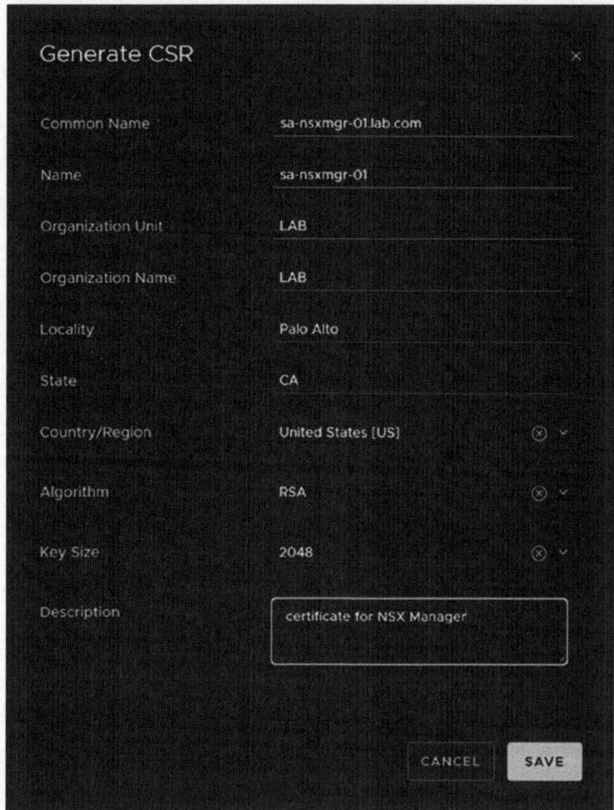

***Figure* 14.24**: *Generating a CSR*

Step 4: Click on **`SAVE`** to create the CSR. Click on three dots against the CSR name to download CSR PEM, which needs to be provided to Certificate Authority to generate a signed certificate.

Note: Self-signed certificates can also be generated against created CSR by clicking on Self-Sign Certificate for CSR.

Importing CA-Signed Certificate

After a signed certificate has been obtained from the Certificate Authority by providing previously generated CSR, follow the following steps to import it into NSX Manager:

Step 5: While present in **`Certificates`** with enterprise admin privileges from the previous section **`Generate a CSR,`** click on **`Certificates`** and it will provide options to import certificates in NSX Manager.

Step 6: Click on **`Import`** and then select **`Certificate`** to import signed certificate or **`Certificate CA`** to import root CA certificate.

Step 7: Provide the following details to add the certificate in NSX Manager:

a. **`Name`**: Name of the certificate. It is not required if importing against a CSR.

b. **`Service Certificate`**: Slide it to No if the certificate is to be used for Platform external communication, else slide it to Yes.

c. **`Certificate Content`**: Paste the certificate content of the CRT or CER file here.

d. **`Private Key`**: Paste the private key content of the certificate. It is not required if importing the certificate against a CSR.

Step 8: Click on **`Save`** to finish importing the certificate.

Replacing Platform Certificates

API POST command needs to be run to replace the certificate for API and Cluster in NSX Manager.

- To replace the API Certificate for the NSX Manager node, run the following API:

API Method: `POST`

API URI:

```
https://<NSX-Manager IP or FQDN>/api/v1/trust-management/
certificates/<cert-id>?action=apply_certificate&service_type=API&node_
id=<node-id>
```

Here **`<cert-id>`** is the certificate ID generated by NSX Manager when it was imported and **`<node-id>`** is the UUID of the NSX Manager node.

- To replace the cluster VIP certificate, run the following API:

API Method: `POST`

API URI: `https://<NSX-Manager IP or FQDN>/api/v1/trust-management/certificates/<cert-id>?action=apply_certificate&service_type=MGMT_CLUSTER`

Here **`<cert-id>`** is the certificate ID generated by the NSX Manager when it was imported.

NSX Multi-Tenancy

NSX has supported multi-tenancy for a long time. However, in earlier releases of NSX prior to version 4.0, it was configured as Tier1 gateways for dedicated tenants or using principal identity. In version 4.0, NSX introduced the concept of projects, but it was configured using API. In version 4.1, NSX extended the functionality of projects into NSX UI as well. Projects in NSX are similar to tenant by providing isolated networking and security objects between different projects in a single NSX deployment.

Projects

NSX implements a multi-tenancy model with the help of projects. A project provides the following features:

- Isolate networking and security configuration between different projects.
- Delegate the task of creating and managing networking or security configurations for each project to a specific set of NSX users with a scope limited to a specific project.
- By default, VMs are allowed to communicate with each other in the same project.
- By default, any communication outside of the project is blocked and requires modification to default security policies.

NSX achieves all these features with the help of two different branches under the policy data model. *Figure* 14.25 shows the hierarchical policy data model with two branches. One is /infra, which is the default space branch and is managed by the enterprise administrator. Another is /org/defaults/, which holds different projects such as project1 and project2, as shown in *Figure* 14.25.

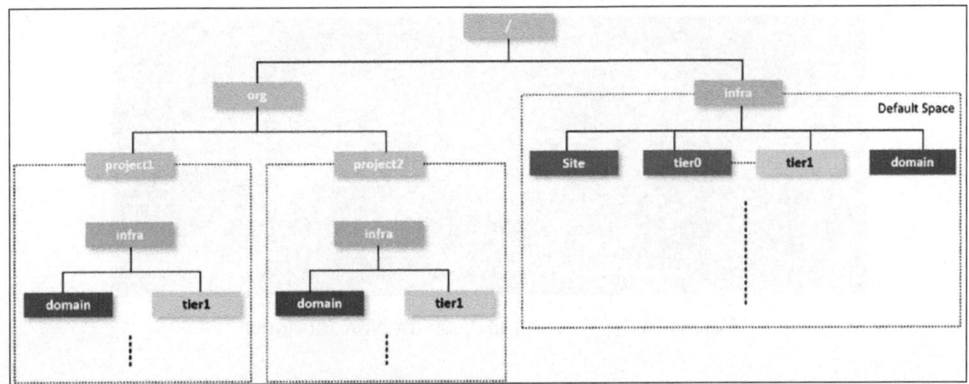

Figure 14.25: NSX Policy Data Model

Figure 14.25 shows the partial policy data model, and the full model is available on official VMware documentation at link https://docs.vmware.com/en/VMware-NSX/4.1/administration/GUID-52180BC5-A1AB-4BC2-B1CE-666292505317.html. This model lists two main branches as follows:

- **`/infra:`** This is the default space branch and is managed by enterprise administrators. Users under this branch have system-wide access under the Default view. Tier0 gateway and edge clusters are owned by default space only and cannot be created inside a specific project.
- **`/orgs/default:`** This branch holds different projects, as illustrated in *Figure* 14.25, which holds project1 and project2. Every project has a dedicated tier1 gateway and domain to hold its own specific objects.

Figure 14.26 shows the default space or **`Default`** view in the NSX Manager. This can be viewed by enterprise administrators or other users not assigned to specific projects.

Figure 14.26: *Default view in NSX Manager*

Adding a Project in NSX

This section provides steps to add a new project in NSX Manager as follows:

Step 1: Login into NSX Manager as an enterprise administrator. Click on the **`Project Switcher`** menu to expand it and then click on **`Manage`**, as shown in *Figure* 14.27.

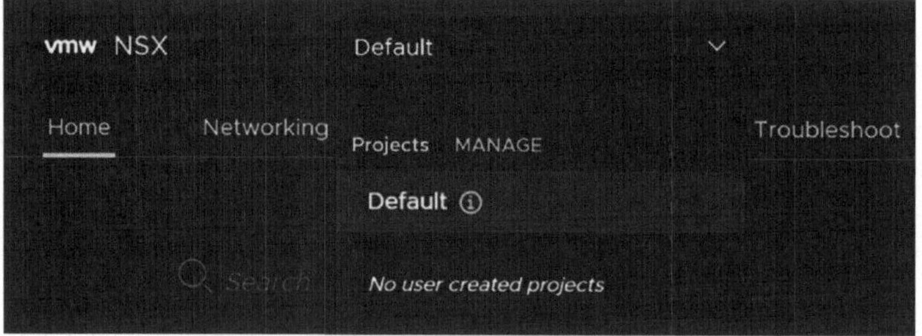

Figure 14.27: *Viewing projects in NSX Manager*

Step 2: Click on **`ADD PROJECT`** to add a new project. Provide a name for the project. Optionally, you can select **`Tier0`** gateway and **`Edge`** cluster to provide North-South connectivity to workload VMs and host centralized services such as NAT, as shown in *Figure 14.28*.

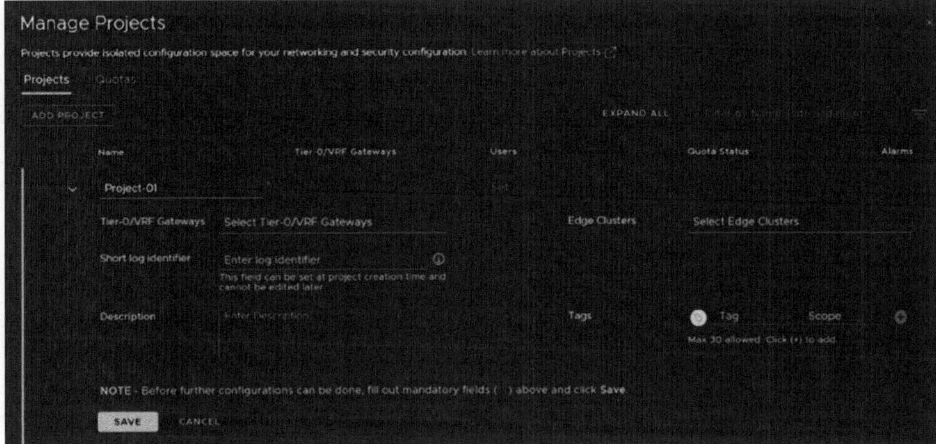

Figure 14.28: *Adding a new project in NSX Manager*

Step 3: Click on **SAVE** to finish creating the project. Optionally, you can create Quotas as well which can be assigned to projects to limit the number of networking or security objects that can be created in a specific project. Click on the tab **c** and then click on **ADD QUOTA** to create a new Quota. Click on **Set** under **Limits** to specify limits for different objects. Select the desired project under the **Applied To** field. *Figure* 14.29 shows a quota with the name Quota-01 applied to project Project-01 with the limit of one Tier1 gateway and 100 distributed firewall rules.

Figure 14.29: *Adding a quota to projects in NSX Manager*

Step 4: Click on **SAVE** to finish changes and then click on **Close** to finish managing projects.

Step 5: While in the **Project** Switcher menu, click on the newly created project to switch to a specific project, as shown in *Figure* 14.30.

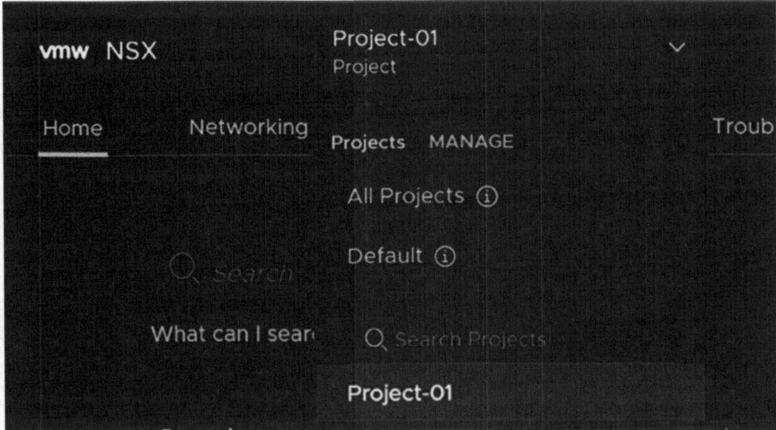

Figure 14.30: *Switching to a specific project in NSX Manager*

Assigning Users to Project

There are two ways to add user assignments to a project as follows:

- **Through User Management menu**: As covered in the earlier section under user assignment, as an enterprise administrator you can assign roles to users through User Management. While assigning roles to the user, check the Scope tab. Instead of selecting scope as All, select a specific project to assign the user to a specific project, as illustrated in *Figure* 14.31.

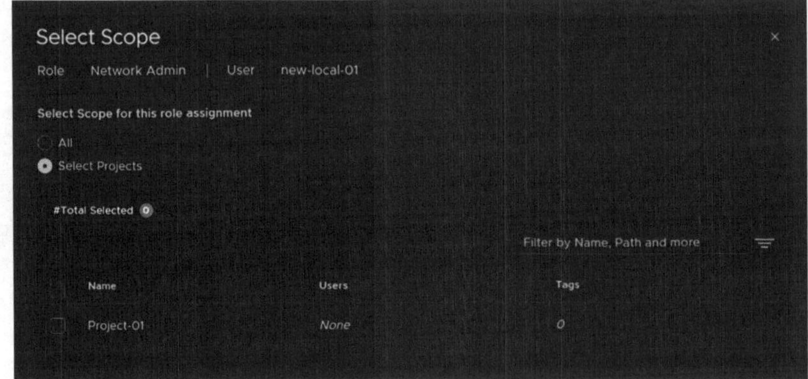

Figure 14.31: *Selecting a specific project in User Role Assignment*

- **Through Project Management menu**: Through project management, if a user has project admin privileges, then they can also manage permissions on the specific project. While in the project management menu, edit the specific project and click on Set under users to assign roles to users for a project, as shown *in Figure* 14.32.

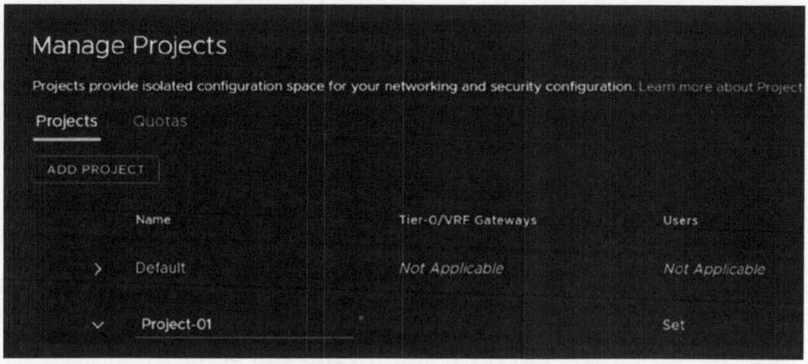

Figure 14.32: *Setting a role for the project through the Manage Projects menu*

The advantage of the second approach is the delegation of responsibilities. Instead of enterprise administrator managing permissions for different projects, they can delegate permission management through the Project Admin role to individuals in a specific project who in turn can manage permissions for their projects.

Figure 14.33 shows user **`new-local-01`** logged into NSX Manager UI and have access to Project-01 with limited access to NSX UI interface options. There is no Tier-0 Gateways as Tier0 gateways are out of scope from projects, similarly no existing Tier-1 Gateways present in Default view are visible in `Project-01` view. This shows clear isolation of management between different project and default view providing administrators to delegate some functionality of NSX to respective tenants.

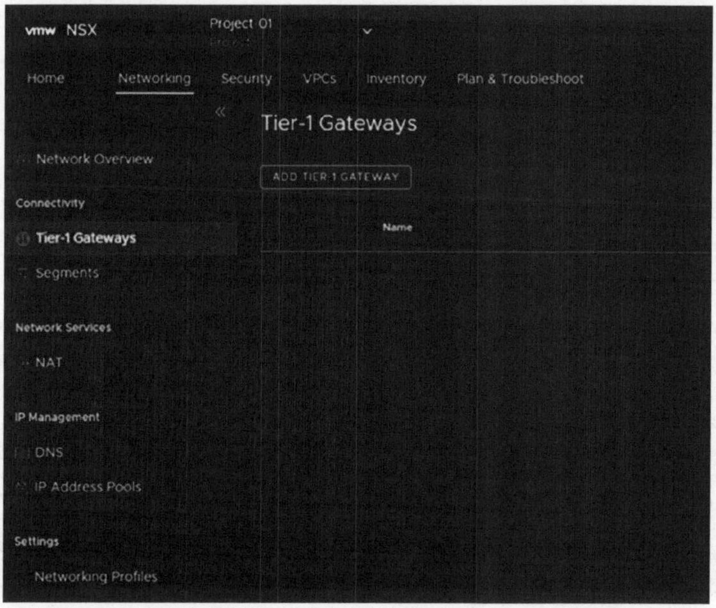

Figure 14.33: *Logging into NSX with project scope*

Monitoring NSX Environment

NSX provides multiple inbuilt tools for monitoring and troubleshooting. These can be used to monitor the health and performance of the NSX environment or troubleshoot network topology in the NSX environment.

When first logging into NSX Manager, the **Home** page provides a quick summary of the NSX Environment. As illustrated in *Figure* 14.34, the **c** tab displays the different objects configured in the NSX environment and their counts. If there are any issues in the environment, it highlights the same with an encircled red exclamation mark against the object in the **system** section.

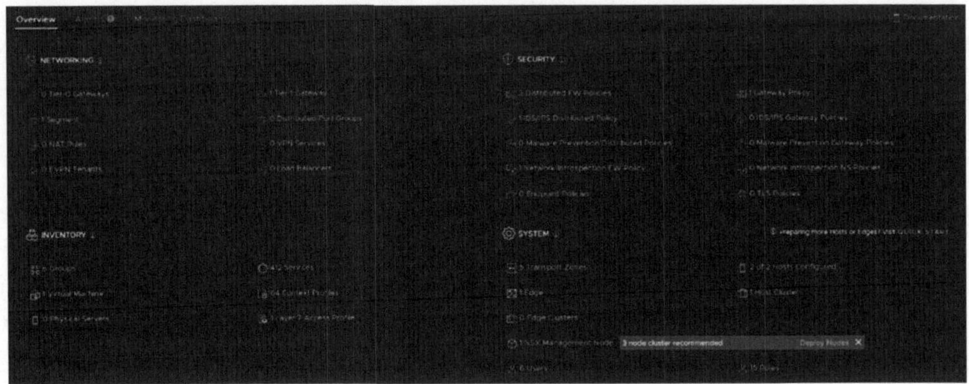

Figure 14.34: *Overview tab in NSX Manager*

Next is the **Alarms** tab, located just next to the **Overview** tab. This tab lists all the open and resolved alarms that occur in the NSX environment. If there are any issues in the NSX environment, Alarms should be the first tab to visit to see if there are any alarms in an open state, which may provide symptoms of an issue. *Figure* 14.35 shows the **Alarms** tab in NSX Manager. It not only provides a list of alarms generated in the environment but also provides different graphical charts based on top alarms.

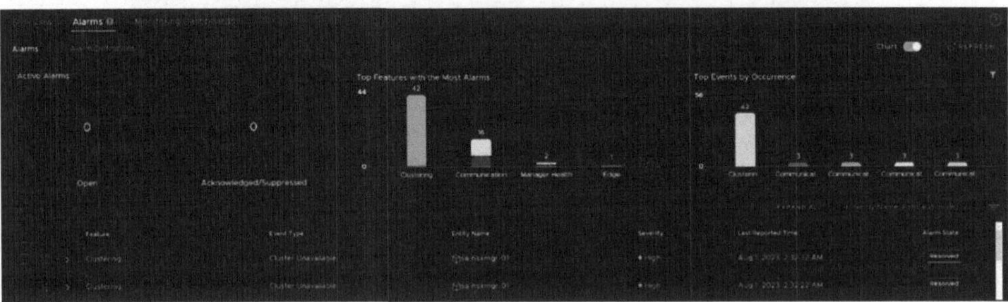

Figure 14.35: *Alarms in NSX Manager*

If required, one can enable or disable specific alarms as well by going to **`Alarm Definitions`** and editing the required alarm.

Next are the **`Monitoring Dashboards`**. There are four different monitoring dashboards available in NSX Manager, as shown in *Figure* 14.36:

***Figure 14.36:** Monitoring Dashboards in NSX Manager*

- **`System`:** This tab shows widgets for overall NSX infrastructure components, such as ESXi host, Edge Nodes, etc., and lists any alarms or issues with them.
- **`Networking & Security`**: This tab shows widgets for Network and Security objects, e.g., Tier1 gateway, Tier0 gateway, or DFW rules, and shows if there is any problem with a specific object.
- **`Compliance Report`**: This tab generates different compliance reports based on industry standards, e.g., HIPAA to validate if the NSX environment is in compliance with said security standards.
- **`Custom`:** This tab shows a custom dashboard created through API with different widgets placed on it.

Configuring SNMP for Alarms

NSX supports configuring SNMP (Simple Network Management Protocol) to monitor the NSX environment, such as NSX Manager or NSX Edge nodes. NSX supports both SNMP v1/2 and SNMPv3. SNMP manager administrators need to upload MIB files to correctly interpret SNMP messages sent by NSX. You can use KB1013445 to download MIB files and provide them to your SNMP manager administrator. By default, SNMP services are in a stopped state on both NSX Manager and Edge nodes, so follow the following steps to configure the same:

Step 1: Login into NSX Manager or Edge Node via SSH session or console to access CLI.

Step 2: Run the following commands to configure SNMP v1/v2:

```
set snmp community <community-string>

start service snmp
```

Here, **< community-string >** will be provided by the SNMP manager administrator.

Step 3: Run the following commands to configure SNMP v3:

```
set snmp v3-users <user_name> auth-password <auth_password>
priv-password <priv_password>

start service snmp
```

After running these commands, check with the SNMP administrator if they are able to see messages being received at their end.

Configuring Syslog in NSX

Remote logging is configured in the NSX environment by configuring the syslog server to forward logs to a central syslog collector, which can help in correlating events from different sources such as Aria Operations for Logs or Splunk. This section covers the commands necessary to run to configure syslog on different infrastructure components, such as NSX Manager, NSX Edge Nodes, and ESXi hosts.

In order to configure logging on NSX Manager or NSX Edge nodes, first login into NSX Manager or NSX Edge node through SSH to access NSX CLI and then run the following commands:

- Configure unsecure remote logging:

```
set logging-server <hostname-or-ip-address[:port]> proto <proto> level
<level> [facility <facility>] [messageid <messageid>]
```

where **<hostname-or-ip-address>** is the fqdn or IP address of the remote logging server.

<proto> specifies whether TCP or UDP to use.

<level> specifies the different levels of logs such as WARN, ERROR, or INFO.

<facility> NSX uses facility local6 to save logs and audit to save audit logs.

<messageid> specifies different components such as SWITCHING, ROUTING, FABRIC, and so on.

- Configure secure remote logging:

```
set logging-server <hostname-or-ip-address[:port]> proto li-tls level
<level> messageid <messageid> serverca <certificate file>
```

where **<hostname-or-ip-address>** is the fqdn or IP address of the remote logging server.

<level> specifies the different levels of logs such as WARN, ERROR, or INFO.

<messageid> specifies different components such as SWITCHING, ROUTING, FABRIC, and so on.

<certificate file> is the path to the root certificate chain file.

- Validate remote logging configuration:

```
get logging-server
```

The preceding command provides the output of the currently configured logging servers in the NSX appliance.

Remote logging in the ESXi host is configured through esxcli commands, which is different from nsxcli. If the vSphere environment is configured with Aria Operations for Logs, then syslog configuration is taken care automatically. However, if required to configure syslog manually, then login into ESXi host through SSH and run the following commands:

```
esxcli network firewall ruleset set -r syslog -e true
esxcli system syslog config set --loghost=udp://<hostname-or-ip-ad-
dress[:port]> --log-level=info
esxcli system syslog reload
esxcli system syslog mark -s "This is a test message"
```

where **<hostname-or-ip-address>** is the fqdn or IP address of the remote logging server.

By default, logging for NSX IDS/IPS is not enabled and requires to run API query to configure syslog for NSX IDS/IPS. Run the following GET query to retrieve status of NSX IDS/IPS logging to syslog server.

```
GET https://<Manager-IP>/api/v1/infra/settings/firewall/security/
intrusion-services/
```

where <**Manager-IP**> is the FQDN or IP address of NSX Manager or cluster VIP.

If output of above query shows **"ids_events_to_syslog": false,** then run following PATCH query to enable syslog for IDS/IPS.

```
PATCH https://<Manager-IP>/api/v1/infra/settings/firewall/security/intrusion-services/
```

where <**Manager-IP**> is the FQDN or IP address of NSX Manager or cluster VIP.

Also, NSX IDS/IPS syslog events are directly exported from ESXi hosts so please ensure remote logging has already been enabled on ESXi hosts. ESXi host uses below files to save IDS/IPS syslog messages conforming with RFC 3164 in `/var/log/nsx-idps` directory.

- `fast.log`: This file contains internal logging of `nsx-idps` process events and is used for debugging purposes.
- `nsx-idps-events.log`: This file contains detailed information about all events including all alerts, drops or rejects with NSX metadata.

This completes the syslog configuration in the NSX environment for different NSX appliances and ESXi hosts.

VMware Aria Operations for Logs

After configuring syslog in NSX Manager, Edge Nodes, and ESXi host to forward logs to a syslog collector, these can be analyzed to provide more useful information. One such example of a syslog collector provided by VMware is Aria Operation for Logs. There is an NSX-specific content pack provided by VMware, which provides a different set of dashboards to quickly review the NSX environment and find any anomalies in the environment. *Figure* 14.37 shows different dashboards present in Aria Operations for Logs for NSX Content Pack.

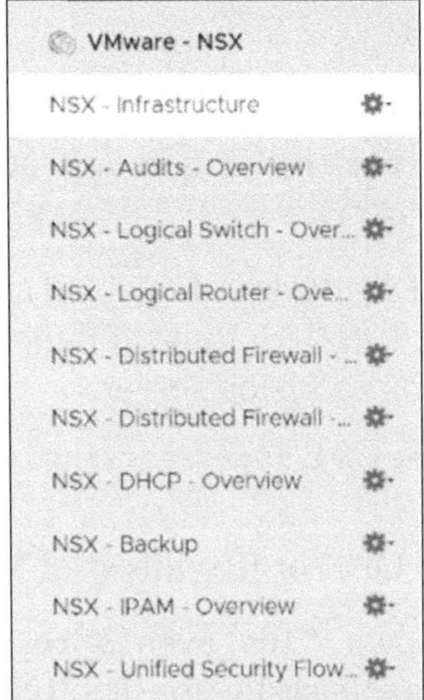

Figure 14.37: *Dashboards in Aria Operations for Logs*

Not only dashboards, but Aria Operations for Logs also provides Log Analytics to deep dive into logs and troubleshoot issues more efficiently. The deployment and configuration of Aria Operations for Logs are beyond the current scope of this book, but if you are interested in reading more, you can find additional information on docs.vmware.com.

Conclusion

This concludes the different tools provided by NSX Manager to effectively manage and monitor the environment. We covered how to integrate different authentication providers, such as Directory services, VMware Identity Manager, and Principal Identities, with NSX Manager, and how to use roles to assign specific permissions to different user accounts. We also touched on how to take backups, manage certificates, and monitor the NSX environment, with the help of alarms, SNMP traps, and syslog collectors.

Key Terms

- **Authentication:** It is a process of verifying the identity of the user or application.
- **LDAP (Lightweight Directory Access Protocol):** LDAP is a vendor-neutral protocol to look up information in directory servers such as Microsoft AD or openLDAP.
- **WS1/vIDM:** Workspace One or VMware Identity Manager is an Identity as a Service platform, which provides users access to SaaS, web, or mobile apps with multi-factor authentication, conditional access, etc.
- **Principal Identity Users:** Principal Identity referred to a third-party application that can use certificate-based authentication to connect to NSX Manager.
- **RBAC:** Role-Based Access Control defines the level of access a user has in the environment.
- **NSX Application Platform:** A distributed platform that provides hosting resources for different services, such as NDR, Intelligence, and Malware Prevention.
- **CSR:** A certificate signing request provides details for the certificate such as Common Name based on which the certificate authority issues the signed certificates.
- **Project:** A project in NSX is equivalent to a tenant, which provides isolated networking and security for different tenants.
- **Syslog:** Syslog is a protocol used by devices to send event data logs to a central location such as VMware Aria Operations for Logs.

Index

B

C

D

E

F

G

H

I

K

L

M

N

T

U

V

Z